Manchester Medieval Sources

series advisers Rosemary Horrox and Simon MacLean

This series aims to meet a growing need among students and teachers of medieval history for translations of key sources that are directly usable in students' own work. It provides texts central to medieval studies courses and focuses upon the diverse cultural and social as well as political conditions that affected the functioning of all levels of medieval society. The basic premise of the series is that translations must be accompanied by sufficient introductory and explanatory material, and each volume, therefore, includes a comprehensive guide to the sources' interpretation, including discussion of critical linguistic problems and an assessment of the most recent research on the topics being covered.

also available in the series

Mark Bailey *The English manor c. 1200–c. 1500*

Malcolm Barber and Keith Bate *The Templars*

Simon Barton and Richard Fletcher *The world of El Cid: Chronicles of the Spanish Reconquest*

Andrew Brown and Graeme Small *Court and civic society in the Burgundian Low Countries c. 1420–1520*

Samuel K. Cohn, Jr. *Popular protest in late-medieval Europe: Italy, France and Flanders*

Trevor Dean *The towns of Italy in the later Middle Ages*

P. J. P. Goldberg *Women in England, c. 1275–1525*

Martin Heale *Monasticism in late medieval England, c. 1300–1535*

Rosemary Horrox *The Black Death*

David Jones *Friars' Tales: Thirteenth-century exempla from the British Isles*

Simon MacLean *History and Politics in Late Carolingian and Ottonian Europe: The Chronicle of Regino of Prüm and Adalbert of Magdeburg*

Anthony Musson with Edward Powell *Crime, law and society in the later middle ages*

I. S. Robinson *Eleventh-century Germany: The Swabian Chronicles*

I. S. Robinson *The papal reform of the eleventh century: Lives of Pope Leo IX and Pope Gregory VII*

Michael Staunton *The lives of Thomas Becket*

Craig Taylor *Joan of Arc: La Pucelle*

Elisabeth van Houts *The Normans in Europe*

David Warner *Ottonian Germany*

Diana Webb *Saints and cities in medieval Italy*

ROGER II AND THE MAKING
OF THE KINGDOM OF SICILY

MANCHESTER
1824

Manchester University Press

MedievalSources*online*

Complementing the printed editions of the Medieval Sources series, Manchester University Press has developed a web-based learning resource which is now available on a yearly subscription basis.

MedievalSources*online* brings quality history source material to the desktops of students and teachers and allows them open and unrestricted access throughout the entire college or university campus. Designed to be fully integrated with academic courses, this is a one-stop answer for many medieval history students, academics and researchers keeping thousands of pages of source material 'in print' over the Internet for research and teaching.

titles available now at MedievalSources*online include*

Trevor Dean *The towns of Italy in the later Middle Ages*

John Edwards *The Jews in Western Europe, 1400–1600*

Paul Fouracre and Richard A. Gerberding *Late Merovingian France: History and hagiography 640–720*

Chris Given-Wilson *Chronicles of the Revolution 1397–1400: The reign of Richard II*

P. J. P. Goldberg *Women in England, c. 1275–1525*

Janet Hamilton and Bernard Hamilton *Christian dualist heresies in the Byzantine world, c. 650–c. 1450*

Rosemary Horrox *The Black Death*

David Jones *Friars' Tales: Thirteenth-century exempla from the British Isles*

Graham A. Loud and Thomas Wiedemann *The history of the tyrants of Sicily by 'Hugo Falcandus', 1153–69*

Simon MacLean *History and politics in late Carolingian and Ottonian Europe: The* Chronicle *of Regino of Prüm and Adalbert of Magdeburg*

Anthony Musson with Edward Powell *Crime, law and society in the later Middle Ages*

Janet L. Nelson *The Annals of St-Bertin: Ninth-century histories, volume I*

Timothy Reuter *The Annals of Fulda: Ninth-century histories, volume II*

R. N. Swanson *Catholic England: Faith, religion and observance before the Reformation*

Elisabeth van Houts *The Normans in Europe*

Jennifer Ward *Women of the English nobility and gentry 1066–1500*

Visit the site at *www.medievalsources.co.uk* for further information and subscription prices.

ROGER II AND THE MAKING OF THE KINGDOM OF SICILY

selected sources translated and annotated

by Graham A. Loud

Manchester University Press
Manchester and New York

distributed exclusively in the USA by Palgrave Macmillan

Copyright © Graham A. Loud 2012

The right of Graham A. Loud to be identified as the author of this work has been asserted by him in accordance with the Copyright, Designs and Patents Act 1988.

Published by Manchester University Press
Oxford Road, Manchester M13 9NR, UK
and Room 400, 175 Fifth Avenue, New York, NY 10010, USA
www.manchesteruniversitypress.co.uk

Distributed exclusively in the USA by
Palgrave Macmillan, 175 Fifth Avenue, New York, NY 10010, USA

Distributed exclusively in Canada by
UBC Press, University of British Columbia, 2029 West Mall,
Vancouver, BC, Canada V6T 1Z2

British Library Cataloguing-in-Publication Data
A catalogue record for this book is available from the British Library

Library of Congress Cataloging-in-Publication Data applied for

ISBN   978 0 7190 8201 6 *hardback*
        978 0 7190 8202 3 *paperback*

First published 2012

The publisher has no responsibility for the persistence or accuracy of URLs for any external or third-party internet websites referred to in this book, and does not guarantee that any content on such websites is, or will remain, accurate or appropriate.

Typeset in Monotype Bell
by Koinonia Ltd, Manchester
Printed in Great Britain
by TJ International Ltd, Padstow

CONTENTS

PREFACE

The Norman kingdom of Sicily is one of the most fascinating and unusual areas of interest within the discipline of medieval history, but until a few years ago those in the anglophone world who wished to study it in any depth were hamstrung by the lack of appropriate literature in English. For many years the only professional historian writing in English on Norman Italy was Evelyn Jamison (1877–1972), to whose pioneering researches on the royal administration and the south Italian nobility we are still indebted. She, however, ploughed a lonely furrow. That lamentable situation has begun to change thanks to the sterling efforts of a number of contemporary scholars, notably David Abulafia, Joanna Drell, John Howe, Jeremy Johns, Donald Matthew, Alex Metcalfe, Paul Oldfield, Chuck Stanton, Valerie Ramseyer and Patricia Skinner, to all of whom I am most grateful, both for their work and for their friendship and collaboration over many years.

But to understand and appreciate the topic, one also needs to read the primary sources, which are often bristling with technical difficulties (and not just linguistic ones). Until recently, none of these had appeared in English translation. In an attempt to remedy this situation I published in this series, twelve years ago, in collaboration with the late Thomas Wiedemann, *The History of the Tyrants of Sicily by 'Hugo Falcandus', 1154–69*. This present book is a companion volume to *Falcandus*, covering the immediately preceding period that saw the foundation of the kingdom of Sicily. It is a substantial volume, for which I must beg the forgiveness both of my readers and of my publisher, but I hope the interest and completeness of the subject matter justifies this. I have always believed that where possible it is better to read, and try to understand, the whole of a text rather than extracts chosen at an editor's whim. One must, obviously, compromise to some extent, especially when dealing with lengthy chronicles only a little of which are about the reign of King Roger, but I make no apology for presenting the complete texts of Alexander of Telese and Falco of Benevento, the principal historians contemporary with the king's reign. It is, for example, impossible to understand the way Falco wrote his chronicle, or his concern with the well-being of his native city, if one omits his account of events before 1127.

These texts were the first two that I translated for my undergraduate special subject on the Norman Kingdom of Sicily, and I must begin by thanking all the students who have studied and discussed them at the University of Leeds since 1989. I am also most grateful to the staff of the Brotherton Library at Leeds, and especially to Neil Plummer and Jane Saunders for their careful stewardship of the History shelves, and to my colleagues in the School of History for allowing me a semester's study leave to complete this book. In preparing it I have received help from many people, but especially Dione Clementi and Edoardo d'Angelo who presented me with copies of the modern editions of Alexander and Falco; the latter also patiently answered innumerable queries over the years, about Falco and many other matters too. My debt to the late Dr Clementi's commentary on Alexander will be apparent from the footnotes, and it was her contacts that first introduced me to the pleasures of archival work in Italy, for which, I fear, I never properly thanked her in her lifetime.

I am also grateful to Dott. Marino Zabbia for advice regarding the chronicle of Romuald, the new edition of which he is preparing. My work at Montecassino was made possible by don Faustino Avagliano, at Cava by the late don Simeone Leone, don Leone Morinelli and Signor Enzo Cioffe, and at Benevento by Prof. Elio Galasso. Prof. Vittorio de Donato allowed me to consult his unpublished thesis while I was working at the British School in Rome in 1990, during which time and on earlier visits too I was much helped by the kindness of the then Director, Richard Hodges, and the Librarian, Valerie Scott. My colleague Ian Moxon has been, as ever, invaluable in assisting me with translation problems, and has saved me from many egregious mistakes. My former research student Paul Oldfield, now a considerable scholar in his own right, and my current PhD students Isabella Bolognese and Benjamin Pohl have all been a great help and even greater encouragement – Isabella not least in meticulously proof-reading the translation of Falco's Chronicle. Hubert Houben, Alex Metcalfe and Paul Oldfield have all read and commented upon the introduction, and Alex has also checked my translation of the selections from al-Idrîsî. To all of them I am most grateful – needless to say, the faults that remain are entirely my own responsibility. And, as ever, Kate has been the prop and mainstay of this work, as well as the ever resourceful solver of computing problems.

G.A. Loud
Leeds and Lyme Regis
August 2010

ABBREVIATIONS

Al. Tel.	*Alexandri Telesini Abbatis Ystoria Rogerii Regis Siciliae atque Calabriae atque Apulie*, ed. Ludovica de Nava, commentary by Dione R. Clementi (FSI 1991)
Annalista Saxo	[*Die*] *Reichschronik des Annalista Saxo*, ed. Klaus Naß (MGH SS xxxvii, Hanover 2000)
Bertolini, 'Annales'	Ottorino Bertolini, 'Gli Annales Beneventani', *Bullettino dell'istituto storico italiano per il medio evo* 42 (1923), 1–163
Catalogus Baronum	*Catalogus Baronum*, ed. E.M. Jamison (FSI, Rome 1972)
Cava	Archivio della badia della Santissima Trinità, Cava dei Tirreni
Chartes de Troia	*Les Chartes de Troia (1024–1266)*, ed. Jean-Marie Martin (Codice diplomatico pugliese xxi, Bari 1976)
Chron. Cas.	*Chronica Monasterii Casinensis*, ed. Hartmut Hoffmann (MGH SS xxxiv, Hanover 1980)
Chron. Casauriense	*Chronicon Casauriense*, ed. L.A. Muratori (RIS ii(2), Milan 1726), 775–916.
Chron. S. Sophiae	*Chronicon Sanctae Sophiae (Cod. Vat. Lat. 4939)*, ed. Jean-Marie Martin (2 vols, FSI, Rome 2000)
Cod. Dipl. Aversa	*Codice diplomatico normanno di Aversa*, ed. Alfonso Gallo (Naples 1927)
Cod. Dipl. Barese	*Codice diplomatico barese* (19 vols, Bari 1897–1950)
Cod. Dipl. Verginiano	*Codice diplomatico verginiano*, ed. P.M. Tropeano (13 vols, Montevergine 1977–2001)
Ekkehard	*Frutolfs und Ekkehards Chroniken und die anonyme Kaiserchronick*, ed. F-J. Schmale and I. Schmale-Ott (Ausgewählte Quellen zur deutschen Geschichte des Mittelaters, Freiherr von Stein Gedächtnisausgabe, 15: Darmstadt 1972)
Falcandus	*La Historia o Liber de Regno Sicilie e la Epistola ad Petrum Panormitane Ecclesie Thesaurarium*, ed. G.B. Siragusa (FSI, Rome 1897)

Falco	Falco of Benevento, *Chronicon Beneventanum*, ed. Edoardo d'Angelo (Florence 1998)
FSI	Fonti per la storia d'Italia
Garufi, *Documenti inediti*	*I Documenti inediti dell'epoca normanna in Sicilia*, ed. Carlo Alberto Garufi (Documenti per servire alla storia di Sicilia, Ser. I.18, Palermo 1899)
Gattula, *Accessiones*	Erasmo Gattula, *Accessiones ad Historiam Abbatiae Casinensis* (Venice 1734)
Italia Pontificia	*Italia Pontificia*, ed. P.F. Kehr (10 vols, Berlin 1905–74: vol. ix, ed. W. Holtzmann, 1963; vol. x, ed. D. Girgensohn, 1974)
J-L	*Regesta Pontificum Romanorum ad annum MCXCVIII*, ed. P. Jaffé, S. Loewenfeld *et alii* (2 vols, Leipzig 1885–8)
Lothar, *Diplomata*	*Lotharii Diplomata*, ed. E. von Ottenthal and S. Hirsch (MGH Diplomatum Regum et Imperatorum Germaniae, viii, Berlin 1927)
Loud, 'Calendar'	G.A. Loud, 'A calendar of the diplomas of the Norman Princes of Capua', *Papers of the British School at Rome* 49 (1981), 99–143
Malaterra	*De Rebus Gestis Rogerii Calabriae et Siciliae Comitis, auctore Gaufredo Malaterra*, ed. Ernesto Pontieri (RIS, 2nd edn, Bologna 1927–8)
Mansi, *Concilia*	G.D. Mansi, *Sacrorum Concilium Nova et Amplissima Collectio* (31 vols, Venice 1759–98)
MGH	Monumenta Germaniae Historica, following the usual conventions, e.g. SS = Scriptores; SRG = Scriptores Rerum Germanicarum, etc.
MPL	J.P. Migne, *Patrologia Latina*, 221 vols, Paris 1844–64
Necrologio del Cod. Cas. 47	*I Necrologi Cassinesi* I *Il Necrologio del Codice Cassinese 47*, ed. Mauro Inguanez (FSI, Rome 1941)
Necrologio di S. Matteo	*Necrologio del Liber Confratrum di S. Matteo di Salerno*, ed. C.A. Garufi (FSI, Rome 1922)
Orderic	*The Ecclesiastical History of Orderic Vitalis*, ed. and trans. Marjorie Chibnall (6 vols, Oxford 1969–80)
Reg. Neap. Arch. Mon.	*Regii Neapolitani Archivii Monumenta* (6 vols, Naples 1854–61)

RIS	Rerum Italicarum Scriptores
Roger II Diplomata	*Rogerii II Regis Diplomata Latina*, ed. Carl-Richard Brühl (Codex Diplomaticus Regni Siciliae, Ser. I.ii(1), Cologne 1987)
Romuald	*Romualdi Salernitani Chronicon*, ed. C.A. Garufi (RIS, 2nd edn, Città di Castello 1935)
Tyrants	*The History of the Tyrants of Sicily by 'Hugo Falcandus' 1154–69*, trans. G.A. Loud and T.E.J. Wiedemann (Manchester 1998)
Ughelli, *Italia Sacra*	*Italia Sacra*, ed. F. Ughelli (2nd edn by N. Colletti, 10 vols, Venice 1717–21)
William I Diplomata	*Guillelmi I. Regis Diplomata*, ed. Horst Enzensberger (Codex Diplomaticus Regni siciliae, Ser. I.iii, Cologne 1996)

The family of King Roger

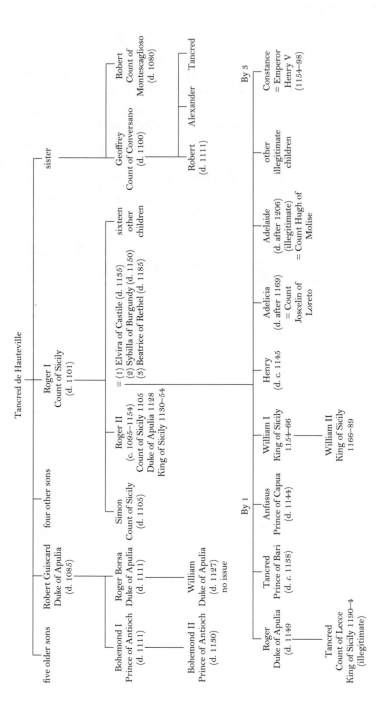

The family of the Norman princes of Capua

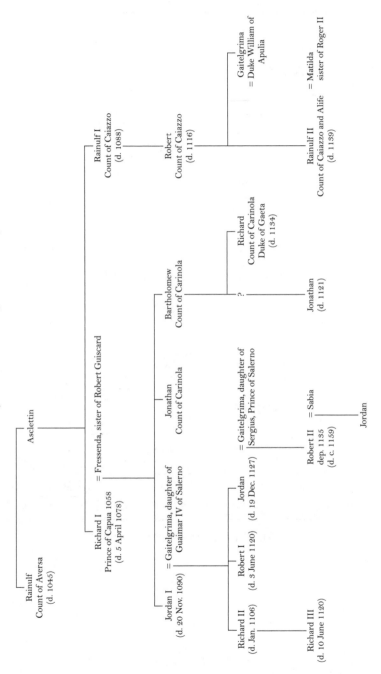

Map 1 Sicily and southern Italy

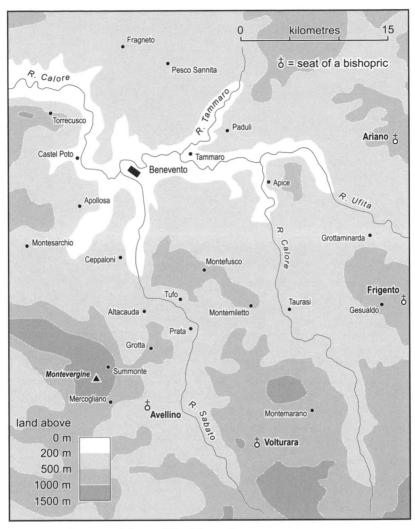

Map 2 The Terra Beneventana

INTRODUCTION

Count Roger II of Sicily was crowned as the first king of the new kingdom of Sicily in Palermo cathedral on Christmas Day 1130. The consequences of that action were profound. The unification of the island of Sicily with the southern Italian mainland in the years after 1127 altered the balance of power in the Mediterranean and had a major impact on the power politics of Europe in the central Middle Ages. Furthermore, the kingdom thus created lasted, despite terrible and prolonged internal conflicts in the later Middle Ages, for more than seven hundred years, until its incorporation into the *Risorgimento* kingdom of Italy by Giuseppe Garibaldi in 1860. One could therefore hardly deny that the process by which this new political entity was erected and consolidated was one of great importance and interest for the history of medieval Europe. Furthermore, the contemporary sources which describe the creation of the kingdom (here translated into English for the first time) are of unusual interest, not least in that the two principal narrative texts, the 'History of King Roger' of Abbot Alexander of Telese and the Chronicle of Falco of Benevento, reveal diametrically opposing views of King Roger and his state-building.

The reputation of King Roger

King Roger was a controversial figure, in his lifetime and afterwards. Most contemporary commentators had a high opinion of his character and abilities, but not necessarily of his rule. In part, this was a product of the circumstances in which the kingdom was created, and of the endorsement of that creation by a schismatic pope whose pontificate was deemed illegitimate. German writers were hostile because in their eyes the erection of the kingdom, in territory which they considered to be subject to their empire and without the sanction of the emperor, was illegitimate under any circumstances. Bernard of Clairvaux seized on this issue when he wrote to Emperor Lothar during the papal schism.

> It is the duty of Caesar to uphold his own crown against the machinations of that Sicilian usurper. Just as it is to the injury of Christ that a man of Jewish

race has seized for himself the See of Peter, so it is against the interests of Caesar that anyone should make himself the king of Sicily.[1]

Others were critical of how Roger ruled. Even in an age of stern, centralising monarchs anxious to strengthen their rule and consolidate their kingdoms, his harshness seemed to many to stray beyond the bounds that were generally acceptable. Orderic Vitalis, writing in Normandy in the early 1140s, encapsulated this view.

> He [*Roger*] took possession of the duchy of Apulia against the wishes of the inhabitants. Later he fought against all who attempted to resist him and cruelly suppressed them with great forces; he spared no man, but struck down kinsmen and strangers alike and, stripping them of their wealth, crushed and humbled them. ... So with passionate violence he destroyed men near and far and, by cruelly causing much bloodshed and mourning, grew to greatness.[2]

Otto of Freising – half-brother of King Conrad III and thus virtually official spokesman of the German crown, a man of deep learning and historical sensibility – went further still, comparing his 'works of cruelty' to those of ancient Sicilian tyrants. Another contemporary German historian wrote that Emperor Lothar in 1137 refused Roger's offers to negotiate a settlement whereby he or one of his sons might hold Apulia from the emperor: 'he flatly refused to hand over that province to a semi-pagan tyrant'. (Quite what gave rise to this accusation is uncertain: was it Roger's support for the anti-pope, or his toleration of non-Christians, or his employment of Muslim soldiers?) Falco of Benevento, who saw his actions from much closer to hand than these writers north of the Alps, waxed lyrical and wrathful over the cruelties inflicted by the king and his troops, exclaiming at one point 'not even Nero, the cruellest emperor among the pagans, had inflicted such slaughter among Christians'.[3]

And yet there was another side to the coin, for shrewder and less biased commentators recognised that Roger's actions were a product of the circumstances of his time. To his credit, much as he disliked Roger and his kingdom, Otto of Freising did admit that there were divergent views about the king.

---

1 *The Letters of St. Bernard of Clairvaux*, trans. Bruno Scott James (London 1953), 210 no. 142. Anacletus II, the pope whom Bernard opposed, was descended from a family of Jewish converts.

2 *Orderic*, vi.432–5.

3 Below, 208, 275. For a wider examination of this theme, Wieruszowski (1963).

There are, however, those who say that he acts rather out of a concern for justice rather than from tyranny, for they say that he loves peace more than all other princes, and it is for the preservation of this that they wish him to repress rebels with such severity. Still others say he is moved by love of money, in which indeed he exceeds all other western kings, rather than peace and justice.[4]

Yet to churchmen, such as Otto, the bringing of peace was the justification for secular government in an imperfect world. As we shall see, that was good enough reason for Alexander of Telese to support King Roger.

Perhaps most interesting was the verdict of a historian writing some years later, probably in the time of Roger's grandson William II (king 1166–89), whose moral outlook appears to have been formed less by conventional Christian ideas than by his reading of classical texts, the so-called 'Hugo Falcandus'. We do not know who this writer may have been, and while he was probably a native of southern Italy not all modern scholars concur in this opinion.[5] He was, however, a well-informed insider at the Sicilian court, and no admirer of the later Sicilian kings and their rule. However, his opinion of King Roger was notably balanced.

Some writers categorise many of his actions as tyrannical and call him inhuman because he imposed on many men penalties that were severe, and not prescribed by the laws. It is my opinion that as a prudent man who was circumspect in all things, he intentionally behaved in this way when his monarchy was recently established so that wicked men should not be able to wheedle any impunity for their crimes; and that while those who deserved well (to whom he showed himself mild) should not be discouraged by excessive severity, there should nevertheless be no place for contempt as a result of excessive mildness. And if perhaps he acted somewhat harshly against some, I suppose that he was forced to it by some necessity. For there was no other way in which the savagery of a rebellious people could have been suppressed, or the daring of traitors restrained.[6]

4 *Otto Episcopi Frisingensis Chronica sive Historia de Duabus Civitatibus*, ed. Adolf Hofmeister (MGH SRG, Hanover 1912), VII.23, pp. 346–7.

5 There have been several attempts to identify 'Hugo Falcandus'. Franke (2008) suggests the author was the well-known Anglo-Norman scholar Peter of Blois, known to have been in Sicily in 1167–8; D'Angelo (2009) puts forward the claims of Peter's brother, William, who was for a time abbot of the monastery of S. Maria of Matina in Calabria. D'Angelo's case in particular is carefully and persuasively argued, but hardly conclusive; there remain grounds to suggest Falcandus was a native of the *regno*, not an incomer whose stay there was relatively brief.

6 *Tyrants*, 58.

Alexander of Telese suggested that Roger deliberately cultivated an image of restraint and remoteness, that he might be feared by evildoers (which in this context meant above all potential rebels and political opponents), and the chronicle attributed to Archbishop Romuald of Salerno said that he was more feared than loved by his subjects. But 'Romuald' added, echoing Alexander and Falcandus, that he was 'in private kindly, generous with honours and rewards to those faithful to him'.[7]

Therefore, insofar as we can approach the king's character and behaviour, the picture given by contemporaries is surprisingly consistent – and one should stress that there is no indication of interdependence between these various sources. That his rule was often harsh was a product of the circumstances in which the kingdom of Sicily was created, and the long struggle that King Roger waged against those who opposed him. For, though crowned in 1130, he was only securely in control of his kingdom from 1139 onwards. Even then, the external relations of the new kingdom remained difficult: the German Empire remained consistently, and the Byzantine Empire intermittently, hostile, and this hostility was kept simmering by political exiles. It was not in fact until some way into the reign of William II that the kingdom of Sicily was absolutely secure against its external enemies. While, to begin with, Roger was prepared to be flexible and to conciliate his opponents, he found, as did other contemporary rulers, that mildness could too easily be interpreted as weakness. Harsh measures, however regrettable, therefore became necessary if the new kingdom created in 1130 was to survive.[8]

The historical background

The new kingdom that emerged was a polyglot one, embodying a mixture of different peoples, cultures and even religions. Mainland southern Italy was divided between a majority who called themselves 'Lombards', thus literally descendants of the Germanic invaders of the

---

7 *Al. Tel.* IV.4 [below, 122]. 'Romuald' [below, 266] also agreed with Otto of Freising about the king's concern with money. Given the potential problems of the authorship of this work, which will be discussed below, I have preferred to adopt this neutral terminology to describe it, to avoid pre-judging the issue.

8 The modern historian inevitably makes a comparison with his exact contemporary King Stephen of England (ruled 1135–54): 'a mild man, and gentle and good, who did no justice', whose reign was 'nineteen long years when God and his saints slept', *Anglo-Saxon Chronicle*, ad. an. 1137, in *English Historical Documents*, ed. D.C. Douglas and G.W. Greenaway ii *1042–1189* (London 1953), 199–200.

peninsula in the later sixth century, but who in our terms may be considered native Italians, and a minority of Greek-speakers, especially in the Salento peninsula of southern Apulia and in Calabria. The *longobardi* of southern Italy – few of whom were really derived from the Lombards of late Antiquity, since the latter, like the other 'barbarian' invaders of the Roman Empire were only a relatively small élite (and themselves an amalgam of different peoples) – had developed a strong sense of their own identity, sustained by the traditional law codes of the early medieval Lombard kings, but separate from the *lombardi* or inhabitants of northern Italy. They were, however, like the northerners Latin Christians, loyal to the Church of Rome.

On the island of Sicily, conquered by the Arabs in the ninth century, much of the population had in the next two centuries converted to Islam, but there remained a substantial Christian minority, especially in the north-east of the island, which was for the most part graecophone, who observed the rites of the Orthodox Church of Constantinople, as did their Greek compatriots on the mainland. In addition, there were a few – we do not know how many – Arabic-speaking Christians on Sicily, and indeed many of the Christian inhabitants of the island may in practice have been bilingual in Arabic and Greek.[9] At the end of the twelfth-century a poet, writing in Latin, could still celebrate the kingdom's capital, Palermo, as being 'endowed with people of three languages',[10] even if by this time the Latin element was becoming dominant. Indeed, the society of southern Italy was, if anything, even more complex than the above summary may suggest. There were on the mainland coastal cities, Amalfi, Naples and Gaeta, that had never been conquered by the Lombards, the inhabitants of which still considered themselves to be distinct from the rest of southern Italy, not least in the observance of Roman (i.e. Byzantine) law, but who were also Latin Christians and who were economically, and to a considerable extent culturally, increasingly interwoven with the general 'Latin' population of the south.[11] Politically, the region had been chronically divided, the mainland between Lombard princes, independent duchies and provinces of the Byzantine Empire, the island from the early eleventh century between rival Muslim rulers.

Into this maelstrom of contending parties a new element had begun to intrude itself from about the year 1000 onwards. Over the course of the

9 Bresc and Nef (1998); Metcalfe (2009), 247–8.
10 Peter of Eboli, *Liber ad Honorem Augusti*, ed. G.B. Siragusa (FSI, Rome 1906), 9, line 56.
11 For these, see especially Skinner (1995); Skinner (2002), and for Naples, Arthur (2002).

eleventh century almost the entire region, with the exception of a few larger towns, was step by step conquered by warriors from France, most of whom described themselves and were known to their contemporaries as 'Normans' (*normanni* in the Latin texts). Many of these were indeed from the duchy of Normandy, even though there were others, perhaps as many as a quarter or even a third of the invaders, who came from other parts of France (mainly from the north).[12] The first of these Normans had arrived in the south as pilgrims. They had soon been employed as mercenaries by the various warring princes, and even by the Byzantine governors. Their establishment in the south was undoubtedly assisted by the fragmentation of authority there and the number of rival political leaders who sought their services. From the early 1040s onwards the Normans began to take over the southern mainland.

By 1059, even though some of Apulia still remained in Byzantine hands, most of the mainland lay under Norman rule – something that was recognised by Pope Nicholas II when in August of that year he formally and publically invested the Norman leader Robert Guiscard as Duke of Apulia and Calabria, to be held as fiefs from the pope as his overlord. At the same time, or perhaps a few months earlier, the other principal Norman leader of the south, Count Richard of Aversa, had been recognised by the pope as Prince of Capua, which city and much of its dependent principality Richard had captured in the previous summer. The two Norman leaders were, it should be noted, closely linked, since Richard was married to Robert Guiscard's sister, and the later Norman princes of Capua were descended from this union. Furthermore, when Pope Nicholas invested Robert as duke at Melfi in August 1059, he not only confirmed him as ruler of the former Byzantine provinces of the mainland, but in addition as 'Duke of Sicily, when it shall be conquered'. Clearly the prospect of recovering Sicily for Christianity was a powerful reason for the pope to ally himself with the new Norman ruler, although this was only one reason among several – the need for political and military support at Rome was at this time an even more compelling one.[13] However, this wish to recover former Christian territory no doubt coincided with the intentions of the Norman leaders, Robert Guiscard and his younger brother Roger, who launched the invasion of Sicily in 1061.

Although Messina and the north-east of the island were soon captured, and Palermo fell in January 1072, the conquest of Sicily was a lengthy

12 Ménager (1975a), especially 202–7; Loud (1981a).
13 See Loud (2000b), 186–94.

process. The last few towns remaining in Muslim hands, in the south-east of the island, were taken only in 1091. While Robert Guiscard, as duke, had been nominally in charge of this conquest, in practice he could rarely spare time and resources for military operations on the island. After the capture of Palermo, he never returned to Sicily. His brother Roger was thus left in *de facto* control of the island, although the duke retained a half share of Palermo and Messina, the two principal towns, under his direct rule.[14] In the late 1080s, at which time most of the island was in Christian hands, Roger I began to enfeof his principal supporters with lands in Sicily, a process that was greatly extended after 1091.[15] Similarly, once the island had been completely conquered, Count Roger established new bishoprics, entrusted to Latin Christian prelates. He also founded, or encouraged the foundation of, monasteries; several were Latin, but the majority of these new houses were Greek, reflecting the overwhelming preponderance of those observing the Greek rite among Christians on the island. By the time of his death in 1101 Count Roger had himself founded three Latin monasteries and one nunnery, but he had also either personally founded or been involved in the foundation of over twenty Greek houses.[16]

By 1101 the balance of power within Norman Italy had been considerably altered. Robert Guiscard had progressively extended and consolidated his power within his dominions, as well as conquering the hitherto-independent Lombard principality of Salerno, the capital city of which fell to him in December 1076. In his last years he had, in addition, led two major expeditions into the Balkans against the Byzantine Empire. However, after his death in the course of the second of these expeditions in 1085, the authority of his successors as dukes of Apulia had progressively diminished. Admittedly, his son Roger Borsa ('the Purse') was by no means as ineffectual as an obituary notice, included by the compiler of the 'Romuald' chronicle, suggested.[17] However, it should be

---

14 *The History of the Normans by Amatus of Montecassino* [hereafter *Amatus*], trans. Prescott N. Dunbar and G.A. Loud (Woodbridge 2004), VI.21, pp. 158–9. For discussion, Loud (2000b), 165.

15 For details, Tramontana (1977), Loud (2000b), 173–80.

16 For the latter, Scaduto (1947), 80–143, who discusses the evidence in detail; Becker (2008), 206–17.

17 *Romuald*, 205–6: 'Duke Roger was of distinguished appearance and illustrious in his behaviour, restrained in matters of ostentation, polite, affable, the governor of churches, behaving humbly to the priests of Christ and greatly honouring the clergy, receiving all who came to him fittingly, pardoning those sentenced to death by him, a nurse to his people, a lover of peace, merciful to sinners, kind to his own men, peaceful to foreigners, amiable to all, and generous in providing gifts. For he was charming and pleasant to all and tried to win the love rather than the fear of both his own people and foreigners.'

remembered that his father had faced repeated revolts, largely from his own relations and his Norman vassals. While these had been success-fully overcome, and towns and lands confiscated from the rebels had increased the duke's resources, Guiscard's rule in Apulia had always been problematic. In addition, Roger Borsa faced the challenge of his elder half-brother Bohemond, the son of Guiscard's first wife, whom the latter had repudiated on grounds of consanguinity.[18] Despite the support of his uncle, Count Roger of Sicily, Duke Roger was forced to make a series of territorial concessions to Bohemond in the years 1088–90, granting him a number of towns in southern and central Apulia, including the important ports of Taranto and Bari. Although Bohemond was largely an absentee after 1096, when he joined the First Crusade, the creation of his lordship began a process whereby the most important seigneurs of that region largely escaped from ducal control. While Duke Roger continued to rule effectively over the principality of Salerno and most of inland Apulia – the towns of Melfi and Troia remained as foci of ducal rule in that region – much of the rest of Apulia (the Salento peninsula in the south, the central coastal region and the northern frontier of the Capitanata) became effectively independent. When Duke Roger and Bohemond both died within a fortnight of each other early in 1111, the former leaving as his heir a boy of 13 or 14, and the latter a small child, the decline of central authority and the growth of noble independence in Apulia accelerated. Furthermore, a similar process of fragmentation had been under way in the principality of Capua since the death of Prince Jordan I in 1090. The maintenance of princely authority was here also hampered by a revolt, or perhaps series of insurrections, by the townspeople of Capua, the resistance of whom was only eventually overcome with the help of Duke Roger Borsa and Count Roger of Sicily in 1098. But, despite recovering their capital, the later princes of Capua only effectively controlled the southern part of their principality, in the plain around the city of Capua; the nobles of more peripheral regions, like their counterparts in Apulia, became more and more autonomous.[19]

What the Norman Conquest had therefore *not* done was to unite southern Italy, and whereas up to c.1085/90 the region was divided into three principal spheres of influence, each controlled by a relatively powerful local ruler, thereafter authority became more and more fragmented. Local territorial lords such as the counts of Conversano and Loritello

---

18 Loud (2000b), 113–14, 127–8, suggests that this was not necessarily simply an excuse.

19 Loud (1985), 86–95.

in Apulia, and the counts of Caiazzo and Carinola in the principality of Capua, even though in all these four cases they were cousins of the ruler, were to all intents and purposes independent. Conflicts emerged between regional potentates – notably Bohemond, and after his death his widow Constance – and the counts of Conversano in southern Apulia. Some of the larger towns sought to assert their independence also. Gaeta as well as Capua revolted against the prince in 1091/2, while Amalfi proved increasingly restive under ducal rule, and in 1096 withstood a full-scale siege from Roger Borsa, whose rule over that city was only restored c.1102.[20] Bari threw off the rule of Bohemond II in 1113; five to six years later, after considerable factional dispute, a local patrician named Grimoald Alfaranites emerged as 'Prince of Bari', apparently as leader of a local civic regime.[21] Furthermore, incidents such as the murder of Archbishop Riso of Bari in 1117, the capture of Constance by treachery at Giovinazzo in August 1119,[22] and the conflict between counts Rainulf of Caiazzo and Jordan of Ariano for dominance in the region around Benevento in the years 1119–21, suggest that this diminution of regional authority had led to a significant breakdown in law and order.[23]

While one should be careful not to exaggerate the extent of this, as Alexander of Telese did when describing the situation after the death of Duke William of Apulia in the first chapter of his *History* – for some parts of southern Italy, notably the principality of Salerno, seem to have remained peaceful and untroubled – the decline of authority in the southern part of the peninsula during this period was marked. One symptom of this was the proclamation by successive popes of the Truce of God at a series of councils (at Melfi in 1089, and at Troia in 1093, 1115 and 1120). The Church sought to enforce peace through spiritual sanctions, precisely because lay authority was weak; the duke was present at all four of these councils, which were held in towns that were part of his fisc, so the proclamation of the Truce was certainly not part of an attempt to undermine his authority, but rather meant to support it. The popes, as nominal overlords of southern Italy, clearly recognised

---

20 Skinner (2002), 78–80.

21 In June 1123, Grimoald issued a charter dated in his fifth year as prince, although in October 1122 another document called him simply *dominator* of Bari, *Codice Diplomatico Barese* v *Le Pergamene di S. Nicola di Bari. Periodo normanno (1075–1194)*, ed. F. Nitti di Vito (Bari 1902), 115–17 no. 67, 121–2 no. 69. This may suggest that he had consolidated his authority by stages. Cf. Oldfield (2009), 46–9.

22 *Romuald*, 210.

23 For these, see *Falco*, below, 147, 152–4, 157, 162.

the weakness of temporal authority there. Hence Gelasius II in 1118 and Calixtus II in 1120 received fealty (and in 1120 also homage) not just from the duke and the prince of Capua but also directly from some of the other leading nobles in the region: in 1120 from counts Rainulf (II) of Caiazzo, Jordan of Ariano and Robert (II) of Loritello, as well as 'innumerable others', or so the papal biographer Pandulf claimed.[24]

The exception to this picture of fragmenting authority was in the dominions of the Count of Sicily. Admittedly, there are hints in the (for this period exiguous) sources that even here there were problems after the death of Roger I in 1101. His successors, his eldest legitimate son Simon (1101–5) and his second son Roger, both succeeded as children[25] with their mother, Adelaide, as regent, and minorities were almost inevitably problematic in the Middle Ages. A later document from 1141 mentioned 'a rebellion in Calabria and Sicily' during this regency, in which the village of Focerò in north-east Sicily was destroyed twice, or perhaps three times. Furthermore, a Greek abbot from the same part of Sicily petitioned the young Roger II in 1109 requesting that his church's land be surveyed afresh, since the document recording their boundaries had been lost in the troubles that had recently affected the island.[26] But while his minority may have had its problems, once he attained his majority and took personal control in 1112 Roger II appears to have been firmly in command of his dominions. Furthermore, both Roger I and his son were able to extend their power in return for the military assistance they rendered to the dukes of Apulia. Robert Guiscard had granted his younger brother the southern half of Calabria in 1062. A number of strongholds in Calabria were apparently held by duke and count together. In return for the count's support for his accession as duke, Roger Borsa granted these in full possession to his uncle. He subsequently added a half share in the confiscated lordship of the Falloc family around Catanzaro in 1088/9, and a half share in Cosenza in 1091, thus extending the count's territory into central Calabria.[27]

24 *Liber Pontificalis*, ii.315, 322. For discussion, Loud (2007a), 145–9.

25 The 'Romuald' chronicle claimed that Roger died at the age of 58 years, two months and five days on 27 February 1154 [below, 266]. Taken literally this suggests he was born on 22 December 1095, and that he was deemed to be of age when 16½ years old. A probably later interpolation in Malaterra's history would suggest that he was born early in 1099; *Malaterra*, IV.26, p. 106. Since his elder brother Simon appears to have been born in 1093, that Roger was born late in 1095 appears quite feasible, Becker (2008), 229.

26 S. Cusa, *I Diplomi greci ed arabi di Sicilia* (Palermo 1868–82), 403–5, 532–5. I am grateful to Alex Metcalfe for drawing my attention to the Focerò document. For other evidence, Houben (2002), 24–5.

27 *Malaterra*, II.28, III.42, IV.11, 17, pp. 39, 82, 92, 96–7.

In 1121/2 Roger II was able to make much more significant gains at Duke William's expense. He apparently sought to achieve this first by conflict – several sources refer to a war between the count and the duke that was brought to an end through the arbitration of Calixtus II, who made a lengthy visit to Calabria that winter. Later Duke William sought military aid from his cousin against Count Jordan of Ariano, who according to Falco of Benevento was openly defying his authority. In return for military and financial assistance, William transferred to the Count of Sicily rule over the northern half of Calabria, and the half shares that up until then the dukes had retained in Palermo and Messina. The 'Romuald' chronicler also claimed that William, who was childless, recognised Roger as his heir, in return for a large sum of money.[28] In the years immediately after this, Count Roger consolidated his control over Calabria and advanced his power northwards into Lucania, notably in claiming the lordship of Montescaglioso, which had been held by his widowed sister Emma.[29]

Underpinning these political advances was the wealth of the island of Sicily, which its ruler was able to exploit to his own benefit; hence the substantial sums of cash with which Count Roger could (in effect) purchase land from his cousin the duke. Some sixty years later a Muslim traveller who visited Sicily wrote that

> the prosperity of the island surpasses description. It is enough to say that it is a daughter of Spain [*his native land*] in the extent of its cultivation, the luxuriance of its harvests, and in its well-being, having an abundance of varied produce, and fruits of every kind and species.[30]

The Arab geographer al-Idrîsî, whose description of the known world, written at Roger's behest, was completed shortly before the king's death, again and again praised the fertility and prosperity of different places in Sicily. Even if there may have been an element of flattery in such descriptions, they were unlikely to be entirely fictional. The territory of Syracuse, for example, 'is vast, covered with farming estates and villages, it is fertile and its fields are perfectly cultivated. Boats loaded with wheat and other products set off [*from there*] for the rest of the world'.[31]

---

28 *Falco* [below, 165], and *Romuald*, 212, and below 250; *Liber Pontificalis*, ii.322–3.

29 *Roger II Diplomata*, 16–17 no. 6 (September–December 1124), in which Roger confirmed a privilege of his sister, who was referred to in the past tense, being 'of blessed memory'. She had held the lordship in right of her son Roger, as widow of its hereditary lord Rodulf Maccabeus, *Reg. Neap. Arch. Mon.* vi. 191–3 no. 23 (July 1119). Cf. Houben (2002), 38–9.

30 *The Travels of Ibn Jubayr*, trans. R.J.C. Broadhurst (London 1952), 339.

31 *Idrîsî. La Première Géographie de l'Occident*, trans. H. Bresc and A. Nef (Paris 1999), 315 [see also below, 358–62]. Among the other products exported from Syracuse were hides; Goitein (1967), 111.

Sicily was a source of wheat and other foodstuffs, not least for the Muslim towns of Tunisia, and of other commodities, such as silk and cotton textiles, wood and even cheese, which were exported to Egypt. It was also a market for spices from the east.[32] The count was able to profit directly from this prosperity, not least because while Roger I had endowed his principal supporters with lordships after the conquest, he had retained a substantial part of the island, including much of the centre (the main wheat-growing area) and the west, in his own hands. Thus he profited not just through tolls and levies on trade, but as the main proprietor of the agricultural surpluses that were exported.[33] Other valuable commodities, notably the tuna fisheries around the coast, were reserved for the ruler to exploit as a monopolist, even though a few favoured churches might occasionally be granted a share in these. These fisheries were not simply a useful source of foodstuffs – they were increasingly large-scale commercial operations.[34] Sicily was also already an entrepôt and exchange point for trans-Mediterranean trade from Byzantium and the Islamic countries through to northern Italy. Jewish merchants in Egypt sent and received cargoes to and from Sicily, both before and after the Norman conquest.

Sicily was, indeed, a principal hub of Mediterranean trade routes, for Jewish, Muslim and (increasingly) Christian merchants.[35] The first reference to Genoese traders on the island comes from 1116, and since this mentions the rebuilding of a merchants' hostel at Messina it is clear that this was not by any means the first such contact. In 1127–8 Roger concluded a treaty, or more properly a series of agreements, with Savona, a Ligurian port allied to Genoa, which suggests that there was already considerable commercial contact between this town and Sicily.[36] Idrîsî noted that many men from Ifrîqiyya (Tunisia) were accustomed to come to Marsala in western Sicily, and presumably these were traders for the geographer also noted the number of markets at Marsala and the abundant tax renders from the town. Similarly, he recorded of Sciacca, on the south coast, that 'its port is frequented by numerous ships arriving without cease from Tripoli and Ifrîqiyya', while at Scicli

32 Goitein (1967), 45 (pepper), 46 (cheese), 102 (silk); Goitein (1983), 114, 144, 157, 168–9, 251–2; Abulafia (1985), 27–30.

33 Abulafia (1983), especially 4–5.

34 Bresc (1987), especially 279–80. Idrîsî noted the tuna fishery at Castellamare del Golfo, west of Palermo, Idrîsî. La Première Géographie de l'Occident, 320.

35 Goitein (1967), 211–17.

36 Cusa, Diplomi greci ed arabi, 359–60; Roger II Diplomata, 24–8 no. 10. Abulafia (1977), 62–9.

in the south-east people came by sea from 'Calabria, Ifrîqiyya, Malta and elsewhere'.[37]

The Count of Sicily possessed the administration to exploit this burgeoning wealth, largely staffed by Greek officials. Registers of lands and boundaries, and lists of serfs, were compiled for Sicily and in Calabria. Commercial tolls were levied on shipping at the ports.[38] To begin with, many of the officials may have come from Calabria, but after Countess Adelaide moved the centre of government from Mileto in Calabria, first to Messina and then to Palermo during Roger's minority, they were recruited both from the island and further afield. These Greek officials were clearly very close to the count, notably George of Antioch, an Arabic-speaking Greek, previously an official of the rulers of Mahdia in North Africa, who fled to Sicily c.1109.[39] When in the autumn of 1124 Roger II moved to establish his foothold in Lucania at Montescaglioso, he was accompanied by his principal minister Christo-doulos (who can be attested from 1105 onwards) and by George of Antioch, who a couple of years later succeeded Christodoulos.[40] The expertise of such administrators enabled the count to build up his financial resources, and to develop a fleet and army (including Muslim soldiers from Sicily) that would enable him to extend his rule to the mainland.[41] Thus, when Duke William died childless on 28 July 1127, Roger II was the wealthiest and most powerful figure in southern Italy, and in an excellent position to claim the succession to the duchy.

The takeover of the mainland

According to Alexander of Telese, Duke William's death was unex-pected, and – though he had promised formally to designate Roger as his heir, and thus as successor to the duchy, in the event of his not having a son – he had not actually done this, and thus 'he did not on his death leave any heir lawfully to succeed him'.[42] Since William was only

37 Idrîsî. La Première Géographie de l'Occident, 316, 318–19.

38 This is implied by the exemption granted in the 1116 charter above, and made more explicit in Cusa, Diplomi greci ed arabi, 554–6 (1125) for the Bishop of Catania.

39 von Falkenhausen (1977), 351–6; von Falkenhausen (1980), 147–51; Takayama (1993), 31–46.

40 See above, note 29. For George, see also Al. Tel. II.8 [below 00, and note 53].

41 The use of Muslim soldiers was by no means new. Roger I had employed these as far back as at the siege of Salerno in 1076, before the conquest of the island was completed: Amatus, VIII.14, p. 194.

42 Al. Tel. I.1, 4 [below, 64, 66].

Example

30 when he died, it seems possible he had not yet despaired of having a male heir, although he had been married as far back as 1116 to a daughter of Count Robert of Caiazzo, and after eleven years of wedlock the prospect of having a son must have been unlikely.[43] 'Romuald', by contrast, claimed that William had, from the account clearly at some point after 1122, appointed Roger as his heir. The question here may well be when this latter version was written: whether it was a contemporary notice incorporated into the later chronicle, or whether, as Houben has suggested, merely an assumption by the later writer, perhaps Archbishop Romuald himself, that because Roger in the end succeeded he therefore must have been the designated heir.[44] Moreover, Fulcher of Chartres, writing in Jerusalem very soon after the events in question (probably c.1127/8) noted that the duke had made an agreement with his first cousin Bohemond II, Prince of Antioch, that whichever of them should survive the other would be his heir. This had taken place, Fulcher said, 'in the presence of the leading men on both sides, who acted as witnesses', immediately before Bohemond left southern Italy to become the ruler of Antioch in the summer of 1126.[45] On the other hand, another contemporary writer, Walter, Archdeacon of Thérouanne, who was in Rome during the summer of 1128, claimed to have heard from Pope Honorius II himself that Duke William on his deathbed had left his dominions to the papacy.[46] And in the event, Pope Honorius refused to accept Count Roger as the new duke and would not grant him investiture despite, so Falco claimed, the considerable bribes, or presents, which the count offered him. It was only a year later, after a military campaign and when his local allies had failed him, that Honorius, very reluctantly, invested the Count of Sicily as the new duke in August 1128.

How do we make sense of all this? The deathbed designation is perfectly feasible, since we know that as he lay dying Duke William made an extensive donation for the good of his soul to the abbey of Cava,

43 *Romuald*, 207.

44 Houben (2002), 42.

45 *Fulcher of Chartres, A History of the Expedition to Jerusalem 1095–1127*, trans. F.R. Ryan and H.S. Fink (Knoxville 1969), III.57, p. 297 [Latin text: *Historia Hierosolymitana (1095–1127)*, ed. H. Hagenmayer (Heidelberg 1913), 805–9]. This was repeated in the later account of William of Tyre, *A History of Deeds done beyond the Sea, by William Archbishop of Tyre*, trans. E.A. Babcock and A.C. Krey (2 vols, New York 1941), ii.32 [Latin text: *Chronicon*, ed. R.B.C. Huygens (Corpus Christianorum, Continuatio Medievalis 63,Turnhout 1986), i.613: lib. XIII.21]. See below, *Al. Tel.* I.12.

46 Walter, *Vita Karoli Comitis Flandriae*, cc. 1–2, MGH SS xii.539–40. Discussion of these various accounts, Deér (1972), 175–80.

although the document that attests this – which records the sworn testimony of several witnesses, including two of the duke's doctors – says nothing of any other bequest, let alone of one so momentous as that of the duchy itself.[47] On the other hand it could have been no more than papal propaganda. Certainly, if William had made such a bequest, it is odd that there was no other later mention of this, when it surely would have strengthened later papal claims over southern Italy.[48] One might suspect, however, that Duke William had at various times offered the possible succession to the duchy of Apulia, or dangled the possibility of the succession, to more than one possible claimant, while still hoping that he might himself have a son. (There are parallels to this in the careers of other childless medieval rulers, not least Edward the Confessor of England). If at the end William did leave the duchy, or the arrangement of the succession to the duchy, to his papal overlord, that does not necessarily disprove one or more earlier promises. But from the point of view of Count Roger, his claim could only ultimately be based on his alleged hereditary right, as enunciated by his partisan Alexander of Telese. And while Bohemond II arguably had a better hereditary claim, he was far away in Antioch, and in no position therefore to intervene.

However, if we leave these somewhat speculative considerations, a more significant question is why Count Roger's claim to the duchy faced such opposition. Some scholars have argued that the pope's refusal to countenance his succession was essentially based upon legal considerations: either that with the death of the childless duke his fief reverted to his overlord, the pope, to allocate as he saw fit, or that the papal investiture of the south Italian Norman leaders had always been conditional, and it was up to the pope whether or not he chose to grant the duchy as a fief to any new claimant.[49] Neither interpretation is particularly convincing. The stress on the 'legal' aspects of relations between the popes and the Norman rulers is misplaced, and misunderstands the essential dynamic of the relationship since the original investiture of 1059. The bond between the two had always been an alliance rather than a relationship between overlord and dependant, and the overriding priority for

---

47 Cava, *Arm. Mag.* F.40 [printed by Guillaume (1877), xxviii–ix appendix I, and L. von Heinemann, *Normannische Herzogs- und Königsurkunden aus Unteritalien und Sizilien* (Tübingen 1899), 33–7 no. 20].

48 Chalandon (1907), i.381.

49 The former was suggested by Kehr (1934), 37, and Houben (2002), 42–4; the latter by Deér (1972), 126–84. What is essentially a summary in English of Deér's arguments is presented by Robinson (1990), 367–83.

the papacy had been the military and political assistance that could be secured from the south Italian princes. There is no evidence that under normal circumstances either popes or Norman rulers had considered papal approval a necessary concomitant for the ducal succession – or that of the princes of Capua. Indeed, while rulers swore fealty to each new pope and received investiture with their lands, that investiture was often delayed for several years after the new prince succeeded. (Duke William succeeded his father in February 1111; he received investiture from the incumbent pope, Paschal II, only in October 1114).[50] Admittedly, the balance in the relationship had shifted in the years immediately before 1127, as the authority of the Norman rulers in their dominions had weakened, while with the end of the Investiture Contest, with the popes securely establishing themselves in Rome after 1120 and then consolidating control of their (until now nominal) territory around Rome, Honorius II was in a stronger position than his predecessors had been.[51]

Roger certainly had a claim to succeed his cousin, especially if some sort of promise or designation had been made – although the fact that Alexander of Telese more or less admitted that any promised designation had not been formally proclaimed is significant, given that this author sought throughout his work to bolster the legitimacy of Roger's rule. Indeed, he even said in his first chapter that William had died without an heir. One might also note that in some twelfth-century enfeoffments in the papal states, succession was limited to the direct heirs of a fief holder.[52] But had Roger been otherwise acceptable, it is unlikely that the pope would have hesitated to recognise him as duke purely because he was a collateral, and not a direct, heir. To Honorius II, however, his succession as duke must have seemed a potentially unwelcome development. First, as ruler of Sicily, Calabria and Apulia he would have had control of the majority of southern Italy – hardly something desirable at a time when the pope was taking a closer interest than hitherto in the affairs of the south of the peninsula.[53] Secondly, Roger had already on several occasions shown that he intended to exercise close control over the Church in his dominions and that he was not necessarily

50 *Falco* [below, 143]; *Chron. Cas.* IV.49, p. 516; *Annales Ceccanenses*, MGH SS xix.282 ; *Romuald*, 207.

51 The interpretation here has been developed at greater length in Loud (2007a), 135–51. For the papacy and Rome at this period, see especially Partner (1972), 158–68.

52 Loud (1985), 140.

53 Matthew (1992), 29, points out that more than 500 papal documents relating to southern Italy survive from the period 1088–1130. Cf. Kamp (1980), 107–10; Loud (2007a), 219–23.

amenable to papal instructions. In 1117 Paschal II had sternly rebuked his interference in Church affairs and his control over the bishops of his dominions, which in that pope's view clearly went well beyond any special powers that might have been granted by his predecessor Urban II to Count Roger I [see the chapter here on 'Roger II and the Papacy', document 1]; and in 1121/2 Roger had treated papal attempts to mediate between him and Duke William with scant respect. The pope and several of his entourage had fallen ill (indeed several cardinals had died while Calixtus II was in the south that winter), and according to his biographer 'with the pope half-dead, Count Roger had done as he liked'.[54] The latter cannot therefore have seemed an ideal candidate to receive papal investiture with the duchy, but the denial of his claim was a pragmatic rather than a 'legal' decision.

It is a good question, which the surviving sources do not clearly answer, what Honorius II's intentions were for the government of southern Italy in 1127. He may have envisaged a loose federation of towns and nobles under papal suzerainty – certainly Falco suggests that he sought to receive oaths of fealty not just from the Prince of Capua but also from other leading nobles,[55] perhaps extending the precedent established in 1118 and 1120. This reminds us that the pope's opposition to Roger's succession was only feasible because there was considerable opposition to the count in southern Italy – from the principality of Capua, led by the new prince, Robert II, and his cousin Count Rainulf of Caiazzo (despite Rainulf being married to Count Roger's sister), from a number of leading nobles in Apulia and from some important towns of the mainland. All three groups feared that, if Roger became duke, backed by the financial and military resources of Sicily, he would substantially limit the independence they had hitherto enjoyed or (in the case of some towns) would have liked to enjoy. Alexander's account suggests that even the citizens of Salerno, hitherto the ducal capital, were reluctant to accept Roger as their ruler, and delicate negotiations and concessions were required before they did. Pope Honorius encouraged this opposition, by repeated excommunications of the count, by playing upon the fears of those who were apprehensive that his rule would be much more forceful and effective than that to which they had been accustomed (as in the speech he made at the inauguration of Prince Robert II of Capua, as reported by Falco), and by offering remission of sins to those who fought against him, drawing here on the holy war ethos of the so-called First

---

54 *Liber Pontificalis*, ii.323.

55 Below, 178.

Crusade. By 1127 this had been extended to include campaigns against the Muslims in Spain, but the offer reported by Falco is the earliest known example of spiritual rewards being expressly offered for warfare against Christians. Honorius also offered tangible benefits, notably in his privilege of December 1127 confirming and extending the rights and liberties of the citizens of Troia, effectively offering the town self-government under papal overlordship.[56] The terms of this document indicate the aspirations of burgesses of one of the more important towns of the region. One notes their aversion to a citadel held by troops of an outside ruler – a key issue in earlier negotiations between Roger and the Salernitans, and later in relations between the king and the citizens of Bari in 1132 – and the dislike of military service being exacted from the town, equally unpopular in Bari and Benevento in 1132.[57]

However, the weakness of the opposition to the count was that it was a coalition of divergent interests. When Count Roger confronted the pope in the summer of 1128, the latter's army melted away. Falco's account blamed the lack of enthusiasm or staying power of the nobles, and particularly Count Rainulf and the Prince of Capua, the former making excuses, the latter 'unable to sustain hard work', even going so far as to blame 'the deceitfulness of the prince and the other barons'. It was the royal partisan Alexander of Telese who ascribed the collapse of the allied army to its arrears of wages and supply problems.[58] (This brief mention of the *stipendii* paid to troops has important implications for military organisation in the south, an issue which requires fuller investigation than there is space for here). In the end, the pope had no option but to grant Roger investiture as duke. While what the chroniclers tell us suggests that the investiture and the oath of fealty followed the pattern that was by now traditional, Falco added another element – that Roger swore to respect the integrity of Benevento and the independence of the principality of Capua. While the former detail might have been something added by the chronicler, always anxious to stress the freedom of his native city, neither of these provisos is intrinsically unlikely, as Honorius sought to maintain some sort of counterweight to Roger's power. The maintenance of Capuan independence, and the continued presence of a papal enclave within the south, were the best means of securing this.

---

56 *Chartes de Troia*, pp. 182–5 no. 50. See Oldfield (2009), 56–8.

57 *Al. Tel.* II.34 [below, 90]; see also the privilege issued in the king's name to Bari in June 1132, *Roger II Diplomata*, 54–6 no. 20 [= *Cod. Dipl. Barese* v.137–9 no. 80], clauses 13 and 19. For discussion, Martin (1980), especially 88–96. For Benevento, *Falco* [below, 94].

58 *Al. Tel.* I.14 [below, 71, and 181]

In the event, however, neither attempt was wholly successful. Soon after Roger's investiture, and (so Falco tells us) even before the pope had returned to Rome, the papal rector of Benevento perished in a popular uprising and a commune was formed in the city, which thereafter fell victim to renewed factional dispute. Meanwhile the new duke set about consolidating his rule on the mainland. During the course of the campaigning seasons of 1129 and 1130 he forced those nobles who were still recalcitrant to surrender – sometimes they had to buy their way back into his grace by territorial concessions, as did the Count of Ariano. One by one he reduced the towns that held out against him – Troia proving the most obstinate – and in the autumn of 1129 at Melfi he issued an edict forbidding private warfare and forced the assembled nobles to swear to maintain general peace, restrain their vassals, respect the Church and hand over criminals to ducal justice. What Roger did here was to enforce the provisions of the Truce of God through his own authority, and proclaim the superiority of that authority over local judicial rights. We have no other record of this edict than Alexander's, but its provisions were reflected in one of Roger's later laws, where he stated:

> Our royal majesty's providence refuses in any way to permit one of our barons to invade the *castrum* of another within the bounds of our kingdom, or to plunder it, to make an armed attack on it or to take anything from it by fraud.[59]

Duke Roger had thus made unequivocally clear that the government of southern Italy was to be very different from what had gone before. The assembly at Melfi in September/October 1129 was an important step in the creation of the new kingdom. Early in 1130, too, Robert II of Capua formally submitted to him. This was not the first time that a prince had become a vassal of the duke; Prince Richard II had done so in 1098 in return for Roger Borsa's assistance in recovering his rebel capital. But whereas the submission of 1098 had no lasting consequences – the stress in some of the older scholarly literature on its long-term effects is misplaced[60] – that of 1130 was to have enduring results, as almost the final piece in the jigsaw of south Italian unification.

---

59 Vatican Assize xxxi [below, 325]; Zecchino (1980), 153–4; Houben (2002), 48.

60 E.g. Kehr (1934), 32–3, who went so far as to suggest that this precluded any subsequent vassalic link with, or investiture by the pope, on the part of the princes, a misconception which has been followed by Hoffmann (1978), 167–72. See Loud (1985), 97–101; and Loud (2002), 160–1, for a critique of this view.

The papacy and the creation of the kingdom

The creation of the Sicilian kingship followed swiftly on from the unification of the south; indeed, if one were simply to read the account of
Alexander of Telese, the former would seem to be the logical corol-
lary of the latter. Roger's power was now such as to merit a royal title.
Alexander also referred to what was a convenient piece of historical
fiction: that Sicily had once 'in ancient times' had kings who ruled from
Palermo, and therefore what was taking place in 1130 was the restoration of a former monarchy rather than a *de novo* creation. (None of the
Greek kings on Sicily in the pre-Roman period had, in fact, ruled over
the island as a whole). According to Alexander, the new kingship was
also validated by election, or perhaps one should rather say by acclama-
tion. At an assembly at Salerno in the summer of 1130 the churchmen
and barons of the land had 'unanimously' agreed that Roger should
become a king; 'strengthened by their sincere approval' (*veridicis asser-
tionibus roboratus*) he set about organising his royal coronation.[61]

Alexander's account was, to say the least, disingenuous, not in the
sense that such careful domestic preparations and (in modern parlance)
management of public opinion among the politically powerful classes
did not take place, but in what he did not say. For what Alexander
entirely omitted was the role of the papacy. Some modern commentators have suggested that this reflected the king's own wish that his
authority should not be beholden to an external power, or in any sense
be subject to papal approval, but rather held directly from God; or as
later jurists rendered this, he wished to be 'king in his own kingdom'
(*rex in regno suo*).[62] One would not deny that the sense of divine empow-
erment was significant for the new Sicilian monarchy – as expressed,
for example in the famous mosaic of Roger being crowned by Christ
in the church of the Martorana in Palermo, and in his law code, if
that is what the collection in Cod. Vat. Lat. 8782 is (discussed below).
Thus the king described himself in the preface to this code as 'we who
through His grace possess the authority of justice and law'. But while
it is clear that Alexander saw Roger's kingship as divinely ordained,
he did not entirely eliminate the papacy from his account. While he
was critical of the refusal of Honorius II to invest Roger as duke, he
was careful not to accord Roger the ducal title in his account until he

---

61 *Al. Tel.* II.1–3. Cilento (1983), 168–9.

62 Fuiano (1956), followed by, for example, Cilento (1983), 167–71. Brown (1992), 199, seems
  to suggest that this omission was almost accidental, a sign that Alexander 'did not have a
  coherent position' on the legitimacy of the *regno*. This is nonsense.

had received investiture. Roger may have claimed to be the legitimate heir to the duchy, and by implication Alexander accepted that, but until the ceremony of August 1128 he remained in his eyes only 'count'.[63] So Alexander did recognise the papal role. The problem he faced was rather the equivocal status of Pope Anacletus II.

The creation of the kingdom of Sicily was a product not just of the unification of southern Italy but also of the papal schism of February 1130. On the death of Honorius II, splits within the college of cardinals led to a disputed election, in which two rival popes were chosen: Cardinal Gregory of Sant'Angelo (as Innocent II) by some of the younger or more recently-appointed cardinals led by the papal chancellor Haimeric (a group which included nearly all of the non-Italian cardinals), and Cardinal Peter Pierleone (Anacletus II) by those who resented Haimeric's attempts to hijack the election, including most of the older and more experienced members of the college as well as those from Lazio and southern Italy.[64] Roger's kingship was formally recognised by a bull from Anacletus II, issued on 27 September 1130, according to Falco after king and pope had met at Avellino, and presumably there agreed on the terms of the creation [see 'Roger II and the Papacy', document no. 2]. The bull in several ways reflected what Alexander said about the creation of the kingdom, notably about the extent of Roger's authority justifying his promotion to royal status, and recognising Palermo as the capital of the new kingdom.

While harking back to the earlier investitures of Robert Guiscard and his successors as dukes of Apulia, and as in the investitures of Guiscard (for which documentary evidence survives) specifying that an annual *census* be paid in recognition of papal overlordship, now to be in Byzantine *nomisma* rather than in silver pennies of Pavia, in several other respects the alliance (for this is what this was) seems to have been more favourable to the ruler than to the pope. Admittedly, while the bull refers to homage and fealty to be sworn by the kings, no such oath

---

63 E.g. *Al. Tel.* I.13.

64 The literature on the 1130 schism is vast. Schmale (1961), especially 30–56, argued that the party of Innocent and Haimeric was closely connected to the new religious orders, particularly the regular canons, which were developing at this time. They were, so he claimed, part of a new reform movement to which Anacletus and his supporters were opposed. This interpretation has attracted criticism, especially with regard to the supposed links of several pro-Innocent cardinals with the regular canons. But there can be no doubt that most of the cardinals appointed by Calixtus II and Honorius II, who included several Frenchmen (one of whom was Haimeric) supported Innocent, while cardinals surviving from the pontificate of Paschal II tended to support Anacletus. See Bloch (1986), ii.944–51, and especially Robinson (1990), 69–77, for a balanced viewpoint.

to Anacletus survives – if Roger did do this, then his oath might have repeated the clauses in earlier such texts pledging the ruler to bring help to his papal lord – a key feature of the surviving oaths of Robert Guiscard from 1059 and 1080.[65] But Anacletus also said that he and his successors would not necessarily exact such an oath or homage, and that the royal status of the kingdom was not dependent on this ceremony. Indeed, he expressly recognised the hereditary nature of the new kingdom. In addition, he granted Roger authority over Naples, which up to then had been independent, and the help in time of war of the men of Benevento. (This last grant was to prove less than popular with these papal citizens). He also took steps to begin the organisation of a proper ecclesiastical structure on the island of Sicily, something which he continued in other bulls in September 1131 [for one of which, see 'Roger II and the Papacy', no. 3, below].

Since Anacletus faced the challenge of a rival pope, recognition by the ruler of southern Italy was undoubtedly in his interest, and the bull creating the kingdom was the price he paid for Roger's support. But from Roger's perspective, receiving the bull in 1130 was of great value, legitimising his royal status just as, seventy years earlier, Nicholas II had legitimised the seizure of southern Italy by Robert Guiscard. When the bull was promulgated Anacletus could fairly be seen as the legitimate pope. While neither his election nor that of his rival was strictly canonical, and the college of cardinals had been genuinely divided, arguably his election had been more proper than that of Innocent, which was the product of a surreptitious intrigue by a small group of cardinals within a few hours of the death of Honorius II (there was no precedent for the so-called electoral commission that named Innocent as pope). Although the figures given by modern historians may vary slightly, there is no doubt that Anacletus had more cardinals on his side than Innocent.[66] Above all, he was the pope who was in control of Rome and the papal lands round the city, while Innocent had fled first to Pisa and eventually to France. In previous schisms, both during the Investiture Contest and before, it had invariably been the pope who held Rome who had

---

65 English translation of the 1059 oath in Loud (2000b), 188–9.

66 Palumbo (1942), 209–10, suggests that 22 cardinals backed Anacletus, though only 13 were named in the bull announcing his election. Schmale (1961), 32–3, agreed with this figure, but claimed 20 cardinals eventually supported Innocent, including five cardinal bishops. Responding to Schmale's book, Palumbo (1963), 100–1, criticised his figures, suggesting that he overestimated support in the college for Innocent, who he said had initially the support of 17 cardinals, four of them cardinal bishops. The problem was that until promulgation of the bull *Licet de evitanda* at the Third Lateran Council of 1179 there was no canonical procedure for deciding when and how a pope was legally elected if the cardinals could not agree on a candidate.

won the contest. Neither was Anacletus without support elsewhere, notably in northern Italy and western and south-west France, and he expected to secure the loyalty of Spain. Although the King of France and his bishops were certainly sympathetic to Innocent, none of the north European monarchs had yet openly taken sides, and Anacletus still hoped, and was actively working, for their support.[67]

But by 1135/6, when Alexander of Telese was writing, the cause of Anacletus was clearly lost. The north European rulers and their churchmen had all recognised Innocent, who had the vociferous support of spokesmen of the new monastic orders, and benefited from a vigorous, often highly unscrupulous propaganda campaign on his behalf. Many of those who had begun by supporting the Roman pope had now changed sides, as the Milanese did in 1135. Far from ensuring his defeat, Innocent's flight to France in August 1130 had been the first step towards securing him recognition from the Church as a whole. In St Bernard's famous phrase, 'driven from the City, he has been received by the world' (*pulsus ab urbe, ab orbe suscipitur*).[68] While Anacletus lingered on in Rome, still claiming to be pope until his death in February 1138, the schism had effectively been decided several years earlier. In these circumstances, the bull of Anacletus was an embarrassment, and his role in the creation of the kingdom is best ignored. A generation later, Romuald of Salerno, or his amanuensis, did mention Roger's recognition of Anacletus as pope, but like Alexander he suggested that the creation of the kingdom was the product of an internal consensus, without external authorisation, claiming that the king, 'a wise and astute man', had refused to meet Anacletus or to do homage.[69]

---

67 Palumbo (1942), 310–58. Stroll (1987), 66–70, points to Anacletus's excommunication of Emperor Lothar's opponent Conrad of Staufen in May 1130 as one of the key elements in his bid for imperial support. For France, Reuter (1983), on the basis of a letter from Louis VI in response to the announcement of Innocent's election, which he published for the first time, *art.cit.* 415–16, redated the council at Etampes that recognised Innocent to late May 1130. But Louis only actually controlled part of northern France, and arguably full recognition of Innocent did not come until the Council of Rheims in October 1131. A council of some of the German bishops at Würzburg in October 1130 recognised Innocent, prompted by the arrival of his legate Archbishop Walter of Ravenna; but the emperor did not fully commit himself until he attended Innocent's council at Liège in March 1131 (which had a much larger attendance than the council six months earlier), and then was disposed to make conditions for his support. *Die Reichschronik des Annalista Saxo*, ed. Klaus Nass, MGH SS xxxvii (Hanover 2006), 593; *Annales Palidenses*, MGH SS xvi.78; Robinson (1990), 445–6.

68 *The Letters of St. Bernard of Clairvaux*, 188 no. 127, in a letter to Archbishop Hildebert of Tours, who was sympathetic to Anacletus. My translation is more literal than that of Scott James.

69 Below, 255.

The chroniclers thus ignored or down played what may in fact have been quite close links between the new king and Pope Anacletus and his family. It is notable that when the latter issued his bull formally creating the kingdom, that the witnesses included only one cardinal, but several members of the Pierleone family, including two of Anacletus's brothers [see 'Roger II and the Papacy', no. 2, below]. It is, indeed, possible that the coronation *ordo* used in December 1130, which followed the Romano-German Pontifical, was derived from Rome, perhaps sent with the cardinal who was present at the ceremony.[70] In May–June 1131 Roger despatched Prince Robert of Capua and Count Rainulf of Caiazzo to Rome with two hundred knights, something mentioned by Falco (who would appear to have misdated the episode), but not by Alexander, although the latter let slip that it was while Rainulf was at Rome that his wife left him.[71] The despatch of this force to Rome was surely intended to strengthen the position of Anacletus within the city. In the autumn of 1131 Anacletus, undoubtedly at Roger's behest, restructured the Church on the island of Sicily, promoting Messina to be an archbishopric ['Roger II and the Papacy', no. 3], and creating two new bishoprics, Cefalù and Lipari, to be its suffragans, thus dividing the island into two metropolitan provinces.[72] Roger was also allied with, or made use of, Cardinal Crescentius, whom Anacletus had appointed as his rector in Benevento. While we should be cautious in accepting all the chronicler Falco's rhetorical claims that Crescentius wanted to 'place the city of Benevento under the king's power' – the city was after all papal territory, and there is no evidence that Roger sought to annex it – the king was clearly concerned to have the military aid of Benevento, as he was entitled to by the terms of the bull of 1130. So Falco informs us, in summer 1132, that Roger sought that:

> for love of him and their obligation of fealty to Anacletus, they should bind themselves by an oath of alliance and make war against the Prince of Capua and Count Rainulf.[73]

But the clearest indication of the close links between king and pope was the former's privilege to the Pierleone family in January 1134 ['Roger

---

70 Houben (2002), 56. Copies of this pontifical had been made before 1100 at Montecassino, Elze (1973), 440. Loew and Brown (1980), ii.87, 128. But this does not necessarily mean that it was known in Sicily.

71 *Al. Tel.* II.14; for the date, Clementi (1991), 240–2. [See below, 82, 190].

72 *Italia Pontificia*, x.339 no. 23; 357 no. 4, 364 no. 1. Loud (2007a), 225.

73 Below, 193.

II and the Papacy', no. 4], in which the king promised the Pierleone an annual pension of 240 pounds of gold, in return for which they became his vassals. This was a much larger annual payment that that stipulated for the papacy itself in the bull of 1130, and should surely be interpreted as a subsidy to maintain the position of the Pierleone and of Anacletus himself in Rome. Furthermore the particular significance of this document was shown by its physical form: one of only two surviving *diplomata* of King Roger to be written in golden ink on purple parchment, the other being his foundation charter for his palace chapel, in April 1140.[74] Anacletus also spent quite a lot of time at Benevento, both in the autumn of 1134, after Roger's control of the mainland seemed assured, not least through the renewed submission of Count Rainulf, and for a considerable period in 1136, when Roger once again appeared to be victorious in the south. Neither of these stays would have been possible without Roger's support, and during both of them Anacletus issued privileges to several south Italian churches.

He was still, therefore, very much functioning as 'the pope' for south Italian churchmen during the mid-1130s, even if by this stage for very few others.[75] While Roger was prepared, in October or November 1137 to host talks between representatives of the two rival popes, and to provide at least the appearance of an open-minded desire to end the schism, it is striking that even at this late stage he did not abandon Anacletus, asking that the cardinals on each side give him written details of the original election in 1130 for him to consider on his return to Sicily, and that both send one of their number to accompany him. (This was at a time when the supporters of Innocent had long since abandoned arguing about the rights and wrongs of the election, preferring simply to claim that their pope had the overwhelming support of the Christian world and was indubitably the worthier of the two candidates).[76] One cannot help but suspect that the king's procrastination was intentional. With his fortunes on the mainland once again in the balance after the German invasion of 1137, it would have suited Roger to appear to be wavering in his support for 'his' by-now discredited pontiff, if only to calm the churchmen supporting Innocent while he once again took control of the mainland provinces. Not least among these was Abbot Bernard of Clairvaux (Pope Innocent's principal propagandist), at

---

74 *Roger II Diplomata*, 133–8 no. 48. Brühl (1978), 58–9.

75 Loud (2007a), 227–8.

76 Bloch (1986), ii.955–7; Stroll (1987), 93–9, 136. A more unpleasant aspect of this was the explicitly anti-Jewish propaganda directed against Anacletus, for which *ibid.*, 160–8.

whose initiative these talks took place.[77] But whether the king seriously intended to abandon Anacletus, even then, must be open to doubt: in the event he did not, and (at least according to Falco) was even prepared to recognise a successor to Anacletus. We do not know enough of what went on during these diplomatic exchanges to make a definitive judgement, but from the king's point of view the sticking point must surely have been whether Pope Innocent would recognise the legitimacy of the new kingdom – which he only did when forced to do so in July 1139.

The civil war of the 1130s

Although the legacy of his alliance with Anacletus continued to make relations with the papacy problematic for King Roger years after the schism was concluded, the problem of the two popes was not at first a significant issue in southern Italy. Indeed during the first year of the schism Anacletus spent over six months in the south (September 1130– March 1131), travelling through the principality of Capua and Apulia, issuing privileges to quite a few churches, especially the archbishoprics, which he wished to confirm in obedience to him, and holding a council at Canosa in November.[78] And, as described above, the Prince of Capua and his cousin Count Rainulf, later the leaders of the struggle against the king, were prepared to go to Rome to support Anacletus in 1131. The papal city of Benevento also, at this stage, recognised Anacletus as the legitimate pope. The schism therefore only became an issue in southern Italy after large-scale revolt against Roger broke out there in 1132. Neither the schism nor the new kingdom's external enemies created this opposition, which stemmed from the same forces, and generally the same people, as Roger had defeated in 1128/9, though, once what was effectively a south Italian civil war broke out in 1132, naturally the king's opponents sought help wherever they could, including the pope that Roger opposed.

The necessity to enforce his authority over the reluctant mainland provinces meant that King Roger's actions followed more or less the same pattern every year (but one) from 1127 until 1140. Each spring

---

77 It was probably during these talks that Bernard wrote to his monks at Clairvaux, claiming, as was his habit, to be in southern Italy 'reluctantly', dragged there 'by the prayers of the Church and of secular princes', *Letters of St. Bernard*, 214–15 no. 146. We ought to take these remarks, by the twelfth century's most inveterate ecclesiastical busybody, with a large pinch of salt.

78 *Italia Pontificia* viii.38 no. 40.

he arrived on the mainland with an army to wage a summer campaign, and each autumn he would retire to Sicily, leaving garrisons in the main towns and selected strongpoints to maintain his rule. In the early years he crossed the Straits of Messina and marched north through Calabria, probably utilising the old Roman *Via Popilia*. Subsequently, apart from in 1133, he travelled by sea to Salerno; from which port he almost invariably departed back to Sicily in the autumn. Usually he would arrive about May, finish the campaign and withdraw by October; in 1132 he was somewhat later, only returning to Sicily in early December – this was necessary in that Roger had then to remain on the mainland to retrieve the situation after his defeat in a pitched battle at Nocera on 25 July 1132, although even a relatively short voyage so late in the year was very unusual. These summer campaigns were explicable both because of the difficulty and expense of keeping large forces of troops mobilised for longer periods, and because of the problems of both marching, and even more important sailing, during the winter months. So, for example, in 1133 'before the inclement winter should prevent it, he took ship and returned to Sicily'. (Falco dated this journey to 21 October, although we have a charter which suggests that this must have been on or after 24 October, when the king was still at Salerno, but the difference of a few days is hardly significant).[79] Sailors hardly ever sailed in the Mediterranean during the period from November until the end of March.[80] The only year when Roger may not have campaigned on the mainland was 1136, when he was, seemingly, victorious and only the blockade of Naples disturbed the peace of the mainland. The maintenance of this blockade and the governance of the mainland could for this year be left in the hands of the king's lieutenants.[81] Then, in 1137, with

---

79 *Al. Tel.* II.53 [below, 97, 208]; *Roger II Diplomata*, 89–91 no. 32. Idrîsî, for example, noted that ships were accustomed to pass the winter anchored at Trapani, *Idrîsî. La première géographie de l'Occident*, 319.

80 Goitein (1967), 316–17.

81 *Al. Tel.* III.36, suggests that Roger intended to return to the mainland in 1136 to attack Naples, but Falco's brief account of this year does not mention a campaign by the king. The charter evidence too is extremely sketchy. There are only three royal documents for the period, all originally issued in Greek to Sicilian recipients. In March he issued a privilege for the monastery of Holy Saviour, Messina, of which a Greek text survives. (It would anyway have been most unusual for him to begin a campaign this early). The other two are more problematic. On 28 April he made a donation to the nurse of his son Henry; and before the change of indiction in September he issued a privilege to the Greek monastery of St Philip of Fragalà. The former survives only in later copies; the latter has been lost, though it is mentioned in a later document of this monastery from March 1145, itself surviving only in later Latin translation, Caspar (1904), appendix nos. 108–10, 191. On 10 October he was definitely in Palermo, when he issued a privilege for the Hospital of St John, *Roger II Diplomata*, 119–23 no. 43. The consensus among modern historians is

the invasion of the *regno* by the German emperor, Lothar, the pattern varied, in that Roger then did not seek to meet the (very large) imperial army in battle, relying on his garrisons to hold it up and frustrate it, and he only came to the mainland in September, once the imperial army was withdrawing, to recover what had been lost, returning to Sicily right at the end of the year. Thereafter the traditional timing reappeared. In 1139, for example, so Falco tells us, the king arrived at Salerno on 25 May and embarked from there for Sicily on 5 November.

To begin with, Roger's attitude towards those who opposed him was quite moderate. His aim was above all to be recognised as the legitimate ruler of southern Italy, first as duke and then as king. To that end he sought the surrender of those who opposed him and their fealty, but rarely exacted other penalties. When, for example, Tancred of Conversano surrendered in August 1129, the king returned his lands to him, and even though Alexander of Telese said that Roger particularly disliked Count Roger of Ariano, and the latter was one of the last mainland nobles to submit to him, nevertheless he was allowed to keep most of his extensive lands, even if he had to surrender two *castra* as the price of recovering the king's grace.[82] Before Roger became king the only disobedient noble subject to exemplary punishment was his cousin Robert de Grandmesnil, a baron from Calabria – that is, someone who was already one of Roger's vassals – who lost his lordship and was forced into exile, after deserting Roger's army at the start of the 1129 campaign, before it had even entered Apulia. Even then, Alexander's account (our only one for this incident) not only says that Roger first tried to persuade him to stay with the army by promises of future reward, but seems to imply that it was Robert's truculence and his threats to return to Normandy that exhausted the duke's patience. Furthermore, while Robert's subsequent revolt did not save his lands, and Alexander writes of the duke's 'fury' at this behaviour, he does not mention any other punishment apart from Robert's loss of his lordship, which had already been decided.[83]

But if Roger was unwilling to tolerate any disobedience from someone already under his authority, he was more flexible when faced with

---

that he did not campaign that year, e.g. Caspar (1904), 180; Clementi (1991), 335. Matthew (1992), 49, simply says that Roger's movements in this year 'remain a mystery'.

82 *Al. Tel.* I.18, 23. In southern Italy, the word *castrum* usually denoted a fortified village rather than a castle. In this case, charter evidence clearly reveals the two *castra*, Paduli and Montefusco, to be centres of habitation.

83 *Al. Tel.* I.17, 20–2.

those from Apulia who had opposed his takeover, and even recognised the pretensions of Grimoald to be hereditary Prince of Bari.[84] Roger was equally flexible, or merciful, in gaining the obedience of mainland towns. Not only was he prepared to make concessions to the Salernitans in 1127, a very necessary step to secure what was to become his principal base on the mainland, but even towns that opposed him, like Troia in 1128–9 and Amalfi in 1131, seem to have escaped unscathed provided that they surrendered and recognised his authority – and even if, as in both these cases, he had been forced to undertake a major siege to subdue them. One or two places were not so lucky, notably Nardò which was sacked by Roger's army in 1129, but although the author of a brief set of Lucanian/south Apulian annals that were appended as marginal notes to Romuald's chronicle complained about the excesses of the Muslim troops in Roger's army, what occurred was hardly unusual when a town was taken by storm.[85] By contrast those towns which agreed to surrender came off lightly.

The most striking example of this came in 1132, when Bari fell to the king after a short siege – according to Falco, surrendered by its citizens who abandoned their prince. Grimoald and his family were sent as prisoners to Sicily – Alexander says he went in chains. However, in return for their surrender, the king made generous concessions to the citizens. He, or rather his representatives on his behalf, swore to a lengthy list of terms guaranteeing the rights and privileges of the town: promising to respect the rights of the city's churches, not to appoint outsiders as archbishop, as head of any principal monastery of the city or as a city judge; to allow the citizens their own laws and customs, especially on inheritance; not to levy taxes on them; not to exact military service without their consent; not to install a royal citadel in the town; and, perhaps most important from their point of view, not to punish anyone for the recent insurrection apart from six named persons. A final clause said that, if the king installed one of his sons as prince, the son would swear to observe these terms.[86] The similarity of many of these terms to those granted by Honorius II to Troia in 1127 is striking. Roger appears to have offered similar, if less

---

84 In November 1130, Pope Anacletus granted the Archbishop of Bari *inter alia* the right to consecrate Prince Grimoald and his sons, *Cod. Dipl. Barese*, i.80–1 no. 42. As Houben (2002), 53, notes, this must surely have required Roger's consent.

85 Below, 253.

86 *Cod. Dipl. Barese*, v.137–9 no. 80. It was considered demeaning or improper for kings to swear oaths in person, especially to subjects; a view based on Christ's disapproval of oath-taking in Matthew, v.33–7.

generous, terms to the citizens of Trani in 1133 – by then his policy was changing, but one should note that Trani does not appear actively to have opposed the king, so he was still prepared to offer concessions, though he had the town's defences demolished. Urban customs were already well-established in many towns of southern Italy, and the king was prepared to tolerate them if his rule was accepted.[87]

By 1132, he was less forgiving to nobles who opposed him, hence the arrest and dispossession of Grimoald of Bari and Count Godfrey of Andria, both of whom had joined the coalition formed against him in the spring of that year. Yet there are some apparently puzzling features of the rebellion that broke out then. Most notable of these is the series of incidents that led to the revolt of Count Rainulf of Caiazzo, the king's brother-in-law, who soon became the real leader of the king's enemies.[88] Both Alexander and Falco attributed the breach with the king to a quarrel between the count and his wife Matilda, the king's sister, though the two chroniclers differed about the reason for this: Falco attributed it somewhat vaguely to the 'many insults and injuries' (*convicia multa et afflictiones*) the count had inflicted on his wife, while Alexander referred specifically to his seizure of her dower lands. The thirteenth-century Ferraria chronicle claimed that Matilda complained to her brother that her husband had taken a mistress – but, though this author used the chronicle of Falco, this piece of information was not from Falco. Alexander also referred to attempts by the count's brother to claim the town of Avellino and the nearby *castrum* of Mercogliano for himself. Alexander implied that this was a blatant act of aggression and it seems he was correct, for there is nothing in the quite abundant charter evidence for these two places to suggest he had ever held them. It would appear that Matilda's desertion of her husband took place during, and took advantage of, his absence in Rome during the summer

---

87 *Al. Tel.*II.49. Martin (1980), especially 88–96; Oldfield (2009), 74–7. The privilege for Trani no longer exists; however, that the king did give such a charter to Trani can be inferred from a later privilege of his eldest son Duke Roger of Apulia in June 1139, *Roger II Diplomata*, 237–8, appendix no. I.

88 Most authorities follow Chalandon (1907) in calling Rainulf the Count of Alife, though Caspar (1904) rather perversely referred to him as Count of Avellino, a title he certainly never used and was never referred to by. While the *Liber Pontificalis*, ii.322, called him Count of Airola, both he and his father in their own charters generally used the formula 'Count of the Caiazzans and of many others', Gattula, *Accessiones*, 222–3 (January 1105); *Le Pergamene dell'Archivio Vescovile di Caiazzo (1007–1265)*, ed. C. Salvati, M.A. Arpago *et alii* (Caserta 1983), 46–8 no. 7 (April 1117), 57–9 no. 13 (April 1129). His father Count Robert also sometimes described himself as 'Count of Sant'Agata and of many other towns', *Cod. Dipl. Aversa*, 15–16 no. 10 (1097); *Chron. S. Sophiae*, ii.734–6 (August 1099). But a title they did not use was 'Count of Alife'.

of 1131.[89] What is more puzzling is Roger's refusal to return his sister to her outraged husband, even though the consequence was to drive him into rebellion. Was this simply love for his sister, as Alexander suggested? Or did he hope to use her and her children as hostages, or bargaining chips, to ensure the count's good behaviour? For Rainulf had already opposed Roger not once but twice, and showed clear signs of his ambitions first in seeking overlordship over Count Roger of Ariano, his major local rival in the Benevento region, and then in trying to gain lordship over the ducal town of Troia. If so, the king appears to have miscalculated spectacularly. However, one should add that Falco, by postdating the origins of the quarrel, implies that it blew up very quickly, while in fact it appears to have taken the best part of a year before hostilities arose, which suggests that it might at first have seemed as though the king's ploy was effective, and perhaps also that there were some quite lengthy negotiations before the revolt began in earnest.

The quarrel with Count Rainulf embroiled his cousin and nominal overlord Prince Robert of Capua. Alexander stressed this role of the prince – saying that the latter described Rainulf as his *homo* – although one should note that both Rainulf and his father had in reality been largely independent for many years, and in their documents tended to exalt their own God-given authority, while omitting the regnal years of the prince.[90] But once the prince became involved, then increasingly the conflict became a battle for Capuan independence. Whether, and how far, the rebellion of the prince and Count Rainulf was co-ordinated with that in Apulia by the counts of Conversano, the Count of Andria and the Prince of Bari is uncertain, nor indeed do the chroniclers' accounts make clear whether these Apulian nobles had actually rebelled, or whether the king was working off old scores (or eliminating potentially dangerous figures) by taking pre-emptive action against them. So, in Alexander's account, Count Godfrey of Andria met the king at Taranto (in May 1132) and was then arraigned before the royal court and forced to hand over most of his lands.[91] In at least one other case the chroniclers' account is clearly deficient. For while Falco said that Tancred of Conversano had rebelled, and Alexander had joined with Godfrey and Grimoald of Bari against the king, Tancred and his brother Alexander

---

89 *Falco*, 120; *Al. Tel.* II.13–15; *Chronicon Ignoti Monachi Cisterciensis Sanctae Mariae de Ferraria*, ed. A. Gaudenzi (Naples 1888), 18.

90 Loud (1981b), especially 199–207.

91 *Al. Tel.* II.18.

were two of the four noblemen who swore in the king's name to uphold the rights and privileges of Bari on 22 June 1132 (the other two being Count Geoffrey of Catanzaro, a cousin of the king, and Robert, lord of Gravina). So at that point, presumably, Tancred was either still in favour, or hoped for forgiveness from the king. It must have been within a few days of this that the king made him a substantial payment in return for his renouncing his lands and agreeing to go on pilgrimage to Jerusalem.[92] And why was he not simply sent a prisoner to Sicily as was Grimoald? Was this because he was, as yet, not so fully compromised or committed to opposing the king, or because while Brindisi was in the king's hands, others of his and his brother's territories were not, and drastic measures would have encouraged rather than quelled resistance? Here it is difficult to do more than speculate. However, Alexander said somewhat later in his account that after Roger's defeat at Nocera in late July, Tancred, Alexander and Godfrey of Andria 'now openly betrayed the king' and made a sworn alliance with the Prince of Capua and Count Rainulf.[93] One might well interpret this to mean that earlier the king had been taking action against men whom he distrusted, but who had not yet risen in open and avowed rebellion.

What is clear is that from 1133 the nature of the campaign changed. Thereafter the king took increasingly brutal reprisals against those who opposed him. Towns were sacked and some, like Troia in 1133 and Aversa in 1135, laid waste and their surviving inhabitants driven out to settle elsewhere. Captured opponents were sent in chains to Sicily or sometimes executed, undoubtedly as a salutary example to others. Such reprisals, as with the hanging of five of the leading men of Troia when that city was captured in August 1133, were clearly designed to intimidate others to surrender without resistance, and during that same campaign the king had the walls and towers of other towns demolished, even if they had not openly opposed him, to ensure that resistance in the future would be futile. It is notable that, while Falco was always an opponent of the king, his criticism remained relatively measured until 1133 – from then onwards it became strident, comparing Roger to Nero, the quintessential 'bad' Roman emperor, whose name was a byword for wickedness in the Middle Ages, and accusing him of 'such cruelty towards Christian people as has scarcely or ever been heard of in our century'.[94]

92 *Al. Tel.* II.21.
93 *Al. Tel.* II.36.
94 Below, 205.

Cruel as such tactics may have been, they appear to have worked. From 1133 onwards, until the German invasion four years later, Apulia remained securely in the hands of the king. The campaigns of 1134–5 were conducted in the principality of Capua. Twice it appeared that King Roger had defeated his opponents: in the autumn of 1134 when Count Rainulf surrendered to him while the prince of Capua was in exile, and again in autumn 1135 when the king decided formally to annex the principality and appoint one of his sons as prince in place of the existing dynasty. By that stage only Naples was holding out against him, and it must have seemed as though its surrender was only a matter of time. It was during this latter period, probably over the winter of 1135/6, that Alexander of Telese wrote his account of the king's campaigns, concluding with a series of prophetic dreams showing that the king's triumph was divinely ordained, and referring in the concluding address to the king to 'the story of your most famous victory'.

That this was not, in fact, the end of the civil war, and that Roger was unable completely to subjugate southern Italy in the mid-1130s, was due to three factors. First, the death of the king's wife early in 1135, and what would appear (reading between the lines) to have been his consequent breakdown, sparked rumours of his death and a renewed revolt on the mainland. This not only encouraged Prince Robert of Capua and Duke Sergius of Naples, neither of whom had submitted to the king, but led Count Rainulf to a renewed bid for independence. Admittedly, the 1135 revolt was speedily defeated, and the ringleaders took refuge in Naples. But it appears to have been this renewed revolt that led the king to seek a more permanent solution to the problems on the mainland, redistributing confiscated lands to new holders, replacing the Prince of Capua with one of his sons, and starting to create an administrative structure for the mainland by appointing justiciars and a chamberlain in the principality of Capua and in Lucania.[95] By doing so, he also created irreconcilable enemies, who could no longer hope for pardon and re-integration into the new kingdom. Secondly, Naples, which the king had been unable to take, remained as a base for these men. And the invasion by the German emperor, encouraged by Innocent II and his supporters, cost the king much of his hard-won gains of the preceding years.

Roger wisely did not seek directly to oppose Lothar's invasion. Given the size of the German army and the hazards of pitched battle, this would have been risky indeed. The king preferred to rely on his

---

95 For the latter, Gattula, *Accessiones*, 254; Jamison (1913), 411–12 no. 6.

garrisons to hold up the invading forces. The attempt over the winter of 1136/7 by the chancellor Guarin and other royal officials to take over the abbey of Montecassino, described by the contemporary account of Peter the Deacon [*below, 281–5*], was clearly so that the monastery on its mountain top could act as one such fortress to obstruct the invasion. (Whether they were already aware that the imperial army was to be split into two, with Henry of Bavaria leading one part along the *Via Latina*, while Lothar led the other along the Adriatic coastal route to join the *Via Traiana* in Apulia, we do not know.) In the event, the emperor spent five months in southern Italy – much longer than the imperial expeditions a century earlier – but his time in the region was inevitably finite, not least because his army would wish to return home, particularly so since he had actually entered northern Italy in September 1136, and thus the whole expedition took some fifteen months. While the imperial army penetrated as far south as Melfi and Lagopesole on the border between southern Apulia and Lucania, and secured the surrender of almost all the towns of coastal Apulia, it never threatened Roger's original dominions of Calabria and Sicily. But by removing the royal garrisons in Apulia, re-installing Prince Robert in his principality and appointing Rainulf as Duke of Apulia, and thus the titular as well as the *de facto* leader of the opposition, Lothar's expedition had reinvigorated the king's opponents in the south. It seems that some nobles who had hitherto supported the king or perhaps stayed neutral, notably counts Roger of Ariano and William of Loritello, had now joined the rebels.[96] Though Roger recovered the southern part of the principality of Capua relatively quickly once the German army had withdrawn, apart from Count Rainulf's own lands, and the rest of the principality in a rapid attack in the summer of 1138, most of the campaigning over the next two years took place in the region around Benevento and in northern Apulia, areas which before 1137 had been in the king's hands. And in October 1137, soon after the German withdrawal, Roger suffered a second defeat in a pitched battle, at Rignano near Monte Gargano, where according to Falco three thousand men were killed.

What is notable about all this is how little damage even such a bloody check as Rignano did to the king's cause. Indeed, in one respect it may have made King Roger's task easier, since the death in this battle of Duke Sergius of Naples, apparently without leaving an heir, facilitated his subsequent takeover of that city. In the months after the battle

---

96 Roger of Ariano was on the king's side in 1135, *Al. Tel.* III.6. For the Count of Loritello's surrender to Lothar, see below 272.

Count Rainulf was able to recover some of his own lands and towns, but not much else. And once he died, on 30 April 1139, and the king secured recognition of his rule by Innocent II in July of that year, the opposition to him collapsed.

This raises a further question about the chronicle accounts of the civil war of the 1130s. Falco did list the names of several nobles from the Benevento region who like Duke Sergius died fighting for the king at Rignano. But, for the most part, he and Alexander (and the much briefer account in the 'Romuald' chronicle) went into more detail about the king's opponents than about his supporters. Only when Alexander discussed the measures taken to defend the Terra di Lavoro and blockade Naples late in 1135 did he name several counts 'in whom he [*Roger*] had particular confidence', two of whom were royal relatives from Sicily.[97] Yet it is clear that the king must have had considerable support on the mainland. Thus within a month of his defeat at Nocera in July 1132, the king was able to travel without difficulty from Salerno and across northern Apulia to Bari, something which seems unfeasible unless he had considerable local support in the intervening territory.[98] Similarly, the king's forces in the principality of Capua were reinforced by troops from Apulia in April or May 1135, even before the king himself had arrived from Sicily to lead the campaign.[99]

We cannot therefore assume that, because the Prince of Bari, the Count of Conversano and the Count of Andria opposed the king, all the other nobles of Apulia did so too. Above all, although none of the narrative sources expressly state this, it seems clear that the king enjoyed the almost complete support of the principality of Salerno, in which, apart from the border district around Nocera, he never had to wage a campaign. It is notable too that the most important noble of this region, Count Nicholas of the Principato, survived in possession of his lands into the 1140s – he can hardly therefore have opposed the king, and we must presume had furnished him with assistance. Yet the narrative sources do not mention him. Nor do the chroniclers always furnish much information about the changes of side of some participants; indeed, the fact that they changed sides at all usually only emerges by inference. We can rarely deduce the circumstances of such vacillation. For example, Count Roger of Ariano, who had resisted the king in 1128/9, was captured fighting on his side at Nocera in 1132 –

97 *Al. Tel.* III.32–3.
98 *Al. Tel.* II.34. Clementi (1991), 300–1.
99 *Al. Tel.* III.6.

something revealed not by the chroniclers but in a letter describing the battle.[100] He appears still to have been on the king's side in 1135, but then Count Roger joined the rebels once more – probably during the German invasion of 1137, although Falco makes no mention of this. He was sent as a prisoner to Sicily in 1139 and his county taken into the king's hands. Similarly Duke Sergius of Naples, who opposed the king in the early 1130s and rebelled again in 1135, when Roger allegedly considered him 'absolutely unworthy of pardon',[101] then died fighting on his side in October 1137. Falco once again says nothing of when and why he rejoined the king's side – we only know from 'Romuald' that it was when the German army withdrew late in the summer of 1137. Valuable as the accounts of our narrative sources are, we need to be aware of their limitations too.

However, the account in Falco's Chronicle, in the imperfect form in which it survives, ceases abruptly at the end of 1140; thereafter we have to rely on the brief (and probably much later) account of the 'Romuald' chronicle, whose author concentrated on external affairs, the fragments of the last parts of Falco's work preserved by the later Ferraria Chronicle, a few pages of the late twelfth-century Casauria Chronicle, devoted exclusively to the affairs of that monastery, and the relatively few and decidedly problematic royal charters from this time. In that light, one realises how significant the accounts of Alexander and Falco are, for all their faults. But before we turn to examine the sources translated in this book in more detail, some brief discussion is needed of the later years of the king's rule, from the time when he was fully in command of his kingdom in 1139 onwards.

The consolidation of the kingdom

Despite the death of Anacletus and the capitulation of his short-lived successor, the legacy of the papal schism still caused problems for the new kingdom. Innocent II excommunicated Roger again at the Second Lateran Council of April 1139; although Falco's account suggests he was prepared to negotiate with the king, at first the pope's insistence on recovering the inheritance of his ally Robert of Capua, with whom he had worked closely for some years, prevented agreement. It was only after the pope's disastrous invasion of the kingdom had come to grief

---

100 *Falco*, note 155.
101 *Al. Tel.* III.10.

that he was forced formally to recognise it, at Mignano in July 1139.

The bull Innocent issued purported to create the kingdom of Sicily *de novo*, for of course the actions of the 'antipope' Anacletus could not be recognised. Nevertheless, the terms of the 1139 bull ['Roger II and the Papacy', document no. 6] were not dissimilar to those issued by his rival nine years earlier. The bull of Innocent offered a somewhat more elaborate rationale for the creation of the kingdom, recalling the services of Roger's father and uncle, Duke Robert, to the Church and the Faith, citing the precedent of Roger's investiture as duke by Pope Honorius, and repeating the legend, to which Alexander had made reference, that Sicily had once long ago been a kingdom. This last element reflected, one suspects, the influence of the king and his advisers – as indeed may the praise of Robert Guiscard and Count Roger as a justification for the kingship, for the same sentiments were expressed less than a year later in the foundation charter for the king's palace chapel, a document which was (as described above) redacted in luxury format as a symbol of the prestige of the new monarchy.[102] Although, in contrast to the 1130 bull, no mention was made of Naples or of military service from Benevento (which both pope and king must have been aware was highly unpopular in that city), otherwise almost all the king wanted was granted: possession of the principality of Capua, the hereditary status of his title and possession of the kingdom that was not expressly linked to fealty or homage, though they were required. The same, very light, *census* as in 1130 was stipulated. The royal title, king of 'the kingdom of Sicily, the duchy of Apulia and the principality of Capua', was the same as that already employed by the royal chancery.[103]

Yet while the bull of investiture of 1139 might have been thought to legitimise the new kingdom and its ruler, and to place Roger's relations with the victorious party in the papal schism on a secure footing, this was far from being the case. Relations with the papacy remained fraught until William I's treaty with Pope Adrian IV at Benevento in 1156, and the kingdom remained under threat, for several reasons. The bitterness engendered by the schism, shown by the summary deposition of the former Anacletan cardinals in 1139, even those who had transferred to Innocent while the schism was still under way, continued. Several south Italian archbishops consecrated by or closely associated with Anacletus were also deposed.[104] The way Innocent had been forced to bless the

---

102 *Roger II Diplomata*, 133–7 no. 48, at 136.

103 Brühl (1978), 81–4; Houben (2002), 132.

104 Loud (2007a), 228–9.

kingdom's creation, in return for his freedom from captivity, particularly rankled. 'Romuald' claimed that when Innocent II died in 1143 his
successor refused to recognise the peace treaty with King Roger, and as
late as 1154 Adrian IV caused grave offence when he addressed William
I as 'lord of Sicily' rather than 'king'. It was even alleged that the papal
ban on the consecration of new bishops in the kingdom in the later
1140s (which appears to have really occurred) was 'as a penalty for the
captivity of Pope Innocent'. This last may be questionable, but the fact
that the charge could be made at all, by a well-informed source writing
as late as the 1160s, shows how deep the memory of this event was.[105]
Nor were the popes enamoured of what they considered King Roger's
high-handed control of the Church within the kingdom: the Ferraria
Chronicle, here almost certainly based on the now-lost concluding
pages of Falco, said that Innocent II complained about royal appointment of bishops in 1142, and received no satisfaction from the king.[106]
In addition, the reorganisation of the Sicilian Church by Anacletus
was left in limbo after 1139, and the status of the two new bishoprics
founded in 1131 in doubt – which was of considerable concern to the
king since he intended one of these, Cefalù, to be his burial church. The
king's expansion of his power into the Abruzzi in 1140 was seen as the
annexation of papal territory, even if the popes had never in practice
exercised effective rule in this region – which was anyway traditionally part of the kingdom of Italy, and thus imperial territory. Finally,
the papacy had since the conclusion of the Investiture Contest in 1122
enjoyed good relations with the German emperors; the popes wished
this state of affairs to continue, not least since they hoped for imperial
assistance to quell the increasingly strident claims of the citizens of
Rome for self-government, and the rulers of Germany remained impla-
cably opposed to the new kingdom of Sicily.[107]

This is not to say that relations between the Curia and King Roger were
uniformly hostile. There were periods of détente – 'Romuald' claimed that
the king welcomed the election of Cardinal Gerard of S. Croce as Lucius
II in 1144, but (significantly) the two found difficulty in concluding
a treaty because of the hostility of the cardinals. Lucius eventually
concluded a seven-year truce with the king while complaining about
his 'violence', clearly referring to the invasion of the papal Campagna

---

105 *Romuald*, 237 [*Tyrants*, 222]; *The Historia Pontificalis of John of Salisbury*, ed. and trans.
    M. Chibnall (London 1956), 66. Kamp (1980), 121–4.

106 Below, 247.

107 Loud (2007a), 156–60; for the annexation of the Abruzzi, also Clementi (1968), 191–7.

by the king's son ['Roger II and the Papacy', document no. 7]. In 1150 Eugenius III concluded a treaty with the king, which went some way to solve the outstanding issues, although the pope refused to accept the king's homage and the status of the Sicilian bishoprics remained in doubt, an issue which was in fact to remain unsolved until 1166. Furthermore any goodwill thus created was rapidly dissipated by the coronation of the king's only surviving son as monarch in his father's lifetime at Easter 1151, an action which taken without papal permission or knowledge was deemed to infringe the pope's rights – and suggests that lingering resentment at the very existence of the kingdom was still present at the Curia.[108] The papacy remained committed to its alliance with Germany, re-asserted at the Treaty of Konstanz in 1153, although one should note that this alliance was as much directed against the Roman Commune as it was against the kingdom of Sicily ['Roger II and the Papacy', document no. 8]. But it was only after the German nobles had made clear that they would not take part in another invasion of the Sicilian kingdom, at the imperial coronation of Frederick Barbarossa in 1155, and the new king, William, had demonstrated the strength of the kingdom by defeating the combined attack of internal rebels and a Byzantine expedition, that the papacy finally concluded a lasting peace with the King of Sicily in 1156.[109]

The rebellion of 1155 occurred after King Roger's death, and from 1139 onwards the kingdom enjoyed internal peace. In the words of 'Romuald', the king

> established peace and good order in his kingdom, and to preserve that peace instituted chamberlains and justiciars throughout the land, promulgated good laws which he had newly drafted and removed evil customs.[110]

Here the chronicler encapsulated the internal reforms undertaken by the king to consolidate his authority and the continuance of his kingdom. Nevertheless, this succinct summary was a considerable simplification of a complex process. Whereas 'Romuald', for example, implied that the establishment of a provincial administration on the mainland, staffed by chamberlains and justiciars, came only after peace had been established in 1139/40, the process had begun while the conflict was still under way, although this may not have been the case in every region. Some of

---

108 *Historia Pontificalis of John of Salisbury*, 69. See Kamp (1980), 121–30.

109 *The Deeds of Frederick Barbarossa. Otto of Freising and his Continuator Rahewin*, trans. C.C. Mierow (New York 1953), 154–5. Loud (2007a), 163–6. For the treaty of 1156, *Tyrants*, 248–52.

110 Below, 259.

the personnel employed had been officials of the previous rulers; thus Joscelin, the chamberlain appointed in the principality of Capua in 1135 had previously served Prince Robert, and John Mansellus, chamberlain in the Valle Caudina in 1139, was a former chamberlain of Duke William of Apulia.[111] These officials were invariably drawn from the local nobility – the justiciars, responsible for the maintenance of law and order, judgement in serious criminal cases and in disputes between landholders, were generally men of greater social importance than chamberlains, who administered the crown lands, collected revenues and presided over minor civil cases. Thus the son of Henry de Ollia, justiciar in the Monte Gargano region in the 1140s, was promoted to comital rank by William I c.1156/7,[112] as was the nephew of Gilbert de Balbano, justiciar in southern Apulia and constable in the principality of Salerno,[113] while by contrast the royal chamberlains included men like Leo of Foggia, recorded as offering the service of a single knight to the king's army. But not all the justiciars were particularly powerful: for example Lampus of Fasanella, a justiciar in the principality of Salerno, from an aristocratic Lombard family, held only five knights' fees.[114] Nor was the overall structure of the royal administration on the mainland fully established under King Roger. The king's sons may have been nominal rulers of the various provinces to which they held title, but it would appear that the royal chancellors, successively Guarin (d.1137) and Robert of Selby (d.1151) played an administrative role on the mainland, and the latter in particular may have had overall charge of the provincial administration, given that after 1140 the king's visits to the mainland became increasingly rare. But it was only under William I that institutional provision was made for a mainland viceroy, with the creation of the office of Master Captain of Apulia and Terra di Lavoro. Nor is it clear that there were fixed territorial jurisdictions for justiciars and chamberlains until the reign of William II.[115]

The central royal administration at Palermo was also reformed and developed. Prior to 1127 most of the functionaries of this nascent

111 For Joscelin, *Al. Tel.* III.32, note 156; for John: Cava, *Arm. Mag.* F.34 (January 1125); Loud (1996), 336–7.

112 Cuozzo (1984), 97–8.

113 Cuozzo (1980), especially 64–5, 72–3. Takayama (1993), 107, is wrong to suggest that Gilbert himself ever had a comital title.

114 *Catalogus Baronum*, arts. 401, 442 [below, 335, 340]. For chamberlains generally, Jamison (1913), 384–5.

115 Jamison (1913) remains fundamental for this subject; see also Matthew (1992), 242–54; Takayama (1993), 78–81, 104–14, 159–60. There is a very brief, but clear, survey by Houben (2002), 147–9.

administration had been Greek, and the counts' documents had been almost all written in Greek. Once the king had extended his rule to the duchy of Apulia, it became necessary to issue charters in Latin, although for some years only one full-time Latin notary was employed by the royal chancery – from 1132 to 1136 this was a man called Wido. However, in the last decade of the reign, when the chancery was under the day-to-day direction of Maio of Bari (later William I's chief minister) there seem to have been at least three chancery notaries writing in Latin, and after 1144/5, when there was a flurry of activity as previous privileges were confirmed or revoked, the number of Greek documents became markedly fewer.[116] At about the same time, and quite possibly connected with the revocation of privileges, George of Antioch re-organised the royal court on the model of the Fatimid caliphate of Egypt, with which the Sicilian court had for some time enjoyed friendly contact. His principal innovation was to create the *Dīwān al-Taḥqīq al-Maʿmūr*, the office of land administration, which kept registers of boundaries, fiefs and serfs, and generally oversaw property matters on the island of Sicily, and perhaps also Calabria. The officials who staffed this organisation, and played an increasing role in overseeing the crown's finances, were mainly Arabic-speaking Christians – most of whom were probably converts from Islam. These Arab officers might also undertake other duties, as for example Philip of Mahdia, who commanded the fleet which captured Bône in 1153.[117]

The evidence for these changes to the central administration at Palermo comes in only a handful of documents in Greek and Arabic, especially the latter, the interpretation of which has until recent years proved very difficult. 'Romuald' said nothing of these developments; although, if the archbishop himself was the author of this section of the chronicle, he must with his close connections to the court have had knowledge of them – he was indeed briefly one of the royal *familiares*, the governing council of ministers, in 1168.[118] The chronicler did, however, refer to 'the promulgation of laws'; for which we have more evidence, though

---

116 See now, Loud (2009), especially 792–4; Brühl (1978), 38–51. On the documents of Roger I, Becker (2004); on the Greek documents, von Falkenhausen (1998); on the revocation of privileges, Johns (2002), 115–43. The inquiry into privileges may have been limited to Calabria and Sicily, although the phraseology of the documents concerned implies that it was of general application. The survival of documents from the royal chancery is notably poor: in total 200 charters of King Roger, 114 originally in Greek (many of which now exist only in Latin translation), 86 originally in Latin, no less than 37 of which are forgeries.

117 Takayama (1993), 81–93; Johns (1993); Johns (2002), 193–8. For Philip, below 266.

118 *Tyrants*, 214; for the *familiares*, Takayama (1989); Takayama (1993), 98–101, 115–25.

once again its interpretation has pitfalls. We possess two manuscripts containing copies of laws issued by King Roger: Codice Vaticano Latino 8782 and Codice Cassinese 468. The former dates from the mid-to-late twelfth century, the latter perhaps from the early years of the thirteenth. Both collections are arranged as though they were law codes. While they contain much of the same material, they are not identical: the Cassinese collection shows textual variations, sometimes abbreviates particular sections, significantly re-arranges the order of the various laws or 'assizes', omits some material and also introduces seven new assizes.[119]

It was once generally believed that the Vatican collection, thought to be the earlier of the two (it contains a preface suggesting that this was a group or code of laws promulgated at an assembly), represented the laws issued at Ariano in August or September 1140, when according to the chronicler Falco, the king promulgated an edict on withdrawing the existing coinage and issuing new money.[120] However, as Léon-Robert Ménager pointed out, this is unlikely, since there is nothing in the Vatican laws about coinage, and Roger held a number of assemblies on the mainland, notably one at Silva Marca, near Ariano, in July 1142.[121] Ménager indeed went further, and suggested that, far from being contemporary law codes or collections of Roger's assizes, these two manuscripts were in fact retrospective collections, to identify and preserve what laws Roger may have promulgated, compiled as part of the preliminary work for the issue of the much more extensive law code of Frederick II, the *Liber Augustalis* of 1231.[122] But, while most of these laws did appear in the 1231 code, correctly ascribed to King Roger, and the French scholar was undoubtedly correct in his scepticism about the so-called 'Assizes of Ariano', both the probable date of the Vatican manuscript and a number of contemporary or late twelfth-century references to individual laws suggest that these collections were actually earlier than the thirteenth century, and indeed probably do date from the time of King Roger. In particular, the list of pleas of the crown appended to the Cassinese text was repeated in a charter of Count Hugh of Molise of July 1153; and the account by 'Hugo Falcandus' of the trial of Hugh's successor as Count of Molise, Richard of Mandra,

119 For discussion, Zecchino (1980), 109–19; Trombetti Budriesi (1992). Strictly speaking, only the Cassinese MS uses the word 'assizes', but for the sake of convenience the traditional usage will be retained here.

120 Below, 245.

121 *Roger II Diplomata*, 149 no. 53.

122 Ménager (1969).

early in 1168, made explicit reference to the law about judgments of the crown (assize xvii in the Vatican collection, assize 11 in the Montecassino one).[123] The presumption therefore is that the laws found in these two manuscripts represent genuine legislation of King Roger, and it seems probable from its format that the Vatican collection [*translated below, pp. 314–28*] was indeed a set of laws issued by the king at some stage in the 1140s, albeit not at Ariano in 1140. But it is also possible that we are dealing with not an original version of such a code but a copy of such a version. Some textual variations between the Vatican and Montecassino MSS would be explicable if each collection was derived at second hand from another manuscript. Whatever the case, these were laws issued by the king.

However, relatively little of this legislation was original. The majority of Roger's laws, about two thirds of those found in both manuscripts, were reworked versions of the Roman Law of Justinian.[124] Since all these citations came from only three sections of the *Corpus Iuris Civilis* – *Codex* books I and IX and *Digest* book XLVIII – it might at first sight seem as though these were derived not from full use of the *Codex* and *Digest*, but from a collection of extracts. However, it has been suggested that these laws were drawn up by one or more Bologna-trained jurists, who would undoubtedly know the entire *Corpus*, and some of this wider knowledge is reflected in the laws. This in turn suggests that the king was at pains to secure the services of outstanding legal experts,[125] though it may be noted that three of the laws here also appeared in the *Prochiron Legum*, a tenth-century south Italian compilation of Roman Law; so these at least were apparently already known in the Byzantine provinces of southern Italy.

The scope of this legislation of King Roger is limited: it concerns only the powers of the Crown, the rights of the Church, treason, some criminal activities and marriage – seen here, following Byzantine precedent, as a matter where the state should legislate rather than the Church. This has led some commentators to suggest that

123 Jamison (1929), 557, document no. 2; *Tyrants*, 194.

124 Caspar (1904), 251.

125 Pennington (2006), to which my attention was drawn by Hubert Houben, who refers to this article in Houben (2010), 191–2. Pennington suggests that the compilers were aware of the legal work on procedure of Bulgarus at Bologna, completed between 1123 and 1141, and that this reinforces the case for the promulgation of these laws under King Roger, and probably not much later than the traditional date of 1140, not least in that the work of Bulgarus was rapidly superseded. But, *contra* Pennington, one must doubt whether King Roger would have had access to Bolognese lawyers before his peace with the papacy in 1139.

this 'code' (if it is a code at all) must be incomplete;[126] but few if any medieval law codes were comprehensive. Furthermore, we should note that the first assize expressly confirms 'the usages, customs and laws' already existing among the different peoples of the kingdom, provided these did not contravene this new royal law. So we should view this royal legislation as being intended as a supplement to the law already present: that of the Lombard kings, French customary law, the Roman Law already observed in the former Byzantine provinces (and, for example, at Amalfi) and Islamic law administered locally, at least on minor issues, by the headmen of Arabic communities in Sicily under the supervision of a royally-appointed *qāḍī*.[127] What this legal 'code' does show, though, is both the commitment to law and equity that 'Romuald' praised and a stress, derived from Byzantium, on the prerogatives and authority of the Crown. It is no coincidence that in the surviving ceremonial portraits of Roger, notably the mosaic in the church of S. Maria dell'Ammiraglio in Palermo, a church founded by George of Antioch, on the one surviving golden seal appended to a document and on his new coinage of 1140, the king was shown wearing the ceremonial regalia of a Byzantine *basileus*.[128] And it was his use of this title that led the peace negotiations with the Byzantine Empire to break down c.1143/4, for the Emperor Manuel Komnenos refused to tolerate another ruler using the title which, in his eyes, pertained to him alone.[129] Byzantium was thus a powerful influence on the ethos of the new Sicilian kingship. Another mark of this influence was that the king took advantage of the brief period of détente with the emperor at Constantinople in the early 1140s to obtain skilled craftsmen to make mosaics for his new cathedral at Cefalù and his palace chapel.[130] But while the assizes that laid such stress on the powers of the crown were derived from Roman Law, one might suggest that it was the continued opposition on the mainland, which had taken so long to overcome, that made such an autocratic ethos seem necessary to the monarch.

---

126 Caspar (1904), 257–9; Houben (2002), 142–3. It should be stressed that Houben (2002), 135–47, is the most balanced consideration of the problems of this legislation. Matthew (1992), 184–8, also has an interesting discussion, but he considers the two MSS were private collections of royal laws and not in any sense 'codes'.

127 Johns (2002), 292–6.

128 Houben (2002), 113–22. The gold seal (*bulla*) is attached to *Roger II Diplomata*, 45–8 no. 16, issued to the abbey of Cava in February 1131.

129 *The Deeds of John and Manuel Comnenus, by John Kinnamos*, trans. Charles M. Brand (New York, 1976), 75–6.

130 Demus (1950), 51–8.

The struggle in the 1130s, and the continued external threat thereafter, had further administrative consequences. Even while the conflict was going on, the lands of rebels were being confiscated, and in some cases re-granted to men loyal to the Crown. Thus the county of Conversano was given, if we are to believe Alexander of Telese, to the king's brother-in-law Adam, in 1134, and then, as the charter evidence makes clear, to another brother-in-law, Robert de Bassonville, although the lands of the post-1134 county were less extensive and more scattered than those held by the original comital family.[131] Similarly, in 1135 the title of Count of Boiano was transferred from Count Hugh, a former royal supporter who had joined the rebels, to Robert son of Richard, who had already been granted some of Hugh's lands.[132] After 1139 there were further and more extensive changes among the higher nobility. Three of the largest and most powerful mainland counties were suppressed, those of Ariano, Caiazzo and Loritello, and their lands taken into the hands of the king. He confiscated the county of Manopello in the Abruzzi and re-granted it to a Calabrian baron, Bohemond of Tarsia. The counts of Aquino in the principality of Capua, a family of Lombard aristocrats who had survived the Norman conquest, were deprived of their comital title, as punishment for submitting to Emperor Lothar in 1137, although they were allowed to retain their lands.[133] Somewhat later, but before 1144, Count Hugh of Boiano was restored to his former position, although his county was now known by his family name of Molise, and Robert's son Richard transferred to a new county of Civitate.[134] Other new counties were created at Avellino on the southern border of the principality of Capua, and Conza, Marsico and Policastro in the principality of Salerno, the latter two given to relatives of the king. A lordship which was later treated as a county was also established at Gravina in southern Apulia c.1141, and entrusted to a relative of Roger's mother.[135] About 1146 the county of Andria, confiscated from the rebel Count Godfrey in 1132, was given to a Norman called Richard of Lingèvres, apparently newly arrived from his homeland.[136] Finally,

---

131 *Al. Tel.* III.28, and note 149 for the problems with this passage. For the later county, Martin (1993), 775–6.

132 *Al. Tel.* II.64, IV.2.

133 Scandone (1956), 68–72.

134 Jamison (1913), 418–19 no. 17; Jamison (1929), 531.

135 Martin (1993), 777. The lords of Gravina used the title of margrave, derived from their north Italian family, the margraves of Savona, e.g. Cava, *Arm. Mag.* H.21–2 (both November 1155).

136 Cuozzo (1984), 159–61, 181–2; Cuozzo (1995), 281.

at some stage before 1150 a part, though only a small part, of Count Rainulf of Caiazzo's lands was used for a new county called Alife, given to a Count Mauger;[137] and c.1152 another new county was created, with its *caput* at Montescaglioso in Lucania, and entrusted to a scion of an existing noble family from Lecce in the Terra d'Otranto with close connections to the Crown.[138] In addition, several counts ruling over lordships already existing in 1130 were encouraged to marry women from the royal family, clearly as a means of fostering their loyalty to the king.[139] Thus over some years there was a wholesale re-organisation of the most important lordships on the mainland, with the intention of creating a group of feudatories entirely loyal to the king, and none with quite such a consolidated powerbase as Rainulf of Caiazzo had once possessed.[140]

It should be stressed that these 'counties' were not all consolidated territorial units, nor were they necessarily intended as administrative jurisdictions. Counts might sometimes act as justiciars, but then they were specifically designated as justiciars in addition to their comital titles.[141] Although the county of Molise, for example, comprised a substantial and coherent block of territory, the lands and fiefs of other counties were quite scattered. The county of Andria had two distinct foci, one on the coast of northern Apulia and the other 100 km to the south in the Val d'Agri in Lucania.[142] It would seem the intention was to create a network of counts rather than of counties, and the purpose of this, apart from distinguishing the top rank of the nobility and enhancing the prestige of loyal supporters, was primarily military. These counts were the men who would lead the defence of the *regno* in case of invasion, a threat which, given the continued hostility of the German Empire and the intermittent threat from Byzantium, was always to be considered. The appointment of new counts and the creation of new counties was

137 *Catalogus Baronum*, arts. 959–60. Cuozzo (1984), 266–7.

138 Antonucci (1933); Martin (1993), 778. Godfrey of Montescaglioso's sister had been mistress of the king's eldest son, Duke Roger of Apulia, and mother of his children Tancred (the future king) and William; Reisinger (1992), 9–12.

139 For example, Hugh of Molise married an illegitimate daughter of the king c.1150; Count Richard of Avellino (holder of a new county, but from a long-established family) married the king's great-niece Magalda.

140 A full study of the aristocracy after 1130 is urgently needed. For brief discussions on which the paragraph above is based, Cuozzo (1989), 105–20; Martin (1993), 768–79.

141 In the dispute between the abbot of Montecassino and the bishop of Aprutium in April 1148, the royal justiciars present included Count Bohemond of Manopello and Count Robert of Aprutium, Jamison (1913), 458–61 no. 5.

142 Martin (1993), 774–5.

part of the creation of a consolidated system of military defence, which was recorded c.1150 in the *Catalogus Baronum [for extracts from which, see pp. 329–54 below]*. The Catalogue was a list of fief holders and the military obligations they owed from their fiefs, from Apulia, the principalities of Salerno and Capua, and the Abruzzi region which Roger and his sons had conquered in 1140. But it was not, or not simply, a record of existing military obligations, now made subject to the Crown.[143] It was the creation, for the first time, of a unified system of military service owed to the king, and many of the military quotas were new – and quite possibly the subject of negotiation. Obviously they reflected the realities of the existing situation – there was no point in having quotas that fief holders could not fulfil, and no doubt they reflected the number of vassals who had actually been enfeoffed. There may have been some financial element in these obligations – fief holders were presumably liable to the payment of aids – but given how few obligations were recorded as fractions of a knights' fee, the military system was not, as that in Anglo-Norman England was, primarily a means of raising money to hire troops.

One of the peculiarities of the *Catalogus Baronum* was that it revealed two different quotas of service, a 'normal' quota and the *augmentum* – usually twice the knight service of the first quota, and sometimes adding the service of further soldiers, generally sergeants and occasionally crossbowmen. The most plausible explanation for this is that the first figure was the usual quota when military service was required from feudatories, and the *augmentum* was the emergency *arrière ban* to be demanded if the kingdom was invaded, when every armed man available would be needed.[144] Whether all of these would be men directly dependent on the feudatory, or if they would in some cases include other people whom he might pay, is impossible to say. Where the feudatory's fief was very poor – as for example with John de Boctio, who had twenty commended men at Castiglione in the territory of Troia and who with the *augmentum* offered one knight – the presumption would be that the property owner would themselves provide the service. In one other similar instance this was explicitly stated.[145] The Catalogue invariably says that someone 'offered' or 'proffered' (*obtulit*) so many knights and other men for the *augmentum*: this would suggest that there

---

143 As, for example, suggested by Matthew (1992), 145–6.

144 Cahen (1940), 119; Jamison (1971), 4–7; Cuozzo (1995), 271–2.

145 *Catalogus Baronum*, arts. 400 [below 334], 990: 'Hugolecta holds a poor fief in Tocco (Caudina), and with the *augmentum* he offers himself'.

was some negotiation about the figure, and quite possibly – certainly when the *augmentum* service was a large figure – that it represented an approximation of the forces available.

The 'Catalogue of the Barons' is a source of great importance for the study of the kingdom of Sicily in the mid-twelfth century, both for the military system and for the structure of landholding in the mainland provinces, but it is a problematic text. The only manuscript, which was destroyed in 1943, dated from more than a hundred years after the original compilation and was therefore a second- or third-hand copy of that original. There were omissions and inconsistencies, and one whole section was repeated,[146] although these faults were more probably those of the scribes of the earlier archetype(s) than of those who copied the late thirteenth-century manuscript.[147] Several churches were named without any contingents being listed for them; indeed, the significance of the Church in the new military system is especially hard to assess. The Casauria chronicle would certainly suggest that royal authorities were keen for churches to contribute to the defence of the kingdom. Bohemond, the new Count of Manopello, brusquely informed the abbot of Casauria: 'the lord king has many people who pray in his kingdom, but he does not have many to defend it'.[148] But why were some bishoprics and abbeys included in the Catalogue, but not others from the same region?[149] In some cases men named were actually vassals of others, but the overlord was not named – this applied to a number of fiefs held from churches, as in the case of John de Boctio (mentioned above), who held his exiguous property from the abbey of Montecassino.[150] And what in particular makes the Catalogue a pitfall for the unwary student is that it was revised in the minority of King William II, c.1167/8, probably during an overhaul of the provincial administration at that time,[151] but revised partially and imperfectly, so that in some places the names of new feudatories have been inserted, but in many others not. (The footnotes draw attention to such problems in the entries translated in this book).

If the compilation of the Catalogue was primarily intended to provide for the defence of the kingdom, the organisation of its military

---

146 *Catalogus Baronum*, arts. 1053–84, repeated by 1230–62, with one extra entry and minor textual variations.

147 Jamison (1971), 29–30.

148 Below, 301.

149 Cahen (1940), 127–32; Loud (2007a), 340–62.

150 Below 334, note 27.

151 For which, Takayama (1993), 143–57.

resources was also necessary to facilitate more aggressive activity, for after 1140 King Roger sought actively to expand his power. Admittedly, the conquest of the Abruzzi region might be seen as partly defensive, creating an extended northwards defensive zone to obstruct any potential imperial invasion and denying this province as a possible base from which political exiles might attack the kingdom,[152] but Roger had already, even before becoming king, used Sicilian naval power to increase his dominions, launching an attack on Mahdia in North Africa in 1123, albeit unsuccessfully, and claiming the North African coast to be a sphere of Sicilian influence in his treaty with Savona in 1127.[153] The continuing political and economic weakness of the coastal towns of Tunisia and Libya, with their hinterlands under pressure from Bedouin and Berber nomads, and their increasing dependence on Sicilian grain, encouraged further intervention.[154] The island of Jerba was captured in 1135 (partly to eliminate a base for pirates), and that of Kerkenah in 1145. Sicilian expeditions took the ports of Tripoli in 1146, Mahdia, Sfax and Sousa in 1148, and finally Bône a few months before King Roger died. Other towns along this coast paid tribute to the Sicilian king. Attempts were made to conciliate the Muslim inhabitants of these towns, and to encourage the indigenous Christians who were still living there at that period, but no real effort was made at settlement. Some towns such as Bône were left in the hands of local governors, under a very loose suzerainity.[155] One suspects that the primary motive for these conquests was economic, to levy dues and taxes from these ports and their inhabitants, to safeguard the lucrative trade between North Africa and Sicily, and if possible to control the aptly-named Narrows between Tunisia and Sicily.[156] But whether even in the short term these economic gains were very significant is doubtful – certainly Idrîsî remarked that, while the trade of Mahdia had been immense, 'in our times it has begun to diminish'.[157] Unfortunately the Latin sources say little about these expeditions; most of what is known about them comes from later Arabic historians, notably the Mosul chronicler Ibn al-Athir (d.1233).[158]

---

152 Feller (2002), 64–70.

153 *Roger II Diplomata*, 24–8 no. 10.

154 One symptom of the economic weakness of the region was the debasement of its currency from the mid-eleventh century, Goitein (1967), 235–6.

155 *Idrîsî. La Première Géographie de l'Occident*, 193.

156 For relevant literature, *Romuald*, below 260, note 18.

157 *Idrîsî. La Première Géographie de l'Occident*, 184.

158 This account is of value since its author used a much more contemporary history by an

Similarly the renewal of hostilities with Byzantium in the late 1140s was directed not at conquest of the empire proper – far stronger under the Komnenan emperors than when Robert Guiscard attacked it at the nadir of Byzantine fortunes in 1081 – but at the capture of strategic bases, control of the mouth of the Adriatic, and plundering raids on coastal cities. Corfu and Cephalonia were taken in 1147, but this in turn led the Venetians to intervene on the Byzantine side, and to the eventual recovery of these islands by the eastern empire. To what extent the Sicilians hoped for long-term strategic and territorial gains, or whether the intention was to force the Byzantine emperor to make peace and recognise the validity of the new kingdom, which Manuel Komnenos eventually did in 1158, is a good question. Certainly these naval campaigns, and the North African conquests carried out during the same few years, show the considerable strength of the Sicilian fleet; and, though we know nothing of where the military contingents to capture and garrison these conquests came from, they suggest that the kingdom's military recruitment was working effectively. These ambitious operations were also possible because the German ruler Conrad III was absent during 1147–9 on the Second Crusade, ensuring that the kingdom of Sicily would not face an attack from the north. Once the crusade was over, Roger took pains to entertain one of the most powerful German princes, Duke Welf VI of Spoleto, on his way home from Palestine, and bribed him lavishly to rebel against Conrad.[159] But the compilation of the *Catalogus Baronum* at precisely this time suggests that the potential threat from the north was still a major concern.

The king's legacy

King Roger died on 27 February 1154, at the age of (probably) 58. 'Falcandus' attributed his end to exhaustion after his immense efforts, and over-indulgence in sexual activity, although whether the king was any more prone to the latter than most medieval rulers is impossible to know.[160] Contemporary observers, even those who disliked him, were

---

émigré from Tunisia, Abd al'Azīz ibn Shaddād, which was known to a number of Arabic historians, including the important fourteenth-century chronicler Ibn Khaldūn, Bresc (1999), 349.

159 *Historia Welforum Weingartensis*, MGH SS xxi.468–9 cc. 27–8.

160 *Tyrants*, 59. To judge by his reaction to his first wife's death, he was genuinely fond of her, Houben (2002), 65–6. The later Muslim historian Ibn al-Athir claimed that he died of diphtheria, aged 80, *The Chronicle of Ibn al-Athir for the Crusading Period, from al-Kāmil fi 'l-ta'rīkh*, Part 2, *The Years 541–589/1146–1193: The Age of Nur al-Din and Saladin*, trans. D.S. Richards (Crusader Texts in Translation 15: Aldershot 2007), 64.

unanimous in praising his great talents as a ruler and his unremitting endeavour in building his new kingdom. Even Falco, who hated him, so far forgot himself as at one point to describe Roger as 'sagacious of mind and far-seeing in counsel'.[161] In retrospect, his role as the ruler who brought peace and unity to southern Italy was greatly appreciated by his subjects – for example John Berard, the chronicler of Casauria, who contrasted the era of peace in the Abruzzi after 1140 with the time of chaos and violence that preceded Roger's takeover.[162] The creation of a new and powerful kingdom, despite so many obstacles, was no mean achievement.

Nonetheless, a dispassionate view of King Roger's legacy might suggest that the kingdom which he bequeathed to his only surviving son in 1154 still faced considerable problems, and, impressive as Roger's state-building had been, his work had been left incomplete. Apart from good relations with the king of France, Sicily was diplomatically isolated, facing the hostility of both eastern and western empires, and the papacy, and uncertain relations with the maritime cities of northern Italy.[163] Exiled noblemen posed another significant threat, and in 1155–6 this combination of enemies came close to toppling William I from his throne. The newly conquered North African coastal towns were restive under Christian rule, and their Sicilian garrisons were soon to be swept away by the Almohads of Morocco. There were also internal tensions in the kingdom, among the aristocracy and on the island of Sicily, where immigration from the mainland was changing the demographic and religious balance. It may be, too, depending how one interprets the hints in 'Falcandus' and 'Romuald', that the king in his last years was either becoming less tolerant towards his Muslim subjects or was relaxing his grip and allowing court factions to flourish. Either explanation might explain the downfall and execution of Philip of Mahdia about three months before the king himself died.[164] In fact, despite the snide and unfair criticism of 'Falcandus', who loathed them, the survival of the kingdom of Sicily owed much to the military and diplomatic successes of King William I and his minister Maio of Bari, who were able to overcome the crisis of 1155–6 and within a very few years negotiate long-term

---

161 During the negotiations between representatives of the rival popes at Salerno in November 1137, below 229.

162 Below, 298.

163 Reuter (1996), especially 53–4, where he went so far as to compare attitudes towards Roger and his kingdom (somewhat fancifully) to modern ones towards Saddam Hussein.

164 Below, 245–8. Houben (2002), 109–13; Johns (2002), 213–18.

peace agreements with the papacy, Byzantium and the Italian maritime cities.[165]

An analysis of the contemporary historians

The major south Italian narrative texts of the twelfth century present significant contrasts, not just (as has already been made clear) in their attitude to the king, but also in their authorship, purpose, mode of composition and subsequent transmission.

The work of Alexander, Abbot of the monastery of Holy Saviour near Telese, fits the medieval definition of a history, in being a coherent historical work written apparently at one time, with a clear theme, the inevitability and divinely-approved rightness of the king's triumph. (The work of Falco of Benevento is, by contrast, a chronicle, written as a series of year-by-year entries.)[166] Alexander wrote probably in late 1135/early 1136, before Emperor Lothar's invasion of the *regno*, to which it makes no reference. We know nothing of the author apart from what we can glean from his work, though he was either dead or had resigned by November 1143, when his successor Stephen, presumably the man whom Alexander mentions as prior in 1135, was in office.[167] The first record of his abbey comes in 1075, when its abbot attended a synod of Archbishop Milo of Benevento;[168] it has been plausibly suggested that the house was founded shortly before this date, probably by Rainulf, younger brother of the first Norman Prince of Capua, Richard I, grandfather of the Count Rainulf who so plagued Roger II. The ruins of the abbey church appear to date from c.1100 or slightly earlier; the French-inspired Romanesque design is not altogether surprising since the abbot at this time, John, was a former monk of Bec, but it also supports the theory that this house was a Norman foundation.[169]

Alexander was a man of some learning, within conventional monastic parameters. His reading included familiar monastic texts like the *Libri Miraculorum* of Gregory of Tours, the works of John Cassian and probably

165 Loud (1999c).

166 On the difference between 'histories' and 'chronicles', see especially Guenée (1973).

167 *Roger II Diplomata*, 166–70 no. 59. *Al. Tel.* III.36.

168 *Chronicon S. Sophiae*, ii.686.

169 Cielo (1995), especially 35–62. For Abbot John, see *The Life of St. Anselm, Archbishop of Canterbury, by Eadmer*, ed. and trans. R.W. Southern (London 1962), 106. Before October 1100 he became Cardinal Bishop of Tusculum, which suggests that he was highly esteemed, and implies his monastery was, Hüls (1977), 141.

works of Christian history such as those by Eusebius and Orosius, but although his Latin included some classical syntax and usages, probably derived from standard schoolbooks, the only classical texts to which he seems directly to refer are the *Aeneid*, the *Georgics* and perhaps Seneca's *Naturales Quaestiones*; and it is quite possible that his occasional quotations from these works may have come from a *florilegium*.[170] As with most monastic authors his principal citations were Biblical. His work ends with a series of dreams foretelling Roger's inevitable victory, but it is not clear that he directly knew the standard text on this, the commentary of Macrobius on Cicero's *Somnium Scipionis*.[171]

Alexander saw Roger as divinely appointed to bring peace and order to southern Italy. His motives may have been in part dictated by the interests of his monastery, for he contrasted King Roger's generosity and favour towards that house – to whose confraternity he and his son Anfusus, now Prince of Capua, were admitted – with the depredations of Count Rainulf, who had taken even the ornaments from the high altar in his desperation to pay his troops.[172] But by his own account he was also writing at the request of Roger's sister, and Rainulf's estranged wife, Matilda. This may explain why Alexander's attitude to the count remained equivocal, treating his repeated revolts with discretion and without outright condemnation until quite late in his account, when finally – describing the aftermath of the renewed revolt in 1135 – he attributed a bitter speech to the king, stigmatising Rainulf for his repeated breaches of faith: 'how can his good faith be trusted any more after he has violated his oath?'[173] Here Alexander repeated one of his principal themes. Not only was Roger doing God's work in bringing peace to southern Italy, but those who opposed him were guilty of perjury, since they had all sworn fealty to him, in some cases several times. Hence they merited God's punishment, just as in the Old Testament King Zedekiah had merited the retribution inflicted upon him by Nebuchadnezzar; and, where Falco criticised the king's cruel treatment of rebel nobles or towns, Alexander adopted a didactic tone: 'So let the wise reader now reflect how great a crime it is to commit the sin of perjury'.[174]

170 *Al. Tel.*, introduzione, xviii–xxiv, xlv.

171 While noting similarities with Macrobius in Alexander's treatment of these dreams, Clementi (1991), 186–7, also points to differences in vocabulary, which suggest that Macrobius had not been used directly.

172 *Al. Tel.* II.65, III.29–30.

173 *Al. Tel.* III.10.

174 *Al. Tel.* II.46.

Apart from the position of Count Rainulf, and the involvement of Pope Anacletus (which Alexander solved by omission), the other main problem facing the abbot was the reverses that Roger suffered, especially his defeat at Nocera in 1132. How could these be explained if the king's victory was part of the divine plan? The answer, the abbot said, was to teach the king humility and so make him a better Christian ruler, rendering him worthier to receive God's help, a theme to which he returned in his *alloquium* to the king that ended the History.[175]

The prophetic dreams recounted in Book IV, presaging the triumph of the king and showing the folly, as well as sin, in opposing him, were thus an integral part of, and a fitting conclusion to, the account. They were, however, omitted from the first published edition of Alexander's History, in 1578, by Jeronimo Zurita y Castro (1512–80, otherwise notable as the historian of the medieval kingdom of Aragon), and from the five subsequent editions, all entirely derivative from the *editio princeps*, until published for the first time in the 1960s.[176] And it was only with the modern edition by Ludovica de Nava (1991) that the *alloquium* addressed to the king was placed in its correct position, as the conclusion to the work, rather than at the front, as (apparently) a second preface, as it had been in the earlier editions.[177] The restoration of the full text of the History reveals it to be a much more coherent, and complete, work than was thought when historians only had access to the incomplete and misleading earlier editions. Yet while it also shows the History to be even more propagandist than was earlier believed, it certainly did not serve as such. Only one manuscript survives, Barcelona, Biblioteca Central, ms. 996-8-III, fols. 97–140, dating from the later fourteenth century, part of a composite manuscript containing several other historical works, including the Deeds of Count Roger by Geoffrey Malaterra. This manuscript may have come from the library of S. Nicolò d'Arena, Catania, which Zurita appears to have plundered when he visited Sicily in 1550.[178] How this may have been copied, we do not know – but the work can never have had much distribution. Massimo Oldoni has suggested that it was intended to be read aloud

---

175 For a development of these arguments, Loud (2007b), 30–6.

176 Reichenmiller (1963); Clementi (1965), apparently published independently of each other. Clementi (1991), 179–80, noted that Zurita had originally prepared these chapters for publication; were they eventually omitted because they were considered simply to be instances of popular superstition? Zurita was appointed official historian of the Crown of Aragon in 1548, and became secretary to the privy council of Philip II in 1567.

177 Oldoni (1980), 277, for example, was still under the impression that the *alloquium* began the work, which was where it was located in the edition he used, that in Del Re (1845).

178 *Al. Tel.*, introduzione, xi.

in public, but if so it is possible that the monks of Telese were the only audience.[179]

The transmission of the Chronicle of Falco of Benevento was somewhat different, but equally tenuous. No medieval manuscript survives: there are four manuscripts (one of which is a copy of another, and a third is only a part), but the earliest of these dates from c.1600, while the *editio princeps* of 1626 appears to have been taken from a separate manuscript, not from any of those now surviving. All these different versions may well have been derived from a single archetype, since by the time they were copied the work was already incomplete, missing both beginning and end.[180] This is clear, not just because of the abruptness of the beginning and end, both in the middle of a sentence, but because another work, the thirteenth-century chronicle of the Cistercian monastery of S. Maria di Ferraria, in the diocese of Teano, which utilised (albeit rather carelessly) Falco's Chronicle, contains further material relating to Benevento [*translated below, pp. 130, 247–9*]. This extra matter suggests that Falco began his work with the papal siege of the city in 1101, and probably concluded it in 1144 with an entry on Benevento during the pontificate of Celestine II, who died in March of that year. (The Ferraria monks may have obtained a copy of Falco's chronicle from the monastery of St Maria in Gualdo, near Benevento, an eremitic house reformed by the Cistercians in 1220).[181] This date of 1144 also fits with what is known from charter evidence of Falco's career. The chronicle reveals that its author was a notary, who in 1133 was promoted to be one of the city's judges by Innocent II's rector of Benevento, Cardinal Gerard (later Pope Lucius II). Ten charters written between November 1107 and January 1128 by a notary Falco can be identified, and a further six witnessed by him as judge between July 1137 and September 1143. The practice at Benevento of notaries and judges authenticating their documents with their sign manual shows that these were all written or witnessed by the same man, and the dates clearly fit the career revealed by the author of the chronicle. Furthermore, in September 1161 a notary called Trasemundus, son of the late judge Falco, made two separate donations to the abbey of St Sophia in the city: since this Trasemundus was the notary who wrote all six of the charters witnessed by Falco as judge, it appears that he was the son of the chronicler.[182]

179 Oldoni (1980), 279.

180 Gervasio (1939), 76–102; D'Angelo, *Falcone*, introduzione, lii–lv.

181 *Chron. Ferraria* [above, note 89], 37. Schmeidler (1905–6), especially 37–8, 47–8, 53–7.

182 Loud (1993), 184–5, and 194–5 for a consolidated list of these charters.

The last mention of Falco the judge in September 1143 fits with the apparent conclusion of his chronicle in 1143/4, and it is probable that he died soon afterwards. But, in contrast to the History of Alexander, it is unlikely that his chronicle was written as a single continuous work around that time – it would, indeed, appear to have been written in several stages, probably beginning during the early 1120s, and continued on and off (though not necessarily always contemporaneously, or in individual entries for each year) until 1143/4. This seems clear from the variations in coverage of individual years, from changes in the author's attitude to various protagonists and from occasional interjections which suggest either that Falco was writing soon after the events he was discussing, or alternatively in other passages that he was writing some time after the events in question. Thus when he described the double papal election of February 1130 he went on to mention immediately afterwards the council which Innocent II celebrated at Rheims, which took place in October 1131. This entry must therefore have been written some time later. On the other hand, in 1133 he mentioned the Prince of Capua's journey to Pisa to seek help against the king, and added: 'how he dealt with the Pisans has not yet come in any detail to our notice', which suggests that he was writing this passage soon after that time.[183] The early parts of the chronicle, up to c.1119, appear to be a compilation from several sources, not all of which were necessarily written by Falco. The sketchy annals up to 1112 would seem to be a variant of the independently surviving annals from the abbey of St Sophia, two other versions of which are known.[184] The description of events at Benevento in 1113–14 and the pope's dealings with Archbishop Landulf II, which culminated in the latter's deposition in October 1114, may also have originated as an independent account, while the brief notice at the end of the 1114 entry to the archbishop's deposition (which had already been described in detail) would appear to come from a separate annal. Falco also seems to have had access to an account of events at Rome and the papal court from 1116–19. It was probably about 1122 that Falco combined all this material, adding some of his own comments and memories. Thereafter he continued the chronicle in stages. The first of these was probably completed in 1125 – hence the relatively full entries for this year and those immediately preceding, in contrast to the one sentence on the death of the Emperor Henry V for the next year, which appears to be an afterthought. (One

183 Below, 184, 207.
184 Bertolini (1923), 39–42, 74–6.

should note, incidentally, that Falco began the year on 1 March, which was probably general practice at Benevento).[185]

Until 1125 the focus of Falco's chronicle was the city of Benevento and events there, even though he also included material about the papacy, the overlord of the city (perhaps originally by another hand). But from 1127 onwards, while Benevento was still the centre of his account, the arrival of Roger of Sicily on the mainland led Falco increasingly to broaden his narrative to discuss the latter's campaigns and to spread his geographical focus to take in what took place in Apulia and the Terra di Lavoro, as well as the immediate environs of his native city. But he was still writing in stages, rather than either year by year or in one go in the early 1140s. Although some entries may have been written contemporaneously, that for 1130 seems to be somewhat later, whereas the section for 1133 would appear once more to be more or less contemporaneous. The brief entries for 1135–6, which contain nothing about Benevento, were probably written in 1137, after Falco returned from exile – to which he refers, in studiously impersonal terms, when describing Benevento's surrender to Pope Innocent and Henry of Bavaria in May 1137.[186] However, the long section for 1137 (the longest yearly entry in the whole chronicle) may have been written in two stages, the majority of this immediately after the event in the autumn of 1137, and the last part, describing the conference at Salerno to solve the papal schism, somewhat later. Certainly the hostile attitude to King Roger in the main part of this entry seems at variance with the more measured comments during the account of the Salerno conference. The sections thereafter may have been written relatively contemporaneously.[187]

Falco's style is not quite as artless as it might seem at first reading, despite such banalities as his repeated 'What more?', or 'O reader, if you had been there', and even the latter does remind us that he was an eyewitness to much of what he described. His writing was generally unadorned, although he occasionally employed alliteration to emphasise particularly dramatic moments in the narrative, such as the earthquake at Benevento in 1125 and the speech of Honorius II against Count Roger at Capua in December 1127. As a notary, he had mastered the rhythmic clauses of the *cursus*, which he often varied quite artfully

---

185 Poole (1934), 6–7, who notes that this practice was otherwise only known at Venice.

186 Below, 219.

187 The arguments summarised here have been discussed in much greater detail in Loud (1993), especially 180–91. The modern editor of the Chronicle, D'Angelo, accepts this reconstruction, at least in general terms, *Falco*, introduzione, xxi–xxv.

in his chronicle, employing not just the three 'standard' elements of the *cursus* (*velox*, *tardus* and *planus*), but also the *trispondiacus* rhythm.[188] But although clearly familiar with the Bible, for example comparing the king's opponents with the Maccabees, his reading otherwise probably did not extend beyond local annals and hagiography.[189] Nevertheless, the chronicle is not only a most valuable and informative source for the reign of King Roger, but also significant as more or less contemporary with the work of Caffaro of Genoa as the first civic chronicle written by a layman in medieval Italy.

Two further contemporary, or near-contemporary, chronicles are also of considerable value for this subject, although neither is without its problems. These may be dealt with fairly briefly. The chronicle attributed to Romuald Guarna, Archbishop of Salerno 1153–81, is a 'world chronicle', from the Creation until 1178, concluding with a very detailed account of the peace conference at Venice that concluded the conflict between Pope Alexander III and the emperor, Frederick Barbarossa, and also finally ended the hostility between the German empire and the kingdom of Sicily; at this conference, Archbishop Romuald was head of the Sicilian delegation. As with other works of this type, the early parts of the chronicle are simply a compilation of existing authorities such as Orosius, Bede's *Chronica Minora* and Paul the Deacon's *Historia Romana*, as well as several Frankish sources.[190] The eleventh- and early twelfth-century sections are also a compilation, from local annals, notably from a version of the surviving Amalfi chronicle, and the section from 1080–1125 appears to have been primarily derived from a lost set of Apulian annals, perhaps from Troia.

The question remains how much if any of this chronicle was actually written or compiled by Archbishop Romuald, who was after all a busy metropolitan and a political figure of considerable importance in the kingdom. It has been suggested that the only section of this work that Romuald himself wrote was the account of the Venice peace conference, where he did expressly acknowledge his authorship.[191] However, the

---

188 *Falco*, introduzione, cxxxiv–v, cxxxvii–cxli.

189 *Ibid.*, cxliv–clxiv. D'Angelo wonders whether he might have read Paul the Deacon, for example, but it is hard to see any sign of this.

190 Matthew (1980), 258–67.

191 'All that is said above was indeed done, and no scrap of doubt or disbelief should be raised about it, since Archbishop Romuald II of Salerno, who was present and saw it, wrote this; and thus you should know it to be true testimony', *Romuald*, 293–4. Cf. Matthew (1980), 239–40.

three surviving manuscripts of this chronicle do preserve an otherwise original account of King Roger's reign, whoever the author may have been, which, although brief, is particularly useful in that it extends beyond 1140 when the chronicle of Falco in its present incomplete form ceases, until the end of the reign, as well as covering the reigns of Roger's son and (up to 1178) grandson.[192] The section of the 'Romuald' Chronicle after 1125 contrasts with what came before in at least three respects. First, while some dates are still given, the structure is less rigidly annalistic than in the previous part of the chronicle. Secondly, the geographical focus within the *regno* is on Salerno, not as hitherto Apulia, and finally the brief account of events after 1140 is as much concerned with external affairs as with those within the kingdom. Hence, while it discusses the Sicilian acquisition of the North African littoral, it also gives a brief account of the Second Crusade, and displays considerable interest in the papacy. These *were* matters that concerned the kingdom, but the focus is somewhat diffuse. Donald Matthew suggests that this section of the chronicle was therefore written at Salerno, probably after King Roger's death – since it involves some *ex post facto* justification of his policy, especially with regard to the papacy – and perhaps as late as 1177. This was grafted on to an earlier world chronicle, which may have been compiled in Apulia about 1125.[193]

The chronicle of 'Romuald' is also interesting in that two of the three manuscripts contain significant marginal additions concerning Roger's reign. The more contemporary is a group of entries on Roger's campaigns on the mainland in the years 1127–31, which appear to be derived from a separate (and quite possibly contemporary) set of annals, which seem to show a particular interest in the Bradano valley in the border region between Lucania and southern Apulia, and may be derived from that area. These are of considerable value in fleshing out the accounts of Alexander and Falco for this early period.[194] The other addition is an account of the trial and execution for apostasy of Philip of Mahdia, one of the king's Arabic Christian officials, shortly before the king's death, which may date from the early thirteenth century. Matthew dismisses this addition as 'a highly improbable story', though we know from Arabic sources that Philip was indeed tried and executed in November/December 1153. Others have given this version much

---

192 Romuald's account for 1154–69 is translated in *Tyrants*, 219–43.

193 Matthew (1980), 252–5, 267–9.

194 Clementi (1991), 270–7, 337–44 (giving the Latin text of these annals). These are trans- lated in the notes to *Romuald*, below 251–4.

greater credence, suggesting that even if it was written later it was
based upon a contemporary report.[195]

A purely contemporary south Italian witness to the reign of King
Roger comes in the closing pages of the Montecassino abbey chronicle,
as contained in the one and only manuscript of the full text of that
work, Cod. Cas. 202. The authorship of the later parts of this chronicle,
begun by Leo Marsicanus, later Cardinal Bishop of Ostia (d.1115), is
a complex and much-discussed issue, but is of little direct relevance
here.[196] There can be no doubt that this final section of the chronicle,
a lengthy discussion of the abbey's affairs in the years 1136–8, was
written by Peter the Deacon, who was at that time the librarian and
archivist of the abbey. Peter's account of these years was tacked rather
uneasily on to the earlier continuation of the abbey chronicle, much of
which was probably written by a monk called Guido, who was Peter's
teacher and mentor, but whose authorship Peter ungratefully tried
to conceal, mendaciously claiming in his prologue to Book IV of the
chronicle to have himself written the entire continuation from the point
in the account (in 1072) where Leo laid down his pen.[197] In fact, the
break between the different parts of the chronicle continuation is very
obvious, since the period between 1127 and 1136 is covered in two brief
chapters (Bk IV, cc. 96–7), before Peter began his detailed account of
the problems the abbey faced in 1136–7, first with the officials of King
Roger, anxious to ensure Montecassino's loyalty and incorporate it in
their defensive measures against the impending invasion by Emperor
Lothar, and then with Pope Innocent II, angry at the monks' earlier
support for his rival Anacletus.[198] Much of this section was taken up
with a lengthy, at times *verbatim*, account of a stormy meeting between
Abbot Rainald and a delegation of Cassinese monks and Innocent and
his *Curia*, in the presence of Lothar III, at Lagopesole in Lucania over
ten days in July 1137 [*not translated here*]. Peter based his description
of this meeting (written in the early 1140s) on an earlier propaganda
tract, 'The case on behalf of the Monastery of Montecassino', which he

195 Matthew (1980), 242; but cf. Caspar (1904), 432–3, who argued that it was based on an
    official record of Philip's trial; Houben (2002), 110–12; Johns (2002), 215–18; Metcalfe
    (2009), 166–9. By contrast, Chalandon (1907), ii.104, 166, seems to have been more
    sceptical as to the value of this account, while Garufi, in his edition of *Romuald*, 234 note
    2, suggested that this addition dated from c.1250 or later.

196 Bloch (1986), i.113–17, provides an excellent summary in English, while Cowdrey
    (1983), 239–62, adds valuable insights on the sources and composition of the first stage
    of the continuation to Leo's work. Hoffmann (1973) is, however, still fundamental.

197 *Chron. Cas.* 459.

198 For this, Bloch (1986), ii.960–9.

had written very soon after the event. In this account, he himself was the principal spokesman and defender of the abbey against the charges brought against it by Cardinal Gerard of S. Croce (the future Lucius II) and 'a certain Cistercian abbot' – almost certainly Bernard of Clairvaux, who was in the papal entourage at this time. But how much, or indeed whether any of this, was true is another matter. Claims that, for example, the emperor had specifically requested Peter to be included in the Cassinese delegation, or that Peter had somehow got the better of St Bernard in a debate about monastic customs, seem singularly implausible.[199]

Peter the Deacon's role as the alleged champion of his abbey is on a par with his notorious career as perhaps the most inventive and outrageous forger of the twelfth century, but that is hardly our concern here.[200] However, what the narrative in the chronicle of events before and after the Lagopesole conference does provide is a vivid account of the dilemma with which the abbey was faced in 1137 when the arrival of the imperial army threatened to overturn the recently established royal government in the south, and of the problems that the schism had left for south Italian churchmen. If the German sources, especially the so-called 'Saxon Annalist', show the expedition of 1137 from the viewpoint of the invaders, and Falco from that of their local allies, the Montecassino chronicle depicts it from that of the recipients, trying to safeguard their own interests in the face of conflicting pressures on them. Emperor Lothar, at least by Peter's account, proved surprisingly sympathetic to Montecassino: Pope Innocent did not, and the abbot elected with the connivance of the royal officials and the approval of Anacletus was the sacrificial victim. But the monks' choice of a German abbot to replace him (or perhaps Lothar's imposition of him) brought them the wrath of King Roger when the Germans withdrew, something which the abbey never quite lived down.[201] While the view from Montecassino may have been parochial, it does nonetheless provide an extra viewpoint of the crisis of King Roger's reign, albeit one in which the king himself is no more than a distant, largely offstage figure.

199 The *Altercatio pro Coenobio Casinensi* is edited in Caspar (1909), 248–80; *Chron. Cas.* IV.108–17, pp. 572–91. For these two specific claims, *Chron. Cas.* IV.108, 114, pp. 570, 587–8. The account of the debate with the Cistercian is considerably abbreviated in the chronicle from that in the *Altercatio*, 263–78.

200 For a helpful brief account of Peter's career and work, Bloch (1998), 15–28.

201 Thus several of the abbey's *castella* were burned during the campaign of 1139, others confiscated in 1140, and the abbey's treasures removed in 1143, *Annales Casinenses*, MGH SS xix.309–10. And a royal privilege to the abbey of 'December 1147' is actually a thirteenth-century forgery, *Roger II Diplomata*, 211–14 no. †74. Brühl (1978), 169–72.

Finally, one later monastic chronicle, from the Abruzzi abbey of St
Clement, Casauria, which was completed about 1182, gives a brief but
vivid account of the king's takeover of that region in 1140 as it affected
the abbey. Here the view of King Roger was much more favourable.
The Abruzzi in the early twelfth century was a disturbed and lawless
region, and the abbey of St Clement, an ancient and wealthy house
founded by Emperor Louis II in the 870s, tended to be a victim of the
acquisitive instincts of competing local nobles.[202] The king restored
order, and at least up to a point favoured the abbey, even if his agents,
the chancellor Robert of Selby and Count Bohemond of Manopello
were keen to make the abbey contribute to the defence of the kingdom.
According to the chronicler, the king intervened to protect the abbey
from their demands. Here, almost a generation after the king's death,
he was commemorated as a strong but pious ruler, who brought peace
and favoured churchmen. Alexander of Telese would have doubtless
concurred in this verdict.

202 On the region, Feller (1998), 746–63. On the Casauria chronicle, which was actually
   written in the margins of the abbey's chartulary, see Loud (2005), 106–28.

ABBOT ALEXANDER OF TELESE
THE HISTORY OF THE MOST SERENE ROGER, FIRST KING OF SICILY

Here begins the preface

Alexander, unworthy Abbot of the monastery of Telese, greets all those *and.*
believing in Christ. I think that it is not unsuitable if things once done
are recorded in writing for posterity. For it is acknowledged that there
is much in them that it is desirable either to imitate or to avoid. Even
acts of war, although they are recognised not to be good things, will
nevertheless be written down since these acts in some ways suggest,
indeed order, that they should [in future] be avoided, and that the bond
of peace be strong in us, because it is much more desirable and should
not easily be dissolved. I ought not to be blamed if I, a monk, have
taken up my pen and brought to the notice of posterity warlike deeds
which have happened in modern times, since even in old and holy histories many similar stories are told of Saul and David and other kings.
These are allowed to be read in every Church throughout the world
for the profit of those listening. I have therefore preferred from time
to time to turn away from the cares of monks without any sin rather
than that these deeds be suppressed in pointless silence and remain
utterly without fruit. Indeed, it was the continued request of Countess
Matilda, sister of King Roger and wife of Count Rainulf that led me *patron*
to finish this little work. Even though at first I wanted to escape her
petition because of the rules of my order, afterwards I regretted not
having accepted her request. For I thought that what had been asked
by her would undoubtedly not lack advantage for future centuries. Now
therefore the deeds of the said king are taken up to be written down to
be remembered for ever; first of all the deeds he did as a child, then after
he had received the honour of the county of Sicily, how he was raised to
the high title of duke, and then to the dignity of king. [I shall describe]
the extent to which his power was outstanding in the days of our own
century, and with how much terror he controlled all the provinces from
Sicily as far as Rome, grinding them down in a short time. Only a select
summary of this can be put forward in this volume. This man's virtue
was outstanding, even if it was shown in bringing so many territories under his control. Nevertheless, in order that the iniquity which
greatly overflowed in many people might be brought to an end, it had

to be ground down by the whip of this man according to 'the secret judgement of God'.[1] For just as the great sin of the Lombards was once overcome by the violence of the Normans when they came, according to God's plan or at least with God's permission, in the same way today it is also certain that it was given, or at least permitted, to Roger by Heaven to coerce the immense malice of these regions by means of his sword. For what sin was not exercised among these people? Having thrown away all fear [of God] they did not hesitate to slaughter men, steal, commit sacrilege, adultery, perjury, even the oppression of churches and monasteries, contempt for men of God and many things similar to these. Some pilgrims travelling on God's behalf were robbed, others indeed, instead of having their property stolen, were assassinated in distant places. God, greatly offended by these crimes, drew Roger from the sheath of the province of Sicily, so that holding him in His hand as though a sharp sword He might repress those who had committed these crimes, stabbing them by means of Roger, that those whom He had long considered incorrigible should be frightened by fear of Roger and brought back to the path of justice. Having said these few things in my preface now we shall go to the beginning of my story.

Book I

(1) Duke William of Apulia, taken by death, passed from human affairs.[2] He had been the grandson of the most mighty Duke Robert Guiscard, the son of the latter's son Roger who had succeeded him and been the second to undertake the ducal office. After this, however, the above-mentioned province and the other regions round about were in the grip of great travail since they were left without the guidance of ducal rule. For since the duke had no legitimate child he did not on his death leave any heir lawfully to succeed him.[3] Hence it happened that some of the ducal cities such as Salerno, Troia, Melfi, Venosa and the rest, which had been left without duke or lord, were seized by someone's tyran-

---

1 II Maccabees, 7:36.

2 On 28 July 1127. *Necrologio di S. Matteo*, 102; *Necrologio del Cod. Cas.* 47, 38; *Il "Libro del capitolo" del monastero della SS.Trinità di Venosa (Cod. Casin. 334): una testimonianza del Mezzogiorno normanno*, ed. Hubert Houben (Galatina 1984), 134–5; Romuald [see below, 250]. His deathbed bequest to the abbey of Cava, granting it lands between the rivers Tusciano and Sele south of Salerno, was legally recorded on 8 August 1127, Cava, *Arm. Mag.* F.40, ed. Guillaume (1877), xxviii–xxix, appendix I.

3 *Heredem iure sibi succedentem moriens non reliquerat*: for the significance of this phrase, see the introduction, above 16.

nical ambition. Some persons who were pleasing to their eyes were able to do as they liked without hindrance. Nobody any longer feared bodily punishment, therefore everyone was more and more inclined to do evil, so that not only were travellers oppressed by fear, but that even peasants who wanted to cultivate their fields lacked peace and security. What more [is there to be said]? If God had not preserved a scion of the Guiscard's lineage through whom the ducal power might quickly be revived, almost the whole country, burdened with unbelievably horrible crimes, would have rushed headlong to destruction. Who this scion was shall now be made manifest. This descendant was Roger, son of Roger Count of Sicily, brother of the above-mentioned Guiscard, who at the time that these events were taking place was ruling the county of the Sicilians. I have thought it suitable to relate here, albeit briefly, who he was and what his deeds were when a boy.

(2) He had an older brother called Simon, who on their father's death succeeded him in the lordship of this province.[4] As is the way of children, they were playing at 'coin' [*nummus*] which was their favourite game, and this degenerated into fighting. When they fought, each with a group of other boys whom they had gathered together, the younger, Roger, was the conqueror. As a result he mocked his brother Simon, saying; 'it would be far better that I should have the honour of ruling triumphantly after our father's death than you. However, when I shall be able to do this I shall make you a bishop or even Pope at Rome – to which you're far better suited'. And hence I believe that through these insulting words he foretold that he already intended to be truly the ruler after his father, and, as will be shown below, to extend his lands far and wide, as he was to do following his victories.

(3) It happened that, after both Simon and their father Roger had died, Roger the younger succeeded as heir to the county.[5] But, since he was still of tender age and unable to rule personally, his mother Adalesia, a most prudent woman, exercised the cares of government and ruled over the county until he came of proper age.[6] While he was still a boy living under his mother's tutelage, he was so greatly and frequently

---

4 Simon was recorded as Roger I's designated heir in June 1094, while still only a baby, Becker (2008), 227.

5 Roger I died at Mileto on 22 June 1101; Simon died on 28 September 1105, aged about 12, Chalandon (1907), i.354, 358.

6 For Adalesia (Adelaide)'s regency, see now Becker (2008), 228–35. She was a member of the Aleramici family, the margraves of Savona, whom Roger I had married as his third wife in 1090, *Malaterra*, IV.14, p. 93. On Adelaide, and for a comprehensive list of Roger I's numerous children, legitimate and illegitimate, Houben (1996), 81–113.

moved by piety that hardly ever did a poor man or pilgrim leave his presence without reward. When he had nothing more to give he would go in search of his mother, asking that she give to him what he would then give to the poor, and he would entreat her that whatever he himself had done, she should do more.

(4) When he had become a young man and been made a knight, and was thus in a position to exercise his rights as lord,[7] he showed such activity and demonstrated such admirable firmness, ruling the whole province of Sicily so well and strongly, and exercising such terrible authority over all that no robber, thief, plunderer or other malefactor dared to stir out of his lair. He was most richly endowed with gold, silver and other goods, and this led all to hold him in the greatest awe. Not only his own people but foreigners from faraway lands feared him greatly. He conquered other islands, one of which was called Malta.[8] It was his firm intention to occupy other islands and lands. Suddenly he was informed that Duke William had departed this life at Salerno. He greatly lamented that he had died without his [Roger's] knowledge and without, as he had promised in his lifetime he would if he had no son, making him his heir. Hence he would brook no delay, and prepared to travel by ship, to reach Salerno as fast as possible.

(5) When he was not far from Salerno he ordered his ships to anchor, and sent messengers to the citizens of Salerno ordering them to surrender to him; for lordship over the city belonged to him rather than to any other both by right of relationship, and because in his lifetime Duke William had conceded it to him if there should be no heir born of his wife.[9] But to these messengers the citizens replied thus, saying that, 'we shall in no way and for no reason whatsoever submit to him, since we have suffered many ills from Duke William and his predecessors, and we fear that we should receive the same from him if he should undertake rule over us'. After these and other similar and important things had been expounded with impertinent pride, one of those who had been sent as ambassadors from the count's side, called Sarolus,

---

7 Roger had come of age by 12 June 1112, when his new knightly status was expressly mentioned in a privilege he and his mother granted to the archbishopric of Palermo, *Roger II Diplomata*, 6–8 no. 3.

8 Roger I had conquered Malta in 1090, *Malaterra*, IV.16, pp. 94–5, although whether this was an attempt at colonisation or simply a large-scale raid is unclear, but Arabic sources ascribe the conquest of the island to Roger II, and even thereafter there is no evidence of Latin colonisation before the thirteenth century, Luttrell (1975), 30–4.

9 According to *Romuald*, 213–14, [below, 250] this took place at Messina in 1122, and was done in return for a substantial cash payment. Houben (2002), 42–3, is sceptical, suggesting that at best 'this was a verbal promise that was not put into effect'.

argued back fiercely against them. Soon they stirred up an attack on him, and though the unlucky man attempted to take refuge in flight he was struck down and died by the sword.

(6) When these events were related to Roger, although he was greatly annoyed, he concealed his feelings because of the serious situation, and sent further messages requesting the citizens not to deny him that which he was justly entitled to have. After a long series of discussions amongst themselves about this, finally they replied in this vein: 'Let the fortified citadel be conceded to us to guard, and after this we shall submit to your rule'. On hearing this, although he was much annoyed by the proposal, he agreed that they might keep the said castle for their protection, in order to secure the citizens' submission.[10] *gave in/authority*

(7) Meanwhile Count Rainulf, who had previously married his sister Matilda, hearing that he had arrived in Salerno, and travelling fast, met him at sea at the place where he had first of all anchored. There, after long discussion, Roger requested him to render him homage. He however refused unless he should be given something by Roger for which this ought to be done. Roger then asked him what he wanted to have given to him in return for this. He then said: 'If you seek to augment your honour by receiving my homage, then in a similar way I want the honours of Count Roger of Ariano to be made subject to me'.[11] On hearing this, Roger received it badly, being unwilling that one equal should make submission to another. As a consequence they had a long and acrimonious dispute between them. Then Count Rainulf, filled with indignation, wanted to depart. Roger however did not want him to leave, and finally, because of his marriage to Matilda, of whom he was very fond, and because Rainulf had the reputation of great prowess, which Roger hoped would be very useful to him in the conquest of Apulia, he

bartering for more power

10 *Romuald* [below 251] suggests that this was among a number of concessions granted to the Salernitans. Matthew (2004), 29–32, argues that the surviving fifteenth-century liberties of the city preserve the substance of those granted in 1127, a view accepted by Oldfield (2009), 58. The citadel, the ruins of which survive today, was on the hill overlooking the city. The first surviving document from Salerno to be dated by Roger's regnal years is from December 1127, Cava, *Arca* xxii.42. Three other documents in the same archive, from September and November 1127, have no regnal years in their dating clauses.

11 This Roger was the son of Count Jordan of Ariano (1112–27), who had just been killed while besieging Fiorentino [see *Falco*, below, 174]. The county of Ariano (a hill town 25 km. E of Benevento) was one of the earliest lordships established by the Normans in southern Italy – Errico Cuozzo suggests it was the earliest – but certainly founded by Roger's great-grandfather Gerard of Buonalbergo (d.1086), perhaps a relative and certainly a principal ally of Robert Guiscard, Cuozzo (1998), Loud (2000b), 112–13, 244, 250.

received his homage and in turn made the other count subordinate to him, as he had requested. Then, receiving the oath of fealty, he entered Salerno. The Amalfitans, seeing that the Salernitans had submitted to the count's yoke, submitted similarly, retaining their fortifications [in their own hands].[12]

(**8**) At this time Pope Honorius II ruled as Pontiff of the Roman Church. When he heard at Rome of the death of Duke William, and knowing of the intention of the Count of Sicily to take on the rule of the duchy, he lamented greatly, and left the city without delay. He hastened to Benevento and there, during the solemn celebration of the Mass, he publicly threatened Roger with the javelin of anathema if he should make any further effort to obtain rule over the duchy; and he extended this punishment to anyone who might join, help or advise him in this.[13] After this had been done Count Rainulf, being badly advised, deserted him completely, and did everything in his power to hinder him and prevent him gaining the ducal throne.

(**9**) Roger was still at Salerno when he heard that the pope was at Benevento and had launched the javelin of excommunication against him. He sent to him requesting that the Church should not hinder him from seeking to rule the duchy, an honour which was his by hereditary right; and that, as was right, he would as duke willingly be obedient to him. But hearing this, the pope was quite unwilling to agree, and neither argument nor condition could move him; and once again he launched a further excommunication against him. Roger however suffered his anger patiently, and sent again and again, requesting that he be received, and not denied that which he ought to have by right. But by contrast the Pope's mind remained fixed most obstinately against him, and he absolutely refused to accede to his wish.

(**10**) After this the Pope was invited by the citizens of Troia and on their request received their homage.[14] There all the magnates of Apulia came

---

12 An Amalfitan will on 1 November 1129 was dated in the third year of Duke Roger, *Le Pergamene degli archivii vescovili di Amalfi e Ravello*, ed. J. Mazzoleni (Naples 1972), i.53–5 no. 36, which confirms the submission of Amalfi in the summer or autumn of 1127.

13 Honorius was at Benevento on 18 October 1127, when he wrote to Bishop Otto of Halberstadt, who had been accused of gaining his see through simony, J-L 7293.

14 In return for this, during his second stay at Troia in early December, Honorius granted the inhabitants a wide-ranging charter of liberties, including *inter alia* the promises that a papal rector would only be installed with their agreement, and that the citizens would be freed from military service, unless they performed this of their own free will, and from external taxation, *Chartes de Troia*, 182–5 no. 50; helpful discussion by Oldfield (2009), 56–8. A sign of the town's *de facto* independence was that a charter written in that same month was dated by the pontifical years of the bishop, *ibid.*, 185–8 no. 51.

to him, and on his suggestion joined together with him in an alliance against Roger, not only in order to drive him from the land, but, if they could, to kill him in battle. Among them were numbered Prince Grimoald of Bari,[15] Count Godfrey of Andria,[16] Tancred of Conversano[17] and Count Roger of Ariano, as well as others all of the same mind; and with them, by the Pope's encouragement and the persuasion of Count Rainulf, was associated Robert, Prince of the Capuans. Without delay the Pope returned to Benevento, and after a short stay there he came back once more to Troia where he held a council of bishops. Here he once again excommunicated Roger and cast him forth from the Church, along with anybody who might consent to or assist him in the acquisition of the duchy. After doing this he withdrew to Benevento once again.[18] Roger once more directed an embassy to him, begging him humbly to remove the sentence of anathema, to concede him the ducal dignity and to receive his service. But just as before the Pope remained fixed and unmovable, and refused to accede to the request.

(11) Seeing such great insolence, and realising how inflexible his mind was, Roger set sail back to Sicily; what he could not obtain by humble words he would now wrest by force of arms. When the Pope knew of his absence he returned to Rome as fast as he could so that he, along with the princes mentioned above, could raise an army against him if he should return and invade the duchy in force. I have here omitted much since, as I said in my introduction, it is my intention to narrate above all the most important and significant matters.

(12) Roger remained in Sicily until the usual campaigning season, and then, having gathered together a huge army, crossed the Straits of

---

15 Grimoald Alfaranites had been ruler of Bari from the early months of 1119, as can be deduced from the dating clauses of *Cod. Dipl. Barese*, v.121–4 nos. 69–71 (June and November 1123), both dated in the fifth year of Grimoald. He was a member of one of the patrician families of the city.

16 Godfrey of Andria was probably a descendant of Peter, Count of Andria (d. 1058/64), one of the 'sons of Amicus' kin group, the Hautevilles' chief rivals in Apulia, who had often revolted against Robert Guiscard, Jahn (1989), especially 203–5, 212–13; Martin (1993), 731–3, 860; Loud (2000b), 249–50, 304 (genealogical chart).

17 Tancred was one of the sons of Count Geoffrey of Conversano (d. September 1100), a nephew of Robert Guiscard, but still one of the Apulian nobles who had tried to throw off his rule. Tancred appears to have been lord of Brindisi, and to have held lands in the Gargano region (see below, I.12, II.38), while his (probably older) brother Alexander was Count of Conversano, Jahn (1989), 234–65, especially 263–5; Martin (1993), 737–9; Loud (2000b), 237–9, 241–2, 247 (on Count Geoffrey).

18 Honorius was present at Benevento from 6 to 20 December 1127, J-L 7294–6.

Messina.[19] Moving from there he started to besiege Torre Umfredo, which he quickly captured and demolished.[20] Then he came to Taranto, and rapidly gained possession of this through the surrender of its citizens. After this siege the terrified citizens of Otranto surrendered their city and themselves. These cities had formerly belonged to Bohemond, who had committed them and all his lands to papal tutelage when he had set out across the sea to obtain the Principality of Antioch. However, after he had been crowned prince of that city, only a brief time had passed before he and his men fell victim to a surprise attack by the Turks in a place where they had thought themselves safe, and he and many others were cut down and killed.[21] Then Roger came to Brindisi, a city belonging to Tancred, and besieged it closely for so long that the townsmen were unwilling to endure it and rendered up the city and themselves. Having done this he hastened to besiege the town of Castro, which he captured without delay.[22] After this he went to another town called Oria, and immediately attacked it.[23] Furthermore he also captured other *castra* whose names I do not recall, and must therefore be ignored.

(13) Meanwhile Pope Honorius, knowing that the Count of the Sicilians had crossed the sea and occupied the lands of Bohemond and some of those of Tancred, returned with some 300 knights, ordering Prince Robert, Count Rainulf and the other above-mentioned princes of Apulia to gather together as many troops as they could and to march with him against their enemy Roger who was fast approaching. Therefore Count Roger, discovering that this army was advancing to fight him, moved to the River Bradano and ordered camp to be pitched at a place called Guazzo Petrose.[24] On the other side the Pope and his men approached

---

19 This was in May 1128, according to a marginal note in Romuald's chronicle, *Romuald*, 216; Clementi (1991), 339, translated below, 252.

20 On the River Basento, along the border between Lucania and southern Apulia.

21 Bohemond II set off for Antioch during the late summer of 1126. Both Fulcher of Chartres and the later Jerusalem chronicler William of Tyre said that he and Duke William had made an agreement by which whoever survived the other was to be his heir, although what Alexander says would appear to contradict this [see introduction, 14 above]. Bohemond was, however, killed in February 1130, after Roger's takeover of his lands in southern Apulia. [William of Tyre,] *A History of Deeds done beyond the Sea*, trans. Babcock and Krey, ii.32–3, 43 [Latin text, *Chronicon*, ed. Huygens, XIII.21, 27, pp. 617, 623–4]; Asbridge (2000), 89–90, 127. For Bohemond's lands in southern Italy, Martin (1993), 742–3.

22 Castro (modern Mesagne) is 13 km. SW of Brindisi.

23 Oria is 15 km. SW of Castro. The canons of the collegiate church there had a long-running dispute with those of Brindisi as to which church should be the seat of the archbishopric, Loud (2007a), 195–7.

24 A ford on the River Bradano near S. Fele, Clementi (1991), 273. Honorius was 'in the territory of Bari' on 8 July when writing to the Patriarch of Jerusalem about the new

so closely that only the river flowed between them. However, when Roger found out that the lord Pope himself was a part of this force, he showed proper reverence to him and tried to avoid being seen to fight against God, or even His Vicar. Therefore he sent another embassy to him, once again requesting that he be absolved from the bond of anathema and be allowed to receive the duchy which belonged to him by hereditary right.

(14) While both sides remained there for a long time without accomplishing anything, Prince Robert's magnates, with their wages in arrears [*deficientibus sumptuum stipendiis*], began to be in such distress that many of them were compelled to remove their surcoats and sell them for food.[25] And it happened that some of them could bear this lack of provision no longer and speedily deserted. The Pope realised that the barons and knights were complaining because they had had to sustain themselves under arms for such a long time that they were suffering want, and that they wished to be dismissed and leave. Thus he took advice and sent to Roger, quickly and secretly, promising to grant the duchy to him; however he requested him first to come to Benevento and render his homage to him, and afterwards he would receive the duchy from him as was customary [*sicque postea ipsum a se ducatum ex more acciperet*]. Once this grant had been made, and agreed by both sides, and the Apulian lords had discovered it, they soon dismissed their forces and returned home in disgust, blaming the untrustworthy Pope who had, without their consent, made an agreement with their enemy Roger.

(15) Thus when the Pope had returned to Benevento, lo Roger came to Monte S. Felice (not far from Benevento), climbed up it and deployed his army on the slopes of that mountain. On the third day the Pope, on his invitation, went out a little way from the city and, as is customary, received his homage and then invested him with the ducal rule by banner [*cum vexillo ducale eidem tradidit regimen*].[26] Roger was constituted duke by Apostolic confirmation, as had previously been agreed between them, and made the oath of fealty to him to serve him in everything

---

archbishopric of Tyre, so this confrontation would be shortly after, William of Tyre, *History*, ii.37 [*Chronicon*, ed. Huygens, XIII.23, p. 617].

25 This is an important passage for the use of paid troops in southern Italy, cf. later references by Alexander, below, III.2, III.23. We only have occasional earlier evidence, e.g. the *milites stipendiarii* who garrisoned Petralia in Sicily in 1062, *Malaterra*, II.20, p. 35.

26 Traditionally the popes used a banner to invest the dukes, here following imperial practice for border fiefs, Deér (1972), 13–36. Homage appears to have been introduced to the investiture ceremonial for the first time in 1120, probably due to the French pope, Calixtus II. Previous ceremonies had involved fealty, but not homage, Loud (1985), 107. Falco gives the date 23 August for this investiture.

[*sacramentum ei fidelitatis per omnia servandum exhibuit*].[27] After this had
been done, the Pope returned to his palace, while the duke marched
rapidly to Troia to start the siege. However, although the city was
very closely besieged by him, its citizens resisted him stoutly. For the
Troians had anticipated that he would besiege them and had carefully
fortified their city, hence they were audacious enough not to be intimi-
dated by his siege. When the duke had been there for some considerable
time he realised that the city was very strongly fortified, and he saw
that he could do nothing to capture it – and winter was approaching.
He raised the siege and then moved rapidly to recapture Melfi and the
other ducal towns, to which he had already sent messages ordering
them to submit to him. After receiving their surrender, he commanded
his expeditionary force to return to their homes, while he went back
to Salerno, where he remained for a brief period, and then returned to
Sicily – ready to come back once more with a great army. While he was
staying in that province and was absent from Apulia, Tancred by his
intrigues recovered the city of Brindisi and the [other] towns which he
had lost in Roger's invasion.

(16) However, it happened that when the campaigning season came
round once again, Duke Roger gathered his army together and crossed
the Straits of Messina once again. His army began to occupy all these
lands by brute force. He recovered most of the towns that Tancred had
occupied in his absence, and at length once again besieged Brindisi,
intent on its recovery. The siege dragged on however, and he could see
that he was managing to do nothing to capture it. He left it for the time
being, and moved on to attack other towns.[28]

(17) Coming to Castro, already mentioned above, which had deserted
him and supported Tancred, he quickly destroyed it. Then, while he
was besieging Montalto,[29] Robert de Grandmesnil approached him and

---

27 The papal biographer Pandulf alleged that Honorius appointed Roger to the duchy 'shame-
    fully [and] without any service'. He also claimed that: 'this was not so much his fault as
    that of Cencius Frangipane, the lord Haimeric the chancellor and Bishop John of Ostia,
    who greatly loved the duke, and this was all done for his love and grace', *Liber Pontificalis
    prout exstat in Codice Dertusensi*, ed. J.M. March (Barcelona 1925), 206–7. John, Cardinal
    Bishop of Ostia 1126–1133/4, was a former prior of Camaldoli in Tuscany, Zenker (1964),
    11–12; Hüls (1977), 108. One should remember that Pandulf was a supporter of Anacletus
    II and deeply hostile to both Honorius and Haimeric.

28 Another marginal note in *Romuald*, 218; Clementi (1991), 341 [translated below, 253],
    dates the siege of Brindisi to June 1129, and says that Roger's army had previously
    stormed Nardò, in the Terra d'Otranto.

29 Montalto, appropriately named, is atop a 938m mountain above the upper Bradano, 4 km.
    E of Lagopesole.

requested that he be given permission to return home immediately.[30] Roger said, 'Why do you ask this?' To which he [Robert] replied: 'I seek to leave because I am hampered by this army's lack of supplies and I am unable to bear this burden any more. The fief which I have is not very large and cannot sustain my troops for very long. Let us be clear therefore that if it is not in some way increased, I shall be unable to sustain the burden of military service to you any more; and instead I shall travel across the Alps to the land of my kinsmen. There I shall certainly be able to stay without this poverty'. To which the duke replied, 'I am unwilling to agree to this request. But remain for a little while until all of Apulia has been subjugated to me, but after this what you seek will undoubtedly be fulfilled'. But he, seeing that what he sought was being postponed, as was his habit rapidly became very angry and said: 'If you do not now grant me what I seek, I shall not wait until some later time for you to give it to me, nor do I desire to hold any longer that land which I now hold, since it is so little'. After saying this and other similar things he left, and soon without permission he ill-advisedly deserted the host. This greatly displeased the duke, as will be apparent from what follows.

(18) After the capture of Montalto he hurried to attack Ruvo, a city belonging to the afore-mentioned Tancred.[31] When this was captured Count Alexander, Tancred, Prince Grimoald of Bari and Count Godfrey of Andria, having experienced his formidable power, had more sensible discussions with each other, and soon they surrendered to him. The duke's anger against Tancred was appeased and he returned to him those of his lands that he had seized.[32] Then he ordered them to join him at the siege of Troia as fast as was feasible. The Troians, seeing that these magnates had surrendered themselves to the duke's rule, were thrown into confusion, and since they found themselves without a protector sent to Robert, Prince of the Capuans, asking him to come speedily, undertake lordship over them and protect them from the duke,

---

30 Robert was the younger son of William de Grandmesnil, of the celebrated Norman family from near Lisieux, and Mabel, a daughter of Robert Guiscard. William took part in Guiscard's attack on Byzantium in 1081 and in the First Crusade. He married Mabel c.1090, and had revolted against Duke Roger Borsa in 1093, for which rebellion he was temporarily deprived of his lordship in the Val di Crati. He died before 1114; Robert had succeeded to the lordship on the death of his elder brother William, after 1117. *Orderic*, iv.16, 168, 338; *Malaterra*, IV.21–2, pp. 99–101. Jamison (1939), 199–200; Ménager (1975), 318–20.

31 Ruvo in central Apulia, 14 km. SW of Molfetta and 18 km. SE of Trani.

32 Another marginal note in *Romuald*, 216; Clementi (1991), 342, dated this to 10 August 1129 [translated below, 253].

who was already near at hand. The prince was however unwilling to go
to [aid] them – fearing to exchange a secure position for a decidedly
insecure one. To this the infuriated Count Rainulf responded: 'If you
don't go', he said, 'I will not follow your example but rather will hurry
to bring help to them'. When he entered Troia he spoke to the citizens,
they swore mutual fealty to each other, and he promised that he would
be their most stalwart protector against King Roger.

(**19**) The approaching duke came to Salpi and soon gained possession of
it.[33] Hearing that Count Rainulf wished to defend the Troians against
him he was extremely annoyed, saying: 'If Count Rainulf takes my land
then I shall leave Troia for the moment and go and take his from him'.
Therefore he bypassed Troia and came to the *castrum* of Greci.[34] Count
Rainulf thought that the duke wanted to invade his own lands, as he
had said he would. Fearing to lose them, he sent messengers after him,
requesting that peace be speedily be made between them. And when
the duke promised that there would be peace between them if he [the
count] was willing to hold Troia from him, he immediately abandoned
the Troians and went to his camp which had remained in the same
place mentioned above. They then had talks there and a peace treaty
was concluded between them, after which the count returned home.
The duke returned to besiege Troia, and, as they had been ordered,
the above-mentioned barons [*proceres*] marched to join the siege. What
more is there to say? The city was so closely besieged that within a few
days, like it or not, the inhabitants submitted to the duke.[35] Once Troia
had been captured the other ducal cities, by now very afraid, humbly
surrendered to him, and all Apulia was without exception subject to
him.

(**20**) After this Roger brought his army to the town which is popularly

---

33 Salpi no longer exists, but was near the salt pans along the coast, about 20 km. NW of
   Barletta.
34 Greci in Irpinia, c. 16 km directly NE of Ariano (though considerably further by road),
   held by a family of Breton descent who were vassals of the counts of Ariano, for whom see
   below, 161 note 91).
35 It was probably immediately after this that Roger issued a privilege to the cathedral of
   Troia, confirming its tithes and other income (largely repeating an earlier privilege of
   Robert Guiscard of April 1081), *Roger II Diplomata*, 35–8 no. 12. This was dated 1129,
   indiction VIII, thus September or later. Brühl suggested a date of November, accepted
   by Houben (2002), 48, but this is difficult to reconcile with Alexander's account, and
   September seems more likely, although Clementi (1991), 236, argues for the summer of
   1130 (which would fit the indiction number, but not the year of the Incarnation). A charter
   of sale for a church in Troia of September 1129 noted in the dating clause that Duke
   Roger was ruling Apulia, confirming that the city must have submitted to him by then,
   Pergamene Aldobrandini, Cart. I no. 39.

called Lagopesole, where Robert de Grandmesnil was to be found.[36] He charged him before all with deserting the army without permission at the siege of Montalto – an action which had been very damaging to him. The latter replied, 'Let me be free from this charge and I shall go away, across the mountains to the land of my relatives'. The duke said: 'You want to hurry across the Alps. Now, in front of all, renounce those lands which you now hold and which you have claimed that you don't want to hold any more'. To this he replied, 'You can have them back now provided that I can depart in safety'. What more? The duke recovered his lands on the spot, and then gave him permission for immediate departure.[37]

(21) Once this had been done the duke went to Melfi, and ordered all the great men [*optimates*] of Apulia to gather there in his presence.[38] He then laid down for them this edict (amongst others): that they should be permanently at peace and not fight among themselves. At the same time he ordered them to swear that from this time and henceforth they would keep the peace and maintain justice, and assist in its mainte-nance. They would not maintain on their lands men who would rob or plunder, nor would they allow this to happen. And if any malefactor of this type was found there, they would, without any sort of trickery, produce him at his [Roger's] court at a place designated by him to receive justice. They should keep and observe the peace for all ecclesias-tical persons, namely archbishops, bishops, abbots, monks and all clerics and their property, and for all peasants, villeins and all the people of the land under his rule and their property, as well as pilgrims, travellers and merchants, nor should they molest them, nor permit them to be molested on their land. Therefore it is no wonder that he was able with the aid of God to bring all these lands under his power, since every-where he ruled he promulgated such mighty and thorough justice that continuous peace was seen to endure. As the Psalmist says, 'His place is made in peace'.[39] For how could the benefit of peace be absent when

---

36 Lagopesole, c. 20 km. N of Potenza and 20 km S of Melfi.

37 This incident may well be reflected in the drastic provisions of a later assize of the king, Cassino Assize 34 (not in the Vatican MS of Roger's laws), that said: 'If anybody shall falsely or dishonestly not come to [the muster of] the great army, or after they have come shall abandon the army without permission of the court, he shall suffer a capital sentence, or shall be given into the hands of the court, so that he and his heirs shall become unfree'. Monti (1945), 158; Trombetti Budriesi (1992), 79.

38 Melfi had always been a ducal possession and a centre of ducal authority, Jahn (1989), 155. Alexander's account is confirmed by another marginal note in Romuald's chronicle, *Romuald*, 217; Clementi (1991), 342–3 [translated below, 254].

39 Psalm 76:2.

no malefactor dared to misbehave due to fear of his vigour?[40] When the duke had stayed here for some considerable time and made these and other similar dispositions for the common good, the barons returned home, and he marched to Taranto. Fearing that the above-mentioned Robert might not observe his word and plot something against him, he compelled him before his departure to swear that when he went beyond the mountains he would remain there in perpetuity and never seek to live in Apulia again. Since he confirmed this by his oath he was in consequence allowed to depart freely. After this the Duke returned to Sicily.[41]

(22) Here he remained until the season was suitable. He heard that the said Robert had returned, violating his oath, had recovered the towns of Oriolo and Castrovillari and was ready to fight against him. Annoyed, he sailed with an army of Sicilians across the Straits of Messina.[42] Then, gathering also warlike squadrons of Calabrians and Apulians, he advanced against him with fury in his heart, besieged him most fiercely and within a few days forced him, willing or not, to submit and to hand back these towns. After this Roger went to Salerno, and blockaded it with a stringent siege until the citizens returned their citadel, which at their request [he had] most unwillingly given them to hold, to his custody. For he realised that he would [only] control the town for as long as the citadel was not subject to them. Seeing that there was no way that they could resist him, they acceded to his demand without delay.

make sure noun and power

(23) Having finished with this, not long afterwards he moved his army, bringing it into the land of Count Roger of Ariano and pitched camp at a town called Apice; here he remained for a long time of set purpose.[43] The count's land was almost entirely plundered by his foragers. The

---

40 The oath sworn at Melfi, in September/October 1129, has always been seen as one of the most fundamental and important steps whereby Roger established his authority on the mainland, e.g. Caspar (1904), 84–5, who considered this a continuation of earlier papal proclamations of the Truce of God; Chalandon (1907), i.401–2; Jamison (1913), 238–43; Matthew (1992), 174–5.

41 The marginal note in *Romuald*, 217, said he returned to Sicily in October; Houben (2002), 48, posits a return to Troia in November, based on *Roger II Diplomata*, 259–61, appendix II no. 1, whose dating is problematic. Roger was at Palermo on 30 December 1129 when he issued a privilege to Montecassino, confirming the donations of his predecessors as dukes of Apulia, *Roger II Diplomata*, 40–2 no. 14.

42 Castrovillari is about 30 km. NNW of the mouth of the River Crati in northern Calabria, and about 60 km. N of Cosenza. Oriolo is near the headwaters of the River Ferro, some 35 km. NE of Castrovillari. Clementi (1991), 237, tentatively suggests that Roger arrived in May 1130.

43 Apice is some 15 km. E of Benevento as the crow flies, about 18 km by road.

duke had a very great hatred for the count, for he had learnt by report that the latter had not behaved towards him in a properly faithful manner. He made inquiry about this in the presence of all, and since the count was unable to clear himself judicially he was forced to surrender two important *castra*, Paduli and Montefusco.[44] Once this had been done then the duke's hostility was appeased.

(24) From here he marched on Troia and once again closely besieged it, for the citizens had acted just as those of Salerno had done, and his response was also exactly the same. They agreed to rebuild the citadel [*castrum*] which they had destroyed at the death of Duke William.[45] After achieving such great and numerous successes the duke promptly left Troia, rejoicing, and went to Melfi. Here he ordered that the fortress which the citizens on the order of the former duke had demolished be restored. And at this time Robert, Prince of the Capuans, constrained solely by the terror of his name, submitted to his lordship.[46] Not long afterwards he returned to Salerno and from there sailed back to Sicily.[47] And now at this point Book One, about his time as duke, ends. The pen will turn to record what he did after becoming king.

Book II

(1) With so many successes achieved, all the lands of Bohemond and the whole duchy seemingly in his power, the Prince of the Capuans, the *Magister Militum* of Naples[48] and all the land up to the borders of the city of Ancona subject to him, and his opponents in war subdued, those close to Duke Roger, and particularly his uncle Count Henry by whom

44 Paduli is on a hill overlooking the River Tammaro, about 10 km. NE of Benevento; Montefusco is 13 km to the SE of Benevento (but considerably more by the winding road), on a 700m. mountain top.

45 Clementi (1991), 236, would date Roger's privilege to Troia cathedral [above, note 35] to this point.

46 In January 1129 Robert II was still styling himself 'by provision of the mercy of God alone prince of the Capuans', *Le Pergamene di Capua*, ed. Jole Mazzoleni (2 vols. in 3, Naples 1957–60), i.61–3 no. 24 [Loud, 'Calendar', no. 140]. Loud (1985), 143. Falco [below, 182] said that Pope Honorius insisted upon the independence of Capua when he granted Roger investiture as duke.

47 This sentence anticipates: in fact Roger returned to Sicily after the assembly at Salerno (below, II.2–3).

48 Sergius VII, Duke of Naples 1123–37. *Magister Militum* (Master of the Soldiers) was the traditional title of the dukes of Naples. His peace treaty with Gaieta in April 1129 may, as Chalandon (1907), ii.13, suggested, have been a reaction to the encroaching threat of Roger's power, *Codex Diplomaticus Caietanus* (2 vols., Montecassino 1887–92), ii.242–3 no. 318.

he was loved more than anyone,[49] began very frequently to suggest to him the plan that he, who with the help of God ruled so many provinces, Sicily, Calabria, Apulia and other regions stretching almost to Rome, ought not to have just the ducal title but ought to be distinguished by the honour of kingship. They added that the centre and capital of this kingdom ought to be Palermo, the chief city of Sicily, which once, in ancient times, was believed to have had kings [who ruled] over this province; but now, many years later, was by 'the secret judgement of God'[50] without them.[51]

(2) After turning over in his own mind their well-intentioned and praiseworthy suggestion, he wanted to have sure and certain counsel. He journeyed back to Salerno, and just outside it he convoked some most learned Churchmen and most competent persons, as well as certain princes, counts, barons and others whom he thought trustworthy to examine this secret and unlooked for matter. Examining the issue carefully, they unanimously, as if with one voice, praised [this proposal] and conceded, decided and insisted with mighty prayers that Duke Roger ought to be promoted at Palermo, the chief city of Sicily, to the royal dignity since he held not only Sicily, his hereditary patrimony, but also Calabria, Apulia and other lands – not just obtained by military prowess, but which had devolved to him by right of his close relationship to the preceding dukes. For it was certain that kingship had once existed in that city, governing all Sicily; it seemed to have been in abeyance for a long time, but now it was right and proper that the crown should be placed on Roger's head and that this kingdom should not only be restored but should be spread wide to include those other regions where he was now recognised as ruler.

(3) Once the duke had taken counsel with them and been strengthened by their sincere approval he went back to Sicily, ordering that all the men of dignity, power and honour from his lands and provinces should gather together at Palermo for his coronation, which would take place on Christmas Day. At the constituted day all they and a numberless

---

49 Henry was the brother of Roger's mother, Adelaide, from the del Vasto family in Liguria. He was present in Sicily from 1094, and was married to Flandina, a daughter of Roger I by one of his first two wives. He subsequently became lord of Butera and Paternò in SE Sicily, but probably only during the regency of his sister, during Roger II's minority, and the grant of the comital title may indeed have come after 1127; see Garufi (1910), especially 49–50; Loud (2000b), 177, 180; Houben (2002), 22, 26.

50 II Maccabees, 7:36.

51 This phraseology, with its reference to the classical 'kings' of Sicily, was also employed in Innocent II's bull granting Roger the kingdom in July 1139 [see below, p. 311].

populace 'both small and great'[52] flocked together. All were once again solemnly asked the same question and answered in the same way as above; to the glory of God and the advantage of His Church all in the royal city of Palermo approved the promotion to the Kingship for him to whom so much power had been given by God and who had already greatly extended the lands of his family, that he might exercise it to punish the evil and to preserve justice.[53]

(4) When therefore the duke had been led to the archiepiscopal church in royal manner and had there through unction with the Holy Oil assumed the royal dignity, one cannot write down nor indeed even imagine quite how glorious he was, how regal in his dignity, how splendid in his richly-adorned apparel. For it seemed to the onlookers that all the riches and honours of this world were present. The whole city was decorated in a stupendous manner, and nowhere was there anything but rejoicing and light.[54]

(5) The royal palace was on its interior walls gloriously draped throughout. The pavement was bestrewed with multi-coloured carpets and showed a flowing softness to the feet of those who trod there. When the king went to the church for the ceremony he was surrounded by dignitaries, and the huge number of horses which accompanied them had saddles and bridles decorated with gold and silver.

(6) Large amounts of the choicest food and drink were served to the diners at the royal table, and nothing was served except in dishes or cups of gold or silver. There was no servant there who did not wear a silk tunic – the very waiters were clad in silk clothes! What more [is there to say]? The glory and wealth of the royal abode was so spectacular that it caused great wonder and deep stupefaction – so great indeed that it instilled not a little fear in all those who had come from so far away. For many saw there more things even than they had heard rumoured previously.

---

52 Revelations, 13:16; 19:5.

53 Ménager (1959), 446–7, suggests that there was a formal tripartite process of *consensus* and *collaudatio*, which took place at Salerno, and then *acclamatio* before the coronation. He also argued that Roger took a coronation oath similar to that described by John of Salisbury for the coronation of King William I in his father's lifetime in 1151, *Historia Pontificalis*, 68–9; *art cit.* 458–9. But these arguments, which were part of Ménager's larger thesis that the kingdom of Sicily followed essentially western models of a monarchy mediated by consent of the baronial class, have been criticised by, among others, Caravale (1966), 66–8.

54 The coronation *Ordo* that was almost certainly used for this ceremony, which survives in four south Italian MSS, all post-1200, followed that of the Romano-German pontifical for the coronation of an emperor, with slight variations; for discussion and edition, Elze (1973), 440–2, 445–52.

(7) When the king's coronation celebrations had finished everybody returned to their homes. The king began to consider carefully the problem of how he might strengthen his kingdom in that perpetual peace which he greatly desired, and how to prevent anybody having the opportunity to resist him. Thus he began to demand urgently and peremptorily from the Amalfitans that they hand over to him all those fortifications which had been left in their hands to guard, for he would in no way consent to nor allow any further agreement by which they might hold these while serving him. The Amalfitans unanimously refused this demand and remained most obstinate in this matter. The king was furious and refused to accept their fealty to him [*a fidei suae consortio dissociavit*].

(8) He called to him the Emir [*Ammiratus*] John, a man most prudent and active in warlike matters, and placed under his command all those who were to go to besiege rebel Amalfi, and to these forces he intended to unite all the warriors of Calabria and Apulia once John had crossed the Straits of Messina.[55] Meanwhile the Grand Emir George, a man most faithful to the King and most accomplished in secular matters, in obedience to the King's orders blockaded Amalfi from the sea, so that he could capture any Amalfitan who might be at sea and prevent aid from anywhere else coming by that same route.[56]

(9) While he was patrolling the Gulf he happened to capture by storm a little island base of the Amalfitans called Li Galli. Then his ships surrounded another island base called Capri, attacked it in strength and captured it. And then on royal orders he moved with his forces to

---

55 John came from a family of Greek officials. His father, the Emir Eugenius, had worked for Roger I in the 1090s. He was first mentioned in June 1117, when he already held the title of emir, Houben (1995), 327–8 no. 92. This was a badge of rank rather than signifying an office. John was last attested in 1142, and was apparently dead by 1154. Ménager (1960), 59–61; Takayama (1993), 67–8, 90–1. His son Eugenius was a financial official, Master of the *Duana Baronum* (the royal finance office on the mainland) from 1174, and a principal minister of King Tancred after 1190, as well as a considerable scholar, Jamison (1957), especially 35–9, 56–9.

56 George of Antioch, *magnus ammiratus*, was a Greek Christian who had previously been an official of the Zirid rulers of Mahdia in Tunisia, but who after losing favour with the new Sultan, Yahyā, had offered his services to the Sicilian court, between 1108 and 1113, by when he was the royal administrator of the Iato district in western Sicily. He was one of the commanders of an unsuccessful attack on Mahdia in 1123, and at some point in the late 1120s, probably c.1127, became Roger's principal minister, which he remained until his death between April and August 1151, Amari (1933–9), iii.368–71; Ménager (1960), 44–54; Takayama (1993), 53, 66–7, 90; De Simone (1999), 276–80; Johns (2002), 80–8; Kislinger (2009) especially 48–50; Metcalfe (2009), 125–8.

besiege the Amalfitan town of Atrani[57] which was already being closely blockaded by the John mentioned above with the royal army which had arrived.

(10) Against them John called Sclavus who governed this *castrum* devoted all his attention and forces to oppose them. But the royal soldiers, seeing that the *castrum* was very strong, built a siege tower [*molimenum*], intending to attack the place with stone throwers [*tormenta*]. Lastly, with a very large battering ram topped with a metal head, used with the utmost power, they levelled the antemural fortification, popularly called the barbican. While those outside were labouring actively at its demolition, the above-named John, seeing this, was struck with fear. Thinking that he would be able to find no way of escape, he surrendered himself and his *castrum* to the king. Once Atrani was captured the royal formations began to besiege another town of the Amalfitans called Ravello. While this was being attacked by a wooden siege tower which had been prepared by them, not long afterwards the king himself arrived by sea.[58] With not just this [Ravello] but all the other towns of the Amalfitans besieged by detachments of the army, they were terribly threatened.

(11) It happened that the tower of Ravello, on which above all the other towns the hope of the Amalfitans lay,[59] was struck by a large number of stone missiles and much of it was as a result knocked down. The inhabitants of Ravello and the Amalfitans themselves, seeing this, rapidly lost heart and with their strength ebbing through fear soon requested peace terms from the king. King Roger, as he wanted, was offered and accepted the [right] hands of the men of Ravello, Scala, Agérola, Pogérola and the other Amalfitan towns; and having subjected Amalfi to his will returned the victor to Salerno.

(12) While he was staying there the *Magister Militum* of the city of Naples, by name Sergius, realising that in Roger there was such mighty strength and valour, went to him, constrained not by warlike means but by fear alone, and surrended to him lordship over this city

---

57 The text reads *Tramuntum*, which at first sight suggests Tramonti, in the mountains inland from Amalfi. But, as Clementi (1991), 288–9, points out, Atrani on the coast makes more sense as the target for a naval attack.

58 Roger was still in Palermo in (early?) February 1131, *Roger II Diplomata*, 45–8 no. 17. A later document from Atrani, dated 5 February 1136, was also dated 'in the fifth year of King Roger's rule over Amalfi', *Codice diplomatico amalfitano*, ed. R. Filangieri di Candida i (Naples 1917), 236–8 no. 138; which confirms that Amalfi submitted to the king after 5 February 1131.

59 Ravello is situated on a cliff, 350m. high, overlooking Amalfi.

which, amazing to say, after the Roman Empire had scarcely ever been subjected by the sword.[60] Now he surrendered it to Roger, constrained by word alone.

(13) King Roger then took seriously and very ill that Richard, the brother of Count Rainulf, was led astray by pride into claiming to possess for himself the city of Avellino and the *castrum* of Mercogliano,[61] with neither the king nor any other lord above him and rendering no service for them. He sent an embassy to him ordering him to subject himself to his lordship. Such was his reputation for valour that his word alone directed to almost any *castrum* or city was enough to ensure its surrender without delay. When however this was made known to Richard 'his anger burned in him'[62] and he madly resolved on war. He hurled the messenger to the ground, cut off his nose, and then ordered him to be blinded.

(14) Meanwhile Countess Matilda, of whom mention was made a long time previously, heard that her brother King Roger had arrived at Salerno, and travelled there from Alife. She left and journeyed to him without the knowledge of her husband Count Rainulf, who was absent.[63] She said that she would on no account and by no agreement return to his bed unless all her dower lands were restored to her, namely the whole of the Caudine Valley with all the towns within it. When the king realised the just cause for her arrival, and desiring to provide protection for her, he permitted her to stay with him as she wished. For he saw what she asked as by no means unjust, and he realised that there was no other means for her to obtain justice unless she was given the opportunity to remain with him for some time.

(15) When the count returned from Rome where he had gone and found that his wife had left, and that Avellino and Mercogliano had been taken away from him, he was very much upset, not so much because he had lost the aforesaid lands but that he appeared to have been abandoned

---

60 Throughout the early Middle Ages Naples had remained an independent duchy, acknowledging the purely nominal overlordship of the Byzantine Empire; it had never submitted to the Lombards and successfully resisted a siege by the Normans in 1076–7.

61 Mercogliano is 4 km. W of Avellino.

62 Esther, 1:12.

63 Clementi (1991), 240–2, suggests that Rainulf, and Prince Robert of Capua, were escorting Pope Anacletus back to Rome, which is certainly plausible, if unprovable. Alexander never mentions Anacletus. Clementi also convincingly argues that Falco wrongly places his account of these events [below, 190] in spring 1132, rather than a year earlier as Alexander does.

by his wife. Because of this he sent to Montefusco[64] where the king was, requesting most fervently that his wife, together with Avellino and Mercogliano, should be restored to him. But he [the king] replied to those who had been sent saying: 'I do not hold the count's wife, nor shall I force her to return since I did not take her. Thus her consent is required. If she wants to return, then I shall not stop her. However, what she seeks seems to be just, nor should she be denied this when it was, as she says, by reason of this dower that he, with my agreement, married her. Nor is there any reason on this account for me to return Avellino and Mercogliano, since his brother Richard, in his hearing and with him being silent, claimed that these were his own property, that he acknowledged no lord over him nor should he owe any one service for them. If they are therefore rightfully his, as he alleges, how is it that Richard testified in his hearing that he had no lord? Has he not shown with his own mouth that they are not of his right? And there is another reason why what he seeks ought not to be returned to him, since when I was in Palermo and in his presence complained about his brother's pride, in that he was unwilling to be subject either to me or to anyone else with respect to the lands he appeared to hold, he himself was completely silent.[65] By this he seemed to be agreeing with the dishonest words of his brother rather than with what was said by me. Nonetheless, let him come to me at Salerno with any of his leading men he shall choose, and whatever he shall rightfully ask of me, I am ready freely to grant – however on condition that he shall do justice to me with regard to those matters on which I rightly charge him'.

(16) The count's messengers returned and recounted what they had heard. He however ill-advisedly, as was his custom, failed to go to the king as he had been ordered, but rather chose to send to him those [who had returned] requesting that what seemed to have been taken away be given back. The king was extremely annoyed that he had been so contemptuously unwilling to come, and he took his sister Matilda and her son Robert, whom she then had with her, back to Sicily by ship with him.[66]

(17) Hearing that his wife and son had gone so far away, the count became very sorrowful; he thought it certain that, because the king's heart was so totally turned against him, when summer came around

64 Montefusco is 13 km. SE of Benevento.

65 This was presumably at the time of the king's coronation.

66 Roger was back in Sicily by 7 June 1131, when the foundation stone of his new church at Cefalù, shortly to be the seat of a bishopric, was laid, Caspar (1904), 511 no. 70a.

again, he would undoubtedly mount an armed attack against him. For
this reason he acted in the meanwhile to strengthen the defences of all
his fortresses and made every preparation to oppose the royal attack if
it should happen to be directed against him.

(18) After returning to Sicily King Roger stayed there for some time
until the start of the [next] campaigning season.[67] Then he crossed the
Straits of Messina and came with a powerful army to Taranto. There
Count Godfrey of Andria came, as was customary, to his court, and the
king there accused him of certain misdeeds and insisted that justice be
done regarding them. The count realised that he would be unable to
excuse himself judicially for clearly-established crimes, but felt that he
would secure pardon by handing over to him a great part of his lands.[68]

(19) After this, because Prince Grimoald of the Bariots, breaking his
fealty, had made an agreement with his enemies, the king came to Bari
and besieged it by land and sea. But Count Rainulf, as he knew that
the king was besieging Bari, was led by his zeal to collect a multitude
of cavalry, desiring to assist the afore-mentioned Grimoald. However
soon afterwards his lord the prince [of Capua] summoned him and
with difficulty persuaded him that he should abstain from warlike action
and should not invade the king's lands for this reason intent on battle:
unless first of all he had summoned him by messenger to restore what
had been taken away from him. Thus, while this message was being sent
to the king, the count ordered the knights whom he had mustered to
return home and remain quiet in the meanwhile.

(20) Grimoald in the meantime devoted all his care and warlike endeavours to protect the besieged city from the king, but in vain; for the
latter obtained justice so quickly that it was captured very speedily – no
more than three weeks were taken up in the siege of a city that Robert
Guiscard, the most mighty duke, had scarcely been able to attack
during a siege of three solid years.[69] Once captured Grimoald was sent
in chains to Sicily.

(21) Tancred of Conversano, one of the most important magnates of
Apulia, knowing that Grimoald had been defeated and that Godfrey

---

67 Roger was at Palermo in March 1132, if Brühl's dating of *Roger II Diplomata*, 52–3 no. 19,
    is accepted.

68 Roger was at Taranto on 13 May, when he confirmed several earlier privileges of the
    Greek monastery of SS Elias and Anastasius, Carbone, Robinson (1929), 273–5 no. 31 [=
    Caspar (1904), 513 no. 76]. Some authorities have considered this document a forgery, but
    it was in turn confirmed by William I in October 1154, *William I Diplomata*, 7–8 no. 2.

69 October 1068–April 1071, Loud (2000b).

had already lost most of his lands, began to be greatly afraid, thinking that he had been most unwise to have joined with them against the king. Before he was investigated over this and judged in the royal court, he preferred rather to go abroad by sea and use this as an excuse freely to hand over Brindisi and the other cities and towns of which he was lord to the king, fearing that otherwise they would be judicially confiscated. What more need be said? Tancred received 20,000 *schifati* from the king and renounced his lands with the intention of hastening to Jerusalem within a fixed time.[70]

(22) The envoys of the prince to the king, who have already been mentioned, arrived after the attack on Bari. The prince had ordered them to convey his request that the king restore to his baron Count Rainulf Avellino and Mercogliano, and his wife and son, otherwise he would undoubtedly withdraw his service. On hearing this, the king was angry and said to them, 'I am very much amazed that the prince dares to importune me about matters which are none of his business. He sends such a message so that he might find an excuse not to serve me. Return then to him with this announcement first of all, that I shall send envoys to him without delay who shall bring my exact reply to his message. The one thing that we wish you to convey to him is this: he is to know for certain that if for this or for any other reason he withdraws his service from me, he shall be instantly charged with the crime of perjury'.

(23) Without delay they returned and the king sent [envoys] to the said prince, who was collecting an army that he might go to Rome to aid the Roman Church against its enemies. To these men he gave the following response. 'I shall in no way submit to the king's orders unless my vassal [*homo*] Count Rainulf has his property returned to him. After hearing this answer the envoys quickly returned to the king to inform him of all that they had been told.

(24) Meanwhile the prince and Count Rainulf, fearing that the message despatched back to him would displease the king, rushed into arms against him and occupied the Caudine Valley with a large force of cavalry. Here they decided to remain, that the king should not find them unready for battle if he should move against them. On receiving the prince's reply the king was far from being left in an even frame of mind. Knowing that the count was recruiting a large number of infantry and

---

70 Tancred and his brother Alexander had been among those who swore in Roger's name to respect the rights of the people of Bari on 22 June 1132, *Roger II Diplomata*, 54–6 no. 20. Presumably his disgrace occurred after this date.

knights and preparing for war against him, he was extremely annoyed, and moved his army to a town called Crepacuore, where he ordered camp to be pitched.[71] Knowing that he was very close to them and thinking that he was indeed about to hasten against them, the prince and Count Rainulf devoted all their attention and efforts to preparations to defend themselves.

(25) However, the king moved camp again and placed it below the town of Montecalvo.[72] He then sent to the prince, who had left the aforementioned valley and was with the count staying at a place called Tressanti; [requesting] that he be permitted to march through his land to go to Rome against the enemy, and also that the prince accompany him. To this the latter is said to have made this reply: 'I will not allow him to go through my land to Rome, nor will I come with him, unless my baron has his property returned to him'. The envoys of the king returned and reported what they had seen and heard. The king listened to this and took it badly. Moving his camp he placed it on the hillside below the town of Paduli. Then he sent to the prince once more, requesting him to consent as before to his crossing his territory to go to Rome against the enemy. After fifteen days, when reply had been made as to what he might do, he made an appearance at Ponte S. Valentino.[73] But the other, filled with anger and disgusted at what the king had done to him, renounced the oath of fealty which he had made to him, saying that 'Unless he first return Avellino and Mercogliano to Count Rainulf, and also his wife and son to him, by no reason or agreement shall I be loyal to him, nor shall I obey his orders, nor suffer him to traverse my land to go to Rome as he wishes'.

(26) Realising that the prince's mind was most obstinately set against him, King Roger sent to the rector of Benevento, named Crescentius, and the archbishop, who was called Landulf, [ordering] that all the populace of the city, saving their fealty to the pope, should pledge their fealty to him by oath.[74] They, with other agents of the king, began to force the people to swear, and because of this great dissension arose

---

71 Clementi (1991), 298, has identified this place, which no longer exists, as being near Orsara di Puglia, some 40 km. NE of Benevento, thus very close to the main route from the Capitanata to Benevento.

72 Montecalvo is 24 km. E of Benevento.

73 According to Falco, this was on 13 July. Ponte S. Valentino was on the River Calore, 6 km. E of Benevento, and not far from Paduli.

74 Crescentius, cardinal–priest of SS Marcellino e Pietro [for whom see *Falco*, below 166 and note 107]; Landulf (III), Archbishop of Benevento 1130–2, for whose election see *Falco*, below 184.

in the city – to the extent that almost the whole people were roused against them, since they were unwilling to render their oath of fealty to the king. Indeed the archbishop and the rector, fearing the revolt of the people, were forced to flee from the city.

(27) Since the citizens were all firmly opposed to taking the oath to the king, they now sent an embassy to the prince and the count, who had remained with their army in the place mentioned above. Realising that the Beneventans were wholly unwilling to adhere to him and that the mind of the prince was, as already said, set most obstinately against him, the king sent to the prince, maintaining to him most forcefully that he should not take up arms against his lord who had done nothing to injure him. But he ordered his defiance to be sent to Count Rainulf, whom he believed had stirred up the prince against him.

(28) Ignoring these threats, the prince and count then took counsel as to where they should move their army and approached the city of Benevento, so that by being stationed more closely to it what had been promised by the citizens might more easily come to pass. Thus leaving where they had been, they came to pitch camp at Castelpoto not far from the River Calore,[75] so that each army was able to see the other, with the city in between them. Then the prince and count entered Benevento, harangued the citizens, and a pact was concluded between them. They agreed under oath that each would be faithful to the other against the king.

(29) On the other side, when the king had found out about this agreement between them and that the prince had already absolutely repudiated his service, moved by anger he ordered that at a given signal his camp be struck, and marching to Nocera, a most important town of the prince, he started to besiege it.[76] But the prince and count, not knowing that the king had moved off, intended to remain where they were for as long as possible; until however they realised that he had departed. The next day they learned that the king was besieging the *castrum* and already launching fierce assaults upon it. They immediately marched off with their army, that they might rapidly bring help to those besieged. When though they came to the River Sarno at a place called Scafati,

75 Castelpoto is 7 km. directly W of Benevento, although further by road.

76 Nocera, 14 km. NW of Salerno, on the border between the principalities of Salerno and Capua, had been the lordship of Prince Robert's father Jordan, before the latter became prince in 1120; Cava, *Arm. Mag.* E.8 (May 1109), E.9 (October 1109), E.20–1 (both September 1111), E.45 (January 1115), and *Reg. Neap. Arch. Mon.* v.373–5 no. 549 (November 1113) [Loud, 'Calendar', nos. 115–120].

thinking to cross the river quickly since there was no other feasible place to traverse it, they found that the wooden bridge there had already been destroyed the previous day by the royal scouts, the timbers flung into the stream and swept away by the waters. Lamenting that they were unable to cross, they were forced to remain there for some time until the bridge had been rebuilt with other timbers and they were thus given the opportunity to cross. Once the bridge had been repaired, and when the king had discovered that his enemies were preparing to cross, the siege was abandoned and he ordered his men to arm themselves, that they might commence battle by charging down upon them.[77]

(30) The prince and the count heard that the king was gathering his forces to make a charge against them. Thus they began to cross the river as quickly as possible for they saw the enemy's attack fast approaching. When they had donned their armour, crossing [the river] they drew each unit up in its appointed place as is done in war and were ready for battle. When each side had slowly approached the other the king's first battleline, lowering their lances and spurring their horses, charged the front line of their adversaries and crashed fiercely into them with such a mighty charge that their formation immediately turned tail. Seeing this, the second rank took fright and because of this also turned about and fled. The infantry placed in formation to the rear as a reserve saw this and were struck by the same fear, and they also retreated. While those who had first turned tail were pursued by the royal knights, a part of them, seeking their means of escape by flight, rushed into the waters of the river and perished in them. Another part fled cross-country, avoiding the river, others were hurled from their saddles by the lances of their pursuers. A great part of the infantry who had taken flight, while in their fear seeking a place of safety, were pushed with many others over the the river bank and fell into the river to drown.[78]

(31) Count Rainulf was placed on the right wing. He was a most doughty warrior, and when he saw his men driven back he was the first to throw himself, spear in hand, into the royal battle line facing him. Observing this, his men, who had been entrusted with the right and left flanks, were spurred into valour, and followed him in resisting their adversaries. When they had broken their spearpoints upon one another they drew their swords and struck out with them. After the count had

---

77 On 25 July 1132, according to Falco [below 199].

78 One of those who drowned, Gilbert the Amalfitan, a burgess of Aversa, had before leaving on the expedition left a will leaving a half-share in his house to Aversa cathedral, the other half to be sold to pay his debts. Bishop Robert, with the agreement of the prince, bought the other half. *Cod. Dipl. Aversa*, 52–4 no. 32.

shattered his spear by the force of his charge, he immediately drew his sword and inflicted a terrible blow on the helmet of the horseman opposing him, so that the knight, reeling from his wound, turned tail from the melee. When the others who were positioned round about saw him running away, they quickly one after another followed him in flight. Then others who were stationed to guard the right and left flanks, seeing their men turn tail, soon became afraid, and immediately turned their backs also.

(32) Let the prudent reader therefore at this point consider[79] by what judgment of God it happened that King Roger, who previously had been the victor in everything, should now not have been granted the victory. Indeed it seems to me that, even if it appears unfair to the king, it was however for his correction – I say this deliberately – since he was not permitted in this instance to secure the fulfilment of his wishes; for he had always been able to achieve success, and his mind was as a result exalted, though it should rather have been humbled. The Bible urges this when it says: 'Everyone that exalteth himself shall be abased'.[80] For now, as was related later, the king did as was written and accused himself with his own mouth, and confessed with humble voice that what had happened had done so deservedly. However he remained at Salerno with a joyful face, showing himself to be resolute in mind, knowing for certain that this setback would be replaced by God's gift by some happier outcome.

(33) Tancred, who has already been discussed, heard that the king had fought a battle with Prince Robert and Count Rainulf on the plain of Nocera, and that there the fortune of war had not granted him success. He regretted that he had sought to travel across the sea and had alienated and abjured his lands. Thus, in his attempt to recover his property, he dared to raise soldiers at Montepeloso, where he was invited to enter by the inhabitants, who were opposed to the king.[81] With these men he made sorties hither and thither and savagely raided the lands of the king. There was a city called Acerenza which was strongly fortified not just by human hand but by nature itself; its citizens expelled their lord, a man named Polutinus, because he had submitted to the king without their consent, and in his place they received Tancred to rule over them

---

79 De Nava in *Alexandri Telesini*, FSI 1991, p. 38n.1, suggests this draws on John Cassian, *Collationes*, 7.28 (MPL 49:707), but apart from the use of the verb *perpendere* it is hard to see any connection.

80 Luke, 18:14.

81 Montepeloso, modern Irsina, in the Bradano valley, about 30 km. NW of Matera and 40 km. NE of Potenza.

and to defend them against the king.[82] After this, feeling that an opportune time was coming for him to recover his lands, he journeyed to Count Godfrey of Andria and to Alexander. These men, committing open perjury against the king, bound themselves in a wicked treaty of alliance to fight against him, and they also sent to Robert, Prince of the Capuans, and Count Rainulf [to ask] that they make no pact or agreement with the king without them, for they themselves would make no treaty or peace with him without their agreement.

(34) While this was taking place the king remained at Salerno. He was informed that the citizens of Bari were about to desert him because they had in their anger killed some Saracens whom he had sent there to build a fortress. They had done this because the son of a certain nobleman had been murdered by these same Saracens. And on this account the hostility of the citizens had already stopped work on the royal castle which was being constructed just outside the city. The king took warning from this worrying news and, having garrisoned his towns round Benevento, travelled to Bari.[83] Since this was threatened by Tancred and other enemies, he was unwilling for the moment further to annoy the people of Bari and so he took the prudent path, consented to their petitions and left them for the time being in peace.

(35) After this the king deployed his knights to combat Tancred and the latter's accomplices in his plot, and having garrisoned all his cities and towns in Apulia returned once more to Salerno. Then, having sent particularly large forces of troops to the towns of Montefusco and Paduli, he ordered that they ravage the countryside round about to blockade the citizens of Benevento, who had preferred to side with the prince and count rather than himself, to prevent anyone bringing anything from Apulia to Benevento to be sold there. Not long afterwards he returned to Sicily, without a doubt to return with his army at a suitable later season to attack and subdue the rebels.[84]

(36) While he tarried in that province he meditated carefully and unceasingly on the means by which he might destroy his enemies. And on the other side Prince Robert of the Capuans, and especially Count Rainulf, sought continually and assiduously how and by what means they might

---

82 Acerenza, about 24 km. NW of Montepeloso.

83 *Falco* [below, 199] suggests that his journey took place after the death of Archbishop Landulf of Benevento on 12 August 1132. As Clementi (1991), 300, observes, the king must, despite his defeat at Nocera, have retained plenty of support in northern Apulia to make crossing through the region possible.

84 On 8 December, according to Falco (below, 200).

act against him, for they desired that, having defeated him, they might deprive him of the rank of king, and even, if they could, drive him from the land. Thus it came about that the count, on the prince's advice, travelled into Apulia and had a meeting with Tancred, Count Godfrey, Alexander and the other magnates who had now openly betrayed the king [*regis scilicet iam manifeste periuriis*], that they all might be united in an alliance against him. And when they had confirmed this conspiracy among them with an oath, he heard that the King of the Germans, Lothar, had come to Rome. This news made him very joyful, and he returned in haste to his own lands. After he had consulted with the prince, they both hurried to join the king, that they might seek help from him against King Roger. However, although they were honorably received by him, they were unable to secure his help, for which they were hoping, against the king.[85]

(37) While they stayed in Rome with the king they heard that King Roger, with a huge army of both cavalry and footmen, had already crossed the Straits of Messina, and they sought and received from the king [Lothar], even if not freely, his permission to return to their homes. King Roger had discovered that the prince had perjuriously made a conspiracy with the others named above against him, and he was thus filled with such great indignation against them and was so furiously angry that he was hardly willing to spare any count, magnate or even knight who had raised his head in perjury against him. Indeed Count Alexander was so exceedingly afraid because of the perjury he had committed against the king that he fled to Count Rainulf, leaving the heavily-fortified town of Matera to his son, whose name was Geoffrey.[86] Meanwhile Prince Robert, realising that he would be unable to obtain German help, sailed swiftly to Pisa so that he might raise a force of soldiers [there] and bring them back to help him against the king.

(38) After the king had occupied the lands of the perjured pair, Count Godfrey of Andria and of the above-named Tancred, namely Acquabella, Corato, Barletta, Minervino, Grottole and other places, then he set out to besiege the already mentioned *castrum* where Geoffrey, Count Alexander's son, was.[87] He closely besieged it for a long time, captured

---

85 Lothar arrived in Rome on 30 April 1133 and stayed there for six weeks, *Annalista Saxo*, 595.

86 Named after his grandfather, Count Geoffrey of Conversano, Robert Guiscard's nephew (d. 1100).

87 Assuming that Alexander's sequence was correct, the king appears to have begun by overrunning the Count of Andria's lands on the north coast of Apulia, then returning south along the Murge ridge to attack Matera and other towns along the border with Lucania.

the town and forced Geoffrey to surrender to him. On hearing this Count Alexander, who had previously fled in fright, was for a long while prostrate in his great grief, and then fled [again] to Dalmatia, not only deprived of his patrimony but forced to remain in exile from his native land. Not long afterwards he set out to journey to the emperor, and passing through a forest 'he fell among thieves',[88] who plundered him and his men of all they had. Then, left in Avlona, he was seen there, according to those who told of these things in our hearing, living in a very poor and hungry fashion.[89]

(39) Having captured Matera the King came to Armento, a heavily-fortified town in which was Robert, brother of the above-mentioned Geoffrey.[90] This was quickly reduced by siege, and Robert surrendered both himself and the *castrum* to the King. Then, since he was unwilling to give a hostage for himself, as the king demanded, he was sent to Sicily in chains.

(40) After this the king struck his camp and marched to a certain strong and powerfully fortified *castrum* called Anzi held by Count Godfrey, and besieged it fiercely for a long time.[91] When the count was captured he was despatched into exile in Sicily as a punishment for his perjury.

(41) Once this had been done they hurried to the siege of Montepeloso. However Tancred, hearing that the king was marching swiftly against him, soon abandoned a fortress [*municipium*] called Irsi which he was then besieging,[92] and returned as fast as possible to safeguard the said city. Count Rainulf had already directed forty or more knights to go to its aid under the command of a most valiant knight called Roger de Plenco[93] who was a great enemy of the king. With siege works set up around Montepeloso Tancred prepared to defend it with all his forces.

---

88 Luke, 11:30.

89 Avlone, modern Vlorë (Albania): the emperor in question was the Eastern Emperor John Komnenos (1118–43). Alexander did, however, have a long subsequent career as one of the principal intermediaries between the German and Byzantine courts, and he played an important part in the Byzantine attack on Apulia in 1155. Conrad III described him in 1150 as a man 'accustomed to serve both empires with unbroken loyalty', *Monumenta Corbeiensia*, ed. P. Jaffé (Bibliotheca Rerum Germanicarum 1, Berlin 1864), 365. Cf. *The Deeds of Frederick Barbarossa by Otto of Freising and his continuator Rahewin*, 59, 123–4.

90 Armento is in Lucania, to the north of the River Agri, some 45 km. SE from Potenza.

91 Anzi, about 20 km. SE of Potenza.

92 On Monte Irsi, some 8 km. E of Montepeloso.

93 Plenco has not been certainly identified; *Falco* [below, 205] has Pleuto. Clementi (1991), 304, suggests it could be Plauto, near the River Melfa in the north of the principality of Capua. A more probable identity is *Pleucto*, or Chieuti, on the north side of Monte Gargano; cf. *Catalogus Baronum*, art. 384.

Now in front of the barbican of the city was a place called Catuvella which had been provided with substantial earthworks, and in which nearly all the city stood gathered to repel attack. When the royal army launched a violent attack on this place they were driven back, and Tancred counter-attacking hard with his men forced them to abandon the earthwork and turn tail. But then the king's warriors took heart once again. They launched another attack on Tancred and his men, drove them back and regained the earthwork. Tancred and his men retreated from there and took refuge in the barbican.

(42) However, realising that the city was strongly fortified and possessed a warlike garrison, the king turned to artifice; namely to attack with siegecraft a city which could not be stormed. Thus a siege engine was constructed and the king ordered it to be brought by slow stages to a place where the city seemed to be less strongly defended. By this means those outside could fight face to face with the citizens, with each side throwing missiles at the other. Meanwhile, however, while they were fighting each other, by means of this machine the Saracens hurled wood to fill up the ditch, and others with great energy dragged the earth from the rampart by using iron rakes and tried to level its stockade by pulling it over.

(43) When Tancred saw the ditch being filled in, he had a fire kindled so that the debris might be burned, and hastened to send out [men] to set fire to the wood. But to counter this water was poured down a wooden pipe and the fire was extinguished. Once it had been put out, those who were in the machine began with the utmost deliberation to level the barbican with a long pole at the end of which was a huge iron hook. Those who were defending the barbican, seeing the pole destroying their barbican, cut the ropes holding it. And when other hooks were for a third time extended to level it, then for a third time they were cut by the defenders, but when the attackers pushed them out again they destroyed quite a large part of the barbican.

(44) When they saw this the citizens were terrified; they all turned tail and going through the gate took refuge in another part of the city which was better defended. The royal army immediately carried the gate and followed them, putting anybody they met to the sword. When the citizens who had taken refuge in the aforementioned part of the city saw that they could find no means of escape, they offered a very poor resistance and allowed the enemy to enter that part of the city.

(45) After the royal troops had entered the city they sacked it furiously. Roger of Plenco, who was mentioned above, was captured with others

and led to the king to be put to death. Tancred meanwhile was hiding, and a search was made for him on the king's express order. At length someone betrayed him, and he was led before the king for his inspection. On his discovery the king was exceedingly glad.[94]

(46) Then the wretched Roger, who had for a long time been most bitter in his opposition to the King, was, despite his pleading, horribly put to death by hanging. Although Tancred too had merited a death sentence, he was however sent to Sicily in chains. Of the knights one part left behind their arms and horses and changed into humbler garb, lest anyone should guess their rank, and escaped by fleeing along the byways. This group came in their flight to the city of Acerenza which adhered to Tancred, and thus evaded capture. Others, however, who were captured in one place or another were ordered to be held in chains. Then the city itself was plundered and given over to the flames, and finally demolished. So let the wise reader now reflect how great a crime it is to commit the sin of perjury, and particularly when someone guarantees on oath the life, limbs and honour of his lord, and that capture will not afflict him, and then does not keep to what he swears.[95] Hence Grimoald, Godfrey, Tancred, Count Alexander and others who accepted Roger's lordship over them and then did not observe their oath of fealty, were rightly exposed to the vengeance of divine justice and suffered appropriate retribution for their crimes. For the same thing happened to them as did to King Zedekiah, who swore to a certain pact with King Nebuchadnezzar, and then perjured himself by breaking that pact. Nebuchadnezzar came to Jerusalem, which belonged to Zedekiah, and besieged it. Seeing that there was no way that he could stop the siege, the latter left the city and sought to escape by flight, but was followed by soldiers of the former's army and was captured along with his sons who accompanied him. And when father and sons were brought to King Nebuchadnezzar he immediately ordered the sons to be killed in front of their father, and then the father had his eyes put out and was led bound with many other captives to Babylon.[96] This most wretched of stories makes clear the total ruin that perjurers ought to fear, because whosoever thinks as nothing this practice which should be shunned, shall be thought equally little of by God, so that he shall receive a worthy punishment, as happened to these

---

94 Tancred's capture was noted by *Orderic*, vi.434, who rendered Montepeloso as *Mons Petrosus*. Chibnall wrongly translates this as Montescaglioso.

95 Alexander was here quoting the wording of a vassalic oath.

96 II Kings, 25:1–7.

people. Now therefore we shall return to the course of our narration, from which we have strayed a little.

(47) Having burned and destroyed Montepeloso, King Roger hastened to besiege Acerenza. But then, thinking that he might not be able to capture it, he promised a peace treaty to the citizens, provided that Polutinus, whom as was mentioned before they had expelled, was restored to lordship over them and they submitted themselves to his rule.

(48) When indeed Count Rainulf heard of the capture of Tancred and of the shameful hanging of Roger he was afflicted with great grief, not so much for their ill fortune as for the great assistance from them which would now be lacking. He also considered that after having overcome them the king would undoubtedly be about to launch an attack on him. At length he overcame his sadness, and turned all his attention to defending himself. Journeying to Benevento, he there renewed the alliance with the citizens which had formerly been agreed between them, and then returned without delay. Then he collected no small force of foot and horse in the Caudine Valley, expecting battle with the king who, he thought, would be advancing upon him. The *Magister Militum* Sergius and Count Hugh of Boiano took part in this expedition.[97]

(49) The king however came to the coastal town of Bisceglie, immediately attacked it and destroyed the walls which surrounded it. Moving off he pitched camp at Trani; that city was so struck with terror that it immediately surrendered to him. All its towers were on his order demolished. Coming from there to Bari, whose citizens he had previously left to their own devices, he now destroyed all their towers and had the citadel there, the construction of which had been previously interrupted, rebuilt.[98] Then he went with his army to Troia, a city which, because it was so well fortified, had often rebelled against him. He strengthened it [further] while dividing the great part of the populace among several *casales*.

97 Hugh of Molise, Count of Boiano, ruled an extensive lordship in the north-east of the principality of Capua, stretching across the Monti di Matese watershed into the duchy of Apulia. His family derived from Moulins-la-Marche (département Orne), Ménager (1975), 332–6. His father, Count Simon, had been killed in an earthquake at Isernia in 1117, *Chron. Cas.* IV.62, p. 525. On the counts and their county, de Francesco (1910), 78–90; Jamison (1931), especially 73–9; Schütz (1995), 398–402.

98 Alexander's account of 'all the towers' being destroyed at Trani and Bari probably refers to the city walls; but the phrase is ambiguous and could also refer to towers attached to the homes of individual families. Roger had now marched northwards across the Murge ridge into coastal Apulia. Bisceglie is 8 km. SE of Trani and 35 km. NE of Bari. Clementi (1991), 250, would date this part of the campaign, not implausibly, to August 1133.

(50) Hearing of the king's approach so near to him, and suspecting that he would indeed be moving against him, Count Rainulf devoted himself even more energetically to his defences. On this account he went to Naples where he harangued the *Magister Militum* and citizens, begging them all to help him; then he went on to Aversa where he encouraged all those who were capable of bearing arms to join him against the enemy. After that he returned to the Caudine Valley where he had left his army, waiting there for the *Magister Militum* and all those as yet absent.

(51) Meanwhile, during the king's stay in Troia,[99] Richard son of Hoel handed over his town called S. Agata to be held by whomever the King wished, receiving another in exchange for it.[100] The king very much desired [to have] this *castrum*, which was situated on a steep hill overlooking almost all Apulia, and could therefore play a crucial role in guarding it for him.[101]

(52) With Troia overthrown the king left there and journeyed to Melfi, and while on his way there he toppled the pride of the city of Ascoli, for completely demolishing it he established its populace in three separate *casales* on the plain. When the count thus realised that the king was not intending to march against him but was remaining at Melfi, he and his army returned to their homes.[102]

(53) The king, however, left Melfi and went to the city of Gravina where he remained for a little while; afterwards he returned to Salerno, happy and rejoicing that all Apulia had been conquered, and that only Benevento, Prince Robert, Count Rainulf and Naples remained for him

99 Alexander omits discussion of the king's treatment of Troia, for which see Falco, below 206.

100 S. Agata di Puglia, 50 km. E of Benevento, and overlooking one of the main east–west routes through the mountains in the centre of the peninsula, had been given to Richard's grandfather, Rainulf, a Breton, by Robert Guiscard c.1080, Loud (2000b), 243. Rainulf and Hoel (d.1121) had been ducal constables under Roger Borsa and Duke William; for the latter's will (August 1121), Cava, *Arm. Mag.* F.20, ed. Martini (1915), 48–50 no. 10. Richard was a benefactor of the abbeys of St Sophia, Benevento, Cava and St Lawrence, Aversa, respectively Pergamene Aldobrandini, Cart. I no. 41 (November 1122); Cava, *Arm. Mag.* F. 25 (February 1125); *Reg. Neap. Arch. Mon.* vi.109–10 no. 601 (December 1127). In exchange for S. Agata, Richard was granted the *castello* of Rutigliano, near Bari, cf. *Cod. Dipl. Barese* v.139–42 nos. 80–1 (September 1133, May 1134).

101 *Romuald,* 188, describing the siege of Sant'Agata in 1076, called it 'impregnable against attack'.

102 The king was thus marching almost due south back towards the border with Lucania where he had begun his campaign. Ascoli Satriano is about 22 km. SE of Troia, and Melfi a further 25 km S of Ascoli. On 28 September Roger was at Rapolla, 5 km. S of Melfi, where he issued a charter for the nuns of St Maria, Brindisi, *Roger II Diplomata,* 81–3 no. 29.

to overcome in battle.[103] To this end, the king gave his knights who were stationed around Benevento and Capua strict instructions that until he should return from Sicily with his army they should continually plunder the areas round about these places. After this, however, and before the inclement winter should prevent it, he took ship and returned to Sicily.[104]

(54) And when the customary campaigning season had once more arrived, he once again arrived at Salerno by ship, and ordered a host of troops gathered from all parts to join him at the town of Apice.[105] Then, when it was thought that he was about to besiege Benevento, suddenly he moved his army to attack a *castellum* called Prata, set it ablaze and more or less completely destroyed it. Then he captured three other *castella* one after another, all of which the terrified inhabitants surrendered to him; these however he spared because they had submitted to him. These *castella* had been ruled by Radulf de Fragneto under the lordship of Count Rainulf – one was called Grotta, the second Summonte and the third Altacauda.[106]

(55) Meanwhile Count Rainulf remained with a few men with him at a place called Tressanti; he was in great agony of spirit, for he was unable with only a small number of warriors to march out against him [the king] as he wished. Thus he sent urgent messages to all his princes and barons encouraging them to hurry to him that they might do battle. But while he waited for their arrival he was taken by surprise because the king, who he thought would once again return to besiege Benevento,[107] [instead] attacked with great speed a town called Palma, belonging to

103 Roger was at Gravina on 30 September 1133, having covered the 65 km. E from Rapolla in two days' forced march, and was subsequently at Salerno 16–24 October, *Roger II Diplomata*, 84–91 nos. 30–2.

104 Falco dated this to 21 October, but the charter evidence suggests he erred by a few days. A charter which purports to show the king at Palermo on 24 November 1133 is unfortunately a thirteenth-century forgery, *Roger II Diplomata*, 92–5 no. †33.

105 Roger was still at Palermo on 29 April 1134, *Roger II Diplomata*, 101–3 no. 36. Clementi (1991), 251, suggests that he crossed to the mainland in May. Apice is 14 km E of Benevento.

106 Roger's army was moving south from the Benevento area. Prata is 16 km. SE of Benevento; Summonte 10 km. SW of Prata, Grotta (modern Grotalella) about halfway between them. Altacauda (modern Altavilla Irpinia) is 6 km. W of Prata and 16 km. N of Avellino on the main Benevento–Avellino road (cf. *Catalogus Baronum*, art. 955). For Radulf (Raoul) of Fragneto (Monteforte), who plays an important role in the account of Falco, see below 167.

107 De Nava, 49, followed the *editio princeps* in amending the reading of the verb in this clause to a passive form, *putaretur* ('it was thought'), but the MS has the active *putaret*, which also makes more sense.

one of the prince's magnates called Annonius.[108] After this he quickly began to besiege another place called Sarno, whose lord was one of the prince's magnates called Henry.[109] When the count realised this he stoutly concealed the sadness in his heart. He soon moved with the men who were with him to Marigliano, a town belonging to Robert de Medania.[110] Here he started to wait impatiently for Prince Robert, who had recently returned from Pisa and was expecting help from the Pisans, the *Magister Militum* Sergius, all the magnates of the prince, and for his own men.[111] He intended that he and they together should move to the River Sarno, and by capturing that *castrum* provoke the king to battle.

(56) Thus when most of them had mustered there they waited impatiently for the others because they were still too few in numbers; but lo it was announced that the above-mentioned town had been captured by the king. Then the tower in the said river which was called Scafati was captured when its garrison were seized with fear and surrendered. The wooden bridge which was there was totally destroyed and its timbers thrown into the waters. By doing this it was ensured that nobody could cross the river to attack the king since the bridge was the only means of finding a way over, and the army of the Terra di Lavoro had, as was explained above, thought to cross it and oppose itself to the king. As a result they were not a little downcast with grief, not just for the capture of the town but even more because they by losing the tower to the king they had lost the opportunity to cross the river. When the prince discovered that the tower had been taken, and realising that the help of the Pisans, for the speedy arrival of which he was hoping, had been for a long time delayed, he put to sea once again and returned in haste to Pisa, that he might bring to his aid as fast as possible those whom he had already recruited with wages of many thousands of marks of silver which he had promised to them.

(57) After taking Sarno and garrisoning the tower to prevent the river being crossed the king suddenly flung his siege lines round Nocera, a

---

108 Palma, 25 km. E of Naples, halfway between Naples and Avellino. Anonius is not other-
    wise known.

109 Henry, son of Count Richard of Sarno (d.1125), for whom see below, *Falco*, note 224.

110 Marigliano, 19 km. NE of Naples and 6 km. W of Nola. Robert de Medania, lord of
    Acerra, whose family came originally from Anjou, succeeded his father Geoffrey after
    1118 and died before 1154. His mother Sica was a grand-daughter of Prince Guaimar IV
    of Salerno, and through her second (?) marriage he was the half-brother of Henry of S.
    Severino, the most important seigneur of the Avellino region. See below 343, *Catalogus
    Baronum*, art. 806, for references.

111 According to Falco [below, 212], Robert had returned on 26 February.

very large town belonging to the prince, whose defences were strengthened not only by its site but were also marvellously sustained by the
spirit and strength of its fighting men. Thus, when a fierce assault was
made by those outside, the men inside made a most spirited defence,
aided also by the natural strength of the site.

(58) Meanwhile the army of the Terra di Lavoro, remaining in the place
mentioned above, had sought for some means or other to cross the river
and foil the king by provoking him to battle and making him lift the
siege. To this end Count Rainulf gathered together no small number of
troops and, moving to Scafati, sought there for some opportunity for
him and all the others to cross over safely. But since all the ways across
were heavily guarded by the king's men there was no chance for them to
traverse the river, and he soon returned to his fellow soldiers and all of
them were very downcast since they were forced to remain there with
no opportunity of putting up a fight.

(59) Meanwhile King Roger, realising how very difficult attacking the
town was, carefully furnished himself with siege-engines, that he might
acquire by cunning use of machines what he could not gain by force
alone. He ordered a wooden machine to be prepared and stationed it
at a suitable place situated not far away [from the town]. When it had
been moved close enough for rocks hurled from it to start to strike
the walls of the town, the townsmen soon lost heart and were filled
with fear, and wanted peace from the king. To gain this some of the
most important among them, all with the same intention, went outside
to the king, requesting that he promise quarter to both townspeople
and garrison and to leave the town unscathed, and then they would
willingly surrender themselves and the town to him.

(60) The king's agreement to this promise was secured, and they
returned inside, where they quickly consulted the commander of the
knights, a man called Roger of Sorrento, and the other members of the
garrison about the surrender of the town, and particularly with regard
to the count, who was seen not to have come to relieve them. Surely it
would be better for them, they said, to surrender to the king than that
they run the risk of the town being attacked and destroyed. Having
heard this, everyone at first opposed this course of action, but afterwards, constrained by fear of the king, they consented to the place's
surrender. The king thus received the town in the manner specified.
Roger (mentioned above) and the others who had gathered there for its
defence were captured, but, as the king had promised they were granted
quarter, and after they had been bound by oath were allowed to leave.

(61) After Nocera had been captured and a garrison left to guard it, the king turned his full attention to the invasion of Count Rainulf's land. So having concentrated his army he marched to Paduli, and from there hastened to secure a town called Ponte which was held by a baron called Baldwin under the lordship of Count Rainulf.[112] When its inhabitants saw from afar the immense army they were immediately struck with terror, and offering no resistance they allowed it entry. On the same day as its capture the king went on to attack a *castrum* called Limata which was quickly taken and sacked, and then given over to the flames and completely destroyed, for it belonged to another of the count's leading barons called Radulf de Bernia.[113]

(62) Meanwhile Count Rainulf still remained at Marigliano. When he discovered from the messages which he received that he had lost so many of his lands he marched out in haste and with a heavy heart to recover his property, with only a few troops accompanying him. While he was near the fortress [*municipium*] of Dugenta he decided on the plan – and his own men advised him to do this with all haste – of trying to come to a peace with the king before he was stripped of all that he had.[114] Therefore an embassy was speedily sent to the king and he asked for peace terms, promising to submit himself completely to the royal will. On hearing this, the king reined in his anger, stopped any further occupation of his lands, and then set out a peace agreement. He sent to him [to say] that, following his offer, he would in consequence receive him in peace and restore his wife and son to him; on this condition however, that the dower lands, on account of which they had left him, should be restored to her, and that he must leave him [Roger] in peace in possession of all the lands which he had obtained from him by force. Although he found these terms very burdensome, the count decided to submit to the king as the latter had ordered, lest otherwise he incur the loss of all his property.

112 Ponte (S. Anastasia) is on the River Calore about 14 km. NW of Benevento. A Baldwin son of Roger, lord of Ponte, who was a vassal of Count Rainulf I (grandfather of our Count Rainulf), gave a church there to Montecassino in 1089, Hoffmann (1971b), 201–5 appendix II. It is unlikely, however, that the holder in 1134 was the same man 45 years later, though he might have been the son of the 1089 incumbent.

113 Limata was 5 km. N of Telese. Radulf is not otherwise attested; from his surname his family probably came from Bernay (dépt Eure), Normandy. Surprisingly, he is not in Ménager's list of Normans in southern Italy.

114 Dugenta is on the River Volturno, some 21 km. NE of Caserta. 'With only a few troops accompanying him' is in the Latin *paucis galeis comitantibus.* Clementi (1991), 312, interprets this as 'a few galleys', in which case these would have had to sail around to the mouth of the Volturno and rowed up the river, but *galea* actually means a helmet – thus literally 'with only a few helmets'.

(63) Thus coming to him on bended knee, he wanted to kiss the king's feet. When the king had raised him with his own hands from kissing his feet, for he wished to receive the kiss [of peace] on the mouth, the count first prayed him to cast all anger out of his heart. The king replied to him that: 'I do indeed cast it from my heart'. Then Rainulf said: 'I would also wish that, as I shall be thenceforth a servant to you, you shall therefore cherish me'. To this the king said: 'And this too I concede'. Again he said: 'Of these promises which we have made to each other, I wish God to be a witness between you and me'. The other then said, 'So be it'. When this had been said the king immediately gave him the kiss [of peace] and was seen to embrace him for a long time. In consequence joyful tears were seen to flow from the eyes of all who were round about them.

(64) The king also proposed to receive the prince in his peace on the following conditions: that if he should return before the middle of the month of August he should not be deprived of his *honor*. However, according to the terms written into the agreement, if he wished to yield himself to be his subject, the king would retain under his direct rule whatsoever he had obtained by force in the war. If however his mind was dead set against returning, the king would concede the principality to his little son Robert, though with the proviso that he himself would exercise authority therein until the boy had reached the age of majority and could undertake knighthood [*exercere militiam posset*]. If he allowed the said deadline to lapse by remaining absent then the king would take the principality under his direct lordship and would quite properly receive the homage of all its barons. Then Count Hugh of Boiano, seeing the king moving on him in his wrath because he had joined the prince and count against him, came to him begging for his pardon with many prayers. But he was unable to secure this until he had surrendered to him all his lands to the east of the Biferno River and also the Castello Maris situated at the mouth of the River Volturno.[115] However Sergius, the *Magister Militum*, refused what the King demanded, which was that he recognise the King's lordship over him and do him service. Afterwards he was joined by Rolpoto, commander of the knights of Benevento, who hearing of the Count's peace treaty, fled fearfully from the city accompanied, so it is said, by a hundred or more men-at-arms.[116]

115 The lands east of the Biferno were the Apulian part of Hugh's lordship. Castello Maris was physically quite separate from the rest of the county, but had long been a family possession. In February 1097 Count Hugh's grandfather, also Hugh (I), granted the monastery of St Angelo in Formis, near Capua, fishing rights at Castello Maris, *Regesto di S. Angelo in Formis*, ed. M. Inguanez (Montecassino 1925), 47–50 no. 17.

116 The MS calls him *Ranipotus*. Falco dates his flight to 1 July 1134 [below, 214].

(65) Meanwhile, finding himself to be near the monastery of Telese, the king desired to visit it and to commend himself to the prayers of the brothers. And when he had come to the monastery he was honourably received, as was proper, by the brothers who went out to meet him with hymns and *laudes*.[117] After the prayer at the altar was completed he entered the chapterhouse and kissed the brothers. Afterwards he humbly and reverently received the holy grant of their confraternity from the hand of Alexander, abbot of the congregation. He promised that he would increase the property of the monastery, and then, with the good wishes of the brothers, left them joyfully to return to the army from which he had come.

(66) Three days later, he arrived very early in the morning at the most illustrious city of Capua and received the surrender of its citizens and of all the magnates of the Terra di Lavoro. This city is indeed a real metropolis, and as is recorded from ancient times was called by this name either because it is the capital of Campania or because it is surrounded by a long and wide plain [*campus*] or, so it seems to some people, is called Capua from its founder Capy.[118] It is a most extensive city, fortified by a circuit of walls and towers, and the River Volturno flows through the middle of these walls. On this river there are many water mills tied together with hempen ropes. A bridge of great size and wonderful workmanship has been built across it, which allows people to go in and out from one part of the city to the other where there is an extensive suburb.[119] And it is a city overflowing with [the fruits of] Ceres and Bacchus,[120] and meat as well as with all sorts of other merchandise, nonetheless a great many people frequent it. What is more, it is above all distinguished by its dignity as the princely capital.

(67) When the city had submitted to him and the king was about to enter, he was honourably received, as was proper, by a procession organised in advance of the clerics and all the townspeople, and was led to the archiepiscopal church with hymns and *laudes*. Then immediately afterwards he marched out with his army, and commanded Sergius the *Magister Militum* to come and surrender to him immediately, otherwise he should know that his city would undoubtedly be placed under siege.

117 The *Laudes Regiae*, the ceremonial acclamations of a king.

118 Vergil, *Aeneid*, 10.45.

119 'The bridge called Casolini' leading to the suburb was mentioned in a charter of December 1165; an earlier charter of September 1136 referred to the church of St Peter *ad Pontem*, *Le Pergamene normanne della Mater Ecclesia Capuana*, ed. G. Bova (Naples 1996), 102–5 no. 8; 116–19 no. 12.

120 That is grain and wine. The phrase comes from Horace, *Georgics*, 2.221–5.

And indeed Sergius was afraid that if he declined to do this the king would march upon him and attack his city. Thus he decided to yield, came to the king and on bended knee placed his hands between his, rendered homage to him and swore fealty. This was indeed an amazing thing, for as we have already said [earlier] in book two Naples had after the time of the Roman Empire never been subjected by the sword, and now it seemed to be constrained by word alone.[121]

(68) After this Roger collected his army without delay and pitched camp between Morcone and Pontelandolfo,[122] so that he might give all the lands which the Count of Boiano had surrendered to him (as was described above) to Robert son of Richard. For, while he was at war with the count and the others, he had promised these lands to him if, victory being secured, he should acquire them, and provided that, while he was at war, he should not find him unfaithful.[123]

(69) While the king remained here, the lords of the Borell family, fearing that he might soon march against them, hurried before him to secure his favour by doing homage to him without delay.[124] Then the king returned to Benevento and pitched his tents outside the city. The citizens rendered fealty to him, saving their fealty to the Pope.

(70) Meanwhile Rolpoto realised that the *Magister Militum* of Naples was about come to an agreement with the king. He quickly took ship, intending to take flight to Pisa, but [his ship] was overwhelmed by a storm, and he and his son drowned in the waves. Then the King, realising that everything was prospering as he would wish and that all his subjects were as he desired obedient to his authority, therefore dismissed his army and allowed all his men to return to their homes, retaining with him only those knights whom he was sustaining from his own treasury. Then he went back to Salerno, remained there for a

---

121 II.12 above.

122 Pontelandolfo is on the River Lenta, about 20 km NW of Benevento; Morcone is some 6 km NW of that.

123 Robert was also given the title of Count of Boiano, see below *Al. Tel.*, IV.2. For references to him, Clementi (1991), 331–2. However, here she was unduly cautious in what she surmised of his subsequent career: Robert is surely to be identified with the later Count Robert of Civitate, to which position he was transferred when King Roger restored Count Hugh to his favour in the early 1140s, Cuozzo (1984), 66–7.

124 The Borell family was a large kin group of Lombard descent, who during the eleventh century took over much of the Sangro valley and part of Molise, profiting in the latter region especially at the expense of the monastery of St Vincent on Volturno. Their leading figures in the 1130s were Count Todinus of Sangro, his cousin Borell IV, lord of Agnone, and the latter's sons Oderisius and William. For this kin, see Rivera (1919), Jamison (1959), especially 445–6, and also *Catalogus Baronum*, arts. 758, 761, 780, 1079–85.

little while,[125] and afterwards returned to Sicily, joyfully crowned with the glory of his triumph. Here the second book is completed, and after a brief pause the powers of speech will be restored to start and to bring to a conclusion the third book.

Book III

(1) It happened in the same year not long after King Roger returned to Sicily that he was afflicted with a serious illness. But while with God's aid he rapidly recovered, his wife Queen Elvira soon became very ill indeed and died.[126] This woman was during her lifetime distinguished by the grace of religion and by the generosity of her almsgiving. On her death the king was afflicted by such bitter grief that for many days he shut himself away in his chamber, and was only seen by a few of his personal attendants. Hence little by little the rumour spread, not just to those who were far away but even to those who were close by, that he himself had died. As a consequence of this rumour Prince Robert (who had fled to Pisa) travelled by sea with a very large force of troops and was welcomed in Naples with the agreement of Sergius, the *Magister Militum* of the city, who had already been conspiring with him against the king – for these two had been sending messengers to each other.[127]

(2) Count Rainulf was deceived by this rumour and believed that the king had really died. When he found out that the prince had returned with a huge armed force he took heart and rejoiced greatly. For it seemed that, with the king dead, an opportune time had arrived for the prince to recover Capua and his lost principality and for him to get back those of his lands of which he had been deprived. Thus, not fearing to commit perjury against King Roger, without a moment's delay he used his money to collect about 400 knights and with these he marched close to the walls of Capua, expecting perhaps that the city would be surrendered to him by the inhabitants since they ought to restore it to the prince for whom they seemed to have a very considerable affection.

125 He was at Salerno on 21 July, when he issued privileges for Bishop Ursus of Giovi-nazzo and for St Sophia, Benevento, *Roger II Diplomata*, 104–8 nos. 37–8, the latter privi-lege also published in *Chron. S. Sophiae*, ii.799–801. Brühl (1978), 106–7, confirms this document is genuine, despite some earlier suspicions.

126 She died on 6 February 1135, *Necrologio di S. Matteo di Salerno*, 18. She was a daughter of King Alfonso VI of Castile, whom Roger had married c.1117, Houben (2002), 35.

127 Alexander later (III.7) makes clear that these troops were Pisan, or at least had been recruited there. Falco [below, 215] says that he arrived at Naples with twenty ships on 24 April.

However, when he discovered that his treason had had no effect, he was very heavy at heart. When the next day dawned he ranged through the fields, seized a host of animals and plundered all sorts of property in the outskirts of the city, and then he returned in low spirits to Caiazzo, the heavily-fortified town of his from which he had set out. It was in this manner that war against the king was started, and some of his barons secretly joined the count in his manifest perjury against the king, for they had sworn to the king that if and when the count should wish to revolt against him a forty-days breathing space should be granted during which they should persuade him to return to his obedience to the king. On the expiry of this period they should instantly declare war against him until such time as he should be forced to surrender.

(3) At this time the royal chancellor Guarin, a man most erudite in learned matters and most prudent in secular business,[128] and the Emir [*Ammiratus*] John, whose formidable character has already been mentioned, had been left in charge of all the Terra di Lavoro. When they found out about the prince's return and the count's immediate rebellion they immediately and with the utmost diligence began to furnish the city of Capua, the *castra* of Maddaloni, Cicala, Nocera and other places, and the Terra di Lavoro itself, with armed garrisons.[129]

(4) There was in that same Terra di Lavoro a city called Aversa which had been founded by the Normans at the time when they had attacked Apulia and which was distinguished by a population comprising twelve barons [*magnates*], knights and an immense number of other people.[130] Furthermore the city was surrounded by a wall circuit from which they could, if necessary, resist their enemies. When the Emir John and Guarin the chancellor arrived there, they began emphatically to warn the barons, knights and all those who dwelt there that they should never relinquish their fealty to the king whether from love or fear, and that they should not allow the exigencies of the moment to cast any blemish on their good name, which up to now they had distinguished by their careful observation of law and the rigorous purity of their faith. And when they had addressed them at sufficient length with these and

---

128 Guarin had been chancellor from 1132, and had been previously recorded in his charters as 'Master chaplain', *Roger II Diplomata*, nos. 7 (July 1126), 14 (December 1129), 19 (March (?) 1132). He was also dean of Mazara cathedral. See Brühl (1978), 38, 44–5.

129 Maddaloni is 18 km. SE of Capua and 21 km. N of Naples, Cicala just E of Nola and 25 km. NE of Naples.

130 Aversa had been founded, or at least established as a town, in 1030, after it had been granted to the Norman leader Rainulf by Duke Sergius IV of Naples, Loud (2000b), 74–5. For the clearly-delineated 'barons' and 'knights' of Aversa, Gallo (1938), 113–20.

other speeches of encouragement, John sent [messages] to Apulia in
the king's name begging everyone to hurry to the defence of the Terra
di Lavoro as fast as they could.

(5) Prince Robert was still uncertain about the king's death, but he
did not desist from formulating plans through which he could recover
his lost principality. Thus he sent to Count Rainulf [asking] that he
hurry to him since he would be quite unable to do what had to be done
without his valour [*strenuitas*]. The latter indeed, as has already been
said, had never had any doubts about the king's death, and with those
forces he had collected hastened enthusiastically to him in Naples. With
his arrival the prince and Sergius the *Magister Militum* regained greater
boldness and were imbued with greater vigour, thinking that through
him, because he was a man of the most warlike mettle, they would
achieve a happy result in what they desired. Their mutual conspiracy
was therefore confirmed, and thus it was at length decided that the
prince and count should restore to themselves all their lost possessions
and the *Magister Militum* should retain in security Naples and all the
other property which legally belonged to him. The king was still, as
before, believed to be dead, and many even of his faithful supporters
despaired of his life, especially since he delayed his arrival more than
usual in the face of declared enemies. Indeed if anyone should appear
claiming that he was alive or about to arrive, then he was heard with
disbelief since many who had come before and asserted the same thing
had been believed in vain, and the month of May had already reached
half its course.

(6) Although the leaders and people of Aversa had been informed by
various persons that the king was really alive and was about to put in
an appearance, they were however driven to such insanity that, forgetting the warnings that they had had from John and Guarin, threw
off their obedience to the king and, despising his lordship, submitted
to the prince without making any previous resistance. However, the
Chancellor Guarin and the Emir John, foreseeing that they might
do this, had already retired to Capua to avoid being made prisoner
by them and handed over to their enemies. The Chancellor remained
there with a large number of knights to defend the city. John moved
swiftly to garrison Maddaloni, Cicala and other towns. A large army
from Apulia of both horse and foot joined him at Cicala as he had
ordered. They remained there under John's command to defend the
Terra di Lavoro until the arrival of the king, and among those present
were Robert *filius Ricardi*, a man most faithful to the king (as was

described above in the previous book), and Count Roger of Ariano, as well as many others. After this the army, when combined with the knights who were in Capua but excluding the footsoldiers, numbered nearly 2,000.

(7) After the city of Aversa had been recovered by the prince, the Pisan army which had come with him and which was said to number around 8,000, did its best to encourage the prince, Count Rainulf and the *Magister Militum* Sergius to hasten onwards and launch an attack on Capua. They asserted that it should undoubtedly be occupied as fast as possible. But recognising that the city was defended by a very large garrison, more prudent counsel led them to refrain from attacking it and they pitched camp near the River Lagno at a place called Ponte di Selice.[131] There they waited a little while to see whether the city might in some way be betrayed by those who more than others loved the prince. But the chancellor, who was cautious and careful, found out who favoured the prince more than the others before his army could be admitted to the town and ordered that those who were most suspected of trying to betray it be arrested and held under guard at Salerno.

(8) The prince remained at that place until he lost hope of the city being betrayed to him, then he moved once again to another spot and pitched his tents next to the waters of the river. On the other bank was the royal army commanded by the afore-mentioned John. Count Rainulf indeed was very heated in spirit because, with the river in between, there was no possibility of destroying them by launching a secret and sudden attack. The Emir John, a most sagacious man who guarded against unlucky encounters, led the army cautiously, and prevented them from undertaking an unnecessarily reckless attack. And when both sides had remained there for some time the prince's forces began to be worried by a scarcity of bread and were unable to maintain themselves there. For such was the shortage in that place that one small loaf could scarcely be bought with a coin of Rouen, and on this account the prince and the *Magister Militum* of Naples retreated.[132] However Count Rainulf was despatched to guard Aversa.

---

131 The Lagno flowed into the Lago di Patria, near the coast west of Aversa, rather than directly into the sea as it does today – its course was diverted northwards in later centuries. Ponte di Selice is north of Aversa.

132 That such pennies still circulated in the 1130s is evidence that links continued between southern Italy and Normandy. Archaeology supports this: 176 pennies of Rouen were found at Aversa in the 1890s, 36 in the citadel at Salerno in the 1970s and 18 at the citadel in Bari in 1976–81. Grierson and other numismatists identify these coins with Falco's *romesinae* [below, 245]. See Travaini (1995), 56–8, 210, 297–9, 370.

(9) While all this was going on King Roger, whom his own men had been ardently expecting and whose enemies believed no longer to be alive, crossed the sea and sailed into Salerno on 5th June. When he left the ship the whole city population rushed out together, all filled with joy and rendering thanks to God for him. Hearing of his arrival the inhabitants of Benevento were overwhelmed with joy, and, while I was present and listening, sounded the bells of the city's churches and the body of the clergy processed from the cathedral right up to the monastery of St Sophia with hymns and *laudes*.[133] The king meanwhile ascertained the state of affairs from all those present individually and, once informed, rapidly sent messages through all those lands under his authority, ordering every man who could bear arms to hurry and prepare themselves for battle.

(10) When he joined the army which had been gathered together from all sides, the king much lamented that the inhabitants of Aversa, whom formerly he had praised for their law-abiding nature and the sincerity of their loyalty, had in time of need been found wanting in those things for which he had once commended them. He was also particularly upset about Count Rainulf, and complained about him saying: 'How can Count Rainulf in future be received or believed by me, for he has always done me harm, and neither blood relationship nor, after I received his homage, the oath of fealty has restrained him? How can his good faith be trusted any more after he has violated his oath? That love by which I was united and bound to him as a relation, because of his marriage to my sister, shall be wholly sundered. But even now, if he should return to my fealty and seek my glory and honour, I shall forget all those injuries which he has done me and he need not doubt that in consequence he will be greatly honoured by me. The *Magister Militum*, who has abandoned my fealty to adhere to my enemies, is absolutely unworthy of pardon and will surely lose his rule over Naples. However the prince, who has fled from my wrath more for escape [than anything else], since he has not in this transgressed very seriously, ought to be shown mercy and will not be deprived of his whole *honor*, provided however he is willing to disassociate himself from my enemies, namely the *Magister Militum* and Count Rainulf. In consequence let him be sent to immediately and

---

133 St Sophia, founded as a nunnery in the eighth century and converted to a male monastic house before 945, was the richest and most important of the several monasteries in Benevento; for its history see especially Loud (1997). The medieval town of Benevento was built on a steep ridge rising from west to east; the cathedral is about halfway along the main street on the south side, the abbey of St Sophia was at the eastern end near the 'top gate', the Porta Somma. Hence one indeed went uphill from the cathedral to St Sophia.

let us prove whether my words are pleasing to him – namely whether he abandons them'. But when the prince and count realised that he had arrived they were thrown into such depths of despair that they would have preferred death to life, seeing that they had been deluded by an untrue rumour.

(11) When therefore the prince decided to disdain the message sent to him, the king mustered in one place the huge force of knights and footmen which was greater than any he had previously had. He decided to attack Aversa which Count Rainulf had remained behind to defend, and devoted his whole attention to this. Fearing the ferocity of his attack, the Aversans all began as best they could to seek flight and to hasten to Naples to save themselves. The count realised that he was being abandoned by everyone in this timorous flight, that the king would undoubtedly immediately commence operations aganst him, and at length he too fled with scarcely a handful of men. He retired in confusion to the walls of Naples, where the prince and the *Magister Militum* had joined forces, and once shut up there he did not dare to stir forth, and in the depths of his mind was cruelly tortured with regret by the thought that he had been ill-advised to have begun the war and never to have given credence to those who had advised him towards peace. What then should he do? He realised that he would be the next one to lose his lands which he had left his brother Richard to defend. But the latter was similarly terrified by the king's advance, and abandoning also his son whom he had surrendered to the king as a hostage; since he was unable to return to his brother the count, he immediately fled by 'secret routes'.[134]

(12) While the king was advancing on Aversa he learned that the count had escaped by flight and greatly lamented that the latter, by escaping his net, had not met with the punishment that he deserved. The king was then so furious that the whole city, having first had its people driven forth, was then given over to the flames. This city, not only within in it but also outside, had had a most abundant population and 'all its fields were fertile'; indeed it had no reason to be jealous even of its neighbours Capua and Naples. It was more fruitful in 'foodstuffs such as corn, wine and meat',[135] so that nobody living within it lacked sustenance; and in consequence almost all its inhabitants gave way to a shameful pursuit of pleasure, and failed to restrain this vice, which was, I feel, so offensive to God that he decreed that Roger should destroy the city.

134 Vergil, *Aeneid,* 5.610; 6.676; 11.515.
135 Vergil, *Georgics,* 2.228–9.

(13) When Aversa had thus been destroyed, the king afterwards ordered its suburban area [also] to be burned. Then approaching Naples between the town called Cuculo and the Lago di Patria[136] he pitched camp and remained here for some time, from whence he had all this part of the suburbs of Naples consumed by fire and all the fields were laid bare by his army's foragers. Prince Robert, Count Rainulf and the *Magister Militum* Sergius were kept by their fear of him inside the city and did not dare to make a sortie outside the gate. And when all had been consumed the king once again had Aversa laid waste, and he ordered that matters be conducted so diligently that if there was anything between Aversa and Naples that might be burned which had [so far] remained unburned then it was to be consumed. After thus staying for a long time, until the crops which had been abundant had been totally destroyed, the whole region was left a desert.

(14) After this had taken place the king took counsel and sent his chancellor, Guarin, with a large force of troops to secure the surrender of those cities which Count Rainulf had held under his own rule, failing which he was to fall on them without mercy, drive out the populace and then burn them to the ground. Thus when the chancellor came to the city called Alife the whole populace surrendered without hesitation to the king on the day of his arrival. The next day he went to capture the town of S. Angelo, called Rabicano, of which Richard, the count's brother, was the lord.[137] But he, terrified by the king's arrival, as has already been described, abandoned that *castrum* and fled off into the Campagna.[138]

(15) Then the chancellor retraced his steps to Caiazzo, remaining however three miles away along the River Volturno. The inhabitants, and particularly those who were most important in the *castrum*, were ordered to accept the king's rule over them without delay. However, thinking that they were defended by an impregnable fortress they rashly refused to do this; rather they declared that, if it was necessary, they would resist him. In consequence the chancellor moved on and pitched his camp near the city of S. Agata, urging the citizens to

---

136 Cuculo, modern Villaricca, about 6 km. S of Aversa. The royal army thus approached the duchy of Naples from the north, through the coastal region west of Aversa, despite this area probably being quite marshy.

137 Now Raviscanina, 9 km. NW of Alife.

138 The Latin *Campania* here refers to the Campagna, the southern part of the papal states, rather than classical Campania, the area around Naples and Capua where Roger's army was stationed, and for which Alexander used the phrase Terra di Lavoro. According to Falco (below, 215), Richard subsequently went to Pisa.

surrender of their own accord to the king.[139] But they, like those of Caiazzo, were unwilling to do this and made preparations to resist him. All this was reported to the king, who was then at Aversa, and since both cities were well fortified the king himself was required to march out and capture them.

(16) Hearing of their pride, the king was gravely displeased, and leaving a large part of his army to guard Capua and the other towns of the Terra di Lavoro, hastened angrily to besiege the afore-mentioned towns. Coming to S. Agata, he surrounded it closely on all sides and ordered engines to be made so that it could more quickly be taken. Seeing this, the city's inhabitants were seized with fear. Some of them immediately went outside and with the intention of forestalling the king flung themselves at his feet begging him now to deign to receive their surrender. That they, with their wives, children and property, not be exposed to the horrors of a sack, they humiliated themselves in the hearing of everyone. The king scarcely heeded their prayers and thus received the city unconditionally. On the third day he marched to take Caiazzo. This city is known to be situated as follows: on the east there is a most powerful citadel [*castrum*], fortified not merely by human hand but indeed by the natural excellence of its mountain site. Because this citadel lies at some distance from the city the citizens can scarcely prevail in any way against it. Indeed his siege scarcely seemed to be a threat to it, and if the food supplies to sustain its defenders had not been lacking he would probably never have been able to capture it.

(17) Thus when Roger came to it, wonderful to say, the garrison were struck by terror in the first assault, and could think of nothing except making their peace, and they decided to surrender to him as speedily as possible. Indeed they had received so many missile wounds in that assault that scarcely any of the garrison dared to raise a hand to resist the enemy. For if some hapless man placed as a guard stretched out his arm he immediately received a wound in it from a dart launched from outside. Thus the citadel was attacked once and then the king received its surrender; and after having entered to view it, he confessed himself much struck by its size and strength, and very pleased that it had been handed over for the defence of his crown.

(18) Afterwards he disinherited by due process a nobleman called

---

139 S. Agata dei Goti, seat of a bishopric, 25 km. E of Capua [not to be confused with S. Agata di Puglia, for which see above, II.51] was also part of Count Rainulf's lordship: in October 1097 his father Count Robert had described himself as 'Count of S. Agata and of many other cities', *Cod. Dipl. Aversa*, 15–16 no. 10.

Nicholas for committing perjury by making common cause with his enemies. Then, wishing to secure in perpetuity the benefit of peace, he decreed that [the defences of?] all the towns in the count's lands should be demolished except for the most well-defended fortresses, which it pleased him to keep under his own control for the preservation of peace. After this he came to Alife to inspect it and having done so he was greatly pleased with the amenities of the place and with the abundant waters flowing there. Such was the availability of these waters that whosoever should wish it could divert a rivulet from them into his garden where it would serve his desire to irrigate the plants.

(19) Following this he rejoined his army which he had left at the River Volturno, and set off to besiege Naples where those enemies who had rebelled against him had taken refuge. It was a most ancient city which Aeneas was said to have founded when he had landed there on his voyage: it was of great size and was defended on its southern flank not only by the height of its walls but by the Tyrrenian Sea. On its other sides it was protected by very high walls. Because of this it was considered to be unstormable, and indeed impregnable except for the danger of famine. Once upon a time the ruler of the city, by the order of Octavian Augustus, had been Vergil, the greatest of poets, and in it he had composed a huge volume of verses in hexameters.[140]

(20) Thus when King Roger besieged this city from the eastern side he foresaw that its capture would be very time-consuming.[141] He decided to recruit a vast number of workmen and to build a large [siege] castle, strongly protected by surrounding ramparts, by means of which, provided that it was sufficiently garrisoned, Naples could (even in his absence) be closely blockaded. Thus when Naples was put under siege the ground was dug to raise the rampart for the siege castle; but due to the crumbling of the parched earth the rampart started to collapse. Because of this the work seemed to be in vain, and it was impossible to finish the castle which had been begun while the rampart kept on collapsing. On seeing this the magnates quickly came to the king and began muted complaints. 'This work to build the castle is', they said, 'in vain, since every day the ground is dug to throw up the rampart, but the castle comes no nearer completion. The earth dug is unsuitable for

---

140 Cf. also the *alloquium* [below, 127]. This legend about Vergil may have come from a misreading of Seneca's *Quaestiones Naturales* 6.1, or from Donatus's fifth-century life of Vergil, Comparetti (1908), 266–87.

141 The defences here may have dated from a tenth-century extension of the city walls to include new suburbs; although for the most part medieval Naples preserved its late-Roman defences, Arthur (2002), 34–8.

building the rampart and it is so unstable that it keeps on collapsing. Let's therefore abandon this operation and find another plan which will give us a better chance to abase the pride of this rebel city'.

(21) 'And' [they said] 'there is also another thing which we must greatly lament, since many among the army find the heat of the summer here too much for them and begin to sicken, while others cannot endure the ghastly smell of the corpses of the horses which have died because there is such a lack of water. Furthermore the land on which we are situated, because it is so dry, gives forth an impure heat. On this account we greatly fear the harmful consequences, and indeed that the whole army might fall sick and at the worst be entirely wiped out. Hence, if it is not displeasing to your piety, we ought immediately to move, for by not remaining here and thus recovering our health we could not only blockade Naples in the summer but if it was necessary in the winter as well'. On hearing this, the king felt sorry for them and immediately ordered the siege to be raised. He decided on another way to put pressure on his enemies without endangering his own men, for dispersing the greater part of his army among the various towns closest to Naples he ordered it to blockade the city closely even in his absence, and if the rebels should ever happen to make a sortie they could be driven back by those nearest to them.

(22) After making these dispositions he went to Cuculo which had, while he had delayed his return from Sicily, been in part destroyed by the Pisans whom the prince had brought with him to so little effect. [They had done this] because his order [to do so] had been opposed by the Neapolitans. Since this town was so very close to Naples he ordered that work be started to rebuild it as fast as possible, and stronger than it had been before, as part of his blockade.[142] Then, seeing that the rebuilding of Aversa could restrain the pride of rebel Naples, he went there and ordered that it be rebuilt on the same site as before, and permitted all those who had lived there before to return and settle there once again.

(23) Meanwhile, with this city being energetically rebuilt in the presence of the king and his army, the prince, count and the *Magister Militum* Sergius, trapped within the walls of Naples, had no idea what to do, realising that they were very close to disaster unless help was to be very quickly forthcoming from somewhere or other, for they were all the time menaced by their shortage of supplies, since nothing could

---

142 Cuculo (modern Villaricca) is 10 km. NW of Naples and 6 km. S of Aversa.

be brought in from outside by land to sustain them and their men. Of their knights, who had apparently enlisted for wages, some very much feared capture by the king, and fled from the city whenever they had the opportunity, others were unwilling to lose their property and were prepared to change sides if they were able to gain the king's sanction for its recovery.

(24) Finding themselves blockaded in the city, the princes finally decided, after exhaustive discussion, immediately to send messengers to Pisa to deafen the ears of the citizens with their prayers, and beg their compassion upon them that they might send a mighty army by sea to bring speedy help to those who were at their last gasp. When the immense force which they had sent had crossed the sea and arrived with its ships at Naples the decision was taken to make a sudden dawn attack on the city of Amalfi, with the intention either of plundering it or of seizing it from the king, assuming that ill-fortune did not prevent this.

(25) For at this time Amalfi's warriors were almost all absent; on the king's orders some, with four light vessels[143] filled with men, had gone to raid in coastal waters, and part had gone with the king in his army, while others, seeing the Pisan fleet, thought that it was going to attack Salerno, hurried to defend it and remained there. So when the Pisans arrived at dawn and stormed the city they found no resistance and cruelly sacked it. And when the city had been completely ravaged and all the booty carried down to the fleet they then seized the town of Scala and the other fortresses of Amalfi, and lastly launched an assault on the fortress called Fratte.

(26) Meanwhile King Roger, with a large army, was (as has already been described) intent on the reconstruction of Aversa. He was informed that a Pisan naval squadron had of a certainty seized Amalfi. Galvanised by this news he temporarily abandoned the rebuilding of Aversa, raised camp and marched in force on Amalfi. What more [need be said]? While the fortress mentioned above was under attack [by the Pisans] as described above, the royal army charged down upon them; part of their force were killed, others surrendered to the violent and unexpected assault. The dead and the prisoners between them numbered some 1,500. Of their consuls two were captured and a third was cut down and killed. Those who had remained on the ships or who had returned to them terrified and weighed down by innumerable

---

143 *Liburnae*: the same word (a very classical usage) is employed for the Pisan vessels in the next chapter.

spoils sought safety by flight. Some alleged that the number of vessels was forty-three, others more. The king dispersed the crowd of captives in various places and ordered them to be held in chains.[144]

(27) These pirates returned to Naples with the Pisans whom the prince had brought with him. Then, leaving some of their number there as a garrison, they went back to Pisa with the prince himself, [intending] to return to aid the Neapolitans in the spring. Sergius the *Magister Militum* and Count Rainulf with his son Robert remained in the city to defend it. Robert had been made a knight [*miles constitutus*] in his earliest adolescence, at a time when despite his youth he was already beginning to attract praise for his great courage and daring.

(28) Then the king, re-uniting his forces in one army, returned to cut down all the vines belonging to the Neapolitans which he could get his hands on. Having accomplished this destruction far and wide he returned to Aversa to finish the rebuilding which, as we have said, had for a time been left incomplete. Afterwards, seeing winter fast approaching, and that [therefore] he would not be able to keep his army with him for very long and would himself have very soon to return to Sicily, he thus rapidly made his arrangements for the reconstruction which had to be done and placed garrisons of infantry and cavalry in every town for their defence. He [then] returned to Benevento[145] and pitched his camp below the town of Paduli not far from the River Calore. There he was approached by some of the chief men of Benevento with the archbishop on behalf of all the citizens,[146]

---

144 Cf. *Gli Annales Pisani di Bernardo Maragone*, ed. M. Lupo Gentile (RIS, Bologna 1930–6), 9–10: 'The Pisans attacked Amalfi on 4th August with 46 galleys and captured it that same day. It was burned, along with seven galleys and two [sailing] ships and many other vessels, and thoroughly plundered. On that same day Atrani was captured. The next day, 5th August, with the help of divine clemency the towns in the hills, Pogérola, Ravello, Scala and Scalella, [along with] Maiori and Minori were taken. On the third day, 6th August, the forces of the Pisans besieged the citadel of Ravello with siege-towers and 'cats' [portable shields]. King Roger of Sicily [at first] remained at Salerno with 7,000 knights, 60 galleys, *catti* [scouting vessels] and ships, and a host of footsoldiers, not daring to assist the captured towns. But when the royal expedition climbed up into the hills, it defeated the Pisans besieging the citadel, and set them in flight to the sea, and it captured 596 of them. This took place on the feast of St Sixtus [6 August]. After this the Pisans awaited battle for 23 days, during which time they ravaged the island of Ischia, which was subject to the king. Then they returned to Pisa on 8 September.'

145 This clause is in the Del Re edition, and in the Italian translation of the De Nava edition, but not in the Latin text thereof. However, there is no indication in the modern edition of the alternative reading in the 1845 edition (as is normally the case). This phrase would appear therefore to have been omitted in error.

146 This must be the Anacletan archbishop, Rossemanus, who (Falco says) was in office in 1137 [below, 217].

whom he welcomed in a kindly and friendly manner, that they should not doubt the genuineness of his love for them, [telling them] that they should make every effort to be bound by the bond of peace so that, by avoiding civil dissension they should also avoid rightful censure, and that they should guard their fealty to him devotedly against all others, saving their fealty to the pope.[147] For his intention was firm always to be ready to love, benefit and protect them; provided that they persevered in the fealty to him which they had undertaken. Having heard these and other things along the same lines from him they joyfully responded as follows: 'We, lord king', they said, shall willingly do all that you command and shall adhere to you with all our hearts, nor shall we attempt anything which shall be in breach of our fealty to you, and we shall always be wholehearted and unceasing in your service, after the lord pope, and will never fail in our obedience in such a way that your love and regard will be withdrawn from us'. After saying this they withdrew. The next day King Roger, with the agreement of his leading men and of all the knights, granted the principality of Capua by banner to his son Anfusus, a boy of high promise.[148] Then on the same day he raised to the comital title which had once graced Count Alexander, whom I discussed earlier, his brother-in-law [gener] Adam, a man in the flower of his youth, both affable and most active in knightly deeds.[149] The king had two other older sons, distinguished by their good looks and also by their good conduct, and who had both already come to the age when they had received the belt of knighthood. One of them, Roger, who was the eldest of all the brothers, had already received the ducal title, the other was promoted to the Principality of Bari. He also had two other younger sons, who

147 This of course conveniently leaves out to *which* pope fealty should be shown.

148 The use of the banner followed imperial and papal precedent, for which see note 26 above.

149 The identity of this Adam is uncertain and raises several problems. It is possible he was actually Roger's great-nephew Adam Avenel, son of the king's niece Adelaide, in which case *gener* should be translated as 'relative' rather than its usual meaning as brother-in-law. This identification was suggested by Chalandon (1907), ii.49, but he may have been too young to be the person in question, Clementi (1991), 331. However, there is another possibility. A charter of April 1134, *Le Pergamene di Conversano 901–1265*, ed. G. Coniglio (Codice diplomatico pugliese 19, Bari 1975), 180–1 no. 81 describes Robert de Bassonville as Count of Conversano. Robert *was* actually the king's brother-in-law, having married his sister Judith. Might Alexander have made a mistake with the new count's name, and Robert (rather than Adam) have been the count appointed, somewhat earlier than Alexander suggested? This hypothesis assumes the 1134 charter to be genuine. Alternatively, Adam (whoever he was) must have died soon after his appointment, since by May 1136 the county of Conversano had definitively been entrusted to Robert de Basonville, Garufi, *Documenti inediti*, 33–6 no. 13. Robert de Basonville died before 1142, Petrucci (1959), 113.

were boys still of tender years and who remained in the royal household [*in regia aula*].[150]

(29) At length the king, keeping with him his closest councillors,
allowed all the others with him to return to their homes. After this
he retraced his steps to inspect a fortress which was called Guardia
and a citadel [*arx*] named Dragoni, situated on the summit of a steep
mountain, that he might know how, and how strongly, both were
defended.[151] However, while he was on his journey and before he had
reached the citadel, he turned aside to the monastery of the Holy
Saviour of Telese to pray to the Lord. The aforesaid Abbot Alexander
and the whole congregation of the brothers processed out to meet him
and he was honourably received by them as was proper. [Then] he
was led into the Church amid the chants of the *laudes* to God. The king
prayed on his knees before the altar and then went to their chapter
house and delivered a short and friendly speech to the abbot and all
the brothers. Afterwards, in the king's presence, his son Anfusus,
mentioned above, received their confraternity from the abbot's hand,
the king having already received this on a previous occasion as was
described above.[152]

(30) When the king had gone to his chamber after dining he promised
to restore to the abbot, on the latter's request, the mountain overlooking
the monastery which had been lost [to it] for the space of many years,
and [to give] as much silver as would make a chalice and two thuribles,
for which the brothers appeared to have a particular need for the service
of God. The fulfilment of these promises should be sought from him in
due course when he was in Salerno. How this need had arisen shall be
briefly mentioned here. Count Rainulf pressurised this monastery by
every means that he might be able to continue his war with the king,
and after many gifts of various of its properties did not fear to lay bare
its altar of every one of its ornaments. By doing this he offended God,
and hindered by his sin was unable to prevail over Roger. He acted most
ill-advisedly if he thought that he would receive divine help against
Roger by stealing divine utensils.[153]

150 Roger's sons were 1. Roger, born c.1118, Duke of Apulia (d.1149); 2. Tancred, Prince of
     Bari (d.c.1139); 3. Anfusus, Prince of Capua (d.1144); 4. William, his successor as king,
     who (*Romuald*, 253) died in his 46th year in May 1166, thus born 1120/1; 5. Henry (d.
     before 1145). See Houben (2002), 35–6, 95–6.

151 Guadia Sanfremondi, 8 km. NE of Telese; Dragoni near the River Volturno, about 5 km.
     S of Alife.

152 *Al. Tel.*, II.65.

153 If, as seems possible, Rainulf's grandfather had founded the monastery, as suggested by

(31) The king inspected with great interest Guardia and the citadel of Dragoni, and then leaving instructions how and where their defences should be strengthened he returned to Caiazzo. Climbing the *castellum* and inspecting its entire circuit very carefully he saw how it too might be strengthened on all sides and had work started without delay. He also arranged that all the barons [*proceres*] who lived in the vicinity, with all the knights subject to them who were natives of that area, should build houses in the neighbourhood of Caiazzo and have perpetual residences there so that this *castrum* which was known to be most strongly fortified both by nature and man should be strengthened too by the number of soldiers living there. Some of the clergy and laity of Capua came there, and with the advice of the king elected a cleric named William, a man well-endowed with both divine and secular knowledge, to the office of archbishop; his predecessor had been guilty of the sin of simony and had been sentenced to deposition.[154]

(32) After this the king returned to Capua and the clergy and people of the city processed out and introduced into the city first the archbishop-elect and then, separately, Anfusus the king's son (mentioned above). Then all the barons [*proceres*] of the Principality of Capua who were gathered there made submission to the new prince and swore fealty and [did] homage to him, saving however their fealty to the king and to his son Roger who was to succeed him in the kingdom. Then, that justice should be given to all who had suffered injustice, the king appointed the afore-mentioned archbishop-elect and a certain magnate called Haymo de Argentia.[155] And he constituted as his *procurator* over all the land which was under his own lordship a very energetic man whose name was Joscelin, extremely accomplished in all secular matters.[156] He [the king] had already, when he was at

---

Cielo (1995), 7–8, Rainulf may have felt entitled to use its resources in his hour of need. Clementi (1991), 335n, suggests this may have been early in 1134, when the count and prince needed to pay their Pisan allies; cf. above, II.56.

154 William of Ravenna, Archbishop of Salerno 1137–52. See *Romuald*, 225 [below, 258]. Alexander may not have been entirely truthful about the downfall of his predecessor at Capua, whose real sin may have been his confirmation, and perhaps consecration, by Anacletus, and who was probably deposed before the royal takeover of the principality. See Loud (1985), 165, and a more extended discussion in Loud (2007), 534–6.

155 Aymo or Haymo of Arienzo, lord of Castrocicala and a baron of Aversa, was first attested in 1108. He occasionally witnessed charters of the princes and still recognised princely authority in May 1132, *Cod. Dipl. Aversa*, 379–81 no. 40. After defecting to the king – his donation to Montevergine in March 1136 mentions Roger in the dating clause, *Cod. Dipl. Verginiano* iii.124–7 no. 231 – he continued as a royal justiciar into the 1140s, Loud (1985), 164.

156 Assuming that Joscelin is the Cansolinus of *Pergamene di Capua*, i.61–3 no. 24 (January

Aversa, entrusted the knights who had been chosen for the defence of the Terra di Lavoro while he was in Sicily to several counts in whom he had particular confidence, who were to succeed each other for set terms of office.

(33) The king's brother-in-law Adam was appointed to the first of these periods in command. After him the second was given to Count Robert son of Richard, and after that the third to Count Simon of Sant'Angelo on Monte Gargano, and so on in order. This Simon was the first cousin of the king, the son of the king's uncle Henry and a most worthy knight. And Henry, distinguished by proof of all the virtues and his sweetness and affability, wise in counsel and most active in matters warlike, was a man most highly esteemed. In particular it was said of him that it was by his wise counsel and action, ahead of all others, that the king received first the ducal title and then the royal crown.[157]

(34) When these and other matters had been arranged the king set off for Sicily as quickly as he could. But while his journey took him near to Arienzo he decided to have a look at it because he felt that it was not wholly suitable for defence. After this he directed his journey through the Caudine Valley with a view to inspecting the towns of Arpaia and Montesarchio, for the others [of the area] had been demolished on his orders.[158] On good advice he had despatched his sister Matilda from here to far-away Sicily, in case her husband might in some way seduce her to secure her consent for some future action against him.

(35) Thus, having inspected these towns and ordered what needed to be done there, he hastened to see the *castrum* which was called Tocco, and after inspecting this he ordered its fortifications to be strengthened.[159] He then went to inspect the town of Ceppaloni, and leaving instructions as to how it [too] should be more strongly defended finally came to Salerno.

1129) and *Reg. S. Angelo in Formis*, 129–31 no. 44 (January–August 1129) [Loud, 'Calendar', nos. 140–1], and *Chron. Cas.* IV.98, pp. 558–9, calls him this, then he was another princely *curialis* who had changed sides.

157 For Henry, see *Al. Tel.*, II.1 above. Simon (d.1156) was subsequently known as Count of Policastro, and played a major role in the troubles of the early years of William I. For him, see Garufi (1910), 49–52, and appendix documents nos. 6–8; *Tyrants*, 61–72.

158 Montesarchio, 14 km. SW of Benevento, was a staging point on the main route between Benevento and Capua, *Idrîsî, La Première Geographie de l'Occident*, 380, 397. Arpaia was on the other side of the Valle Caudina 8 km. SW of Montesarchio, near the Forche Caudine, the narrow pass giving access to the Capuan plain (site of the celebrated Roman defeat by the Samnites in 321 bc).

159 Tocco Caudio, in the hills about 5 km.N of Montesarchio, and 13 km. due W of Benevento.

(36) The afore-mentioned Abbot Alexander of Telese, hearing that the king had reached Salerno and not unmindful of his promise, immediately sent the prior of the monastery, named Stephen, with some of the other brothers, to remind him of what he had promised to him.[160] And as soon as they had come to him he joyfully gave them enough silver to make a chalice and two thuribles, and sent a letter directing Joscelin his *vicedominus* to assign the mountain to the said monastery of Telese, since it rightfully belonged to it. Thus when Joscelin received this mandate he sent a letter to Minanus the viscount telling him to have the mountain handed over to the abbot. The abbot and his congregation were overjoyed by this acquisition and rendered thanks to God who had arranged the recovery of this mountain, which had been for so long lost, through Roger's agency. In consequence the abbot immediately ordained that every day at the morning mass in the convent there should be a solemn prayer for the life and safety of the king and his sons. Since it is always right to record good deeds we have in consequence thought it proper to write down this benefaction of the king, both that this king by remembering it should be spurred on to even better deeds and so that others should be encouraged to similar actions. Afterwards the king took ship for Sicily, to return in the spring with an immense army for a new assault on Naples.[161] At this point the third book ends, that in a little while with restored mind, as men say, we shall resume to start the fourth.

Book IV

(1) After the king's departure for Sicily, according to the periods of office which he had arranged (as was discussed above), Count Adam entered Aversa to take command of its knights and conducting himself bravely and well gathered a great reputation by his vigorous military activity. For he launched continual sorties all round the outskirts of the city [of Naples] and was not afraid to penetrate right up to the city gate. The city was already vexed with such a shortage of bread

---

160 Stephen was Alexander's successor as abbot, *Roger II Diplomata*, 166–9 no. 59 (November 1143).

161 According to a diploma issued in favour of the Hospitallers of Messina, Roger was back in Palermo by 10 October 1135 – but this document, known only from a copy of 1510, is at least in its present form a forgery, *Roger II Diplomata*, 113–15 no. †41. This was based on a genuine privilege for the Hospitallers issued on 10 October 1136 (which, if also surviving only in a copy, does at least come from a thirteenth-century one), *ibid.*, 119–23 no. 43.

that a penny of Rouen would scarcely buy two little loaves of millet.[162] The knights whom Adam commanded numbered about 1,000; some of these blockaded Naples, others were placed in the town of Somma and at Acerra, some in the fortress of Cuculo, but the majority were ordered to garrison Aversa.[163]

(2) After no small number of knights had deserted from Naples, either from fear of the king or from shortage of food, barely 300 remained who were unable because of their lack of numbers to wage open resistance by day, although sortying in the silence of the night without the besiegers knowing they managed to burn and rob. While they were busy with this raiding and the besiegers with fighting them Count Adam came to the end of his term of office and returned home. To him succeeded Count Robert son of Richard, a man most faithful to the king and most warlike, and who had been richly rewarded for his great loyalty by the king who had raised him to the honour of the County of Boiano.[164] For the king had this praiseworthy custom that not only did he hold in high regard anyone who seemed to him to have strong and true loyalty but they were not disappointed in his gratitude. By contrast if he found someone unfaithful once, as a consequence of this fault it was scarcely if ever possible for them to secure the sweetness of his love.

(3) Since opportunity is afforded here, his good qualities, and how they showed themselves in him, should not be omitted from record and praise. He was a lover and defender of justice, and a most stern judge of evildoers. He had above all a great dislike for liars, and if somebody who ought to have spoken the truth instead produced a lie, then ever after he could scarcely if ever bring himself to believe them. He was a generous benefactor and protector to churches and monasteries. He hardly ever gave way to idleness or recreation, so much so that if and when it should happen that he was not involved with some more profitable occupation, then either he supervised the public exactions or checked what had been or ought to have been given, or ought to be received, with the result that through studying the accounts[165] he always understood better the revenues which had to be paid to his treasury, and from where they ought to be drawn. To sum up there

---

162 For the use of pennies of Rouen, see above note 132.

163 Somma Vesuviana is 5 km. N of the cone of Monte Vesuvio and 15 km. E of Naples, while Acerra is 10 km. NW of Somma and 14 km. E of Aversa. For Cuculo, S of Aversa, see note 136. The effect was to establish a circle of garrisons around Naples.

164 See above, note 123.

165 Cf. *sub cirographorum ratiociniis*, Tobit, 1:17.

was nothing which was his that was not recorded in written account, neither did he squander anything in empty generosity; hence he never lacked means for any enterprise, for he looked after his property with much care and diligence, fearing to fall into that state which is commonly called thus, 'he who does not live within his means [*ad numerum*] shall live to shame'.[166]

(4) He paid on time military salaries or whatever it had been agreed or promised should be paid. He was never willing to promise what he would not or ought not to pay. In doing things he was not headlong, but before he did anything he was careful always to study it with the eye of prudence. Nor did he seek to punish anybody or to exact any due without proper hearing. If he promised anyone any benefit or threatened them with any ill, according to their merits, that was settled and ratified. But, and this was most admirable in him, when he was campaigning against an enemy he laid his military plans with such foresight that wherever possible he overcame him without bloodshed and thus always tried to avoid risk to his army. In speaking he was quick, in prudence mighty, endowed with gravity of counsel, clear of speech and always prepared to reply wisely and with ready answers. But, since familiarity generally breeds contempt, he himself was both in public and in private restrained in familiarity, affability and mirth, so that he never ceased to be feared. For fear of him grew so much that with the help of God evildoing was almost entirely eliminated from every part of his kingdom and only justice and peace prevailed, thus the words of the Psalmist seemed to be fulfilled in him, 'justice and peace shall be kissed'.[167]

(5) Since we have digressed to picture the admirable character of the king for quite long enough, let us once more turn our pen to the events of our story. When the aforementioned Count Robert took command of the royal troops at Aversa in succession to Adam, he instantly blockaded the borders of Naples with such military prowess and energy that its defenders never dared to sortie to inflict injury on their enemies, except occasionally at night when they could not be seen. After the king had left for Sicily the *Magister Militum* Sergius had sailed to Pisa in an attempt to gain assistance for himself and his accomplices for the moment when the king himself returned to besiege Naples. The king himself, on Christmas Day, promoted his two sons, Duke Roger

---

166 As de Nava points out, *Al. Tel.* 87n, there are theological implications here – *numerus* was often used for the divine order in medieval Latin. For another, very similar description of Roger's character, *Falcandus*, 5–6 [English translation, *Tyrants*, 57–8].

167 Psalm 84:11.

and Tancred Prince of Bari, to knighthood, and that they might be praised and honoured more also decorated forty others with the belt of knighthood.[168] Meanwhile Count Robert, who has been mentioned so many times above, completed his two-month term of duty at Aversa, namely November and December, and returned home. He was succeeded by Simon, Count of [Monte] Sant'Angelo who has already been mentioned, a man, as said, mighty in arms and adroit in stratagem.

(6) It seems suitable at this point, even if apparently it interrupts the order of the narrative, not to omit what was revealed in a dream to a certain priest of the valley of Telese long before Roger's victory and the placing of the crown upon his head. For a long time he kept this dream secret, until Count Rainulf fled to Naples and all his land was made subject to King Roger. Not long after this he revealed it without fear to all. And after the king's departure to Sicily, hearing of this in the monastery where I then was, I had the priest come [to me] and made earnest entreaty to him that he satisfy my wish by narrating his dream about the king.[169]

(7) He told us that just before the death of Duke William, when the king still held [only] the comital title, he was asleep one night when he saw in a dream the said Duke William, Robert, Prince of the Capuans, Count Rainulf and all the barons [*proceres*] of Apulia, Calabria, the Capitanata and many other provinces gather together in Apulia to fight against Roger, Count of the Sicilians. Hearing this Roger himself gathered a multitude of soldiers and crossed the sea to fight them. Thus forces of knights and footmen were drawn up here and there in great numbers and battle was joined on each side. Soon the terrified Count Roger took refuge in flight with all his men. When the duke and the rest pursued him as he fled he tried to escape by throwing himself in the sea. And when he had fled before them through the sea itself for nearly a mile, at length because of the great thirst he was suffering he suddenly drank all the sea.[170] When he had thus drunk, his strength returned, and soon he charged bravely against those who were following him and immediately made them take flight. Duke William fled and completely

168 For the king's sons, see note 150.

169 For discussion of these prophetic dreams, see especially Clementi (1965). Chapters 6–10 were omitted from the first printed edition of 1578 and all subsequent ones; they were discovered and published by Reichenmiller (1963) and Clementi (1965).

170 A very similar prophetic dream, in which Robert Guiscard drank various rivers as an omen of conquest, was recorded by Amatus of Montecassino, *The History of the Normans*, V.3, p. 133. The motif came ultimately from a Scandinavian archetype, where the feat was attributed to Thor; cf. *The Prose Edda*, trans. A.G. Brodeur (New York 1916), 63–4, 67.

disappeared. Prince Robert, Count Rainulf and all the others fell on their faces before him in fear. However, when Count Roger saw that he would be able to kill them all, then restrained by his piety he immediately spared them. After he had done this, behold suddenly two men clad in white robes appeared, and rising from the ground said: 'You can for the moment live, although if he had so wished Count Roger could have killed you all. But since he has spared you and allowed all of you your lives, now approach and with necks bent low show respect for him. For you all know that the Divine Will has disposed that whomsoever shall try to resist him shall be struck dead by his sword'. On hearing this all came forward without delay and putting down their weapons showed respect for him and submitted to him by doing homage. Roger was thus shown as the victor and then immediately climbed up a hillock and planted his spear on the top. The spear promptly grew into a most beautiful tree whose topmost part seemed to extend right up to the clouds. It was filled with beautiful foliage and flowers and innumerable wonderful fruit and had a most elegant and excellent appearance 'set upon the top of the rock'.[171] Then a broad ladder was placed against the tree which led up to a marvellous throne.[172] The two men, those who had appeared in their robes, approached and held him by the hand, one on the right and the other on the left, and they led him with them up the tree by the ladder and placed him on that throne. They crowned him and had him sit there as a king. And then the priest woke up and the vision disappeared.

(8) Another dream about him was told to us which was seen by a certain elderly woman living in the same valley. For she told how one night as she was sleeping the Blessed Mother of God Mary appeared to her in a dream. The woman said, asking her, 'How is it, Lady, that you do not pray for us and liberate us from the harsh oppression of this king?' The Blessed Virgin Mary replied to her, 'Woman, I cannot do this, since two guards have been sent to him by my son the Lord Jesus Christ, who, the one leading him by the right hand and the other by the left, unceasingly guard and protect him. Hence nobody opposing him will be able to resist for very long. He will prevail against all and trample them under his feet until they be fully contrite and "the dross within them shall be purely purged away".'[173] So she asked

---

171 Ezekiel, 24:7.

172 The imagery here was taken from the dream of Nebuchadnezzar, Daniel, 4:4–27. Cf. also Genesis, 28:12, and Isaiah, 61:3.

173 Isaiah, 1:25.

again, saying: 'And who are they, Lady, who lead and guard him?' The Blessed Virgin Mary replied, 'They are the Apostles of my son Jesus Christ, Peter and Paul'. At this the old woman woke up and the vision disappeared.

(9) Thus these two visions undoubtedly show that Roger has triumphed by divine disposition and received the royal crown by divine influence, so that he will never be deprived of it, [hence] let wars be put to sleep and all opposition to him cease. Nor shall anything be accomplished either by someone striving against him or by he who plots since according to the visions, which indeed are apposite, Roger shall be served by the guidance of the Apostles and those who attempt to rebel against him shall undoubtedly be struck down by his sword. Let it be recalled what the saying is of the Apostle, 'Who resists authority resists the ordinance of God'.[174] If therefore it is a sin to resist the ordinance of God it is equally one to fight against him. Indeed if Roger had not received his power from above he could not have done anything. Whosoever is afraid to oppose divine disposition, let him therefore protect himself from Roger's sword, let him not fight against him, nay let him submit to him.

(10) We set forth another dream which a certain priest told to us while staying in a property of our monastery. By writing this down we shall try to teach that everything shows how Roger did not obtain the kingdom's throne by chance but by the workings of divine providence. For he said that in the same year that Duke William died he was asleep one night when he saw a revelation in a dream; namely that he seemed to be in a field outside the town of Paduli and there were a large number of other people there with him. Lo suddenly a most beautiful vine sprang out of the ground and was seen to grow with such speed that it appeared to stretch up into the sky. And when at last it appeared to stand there so sublimely erect, then suddenly a tremendous wind gusted against it and smashed it to the ground so that it was reduced to nothing and completely disappeared. At this immediately, from the spot on the ground where the vine had sprung, a hillock little by little arose, and it began thereafter to raise itself from the surface of the earth until it had reached the height of a full-grown man. Then the mound changed into stone and afterwards grew [once again] up to the height of a lance – finally it appeared to stand still. Indeed all the people who were there, seeing the vine developing from nothing and the hillock rising from the same spot where the vine had emerged, were struck

174 Romans, 13:2.

with amazement, saying 'This vine was certainly destroyed by the wind so that from where it fell the hillock could rise up'. At this the priest woke up from his dream, and wondered greatly at it, not then knowing what was foretold by it. However, after Roger had obtained his victory and crown, the priest remembered his dream and asserted that its contents had been fulfilled without any ambiguity, namely that the vine so quickly appearing and so quickly overthrown was Duke William who had finished his life soon afterwards. The hillock appearing in the vine's place and changing into stone was Roger, substituted in his place and attaining the summit of the kingdom, and signifying fortitude.

We ourselves approving his interpretation [*coniectura*] as the truest one, we think it best that this vision should be described, so that, as already said, it should be known by all that Roger undertook the royal dignity 'not by chance but by grace of divine election'.[175] If however anyone is indeed doubtful about anything from these three dreams, let him turn his mind away from any such doubts since if I was in doubt about anything in connection with these [dreams] then I would not have recorded these letters so accurately and carefully.

Alloquium to King Roger

Lo, my lord King Roger, we have thought to dedicate this little book to nobody else but to you to whose glory and honour it stands devoted. Because we wish therefore something to be made, so that while you read and re-read the story of your most famous victory, you may remember the Lord and Saviour your Eternal King and study to please Him, fortified by whose benevolence [*beneficium*] we do not doubt you have triumphed and obtained your kingdom. On account of this you should not cease to give thanks; and chanting with the Psalmist, say 'Not to us, but to your name give glory'.[176] For we do not doubt that you will rule so much the more perseveringly and firmly in proportion to how much you have received the grace of success and the high dignity of your kingdom from Him, and how much you consciously submit yourself to His orders. Furthermore we pray your magnificence that the effort which we have expended on this little work should be granted the recompense of suitable reward, namely that you allow us who live perpetually in the service of God permanent support, quiet, peace and liberty, so that by following the divine service more freely and securely,

175 Romans, 9:11. The AV translation differs somewhat from the Vulgate text.
176 Psalm 113:9.

we may pray more safely and devotedly for your safety and that of your sons. For if Vergil, the greatest of poets, was esteemed so much at the court of the Emperor Octavian that for two verses which he had written in his praise he received as an earthly reward rule over the city of Naples and at the same time the province of Calabria,[177] we believe it much better that we should be rewarded by you with those things for which we ask for following the divine observance, not however so much for this little work as for the safety of your soul and for the Lord our Saviour, in whose name we are here gathered together, and by Whom you yourself have up to now been preserved safely and have achieved your kingdom. For let us pray our Saviour that you who at present reign will perform such deeds that both at present and in the future you will deserve to possess this kingdom and, if you rule well and justly, I do not doubt that you will gain also that other kingdom which is that to come. For what did it profit Saul to possess the Israelite kingdom according to the Divine Will when afterwards by his contempt for His commands he lost both kingdoms? And what did it profit the Roman emperors Octavian called Augustus, Domitian and Maximian and others to rule over the whole world when as soon as they were buried they would be suffering in hell for all eternity? As these universal torments ought to be feared, therefore from the royal honour with which you are now adorned, you should study to magnify God, to serve Him and to please Him, who gave it to you. For just as it is right that he who owes the debt of service to you for those things which he is seen to hold from you should render it, so also is it right that you should display that service pleasing to the Lord God for those things which He has brought to you or committed to your charge. If perhaps it is asked how the kingdom which God has conceded ought now to be well and justly administered, we shall briefly set this out. The kingdom is rightly and justly administered, when it is ruled justly in both peace and wartime, when by means of laws you drive out iniquity and when you are triumphant after conquering your enemies by force of arms. Remember therefore that you are called by the name of king that all placed under your authority are ruled by the sanction of justice and the bond of peace. That the boon of this peace and justice may be perpetuated in your kingdom, it is greatly to your advantage if you subjugate to your own rule fortifications, impregnable cities and the stronger and impregnable towns. Therefore let the prudence be recalled to your mind of the praiseworthy Emperor of Constantinople, who for the

177 These two verses may be *Georgics*, 3.35–6. See above, *Al. Tel.* III.19.

conservation of this same peace and justice retained for himself the stronger lands and by contrast granted to others, who were inferior in rank to him, the poorer lands to be subject to him and to follow him.[178] While therefore you aim with similar foresight to achieve this precaution, you will be, as Solomon said, as 'a lion which is strongest among beasts, and turneth not away for any':[179] since as the innocents you will sleep securely, you will rest in the day before the night watches and will pass through those night watches without trepidation. Prudent counsel of this sort will lead to all that you desire, and beware lest you ever forget and fail to follow this, for I know that it is in every way pleasing to God, and do not depart from His will. Furthermore let us sway your Serenity with all our entreaties to be mindful of your condition, that you acknowledge as your king He who is the King of Kings, the Lord of Lords, in Whose hands are all the ends of the earth and the hearts of kings, Who has the sole right to dispose of the seasons, to distribute kingdoms, and also to confiscate what He wishes, Who alone is worthy to be honoured, feared and adored, and without Whose grace we would doubtless not exist, live, think or move. Whence the Apostle says: 'For what hast thou that thou did not receive' and 'why dost thou glory, as if thou hadst not received it'.[180] Beware then when the thought surfaces in your mind to make you think that you can do anything without Him, for it is He who gives body and life and without Him you can neither do nor know anything. He gives you everything that you have; even if you seem to be working in these things. Hence in the Gospel the Truthsayer says to His disciples; 'for without me ye can do nothing'.[181] If therefore the disciples Peter, Paul and Andrew and the other Apostles are believed to have been able to do nothing without Him, how much more must this apply to all of us who compared to them are as almost nothing. How many are there who at God's wish or at least with His consent prosper in what they desire in this secular world, who then allow their minds to become forgetful and rush to ascribe this not to God but to themselves. Among these there was Nebuchadnezzar, King of Babylon. He was walking in the royal palace when his heart was filled with pride, and he said 'Is this not Great Babylon that I have built for the house of the kingdom, the might of my power and the honour of my Majesty?'[182]

178 This would seem to be a reference to Alexios Komnenos and the First Crusade.

179 Proverbs, 30:30.

180 I Corinthians, 4:7.

181 John, 15:5.

182 Daniel, 4:30.

With these words he showed that he was sinning by pride against God, when he asserted that Babylon was built not by His strength and fortitude but by his own power. Because of this he quickly (and justly) fell into folly, was expelled from his kingdom, and for seven years dwelt with the beasts of the field and lived as they did. Afterwards, according to God's will he returned to his senses, acknowledged that he had erred by his pride and at length was restored to his former honour, and praised, glorified and magnified the King of Heaven, since just are His works and just His judgments, and He can abase all who walk in pride.[183] Therefore that a descent into pride can be avoided, do not doubt that you have received all glory, honour, rule [*regnum*], courage, wealth, wisdom, prudence and all other things from Him. To sum up therefore, there is no angel in Heaven nor man on the earth who without His consent could either have anything nor have any existence. For God alone has what He has by Himself, since His existence comes from Himself and from nothing else. The holy King David comes to mind. Study to be like him, who while he held the realm of the Israelites without opposition, still despised himself in everything, humbled himself in his own eyes, and while chanting before the altar of the Lord said, 'I will play ... and I will yet be more vile than thus, and I will be base in mine own sight'.[184] Thus it happened that because King David first esteemed himself humbly, he was therefore greatly esteemed by God, and was more deserving of being confirmed in his kingdom which was greatly exalted. So also the Emperor Constantine, who ruled after he had received baptism over the whole world, and showed to God such subjection that He did not abandon his kingdom, and thus like David from his kingdom was brought to the Kingdom, and from his empire merited transfer to the Celestial Empire. In God's time you will be brought to this Kingdom and Empire to reign with them, to stand before Our Lord Jesus Christ, who with the Father and the Holy Spirit lives and reigns for eternity. Amen.

183 Cf. here Daniel, 4:32–7.
184 II Samuel, 6:21–2.

THE CHRONICLE OF FALCO OF BENEVENTO

[From the Chronicle of St Maria di Ferraria, based on the original text of Falco's work][1]

(1101) The pope arrived with a large army before the walls and laid siege to Benevento. Terrified by this Anso, who was ruling over the city in defiance of the pope, fled. The citizens received the pope with the appropriate honours. He appointed Rossemanus as rector there and [then] departed.[2]

(1102) After his departure Duke Roger, along with Herbert and other barons,[3] surrounded the city and blockaded it so tightly that nobody dared to carry supplies into it. Hence the Beneventans were constrained by hunger, and fearing that the duke and his barons would deprive them of their property, because of the feud which John de Cito, then the rector of the city had with them, they drove the latter from the city, and what is more prayed for divine help, that God might snatch them both from the danger of hunger and from their adversaries.[4]

… at the city of Rome he deprived him of his position because, contrary to the lord Pope's instructions, he had frequently urged the Beneventans not to consent to the archbishopric *[sic]*. Finally the citizens, seeing the folly of this proceeding, sent without delay nearly a hundred noble and good men to Rome, to request the lord Pope to grant confirmation to

---

1 *Chronicon Ignoti Monachi Cisterciensis Sanctae Mariae de Ferraria*, ed. A. Gaudenzi (Naples 1888), 15. Extracts from the Ferraria Chronicle that appear to be based on Falco are shown in smaller print with a slight indent, to distinguish the two texts.

2 'Pope Paschal with Duke Roger and a multitude of knights and innumerable [other] men came against Benevento, from fear of whom Anso the son of Dacomirius fled terrified on 22 September, in the tenth [year] of the indiction. The next day he entered the city in triumph and made it subject to his rule', Bertolini, 'Annales', 151, version 1. Cf. also *Annales Cavenses*, ad. an. 1101, MGH SS iii.191. Paschal remained in Benevento until 20 October, J–L 5872–4. Anso had succeeded his father Dacomirius, a local noble who had been ruling Benevento since the early 1080s, at first as the pope's representative, but then increasingly independently, Vehse (1930–1), 108–15.

3 Count Herbert of Ariano, attested from 1079 onwards. For a genealogy of this family, Loud (1997), 296.

4 In the surviving manuscripts the chronicle begins here, abruptly and in the middle of a sentence, the subject of which is Pope Paschal II. D'Angelo suggests that the person deprived, presumably of the position of rector, was Riso, archdeacon of Benevento, who is mentioned a little later, *Falco*, 243, but it could of course be John de Cito.

the pastor-elect.[5] When they arrived there they asked this most insistently in the presence of all at the Synod which he [the pope] had called, but were quite unable to obtain what they wanted. Then seeing this, the envoys retired and worked on the opinions of others, saying 'Our fathers, grandfathers and great-grandfathers never received such an insult'. But what more? Those who seemed to be of the party of Riso installed arms and military equipment on the campanile, for they had heard that Bishop Peter of Porto had hatched a plot, because he wished to seize the treasures and property of the church by force.[6] Then the bishop, seeing these munitions being placed in the tower and being most unhappy about this, ordered his supporters [*fideles*] to be summoned to discuss what ought to be done in this important and weighty matter. Soon battle commenced and because the bishop's party were climbing up the campanile [the other party] fiercely attacked the Palace of Dacomarius, in which the bishop was [then] dwelling, and the bishop's partisans fought back from the Tower of Dacomarius.[7] Both sides fought savagely, and two young men rendered up their souls in this conflict. Finally night intervened, and the bishop, seeing himself surrounded, climbed up with some of his men in the middle of the night to the abbey of St Sophia. He did not however remain here for long. Meanwhile the citizens were afraid, fearing that the bishop would make trouble for them with the pope; so they compelled him to promise them, confirming this by an oath, that he would beg the pope, that when he should send them a Rector this should once again be the monk Rossemanus.[8]

In the year 1103, twelfth of the indiction.[9]

5 This term is problematic: what seems to be meant here is the rectorate. Archbishop Roffred had held office since 1076, so it cannot mean him. Is the word 'pastor' used because the person the Beneventans wanted was a cleric, probably Riso the archdeacon, perhaps Rossemanus the monk? Or is this a problem created by errors that have crept into the transmission of the text in late manuscripts? Vehse (1930–1), 119n.

6 Peter, a leading member of the college of cardinals for some thirty years, became Cardinal Bishop of Porto early in 1102, was Rector of Benevento again 1106–9, Apostolic Vicar in Rome 1118–19 while Gelasius II was north of the Alps, legate to the Holy Land in 1121 and a principal supporter of Anacletus II in the schism of 1130. He died in 1133/4. Hüls (1977), 122–4.

7 The palace of Dacomirius, the former ruler, was next door to the cathedral, and subsequently became the residence of the papal rectors, Vehse (1930–1), 112.

8 Paschal visited Benevento again from late September to 12 December 1102, and may have held a synod there, J-L 5921–5931; Blumenthal (1978a), 130–1.

9 The indiction was the 15-year fiscal period used to date events at Rome, calculated from 312, the presumed date of Constantine's conversion.

In the year 1104, thirteenth of the indiction.

In the year 1105, fourteenth of the indiction, there was much snow in the months of January and February, and the rivers flooded, and a comet appeared from the west; three days later the pope came to Benevento.[10]

In the following year Henry, King of the Germans died.[11]

In the year 1107, in the month of September, first of the indiction, there died the afore-mentioned Roffred, Archbishop of Benevento, who had been in office for thirty-one years, two months and twenty days. In this year, in the month of September, died Abbot Madelmus, and in this same month of September, on the feast of S. Angelo, Abbot Bernard was elected.[12]

In the year 1108, second of the indiction, the wine was unfruitful and many animals died; and Pope Paschal came to Benevento and in the month of November ordained Landulf as archbishop.[13]

In the year 1109, third of the indiction, Formatus died. Easter occurred on 24th April, and on 2nd November the treasury of St Mary was burned down.[14]

In the year 1110, fourth of the indiction, King Henry came to Rome and in the month of February, by fraud and trickery, captured Pope Paschal and the Cardinals.[15] In the same month died Duke Roger and

---

10 Cf. Bertolini, 'Annales', 152, which date the appearance of the comet to 10 February [1106].

11 Emperor Henry IV died on 7 August 1106. His death was also noted by two of the three versions of the Benevento Annals, Bertolini, 'Annales', 153.

12 On 29 September. Version 3 of the Benevento Annals dates the death of Archbishop Roffred to 9 September and that of Madelmus to 27 September. Madelmus became abbot of St Sophia between March 1074 and March 1075, Roffred archbishop after March 1076, Bertolini, 'Annales', 144, 153. Loud (1991), 12.

13 Paschal II was at Benevento 25 September–12 November, then after a visit to Troia he returned there for Christmas, J-L 6205–9, 6214. He held a council in October, where he repeated earlier prohibitions of the investiture of bishops by laymen, Blumenthal (1978a), 102–6. Landulf had been Cardinal priest of S. Lorenzo in Lucina from November 1106, Hüls (1977), 181–2; he was one of a number of cardinals appointed to South Italian metropolitan sees at this period, Loud (2007a), 216–17.

14 This was the cathedral treasury: cf. Bertolini, 'Annales', 153.

15 Henry V had attempted to negotiate a peace in the long-running dispute between papacy and empire, but a compromise peace broke down in the face of the German bishops' opposition; the pope was taken prisoner, eventually forced to conclude a treaty at Ponte Mammolo in April, very much on Henry's terms, and crowned him as emperor. One of the most detailed contemporary accounts is *Chron. Cas.* IV.36–40, pp. 502–9; see also *Ekkehard*, 256–60. For discussion (in English) see Partner (1972), 147–50; Morris (1989), 158–61; Robinson (1990), 424–9; and most exhaustively (in German) Servatius (1979), 214–52.

Bohemond his brother.[16]

In the year 1111, fifth of the indiction.

In the year 1112, sixth of the indiction, Pope Paschal held a Synod at Rome in the month of March and broke the pact which he had made with King Henry.[17] In this year building began on the oratory of St Bartholomew the Apostle.[18]

When these and other things had happened, the Beneventans, seeing that they were afflicted with many violent animosities, took counsel and despatched Archbishop Landulf and John the Judge to the above-mentioned pope, for since the citizens were faced with such a catastrophe, they sought him as their means of safety; particularly since some among the Beneventans caused disturbance within the city with frequent conspiracies.[19] Some sought to make Landulf Burrellus and others Anso the rector of the city without the pope's consent. On hearing this, the pope did not delay and came to Benevento on 2nd December, and called a Synod in February.[20] And when this Synod had commenced sitting in the Sacred Beneventan Palace the plot made on behalf of Landulf Burrellus was uncovered. He ordered the citizens to be called so that it might be properly decided what ought to be done about such a weighty and important matter. This conspiracy was intended, as we have said, to subvert and damage the city. Some of the citizens had after dark seized the towers of the Porta Somma in order to assist this same Landulf, expelled the guards and had defended this fortification for the space of a night. After a while, with God's help and with the aid of the many loyal Beneventans who were of a sounder disposition, these towers were recovered and restored to [the possession of] St Peter. The citizens gave this reply to the lord pope; that he should summon those who he held suspect and do full justice upon them. What more

---

16 Duke Roger died on 21 February 1111, *Necrologio di S. Matteo*, 28; *Necrologio del Cod. Cas.* 47, 59; and the necrologies of Catania cathedral and the palace chapel at Palermo, for which *Libro del Capitolo*, ed. Houben, 133. Bohemond died on 7 March, according to the *Necrologio del Cod. Cas.* 47, 27, which fits with the fourteen days after Roger according to *Romuald*, 206.

17 Paschal was forced to disavow the Treaty of Ponte Mammolo after bitter criticism at the synod from a number of senior clerics, *Ekkehard*, 306–8; William of Malmesbury, *Gesta Regum Anglorum*, ed. R.A.B. Mynors, R.M. Thomson and M. Winterbottam, i (Oxford 1998), 770–5. Blumenthal (1978b); Servatius (1979), 309–25; Robinson (1990), 128–31.

18 Bertolini, 'Annales', 155, version 1, said that building began on 22 July.

19 John the Judge was probably the man later recorded as being exiled in 1128 [below, 158, and note 86, 182].

20 Paschal remained at Benevento until 31 March 1113, J-L 6336–6344.

[need be said]? A court was constituted. Those responsible for these disorders and those under suspicion were summoned. Finally a just sentence was pronounced. We saw some imprisoned, others expelled. Some men's houses were confiscated, others had them destroyed. This was what happened.[21]

In the year 1113, the fourteenth of the lord Pope's pontificate, in the month of March, the sixth of the indiction, the Pontiff, seeing the city of Benevento oppressed by strife on all sides and being informed that the property of the citizens all over the region was every day stolen or plundered by the Normans, called a council. He appointed Landulf de Greca, an outstanding and skilful knight, as Constable of the Beneventans, by whose prudence and the help of God the city might be made safe and kept so in the future from the disorders which so often menaced it and from the frequent conspiracies fomented against the lord pope.[22] He knew him to be a man both prudent and brave, and of quick wits, by whose help and skill he expected that not only the people of Benevento who had been entrusted to his rule but also many other lands of the Lombards would be freed from the Norman servitude with which they had been afflicted. Landulf was indeed of a warlike spirit, would not put up with injuries and menaces, and was every day a threat to his enemies. For if one of his enemies did him injury or harm then he would have preferred rather to die than to allow that enemy to retire unpunished. What more [need be said]? Landulf the Constable was distinguished with every sort of virtue and experience and refused to bend his neck to any who threatened him. After Landulf had received the honour of the Constable's position from the lord Pope Paschal, as has been described above; seeing the *castellum* which had been built on Monte Sableta by Robert, called Sclavus, an evil man devoted to the study of vice, he urged him to have it destroyed.[23] Robert had built this *castellum* on a grand

21 The synod was also discussed by *Chron. Cas.* IV.48, pp. 514–15, but this account concentrated on ecclesiastical matters raised by Montecassino, both its continued claims over the abbey of St Sophia and a dispute with the abbey of Torremaggiore in northern Apulia.

22 Landulf was a landowner at Montefusco, on a 700m. hill 13 km. SE of Benevento (rather more by road, which even today is winding), cf. *Catalogus Baronum*, art. 424, which refers to his son Tadeus, and Cuozzo (1984), 115.

23 Monte Sableta or Saglieta, 5 km. NE of Benevento, near the confluence of the Calore and Tammaro rivers. Robert Sclavus cannot be clearly identified, but in May 1152 a Robert Sclavus was acting as the advocate (legal representative) of the abbey of Tremiti in Apulia, *Codice diplomatico del monastero benedettino di S. Maria di Tremiti* (3 vols, Rome FSI, 1960), iii.294–7 no. 106. While this is most unlikely to have been the same man, he may well have been a relative. Cuozzo (1984), 89–90, suggests the surname was derived from Eschauffour, the Norman toponym borne by some members of the Giroie family so well known to Orderic Vitalis. But this may be hard to reconcile with the John Sclavus who defended

scale and with great labour on account of his war with the Beneventans and the hostility of the city. From those residing in this *castrum* the citizens had suffered much harm and a multitude of injuries, [not least] because as a consequence of its construction some amongst them had lost the lands and properties which they had owned in the vicinity of the mountain. This *castellum* was very strongly constructed; those who lived there, along with Robert's sergeants, sometimes captured men of Benevento. But, what was crueller, on other occasions they deprived pilgrims not merely of their goods but of their lives. Hearing of this at Rome the pope excommunicated Robert, until he should destroy this *castellum* vexing the city, which however Robert refused to do. What more? The Constable Landulf de Greca came to an agreement with Robert that the *castellum* should be destroyed (which he had been unwilling to do for the pope) and levelled to the ground, in return for two excellent horses and 200 *solidi*. Then the Constable Landulf came to an agreement, confirmed under oath, with Count Jordan and [hence] his virtues and good qualities were universally praised.

However Prince Robert and counts Robert and Jordan, seeing this *castellum* thus destroyed and the Constable Landulf daily increasing in fame and wealth, were convulsed with envy and hatred of the Lombards.[24] Thinking that they might through his prudence be dispossessed, they plotted with all the Normans of the neighbouring areas, agreeing to levy war and rapine against the Beneventans as long as Landulf remained as their constable. They confirmed this by oath and then marched against Benevento on 12th August with a large number of knights and footsoldiers. They halted on Monte Guardia for a day and pitched camp there for the night,[25] believing that they would be able to expel the constable and lay waste the city, but on the same day on which they had arrived battle was joined and they were defeated, and some of them were captured. After nightfall they were overcome with fear both of the Divine One and of the Beneventans and fled along the byways like thieves, thinking that they would during the night be captured by the Beneventans and shamefully imprisoned. Indeed, according to the account given by many of them, if the constable, with the Beneventans

---

Atrani in 1131, *Al. Tel.* II.10, and it is possible that it was a fairly common surname/nickname.

24 Robert I, Prince of Capua 1106/7–20; Count Robert of Caiazzo (d.1116), for whom see especially Tescione (1975), also Loud (1982), 200–8; and Count Jordan of Ariano (attested from 1112 onwards, d.1127), whose grandfather Gerard of Buonalbergo (d.1086) had been one of the main allies of Robert Guiscard.

25 Monte Guadia was a plateau about 350m. above sea level, 10 km. S of Benevento.

and his knights, had gone past the church of S. Angelo *ad crucem*,[26] or if the sound of anybody's voice had been heard then [our] enemies and their war gear would have undoubtedly have fallen into the hands of the Beneventan forces.[27]

Once these Normans had retired, the Constable Landulf de Greca was unwilling just to await the assaults of the enemy, and instead of returning to receive these collected together with scarcely a delay nearly 180 well-armed knights and a multitude of some 4,000 citizens, went to the *castellum* called Terra Rubea and razed it to the ground by fire and sword; in the firing of this *castrum* Robert 'of Sicily' was burned and died.[28] A vast number of animals and other goods were brought back to Benevento amid [scenes of] great joy. Not long afterwards Landulf once more raised a force of knights and citizens, attacked the *castellum* of Apice and destroyed it and its mills, returning joyfully bringing with him [its] animals as booty.[29]

After these events, war with the Normans (whom we have mentioned) flared up most fiercely, and in it Landulf distributed vast quantities of gold, silver and many horses. In the meantime, while the constable himself with a force of knights was on guard against the ambushes of the enemy near the bridge of Serratella, there appeared nearly fifty knights of Count Robert who took station threateningly in the gardens of the city. What can I say? Each side having discovered the other's ambush, fighting broke out between them. Finally Divine Mercy intervened and the enemy turned tail and fled. The constable captured twelve of their knights with all their equipment. Thereafter, as we have said, the war was waged fiercely on both sides and there was frequent and widespread plundering. It happened one day that Rao, who was the lord of the *castellum* of Ceppaloni,[30] with Landulf Burrellus, nearly 150 other knights and a large force of infantry came to break down, so I say, the water course. When the constable saw them crossing the River Sabato he was unwilling to permit such audacity and accompanied by a troop of knights rode into the midst of the plain near the the church of the Seven Holy Brothers. Battle was commenced on all sides, but their

---

26 A little way outside the Porta Somma.

27 Bertolini, 'Annales', 155, version 1, confirms the date of 12 August, adding that the Normans were 'shamefully' put to flight by Landulf the Constable.

28 Terra Rubea, now disappeared, but see *Catalogus Baronum*, art. 347.

29 Apice, on a 250m. hilltop site, 14 km. due E of Benevento, although more like 19 km. by road.

30 Ceppaloni is 9 km. S of Benevento. Falco later recorded the death of this Rao, on 9 July 1120.

sins led the constable's party to fall prey to the traps of their enemies; they were driven from the plain and twelve noble knights of the city were captured with all their war gear.

With all these and other things happening, all those enemies who had sworn to wage war together, seeing that the constable would not submit but was even more of a threat to them, and that the Beneventans loyally followed him and his orders, began to harass the city more than ever, instructing [their men] to cut down as many as they could of the vines planted nearby. This was done. Also they were to capture poor men and others when they ran across them; and after this order was pronounced many were indeed made prisoners.

In the month of March of the year 1114, seventh of the indiction, while the vines were being cut and men captured, some of the Beneventans, struck by the sword of envy, sent Archbishop Landulf and Abbot Rachisius of St Modestus to the pope to inform him of the calamities which surrounded them on all sides.[31] They went to the pope, told him of the suffering which they had seen, and tearfully begged him to deign to help them as a good pastor does his flock. Once he had been shown their predicament, the pope ordered them to do the best they could to secure peace for the city and to help the poor, lest the Apostle Peter lose the city which he had by chance acquired; the terms however of the peace treaty they should leave to him. But when the archbishop returned from Rome he did the opposite of what he had been told and sent to Landulf the Constable saying that, constrained by the plight of the poor, he was deposing him as constable until the time when the lord pope should come to Benevento. Afterwards, indeed, either for money and services or by the prayers of the citizens they would request the pope to restore him to his original honour; [he did this] only because the Normans were unwilling to make peace, for they were prevented, as has been said, by their oath.[32] However, on hearing this, Landulf the Constable, in the Sacred Beneventan Palace in front of the *fideles* of St Peter, replied saying that he would never relinquish the constable's position unless he was captured and kept prisoner by main force. Of course he wished to see the Normans desirous of making peace with the Beneventans and

31 The monastery of St Modestus, founded between 758 and 774, was in the 'new city', the eighth-century westward extension of Benevento, between the archbishop's palace and the Porta Rufina, *Le più antiche carte dell'abbazia di S. Modesto di Benevento (secoli VIII–XIII)*, ed. F. Bartoloni (Rome 1950), pp. xii–xiii. Unfortunately most of its many surviving documents date from after 1200, its earliest twelfth-century charter from 1139, but Rachisius can be attested as abbot in January 1108, *Chron. S. Sophiae*, ii.752.

32 See above 135. The Normans had sworn not to make peace while Landulf was constable.

himself bringing news of that peace to the pope. He would do what was ordered, either to secure peace or to lay down the constableship, if the pope ordered him [to do this] in public. This the constable reiterated in the Sacred Beneventan Palace.

When the archbishop had returned from Rome, as has been described, the pope had sent with him to secure peace [two] cardinals of the Holy Roman See, Peter Bishop of Porto and the deacon Romuald.[33] Immediately on their arrival and even before they had found their lodgings the people were whipped up to a fury and mobbed the palace of Dacomarius where the constable lived, crying out: 'If you do not make peace at once as we want, we shall draw our swords and there will be death in the streets'. Furthermore they hurled threats and abuse at the constable, saying that they ought not to suffer a war and so lose their lives wretchedly just to keep one man in the constable's office. On another day the archbishop's party rose up and mustered arms and warlike gear on the belltower, in order to defeat Landulf with missiles and stones and thus expel him. Observing the sedition of the people the Bishop of Porto entered the Prince's Court with the constable and the *fideles* of St Peter. There in the sight of all he spoke as follows: 'You have suffered trouble and famine for a long time because of your loyalty to St Peter, and are suffering it [now]. Our lord the pope has heard this from a variety of people and has been informed of it by the archbishop; as a result you know that his heart is filled with sadness and he greatly laments what he has heard. In consequence he has sent us, along with your archbishop, so that, with God's aid, you may have peace. On that account, we urge and beg you faithful people not to be swayed by pride or wrath while we, along with other wise men, are looking for a way to secure peace for you, for this is so serious and difficult a matter that nobody ought to act precipitately. So no one is to appear armed since, if it be pleasing to God, with anger laid aside we shall be worthy to find peace'. When he had said this and other things similar, the voice of the people was raised to Heaven, saying, 'We shall not listen to these prayers that you make unless you very speedily give us peace'. Then on another day the populace was unable to bear the delays and the truces which they had made and attacked the house of Persicus the judge, totally destroying it.[34] He himself escaped with the help of some friends. The Bishop of

---

33 Romuald, Cardinal deacon of S. Maria in Via Lata from c.1110, who was appointed as archbishop of Salerno in 1121 and died on 21 January 1137, *Necrologio di S. Matteo*, 12; Hülls (1977), 238.

34 Persicus the judge witnessed a donation to the chapel of St Marcianus, inside the cathedral, in March 1105, and an exchange between Archbishop Landulf and the church of St Paul

Porto was unable to calm this uprising by the people, and departed at dawn the next day. He ordered the constable to go up into the Palace of the Prince, and thus escape the howling of the furious people. Following this advice he took up residence in the Sacred Palace. But let us return to our story.

Hearing the words of the constable, the archbishop sent him instructions laying down clearly the conditions on which peace was to be made, as he had asked. Having ascertained the details of the document concerning the peace, the constable said, 'The details of the peace are excellent; now it shall be sent to our lord [the pope], and as he orders so shall we obey'. Meanwhile the archbishop and a man called Fulco frequently gathered many of the citizens together in the cathedral, saying that 'We have notified the lord pope of your need and he has ordered us to make a treaty with the Normans; thus it seems superfluous to send him the full details'. However, certain among the citizens, filled by hatred from other grievances, incited others, saying openly that that they had not suffered the war merely to maintain someone in the constable's office. After discussing it [amongst themselves] inside the cathedral, they swore that they would not agree to Landulf de Greca being constable and that on the advice of the Normans the lord pope should not restore him to that office. After the oath had been taken the archbishop sent the bishop of Avellino and some priests to the constable, [telling him] to lay down the honour, and the latter replied in kind.[35] Then, on Sunday 14th March, the constable marched into the midst of the square with an armed band of his men, saying that 'I wish to see those who are trying to drive me from the palace and my position. It is more praiseworthy to give up one's life like this rather than abandon a post one has received in a cowardly manner or for the promise of a big bribe'. Hearing this the archbishop prepared for war, and with the palace bell sadly tolling, ordered his partisans to be summoned, that the peace they were making with the Normans should be confirmed; and if the constable wished to resist they should be ready for him.

Meanwhile, since he refused to submit to them, the party of the archbishop attacked the house of one of the constable's supporters. Hearing of this, the constable made a sortie to defend that house and

---

in July 1112, *Più antiche carte del capitolo della cattedrale di Benevento (668–1200)*, ed. V. Ciarelli, V. de Donato and V. Matera (Rome 2002), 163–4 no. 53, 167–70 no. 55. He died on 12 April (year unknown), *L'Obituarium S. Spiritus della biblioteca capitolare di Benevento (secc. XII-XIV)*, ed. A. Zazo (Naples 1963), 35.

35 Probably John, attested as Bishop of Avellino in May 1123, *Cod. Dipl. Verginiano*, ii.186–9 no. 145.

thus civil war commenced. Some fought from towers, others from the roofs of houses, others still in the squares. Eventually fortune was reversed and the archbishop's party gained the victory; they chased the constable and his men back to the Palace of the Prince. We saw men on both sides wounded. The constable took refuge in the Palace and remained there for a short time until the archbishop pledged him his word, in his followers' name as well as on his own account. The citizens however would not accept this armistice since they thirsted after a [full] peace settlement. They threatened him with rocks, [saying] that if he did not immediately come down from the Palace then they would seize him and hew him limb from limb. Seeing himself trapped Landulf surrendered to the archbishop and citizens. He swore on oath to them that he would not accept the Constableship, the Rectorate or any other public office [balia] without the agreement of the archbishop, Roffred the archpriest, Alechisius the archdeacon, Roffred son of Gaderisius, Roffred of Porta Aurea, Gervase and Vitalis the son of John Gallus, [36] and that he would not do harm to the Archbishop nor to any Beneventan, and if anyone wished to dispute with him he would respond without trickery or malice. Once this had been done, and a similar undertaking had been received from his followers, everyone returned to their own homes and Landulf himself went home after laying down the constable-ship in the same month of March as he had been appointed, having held the office for a single year.

After this had happened, early one Sunday Count Robert, and [accom-panying him] Rao lord of Ceppaloni and Hugh of Castelpoto, came at the head of a multitude of knights and footmen to the Ponte Maggiore and confirmed on oath the promised peace for their lifetimes.[37] Count Jordan, Robert Sclavus and Gerard de la Marca swore similarly.[38] And

---

36 Roffred the archpriest, later Archbishop Roffred II (1119–30), witnessed a charter of the archbishop in June 1114, *Chron. S. Sophiae*, ii.695; Roffred de Gaderisio was father of his successor, Archbishop Landulf III (1130–2); Vitalis Galli, who witnessed a charter in October 1146, *Più antiche carte della cattedrale*, 211 no. 70, was probably the man mentioned here.

37 Hugh of Castelpoto (13 km. W of Benevento) was perhaps father of the Hugh the Infant mentioned below in 1122, as argued by Cuozzo (1984), 278–9, though the genealogy of this family is confused and Cuozzo is too dogmatic here. More probably they were the same person. Certainly Hugh son of *quondam* Hugh *Infans* made donations to Montecassino in May 1112 and St Sophia in March 1118, *Chron. Cas.* IV.47, p. 514; De Donato (1952), 25–7 no. 4; Benevento, Museo del Sannio, Fondo S. Sofia, vol. 12 no. 38. The Ponte Maggiore bridged the River Sabato, SW of the city, and led to the Caudine Valley and Capua.

38 Gerard de la Marca, or de Marcia as the charters render this name, was son of Rao Pinella, specifically identified as a Norman, who was later a benefactor of the abbey of St Sophia, Pergamene Aldobrandini, Cart. I nos. 51 (March 1122) and 56 (March 1126). He died soon

when, as has been related above, the archbishop had given pledge of security to the constable and to other knights and footmen, as he [the constable] had requested, and the latter had laid down his office and gone home, it was clear both to the archbishop and to the Beneventans that they had gained the long-desired peace.

The constable then, having received [promise of] security, was residing at home, thinking that nothing else was going to happen which was going to threaten his peace of mind. He was then, as we were told, gravely wounded. His friends and the *fideles* of St Peter day and night lamented this unhappy incident and his injuries. They soothed him, though not in public, encouraging him not to be cast down by these events, for what they saw and what had been done to him, he had suffered because of his faithfulness to St Peter. However, on hearing this, the archbishop and his supporters were filled with suspicion, thinking that Landulf was receiving advice on how to recover the constableship. They sent messages to him more and more frequently suggesting that he leave the city and stop consorting with his friends until, as had been laid down already, the lord pope should restore him to his previous office. After receiving these messages the constable openly complained to others among his fellow citizens; 'I am altogether bemused by such words, since I was forced by the full assembly of the Beneventans to lay down the constableship but in no way do I see myself given that security which was promised by the archbishop'. Finally, at dawn on Palm Sunday,[39] seeing the determination of the enraged populace becoming more and more inflamed, and yielding to advice, he left with a handful of knights for Montefusco.

With undiminished untrustworthiness the archbishop's faction [*coniuratio*] still did not observe its word. They forced the judges John and Persicus, and other nobles and *boni homines* [to swear] the same oath that the constable himself had sworn, and abandoning all restraint they bound others of the citizens [as well], wishing them to receive due retribution for their hostility. When matters had been arranged in this fashion and other things done more evil than would be believed possible, news of it came to the ears of the pontiff, who was greatly upset by the expulsion of his beloved son the constable. With, as we have heard, tears flowing, he roared out his anger and immediately and publicly deposed Archbishop Landulf from every office which he had

---

after this donation. He also witnessed a donation to the monastery of St Nicholas, Troia, in November 1123, *Chartes de Troia*, 175–7 no. 46.

39 Palm Sunday was on 22 March.

received from the Roman See, and similarly bound all his followers with the chain of anathema until they should make satisfaction. But, if it is not too much of a strain on the reader's charity, I shall record what ought not to be omitted, namely what happened at Benevento after that excommunication. For God is my witness I have written down nothing except what I have seen or heard [myself].

This sentence of anathema on the enemies of St Peter was published far and wide, and the pope selected [two] suitable cardinals of the Roman See, Anastasius and the Bishop of Albano, desiring to ascertain what the populace of Benevento actually wanted.[40] The cardinals were made welcome there, and three days later the assembly of all the Beneventans gathered in the Sacred Beneventan Palace, and there in the cardinals' presence everything that had happened at Benevento and the root and origin of the civil war [*guerra*] was recounted. After hearing this Anastasius began to speak saying, 'Let it be known, my lords and brothers, that we have been selected to inspect and investigate certain matters which have come to the attention of our lord the pope at Rome. Thus, as best we can and with the help of God, we shall day and night offer advice and help for the promotion of peace and for your advantage'. After this and various other similar speeches everyone returned to their homes. Not many days had gone by when a man of whom we have made mention, named Fulco, departed miserably from this earthly prison still bound by the chain of anathema. Once this had happened, the cardinal himself departed for Rome.

While Cardinal Anastasius was going to Rome, the lord Pope Paschal gathered together the archbishops, bishops and abbots and held a council at Ceprano, in the month of October following his first return. To this sacred gathering came Duke William and Prince Robert with nearly 1,000 knights. The Constable Landulf de Greca appeared there most honourably, summoned to the council by a personal letter from the lord pope. He was received in the most gracious manner by the pope. To avoid any sort of trickery from the Normans, he had travelled in safety by ship.[41] Count Jordan, fearing to put in an appearance at such an important council when burdened by the weight of his many sins, sent his envoys. Archbishop Landulf gathered together his suffragans,

---

40 Anastasius, Cardinal priest of S. Clemente 1102–25, was one of the cardinals who accompanied Paschal to Benevento in January 1113; Richard, Cardinal Bishop of Albano 1101–15, a Frenchman, was a former canon of Metz, much of whose curial career was spent on legations to France, Hüls (1977), 93–5, 161–2.

41 Presumably from Naples to Gaeta – it is unlikely he sailed from Salerno since it was under Norman rule.

raised a huge sum of gold and silver and came to the meeting with Count Robert. When all these great prelates and nobles had been convened, then on the Saturday, in the midst of the council, the pontiff conceded to the above-mentioned duke ducal rule over Italy, Calabria and Sicily.[42] The council was thus splendidly inaugurated, and then the pope tearfully lamented in front of all and made complaint about Archbishop Landulf, because he had expelled his constable Landulf and after being summoned by his letter had refused to come. For the archbishop had been unwilling to put in an appearance at the council before his place and office had been restored, and had stayed at Isola, near Ceprano.[43] When he found out that the pope had made [formal] complaint about him then he ordered some of the Romans and the Prefect to be summoned, that they might, to the best of their ability, beg mercy for him from the lord pope: for the archbishop said that if he made satisfaction to the lord pope for all his charges against him, then in consequence he [the pope] ought to restore to him his place at the council and his office. When the pope heard this he took advice and restored his place and office to him.

Once restored to his place then without delay on the Monday he came to the council, along with Count Robert. What more [need we say]? The pope, through a certain deacon, ordered him, now that he had been restored, to be called into their presence that justice might be done. He rose up immediately and replied in front of them all, saying: 'First of all I thank God, St Peter and you, lord Pope Paschal, for restoring my place and office. Now, holy Father, I implore you to have mercy upon me, whom your Holiness did appoint to the Beneventan See'. However, on hearing this, the pope replied, 'Why do you want us to have mercy upon you?' And the archbishop, 'Lord, because I have heard that you are angry with me since you ordered me by your letters to be summoned, and I did not come to your court'. The pope said, 'Why, as you yourself admit, did you not come to our court when you were summoned'? To this the archbishop replied, 'Lord Father, I did not come when called because I was afraid of your wrath and of certain persons who were making threats, because you would not receive the bishops I sent as my envoys, and because another man whom I had first of all sent was

42 Cf. for the investiture of Duke William, *Romuald*, 207; while he was there William also issued a privilege confirming the property of Montecassino, witnessed by Prince Robert, Count William II of the Principate and the ducal constable Hoel of S. Agata, *Le Colonie Cassinesi in Capitanata* iv *Troia*, ed. T. Leccisotti (Miscellanea Cassinese 29, 1957), 85–7 no. 23; *Chron. Cas.* IV.48, p. 515.

43 Isola dei Liri, 15 km. N of Ceprano.

physically attacked by my enemies'. To this the pope: 'I would not receive your envoys, whom you say were bishops, since they said nothing about doing justice, but came only to seek mercy for you. As to your other envoy whom you claim was attacked, I have neither seen him nor has any report of him come to us'.

When the archbishop saw that the truth of his replies was being doubted on every side he tried another excuse, saying, 'Lord Father, you did not give me a proper deadline for my appearence; thus I was unable to come, nor indeed did I dare because I was afraid'. The pope [replied]: 'Since you disdained our letter, you now claim that you did not come to us from fear. For I did indeed prescribe a proper deadline, namely six months from 13th April'. He ordered the letter of summons to be read in the midst of the assembly. 'However, our people here will discuss [the case] and will decide if what you say in excuse is canonical'. He then ordered certain cardinals and archbishops to act as judges of the Roman See, separating themselves from the others to consider a verdict about the excuses put forward by the archbishop. They went to one side and discussed the verdict for a long time. Then they returned and pronounced their sentence in the sight of all as follows: 'Lord Archbishop of Benevento, you assert that you did not come to the court when you were called not out of contempt but out of fear. We say and judge that this is not a canonical excuse'. Once this verdict by so many and such important Fathers had been pronounced, the pope ordered the canons of the Holy Fathers of earlier times, which had been confirmed by councils and promulgated against those in contempt of them, to be shown and read out. After this was done the cardinals and bishops deliberated for a long time about these serious matters. But what more? The deacon called him once again to do justice, but he immediately rose up and asked, 'By whom and of what am I accused?' The pope [replied], 'You took over the *regalia* of St Peter without our consent, you held the keys of the gates, you invaded the palace, you expelled Landulf, you assumed the helmet and shield, and you forced Fulco into an oath [against his will]'. Hearing this, the archbishop replied; 'Really I received the *regalia* of St Peter for no other reason than fealty to you. For when you were in Benevento you commended the city to me. I did not receive the keys to the gates. Moreover, the man to whom they were entrusted was someone whom we believed to be faithful to you in every respect. I did not carry a shield in the street, and I wore a helmet only to protect my head from being struck by falling stones. I did not introduce the Normans as you say. I allowed sixteen Lombards to enter to assist the people of the city.' He [also] denied that either the oath taken by

Fulco or those taken by other people were administered on his order.

After listening to all this, the pope ordered the cardinals and the afore-said judges once again to give sentence on all these matters and on the question of contempt. When the archbishop heard this, as one might say, terrible command he exhorted Duke William, Prince Robert, Peter Leone[44] and the bishops, saying: 'My noble lords, brother bishops, request, I beg you, our lord Pope Paschal not so to humiliate me in the sight of you all and make me leave in disgrace. If indeed it shall please him to be merciful I shall seek exile and sail across the sea'. Then the nobles came to the feet of the pope to request this of him as the archbishop had asked, but all in vain. The judges, though cowed and unhappy, followed their orders and appeared to pronounce judgment. The pope instructed the judges who were, as I said, delaying giving sentence, to swear by the faith they owed to St Peter and to himself, that what they announced would be canonical. The Bishop of Porto, though distressed and showing visible signs of grief, was the first to pronounce judgment. 'Since', he said, 'you seized the *regalia* of St Peter, held the keys of the [city] gates, invaded the palace, expelled Landulf, and treated a summons to the Curia with contempt, we sentence you to deposition [from office], since you acted against St Peter and our lord the pope'. The Archbishop of Capua and Cardinal Gregory pronounced likewise.[45] The other judges wished to confirm this sentence, while Landulf himself, in the midst of the council, was convulsed by fear and stood up, smitten by the sword of such a verdict. Oh, if you could have been present, reader, and seen the weeping, and looked at Landulf's pallid face when from the judges' mouths he heard his deposition from the Beneventan See with which he had been honoured and which had made him glorious before all. What should I say? Deprived of his position, he left this fearful council as if gone mad.

In this year the cathedral church of St Mary was enlarged on the advice of Landulf de Greca. In this year Archbishop Landulf of Benevento was arrested, and Landulf de Greca, who had been expelled from the city of Benevento, returned and received the constableship.

44 Head of the family of that name and father of the future (anti-)Pope Anacletus II, who died after 1124. Originally Jewish converts, the Pierleone had become one of the wealth-iest families in Rome and were close allies of the reform popes, especially of Paschal II, Palumbo (1942), 98–117; Zema (1944), 170–5; Stroll (1987), 144–5.

45 Sennes, Archbishop of Capua 1097–1118, had been Apostolic Legate in the Principality of Capua since 1113, Ughelli, *Italia Sacra*, vi.486, Loud (1985), 104. Cardinal Gregory cannot be certainly identified, but Gregory, Cardinal Deacon of S. Eustachio 1110–37 is a possibility, Hülls (1977), 227.

After all this and other things had happened, the pope reached Troia on 24th August, where he decreed and confirmed that there should be a council.[46] At this council nearly all the nobles, archbishops and bishops of Apulia were gathered together. Among the other matters which were decided there this council promulgated the Truce of God, which Count Jordan, the Count of Loritello[47] and other Apulian barons who were present confirmed by oath; this Truce to be observed for three years from thenceforth. When this had been confirmed and the council piously concluded, the pope returned to Benevento on 3rd September. The pope gave judgment on various very pressing civic business and returned to Rome on 25th September. It was then that he dedicated the monastery of St Vincent.[48]

In the year 1116 from the incarnation of Our Lord Jesus Christ, and the seventeenth year of the pontificate of Paschal II, Pontiff and Universal Pope, in the month of March, ninth of the indiction, our said lord pope held a synod at Rome.[49] And in March of this year the Prefect of the city of Rome died,[50] and after his death a terrible civil war arose, because the Roman people had heard that Peter Leone, on the pope's advice, wished to make his son the prefect. In consequence the Romans promoted the son of the deceased prefect to that office. Having done this they sent to the said Pope Paschal, humbly begging him that he give his consent to and confirm their choice. The pope absolutely refused to do this. When the Romans realised this they banded together in a sworn association [*coniuratio*] and demolished down to their foundations various towers and other splendid buildings belonging to those who were allied to Peter Leone in what had been done. Then Ptolomey, the prefect's uncle and other barons seized and occupied the *castra* of the pope.[51] It

---

46 This was in the year 1115. Paschal II was in Benevento from 24 May onwards, and then after the Council of Troia from 3 to 25 September, JL 6457–6466; cf. for the council *Chron. Cas.*, IV.55, pp. 519–20.

47 Robert II, Count of Loritello (in northern Apulia) 1095–1122, great-nephew of Robert Guiscard, for whom de Francesco (1910), 281–4.

48 This was the main abbey church of the monastery of St Vincent on Volturno in Molise, rebuilt after 1093, for which Hodges (1997), 171–5. For the dedication, *Chron. Vulternense*, ed. V. Federici (3 vols, FSI, Rome, 1924–38), i.20–1, 99, which confirms the year as 1115.

49 For this synod, which met on 6 March, *Ekkehard*, 318–24; *Chron. Cas.* IV.60, p. 523. There was much dispute about what policy to pursue towards the emperor, before the latter was excommunicated.

50 Pietro Corsi (d. 29 March 1116), Brezzi (1947), 287.

51 Ptolomey I, Count of Tusculum (d.1128/9), was the maternal uncle (*avunculus*) of the deceased prefect. His son, also Ptolomey (d.1153), married Bertha, an illegitimate daughter of Emperor Henry V, probably in 1117, *Chron. Cas.* IV.61, p. 526. For Ptolomey I, see Hoffmann (1971a), 28–36.

happened one day that the prefect, accompanied by a group of nearly fifty knights, made a sortie from the city to observe some knights whom the pope had sent. The Papal Constable spotted this, launched a chance attack, defeated them and captured the prefect. As soon as Ptolomey heard of his nephew's capture he gathered his knights together, attacked the Papal Constable, freed his captured nephew and rejoicing brought him home with him. While these and other events were happening in Rome the pope left the city and took up residence at the *castrum* called Sezze.[52] He had seen that the rebellion was becoming more and more inflamed and that Peter Leone was every day more fiercely attacked. But after a few days had elapsed the pope realised that the rebellion was dying down and matters were becoming calmer, so, acting on advice, he gathered his troops together and re-entered Rome. He went to the Lateran Palace and there celebrated a solemn mass. After his entry to the city the people of the Romans, who had [previously] showed themselves rebellious to him, became more or less obedient to his will and dominion. Thus peace was restored and the pope remained secure in Rome.[53] After all this had occurred, the pope restored Landulf, whom he had [previously] deposed, to his archbishopric on 11th August.

In the year 1117 from the Incarnation of the Lord and the eighteenth of his pontificate, Pope Paschal celebrated a synod at Benevento in the month of April.[54] In this year Archbishop Riso of Bari was assassinated on the road to Canosa by Argyrus, a citizen of Bari.[55]

In this year Pope Paschal died on 22nd January, and Gelasius was elected Pope.

In the year 1118 from the Incarnation of Our Lord Jesus Christ, the first year of the pontificate of the lord high priest and universal Pope Gelasius II, in the month of March, eleventh of the indiction, the said Pope Gelasius was elected to the pontifical throne with the almost unanimous vote and agreement of the Roman people. He ordered the archbishops, bishops and abbots resident near the Roman See, and sent

52 Sezze is in the southern Campagna, about 65 km. SE of Rome, and 30 km. SW of Frosinone.

53 See also *Liber Pontificalis*, ii.301–2; and for discussion, Partner (1972), 151–4.

54 Paschal was at Benevento from 16 March to 24 April 1117, and then went to Siponto where he held another council, J-L 6546–6558.

55 Riso, Archbishop of Bari 1112–17, previously Cardinal priest of S. Lorenzo in Lucina from 1105, was one of the critics of Paschal II at the Lateran synod of 1112, but it is not clear that he was appointed archbishop as a result of this, to remove him from the Curia, since he joined the papal court at Benevento both in January–February 1113 and in May 1115, Hüls (1977), 179. His murder was a result of internal disputes in Bari, for which *Anonymi Barensis Chronicon*, ed. L.A. Muratori (Rerum Italicarum Scriptores v), 156.

envoys to the regions of Apulia, summoning them to the day of his consecration. He was when he was elected, as we have related, deacon and [Papal] Chancellor, and therefore could not be consecrated unless it was done in the canonical time of Lent. In response to his envoys the Bishop of Troia, the Archbishop of the city of Siponto and several others travelled to his solemn consecration.[56] But before the Pope-Elect Gelasius could receive the dignity of consecration, the afore-said King Henry, having laid his plans, made a stealthy night entry into Rome on 2nd March. [57]

Once the pope was aware of the king's entry in secret, and remembering how this same king had by fraud and deceit captured his predecessor the lord Pope Paschal and his cardinals, he gathered the cardinals together without delay, and set forth on the Tiber. Sailing with a favourable wind they came to Gaeta. However when the king realised that the pope had left, he sent to him at Gaeta, requesting him to return to the city since he himself wanted nothing else than to be able to attend and give added authority [*corroborare*] to his consecration. But Pope Gelasius knew well his wickedness and the depth of his untrustworthiness; 'We wonder', he said, 'why we have received so many envoys from this great man when he had informed us that he would be arriving on Easter Day. Now however we gather that he has rather come by night and before the season appointed. I shall, God willing, receive the confirmation of consecration. Then he may find me wherever he likes, ready to negotiate'. On hearing this, the envoys hurried back to the king and repeated to him all that they had heard from the pope. Then at Gaeta, on the day appointed in the month of March, Gelasius was canonically and properly consecrated by the cardinals who had accompanied him. The king however, hearing the pope's answer, held a pestiferous council and set up and had consecrated a certain Spanish archbishop

---

56 Gelasius was a deacon, so it was deemed appropriate to await the Ember Days, the proper canonical period, to confer priesthood, a necessary preliminary to his consecration. A document from Benevento drawn up on 2 February 1118 for one of the cathedral clergy reflects this. It was dated 'in the first year of the pontificate of John, the chancellor of the Holy Roman Church, elected as Pope Gelasius', *Più antiche carte della cattedrale*, 170–3 no. 56. *Liber Pontificalis*, ii.314–15, gives a much longer list of south Italian prelates at the eventual consecration: not only Bishop William II of Troia (1106–41) and Archbishop Gregory of Siponto (1116–18) but the archbishops of Bari, Benevento, Brindisi, Capua, Naples, Salerno, S. Severina and Trani, the abbots of Cava and Montecassino, Duke William of Apulia and Prince Robert of Capua.

57 Falco suggested that the election of Gelasius was generally accepted, but he faced considerable opposition in Rome, not least from the Frangipane family and the counts of Tusculum, Brezzi (1947), 290–3.

as pope, or as one would rather say, as invader of the Church.[58] What an evil and terrible danger! That monarch who ought to have been the defender and helper of the Roman See and the whole Catholic Church instead introduced to the world a new heresy and a cruel sort of death. Thus some of the Romans who remained loyal to the Roman Church, seeing and understanding heresy of this type [for what it was], lamented, 'How miserable we are, since formerly for many years we elected and consecrated as our Pastor whom we wished by the antique custom of our fathers without the interference and permission of any king, but now shall we no longer dare to elect or consecrate anyone unless we have the king's permission!' Then the prefect and other nobles of the Romans sent envoys to Gelasius, who had by now been canonically ordained at Gaeta. They addressed him, 'Let it be known to you, Father and lord, that we and our friends in no way gave encouragement or help to the consecration of this excommunicate to his wicked pontificate. And you should know that, since with God's assistance the machinations and plots of this most wicked man, the king, will soon be frustrated, you, the destroyer of error and evil will be joyfully and honourably returned to your rightful throne'. After these events the said Landulf de Greca, the former Constable of Benevento, sent a letter to Pope Gelasius, announcing to him that Stephen, the Rector of Benevento, by whom he had been deposed, was not acting with justice, and that his own houses and property had been destroyed by the Beneventans.[59]

In this year Pope Gelasius set out for Gaul on 2nd September, and paused at Pisa. As one is informed he went to Pisa and consecrated the archbishop of that city, and then after holding counsel took ship, and assisted by divine clemency and with a favourable wind sailed to transalpine parts. All the archbishops, bishops and other lords there received him with the utmost joy and great honour. After Gelasius had

---

58 Maurice, Archbishop of Braga in Portugal from 1108, previously Bishop of Coimbra 1099–1108, received coronation as Pope Gregory VIII on 8/9 March 1118. He had been at Rome since 1114, having gone there to seek Paschal II's support in a legal dispute with his erstwhile suffragans, especially Diego Gelmirez of Compostella, over Braga's newly-acquired metropolitan status. Apart from the emperor and the Frangipani family, he had little support – even the German bishops were reluctant to recognise him – and he acquired the nickname *Burdinus* (*burro*, 'the Spanish ass'); see Erdmann (1927). However, William of Malmesbury, or his source for Roman affairs, had a high opinion of his learning and said he would have been admired 'had he not chosen rather to achieve notoriety by such infamous conduct', *Gesta Regum*, i.778.

59 For Stephen as rector, *Chron. S. Sophiae*, ii.648. He may have been rector from autumn 1115, Vehse (1930–1), 124.

been thus received he had talks with the king of the English.[60] The pope remained there, and called a synod for the next March to be held with the Fathers of France and the Germans, where the discord which had so long and so gravely existed between the *Sacerdotium* and *Regnum* would with the aid of the Holy Ghost be discussed. If I were to describe in detail the riches and the gifts of gold and silver with which the pope was showered in these parts then I would run out of time before I had fully recounted them. But before the date set for celebrating the synod had arrived he was taken seriously ill at the monastery of St Peter, which is called Cluny, where he was staying. Realising that his illness was very grave, he ordered the Bishop of Palestrina to be summoned without delay and sought to impose on him that highest of honours, the Roman See.[61] For he saw that he was coming to the end of this bodily life, as is the case with [human] frailty. But the bishop, hearing the pope speaking thus, said; 'Let it not be that I, an unworthy and unhappy man, should undertake such a high honour and heavy responsibility, particularly in these times of ours when it is necessary that the Roman See be defended and strengthened with the help of God and the power of worldy riches against the flail of persecution. If you really want to heed my advice, we should elect to this great office the Archbishop of Vienne, a man both religious and prudent, and distinguished too by secular skills.[62] We believe that with God's assistance and by the merits of St Peter and the aid of this man the Roman See, which has for such a long time been threatened by the danger of persecution, can be brought to peace and triumph'. What more? This speech was pleasing to the sick Pope Gelasius, the rest of the cardinals and the other bishops present. Without delay they ordered the archbishop to be summoned, that they match these words with deeds and persevere [in their intention]. Since he who had been summoned opposed this with all his might, claiming that he was unworthy of the responsibility of so

60 Falco or his source seems to confuse Henry I's meeting with Gelasius's legate, Cono of Palestrina (Rouen, October 1118) and his meeting with Calixtus II (Chaumont, November 1119), *Orderic*, vi.202, 282–90.

61 Cono, Cardinal Bishop of Palestrina c.1108–22, was a German who had been a canon of Arrouaise. He was papal legate in the Holy Land 1110–11, accompanied Paschal II to Benevento in January 1113, and was legate to France and Germany 1114–15, Germany and Normandy in 1118 and (after the election of Calixtus) once again to Normandy in 1119, Hüls (1977), 113–16.

62 He was one of six sons of Count William II of Burgundy, and Archbishop of Vienne from 1088. He was one of the most vocal critics of Paschal II's surrender to Henry V in 1111, Morris (1989), 160–1, but despite this continued to be employed as a papal legate in France. For his election, Schilling (1998), 390–403, for a family tree, *ibid.*, 41; and for a far from favourable view of his character, Stroll (1987), 44–8.

great an office, then on the prompting of Divine Clemency, and on the wishes of the sick Gelasius, they imposed the pontifical diadem on him. And at the said monastery, on the next day, 29th January, Pope Gelasius joyfully departed to the Lord from the prison of this earthly life.

The cardinals who were there present took counsel and then immediately notified Peter, Bishop of Porto, whom Pope Gelasius had left as his vicar at Rome, of the pope's death and that they had elected the archbishop as Pope Calixtus. The Bishop of Porto received these letters and tearfully mourned the death of the pope. Then, summoning the cardinals who had remained with him and various faithful men from among the Romans, he went up on the Campidoglio where he displayed the letters which had been sent and ordered them to be read. When they had been read all were in agreement and with one voice they praised the Lord Almighty who had bestowed on them a man prudent and distinguished for his virtues as pontiff.[63] They were very upset however about the death of Pope Gelasius. After this had been done, it was agreed that the bishop should send to Archbishop Landulf of Benevento, Cardinal Hugh the regent of the city and the clergy and people of Benevento to notify them of the death of Gelasius and the election of Calixtus.[64] Immediately [on receipt of this news] Archbishop Landulf had the citizens, all the priests and the cathedral clergy called to the Sacred Palace so that he might announce to them the state of affairs. When they had gathered he ordered the letters to be read and expounded, and without delay all without exception commended the election of the said Calixtus. Then they issued forth singing the *Te Deum laudamus*; and thus the archbishop, Cardinal Hugh, a great crowd of clergy and a multitude of citizens descended singing from the Sacred Palace to the cathedral. Afterwards the archbishop climbed up to a higher position and exhorted the citizens to preserve in perpetuity their fealty to the Roman See. When this had been done they returned to their homes.

In the year 1119, the first year of the pontificate of the lord Calixtus II, supreme pontiff and universal pope, in the month of March, twelfth of

63 The cardinals left in Rome included Cencius, Cardinal Bishop of Sabina, Vitalis, Cardinal Bishop of Albano, John Cardinal priest of S. Cecilia, Rainerius, Cardinal priest of SS. Marcellino e Pietro, and Desiderius, Cardinal priest of S. Prassede, all of whom before the death of Gelasius issued a bull for Abbot Bernard of St Sophia, *Chron. S. Sophiae*, ii.647–8.

64 Hugh, Cardinal priest of SS. Apostoli from c.1116, died 1121/2, possibly during Calixtus II's journey to Calabria that winter. He was originally from Alatri, in Lazio, Hüls (1977), 151, and was the maternal uncle of the papal biographer Pandulf, *Liber Pontificalis*, ii.316–17. He was one of the witnesses of a privilege of Gelasius II for St Sophia, issued at Capua in April 1118, *Chron. S. Sophiae*, ii.646, and witnessed the cardinals' bull (above) as *provisor* of the Beneventan court.

the indiction, the said Archbishop of Benevento, seeing the city beset
and ravaged on every side by various afflictions and the churches of its
diocese every day vexed by plunderers, celebrated a synod on the tenth
day of this same month of March. At this sacred gathering there were
present the Bishop of Tusculum,[65] the above-named Cardinal Hugh,
another cardinal, about twenty suffragans of the see of Benevento and
the abbots of six monasteries. Among the other things which were
enacted in this synod was that all the malefactors of Benevento, and
all those disturbing the merchants coming to or going from the city
would be bound by the chain of anathema. After the assembly had thus
concluded in a pious and orderly manner, everyone returned home.

I shall now, if it be pleasing to your charity, succinctly relate something
of the war [*guerra*] between Count Jordan, who was mentioned above,
and Count Rainulf. When, as was said, the *castrum* of Montemiletto and also Monteaperto had been destroyed, Robert of Montefusco very frequently launched attacks on another *castellum* called
Tufo.[66] He attacked it fiercely using all sorts of warlike strategems
so that its lord and inhabitants would be filled with terror. Then, by
an unheard of and deadly plan, the fields of the peasants and their
vines and woods were ravaged by fire and the sword. And when the
peasants' fields had been newly sown, he ordered something which
had never been heard of in our time, that they be dug once again by
plough and rake and [the crops] laid waste. However Rao, the lord
of this *castrum*, was undisturbed either by these warlike attacks or
by the general confusion, and he bravely and energetically held the
castrum to its loyalty to Count Jordan.[67] Meanwhile the above named
Robert, who was Count Jordan's uncle, every day raised against him
seditious plots and darting attacks, as though he had the heart of a
viper.[68] Furthermore Robert of Montefusco very frequently consulted
with Count Rainulf about Count Jordan's raids and the danger of their

---

65 John (IV), a pupil of Anselm at the monastery of Bec in Normandy, and then Abbot of the
Holy Saviour, Telese, was appointed Cardinal Bishop of Tusculum 1100. He died later in
1119 on his way to join Calixtus II in France, *Orderic*, vi.274. Hüls (1977), 141–2.

66 Montemiletto is 17 km. SE of Benevento, Monteaperto about 2 km. SW of that. Falco had
not previously discussed this destruction. Tufo is 14 km. S. of Benevento and 6 km. due
W of Monteaperto. Montefusco is 5 km. to the NE of it.

67 Robert, lord of Tufo, had witnessed a charter of Count Jordan in July 1114, *Chron. S.
Sophiae*, ii.728.

68 He was the younger son of Count Gerard of Buonalbergo and younger brother of Jordan's
father Herbert. In the First Crusade he acted as standard-bearer for his cousin Bohemond,
and was of some importance in the first years of the new kingdom of Jerusalem, Jamison
(1939), 201–2; Murray (2009), 71–2, 74–5.

doing damage. Finally, revealing what he had always at heart intended, he demanded from Count Jordan the *castellum* of Templano, to ensure that he would remain his *fidelis* and friend all his days.[69] He wished the count to confirm this *castrum* by oath to a natural son of his whom he loved. When the count heard this he was greatly astonished and more upset than one would have believed possible. He immediately had all his barons summoned and carefully sought advice from them over this great and important matter. They were aware of Robert's perfidiousness, and seeing that there was no other way to win him over to the count's fealty, given the overwhelming difficulties [of the latter's position], advised that he should grant Robert's demand. After the council had discussed and decided this then, in the presence of Archbishop Landulf and Cardinal Hugh, as well as other Beneventans and nobles, the count granted all that he wanted. Then he [in turn] became by means of an oath the *fidelis* and dependant of Count Jordan. By this means the latter obtained 100 knights for his service. But he soon took revenge for what evil he had suffered and devastated all the fields of the knights of Montefusco. And it happened that while one day Landulf de Greca the Constable of Montefusco was going to the already mentioned *castrum* of Tufo, attended by a troop of knights, Count Jordan, who was secretly watching, attacked and defeated them and captured twelve of the knights with all their equipment. Among those who were led away captive was a knight called Eternus and another called Brian.[70] Count Rainulf however heard of this disaster to his *fideles* and was reluctant to see them overcome by Count Jordan. He gathered together nearly 400 knights and a multitude of infantry. Once this force had been mustered he many times threatened to invade the land of Count Jordan and to destroy the *castrum* with fire and sword. But when he finally did enter Count Jordan's land with the army of knights and infantry which he had raised; then despite what he had so often said he did not dare to attack the *castellum* or to prepare for the sound of battle. But, to increase the glory of his name and to frighten Count Jordan, he entered the territory of a *castellum* called Pesco, and then returned home without having arranged any attack by

69 Templano cannot now be identified, but a Gilbert of Templano donated land near Montefusco to the church of St Peter de Gualderada in May 1114, so it was probably close to Montefusco, D. Girgensohn, 'Documenti beneventani inediti del secolo XII', *Samnium* 40 (1967), 288–90 no. 4.

70 Falco mentions Eternus of Montefusco (killed at the battle of Rignano, 30 October 1137) much later in his account. Brian may have been related to the lords of Greci, who often used this name (see note 91).

his men.[71] Count Jordan, who was careful and of great wisdom, knew the impudence [*protervia*] of Count Rainulf and that audacity of this sort did not come from the treasures of prudence. Thus he gathered a force of 300 knights about him and remained in this area. He did this not to launch a foolish pursuit of the count, but to provide, if it should be necessary, a powerful defence for his strongpoints.

On 15th May in this year Archbishop Landulf of Benevento, rejoicing in the way of salvation, exhibited before all the bodies of Saints Martianus, Dorus, Potitus, Prosper, Felix, Cervolus and Stephen, which had formerly lain for a long time in unworthy tombs.[72] After these bodies had been thus exhumed, the archbishop ordered that two bones from [each of] them with great reverence be placed on view to all the citizens, that they might believe [in them]. News of this spread through the city and a great crowd of men and women collected and they rushed weeping with gifts to kiss these bones. I indeed though unworthy kissed the bones. Two days after the bones of the Saints had been exhumed the archbishop ordered all the priests of the city to be summoned to the cathedral, where they would discuss what honours should be rendered to such great Saints. After their advice had been sought he speedily commanded that first the priests of the Porta Somma should go down to the cathedral rejoicing with candles and lamps, and should sing the praises of God and these Saints in front of their bones. Secondly [this should be done by] the priests of the Porta Aurea,[73] thirdly by those of the Porta Rufina, fourth by those outside the walls, and fifth by those of the new city. Afterwards the priests and men of the whole city should gather as one in honour of God and the Saints, asking for the mercy of Almighty God, that by their intercessions they should receive pardon for their sins. Hearing the orders of their Pastor the priests carried out what he had ordered, and went down in order to the Saints' bodies singing praises innumerable. A crowd of men and women and of the

71 Pesco Sannita, some 13 km. N of Benevento as the crow flies and about 18 km. by road. This *castellum* was held by Jordan's vassal Gerard de Marca [see above, 140 and note 38].

72 Most of these were early martyrs, who may have been among the 31 martyrs and confessors whose relics were allegedly collected by Prince Arichis 'from various parts of Italy' according to Leo Marsicanus, *Chron. Cas.* I.9, p. 38. Martianus was supposedly Bishop of Tortona in Piedmont, martyred under Emperor Hadrian (117–38); Potitus a boy martyr from Naples; Felix perhaps a bishop martyred at Carthage or at Venosa under Diocletian (though there were several martyrs of this name); Stephen either the Protomartyr (Acts, 7:54–60) or Pope Stephen I, martyred under Valerian in 257. D'Angelo, *Falcone*, 250, suggests that Dorus was Bishop of Benevento c.448, and Prosper a Bishop of Reggio Calabria.

73 The Roman Arch of Trajan, which was incorporated as a gateway on the north wall of the city.

poor went before and behind them singing, and raising lighted candles on high. Reader, if you could have seen them rejoicing so greatly, more than seemed possible for men, and producing from the depths of their hearts a river of tears! You would have seen a most unusual procession, and something unheard of for many years, the city of Benevento moved only by honour and love for the Saints. And I testify to the King of Heaven that if my tongue could give out three [different] sounds and my voice issue forth like an unceasing lyre then I still would be unable to describe the extent of the rejoicing and the scale of the praises sung. Who among the citizens living at that time could remember when the city had been so entirely joyful? Indeed I believe that the city had not been so utterly filled with joy since the coming of its patron, St Bartholomew.[74]

And, that the memory of the Beneventans might be stirred for two generations, the abbots of all the churches built with great care and wonderful artifice machines built of wood. The priests of the new city, that they might seem before all the more devoted, dragged to the bodies of the Saints a wooden float surrounded by candles and huge lamps. On it we saw young men playing drums and blowing flutes. We saw too on this machine large bells and many small ones. Then the priests clad in white with banners and a large number of candles chanted before the bones of the Saints. Finally the archdeacon Alechisius, seeing that there was such unusual and great rejoicing spread through every part of the city and indeed every street of every part, took counsel and ordered a wonderful wooden structure to be built in honour of the church of St Lawrence, over which he ruled, and of the whole city. Oh, if you could have been there, reader, you would have seen many craftsmen, and here a body of watermen working, by whose industry this float was made in the form of a ship.[75] When this was completed he ordered a bell of great weight, many other types of metallic musical instruments, and many lighted candles to be placed upon it. He placed there a man playing the lyre, and trumpets sounding to the heavens, and around it there danced [men with] drums splendidly played, flutes and various other sorts of instrument. Oh reader, if you had seen what exultation, if you

74 The relics of St Bartholomew had been brought to Benevento from Lipari, probably by Prince Sicard in 838, *Chronicon S. Sophiae*, 216 (Bertolini, 'Annales', 114). One of the continuators of Paul the Deacon, however, claimed that this had taken place in 809, after Muslim pirates had profaned his tomb at Lipari, *Pauli Continuatio Tertia*, c. 71, ed. L. Bethmann and G. Waitz, MGH *Scriptores Rerum Langobardorum*, 215. Later tradition favoured the 838 date, *Romuald*, 159. Cf. also Mallet and Thibaut (1984), 123.

75 *Stolii manus operantes*: since Benevento is nowhere near the sea, these were probably watermen working boats on the River Calore.

had perceived what joy spread through every part of the city, if you had been there, you would really have thought and believed yourself to be imitating another life, another type of heart, of eye and of body! After all this music had been played, that the archdeacon's prestige be enhanced [still further] he attached oxen to that structure, and this team dragged it to the church of St Andrew. From there the oxen were unable to drag it to the cathedral because of the number of buildings which encroached on the open spaces. At once the machine was raised by the hands of a multitude of men and carried to the bodies of the Saints. After it had been brought there the archdeacon and a group of clerics clad in white sang the vigils in front of the Saints' bones, and when that had been finished everyone returned home. The next day, 22nd May, the archbishop, with the Bishops of Frigento, Monte Marano and Ariano, interred the bodies of the Saints;[76] and among them he placed the body of the Blessed John, twenty-first Archbishop [sic] of Benevento who, as the inscription [titulus] testifies, had an episcopate of thirty-three years.[77] Similarly [there was] the body of Stephen the Levite and the body of another saint whose name was unknown. The bodies of Bishop John, Stephen the Levite and the other saint were found after the discovery of St Martianus and his fellows, next to the altar where the latter rested. At the venerable dedication of these tombs the archbishop remitted to all those who came to visit the Saints the quarter part of their sins; he gave the same to all those who might come to the dedication up to the eighth day of the Apostles SS. Peter and Paul. But he placed under the bond of excommunication all those who might do harm to those who had come to the dedication of such important Saints.

In this year Archbishop Landulf of Benevento died on 4th August, and Roffred, who was then the archpriest, was elected.

In this year Alferius judge of Porta Aurea died on 22nd February.[78]

The year 1120 from the Incarnation of the Lord and the second year of the pontificate of lord Calixtus, Supreme Pontiff and Universal Pope,

76 A John, Bishop of Frigento, was attested in 1114, and another John in 1144–5, although since the name was so common one cannot be absolutely sure these references were to the same man. The Bishop of Ariano was probably the Bishop Richard who was present at a court in June 1122, which vindicated the rights of St Sophia, Benevento, over the church of St Angelo, outside the walls of Ariano, Cod. Vat. Lat. 13491, document no. 16. He was still bishop in January 1134, Pratesi (1955), 65–6 no. 6.

77 D'Angelo (Falco, 250) suggests this John was a Bishop of Benevento who died in 415. The archbishopric dated only from 969.

78 His family remained prominent as judges and consuls in Benevento through the twelfth and thirteenth centuries, Obituarium S. Spiritus, 259.

the month of March, thirteenth of the indiction. In this year in the month of May, on the third day before the festival of Saint Eustasius, there was a great flood of the River Calore, [something] which nobody living at that time could remember.[79] At the same time Count Rainulf, of whom we made mention, gathered a vast force of knights and footmen and, together with Robert of Montefusco, marched against the *castellum* called Tufo. They rapidly ascended this very defensible mountain, on which the fortifications of the *castellum* itself were very skilfully constructed, surrounded it by a ditch and rampart, on which they placed wooden siege-engines all the way round, and thus entrenched they launched frequent and fierce attacks upon it. However Rao, the lord of the *castrum*, defended it bravely. Furthermore Count Jordan, hearing that Count Rainulf had thrown up siege works round Tufo and had filled them with weapons of war, collected a strong force of cavalry and infantry and marched to the *castellum* called Montefalcone, not far from Count Rainulf's camp.[80] Then he ordered Cardinal Hugh the Regent of Benevento, the Rector Stephen and Roffred the archbishop-elect to be summoned. On their advice he sent them to Count Rainulf, adding by letter that he willingly sought justice from Rainulf, and he would do justice to him. The count hearing this in turn promised that he would accept justice and freely grant it. What more? They left Tufo and a great assembly of nobles congregated at the Ponte S. Valentino. In front of everyone they pledged and received faith and a truce was speedily confirmed, to last from 25th May to 1st September, in which truce the city of Benevento was included.

On 5th May of this year the Capuans appointed as their prince the lord Richard, son of their Prince Robert, because the prince his father was a sick man. Once he had been appointed, the Archbishop of Capua summoned bishops, other prudent men and Roffred the archbishop-elect of Benevento, and on Ascension Day, 27th May, consecrated him as prince. On the eighth day after his son's consecration the prince his father left this world. However the prince his son lived [only] ten days after his consecration. On his death they raised to the princely honour Jordan, the brother of the said Prince Robert.[81]

In this year the above-mentioned Pope Calixtus returned from north of the Alps and entered Rome on 9th June. Whence it happened that

---

79 This was on 7 May.

80 Montefalcone, about 10 km. NE of Avellino and 9 km. S of Montefusco.

81 Cf. the *Annales Casinenses*, ad. an. 1120, MGH SS xix.308: 'Prince Robert died and Richard his son was anointed. He died soon afterwards, and his uncle Jordan became prince'.

Peter Bishop of Porto, then the Vicar, with the other cardinals staying in Rome, and a great crowd of clergy and men and women hurried to meet the Pontiff. Reader, if you had seen the happiness and rejoicing of the Roman people, you would have been amazed and said that never formerly had a pope entered the city in such honour and triumph.[82] Hearing of the pope's arrival Cardinal Hugh, who was then ruling the city of Benevento, hurried to Rome, and with him were various of the citizens. In that same year, on 9th July, Rao lord of Ceppaloni died.

On 30th July of this year Abbot Bernard of the monastery of St Sophia migrated to the Lord. After his death, on 31st July, one part of the monks elected as Abbot a monk named Ademarius who was the nephew of Abbot Madelmus. John the Dean,[83] John the Grammarian, a most praiseworthy man, Rao priest and monk and other wise men among the monks would not consent to his election. Thus it was that there was great discord amongst them. Our lord Pope Calixtus came on advice to Benevento and entered the city on 8th August. However, hearing of his arrival, the people of Benevento who had long wished for this, went out full of joy some two miles from the city. Finally the pope was welcomed gloriously and with great rejoicing by the clergy, the Jews,[84] a crowd of monks and by all the priests and citizens. Further-more the Amalfitans had decorated all the squares with silk cloaks and stoles and other precious ornaments to celebrate his arrival. Among these ornaments they had put gold and silver thuribles with sweet-smelling things and cinnamon. Four citizens led the pope's feet and the reins of his horse from the Ponte Leproso to the Porta S. Lorenzo, and then another four took over from there to the cathedral.[85] From the cathedral four judges brought him to the Sacred Beneventan Palace – these were John, Persicus, Guisliccio and Landulf.[86] Reader, if you had

---

82 Here Falco was describing the formal *adventus* or arrival ceremony of a pope, all the more significant in this case because Calixtus had been elected outside Rome, by only a minority of the cardinals – hence the formal welcome also marked a public legitimisation of his pontificate. Other descriptions of this event suggest that at least some cardinals may have come out to meet him; for these Twyman (2002), 92–7.

83 John the Dean is attested only after these events, remaining in office under the next abbot. He received the gift of a church from Gerard de Marca on the monastery's behalf in March 1122, Pergamene Aldobrandini, Cart I. 51 [above, note 37], and he was one of the witnesses to an agreement between St Sophia and the Abbey of St Lawrence, Aversa, in September 1123, Girgensohn, 'Documenti beneventani', 290–6 no. 5.

84 A generation later, in the 1160s, there were some 200 Jews in Benevento, *The Itinerary of Benjamin of Tudela*, trans. M.N. Adler (London 1907), 13.

85 The Ponte Leproso was the bridge where the Via Appia crossed the River Sabato; the Porta S. Lorenzo was the western, lower, gate to the city.

86 John the judge witnessed an exchange between the Abbey of St Sophia and the church

been in the pope's company and had seen the drums being struck, the cymbals resounding and the lyres playing you would have been certain that no other pope had [ever] entered the city with such triumph and joy.

After a few days had gone by some of the citizens who were friends of Landulf the ex-constable requested the pope to allow him the right to live in the city. (The constable had been living in Montefusco for the last three years). The pope acceded to the prayers of his faithful subjects and gave the permission they had requested. Immediately they, along with Count Jordan who had come as his representative, went out to meet Landulf and brought him into the city. Meanwhile Pope Calixtus, hearing of the discord which reigned among the brothers of the monastery of St Sophia about the election of the said Ademarius, went to the monastery and, gathering the brothers together, had a full and lengthy discussion with them about the election. At length the truth of the matter emerged, that the election was neither canonical nor according to the Rule, and it was thus judged to be null and void by Peter, Bishop of Porto, and the other cardinals who had assembled there. This decision was immediately confirmed by Pope Calixtus. What more? He gave permission to the brothers to elect whomsoever they wished as abbot. Having done this the pope returned to the Palace. Early the next day, 14th August, the whole body of the brothers entered the accustomed place for their chapter, and there, with the help of the Holy Ghost, they had a full discussion about the election. Meanwhile the venerable Dean John selected one of the brothers capable of bearing this great responsibility, and he disclosed who this was to the assembled brothers. Then he interviewed each of them individually to ask if this choice was acceptable. All with one voice proclaimed in agreement that the choice was worthy. The brothers gathered together nearly fifty strong and acclaimed the person chosen, John the Grammarian, whom they knew to be a man of prudence and of good life. He was reluctant to accede to their choice, but rejoicing they made him sit on the abbatial throne,

---

of St John in August 1122 (written by Falco), a donation to St Sophia in May 1124, and another donation, by Gerard de Marca in March 1126, Benevento, Museo del Sannio, Fondo S. Sofia, vol. 34 no. 3; *ibid.*, vol. 12 no. 42; Pergamene Aldobrandini, Cart. I no. 56. For Persicus, see note 34 above. For Guisliccio, *Più antiche carte della cattedrale*, 178–80 no. 59 (June 1121); Archivio Segreto Vaticano, AA Arm. I.xviii.4999, no. 6 (undated but c.1127 and written by Falco, also witnessed by John). Landulf was probably the judge of that name who later witnessed a document of Anacletus II restoring property to St Sophia in March 1135(?), and a donation to the church of St Barbatus in November 1136, *Chron. S. Sophiae*, ii.663; *Più antiche carte della cattedrale*, 191–3 no. 63. Zazo identified him with the judge Landulf of Apice whose death was recorded on 21 October in the *Obituarium S. Spiritus*, 90, 291.

even though he claimed before us all to be unworthy and wretched.[87] Then the venerable and holy ceremony took place, and a monk placed the pastoral staff in his hand, and they stationed him in the abbot's place in the chapter. Immediately first the dean and then the other brothers prostrated themselves at his feet, as is the custom, and each of them gave him the kiss of peace. After the election the congregation sent a messenger to Pope Calixtus, announcing that John the Grammarian had been elected. The pope was pleased to hear that the election had been according to the Rule and confirmed it. After a few days had gone by Pope Calixtus came to the monastery of St Sophia and on 19th August, in a solemn mass consecrated the said John the Grammarian whom the congregation of the monastery had elected as abbot. And on the day of that consecration the dedication of the altar of the Blessed Mercurius was celebrated at St Sophia.[88]

Pope Calixtus had previously imposed a delay on the promotion of Roffred the archbishop-elect, in order that he might be consecrated at the customary Ember time in the month of September. After a little while had elapsed that time arrived, and then the pope ordained him priest with great honour and care in the Sacred Beneventan Palace. On the day after, which was a Sunday, he raised him to archiepiscopal rank in the presence of ten of the suffragan bishops of the Beneventan see. Among those present was Abbot John of the monastery of St Sophia. The feast of St Januarius was celebrated on the day of this consecration.[89]

In this year, two days after the consecration of the said Archbishop Roffred, Pope Calixtus took advice and deposed Stephen who was then rector, and ordained as rector the deacon Rossemanus, son of Rossemanus the monk.[90]

---

87 It was, of course, ecclesiastical custom for the elect to protest his unworthiness, cf. the election of Gelasius II as described in the *Liber Pontificalis*, ii.313, Eugenius III's own account of his election in 1145, Robinson (1990), 78, and the election of Norbert of Xanten as archbishop of Magdeburg in 1124, *Vita Norberti*, MGH SS xii.694. Norbert may indeed have actively sought his appointment, Lees (1998), 28–9.

88 The relics of St Mercurius (martyred under Emperor Decius, c.250) had been interred at St Sophia by its founder, Prince Arichis, *Chron. Cas.* I.9, p. 38; *Translatio Sancti Mercurii*, ed. L. Bethmann and G. Waitz, MGH *Scriptores Rerum Langobardorum*, 576–80. This latter text survives in a twelfth-century copy, probably of monastic provenance, Benevento, Biblioteca capitolare, MS 1, fols 67r–69r, Mallet and Thibaut (1984), 115. Donations to the abbey were sometimes made by placing a symbolic object like a book on the altar of St Mercurius, e.g. Museo del Sannio, Fondo S. Sofia, vol. 12 no. 42 (May 1124).

89 On 19 September.

90 He was son of the rector of 1102, and later became archbishop of Benevento in 1133 (see below, 219, 239–40). Calixtus remained at Benevento until 16 October 1120, JL 6857–6865. Among the business he dealt with while there was a dispute between Archbishop Otto

The year 1121 from the Lord's Incarnation and the third year of the pontificate of the lord Calixtus II, Supreme Pontiff and Universal Pope, the month of March, fourth of the indiction. In this year the lady Labinia, Abbess of the nunnery of S. Maria di Porta Somma became seriously ill. Seeing that she had come to the verge of death, she took counsel and ordered all the handmaidens of God, her sisters, to be summoned. When they had been called she spoke these words to them, 'I believe, my dearest sisters, that it is not unknown to your prudence how much I have laboured for this nunnery and for your charity. And thus, with God's favour and through your prayers the prestige of the nunnery has been raised and it has been brought to the summit of perfection. Now however, as you can see, I am dangerously ill and am certain that I shall soon leave this bodily life. Thus I humbly beg you in friendship that you assent to my request, especially since, as God is my witness, I would never ask you anything which was not to the nunnery's benefit. For I see in my heart that after my death discord would arise about the election [of my successor], and the nunnery would come to harm as a result. Hence, if it pleases your charity, while I still live I shall put an end to this argument and nominate who will be abbess.' What more? She named Bethlem, the daughter of Gerard, Count of Greci. The person named pleased them and they praised her excellent choice. Having done this the lady Abbess Labinia migrated to the Lord. They immediately ordered Archbishop Roffred and Rachisius, Abbot of St Modestus, to be summoned, that they might ratify and confirm what had been done, and indeed these two heeded their request and did confirm it. Not many days later the archbishop came to the monastery and consecrated the abbess as the Rule prescribed, while we and many other men watched. At this consecration on 4th April there were present the venerable Abbot John of the monastery of St Sophia and the said Abbot Rachisius of St Modestus.[91]

---

of Capua and Montecassino, *Chron. Cas.* IV.69, p. 533. He then went to Troia where he held a council in early November, before returning briefly to Benevento where he issued a privilege to St Sophia on 29 November, *Liber Pontificalis*, ii.327; *Chartes de Troia*, 168–71 no. 43; *Chron. S. Sophiae*, ii.778–85. On 1 December he was at Capua, on 3–4 December at S. Germano, and he was back in Rome by 15 December, JL 6869–72. See Schilling (1998), 706–9, for details.

91 Bethlem was abbess from 1121 until at least 1175. For her and her family Jamison (1934), who speculates (40–2) that Gerard of Greci was a relative of the counts of Ariano, and perhaps even the brother of Count Jordan of that name attested in *Chron. S. Sophiae*, ii.727–8 (July 1114). However, Bethlem's brother Dauferius appears in a charter of Jordan for Montecassino in 1116, ed. Loud (1981), 215–16, where he was described as the *fidelis* of the count, but not his *nepos*. Nor did he or other members of this family employ the comital title. Ménager (1975b), 373, suggests that the family was of Breton origin.

In this year on 15th May Robert of Montefusco was, poor man, cut
down at Benevento by the swords of Roger son of Trogisius and his
brothers.[92] Reader, if you could have seen his head horribly cut off,
his limbs hewn one from another and scattered about, you would in
your grief have showered them with a fountain of tears and have been
amazed at this type of assassination. However the venerable Abbot John
of the monastery of St Sophia hurried to the body with some of the
brothers and, seeing it, was quite grief-stricken and even more tearful.
Without delay he ordered that the bloody corpse be carried to the
monastery, where they buried it according to the Christian rite of the
slain. Meanwhile Count Jordan hastened to Montefusco and made an
agreement which placed the *castellum* in his power.

In the same year Pope Calixtus gathered an army and marched on a
town called Sutri, for that Gregory whom the above-mentioned king
had installed as pope was holding that town. Why linger any more?
They made a great effort and captured the town. They beat and bound
Gregory (a man of greater wickedness than it was possible to imagine),
stripped him of his clothes, placed him on a camel and led him thus
into Rome on 23rd April. Pope Calixtus, giving thanks to God and the
Apostle Peter and filled with great joy, made a triumphant entry into
the city. Then, after taking advice, he sent him [the anti-pope] to the
monastery of Holy Trinity which is called Cava.[93]

After these events the said Pope Calixtus took counsel and went to
Salerno, [arriving] on 5th September, that he might establish a lasting
peace between Duke William and Count Roger.[94] The Archbishop of

92 They were members of the San Severino kin group who dominated the Avellino region.
Trogisius [Turgisius], lord of Montemiletto and his sons Roger and Alamus gave men
in the Cilento region to the abbey of Cava in October 1113, and Trogisius and Roger
gave two churches to Cava in August 1114, Cava, *Arm. Mag.* E.26, E.32. Roger's brother
Alamus was lord of Taurasi, 4 km. E of Montemiletto and 21 km. SE of Benevento, *Cod.
Dipl. Verginiano*, ii.337–41 no. 180 (August 1129), 364–6 no. 186 (May 1130). Cf. Schütz
(1995), 523–4, and for a genealogical chart, Loud (1987), 160.

93 The great Benedictine abbey, much favoured by the dukes of Apulia, founded in the
early eleventh century 11 km. NW of Salerno; for its development see especially Loud
(1987). Henry V abandoned Maurice of Braga (Gregory VIII) and recognised Calixtus in
1119; Calixtus, on arrival in Rome, made concessions to buy off the anti-pope's principal
supporters there, the Frangipani, *Liber Pontificalis*, ii.323. Erdmann (1927), 241, 248;
Schilling (1998), 469–71. Maurice's imprisonment at Cava is well-attested, e.g. in *Liber
Pontificalis*, ii.323; *Orderic*, vi.306–8; *Annales Palidenses*, MGH SS xvi.76; he was later transferred to the fortress of Rocca Janula near Montecassino, and then to Fumone in Lazio,
Chron. Cas. IV.68, 86, pp. 532, 547.

94 Calixtus subsequently journeyed south into Lucania and Calabria, both to secure peace
between the duke and count, and to undertake a measure of reorganisation of the Church
there, only returning to Benevento in February 1122, *Liber Pontificalis*, ii.322–3. Schilling

Salerno, named Alfanus, died on 29th August.[95] After his death the above-mentioned Pope Calixtus consecrated the Cardinal-deacon Romuald as Archbishop of Salerno in mid-September.[96]

Robert Sclavus died on 22nd December of this year, and also Abbot Rachisius of St Modestus, to whose deathbed the venerable Abbot John of the monastery of St Sophia hastened with some of the brothers. His corpse was immediately prepared as is customary and brought to the monastery for burial; then after the obsequies it was placed in a marble tomb.

I shall now, if it be pleasing, relate another matter. On 23rd February Agnes, Abbess of the nunnery of St Peter the Apostle, which lies within the city of Benevento, went up into the Sacred Beneventan Palace and made a legal complaint about Bethlem, Abbess of the nunnery of S. Maria di Porta Somma, namely that she had been made Abbess of the said nunnery of St Maria against her [Agnes's] will, and alleging this nunnery was under her jurisdiction and subject to the nunnery of St Peter.[97] Hearing this, the pope ordered the said Bethlem to be summoned that he might do justice on this matter. She came immediately, heard the charges and replied through her advocates that he ought not to believe what had been said unless Agnes could produce written proof for what she had claimed. Then the pope, who was seriously ill and unable to hold court himself, ordered Divizo Bishop of Tusculum, Chrysogonus the Chancellor, Robert of Paris and other cardinals to act as judges of this affair, and, having heard the arguments, to put an end to the discord between the two nunneries.[98] This was what happened. After these preceding events the Abbess Agnes, through her advocate, showed a privilege through which Liutprand, once duke of the city of

---

(1998), 489–99, 710–13.

95 Alfanus II, Archbishop of Salerno 1086–1121; *Necrologio di S. Matteo*, 124, records his burial on 30 August.

96 Romuald, Cardinal deacon of S. Maria in Via Lata, for whom see note 33 above. He was a native of Salerno.

97 There were two nunneries dedicated to St Peter at Benevento, this one within the walls; the one outside the walls on the far, south, side of the River Sabato was very ancient, founded in the later seventh century.

98 Divizo was Cardinal Bishop of Tusculum March 1121–May 1122, and previously Cardinal priest of SS. Martino e Silvestro. Chrysogonus, Cardinal deacon of S. Nicola in Carcere from 1117, had been appointed chancellor by Gelasius and continued in office under Calixtus – for his role at the Council of Rheims in 1119, *Orderic*, vi. 254. Robert of Paris had been Cardinal priest of S. Eusebio 1100–12, but was then deposed by Paschal II as punishment for his criticism of the Treaty of Ponte Mamolo with Henry V. He was restored as Cardinal priest of S. Sabina 1120–2, Hüls (1977), 142, 165, 204–5, 240. All three of these cardinals appear to have died in the summer of 1122.

Benevento,[99] conceded and allowed that the said church of S. Maria with all its possessions should be under the jurisdiction and lordship of the said nunnery of St Peter the Apostle. She then showed other privileges in which Prince Pandulf and his successors confirmed that this same church of S. Maria should be under the power of the said nunnery of St Peter. Furthermore she brought other privileges and muniments belonging to the nunnery.[100] To this the said Bethlem, Abbess of the nunnery of S. Maria, produced through her advocate charters and instruments belonging to her nunnery, and among their contents it was clearly shown that from fifty years ago up to the present day the nunnery of S. Maria had been ruled by an abbess. The first of these had been Labinia, the second Sikelgarda, and there had been others whose names were to be read in these documents. We also remember how Abbess Labinia had ruled over this nunnery in recent years.[101] Similarly it could be read in these muniments how the head of this nunnery had ruled and acted for herself in legal cases and other business. Both sides showed their privileges and muniments and these were read, and then the cardinals who had been designated as judges retired to produce their sentence over these quarrels. Thus, having discussed their judgment, they notified the lord Pope Calixtus of their agreed verdict, that he might confirm the sentence they had passed. Pope Calixtus indeed confirmed their verdict without delay and gave it his authority; and that sentence was this, namely that the said nunnery of S. Maria should have in its own right in perpetuity an abbess, who should be consecrated by the Roman Pontiff, that the congregation of the sisters living at this same nunnery of S. Maria should have the power of electing as abbess whom they wished, saving however an annual census which should be paid in perpetuity on the part of the nunnery to the said nunnery of St Peter, namely four loaves and two wax candles at Christmas, the same on Easter Sunday and the same at the Assumption of the Blessed Virgin Mary. The pope ordered this sentence to be written down and commanded that it be witnessed by all the cardinals who had been appointed as judges in this case. This judicial document the pope signed

99 Liutprand was Duke of Benevento 751–8.

100 The origins of the nunnery of St Peter within the walls are obscure, but since the earliest evidence relating to it occurs only c.1050, one suspects that the charter of Duke Liutprand, at least, and perhaps the other princely charters, were forgeries (unless perhaps they were issued for the other, older, nunnery of St Peter, outside the walls). Unfortunately most of the documentation for St Peter within the walls, a substantial part of which still survived in the early eighteenth century, has now been lost, *Italia Pontificia*, ix.101.

101 A Labinia was abbess in 1086, Jamison (1934), 61–2, appendix no. 1. From what Falco said here, she may well have been the first of two abbesses of the same name.

with his own hand. Thus confirmed and made secure, he entrusted it to the venerable Abbess Bethlem, so backed up by the evidence of the cardinals that from henceforth and in perpetuity the nunnery should remain secure and exist without any disturbance and molestation on the part of St Peter's. Having signed this privilege he confirmed that this same nunnery of S. Maria with all the possessions belonging to it should for all time remain inviolate and flourish without anyone's hindrance.[102]

The year 1122 from the Incarnation of the Lord, and the fourth year of the pontificate of the said lord Calixtus II, Supreme Pontiff and Universal Pope, the month of March, fifteenth of the indiction. In this year Duke William son of Duke Roger came to Count Roger son of Count Roger of the Sicilians, complaining of Count Jordan of Ariano [and asking] that he extend a helping hand to him and be generous with his military power and riches, that by his help he might be revenged on Count Jordan. And when the duke had come to the count he begged him with prayers and tears thus: 'To your power, O distinguished count, I have recourse, both because of the strength of our blood-relationship and because of the magnitude of your riches, in order to make complaint about Count Jordan, begging humbly that with your support and aid I may be revenged upon him. For when one day I had gone into the city of Nusco, Count Jordan and a band of his knights arrived before the gate of that city and brought reproach on me, threatening me with many injuries, such as "I shall shorten your cloak for you". Then ranging all around the city of Nusco he laid everything waste.[103] Since I cannot prevail against him, I have unwillingly sustained this, but I ask for a day when I shall be revenged. And having done this the count dishonours me all the time with numerous and varied aggravations'. What more? The duke conceded to the count [of Sicily] his half of the city of Palermo, and Messina and the whole of Calabria, to secure his help in these affairs. He immediately gave him 600 knights and 500 ounces of gold. Without delay the duke came to the lands of Count Jordan, and on St John the Baptist's day[104] he attacked the *castrum* of Roseto and captured it and much else. Then on the feast of SS. John and Paul[105] he

---

102 However, in 1323 the nuns of St Maria were forced to leave their house, whose site was required for a new fortress and residence for the papal rector; they were transferred to the nunnery of St Peter. So the two houses were eventually combined, Jamison (1934), 36.

103 Nusco, 25 km. E of Avellino, but much further by road, was the seat of a bishopric from c.1080 onwards.

104 On 24 June.

105 On 26 June.

proceeded to assail the *castellum* of Monte Giove, devastated it by fire
and sword and captured fifty knights there, whose arms and the booty
he carried off rejoicing.[106] Then he marched to the *castellum* of Apice,
where the count himself was residing, and laid siege to it. Cardinal
Crescentius, then the Rector of Benevento, hurried to the duke's help
with a force of Beneventans.[107] What more? He gained control over
both the *castrum* of Apice and the count himself. Indeed Count Jordan
threw himself prostrate at the duke's feet, begging him for mercy, as
we who were there saw for ourselves. The duke was constrained by the
prayers of many, and especially of Count Rainulf who was there present,
and allowed him to go free and to dwell where he wished. The count
then hurried to Montefusco, [meanwhile] after these events the city
of Ariano and every part of his county came into the duke's power.[108]
And when Count Jordan had ascended up to Montefusco he dwelt there
for fifteen days. But very soon his enemy Landulf de Greca fomented a
conspiracy and expelled him from Montefusco. Thus ejected he went to
the *castrum* of Morcone and lived there for a year. After accomplishing
this, the duke besieged Montecorvino, near Salerno. And since Fulco,
the lord of this *castrum*, was unable to resist he submitted it to the
duke's authority.[109]

At this time Richard son of Guarin de Formari was murdered by his
own villeins. When the above-mentioned duke heard that Richard had
been thus slain he gathered an army, hurried to Monte Vico and took
an unheard of vengeance for the murder. He consumed the *castellum*
with fire and the sword and hanged two priests who had been parties
to the death.[110] After these and other matters had been resolved, the

---

106 Roseto is now Roseto Valfortore. *Mons Iovis* has not been identified; D'Angelo, *Falcone*,
253, wonders if it might be a copyist's error for *Mons Leonis* (Monte Leone), for which
Catalogus Baronum, art. 432.

107 Crescentius, from Anagni, south of Rome, was made cardinal deacon by Paschal II,
promoted Cardinal priest of SS. Marcellino e Pietro 1121/2, was rector again in the
early 1130s and deposed from his position at the Lateran council of 1139, Hüls (1977),
183–4. He played a major role in Falco's Chronicle.

108 At a court held at Ariano in July 1122, in the presence of the bishop and the duke's
constable, a church over which the count had been in dispute with St Sophia, Benevento,
was handed back to the abbey. This clearly took place very soon after Jordan's expulsion,
Loud (1997), 288.

109 Montecorvino was on the southern slopes of the Monti Picentini, about 20 km. E of
Salerno.

110 Monte Vico = Trevico, 61 km. E of Avellino. Richard's son, also Richard, lord of Trevico
and Fiumeri, became a royal constable after 1140, and was a significant benefactor of
the nunnery of St Maria di Porta Somma. His son Roger (d.1190) later became Count of
Andria and an important figure in the reign of King William II, *Catalogus Baronum*, arts.

duke sent back to Count Roger the knights he had received from him. Count Jordan had, as we have said above, been disinherited; now, on the advice of Hugh the Infant, Rao de Boscone and Rao of Fragneto, he seized the *castellum* of Paduli.[111] Once he heard of its capture the duke raised an army and besieged the *castrum* for three months. Finally, seeing that he was thus unable to capture it quickly, the duke asked Prince Jordan of the Capuans to assist him, and for that help he offered him the *castellum* of Apice and [also] Acerno. The prince immediately gathered an army, marched on the castrum of Apice and pitched camp in the plain nearby. Meanwhile the duke ordered the Beneventans not to bring help either to him or to Count Jordan, and gave and conceded to them all the prestations and income which had [formerly] been exacted from the estates of Beneventans [situated] from the *castellum* of Finicchio to the *castellum* of Montefusco. This pleased the Beneventans and so both sides swore to a peace pact. When Count Jordan saw himself so hemmed in then he submitted himself and the *castellum* of Paduli to the hands of the above-said prince. He himself with his associates left there and returned home, going back to the *castrum* of Morcone.[112] With peace established the prince returned to Capua and he held the *castra* of Apice and Acerno for a long time. Then the duke sent a strong force of knights and infantry against the *castrum* of Morcone, thinking to obtain its surrender and that of the count himself, but he was unable to achieve this. The duke then returned to Salerno, and achieved peace after the many and various travails with which he had been vexed. Thus to the day of his death his duchy was peaceful and warlike clashes were stilled. And in that year, on 12th August, a huge number of fish appeared in the River Calore, so many that men and women could catch them in their hands without nets.

The year 1123 from the Incarnation of our Lord, and the fifth year of the pontificate of the lord Calixtus II Supreme Pontiff and Universal Pope, the month of March, first of the indiction. The above-said Pope Calixtus, on the best of advice, commanded almost all the bishops,

---

291–3, 396; Jamison (1934), 48–9; Cuozzo (1984), 64–6; Cuozzo (1995), 185–93.

111 Paduli is 10 km. NE of Benevento. Rao of Fragneto (Fragneto Monforte, 14 km. N of Benevento), who plays a prominent role in the narrative that follows, is sometimes also (confusingly) referred to as Rao of Ceppaloni, which place he seems to have taken over from the family of his homonym who died in 1120. Rao de Boscone, first attested in 1107, was from a Norman family: he and his son Nibelone took over the lands of Rao of Fragneto after 1139, Ménager (1975b), 264; Cuozzo (1984), 265–6.

112 Jordan appears still to have been resident at Morcone, 25 km. NW of Benevento, in May 1125, when he donated a mill there to the abbey of St Sophia, Benevento, Museo del Sannio, Fondo S. Sofia, vol. 12 no. 43, ed. Loud (1997), 300, appendix no. 3.

archbishops and abbots from north of the Alps, and indeed I say all the pastors of the churches of Italy to come to him, that he might confirm with a holy synod in perpetuity an agreement made with Emperor Henry.[113] Archbishop Roffred of Benevento hastened to attend this holy council. When this great council had gathered the pope ordered the privilege which contained the oath of peace sworn by the emperor to be brought in and read in the presence of all those assembled. It was immediately confirmed and approved by everyone. Among the other things laid down there they decreed the observance of the Truce of God. In addition the pope bound by the chain of anathema anyone who attempted to remove the city of Benevento from the power of St Peter. Many other things were also decreed which it seems to us tedious to narrate in this work, for I think that people would consider me tiresome if I tried to include everything in this little book. You will find everything noted and written down elsewhere. We have heard however and are convinced of an amazing thing, that so strong was the peace established within the city of Rome at the time of the pope's coming that nobody, whether citizen or foreigner, dared to carry weapons as was customary. After the celebration of the council, Pope Calixtus came to Benevento, and dealt with certain business concerning the inhabitants.

In the same year the above-mentioned Landulf de Greca died on 20th November and was buried in the church of St Maximus.[114] And when Pope Calixtus had arrived in Benevento he ordered Archbishop Roffred to be summoned, that he might hear the accusations which some of the citizens had brought against him, for he was accused of gaining the archiepiscopal honour by simony. That prelate called to him some of his suffragans and priests of the city and went up to the Sacred Palace. He heard his accusers, requested a delay, and after receiving this delay he replied: 'I am ready, most Holy Father, to purge myself of these accusations as the canons lay down, and to follow your instructions'. Finally he himself swore that he had not been intruded by simony, and was followed by two bishops and three priests.[115]

---

113 The agreement at Worms in September 1122 ended the Investiture Contest, for which *Ekkehard*, 356–60. As Schilling (1998), 533–4, notes, the First Lateran Council is not well-documented, but the settlement with the emperor was criticised by some. For the canons of the 1123 council, Mansi, *Concilia*, xxi.281–6.

114 Despite Landulf de Greca's overtly anti-Norman stance in 1114, his son Taddeus (d. in or about October 1137) married the daughter of a Norman, Paganus de Archiepiscopo, *Cod. Dipl. Verginiano*, iii.175–8 no. 242, 183–6 no. 244. St Maximus' church was in Benevento near the Porta Aurea, Zazo (1959), 72.

115 Calixtus was in Benevento from 12 September until at least 12 October 1123, J-L 7076–9. By 3 November he was at Ceprano on his way back to Rome, *ibid.*, 7082. For the cardinals

The year 1124 from the Lord's Incarnation, and the sixth year of the pontificate of the Lord Pope Calixtus. In this year the said Roffred, Archbishop of Benevento, after taking counsel, removed the body of our most Holy Father Bishop Barbatus of Benevento from the altar tomb where it had lain quietly for many years.[116] But that altar had not been as worthily looked after as it ought to have been, above all because the structure of the new cathedral had been extended up to where the altar was. Thus it was thought proper that it should be moved away from this building work. The above-named archbishop ordered two of his suffragan bishops to be summoned, that with their advice and help so great and abundant a treasure might [indeed] be found. Archbishop Roffred immediately summoned some of the citizens, lawyers and clergy and in the silence of the middle of the night entered the church and went to the altar mentioned above. In the presence of all and with the encouragement of the bishops, he broke into it, and in the damaged altar relics of Saints, whose names nobody knew, were discovered. These were removed and the order was given to dig deeper, for they were seen as the long-desired proof of [the presence of] the body mentioned. Very soon a precious stone was found, unearthed by the enthusiastic and wonderful work on all sides which powered the iron crowbars. Its discovery made all of them very joyful, and they laboured to remove the stone with all their strength; but since it was held fast by the solidity of the masonry, everyone agreed that it should be broken into pieces. When it was [thus] removed, then, with the help of divine grace, the body of the Most Blessed Barbatus was found. The archbishop entered the place before the others and prostrated himself before the bones and dust, then with great joy and praises resounding he brought them up into their midst. Reader, what joy and enthusiasm you would have seen when those pearls so long desired by our times were discovered! The bones which had been collected were brought to the altar of St Sebastian by clergy singing hymns. Once day had dawned the whole city crowded round and praised God the creator of all who had deemed them worthy to be given so important a body as that of St Barbatus. Indeed we ourselves saw some of his bones and kissed them. After this the archbishop commanded that first the priests

---

who accompanied him during this visit, Girgensohn, 'Documenti beneventani', 290–6 no. 5.

116 St Barbatus, the seventh-century 'Apostle of the Beneventans', was believed to have been responsible for converting the Lombards from Arianism to orthodox Catholicism and eliminating the last vestiges of pagan practice among them; see *Vita Barbati Episcopi Beneventani*, ed. G. Waitz, MGH *Scriptores Rerum Langobardorum*, 555–63, though this text probably dates only from the late ninth century, Martin (1974).

of the Porta Somma with its [other] clergy and laity should descend to the cathedral, and celebrate vigils in front of the most holy body of Barbatus. On the archbishop's order the priests formed up immediately and with candles and torches lighted we descended along with a great crowd of the laity of both sexes and all ages; and every day for eight days each gate [i.e. district] of the city did the same. On the eighth day, which was 31st May, the archbishop accompanied by the two other bishops buried the body of St Barbatus under the stone of an altar, and, after this burial, dedicated the altar in the Saint's honour. A huge crowd of the citizens gathered at this solemn dedication, [asking] that Almighty God might forgive their sins. Once this had been done the archbishop climbed up to a prominent place, that he might see and be seen by all, and, by the favour of divine clemency, he pardoned a part of their sins. He gave the like pardon to all those who came devoutly to the dedication up to the eighth day from the feast of the Holy Apostles SS. Peter and Paul.[117]

I shall now outline to you, as best I can, the miracles which Jesus Christ, the lover of the human race, deemed it worthy to demonstrate to us in the sight of all for the honour and through the merits of our said Father Barbatus. For when, as has been written above, the blessed and vener-able body had remained in full view on the altar of St Sebastian for eight days, a certain man called John the Shoemaker entered the cathedral and prostrated himself before the body of the Most Holy Barbatus, watering the ground with his tears. He was immediately asked by the clergy and people who were present what the reason for this was, and he then explained from the beginning everything that had happened. 'While I was lying in bed asleep in the silence of the night I had a dream. There appeared before my eyes a man venerable in appearance, clad in white garments, who came gradually closer and approached my bed. "And why", he said, "did you not come yesterday with the others to sing vigils in front of my bones?" I replied, "Father, because my right arm and hand have been in the grip of grave illness, and I have languished thus unhappily for six months". I added, "Tell me, Father, by what name are you called?" He said, "Barbatus, once Bishop of Benevento". He added, "Show me your arm and hand now". Since I was riven by my illness I was unable to stretch out my hand quickly, however I extended it and touched him, and in a short space of time my illness disappeared, and it was as if it had never affected my hand and arm. The next morning I rose up and was amazed at my restoration to health. I came to give

117 On 29 June.

thanks and praise to God the creator of all and to Bishop Barbatus by whose merits I was cured'. When all this had occurred and been told, the cathedral bells were ordered to be rung to collect the people of the city to hear and see so great a miracle. Almost the whole city immediately rushed there and we praised and blessed the most glorious doctor of doctors. I, the writer, touched the cured hand and arm, and the man's neighbours testified that they had known him to be infirm for a long time. After seeing this we returned to our homes filled with joy.

I shall [now] relate another miracle worked in our days by the Redeemer of the human race Jesus Christ to the glory of our Father Barbatus. A certain peasant, an inhabitant of the *castellum* of Montefusco, hearing of the fame of so great a Holy Man, came to Benevento. He had been lame for the space of many years because the nerves of his shin and foot had dried up. He was in continuous and terrible pain, as if his foot had been bound to his buttocks, and so the poor man was all the time in torture. He immediately prostrated himself before the basilica of St Barbatus, begging God the Redeemer of all that he might be restored to pristine health. After he had prayed he fell very deeply asleep, and remained for a night as if half-dead. Then in the silence of the night there appeared a man of great age and venerable appearance, who (as we heard from the man's own mouth) spoke to him thus: 'Arise', he said, 'and hasten to the altar which has been consecrated in my name. There, thanks to the clemency of the Saviour, you will find the joy of health which you have desired so much for so long'. And he: 'Who are you', he asked, 'who promise to me the gift of such a great treasure?' 'I am Barbatus', he said, 'Bishop of the city of Benevento'. The cripple summoned up his courage and spoke thus: 'I am unable', he said, 'wretched as I am, to go there. Don't you see how, crippled by this wizened foot, I am stuck here? Hearing the fame of your sanctity I came here as fast as I could sitting on an ass, that by your intercessions I might attain the happiness of health which I desire'. Without delay Father Barbatus stretched out his hand and touched his shrivelled foot and his shin, saying: 'Make haste, receive your health and prostrate yourself before the altar'. Hearing this he who had been a cripple arose cured and in a loud voice praised God through whom the benefits of health had been given to him, through which he had been made joyful. In the morning he entered the church to render thanks to God and Father Barbatus for their actions. The man who had been a cripple told the people who were round about everything which had happened to him from the beginning, and how for a long time he had been crippled with contracted nerves. He recounted how Bishop Barbatus had appeared to him, and how by his intervention he had received the health he wanted. Meanwhile rumour of this great miracle spread through every part and every street of the city, and the citizens crowded hurriedly together to see the man. When they had seen him they returned to their homes praising the maker of all. Only a few days later a certain woman with withered hands and trapped nerves hastened to [implore] the benefits of Bishop Barbatus. She lay in front of the altar and shedding tears invoked the mercy of our Saviour. Almighty God, seeing her tears from on high and wishing to demonstrate the glory of his confessor Barbatus and how he worked triumphantly through him to all those who were there present, made the woman raise her withered hands to Heaven. Then she cried out in a loud voice that she felt health returning to her hands and her nerves moving; indeed she opened her hands and the joints of all her fingers were freed. At this nearly the whole populace hurried there and greatly blessed the King of Heaven and our Father Barbatus.[118]

In this year so great was the abundance of wine that, as we and many others saw, 100 *saumae* were sold for 30 pence. In the same year the above-mentioned Pope Calixtus migrated to the Lord on 12th December. After his death all the cardinals elected Bishop Lambert of Ostia as pope, [under the name of] Honorius.[119] Calixtus governed from the papal throne for five years and nine months. Right after Honorius was ordained pontiff he sent the Cardinal-priest Peter as rector to Benevento.

The year 1125 from the Incarnation of the Lord, the first year of the lord Honorius, the month of March, the third of the indiction. In this year, on the eleventh night of the month of October a new and terrible prodigy occurred at Benevento, and as we have heard also in other cities and towns neighbouring the city of Benevento. That night, when all of us were lying sleeping, there was suddenly an earthquake of unheard of strength, so much so that we were all terrified and expected to die. The people of the city rushed outside immediately, sobbing and tearful, some hurrying to the cathedral, others to the monastery of St Sophia. We hurried to pray to God the Saviour of all. The earthquake was so terrible that turrets, palaces and all the buildings of the city trembled at the concussion; the ground and rocks were opened up into two parts by the great force of the tremor, the walls of the city collapsed, and some of the houses were razed to the ground. We can indeed testify to the

---

118 For the place of these episodes in Falco's mental world, Oldoni (1980), 264–6, although he arguably exaggerates their significance.

119 In fact the papal election of December 1124 was disorderly and bitterly contested until Lambert, Cardinal Bishop of Ostia was eventually chosen as Honorius II, *Chron. Cas.* IV.83, p. 546. Palumbo (1942), 152–60; Partner (1972), 164–5; Robinson (1990), 66–9.

Eternal King that we felt the ground shaking under our feet. What can I say? Stupefied by such a great earthquake and stricken by unaccustomed terror, we thought that we would descend into the depths [of the earth]; so until dawn we stayed in the places of the Saints, groaning and weeping, praying with many tears to the Lord, the good Doctor of bodies and souls, that He grant from His vitals mercy to us unworthy people. There are some who say that three or four earthquakes occurred that night. And on the following day, about noon, another earthquake struck, and reader, had you been there, you would have clearly seen every building in the city tremble and shake. Pope Honorius, who was then dwelling in the Sacred Beneventan Palace, feeling the tremor of the great earthquake in the night, left his chamber and hurried to the basilica of St John. He promptly prostrated himself on the ground, and in front of the altar of the Saviour and with tears streaming down implored God's mercy. This was an extraordinary thing, unheard of by anyone living, which had evidently never happened in our time or at least been recorded by anyone! If indeed we remember and affirm that only one earthquake tremor occurred during that night, however [after that] a tempest of very frequent earthquakes lasted day and night for some fifteen days. The citizens were stupefied by fear of these quakes and hastened, men, women and children, to the cathedral and the church of the Holy Pope Leo clamouring to the Lord with litanies and tearful faces. Similarly Pope Honorius summoned the cardinals and with feet bare poured out many tears and prayers on this account.[120]

The year 1126 from the Incarnation of the Lord, the month of March, fourth of the indiction. In this year Emperor Henry died.[121]

The year 1127 from the Incarnation of the Lord. In this year the above-mentioned Duke William died on 26th July.[122] His wife immediately and in front of all there present cut off her hair, which had grown beautiful and soft, and cast it on the breast of the dead duke with tears and lamentations raised to the heavens.[123] Rumour of the duke's death went without delay round every part of the city of Salerno, and so everyone gathered together in a crowd and rushed to the palace, wanting to view

120 Honorius spent some three months at Benevento, from 11 July until early October 1125, although he left soon after the earthquake – he was back in Rome by 21 November. On his way to Benevento he had made a brief and bad-tempered visit to Montecassino: *Chron. Cas.* IV.86; JL 7212–16.

121 Henry V died at the castle of Trifels in Alsace on 23 May 1125, *Ekkehard,* 374.

122 Actually 28 July [*Al. Tel.* note 2, above].

123 She was Gaitelgrima, daughter of Count Robert of Caiazzo (and sister of Count Rainulf), whom Duke William had married in 1116, *Romuald,* 207.

the duke's body. When they saw it they remembered his humility and piety, and clutching their hair and cheeks they miserably called him their father and lord. The archbishop of the city immediately summoned his clergy and went to bear away the corpse. He placed it on a glorious bier; four of his horses which he had loved drew the bier to the cathedral of St Matthew, similarly they placed four gold banners upon it. Reader, if you had been there you would have seen people of both sexes weeping, and you would have affirmed in wonder that never had any duke or indeed emperor been buried with such lamentation. When the obsequies were celebrated as was customary, they buried the duke in an ornate tomb which had been prepared. And when rumour of the duke's death had spread all through Apulia, the afore-mentioned Count Jordan, whom he had disinherited, climbed up to Montefusco with a force of knights on the day of the duke's burial, and with the aid of some friends therein captured it. Then he seized all the cities and towns of his county, and thus recovered all of what he had lost. After some fifteen days had passed Robert son of Richard requested the count to come to his help to enable him to capture the city of Fiorentino.[124] Count Jordan, who was of an ardent spirit, gathered his knights and hurried there without delay. With trumpets sounding the city was immediately attacked on every side, and the count himself charged to one of the gates trying to force an entry. However the guards of the turret saw this great audacity and began to throw stones and fight back with their swords. Then by the operation of divine justice the count was crushed by a hail of stones and dying miserably lost both his life and the extensive county which he had regained.

When he learnt of the death of Duke William, Count Roger of Sicily prepared seven ships, furnishing them with arms and all the necessary supplies, and came to Salerno. There he remained for ten days, unwilling indeed to go ashore, but remaining night and day in his vessel. He summoned the Salernitan citizens and Archbishop Romuald, and when they had all gathered on the shore Count Roger harangued them thus: 'My lords and citizens, as you know well, my uncle, Duke Robert Guiscard of happy memory, being a man of great spirit and much foresight, attacked and conquered this city which your foresight now preserves. After his death his son Duke Roger, our cousin, held it peacefully and enhanced your prosperity. Then his son and heir Duke William ruled it vigorously [*viriliter*] up to the present time.

124 Robert, son of Richard Fitz Guarin, whose murder in 1122 was described above [166].
   Fiorentino, abandoned in the fifteenth century, was 12 km. NE of Lucera. For a description of the site, Beck (1990).

Now indeed by the judgment of God Duke William has died without a son. Hence I, who have been born a member of his family, implore you, gentlemen, that, if it should please your noble selves, you take counsel, choose me before anyone else and consign to me lordship over you and the bond of your love. Now, with God's help and if I am granted life, you will achieve greater prosperity and the riches which, once upon a time, you had'. What more? The citizens agreed to entrust the city of Salerno in obedience to him. All the citizens swore faithfully that they would never abandon their loyalty to him. Count Roger promptly swore that he would never imprison them, or allow them to be imprisoned, without a crime or without proper judgment, nor would he lead them on any military expedition which lasted longer than two days, nor would he remove the citadel [*castellum*] of Torre Maggiore from their power, and if anyone did remove it from their control he would restore it to them. After this he entered the city and dwelt there honourably. Hearing that the count had gained control of the city of Salerno, the people of Benevento sent some wise citizens to him promising their friendship and obedience. The count was pleased by this, and informed the Beneventans in return that he would, while life was granted to him, render them reward. When these and other things had occurred the count brought the whole of the Duchy of Amalfi under his rule; then he marched to the city of Troia and to Melfi and gained control of almost all of Apulia. He gained the allegience of Landulf of Montemarano, Landulf of S. Barbato, Rao of Fragneto and Hugh the Infant and [thus the support of] all their property.[125] Having done this he returned joyfully and in triumph to Sicily.

Soon pride turned his mind to the seizure of the ducal honour and, after discussing the matter, he ordered all those dwelling in his lands to call him Duke Roger, which was done. Meanwhile he sent presents of gold and silver to Pope Honorius, promising him also the city of Troia and Montefusco in return for granting him the banner and the name of duke.[126] This however Pope Honorius at this time absolutely refused to do, and as a result much discord and bloodshed arose.[127] I shall describe,

125 Montemarano is 18 km. E of Avellino, which King Roger destroyed in 1138 [below, 000], S. Barbato is now part of Manocalzati, 7 km. NE of Avellino, *Falco*, 256. For Rao and Hugh, above 140 note 37, 167 note 111.

126 For the use of the banner, see *Al. Tel.* I.15, note 25, above. That Roger offered the pope a substantial sum of money, ostensibly 'for the restoration of the ancient churches of the City' [of Rome], was also suggested by the papal biographer Pandulf, *Liber Pontificalis Dertusensi*, 206.

127 Despite the refusal of Honorius to grant him investiture, Roger used the ducal title in his treaties with the Count of Barcelona in January 1128 and with the people of Savona in

if life be granted to me, how and when the said Pope Honorius conceded the duchy to him in the following [pages]. When he heard that Pope Honorius refused to accede to his requests, Count Roger of the Sicilians ordered the aforesaid Rao of Fragneto, Hugh the Infant and all his other partisans in the region around Benevento to make captives as many of the Beneventans as they could and inflict as much damage as possible on the city.[128] They indeed did even more than they had been ordered, particularly Rao of Fragneto who had of old greatly hated the city. In consequence when William, who was then ruling as Rector of the Beneventans, had taken in the ferocity of and the harm caused by this said Rao of Fragneto, he took counsel and on St Martin's day stirred up every section of the city to take up arms and march against Rao.[129] They were very willing to do this, to secure vengeance for what they had suffered. But the said Rao lay hidden with almost 500 knights and a large force of infantry, and springing from his ambush he captured many of the Beneventans who had turned to flee and he found others [hiding] shamefully in the River Sabato and elsewhere. And so he led them captive with him to the *castrum* of Ceppaloni, and imprisoned them there [until] he received their gold and silver goods as ransom.

On being told of all that had happened, Pope Honorius realised that the city of Benevento could be of no use or support to him, and, receiving good advice, went to the city of Capua on 30th December. Prince Robert immediately received him most ceremoniously, and joyfully ordered him to be lodged at the palace of the archbishop of Capua.[130] Without delay Pope Honorius summoned archbishops and abbots to gather for the prince's anointing; and they came and gathered in the Capuan church on the appointed day to great rejoicing. The archbishop of Capua anointed and confirmed the said Robert in the princely honour, in accordance with the privilege of his predecessors, in the presence of the great Pope Honorius, a crowd of religious men and an assembly of bishops. Oh, what great exultation and joy was there shown! We attest to the King living in the Heavens that none of the princes his predecessors had

---

May of that year – the latter drawn up at Messina as he was preparing to cross over to the mainland, *Roger II Diplomata*, 22–7 nos. 9–10.

128 In January 1128 the rector, William, compensated one Beneventan for the damage his property had suffered at the hands of Hugh the Infant by granting him a house in the city belonging to one of Hugh's vassals, *Cod. Dipl. Verginiano*, ii.296–9 no. 169, a document written by Falco.

129 On 11 November.

130 Whether the archbishop was Otto, attested 1119–26, or Hugh, attested in 1130, is not clear.

been enobled with such jubilation and joyfulness. Indeed we have heard from those who were there that by their testimony some 5,000 men had gathered for the anointing of this great prince. When Pope Honorius saw this great multitude of bishops and eminent men, once the prince had been anointed, he climbed up to a prominent place and preached as follows.

'My lords and dearest brothers, as you know well it is some time since I left the Roman See and came peacefully and laying aside all animosities to the city of Benevento, which is a special possession of the Roman See. Two days after our arrival there Count Roger, the enemy of the Blessed Peter, without warning brought some 400 knights to the vicinity of Benevento in an attempt to ruin the city and to shame us. These have continually plundered the goods of the citizens and launched frequent attacks on their property. We have sustained all their afflictions, hoping that they will desist from their perverseness. However this Count Roger has allied with Hugh the Infant and Rao of Ceppaloni to the grave detriment of the city, thinking that we shall surrender through fear of him and give way to his wicked requests. Hugh and Rao are so enmeshed in this conspiracy that every day they ravage the surroundings of the city with fire and sword. Seeing all that has been hurled against us, and trusting only in the mercy of Almighty God, we have invoked the help of the Celestial King and the Blessed Peter. To avoid the city of Benevento suffering further disturbances, I have asked the help of knights who are our friends; that, so far as we can, we may resist their perverseness. And when we went to the city of Troia for certain urgent business, the above Rao of Ceppaloni, because of Divine wrath and Heavenly anger, held captive some 200 Beneventan citizens who marched on his lands on St Martin's Day to avenge the outrages which had occurred. He had them bound and naked in the depths of prison. Then he gave some of these captive citizens to Hugh the Infant, a man of evil reputation and horrible tyranny, so that he may inflict torture and suffering upon them. Hugh has had teeth pulled out by the roots and limbs slashed so that he can extract ransoms from them. Those whom Rao himself detains he continues to afflict with both cold and hunger. What more? Every outrage which could be thought of has been inflicted on the captive Beneventans. Meanwhile day and night they threaten that they will lead Count Roger, who has been put under anathema, against the city of Benevento, remove it from the authority of Blessed Peter and place it under his command and power. Thus he menaces all of you who hold lordship over cities and power over *castra* with many terrors and all sorts of storms, for he will take away from

each of you the fortresses and citadels in which you trust, and dispose
of your life as he wishes. As and how he wishes he will make vagrants
of citizens and make rich men poor and needy. We know the wickedness and contrivances of his mind, by interpreting certain evidence and
by those who have up to the present suffered. We shun [him] far and
wide and flee from his promises as though from a deadly disease; we
shall in no way trust in them, nor, as I say, shall we think it worthy to
incline our ears to them. What gold and what great piles of wealth has
he promised if we shall only be willing to grant him the ducal honour.
However I shun these many promises of wealth, both for the reputation
of the Roman See, which I am resolved to preserve, and for your exile
which I have all the time suffered with terror, Almighty God, Maker of
the eternal, who sees the hearts of all: I reject and disdain them! You
may [well] believe that he has promised such great riches [to me] for
your confusion and exile; thinking to bend me to his will and secure
my consent for your exile. I however am bound by the bond of your
love. I would choose rather to die with you rather than give way to his
wicked promises. Dearest brothers and sons, you have the power of
choosing between life and the harshness of death, of deciding whether
you wish to fight and to come forward to defend together the cause of
Right. I am certain of your good sense, and that you will take no other
course than to throw aside sloth and faint-heartedness and defend the
dignity of the Roman See, which has [in its turn] assiduously taken
your side, and tried to preserve for you all and your sons what you
possess. Come forward therefore you mighty men of valour and distinguished warriors! When the time of prosperity has come, we shall raise
up on high the rigour of justice, which we esteem, for all men. For God,
who is the way of justice and the light of truth, helps us every day, and
the intervention of the Blessed Apostle St Peter with his customary
devotion brings us aid from his sacred throne'.

With tears flowing Pope Honorius preached these words and many
other things similar, and the voices of the knights and of all the other
people who had gathered there were raised and they clamoured all as
one that they would give themselves and all that they had in the cause
of St Peter. Lastly Robert, the new prince, stood up and promised in
front of all thus: 'Venerable father, I commit both my person, which
you see, and the power of my whole principality, which you have given
me, to your command, that they shall all lie subject to your rule'.
Count Rainulf and many other nobles and bishops who were assembled
there promised similarly. Oh reader, if you had been there, how many
promises you would have seen, and what tears were shed with these

promises! If I wanted to tell of them all, my audience would become very bored! Hearing this multitude agreeing and giving their consent to his exhortations Pope Honorius rendered thanks to God the Saviour of all and the Blessed Apostles SS. Peter and Paul, who had aided him who trusted in them and every day gave him help. Immediately, by Divine authority, and through the merits of the Blessed Virgin Mary and the Holy Apostles, he set out for them this reward, namely that for all those who had shown penitence for their misdeeds, if they died in that expedition, he would remit all their sins; for all those who did not die, and had made confession, he gave them half [remission].

Hearing the grace of this great benefit proclaimed by Pope Honorius, the said Prince and Count Rainulf became immensely enthusiastic, while all those who had gathered there returned to their homes. Without delay they sent out heralds proclaiming throughout their respective principality and county that everyone should come to the aid of the pope. All the people welcomed their command. Meanwhile the prince and Count Rainulf came to the pope, and intimated to him the best course to follow, namely that first Hugh the Infant should be summoned by the count, since, having given and mutually received security, they were to some extent linked. The pope agreed to what they had told him and commended their loyalty to him. The count speedily summoned some of his barons and sent them to meet Hugh that he might yield justice to him. He added to his message that he would give hostages and guarantors, so that with his security fully guaranteed, Hugh might come to the count's court to receive justice. What more? He neither wanted hostages nor did he come to the comital court. The count straightaway notified Pope Honorius of all this. Then, as they had promised, the prince and count raised a strong force of knights and an innumerable multitude of footmen and marched against a *castellum* of Hugh the Infant called La Pellosa.[131] Hearing that this *castellum* was thus besieged, William the Rector of Benevento proclaimed by herald through every section of the city that they should take up arms and march out on this expedition. The people hastened as fast as they could to make the necessary preparations for the expedition. Three days later the rector marched out against the *castellum* accompanied by nearly 2,000 men. And when that *castellum* was being fiercely besieged, the wood which had been growing for a long time under its protection was swiftly cut down and set aflame. Then the people of Benevento attacked as one the citadel of the *castrum*, and having made their attack fought on bravely.

131 La Pellosa is Apollosa, 10 km. SW of Benevento; cf. *Catalogus Baronum*, art. 982.

They could have captured and burnt it had they been brought help by Count Rainulf, but since the count was unwilling to assist them as he could have done the Beneventans retired exhausted to their camp. The next day, seeing that neither the count nor the prince was exerting any energy to bring them help, as they had promised to the pope they would, the Beneventans were amazed at such delays and became fearful and demoralised. In the morning the prince ordered his tent and his baggage to be moved. Then Count Rainulf started to make excuses to justify abandoning the expedition, such as that it was mid-winter and their situation was dangerous, and so left with the prince. The rector was dismayed by their excuses and ordered all the people to return to the city. As soon as they had heard his order they retreated at the double. This attack took place on 29th January.

The pope, who was staying at Montesarchio,[132] heard that the *castrum* had been thus abandoned and that the promises of the prince and count had not been upheld there, was beset with quite staggering grief, and roared and lamented more than one could possibly imagine. He promptly took the road and retreated to the borders of Rome. Meanwhile the prince and the count made excuses to Pope Honorius for their deceitful tricks. However the pope had heard and knew in his heart all that they had done, and he regarded them, so it is said, with a glance as fierce as mind could conceive, and hurried away. After this he ordered Walter, Archbishop of Taranto, to go to Benevento, deal carefully with matters concerning the city, and lend his assistance to its protection. He also ordered the rector to hand over money from the regalian revenues to the archbishop, from which the knights of the city might be armed and as much help as possible be raised. The rector however refused to hand over the money for troops until he had received the order in a personal letter. Only when he had received this command did he grant the money for the knights.

The year 1128, fourth year of the pontificate of the lord Pope Honorius, the month of March, sixth of the indiction. In this year Pope Honorius came to Benevento with 200 Roman knights, and there he found Prince Robert of Capua and Count Rainulf with a great army, and a multitude of the citizens of Benevento at the *castellum* of Torre di Palazzo.[133] This

---

132 In the Valle Caudina, 14 km. SW of Benevento. The Archbishop of Benevento was an extensive landowner here, see for example *Più antiche carte della cattedrale*, 180–9 nos. 60–1 (June 1124, February 1127), and it is possible that the pope was staying at one of his houses.

133 Torre di Palazzo no longer exists, but was on the River Calore, about 10 km. N of Benevento.

they were besieging and making a fierce attack upon, for it belonged to Hugh the Infant. Hugh himself opposed the said prince and Count Rainulf. The *castrum* was thus besieged and the attack was pressed wonderfully well, and since the Lord who observes all did not wish it to be defended, he gave it into the power of the prince and the count. After this had occurred Pope Honorius heard that Count Roger of the Sicilians was every day acting against his wishes and occupying parts of Apulia; hence he persuaded Prince Robert and the count that they raise an army and hasten against Count Roger. What more? The pope marched into Apulia with the prince and the count, and ordered Grimoald of Bari and Tancred to be summoned, that they all resist the Count of the Sicilians together, and this was what was done. When Count Roger found out that the pope was advancing against him with these barons and a powerful army of knights and infantry, he retreated into the mountains, avoiding the pope's forces lest any sort of misfortune come upon him. Thus for forty days under the burning July sun did the pope blockade the count. Meanwhile the prince, who was delicate of body and unable to sustain hard work, began to waver in his loyalty to the pope, thinking of ways in which he might leave his camp and return home. He had his tents struck and endeavoured to start on his way. When the pope found out about the deceitfulness of the prince and others of the barons he came to an agreement, promising via his chancellor Haimeric[134] and Cencius Frangipane that he would give the duchy to Count Roger, and that when the count came to Benevento he would there confirm the ducal honour to him. After doing this the pope returned to Benevento. The count gathered up his army and [also] came to Benevento, pitching camp on Monte S. Felice. Peace was then made between them and their promises fulfilled, and after sundown on the eighth day after the feast of the Assumption of St Mary the pope conceded the ducal honour to the count, in the sight of nearly 20,000 men on the riverbank at the Ponte Maggiore.[135] Many issues which needed negotiation had arisen and the whole of the day had been taken up with dispute between them. And since the count was reluctant to enter the city of Benevento the pope had, as said, gone out to the bridge mentioned above and [there] conceded

134 Haimeric, Cardinal deacon of S. Maria Nuova and papal chancellor 1123–41, was from Burgundy. It is usually believed he was a regular canon of S. Maria Reno at Bologna before becoming a cardinal, though this has been questioned, Hüls (1977), 236; Malaczek (1981), 33. For his importance in the schism of 1130, see the introduction [above, 21].

135 On 23 August. *Romuald* [below, 253], describes this as a bridge over the River Sabato; it was a Roman bridge, also known as the Ponte Leproso. Monte S. Felice faced this bridge. See Clementi (1991), 275n.

to him the ducal honour. The duke had received his title and sworn an oath that he would do nothing in word or deed that would lead St Peter and the lord Pope Honorius and his catholic successors to lose the city of Benevento, and [also] that he would not seize the Principality of Capua or permit it to be seized. And after all this he returned to Salerno and set out for Sicily.

A few days later Pope Honorius took counsel and returned to Rome.[136] But before he had entered the city of Rome, on 29th September a group of Beneventans unsheathed their swords and killed William, the then Rector of the city, in the Sacred Beneventan Palace. In fact the unfortunate rector tried to escape from their wrath and fled behind the altar of St John in the Palace chapel, hiding at the feet of the priest John who was then celebrating Mass there, but he was unable to get away. He was stabbed there and was then pulled out and thrown down from the Palace. They tied a rope around his feet, and the wretched man was thus dragged under a hail of stones through the city square to the meat market of St Lawrence. After his death the people of the city were roused to fury and destroyed the houses of Poto Spitameta, John and Guisliccio the judges, Transo,[137] Lawrence and Louis the doctor. These men, along with the judge Dauferius, fearing the people's pride, fled to Montefusco.[138] The populace immediately organised a Commune and almost all of them swore that Poto Spitameta and the others named above who had fled from the city should not inhabit therein for seven years and forty days.

In the same year Abbot John of St Sophia died on 8th November, and Franco, who was then the sacrist, was elected.[139] Hearing how the rector had met his death, the pope was grief-stricken and threatened revenge on the city of Benevento for such an infamous deed. The people discussed the matter and decided at once to send envoys to the

---

136 Honorius had reached Rome by 7 October, J-L 7321–2.

137 He was presumably Transo the notary, who acted as advocate for the monastery of St Sophia in November 1120, and witnessed a donation to that monastery in August 1127, a document written by Falco, Museo del Sannio, Fondo S. Sofia, vol. 10 no. 26; Loud (1993), 195–6 no. 1. Transo was dead by March 1141, when his son Romuald acted as guarantor in a charter, *Più antiche carte della cattedrale*, 195 no. 64.

138 Dauferius witnessed documents in August 1122, written by Falco; September 1123; November 1127, also written by Falco; and a document of the Rector William in January 1128, Benevento, Museo del Sannio, Fondo S. Sofia, 34 no. 3; Girgensohn, 'Documenti beneventani', 290–8 nos. 5– 6; *Cod. Dipl. Verginiano*, ii.296–9 no. 169. He was to be active in the 1130s as a supporter of Pope Anacletus.

139 He was Abbot of St Sophia 1128–40, and sacrist since 1123, Girgensohn, 'Documenti beneventani', 296.

pope, saying that the rector's death had been the work of foolish and discontented men, and asking that he send a suitable rector and give peace to the Beneventans. The pope took advice and appointed the lord Cardinal Gerard as rector for us.[140]

The year 1129 from the Incarnation of the Lord. In this year Pope Honorius came to Benevento and in the month of August consecrated the said Franco as Abbot of the monastery of St Sophia.[141] He begged the Beneventans who had made the Commune to recall to the city Poto Spitameta and the other citizens already mentioned, whom they had expelled from Benevento, but he was unable to secure this. As a result the pope was furious and left Benevento himself and went to the village called Leocubante.[142] He requested Duke Roger, who was staying there, to come in the month of May with his army and impose punishment on the citizens of Benevento. The duke swore an oath to do this. Then the pope went to the *castrum* of Ceppaloni, had the city raided and thus returned in a fury to Rome. And in this year Archbishop Roffred removed the bodies of SS. Januarius, Festus and Desiderius from the altar where they had of old lain, for they had not been kept there with the reverence that they ought to have had. Then the bones of the Saints were relocated with great respect and joyfulness in the basilica which Archbishop Walter of Taranto had had built in their honour. We ourselves saw this and kissed their bones.

In the same year, in mid-February, Pope Honorius went the way of all flesh, that is to the Lord, and the lord Innocent was elected. After his election, on the third hour of the same day, Bishop Peter of Porto chose Peter son of Peter Leone with the name of Anacletus. Then, cursing the election of Innocent, they confirmed the election of Anacletus. However when Leo Frangipane heard of the election of Anacletus, he began to urge those Roman citizens who were followers and friends of his to lend their help to Innocent, whose partisan he was. Then Anacletus's brother Leo threw open his treasury and asked the people of Rome to support to the utmost of their ability the election of his brother, which

---

140 Gerard, Cardinal priest of S. Croce in Jerusalem from 1123, originally from Bologna, was a regular canon following the observance of S. Frediano in Lucca. He had been legate to Germany in 1125 and was sent by Innocent II as legate to Germany again in 1130–1, 1133 and 1135/6. He was pope in 1144–5 as Lucius II, Zenker (1964), 129–31; Hüls (1977), 164; Malaczek (1981), 44–5, who stresses the importance of his personal contacts with German prelates in persuading the German Church to support Innocent.

141 On 26 August, according to Bertolini, 'Annales Beneventani', 159, version 3.

142 Leocubante was near Montefusco, about 13 km. SE of Benevento, and belonged to St Sophia.

nearly all of them did. So on both sides a vicious and most intense civil war was begun.[143]

The year from the Lord's Incarnation 1130, the month of March, eighth of the indiction. After Anacletus had been elected, he informed the Beneventans how he had been elected and instructed them to do fealty to him. However the said Innocent, after his consecration as pope, saw the divisions among the Roman people and the civil war growing more serious every day. He took counsel and travelled across the mountains to the King of the French and to other faithful subjects of the Roman See, and he was received properly and with great respect by them. He promptly celebrated a synod at the city of Rheims, at which gathering, as I have learnt, nearly 150 archbishops and bishops were present. There he bound Anacletus and his supporters with the chain of excommunication.[144] In the same year Archbishop Roffred of Benevento died, and Landulf son of Roffred de Garderisio was elected to the archbishopric.

In the same year the said Anacletus came to Benevento; then he went to the city of Avellino and agreed with Duke Roger that he would crown him King of Sicily. After agreeing this Anacletus returned to Benevento and the duke to Salerno, and then went back to Sicily.[145] Anacletus sent one of his cardinals, named Comes,[146] to the duke, and he crowned him as king in the city of Palermo on Christmas Day of the same year. Prince Robert of Capua placed the crown on his head, for which he did not receive a proper recompense! And in that same year Anacletus consecrated the said Landulf as archbishop at Rome. After all this had

---

143 Honorius II died on 13 February 1130. For the disputed election, see especially Stroll (1987), 82–90; Robinson (1990), 69–78.

144 For the enactments of the synod of Rheims (October 1131), Mansi, *Concilia*, xxi.457–62. Innocent also crowned the French king's son Louis (VII) there. The French king and some of his churchmen had already recognised Innocent as the legitimate pope at a council held at Etampes in May 1130; indeed this was the spur for Innocent's departure to France, Reuter (1983), Robinson (1990), 104–5; Grant (1998), 134–6. The reference to the Rheims synod here shows that this section cannot have been written contemporaneously.

145 The bull creating the kingdom was issued from Benevento on 27 September [below, 304–6]. Anacletus then went to Apulia: he was at Trani on 30 October, *Italia Pontificia*, ix.293 no. 9, held a council at Canosa in November, Baumgartner (1897), 576–8, then returned to Benevento 28 November–5 December, J-L 8416–8; *Chron. S. Sophiae*, ii.649–51. After a brief visit to Capua, he returned to Benevento, where he is known to have been on 8 February 1131, *Chron. S. Sophiae*, ii.654–9.

146 Comes, Cardinal deacon of S. Maria in Aquiro from 1110, and Cardinal priest of S. Sabina from 1123, had been legate to Germany in 1129, *Lothar Diplomata*, 19 no. 16. Initially a supporter of Anacletus, he later defected to Innocent II, who made him Cardinal priest of S. Pietro in Vincoli, but like the other Anacletan cardinals he lost his position at the Second Lateran Council, Zenker (1964), 93, 118; Hüls (1977), 205, 231.

taken place King Roger gathered an army and captured Amalfi.[147]

Meanwhile Anacletus, as we said, returned to Benevento after his conference with Duke Roger at the city of Avellino. After some consideration he summoned the judges John, Dauferius and Benedict,[148] and Louis the doctor and Poto Spitameta, and after receiving 200 *solidi* from them brought them back to the city and restored all their property to them. Then he had discussions with them and his other partisans about how to dissolve the Commune which had been set up in the city and sworn to at the time of the death of the Rector William, discussed above. It has indeed very often been related how that Commune had been created in consequence of his oppressions and of the damage done to the city, above all in the time of Pope Honorius. As a result the pope was unable to harm those who had killed his rector. It has also been told how the same Pope Honorius came to Benevento after the death of the said rector and had discussed again and again with the citizens the [question of] allowing the judges whom they had exiled after the death of the rector to return to the city and to be restored to their, albeit destroyed, homes; but he had been unable to secure this. In consequence, as we have said, Pope Honorius was greatly annoyed with the city of Benevento, and negotiated with Duke Roger to secure the city's destruction.

Anacletus was informed of these and many other matters about the Commune. By the advice of these aforesaid judges and of his other supporters, Anacletus immediately ordered Prince Robert of Capua, who then favoured him, to be summoned to march to him with a strong force of troops. The latter received the messengers and hurried to do as he was commanded. They immediately planned the destruction of the Commune, and the pope begged him for his most active assistance. What more? On the appointed day, in the Octave of Epiphany,[149] with the prince and his men present, Rolpoto of S. Eustasius, who seemed to be the most ardent supporter of the Commune, and Benvenutus de Iohanne de Rocca, Roffred de Anselmo, Dauferius di Barba Maggiore and others of his partisans, were summoned. They gathered together at the palace of Dacomarius where Anacletus, who had celebrated a council, was dwelling, to listen to what he had to say. From the other party the

---

147 Amalfi surrendered in February 1131, Clementi (1991), 239, hence by Falco's reckoning in the year 1130.

148 Benedict the judge (not hitherto mentioned) was later attested in March 1141 and June 1144, *Più antiche carte della cattedrale*, 194–6 no. 64, 205–6 no. 68.

149 6–13th January 1131.

then rector, Crescentius, summoned nearly 400 armed supporters, to capture them unawares. Thus armed, and having the support of the prince, the partisans of Anacletus rose up and drawing their weapons shamefully seized Rolpoto and all those who had come with him, holding them as prisoners in the Palace of Dacomarius. Then they captured those of their friends whom they found in the streets. They assailed a certain John 'Jocularius' with more swords and stones than one would have believed possible; cut about and suffering from many wounds he escaped half-dead from their hands, but afterwards lived on for many years. And when Rolpoto and his followers had been thus captured, the said Anacletus ordered the arrest of the judges Persicus and Roffred, who had acquiesced in their actions and by whose advice the Commune had for a long time been governed. However the two judges, learning of this plan from their friends, sneaked out of the city and escaped from the hands of Anacletus and their enemies; they were thus exiled for half a year. Hearing of the flight of Persicus and Roffred, Anacletus was very much saddened and wondered how they had been informed of his plan. For he had intended, if the judges had been captured, to send them prisoner to Sicily, never to return to Benevento. After these events Anacletus was requested by various friends of Rolpoto to free the latter from his chains. Acceding to their prayers he released him from his bonds, after Rolpoto had sworn an oath never to take part in that or any other commune. Anacletus drove his other followers from the city, binding them by oath not to return without his permission or that of his Rector.

After all this had taken place, Anacletus went to Salerno on 1st March, and then took counsel intending to return to Rome. But when Rolpoto escaped from captivity at the hands of Anacletus, he started to mull over in his mind many, various and wonderful plots against the pope and his partisans, who had seized him so shamefully and had caused him to sell his garden for 60 *romanati* which he had given to Anacletus.[150] Indeed Rolpoto said that he wished that he might rather be dead than allow his captivity and that of his friends to remain unpunished. He started to try out new plans every day, and directed always a fierce gaze and uncompromising mind against his adversaries.

In the year 1131 from the Lord's Incarnation, the month of March. After not too many days had elapsed the said Benvenutus and his followers took up arms and on 8th May entered Benevento, went up

---

150 The *romanatus* may have been intended to denote a Byzantine *solidus*, but was more probably a unit of account, equivalent to 30 silver *denarii*, Travaini (1995), 270n.

to the house of Dauferius Basaforte and brazenly stationed themselves there. They sent to their friends to come out into the square and assist them to wreak revenge on their adversaries, on whose advice they had been expelled from the city. Benvenutus and his followers without delay started a vigorous conflict with swords and stones. Hearing that they had so boldly entered the city, the Rector Crescentius was much disturbed and indeed quite amazed. He ordered the Palace bell to be sounded, so that all his partisans would hasten to expel them. What more? Seizing their arms they descended to the house of Dauferius Basaforte, and launched a sturdy defence to prevent the city being subverted by their invasion. However Benvenutus and his associates, seeing that the help from their friends had not arrived, climbed out of Dauferius's house, fled through other houses and the streets and out of the city, and thus escaped unharmed from their pursuers. By so fleeing, they allowed the house of the said Dauferius and [those of] the other people who had abetted them to be destroyed.

From that day on there was much fresh discord between the citizens. The judges Persicus and Roffred were so constrained by fear of their enemies that they did not dare to enter the city of Benevento. Finally, hearing that Anacletus had got as far as the city of Capua on his return journey to Rome, they took counsel and boldly went to Capua. Then they humbly begged Prince Robert, at that time a supporter [*fidelis*] of Anacletus, for his intercession to secure for them Anacletus's love and his permission to return to their property. Prince Robert went to Anacletus without delay and persuaded him to grant them his love. What more? Anacletus acceded to the prince's requests and gave them letters granting them permission to return and live in safety in the city. They returned there and came to the St Lawrence gate, intending to return freely to their homes as they had been permitted to do by Anacletus. But a huge crowd of their enemies appeared along with the said Crescentius, and viciously threatened them to prevent their entry. Realising how reckless these people were and how serious were their threats, they took the course of safety and returned to Anacletus, who was still there at Capua. They immediately flung themselves at his feet, and told him from the beginning all that had been said and done to them. Anacletus was furious about this, and began to make awful threats against the Beneventans. Finally, on the prince's advice he sent them back to the city, giving them one of his cardinals [to accompany them] so that, when the people had seen and heard him, they would trust in this and allow them to return in peace to their homes. Thus they came accompanied by the said cardinal, and once they had heard him the citizens laid aside their anger and permitted them and their other fellow citizens to remain there.

Meanwhile the above-mentioned Rolpoto, relying on the help of his friends, was continually day and night concocting new plans and conspiracies both in public and in private against Crescentius and his allies. Rolpoto sought to secure revenge from Crescentius and his associates, remembering his suffering and captivity, as well as the sale of his garden, and how through them he had lost 60 *romanati*. When Crescentius learned of the activities of Rolpoto and his friends and of their fearful threats, he descended from the Curial Palace and dwelt at the monastery of St Sophia. For he had been told how the former Rector William had come to be murdered in the Palace, and to avoid such a savage and terrible death, he stayed safely within the cloister of the monastery. Crescentius's friends and the said judges came eagerly to him and urged him to come back to the *curia* with them. Crescentius however was totally unwilling to heed their admonishments or advice. For he had indeed often been told by his friends that if he returned to the Palace his enemies would rend him limb from limb and mete out an untimely death; thus, as we have said, he avoided their terrible threats and remained in the monastery up to the Feast of S. Angelo, which falls on 29th September. Realising that Rolpoto and his helpers were day and night plotting and threatening him and clearly wished to rise up against him, the Rector Crescentius began to make careful plans with his supporters how to extinguish the deadly flames of this poison. Rolpoto threatened all the time that, if Crescentius did not return to him the 60 *romanati* of which Anacletus had deprived him, he would without a doubt exact an unheard of revenge on his body. Crescentius therefore called together all his supporters and began to discuss with them what he should do. Some of his friends openly and earnestly urged him to pay Rolpoto the 60 *romanati* from the regalian revenues of the Curia, and by this means they could be safe from this great and fearful danger. To this Crescentius told them that he doubted whether he could pay him the money, particularly since Anacletus had transferred that money into his own treasury. He said fearfully that if he then returned money which was there without Anacletus's permission, then he would undoubtedly incur his anger.

While this and other things were happening at Benevento, Crescentius sent a messenger to Anacletus, telling him of all that had happened and how he and his friends were daily expecting death because of the money taken from Rolpoto. Hence for fear of Rolpoto he had come down from the Palace and had dwelt in the monastery of St Sophia; 'Now indeed you should send word to us as to what should be done about the return of this money and concerning the other matters about which we have informed you'. The said Anacletus received this messenger of ill-omen and was much upset. He had various of his friends summoned and discussed with them what should be done. One part of his friends did indeed support the return of the money about which his rector and the city had been so troubled. But Anacletus, who had the heart of a viper, rejected this advice, and he sent orders to Crescentius not to return the money. If life were granted to him, he would himself come to Benevento and calm this storm. The messenger returned from Anacletus and gave a letter detailing all this to Crescentius, who grew more confident and did as the letter commanded. When the above-mentioned Rolpoto heard what Anacletus had ordered and that Crescentius was unwilling to make restitution, he became even more infuriated and began to plot with Robert, Prince of the Capuans, and Count Rainulf how to be revenged on the Rector Crescentius and his friends who had been the cause of his losses, which afterwards was in fact what happened. Because of these and many other conflicts amongst them, and because many old enmities were once again remembered, an agreement could not be reached which would secure tranquillity. The prince and Count Rainulf listened to the honeyed words of Rolpoto, and to his promises of gold and silver, and they swore common oaths that when time and circumstances permitted they would come to each other's aid.

But lest shortage of time prevents me from describing what is necessary and seems opportune, we shall hurry on succinctly. If life be granted us we shall describe in the subsequent narrative how it happened that Crescentius, the afore-mentioned judges, their friends and nearly forty others came to be exiled from the city. If I should wish to describe truthfully one by one the many things which I myself have seen and cannot be doubted, then time would be lacking and I would grow weary under the strain of such work. For it purposes nothing to lie to the reader or those listening and satisfy one's vanity, when so many things have happened which were, as I have said, true, and which, with the Lord's favour we shall try to bring to the notice of posterity.

Therefore in the year 1132 from the Incarnation of the Lord, eighth of the indiction, in the month of March. The moon lost its original splendour and was turned to the colour of blood, which those of us who saw it believed to presage some prodigy. In this year the said Anacletus came to Salerno. In the same year King Roger, seeing that Tancred of

Conversano, a man both prudent and high-spirited, had rebelled and was resisting him, took counsel, raised an army and marched on the *castrum* of Brindisi, which belonged to Tancred. This he besieged by land and sea, and attacked it so effectively that it fell into his hands. After doing this he gathered together his army and marched on the city of Bari. Without delay he began the attack on the city with all sorts of siege engines; for fifteen days that city was under siege and suffering attack. Finally it was betrayed into King Roger's hands by the flagrant treason of its citizens, and after the city had been captured in this manner then Prince Grimoald, a man of a most admirable and warlike spirit, was made prisoner by some of his fellow citizens and handed over to the power of the king. The latter immediately sent him with his wife and sons captive to Sicily, and thus he subjected the whole of Apulia to his power.

After this had taken place the king threatened to disinherit Prince Robert and Count Rainulf. In the same year the aforesaid king had learned that Count Rainulf had inflicted many insults and injuries on his wife Matilda, the king's own sister, whom he loved more than one would think possible.[151] He took counsel and ordered his sister to be summoned to him, and receiving her honourably he consoled her with kind words and sent her to Sicily. In this same year the king had despatched the prince and Count Rainulf with 200 knights to Rome to assist Anacletus, and as they were going there, as I have said above, he took away the count's wife and son, and the city of Avellino. When the prince and the count returned from Rome they were much disturbed and indeed grief-stricken, and amazed at how the king had seized the count's wife. In particular Count Rainulf, whose wife who was very dear to him and whose son had been taken from him, lamented tearfully both in public and in private that he had lost his wife and son unjustly. Then they asked Anacletus, both in their own names and through their friends, to seek the return of the wife and son from King Roger. Anacletus therefore sent messengers begging the king to return the count's wife and son, but was unable to obtain this. The count in consequence became inflamed by his grief, and called for a time when he would have revenge. What more? He allied himself with the said prince and with the *Magister Militum* of the Neapolitans and other friends, and openly marched out with 2,000 cavalry and a multitude of footmen. He sallied forth with a joyous and intrepid heart, desiring to suffer death before disinheritance

---

151 *Chron. Ferraria*, 18, said Matilda complained to Roger of Rainulf taking a mistress. *Al. Tel.* II.14–15 would suggest this was in 1131 and Falco has postdated the start of the dispute, Clementi (1991), 240–2.

by the king and exile in foreign and unknown parts. Having before his eyes the fate of the city of Bari and the evils which the king had inflicted upon Prince Grimoald and Tancred, whom he had once loved, he preferred to be cut down and die by the sword rather than to bow his head under the great power of such a king. Without delay the prince and count, with (as has been said) 2,000 cavalry and a great multitude of heavily-armed infantry, pitched camp on the plain of Montesarchio ready to fight and to defend themselves from the king's attack. They humbly prayed the King of Heaven to accord them celestial help to escape the king's threats and render them free from fear. Every day the count tearfully begged and advised his men that, having trust in God alone, they should cast away fear and lay down their terror; 'It would be recounted triumphantly to the whole world [he said] how, trusting in justice, we defended our homes and chose rather to perish by the sword than to allow foreign hands to invade our property while we still lived and force dainty citizens to become exiles'. Everyone's voice was raised as one, and they turned to their prayers, keeping vigil day and night, and invoking the celestial victory.

When, as we have described above, King Roger had subjugated the city of Bari to his power and had exiled Tancred of Conversano from the borders of Apulia, he gathered his army with fierce energy, and led it against the frontiers of Benevento. The king pitched his camp on the plain of Ponte San Valentino near the city on 13th July. Then he took counsel and sent envoys to Prince Robert of Capua and Count Rainulf summoning them to him to receive justice with regard to many and varied charges [against them]. The prince however heard the envoys and in full sight of all replied thus, 'Let your revered king know that we shall never accept justice from him, as you say we should, until he restores to Count Rainulf his wife and child, and furthermore restores to his power also the city of Avellino and its castle [*castrum*], which he has taken for himself'.[152] While the envoys were returning the prince ordered all his knights, who numbered nearly 3,000, and the 40,000 infantrymen, whom he had asked to gather around, to devote all their attention to listening to such important matters, and having thus begun his speech talked wisely and carefully.

'My lords and brothers, we acknowledge it as most certainly the case that you have left your homes, wives, sons and all your property and kept only your arms to enhance your liberty, and have gathered here calling

---

152 *Al. Tel.* II.15 [above, 82] would suggest that the *castrum* was Mercogliano, 6 km. to the W of Avellino.

only on the mercy of God the Saviour. For you have heard, and we accept it as the undoubted truth, how the king behaved towards the city of Bari, and how he shamefully deprived the great Prince Grimoald of his glorious position and exiled him in chains. Who remembers Tancred of Conversano and his probity? You yourselves have heard how he deprived him of all his cities and towns by a fraudulent device and sent him to lands across the sea. We believe that it is not unknown to you what affliction he brought to Count Godfrey [whom he deprived] of his cities.[153] He greedily desires to plunder all powerful men of their riches, and if they should resist him then he overthrows them and without a trace of compassion reduces their glory to dust. What an evil man, and most worthy of death! He thirsts thus to consume all our glory, to unsheath his sword and unmercifully expose us all to the peril of death. Come to our aid, you most valiant of men, and, I say, aid yourselves too, while there is still time to help and advise us, that we may be freed from the jaws of such a man and his savage power. Let our trust in all our endeavours be only in the help of God, and take consolation for the loss of all your property by being inflamed to take up arms. One ought then to be consoled by having faith in victory. We are willing to shed our blood to defend our liberty and avoid falling into the hands of strangers. We have thus abandoned our fear of death, and will remain united to defend the right, and the legend of our courage will spread around the world. Brothers, the Lord the King of Heaven will examine our just cause, and He who heard the prayers of the Maccabees will deign to listen to our afflictions. For whom does it profit, my dear friends, to live shamefully in this world and submit to injuries, when, after much misery and peril is inflicted upon us, a horrible death occurs unexpectedly and puts an end to our sufferings and a stop to our riches? It will therefore be more glorious to die for that justice which we seek rather than to watch the ills of our people and close our days in fearful exile. So, brothers, in the meanwhile we suggest to you that for greater security we give each other our sons and close relations as hostages. This should indeed be done to relieve our minds by making each of us feel safer in trusting one another and we should abandon our fears and willingly agree to this'.

After the prince had said this and other similar things, every knight and infantryman, inspired by the Divine Clemency, unanimously gave his consent to his requests, and so every one of the barons gave his sons as hostages into the prince's power. The king's envoys returned from

153 The reference here is to Count Godfrey of Andria, see *Al. Tel.*, II.18 [above, 84], rather than to the sons of Count Geoffrey of Conversano, as suggested by D'Angelo, *Falcone*, 259.

the prince, and immediately recounted all that they had been told. After hearing this the king once again took counsel, and he sent other envoys to the prince, whose message went as follows: 'We are greatly amazed by the message which the prince has sent to us, particularly since I have come into these parts as a consequence of his entreaties and envoys, promising that he would render justice to our charges. We expect him to honour his promises, and we advise him to come on the constituted day tomorrow to receive justice from us. Then, if life be granted, we shall arrange to have these matters dealt with'. But the prince sent back to the king the same message as before. King Roger was much upset to hear what the prince and count had to say, and realising that what was happening was certainly not what he had had in mind, became more and more disturbed.

He next ordered the Rector, Cardinal Crescentiu, and Archbishop Landulf of Benevento to be summoned, that they and some of the wiser Beneventan citizens might hasten to meet him. They received his message, and taking with them the judges of Benevento and thirty other trusted men they went to the king. The king received them properly and honourably, and they had a long and thorough discussion, to the effect that, for love of him and their obligation of fealty to Anacletus, they should bind themselves by an oath of alliance and make war against the Prince of Capua and Count Rainulf. He promised that he would give peace to the city of Benevento, and that he would free the hereditary property of the Beneventans from servitude and tribute to the Normans. What more? After listening to this, the cardinal returned to Benevento along with the archbishop and the citizens. Without delay he ordered a large number of the Beneventans to be summoned, that they be advised about those matters which they had heard from the king. That part of the people obedient to the cardinal's wishes went up into the court of the Sacred Palace; then he explained the matter to them and immediately revealed everything the king had promised to the city, and asked for their advice. He also explained how he had been unwilling to settle this matter without their oath in confirmation. Why delay more? The king's request was heard, and quickly proved pleasing to many of the Beneventans. The citizens who were gathered in the Sacred Palace, and at their head the judges John, Persicus, Dauferius, Benedict and Roffred, immediately swore that they would do nothing by deed, advice or consent through which the king would lose life or limb or be captured, and to make immediate and continued war against the prince and count and to observe the other clauses which were read of the treaty, saving their fealty to the Apostle Peter. Once this had been transacted the cardinal came down from the Palace and bound all those he could find in the city to the same oath. But when these citizens had so sworn, a terrible rumour ran round the city of Benevento and tongues wagged freely; those to whom the oath was displeasing claimed that Cardinal Crescentius, Archbishop Landulf, the said judges and some of the citizens wished to give the city of Benevento to King Roger and place it under his power. They alleged that [in return for this] they had received innumerable ounces of gold from the king.[154] When this rumour had spread round the city arms were seized, and a great crowd erupted into the squares, rising up in fury against Cardinal Crescentius and forcing him to flee. Indeed the cardinal was so afraid that he fled from the city and hastened to the king. He reported everything which had happened at Benevento and how the city mob had risen up against him with stones and weapons.

Seeing the cardinal thus fleeing, Archbishop Landulf went up into the archiepiscopal palace and remained there fearfully. After this the people gathered together, carrying their arms, and shouted publicly that the oath recently made to King Roger would not be observed. 'We are unwilling to be bound to the king, and to be forced by oaths to wear ourselves out on his expeditions and to pant under the burning sun along with the Sicilians, Calabrians and Apulians. We are used to an easy life, and have never been accustomed to military dangers; we will have nothing to do with this agreement with such a king'. The prince and Count Rainulf were notified of these events, and after receiving the envoys they sent words of peace and assurances of security to the Beneventans: 'You should know that we, the prince, the count, Rao de Fragneto and Hugh the Infant remit in perpetuity to the Beneventans all the customary obligations [*fidantiae*] and tributes which you have formerly paid to us, and will swear oaths to this effect, provided however that you never give aid to King Roger, nor [need you] to us. Indeed we do not wish to receive your help at this time, to ensure that the city does not incur harm by such action. We do however wish to pass through it in safety and to remain in safety and free from fear'. What more? Although this agreement was displeasing to Cardinal Crescentius, the Rector of Benevento, the Beneventans were more than happy with it. The prince and Count Rainulf came with their knights to the Ponte Maggiore, and in the presence of Archbishop Landulf and a

---

154 Bishop Henry of Sant'Agata, in a letter to Innocent II, written soon after the Battle of Nocera, seems to suggest that such rumours had been deliberately fomented by the pope's supporters, *Monumenta Bambergensia*, ed. P. Jaffé (Bibliotheca Rerum Germanicarum 5, Berlin 1869), 442.

great crowd of Beneventans swore, together with Rao de Fragneto and Hugh the Infant, according to the tenor outlined above. They swore fealty to St Peter, and they ordered the details of the agreement and the swearing of the oath to be recorded in a sealed charter, and a signed copy of this agreement carefully to be placed on every city gate for the memory of posterity.

When rumour of these oaths and of the agreement made with the prince came to the ears of King Roger, he was more amazed than one could possibly believe. Deeply depressed he exclaimed how he had thought to have the help of the city of Benevento, and now it had adhered to the side of the prince and Count Rainulf. Indeed, as we have learned from many people, it was only for this reason that the king had come to the borders of Benevento at all, to secure the city's help in launching an attack on the prince's power and driving him miserably into flight. Thus he changed his mind about his plan, and thinking furiously, he realised all too clearly that he would be unable to put into effect what he had originally intended. 'Why therefore', he said, 'did I come here from faraway Sicily, when those things which I had planned are rendered so useless by fortune?' And he was rendered so anxious that he split up his army into several parts, and gave instructions to the various divisions and groups as if about to draw up the lines for a battle. The king was indeed of a provident mind, and careful of heart, and sought a position of security ready to fight and to resist [attack] in case the opportunity should be realised by his enemies. On the following night he revealed his intention to his attendants and his wisest counsellors, telling them of his wish to move [camp]. Immediately he ordered, through the strong voice of a herald, that the whole army should watch and follow his banner, which was at its head. Hearing the herald's voice and sensing the king's fear, they prepared to march as best they could. Without delay they thus moved camp, with the squadrons of knights and bands of infantry rather fleeing than resisting. Eternal God, who knows the secrets of hearts,[155] is a witness to record that this retreat of the king in nocturnal flight should be ascribed to fear. This king, whose power had previously shaken the heavens, now hurried apace along byways through the darkness of the night. When morning came he had reached the borders of Salerno, and there, tired out and to some extent less fearful, he stopped near the river at Monte Atripalda.[156] The

---

155 Not a quotation, but an echo of I Corinthians, 14:25: 'thus are the secrets of his heart made manifest'.

156 Atripalda, 4 km. E of Avellino.

king had remained for eight days in the plain of Ponte S. Valentino, and while he was thus staying there his men gathered up a great deal of corn and destroyed a lot of property.

The army of the prince heard how the king had abandoned his position and fled. Rao de Fragneto gathered a band of knights and launched an immediate and energetic pursuit. He followed grinding his teeth, and with the desire for revenge filling his breast. At last Rao attacked some Saracens who were in the king's train, and led them off as captives. He ordered that one of them should have his head cut off, and sent it to the prince as a mark of his triumph. The prince ordered the head to be sent to Capua, there to enhance his reputation. Hearing of the disaster and the captivity of his Saracens, the king lamented long and hard; moved by his grief he threatened that when a time came for revenge he would exact payment for what had happened. Then, striking his camp, he gathered together his army and marched on Nocera, a strongly fortified *castrum* which belonged to Prince Robert.[157] Tents were pitched, and with trumpets sounding he launched an immediate siege, surrounding its walls and turrets with a ditch. King Roger ordered the wooden bridge, which had of old crossed the River Sarno at Scafati, to be broken down, and all the broken parts to be lifted and removed from the site. He was indeed afraid that the prince and Count Rainulf would hear news of this siege and come to attack him with a strong enemy force. Now secure, the king besieged the *castellum* of Nocera, and attacking from every side believed that he would [be able to] force it to surrender. Hearing that Nocera was thus besieged, Prince Robert and the count were amazingly downcast, and gathering together all their men force-marched to relieve the *castrum*. They frequently invoked the victorious Lord, and desired rather to die by the sword than to be made prisoners by such an invader, and so marched on eagerly until they came to the bank of the River Sarno where they pitched camp. They immediately sent out scouts to find out whether the castle really had been besieged, as they had been told. Finding this to be true, they started to discuss amongst themselves how they might best raise the siege of the *castrum*. Finally they decided to throw a bridge across the River Sarno, and then to move as fast as possible against the king's battle line to raise the siege.

Once that bridge had been placed in position, the prince and count ordered all their heavily-armed knights and their vast force of infantry to cross. This happened on a Sunday, which was the fifth day after the

157 See above, 87 and note 76.

siege of the *castrum* had started. Once his men had crossed the river the prince, acting on sound advice, immediately divided his force of 1,000 knights into two sections. Count Rainulf, who was a man of good sense, and who greatly grieved the loss of his cherished wife, similarly split his knights, 1,500 strong, into five squadrons. They sent another 250 knights to defend Nocera, who fought bravely against the king. And while, as has been said, the prince and count thus made ready for battle, news of this suddenly came to the ears of the king. What more? The herald's voice rang out ordering everyone in his army to arm themselves for battle. Rapidly seizing their weapons, they appeared clad in their armour before the king; the latter divided, as we have heard, his knights and infantry into eight sections; each of which then closed up its ranks ready for battle. O reader, if you had been there you would have seen what tears were offered up by each side of armed men, asking God for victory, and that He see from on high the justice [of their cause] and free the blood of the innocent![158]

Suddenly the king's first line charged the prince's division who fought to the best of their power to defend themselves. Both sides battled on for a short time, but while they were fighting a tremendous panic unexpectedly engulfed the infantry of the prince and the count, and they turned tail and fled to the river. Many of them crossed the bridge and escaped, but a thousand others, so we were told, missing the bridge, entered the water thinking to make their escape that way, but with their armour were submerged in the thirsty waters and lost their lives in the torrent. What cries there were, and what mourning for the dead! If I wished to describe all this I would run out of time before I had completed my description. But let us return to the matter in hand. Seeing disaster strike so many knights and infantry, the prince's second division summoned up their courage and charged to his rescue. They encountered the royal battle line going to help the king from the other side, and for a time they fought each other savagely. Indeed, as we have heard told from the mouths of those who were there, the king's side fought so stoutly

---

158 According to Bishop Henry of Sant'Agata: 'Since this day was the day of the Resurrection [i.e. a Sunday] and we were unwilling to fight on that day, we spoke to our men, both great and humble, publicly and in private, to urge them to penitence, and telling them that they were defending themselves in honour of St Peter and protecting the land of the Roman Church, and that they should fight not for revenge nor for money or booty, but for defence of the Church and of their common liberty. Thus by the authority of St Peter and the lord Pope Innocent and of the whole Church we absolved them from the sins which they confessed, should they die in that battle', *Monumenta Bambergensia*, 441. Here the bishop emphasised traditional just war theology, and explicitly linked this with the penitential system, Housley (1985), 22–3.

that the prince's battle line fled from the struggle in confusion. But Divine Providence which never fails to dispose matters looked down from on high on the side of righteousness, or so it appeared to us in our weakness. For Count Rainulf, who was positioned on the other side, and his squadron of 500 knights, seeing that the battle was being lost, spurred their horses and furiously charged the king. By doing this he revived the vigour and constancy of the prince, and as they fought their battle cries rose to the heavens. Then the count's second line charged, and attacked the king who fought back savagely for some time. Why delay longer? The count's third division, burning with enthusiasm and realising that their own men were tiring, charged from the other flank like a lion made savage by a three-day fast and wishing to use his teeth. They poured into the midst of the combatants and, with the help of God, the king was defeated and forced to flee. The cries of the soldiers rose aloft that the king was in flight, encouraging their own side to pursue him so that with victory conceded from on high they might be revenged on such a man. However, wishing to restore the courage and constancy of his knights and prevent them from leaving the field because of this setback, the king seized a lance, stood in the path of those fleeing and called out his name. However this rallying cry profited nothing, nor did it bring help to the fugitives, since the Saviour from his throne on high had granted a complete victory to the prince and count. Hence, seeing his men fleeing in unbelievable disorder, the king threw away his lance and thinking only of flight and saving his life, spurred the fine horse he was riding, and as we have heard fled accompanied by only four knights and made a miraculous if sorrowful escape. So borne down by anxiety was he, and his mind so full of the disaster, that by sunset he had entered the city of Salerno.

Realising that he was in flight, the citizens of Salerno welcomed the king. Meanwhile Count Rainulf and his knights pursued the fleeing king almost to the city. The intrepid count turned back when he heard that the king had entered Salerno. He together with the prince had captured nearly twenty of the king's barons and 700 knights, as well as many others whom we shall pass over in silence; we have heard that others still were cruelly done to death while in flight. What more? The whole royal army, knights and infantry, were either in flight, dead, or led into captivity. I testify to the King of Kings that if I wished to describe every single item of the quantity of gold, the vast amount of silver, the abundance of gold vessels, the infinite variety of vestments, the scores of horses, the great number of hauberks and all the baggage which was captured, my capacity to write would be exhausted before

I had described everything. What more? An incredible quantity of all this baggage came into the possession of the prince and count.[159] They rejoiced greatly in this triumph conceded to them by Heaven. After all this had taken place, the noise of the victory and of the king's disastrous flight resounded through Apulia, Sicily and the whole of Italy, and there was much wonder at the casualties and at the king's terror. Nobody living at this time could remember such a great and savage battle happening between Christian people. When however rumour of the victory reached the city of Benevento the people of the city became all of a sudden full of joy, and gathered jubilantly at the cathedral and the monastery of St Sophia, tearfully giving thanks to God and to the Apostle Peter; then, along with the clergy and priests, they crowded with a great number of candles and lighted torches into the Basilica of St Bartholomew the Apostle and into the monastery of St Sophia joyfully offering up praises and vigils. The whole population of the city was filled with ineffable joy, as though the victory had been achieved by the Beneventans themselves. The day on which this battle was fought was the vigil of St James the Apostle, that is 25th July.

In this year Archbishop Landulf of Benevento died on 12th August. After these events King Roger decided to go to Apulia, and stayed at Melfi for a few days.[160] He promptly had certain of his barons summoned whom he urged to remain faithful to him and [thus] in his favour. He also ordered them to avoid, to the best of their ability, any dealings with Tancred of Conversano; for King Roger held a mortal hatred for him and, as we have already described, had tried to drive him

159 The letter of Bishop Henry of Sant'Agata to Pope Innocent reporting the victory continued: 'They could not list the names of all those knights who were captured, but in truth we believe that they numbered nearly a thousand. Nobody from among our men was captured, nor did anybody die apart from a few who threw themselves into the river, these are not however said to be very many. We impute all this not to man but to Almighty God, who deigned to succour those who trusted in Him with speedy help. The names of the barons of the duke who were captured and held are these: Count Roger of Ariano, Count R(obert) of Civitate and almost thirty others. The tents of the duke and his own chapel, with all its utensils and archives, were captured. Among these was found the privilege by which Peter Leone granted him Rome and all the land as far as Sicily, and appointed him as advocate of the Roman Church, Patrician of the Romans and king,' *Monumenta Bambergensia*, 443–4. One should note that the bishop refused to recognise the validity of Roger's royal title here, only that of duke, with which he had been invested by Pope Honorius.

160 There is a diploma of King Roger, to be dated either 26 September or 11 October 1132 (the dating clause is damaged), issued at Melfi. While forged or interpolated in the thirteenth century, this may be based on a genuine original. Brühl considered both of the possible dates and the place of issue to be credible (*glaubhaft*), *Roger II Diplomata*, 60–2 no. †22.

right out of Apulia. Once he had done this he went back to Salerno, and there, respectfully surrounded by a large number of his magnates, he had full and lengthy discussions about the enmity of the Prince of Capua and Count Rainulf. Every day there was discussion as to how he might overcome them; for, as we have said above, he had already been defeated by them and, as was widely known, driven by their valour to flight.

Meanwhile, when a few days had elapsed, King Roger raided the city of Benevento, acting as we have heard on the advice of Cardinal Crescentius the Rector of Benevento and some others among the citizens. He brought both men and women, and a multitude of animals, captive to Montefusco. Reader, if you had been there you would have heard the Beneventans lamenting, and you too would have lamented and been amazed! The city had been guaranteed security by King Roger, and its people had confidently gone out together to their property and their vines, for it was the time of the grape harvest. On the day when this cruel raid was carried out virtually all the people of the city seized their arms and filled with fury they converged on the monastery of St Sophia where the above-mentioned cardinal was staying. They sent him off, unwilling as he was, forthwith to the king to free the citzens from that monarch's chains and to recover the huge booty belonging to them; for it was said that this raid had been made on the advice of him and his supporters. The cardinal swore publicly on oath that the attack had not been made on his advice. Then he hurried without delay to the king. However, when he arrived there the cardinal was totally unable to secure what he sought, namely the cessation of the raids and the return of the captive citizens. After this the king ordered his knights to harass the city of Benevento round the clock and to capture all its citizens they could find.

After a ship had been prepared, the king set sail for Sicily on the 8th of December. Before the king embarked he sent messengers to persuade Bernard of Fragneto, who was lord of the *castellum* of Balba, to yield it up into his power, which he did.[161] Bernard received from the king, so we have heard, 100 ounces of gold; he then took himself to the city of Salerno. The king immediately ordered nearly a hundred armed men to garrison the *castellum*. In consequence Rao of Fragneto, who

---

161 Balba is 3 km. S of Ceppaloni, D'Angelo, *Falcone*, 260. Bernard son of Radulfus and his lord Rao appear in a charter of April 1120, *Cod. Dipl. Verginiano*, ii.164–7 no. 139. However, there appear to have been three separate persons called Rao of Fragneto active in the Benevento region at this period, see the discussion by Tropeano in *Cod. Dipl. Verginiano*, ii.166n.

was Bernard's lord, and from whom the latter held the *castrum*, was much upset when he thought of its loss. He came to Benevento, and earnestly begged for help as quickly as possible. Then he went to Prince Robert of Capua and Count Rainulf and urged them to come to his aid. The said prince and count, together with the Beneventans, immediately hurried with all their forces to besiege the *castrum*, and there they promptly employed wooden engines to destroy its tower. However, the guards who were watching over that tower were not a bit afraid of their attacks; and the knights and footsoldiers of the king entered the *castrum* safely in full sight of the prince and the Beneventans. In front of them all they brought with them weapons and all the supplies that were needed. Seeing this, and their constancy and bravery, the prince then struck his camp and returned to the city of Capua. Count Rainulf and Rao of Fragneto were much downcast and, along with the large number of Beneventans who were present, retired to their homes. In their fear they left behind the wooden engines which Rao of Fragneto had had brought to the siege. The men from the tower immediately made a sortie and in front of everyone captured these machines, and joyfully pulled them inside. So the *castellum* was lost, and remained ever more securely in the king's power.

At this same time a party in the city of Benevento took counsel and brought into the city the Cardinal priest Gerard, who was with the lord Pope Innocent.[162] He reinforced Innocent's party in the city who held that the election of Anacletus had been against the canons and invalid. In mid-November they made the said cardinal the Rector of the Beneventans in fealty to the Roman Church and to this same pope. The day after his entry into the Sacred Beneventan Palace, in front of a crowd of Beneventans whom he had summoned, he gave the honour and authority of the constableship to Rolpoto of S. Eustasio, who once he had been appointed began with the cardinal to direct the affairs of the Court and energetically to dispense justice to all. He asked knights and sergeants to come to the help of the city and to fight the king's knights who were its enemies – hence he appeared wonderfully active in the city's war. However, the constable appointed by the king at Montefusco ordered all the vines and property of the Beneventans to be ravaged by fire and the sword, in order to strike fear into the city, and this was [indeed] done. In consequence, seeing the great harm which had been done to the city and earnestly desiring to render back payment in kind for what had taken place, the above-mentioned Rolpoto, Constable of

162 For Gerard, see above, note 140.

Benevento, immediately ordered a herald to proclaim through every quarter of the city that everyone should gather with their arms at the church of St Martianus. His commands were obeyed, and on the last day of January, along with Count Rainulf who had arrived with 300 knights, he marched against the *castellum* of Fragneto, which belonged to Rao Pinellus.[163] What more? All the houses of the peasants were destroyed by fire and the sword, and all the inhabitants of both sexes and all ages were driven by fear to flee, leaving their property behind. Hence many men, women and children were plundered and despoiled by the citizens, and a vast quantity of their movables and animals were found in that town [*oppidum*]. The lord of the *castrum* was taken prisoner; and once these events had taken place the Beneventans returned home the same day.

The next day however a great multitude of the citizens, along with the said count, hastened to a *castellum* called Pesco. This belonged to Robert de la Marca, who had installed nearly a hundred armed men there.[164] Seeing their constancy the Constable Rolpoto marched back to the city, and so with the withdrawal of the Beneventans the *castellum* remained secure and unharmed. After these events Count Roger, son of Count Jordan, who was being held prisoner by Count Rainulf (by whom King Roger had been put to flight, as we have said earlier on in this tract), took the advice of his friends and swore an oath that he would be faithful to the Prince of Capua, this same Count Rainulf and the city of Benevento and to join them against the king. Robert de la Marca, Bartholomew of Pietrelcina[165] and other knights swore the same.

After these events, in the year 1133 from the Lord's Incarnation, Tancred of Conversano, a man both warlike and prudent, took counsel with Count Rainulf and the other barons of Apulia, raised nearly 1,000 knights and a vast multitude of footsoldiers and occupied the city of Venosa. The populace welcomed the much desired liberation of their city and accepted Tancred's rule of their own free will. He then secured power over other Apulian cities.

While these and other events were taking place within the borders

163 Fragneto l'Abate (*Catalogus Baronum*, art. 349), not Fragneto Monteforte, held by Rao of Fragneto.

164 Robert was the son of Gerard de la Marca [above, 140 and note 38], and like his father was a benefactor of St Sophia, Benevento, Pergamene Aldobrandini, Cart. I no. 59 (1127), in which he confirmed and put into effect a donation of his late father to the abbey.

165 Pietrelcina, 12 km. NE of Benevento, *Catalogus Baronum*, art. 348.

of Apulia, Pope Innocent and Emperor Lothar arrived at Rome.[166] We did indeed hear that they brought 2,000 knights with them. The pope was honourably received and entered the Lateran Palace, where he stayed to great rejoicing and with much respect. The emperor however boldly pitched camp with his army around the monastery of St Paul. He sent [a message] as we have heard to Anacletus that he was there present by the advice of men of religion and that with the aid of the Holy Ghost he would put an end to this great error and slaughter, but Anacletus, as we understand, made a blank refusal.[167] When they heard of the long and widely desired arrival of Pope Innocent and Emperor Lothar, Prince Robert of Capua and Count Rainulf hurried to Rome, accompanied by a band of nearly 300 knights and by Cardinal Gerard the incumbent Rector of Benevento and some of the more responsible Beneventan citizens. When these last had arrived they recounted from the beginning the whole series of troubles with which the city of Benevento had been afflicted, and tearfully begged them to free Benevento from the continual oppression of Count Roger of Sicily, and restore to it the liberty which had been so deeply and long desired. And while this said Cardinal Gerard was acting as rector of the city he took the advice of Rolpoto the constable and others of the wiser citizens and appointed the notary Falco, scribe of the Sacred Palace and the author of this little work, as one can read at its beginning, to be a city judge. Having appointed him he set out for Rome, as we have previously said. The cardinal and the Beneventan citizens who had gone with him promptly informed Pope Innocent about the affairs of the city and the many perils which we had suffered. Indeed, among other things they told him how the cardinal had, on the advice of the Constable and citizens, appointed the scribe Falco as Judge of the Sacred Palace. What more? The pope assented to their request

---

166 Lothar III had been in northern Italy since September 1132. He entered Rome on 30 April, and spent six weeks there, receiving his imperial coronation at Pentecost, 4 June, *Annalista Saxo*, 594–5; *Annales Magdaburgenses*, MGH SS xvi.183. However, his army was relatively small. He was, so Otto of Freising suggested, 'trusting more in resolution than in military power', and he was unable to secure control of St Peter's, *Chronica sive Historia de Duabus Civitatibus*, vii.18, p. 335. The *Liber Pontificalis*, ii.382, claimed that he left Rome because of the summer heat, although this was probably only an excuse. By 19 July he was at Parma on his way home, and by 23 August he had crossed the Alps and was at Freising in Bavaria, *Lothar Diplomata*, 80–2 no. 50, 83–4 no. 52.

167 Other sources suggest that the initiative in these negotiations came from Anacletus, who even at this late stage sought to secure recognition from Lothar, apparently by asking that the validity of his election compared with that of Innocent be properly examined. His envoys met Lothar near Viterbo, before the emperor reached Rome, according to the *Vita Norberti Archiepiscopi Magdaburgensis*, MGH SS xii.701–2. See Stroll (1987), 70–3.

and signed a privilege which he sent to the city of Benevento via the Archbishop-elect Gregory, who had been at Rome, that confirmed the said Falco as a Beneventan judge.[168]

That same year thirty-two Beneventan citizens who had been held captive in the city of Salerno were with the help of God freed from their chains; the day of their liberation was that on which is celebrated St Eustachius the Martyr.[169] Meanwhile the prince and the count had gone to Rome, but they did not obtain the help from the emperor that they wanted. While they were there King Roger of the Sicilians gathered an army of Saracens and unexpectedly crossed the Straits of Messina; he then marched speedily into Apulia and stormed the city of Venosa (which Tancred had captured) and other towns and gave them over to fire and the sword. In them he killed men, women and children; indeed some of them he had burned. We testify to the Eternal King that he demonstrated such cruelty towards Christian people as has scarcely or ever been heard of in our century. The prince and the count were immediately informed of this while they were staying in Rome and urged to return as fast as possible to resist this great tyrant and to protect both Apulia and their own property from the appetite of such a robber. They did indeed return as soon as the message reached them and had the resounding voice of their herald rouse the whole Princi-pality of Capua and the city of Benevento, to take up arms and manfully resist this perfidy and tyranny; which indeed was done and everything put in readiness. Count Rainulf, accompanied by nearly 1,000 knights, marched towards the borders of Troia. He sent messengers to the city of Troia requesting that the citizens fulfil the oaths which they had sworn to him and to the prince. However, the people of Troia were influenced by their fear of the king, and put their trust in his deceitful words of peace. They refused to accede to the count's wish, principally because the bishop of the city persuaded all the people not to abandon their fealty to the king.[170] Hearing this, the count remained in the area for forty days and then returned to Benevento.

While these and other events were occurring the king besieged a city called Matera. Attacking it fiercely he captured it through the treachery of its people, and there he took prisoner Geoffrey son of Count

---

168 This is the first mention of the Innocentian candidate for the archbishopric, though he was not installed there until 1137. This passage is also one of only two identifications by Falco of his authorship; see 219 below for the other.

169 On 2 November.

170 William [II], Bishop of Troia 1106–41.

Geoffrey, the lord of the city.[171] After doing this he obtained power over another city, called Anzi, where he found the gold and silver treasure of Count Alexander. What more? All Count Alexander's cities and towns submitted to his will. The count, like a shipwrecked sailor, went, poor man, to Count Rainulf and died there.[172] The king then devastated the city of Trani and all Apulia with fire and sword. What shall I say? The king behaved towards Christians in a way that had never been heard of in this century. Moving his army on, King Roger, still not satiated by human blood, besieged Montepeloso where were those warlike and energetic men Tancred of Conversano and Roger de Pleuto.[173] He remained there fifteen days. Tancred and Roger manfully and bravely resisted the king and his army. However, seeing their constancy, King Roger ordered wooden machines and [other] war engines to be built [for use] against Montepeloso. As a result a group of the ordinary people of the city who were aware of the king's harshness and of the horrors of battle refused to fight him; they claimed that they were unable to defend themselves. Why should I delay further? With war engines all round the walls, trumpets sounding and shouts rising to Heaven on every side, he attacked Montepeloso. Seeing this assault Tancred of Conversano and the aforesaid Roger mounted their horses and with their knights fought back to the limit of their powers. Finally however, by the intervention of Divine Judgment and to their awful misfortune the city of Montepeloso was captured. Tancred and the unfortunate Roger threw down their arms and took refuge in dark and hidden parts of the city. However, they were found by their pursuers and brought before King Roger. O what grief and horror hitherto unknown! If you had been there, reader, how dreadfully you would have grieved! The king immediately ordered Roger to be hanged. He also ordered that Tancred should pull on the rope attached to the noose with his own hand. What a wicked thing and how terrible to record! Tancred himself unwillingly obeyed the king's command. The whole army was amazed and horrified by this deed of the king's, praying the King of Heaven to see fit to resist such a cruel tyrant. After doing this he ordered this splendid man Tancred of Conversano to be imprisoned. As we have heard it he was led off captive to Sicily. Without further

---

171 Cf. *Al. Tel.* II.37–8 [above, 91–2].

172 This must be in error. *Al. Tel.* II.38 described his flight across the Adriatic, and Count Alexander was subsequently active as an envoy between the German and Byzantine empires. He was still alive in 1155 when he took part in the Byzantine invasion of Apulia, *Deeds of John and Manuel Comnenus, by John Kinnamos*, 106–9, 115–17.

173 For Roger de Pleuto, see *Al. Tel.* II.41, and note 93 there.

delay the king sacked the city of Montepeloso and its monasteries and slew all its inhabitants, men, women and children, by the sword or in the fire.

He then set his army in motion once again and force marched to the city of Troia. The citizens, who believed his lying assurances of peace, expected him without foreboding. Bishop William summoned all the clergy and monks of the city, clad in white, and went out in procession to meet the king with the *laudes*, thinking as we have heard to soothe his ferocious spirit by carrying before him the bodies of the Saints so as to honour him. However, the furious king entered the city and seeing this glorious procession forgot his promise of security and, being unmindful of the Catholic faith and the enemy of the Christian religion, with burning eyes put an end to that procession. 'I do not want', he said, 'honours of this sort, but if life is granted to me, I shall destroy everything and exile everyone'. The clergy and people who had gone out to meet him were put to flight, and everybody fled as best they could. He immediately arrested many of the Troian citizens and put women and children in chains. He ordered a judge named Robert and four other distinguished men to be hanged.[174] Many Troians abandoned their property and fled with their wives and children to Benevento. He then ordered that the houses and property of the Troians be given over to the sword and consumed by fire. O what a wailing of women and children arose over the whole city of Troia! If my tongue had a hundred voices to narrate everything which happened, then I would still fail to do it justice in writing them down![175] A few days later the king gathered together his army and marched on the city of Melfi, which so we heard he stormed and placed under his power.

In this same year, seeing the ferocity of King Roger and that death and destruction were menacing the whole of Apulia and fearing that the king would then invade his principality, Prince Robert took counsel, went on board ship and hastened to the city of Pisa. He was honourably received there and was asked why he had made such a journey. The prince then described in detail King Roger's ferocity and threats, and the resulting dangers. He humbly begged that the city of Pisa would grant him help and advice, and they agreed between them a treaty, as will be described below in this work. The prince put to sea and sailed

---

174 Robert the judge witnessed a deathbed bequest by an inhabitant of Troia to the monastery of St Angelo at Orsara (in the *contado* of the city) in September 1131, *Chartes de Troia*, 196–7 no. 56.

175 As Oldfield (2009), 63, notes, any depopulation and abandonment of the city was relatively brief, since the urban community was once again functioning by 1137.

to Pisa on 25th June. How he dealt with the Pisans has not yet come in any detail to our notice, so let us return to our story.

After the king had devastated Troia and Melfi, as we have heard, he divided his mighty army into sections and returned to the city of Bari. Meanwhile Count Rainulf raised the whole Principality of Capua and mobilised the help of all his lands and of Rolpoto the Constable of Benevento and every section and street of Benevento, that everyone should club together and bear arms to resist the tyrant king. All unanimously and devotedly obeyed Count Rainulf's wish. They cried out that they would rather suffer death than bow their heads to the rule of such a wicked king. Why delay further? The count gathered together 1,000 heavily-armed cavalry and nearly 20,000 footmen. The Constable Rolpoto roused the city of Benevento by his herald and led out a vast number of the citizens with him rejoicing. They joined together in one force, and while the king was ravaging Apulia they hastened on good advice against a *castrum* called La Pellosa. This belonged to Hugh the Infant who had committed perjury, deserted Count Rainulf and joined King Roger's side.[176] The *castrum* was besieged for four days and fiercely attacked. The count immediately instructed wooden machines to be set up to destroy the walls, and the count and the constable sternly ordered the nearby river and the neighbouring springs to be guarded day and night to prevent the peasants drawing water from them. The knights garrisoning the *castellum* saw the threat from the war engines and that the peasants' houses were being destroyed by their stones, and realised [also] the peril of their growing thirst. Terrified, they surrendered the *castrum* into the count's hands lest otherwise they suffer fire and the sword. They then swore oaths and bound themselves in fealty to the count. After that the said constable took counsel and returned rejoicing with the Beneventans to the city. The count gathered all his men together and gave them permission to return home, after they had taken oaths that they would muster with their arms when necessity demanded. And so everyone returned to his home.

In the same year Cardinal Crescentius, of whom we have made mention above, took counsel with King Roger, advising that they should burn all the vines and property of the Beneventans, thinking that this would induce terror in the city and so force Benevento under the rule of the wicked king. Having received this evil advice the king ordered all the

---

176 In September 1133 Hugh made a donation to the bishop and cathedral of Troia, in a document dated using Roger's regnal years, *Chartes de Troia*, 207–8 no. 60. For La Pellosa (Apollosa), see note 131 above.

property and vines of the Beneventans to be wasted by fire and the sword. Without delay some of the vines and other things were cut down, others were burned. Reader, if you had been there then you would have been absolutely terrified by the cutting down of the vines and the arson of the other property. We lost the wine harvest and were faced with famine, thirst and all manner of deadly perils, but we loudly asserted that we would rather suffer flood or an awful death than serve under his rule.[177] Who at any time hearing of the deadly fury of such an evil king would not be terrified to submit to his lordship? We testify to the Eternal King and Judge of All that according to what we have read not even Nero, the cruellest emperor of the pagans, had inflicted such slaughter among Christians.

When, as have already said, the afore-mentioned King Roger had depopulated the cities and towns of Apulia and savagely massacred their men and women, he went to Salerno. There he ordered certain nobles who lived near the city to be summoned, and when they were met discussed with them how he might ruin the citizens of Salerno and Amalfi as he had with his cruel hand those of Apulia. But, since it did not seem to him to be a suitable time for this, he left unrealised what he had conceived in his heart, thinking to put his plan into effect at a more opportune moment. Then a ship was made ready and he set sail for Sicily on 21st October.[178] Furthermore we have heard that twenty-three ships, loaded with gold, silver and movable property which he had looted from the cities of Apulia, sank to the bottom of the sea, and in these ships were many men, women and children from all the cities of Apulia, who were being taken captive into exile, never to see their homeland or relatives again. They drowned in this shipwreck. O what lamentation and ghastly grief spread through every corner of Apulia! They praised however the King of Heaven who had saved them from all sorts of terrible fates and the peril of exile and had in a single moment taken them from the chasm of this world.

While this and other things which have been recorded were happening in Apulia, in mid-September the above-mentioned Pope Innocent and Prince Robert of Capua on good advice took ship and sailed with favourable winds to Pisa. As we have heard, they sought naval squadrons with

---

177 This meant much more than the loss of one harvest: new vines might take seven to nine years to fruit. Damaged vines might grow back more quickly, but it was still a slow process, Martin (1987), 127.

178 Falco must here have been in error by a few days, since Roger was still at Salerno on 24 October, when he issued a privilege for the archbishopric of Taranto, *Roger II Diplomata*, 89–91 no. 32.

men-at-arms and the strong support of Emperor Lothar, and had the intention, if the Lord favoured them, of rescuing the city of Benevento, which was threatened with many and various calamities, from the jaws of the wicked King Roger. For Prince Robert had gone [already] to the city of Pisa and had had long and detailed discussions with the consuls and wise men of the city, to secure from them the aid of a fleet. They had however been unwilling to promise this without the people of Genoa. Finally the discussions were concluded by a treaty, guaranteed under oath, that they would sail against the wicked King Roger round about the next March with 100 ships filled with troops.[179] We have also heard that the Doge of the Venetians had undertaken to provide assistance.[180] So the prince returned to Rome, and explained in detail to Pope Innocent everything which had been agreed with the people of Pisa and Genoa. Hence he and the pope hastened back to Pisa to confirm the treaty.[181]

And while, as has been related, King Roger was going to Sicily, the above-mentioned Crescentius, the so-called cardinal, realising that he could not place the city of Benevento under the king's power, as he planned, began greatly to lament, along with others among the Beneventans who had been exiled from the city. He then commenced many intrigues and conspiracies, trying to bind men to him with oaths, some through bribes and others by promises. Indeed he made them swear to kill the Constable Rolpoto and as many of his followers as they could find, and to make an armed take over of the city squares, crying out deceitfully in the name of peace. Having bound them on oath to do this, Crescentius then tricked other Beneventans, who had more prudence and good sense, ordering them to provide aid and counsel to his followers. He gave some of them money and promised honours to others. So we have gathered, they planned to assassinate the constable on All Saints Day.[182] But the Saviour of the human race, who disposes of the counsels of men and whose own counsel remains eternal, upset their plans.

179 See *Annales Pisani di Bernardo Maragone*, 9: 'In the year 1134, in the month of September, the Pisans began their dispute with the king called Roger'. (Note that dates in 'Pisan style' are one year in advance of normal reckoning, Poole (1934), 11–13). The Pisans had agreed a ten-year truce with various North African rulers in July 1133: this made it easier for them to devote resources to attacking the kingdom of Sicily, but since they had fought a major sea battle with the Genoese two years earlier they would clearly have been anxious to have peace with them also to allow them safely to undertake an expedition.

180 Pietro Polani was Doge 1130–48.

181 Innocent had reached Pisa by 16 November 1133 (J-L 7636), and remained there until the arrival of Emperor Lothar's army in Tuscany in March 1137.

182 On 1 November.

However Crescentius and his followers laboured unceasingly throughout the month of November, craftily and with the utmost care, for the
invasion and destruction of the city. What more? They arranged a
wicked plan that on St Andrew the Apostle's Day Crescentius would
gather nearly 200 knights and a large force of infantry and would go to
a place called Roseto to cut down the vines of the Beneventans there.[183]
When they saw this destruction, then the citizens of Benevento would
make a sortie to protect their vines, and after they had gone out they
[Crescentius's men] planned to attack the Constable Rolpoto and put
him to flight by the following means. By deceit and a deadly trick they
would first turn tail and leave some of their knights and footmen as
prisoners in the hands of the Beneventans. Because of this the said
constable and the citizens would chase them and become over-confident;
and while they were thus in pursuit some of Crescentius's supporters
among the Beneventans, who were committed to the destruction of the
city, would shut the S. Lorenzo gate. With that gate firmly closed, the
constable and the Beneventans who had gone out with him would be
unable to enter the city, and thus Crescentius and the royal knights
would chase the Beneventans right up to the S. Lorenzo gate –there
they would be certain to capture him and however many citizens they
would find there, and then they would put every one of them to death.
They also planned to conceal 100 knights at the church of S. Angelo
ad Crucem (which is just outside the Porta Somma) who, once they had
heard of the battle and capture, would then enter the Porta Somma
by force and strike down men, women and children by the sword and
consign the citizens' property to the fire, and thus they would place the
city under the power and dominion of the king.

But the Lord Almighty, who chastises and saves, who casts to the depths
and raises up again and after tears and weeping brings joy, prevented
their deadly schemes and wicked plans. He who, I say, 'maketh the
devices of the people to no effect',[184] but whose own designs remain for
eternity, indeed prevented and overturned their malignant machinations. What happened was very different from the plan that Crescentius
had hatched with the enemy. O shame! What a terrible thing to record!
In the alleged name of the Roman See they planned to make the city
of Benevento, which had for a long time flourished in freedom and in
fealty to St Peter, submit to the cruelty of this King Roger, the memory

---

183 On 30 November. Roseto was to the north of the city, on the other side of the River
    Calore, D'Angelo, *Falcone*, 261; Zazo (1956), 182.

184 Cf. Psalm, 33:10.

of which ought, or so I consider, to be execrated. We testify to the Eternal King that, through the jealously guarded liberty of the city of Benevento and the merits of the Apostles Peter, Paul and Bartholomew and the other Saints, we shall hope that wretched Apulia made captive by that wicked king and all the lands up to the borders of the Roman provinces be freed from the hands and the desires of this same king and [hence] undoubtedly restored to a glorious position. This should indeed be hoped for since it should be remembered that Pope Innocent and Prince Robert of Capua were labouring with great effort and much danger to free us all, as we have shown in the narrative above; while the enemies of the city have tried to make us all submit to death, plunder and exile. But let us return to the story.

The partisans of Crescentius, thirsting for the blood of the Beneventans, did not in their haste wait for the arrival of the enemies of the city with whom they had conspired. On the said feast day of St Andrew they immediately seized their arms and went out into the streets. What shall I say? Illogically they struck down those faithful to St Peter, but cried out that they wanted peace. They cut down with their swords the judge Roffred and Abbot Paroaldus. What a wonderful thing! How by killing or mortally wounding people was the cause of peace advanced?[185] We have indeed seen and heard of peace being established and strengthened, but by the laying aside of weapons. However those who rushed out into the streets thought that they would by their actions make the whole city subject to their commands. The Constable Rolpoto was not then in the city, for he had gone out to consult with Count Rainulf. But filled with a sense of loyalty the whole populace of Benevento immmdediately rose up, took hold of their weapons, and valiantly and eagerly took control of the city. What more? We captured those wicked men who were partisans of Crescentius. Meanwhile the constable was drawing near to Benevento, and hearing of the disturbance and the dangerous situation, trusted in the fealty of St Peter and entered the city. He desired rather to die than to see the city so unhappily brought to destruction. Having manfully taken up arms, he and those Beneventan knights he had with him marched valiantly up to the city square, and then he hastened to the Porta Somma, which he found firmly shut and guarded by loyal men.

Meanwhile, the knights of Montefusco and the Beneventans who had been expelled from the city arrived outside the Porta Somma with the intention of entering the city and accomplishing what they had planned

---

185 See below, 219 and note 198, for the possibility that Roffred the judge may have survived this attack.

between them. When they saw the gate itself closed they remained there for a little while; however, those faithful to St Peter climbed up the Porta Somma tower, threw rocks at the knights and loyally defended the gate. The knights turned tail without delay and hastily returned home. The constable immediately ordered the Porta Somma to be opened and admirably followed them with his well-equipped knights. The fugitives retreated absolutely terrified to Montefusco. In the pursuit a man named John Benedict was captured; he was a Beneventan who had been exiled with Crescentius. The constable returned to Benevento with those faithful to St Peter and sternly convened his court. What more? He ordered the said John Benedict to be hanged; then he also ordered the hanging of certain other traitors whom we had captured. He commanded John de Lepore, a partisan of Crescentius of evil reputation, to be sunk head first into a pit with his legs in the air, and thus the miserable man died horribly. After these and other events the city of Benevento remained in peace from disturbance and storm. The constable arrested certain citizens who were under suspicion and ordered them to be held in chains in the fortresses of Count Rainulf.

The year from the Lord's Incarnation 1134, the month of March, twelfth of the indiction. In this year the aforesaid Prince Robert, along with the two wise men and consuls of the Pisans Alzopardus and Cane and nearly a thousand other Pisans, returned to his Principality of Capua on 26th February. He was honourably received by the *Magister Militum* of Naples and Count Rainulf. He made known to them all that had been agreed with the Pisans and Genoese in the presence of Pope Innocent, including that he had committed himself on oath to paying them 3,000 pounds of silver in return for the Pisans coming to their aid. Hearing this, the *Magister Militum* and Count Rainulf greatly rejoiced and pledged themselves to everything which the prince had told them had been done. Without delay the churches of the city of Naples and of Capua were notified and the silver was hurriedly collected. What more? They despatched the silver treasure to the Pisans, asking that they speedily come to their aid. They sent with that embassy Gregory, the Archbishop-Elect of Benevento with some of his priests, to inform the Pisans and the lord pope who was also there of the tribulation of the city of Benevento.

After this King Roger arrived at Salerno with almost sixty galleys.[186] He immediately ordered these galleys to attack the city of Naples. They sailed right up to Naples harbour and battle commenced. The citizens of

186 Probably in May 1134, cf. *Al. Tel.* II.54.

Naples seized their arms and manfully drove the galleys away; the latter then plundered the neighbouring Neapolitan *castella* and then returned to the king. Once this and other things had happened King Roger came to Avellino with his army of Sicilians and Apulians. At dawn he moved his army off to attack a *castellum* called Prata which belonged to William de Abinalia.[187] The latter had thought that this *castrum* would be safe and it was unprepared for such a mighty army. What shall I say? In a moment it was captured and consumed by fire and the sword. We have heard that the knights there were killed, wounded and captured. On the same day he captured the *castrum* of Altacauda, and [also] Grotta and Summonte, all of which belonged to Rao de Fragneto.

While these and other awful events were happening the city of Benevento and the whole Principality of Capua were gripped with fear. We asked the Saviour of all to come to our aid with his accustomed goodness. Reader, if you had been there you would have been amazed how many tears were shed and voices raised on high among the Beneventans, Neapolitans, Capuans and everyone living round about! With disordered hair we invoked God the Merciful, while King Roger turned about and captured Palma and Sarno, *castra* of Prince Robert. However, hearing of the invasion and of this major disaster, Count Rainulf, Prince Robert and the *Magister Militum* were wonderfully roused and made it known by herald's voice and the sound of trumpets throughout their cities, towns and villages that every man of theirs capable of bearing arms should rise up, take hold of his weapons and resist this great tyrant. Why delay more? We testify to the King of Heaven that all the knights, nobles, priests, clerics and men young and old came forward, and a wonderful and very powerful army was gathered. They hastened together most joyfully, saying loudly that 'it is better to die in battle than to see harm done to our people and the Saints'. They mustered at the *castellum* of Marigliano and pitched camp there.[188] Rolpoto Constable of the Beneventans sent forty knights and nearly a thousand [other] Beneventans to assist them.

When the aforesaid king realised that Count Rainulf and the prince had made such preparations, he hastened against the *castrum* of Nocera, thinking to take it quickly as he had the other places, and he placed knights and archers along the River Sarno to prevent the count and

187 William de Avenalia living at Troia in March 1144 may be the same man who migrated after losing his land, but we cannot be certain, *Chartes de Troia*, 215–17 no. 65. For Prata, *Al. Tel.* II.54 and note 106.

188 Marigliano is 6 km. W of Nola and 16 km. NE of Naples.

his men from crossing it. Meanwhile his army furiously attacked the *castrum* of Nocera. Roger of Sorrento had been stationed there by the prince with 150 knights and many archers and loyal men-at-arms. He was not in the least afraid of those who were attacking, and daily defended it bravely. What more? The *castrum* of Nocera was betrayed by some of the king's friends into his hands; and then he gained possession of the *castra* of Sarno and Lauro and all the other towns [of the area]. This capture of Lauro much upset the prince, Count Rainulf and the *Magister Militum*. They gathered together nearly a thousand knights and a multitude of footsoldiers to wrest that *castrum* from the king's grasp, but the barons of the prince and count had been bribed by the king and refused to aid them as they had sworn to do. As a result the prince was stricken by grief, hastened to Naples and sailed to Pisa. Count Rainulf however, realising the treachery of his barons and that he was unable [further] to resist so great a king, surrendered on oath to the king's authority. Rolpoto Constable of Benevento heard that Count Rainulf had transferred to the king's lordship and was horrified. On 1st July he left Benevento and went to Naples, and he was followed there by a thousand and more of the Beneventans. Three days later, fearful that he would fall into the king's hands, the Constable Rolpoto took ship, along with some of his followers and his two sons, and set off for Pisa. But by the judgment of God the ship sank on the voyage, and he, one of his sons and two of his lieutenants drowned in the waves; the other son escaped. The king received the count and occupied Capua itself, Aversa and the whole principality; then he went to Salerno and after remaining there for a few days set off victoriously for Sicily.[189] The 'pope' masquerading under the name of Anacletus came in haste to Benevento and through the king's power obtained command over that city. He ordered the houses of certain of the Beneventans to be destroyed.[190] Meanwhile the Prince of Capua was honourably received by Pope Innocent who was at Pisa, and remained there until the month of March.

189 Cf. *Al. Tel.* II.70.

190 It seems probable that two documents of Anacletus in favour of the abbey of St Sophia, dated 10 and 21 March (no year given), were issued during this visit, *Chron. S. Sophiae*, ii.652–4, 662–6. Anacletus had earlier been in Apulia; he was at Oria on 7 December 1134, *Le Pergamene di San Giovanni Evangelista in Lecce*, ed. M. Pastore (Lecce 1970), 4–7 no. 2. That the party of Anacletus was now firmly in control at Benevento is shown by a charter of sale to the abbey of St Sophia in February 1135, witnessed by Archbishop Rossemanus and the judge Dauferius [for whom above 182] and dated 'in the sixth year of the pontificate of lord Anacletus II supreme pontiff and the one and only pope', Pergamene Aldobrandini, Cart. I no. 55. Cf. also, Benevento, Museo del Sannio, Fondo S. Sofia, vol. 13 no. 2 (March 1135). Anacletus visited Benevento again in October 1136, *Più antiche carte della cattedrale*, 189–91 no. 62.

The year from the Lord's Incarnation 1135, the sixth year of the pontificate of the lord Innocent, the month of March, twelfth of the indiction. In this year the prince arrived at Naples on 24th April with twenty ships and captured Aversa and Cucculo. After their capture he returned to Naples and stayed there with his Pisans. In the same year Count Rainulf arrived at Naples with 400 knights, abandoning his cities and towns. After this the king came to Salerno in the middle of the month of June, gathered an army, marched on Aversa, drove its inhabitants out by fire and sword and confiscated their property. After this act of destruction he went to Naples and besieged it for nine days, but the people of the city and the prince were in no way dismayed. Seeing that he could not capture the city the king abandoned the siege and went to Aversa, which he ordered to be rebuilt. After this the people of Pisa sailed to the city of Amalfi with another twenty ships which had now arrived, captured it and plundered it of all its goods. Then glutted with booty they returned to Pisa along with the prince.[191] However, when the king realised that the Pisan fleet had departed, he once again besieged Naples. On the feast of the Saint Mary's Nativity[192] the king wanted to launch a naval attack on the Neapolitans. Suddenly a storm blew up and all the ships were scattered; they were so afraid of sinking that they returned to harbour in Pozzuoli. Seeing that he could effect nothing against the city either by land or sea, the king ordered his ships to retire, went back to Salerno and then returned to Sicily.

When Prince Robert arrived at Pisa he then, on the advice of the lord Pope Innocent, went in haste with Cardinal Gerard and Richard, Count Rainulf's brother, to the glorious Emperor Lothar.[193] They were honourably received by the emperor and with many tears the prince informed him how he had lost his principality. He begged him for love of Pope Innocent to help him and restore to him what he had unjustly lost. The emperor gave him many gifts and promised that he would be coming during the following year to vindicate the freedom of the

---

191 The *Annales Pisani di Bernardo Maragone*, 9–10, dates the Pisan attack on Amalfi to 4 August [see above, *Al. Tel.*, III.26, note 144, for a translation of Maragone's account].

192 On 8 September. Maragone, *Annales Pisani*, 10, gives this date for the departure of the Pisan fleet.

193 Innocent held a council at Pisa from 30 May to 6 June 1135 in which he excommunicated Roger and all his supporters, proclaiming that those who fought Roger and Anacletus would receive the same remission of sins that Pope Urban had proclaimed at the Council of Clermont in 1095 [below, 310], thus effectively granting a crusading indulgence to the king's enemies, Housely (1985), 23. Cardinal Gerard left Pisa after 7 November, JL 7731, and thus he, Robert and Richard may well have spent Christmas 1135 with the emperor at Speyer, *Regesta Imperii* iv(1), ed. J.F. Böhmer and W. Petke (Mainz 1995), no. 459.

Roman See and to restore his principality. The prince returned and told all this to Pope Innocent. In this same year the *Magister Militum* went to Pisa to obtain help from Pope Innocent and the Pisans. The Pisans gave him a decent reception and freely promised to bring help for him, but on the advice of certain enemies that promise was broken. The *Magister Militum* was as a result much upset and returned to Naples, manfully defending that city.

The year 1136 from the Incarnation of the Lord, the seventh year of Pope Innocent. While these and many other things were happening the said emperor informed Pope Innocent that he should expect him since, with the Lord's help, he planned to arrive as he had promised on the Feast of St James.[194] The pope was filled with spiritual joy and informed the *Magister Militum* of all that the emperor had communicated to him. Then, hearing that Naples was in the grip of famine, the prince went to that city with five ships, but when news of the emperor's arrival was confirmed he returned in haste to Pisa. He immediately went on to the emperor, and found that the latter had crossed the Alps and pitched his camp at the city of Cremona. There he flung himself at his feet, begging tearfully that he help one who had been disinherited. Meanwhile famine in the city of Naples had become so dire that many infants, children, adolescents and persons young and old of both sexes breathed their last in the city's streets and houses. But the *Magister Militum* and his *fideles* who guarded the city's freedom upheld the glorious tradition of their ancestors and preferred to die of hunger rather than surrender themselves to the power of the wicked king. Meanwhile the emperor sent envoys to the *Magister Militum* and the citizens with a letter under his own signature filled with words of encouragement, [begging] that they remain steadfast and loyal since with God's help he would very soon come to their rescue. Indeed the envoys swore to it in front of everyone that they had left the emperor at the city of Spoleto. And only a few days later another envoy appeared carrying a letter from the emperor, containing similar words of encouragement, who maintained that he had left him at the river of Pescara. In the following days the emperor sent yet another letter which said that he would next enter Apulia and that he would rescue Italy from this great peril. In addition Marinus, Archbishop of the city of Naples,[195] Philip of Acerra, a Neapolitan citizen of great prudence, and Count Rainulf, who had gone out to meet the emperor, similarly sent encouraging letters to the

194 On 25 July.
195 Marinus, Archbishop of Naples, attested 1118–40.

Magister Militum. After receiving these letters and relying on what they promised, the Neapolitans, even though grievously afflicted by hunger, waited for the emperor's arrival.

The year 1137, the eighth year of the pontificate of the lord Innocent, the month of March, fifteenth of the indiction. The said Pope Innocent, who had been staying at Pisa, took counsel, left the city of Pisa and went to Viterbo to consult with the emperor.[196] The latter sent his son-in-law Henry with 3,000 knights to meet Innocent, adding that he should then defend the borders of Rome and restore Prince Robert's principality to him. He himself intended to go through the Marche. The pope speedily entered Roman territory and received the fealty of the city of Albano and the whole province of Campagna. He did not wish to enter Rome itself lest he be held up by domestic problems there. The emperor reached the river of Pescara and there celebrated Easter.[197] Then he crossed the river and obtained [the submission of] the city of Termoli and of all the counts of that province. His army marched on and entered Apulia, capturing the city of Siponto and Monte Sant'Angelo on 8th May. So great was the fear which spread throughout Apulia that everyone there right down to the city of Bari acknowledged his rule. While this was happening the pope came to the city of S. Germano which surrendered to him. After that he came to Capua and restored it to Prince Robert, and then the pope arrived at Benevento on 23rd May. He and the emperor's son-in-law Duke Henry pitched camp in the rear of Monte S. Felice outside Benevento. He promptly sent the lord Cardinal Gerard, a prudent and discreet man, to the city to ask the inhabitants whether they wished to conclude a peace treaty with him on oath. Some of the Beneventan citizens came out to meet him and they discussed the question of peace together for some considerable time. After this Cardinal Gerard reported back all that had been said to the lord pope. The next day, which was a Saturday, the pope took counsel and moved camp. He and Duke Henry's army moved from Monte S. Felice into the plain of St Peter the Apostle next to the River Sabato, and there he sternly ordered camp to be pitched. However the people of Benevento [at first] knew nothing of what had been done.

After the pope and the duke had thus placed their camp on the plain of St Peter rumour of what had been done reached the city of Benevento. Rossemanus, the enemy of the Roman See who was then in command

196 Innocent was at Viterbo from 26 March to 17 April, J-L 7832–6.

197 The *Annalista Saxo* [below, 272] says he celebrated Easter (11 April 1137) at Fermo, 80 km. north of the River Pescara.

there, persuaded almost all the citizens to rise up and resist to the utmost the pope's coming. Without delay Cardinal Gerard ordered the judge Landulf of Benevento, Louis the doctor and Abbot Malfridus de Grimaldo to be called to discuss a peace treaty and the surrender of the city to the lord Pope Innocent. The men who had been summoned went out and after assenting to the pope's requests returned to the city. Meanwhile at about the ninth hour some of the Beneventans made a sortie and started fighting with the Germans, thinking to make them afraid and put them to flight. Hearing that the Beneventans had thus rushed out upon him, Duke Henry ordered all his men quietly to arm themselves and leave the camp in sections so that they prepare a trap and surprise those Beneventans who had so foolishly and rashly made this sortie. What more? The Germans charged gnashing their teeth like lions and drove the Beneventans who were opposing them back in flight to the Ponte Maggiore. Some forty of them were captured in this rout and others slain, among whom was Peter de Populo who, poor man, had his head cut off. Another, called Priscian, a city notary, died there of multiple wounds. Ten of the wounded who escaped capture died in the city in the next forty days. With so many of its citizens captured, killed or put to death fear immediately invaded the city of Benevento, and there was such lamentation that, reader, if you had been there, you would have been disheartened by such affliction and thought yourself to die with them. When night fell the captured citizens were held as prisoners in chains. The next day, which was a Sunday, some of the wise and sensible citizens of Benevento came to the lord pope and agreed to all that he sought; the pope promptly ordered the citizens who had been captured by the Germans to be released and returned to their homes. Thus many citizens went out to the lord pope and swore fealty to him on oath.

After these oaths had been sworn, a man called Jaquintus, a citizen of Benevento who had been exiled for three years, thinking to gain revenge for what he had suffered, stirred up the Germans to enter the city, seize whomever they could and carry off the inhabitants' property. The Germans took up their arms and charged in, hastening right up to the Porta Rufina, but since those inside had firmly closed that gate they were unable to force an entry to the city. When the news of this attack came to the ears of Pope Innocent he ordered Duke Henry to be summoned, so that he might curb his army and stop it from this deadly aggression. The duke did this immediately and ordered his army all to return to camp; hence the city escaped this attack. However Jaquintus entered it by the S. Renata drain, hurried with some of his associates to the Sacred Palace of the Curia and captured Pope Innocent's enemy Cardinal Crescentius who was skulking there. They led him out into the square without delay and brought him prisoner to the lord Pope. Then in that same square Jaquintus discovered Bernard, called the Count of the Palace, an opponent of the pope. Audaciously he tried to capture him so that he might send him [too] as a prisoner to the pope, but, seeing himself so shamefully seized, Bernard called out to some of his fellows who were riding with him to come and help him as fast as they could. They rescued him from capture and drawing their swords struck at Jaquintus, inflicting cruel wounds. They knocked him off his horse to the ground, and so Bernard was freed from capture. Abject fear spread round the city and forgetting their property the astonished citizens dreaded unheard of ruin and depredation. Jaquintus, cruelly wounded, was carried by some men to his sister's house and died there after lying in a coma for nine days.

Hearing that Jaquintus's wounds and death had been the result of his own actions, the lord Pope, who was a man of wisdom and peace, raised no charge against the Beneventans who had killed him. Meanwhile Rossemanus, who was then archbishop against the pope's wish and had held the city by violence, fled in fear during the silence of the night. After all this had happened I the aforesaid Falco the judge, Roffred the judge,[198] Falco [son] of Abbot Falco, Saductus,[199] Pando, Potofridus and Adonizebet,[200] who had [all] been exiled for three years, returned to their homeland with the pope's permission, along with the other Beneventans who had similarly been exiled, praising the greatness of the Celestial King who had brought them rejoicing after tribulation and lamentation. The pope ordered the above-mentioned Cardinal Gerard

---

198 Falco had earlier implied, though not expressly stated, that a judge called Roffred, a supporter of Innocent II, had been killed by partisans of Cardinal Crescentius in November 1133 [above, 211], leaving it unclear whether this was the same man, which would mean he had only been wounded in 1133. Roffred was one of several judges who heard a legal dispute involving a man called Samnitus Punianellus and the cathedral of Benevento in July 1138, Museo del Sannio, Fondo S. Sofia, vol. 8 no. 36; he later witnessed a charter of Archbishop Gregory in April 1141, *Più antiche carte della cattedrale*, 196–8 no. 65.

199 Although this man cannot be traced in the extant sources, a number of his relatives later appear in Beneventan documents, notably Alferius Saductus son of John Saductus, *Cod. Dipl. Verginiano*, v.46–9 no. 414 (November 1162); Alferius Saducti son of Alferius Saducti, Museo del Sannio, Fondo S. Sofia, vol. 2 no. 9 (June 1180), *Più antiche carte della cattedrale*, 336–7 no. 122 (August 1189); and a judge Saductus, doctor of civil law, *Più antiche carte di S. Modesto*, 95–7 no. 37 (March 1230).

200 Potofridus and Adonizebet (here spelt Adombazec) both appear in the charter of Archbishop Gregory in 1141, described as being among the patrons of the church of St Festus in Benevento.

to go to the city and receive the fealty of all the citizens, which was done.[201]

Once all this had taken place and Pope Innocent had received the oaths of fealty, he took counsel and started on his way to go to Emperor Lothar on 25th May. Coming up to the Porta Somma the pope spoke as follows to the people of the city who were waiting for him there: 'We thank you, brothers and lords, since you have happily and sincerely performed fealty to us; I ask you all to maintain peace and justice amongst yourselves, and if life should be granted to us we shall provide you with appropriate recompense. We cannot now enter the city due to the many different matters which I have to sort out with the emperor. But once these have, with [the aid of] divine clemency, been settled, we shall return to you and devote ourselves to the interests of the city. Now we have assigned our brother Cardinal Gerard to remain with you, who will watch over your affairs carefully and preserve peace amongst you'. After saying this and other similar things, the pope then started his journey and went to Emperor Lothar, whom he found energetically besieging the city of Bari. On the pope's instructions Cardinal Gerard stayed in Benevento, immediately climbed up to the Sacred Palace and worked for the good of the citizens, establishing peace all around him. Among his other dispositions he especially preached the maintenance of peace to the utmost of his ability both with his voice and in his heart. And before the pope had left the city he had appointed the subdeacon Octavian, a man of prudence and wisdom, as Rector of Benevento, who was to rule the city along with the lord Gerard and carefully maintain peace there.[202]

When the pope arrived with Duke Henry at the emperor's camp he was received by the emperor with marvellous honour and rejoicing. The people of Bari had then been attacking the citadel of the city which King Roger had ordered to be built and very strongly fortified to

201 Soon after returning to Benevento, in July 1137 Falco witnessed a charter written by his son Trasemundus, in which a man called Romuald gave a two-storey house in the city to the abbey of St Sophia. Surprisingly, this was dated by the pontifical years of Anacletus, not Innocent, though the name of Anacletus has subsequently been scratched out (but the 'A' is still clearly visible), Benevento, Museo del Sannio, Fondo S. Sofia, Fondo 13 no. 4. Falco later describes how the city once again recognised Anacletus, but this took place only in late September or early October [below, 225].

202 Octavian of Monticelli, a Roman aristocrat, became Cardinal deacon of S. Nicola in Carcere Tulliano in March 1138, Cardinal priest of S. Cecilia in 1151 and finally the imperially-supported [anti]pope Victor IV 1159–64, Zenker (1964), 66–7. For his family, possibly an offshoot of the counts of Tusculum, and their (distant) relationship with the German emperors, see Kehr (1926). Another theory is that he came of a family of Lombard officials in the county of Rieti, Schwartzmaier (1968); Tillmann (1972), 337–43.

overawe them. After besieging this citadel for forty days with the help of the Germans they captured it most courageously and razed it to the ground. The citadel garrison, who were unable any longer to defend it, were captured and slaughtered, or thrown into the sea. The whole of Italy, Calabria and Sicily resounded with this great victory, giving thanks to the Heavenly King and rejoicing at being rescued from the jaws of so great a tyrant. The whole coastline right down to Taranto as well as Calabria decided to submit itself in fealty to the emperor. After the citadel of Bari had been thus captured the pope and the emperor went to the city of Melfi and manfully besieged it. They captured it after only a few days and obtained its fealty.

At the same time the Pisan fleet, comprising 100 armed ships, arrived as they had promised at Naples. Without delay, they hastened at the emperor's order against the city of Amalfi, thinking to devastate it with fire and the sword.[203] But the Amalfitans on good advice paid out a large sum of money and entered into fealty to the emperor and the Pisans. The latter marched against Ravello and Scala, entered them, plundered the inhabitants of all their goods and ravaged them with fire and sword. They led out men, women and children as captives, deriding them as they rejoiced more than one would have thought possible over their vengeance.[204] Meanwhile the emperor and the pope left the city of Melfi and entered the territory of the city of Potenza. They remained there next to the river of Lagopesole for almost thirty days.[205] All the towns and cities of Apulia acknowledged their rule. After this the emperor ordered that the Pisan fleet should besiege Salerno; he ordered also that Prince Robert and the *Magister Militum* and all their forces should besiege the city alongside the Pisans, which they did from 18th July.[206] In addition he sent Count Rainulf, whom he had kept with him because of his great affection for him, with 1,000 Germans against Salerno. All

---

203 Amalfi had by now definitely recognised Roger's rule: the first surviving Amalfitan document with his regnal years as king comes on 5 February 1136, *Cod. Dipl. Amalfitano*, 236–8 no. 138.

204 *Gli Annales Pisani di Bernardo Maragone*, 11: 'The Pisans sent a fleet against King Roger of Sicily. First they made Ischia a tributary, and similarly Sorrento. After this, on 13 July, St Margaret's day, they came to Maiori, in which there was a great host of people with mangonels and stone-throwers, and with the help of God they were defeated. On that same day they took Ravello, a city in the hills, and they ravaged it for three days, set fire to it and led both men and women down to the sea. During those three days they placed Amalfi, Atrani, the towns of Scala, Scalella, Fratte, Rocca, Pogérola, and the entire duchy of the Amalfitans under tribute'.

205 It was here that Innocent and Lothar met the delegation from Montecassino: see below, 293.

206 *Annales Maragone*, 11, said that the Pisans arrived at Salerno on 25 July.

these were gathered together outside its walls laying siege to it. In the city there were indeed 400 knights guarding it, on them the Pisans and the prince and his men launched daily attacks. One day, so we gather, a fierce battle was fought between them and many of the knights of Roger of Sicily were captured and held prisoners. Meanwhile the consuls of the Pisans, seeing the constancy of the city and that it contained such a powerful force of knights within it, considered the matter and ordered that a wooden engine of wonderful size and more fearsome than one could possibly imagine be built as fast as possible. Once that was completed the people of the city realised their peril and waited for death. The emperor however, hearing of the constancy of the city of Salerno while the Pisans were besieging it with fire and sword, took counsel and, along with the pope, hastened to the city. The next day its elders went to the emperor and made an agreement, surrendering the city to his rule. Some of the knights received permission to leave under safe conduct, the others, along with Roger's barons, fled to the Torre Maggiore overlooking the city. So the city became joyful, exulting to be under the rule of such a mighty empire.[207] The Pisans however, seeing that the city of Salerno had been captured by the emperor without their participation, were much distressed and in their anger burnt their great wooden engine and made ready their ships intending to return to Pisa; but they were persuaded by the pleas and promises of Pope Innocent to return to their obedience to the emperor. So it was that because of this discord the citadel of the Torre Maggiore was lost.[208]

After these events the emperor and the pope moved their camp and went first to Avellino and then to Benevento. There they set up their camp on the Ubiano side by the church of St Stephen next to the River Calore on 30th August. When they had arrived at Avellino Pope Innocent decided to appoint a duke to defend Apulia in his name. The emperor though wanted to ordain one in his name, against the pope's wish. As a result there was discord between them for a month, but this was eventually overcome by good and sensible advice. What more? With the help of Divine Clemency and the agreement of the emperor and all his men the pope chose Count Rainulf, a man both prudent and discreet, to be

---

207 Despite the surrender and Falco's comments, Roger in November 1137 rewarded the Salernitans for their loyalty with a privilege saying: 'at the time when Lothar and the Germans entered Apulia through the perfidy of our traitors, and when almost the whole land was contaminated by the stain of disloyalty, alone in Italy the city of Salerno preserved its loyalty undefiled', *Roger II Diplomata*, 129–31 no. 46, at 130.

208 *Annales Maragone*, 11, said the Pisans went home on 19 September after making peace with King Roger.

duke in his name and in fealty to St Peter, and in the sight of all both
pope and emperor handed to the elect his banner as duke. Nobody now
alive could remember such joy and honour being shown at the election
of a duke. They then remained camped there, and on the third day,
that is on 1st September, the empress Florida accompanied by nearly
a hundred knights entered by the Porta Aurea and came to the church
of St Bartholomew the Apostle.[209] There she heard a solemn mass and
offered a *pallium* and a pound of silver on the altar of St Bartholomew.
The whole population of Benevento hurried joyfully from every part
of the city to gaze at the empress since we had not seen the visit of an
emperor or empress for many, many years, and we exulted and thanked
God since we had seen in our own time what our fathers, grandfathers
and [even] great-grandfathers could not have seen.[210] Leaving the
basilica of St Bartholomew she went up to the middle square of the
city and going out through the Porta Somma returned to her army.
Three days after the visit of the empress the pope entered the city of
Benevento and was honourably welcomed by the clergy and the entire
populace. The next day he entered the Sacred Palace and sitting there in
the sight of the clergy and people invited anyone who wished to object
reasonably and canonically to the person or the election of Gregory,
the archbishop-elect of Benevento, freely to make their objection. But
by the working of Divine Clemency, and since the elect conducted his
life religiously, none of the citizens objected to his election. Seeing this,
the pope gave thanks to God and he himself testified that the person
and life of the elect were honest and religious. He ordered the elect
to make confession of his sins, and then on the following Sunday the
latter would with the aid of the Holy Ghost receive consecration. What
more? On the next Sunday, 5th September, the pope went down to
the cathedral church and consecrated the elect, and at this ceremony
there were present the Patriarch of Aquileia and many other religious
men, archbishops, bishops and abbots of the Germans.[211] Reader, if you
had been there you would indeed have said amazed that never had any
archbishop of Benevento received consecration with so much reverence
and honour! Once the consecration was completed the pope returned
to his palace.

209 *Recte* Richenza, not Florida. St Bartholomew's church was next door to the cathedral,
     Zazo (1959), 76.

210 The last emperor to visit Benevento had been Conrad II in 1038, Bertolini, 'Annales
     Beneventani', 134; *Chron. S. Sophiae*, ii.606–11. Henry III tried to enter the city in 1047,
     but was refused admittance.

211 Pilgrim, Patriarch of Aquileia (in north-east Italy) 1131–61.

After this the judges and wise men of the city begged the lord pope that he intercede with the emperor that the latter free the Beneventans from an old affliction from which the city had suffered greatly and for a long time, namely the *fidantiae* from the vines, the *angariae, terraticum,* and all the other dues which the Normans had been accustomed to exact.[212] 'For we, our fathers, grandfathers and great-grandfathers have prayed to God that he deign to grant the coming of an emperor to these parts, through whose arrival we might secure freedom and security. Now indeed, most holy Father, since the opportunity and power to benefit us has been granted to you, tearfully we all pray that you release the city of St Peter from these burdensome tributes'. Moved by Divine piety and sympathising with the city's long affliction the pope sent the Patriarch of Aquileia and other cardinals, and particularly his Cardinal priest Gerard, a venerable and discreet man, to the emperor, who was camped outside the city in the place mentioned above, requesting that he instruct Count Roger of Ariano and his barons freely to remit the *fidantiae* and all the other dues which they were accustomed to exact from the hereditary properties of the Beneventans. The emperor acceded to the prayers of the pope and without delay had the count summoned, that he come to him with his barons and grant, on oath, the pope's petition. Coming before the emperor the count confessed that he had [already] sworn to and confirmed what was requested on behalf of the city in the time of the Constable Rolpoto. Then he made the barons whom he had brought with him swear what the pope required. These were Alferius Draco,[213] Robert de la Marca,[214] Bartholomew of Pietrelcina,[215] Tadeus de la Greca,[216] Gerard de Lanzulino and Sarolus de lo Tufo, and they swore thus: 'I swear and promise that from this hour forward I shall not seek nor shall I allow to be sought from any hereditary property of the Beneventans *fidantiae, angaria, terraticum,* olive tax, wine tax, *salutes,* nor any *dazio,* whether from vines, uncultivated ground, woods, chestnut trees or churches, and I concede liberty for hunting and fowling in the hereditary properties of the Beneventans and to do with them whatever they want, and I shall not disturb the city market nor shall I allow it to be disturbed. I shall observe all this in good faith and without fraud'.

---

212 *Angaria* = labour services, *terraticum* = a due of a proportion of sown crops.

213 Alferius was lord of Foiano and Deliceto, held in the *Catalogus Baronum,* art. 322, by his son Roger. He probably also had a half share of Baselice, if the Robert Drago listed there was another son, *ibid.,* art. 329; Cuozzo (1984), 76–7.

214 For Robert de la Marca, see note 164.

215 *Catalogus Baronum,* art. 348.

216 For Tadeus de la Greca, see note 114. He died in October/November 1137.

After they had thus sworn the emperor ordered that his other barons from Montefusco be summoned to take this same oath. Once this had been done Cardinal Gerard and the elders of the city recounted all this to the lord pope. This oath was taken on 6th September. The next day Cardinal Gerard and the judges went to the emperor to receive a like oath from the count and his [other] barons. Count Roger was unwilling to take the oath, saying that he had already previously taken it, but he ordered his barons of Montefusco to swear it, namely Rao de lo Tufo, Accardus,[217] Gemundus,[218] Eternus, Humphrey, and the others who had received *fidantiae* from Benevento. For these actions we gave thanks to God the Saviour and Pope Innocent, through whose virtue and grace we had been granted so important an exemption.

After all this had happened the emperor raised his camp and took the road to return to Rome, marching with all his army in front of the Porta Somma. The pope set off with him on 9th September. The emperor pitched his camp at a place called Tressanti, then went to Capua and marched on to Rome. What more? The emperor returned to the lofty heights of his empire and to his palaces. Pope Innocent went to the Lateran Palace.[219] However, hearing that the emperor had taken the way home, King Roger summoned his army and went to Salerno; he immediately marched against Nocera and placed it under his rule, then he took over all Count Rainulf's land. Next he went to Capua and stormed it furiously, devastating it with fire and sword. He ordered all the valuables and wealth of the city to be consigned to the flames or destroyed by main force. He plundered the churches of their ornaments, and women and even nuns were treated with contumely.[220] After such events he gained Avellino and the area right up to the boundaries of Benevento. Sergius, the *Magister Militum* of the city of Naples promptly went over to his side. Then the judges of the city of Benevento went with some other citizens to the king and subjected the city in fealty to Anacletus and alliance with the king, ignoring their fealty to Pope Innocent. After this he gathered his army and in mid-October came near to the city of Benevento, marching by the Porta Somma on his way

217 Accardus had died by December 1139, *Cod. Dipl. Verginiano*, ii.235–8 no. 256. His son Guerrerius was later constable of Montefusco, *Catalogus Baronum*, art. 410 [see below, 337]; *Cod. Dipl. Verginiano*, iv. no. 316 (1153); Cuozzo (1984), 113–14.

218 Probably a copyist's error for Guimund; he may well have been the Guimund son of Paganus listed as holding a knight's fee at Montefusco in the *Catalogus Baronum*, art. 420.

219 Innocent was in Rome by 1 November 1137, J-L 7856.

220 Prince Robert, whose role in the events of this year Falco largely ignored, had issued a privilege for the abbey of Cava from Capua in September 1137, shortly before it was sacked, Cava, *Arm. Mag.* G.28.

to Montesarchio which he placed under his rule. Next he force-marched against the city of Count Richard, which the count abandoned as he fled to Duke Rainulf, and so the king brought that city under his control.[221] Then taking Montecorvino he ordered it to be given over to fire and the sword and plundered of its valuables.[222]

Hearing that the king had entered Apulia intent on attacking him and every day plotted his downfall, Duke Rainulf gathered together the people of Trani, Troia and Melfi, and 1,500 knights, affirming that he wished rather to die than to lead a life of misery, and thus prepared he approached the royal army. Meanwhile the Abbot of Clairvaux, a wonderful and discreet man who had come to the king in order to end this corrosive discord, tried to negotiate a peace treaty between the king and the duke; but they were at loggerheads over many different matters and a peaceful solution did not thus find favour with the power of God the Saviour.[223] What more? The king divided his army and drew it up ready to fight manfully; similarly the duke disposed his men wisely. The king's first battle line attacked and charged into the duke's men-at-arms. There the king's line was defeated. The king, who was with his other lines of men-at-arms, was by God's judgment convulsed with fear and was the first to turn tail and run. Thereafter the whole royal army rushed away in flight, leaving behind all their baggage and wealth, their tents and a vast amount of gold and silver, too much for a mere human to estimate. What more? The duke was thus victorious, and captured or killed much of the royal army. He and the people of Bari and Trani and the other places whom he had summoned carried off all that vast hoard of wealth and returned to their homes rich men; 3,000 men were killed in that battle, so we have heard. Sergius, the *Magister Militum* of the city of Naples died there, so too did Eternus of Montefusco, Gerard de Lanzulino and Sarolus de lo Tufo, as well as many others whose names we pass over in silence because of the difficulty of listing them.[224]

---

221 Presumably Richard of Rupecanina, brother of Count Rainulf: it is not clear which *civitas* is meant here.

222 Montecorvino (not to be confused with its homonym near Salerno), 50 km. NE of Benevento, was a new settlement in the early eleventh century and seat of a bishopric by 1058. This was suppressed in 1454 and the town abandoned. For what little is known of this town and a description of the site, Martin and Noyé (1982).

223 (St) Bernard, Abbot of Clairvaux 1115–53, the spokesman and propagandist of the Cistercian order.

224 One of those killed was Idernus of Montefusco (was he Falco's 'Eternus'?), whose widow Proserpina made a donation to the monks of Montevergine in return for their retrieval and burial of her husband's body, *Cod. Dipl. Verginiano*, iii.179–82 no. 243. The brief notice in the *Annales Cavenses*, ad. an. 1137, MGH SS iii.192, also referred to the heavy casualties at the battle of Rignano.

This battle occurred on 2nd October. The king fled with his followers through the night and the next day came to the *castrum* of Paduli,[225] then he hastened on to Salerno.

A few days later Archbishop Rossemanus took counsel and went with some of the judges and elders of the city, hastening to the king to offer him consolation and the city's service. He was however requested to grant the people of Benevento that free possession of their property which the aforesaid Emperor Lothar had conceded. The king acceded to their prayers and for love of the city had a privilege drawn up and signed which remitted all the *fidantiae* and exactions which we had been accustomed to pay. They received this privilege incredibly joyfully and returned to the city of Benevento. The text of this privilege is as follows.

'In the name of the Lord God and of the Eternal Saviour Jesus Christ, in the year 1137 from the Incarnation of the Lord, in the month of November, first of the indiction. I, Roger, by the grace of God King of Sicily and Italy, the upholder and shield of Christians, son of Count Roger I. Of our Royal Excellence we are roused to liberality to those faithful to us to whom we ought to give generous benefits not only because they have merited well of us and will become even more loyal, but also that others will become more active in our service in hope of reward. Therefore, we clemently consent to the petitions of the venerable Rossemanus, Archbishop of Benevento, who has always been faithful to us in every respect, Bernard, Constable of Benevento, and the judges and many other citizens of Benevento, and since you have always been foremost among those faithful to us, and for love of the Supreme King through whom we live and rule, and for the love and fealty which you have for us and shall have for us in the future, we remit and condone to you everything which we and our Norman predecessors have been accustomed to have from round about the city of Benevento under the name of *fidantiae*, namely renders of money, *salutes, angariae, terraticum, herbaticum, carnaticum, kalandaticum*, wine and olive taxes, reliefs, and all other exactions both from churches and from the citizens.[226] We free you from all of the above, and your property shall be free and undisturbed

---

225 *Padula*: D'Alessandro, *Falcone*, 266, suggests this was the *castrum* of Padula in the Val Diano south of Salerno (for which *Catalogus Baronum*, art. 599). But this makes no geographical sense here, whereas Paduli near Benevento does. Falco earlier used *Paludi* for this place, but later he also used *Padula*.

226 *Salutes* were small payments made several times a year, usually but not invariably in kind; *herbaticum* was a payment for grazing rights, *carnaticum* a due of cuts of meat, from flocks, *kalandaticum* a payment on 1 January; for *angaria* and *terraticum*, see above note 212. For discussion, Martin (1987), 146.

with regard to anything which we have been accustomed to receive. As long as you remain in fealty to us and our heirs, you and your property shall remain free and undisturbed from all of the above. You shall have freedom for hunting, fishing and fowling in your lands. And, that you shall enjoy this privilege securely we have had it sealed with our golden seal. If, may it not happen, any person, great or humble, presumes in anything to violate the terms of this our concession, then he shall pay twenty pounds of purest gold to our Palace to obtain mercy, and this present privilege shall remain as it originally stood. We have ordered this record of [our] concession to be written by Henry, our notary, and to be sealed with our golden seal. In the seventh year of our reign.'[227]

When this privilege was read out to the assembly of the Beneventans, we gave thanks to God the Saviour of all, to the said king and to the archbishop, since Jesus Christ had in his mercy, and not because of our merits, deigned to grant to us a gift of liberty and security which our fathers and grandfathers had never been able to see. What more? With this great benefit conceded and confirmed to us, all the citizens promised service and honour to the said king and to serve him without contradiction.

Meanwhile, hearing that the defeated king had, with his morale shattered, entered the city of Salerno with a few followers, the above-mentioned Duke Rainulf took counsel and gathered nearly a thousand cavalry and a multitude of footmen from Apulia. Leaving Troia he bound all his captives to his cause, and then marched against the county of Count Roger of Ariano; arriving there he immediately secured the submission to his authority of Alferius Draco, Robert de la Marca, Robert of Pietramaggiore, Robert de Potofranco[228] and the count's other barons. Thereafter he forced Count Roger himself to submit to his will. After this the duke camped with his forces near the *castellum* of Paduli on 1st December. The people of Benevento were amazed by the steadfastness of Duke Rainulf, but along with Archbishop Rossemanus remained day and night vigilant in love and fealty to the king and in service to Anacletus.[229]

227 *Roger II Diplomata*, 131–3 no. †47. Brühl considered this document to be a forgery, at least in the form in which it was copied into the chronicle, although undoubtedly replacing the genuine original which was confiscated by Robert of Selby in 1143 (below, 247–8). Certainly some of the formulae cannot be found in other documents from Roger's chancery.

228 See *Catalogus Baronum*, art. 351 (below, 330), which reveals he married a sister of Gerard de Greci.

229 Nonetheless a document issued at Benevento in November 1137 was dated by Innocent's pontifical years, *Cod. Dipl. Verginiano*, iii.183–6 no. 244. This may reflect the opinion of the person it was written for.

I shall describe to you, brothers, another matter which should not be passed over in silence. When the Abbot of Clairvaux, that most admirable and discreet man, had discussions with the king about a peace treaty and the unification of the Church, he and the king agreed that three cardinals from the side of Pope Innocent who had been present at his election should come to the king, along with three from the party of Anacletus, and they should in turn relate to the king the details of each election. After the king had heard each side in turn then he would decide which election had been the more holy and just, and thus with the help of the Holy Ghost he would establish peace throughout his kingdom, insofar as this lay in his decision and ability. For he knew and clearly understood that Christians in every part of the world favoured Innocent and venerated him as pope; he and his kingdom alone disagreed. Messages were immediately sent to Pope Innocent and to Anacletus and they were speedily informed of the king's decision. They agreed, and it was decided that from the party of Innocent the Chancellor Haimeric, the venerable Cardinal Gerard, together with the Abbot of Clairvaux, would come to Salerno for the investigation into the election. Similarly from Anacletus's side there came his Chancellor Matthew, Cardinal Peter of Pisa and another Cardinal called Gregory.[230] After they had gathered together the king, as he was sagacious of mind and far-seeing in counsel, first carefully questioned Innocent's party for four days from morning till night, more closely than one would have believed possible; for the next four days he similarly interrogated the party of Anacletus. After studiously and diligently hearing of the election from each side the king ordered all the clerics and people of the city of Salerno to be gathered together, along with the bishops and abbots of monasteries who had attended, and in their presence he spoke thus: 'My lords and brothers, we believe that it is not unknown to your prudence that I have had these cardinals summoned from both sides in this case. For I had thought, insofar as it lies in our power, to have put an end to this matter and to follow clearly on the path of justice. But since our mind is clouded by many questions and a variety of replies I alone am unable to put an end to so important an affair. Hence, if the lord cardinals agree, each side shall write down the details of the election, and one cardinal

230 Matthew, Cardinal priest of SS. Martino e Silvestro 1130–9, known to have been a papal subdeacon in 1126, Zenker (1964), 89; Peter of Pisa, one of the most experienced and respected cardinals, became Cardinal deacon of S. Adriano in 1113, Cardinal priest of S. Susanna 1117/18, Zenker (1964), 103–4, Hüls (1977), 210–11, 219; see also Stroll (1987), 139–41. Gregory, Cardinal priest of the Holy Apostles 1102–12, and again from c.1122, was originally from Ceccano in Lazio; he was elected (as Victor IV) as successor to Anacletus in March 1138, Zenker (1964), 106–7; Hüls (1977), 150–3.

from each side shall come with me to Sicily where, God willing, we shall celebrate the feast of the Nativity of Jesus Christ our Saviour, and there we shall find wise archbishops and bishops, and other men of prudence, by whose advice I have up to now followed the party of Anacletus. Now by their counsel and that of other wise men, and with the assistance of Divine Clemency, we shall certainly put an end to this business, insofar as it lies within my power'. Cardinal Gerard replied to this: 'You know for certain that we shall on our side write down our party's case, for you have heard from our mouth the details of the election, indeed you have heard everything which has happened concerning us. We shall send Cardinal Guido de Castello, a man both wise and discreet, who will, as you ask, come with you to Sicily.[231] Then let it happen that it shall so please your wisdom that the Holy Ghost, the Paraclete, shall light up your heart, and the light of truth shall lead you sincerely back to the Church'.

After this everyone returned to his home.[232] The next day Cardinal Gerard and his companions departed; only the said Cardinal Guido remained to travel with the king as had been arranged. From Anacletus's side similarly one cardinal was sent. When this had been done a ship was prepared and the king sailed to Sicily. Meanwhile Duke Rainulf manfully besieged the above-mentioned *castellum* of Paduli which he assaulted daily with many weapons and machines. Seeing however that he could not take the *castellum* the duke took counsel and abandoned it, moving into the territory of Alife. He immediately captured that city and its fortified citadel and made it subject to his authority.

In this year Anacletus, who went under the title of Pope, died on 25th January.[233] He had reigned for seven years, eleven months and twenty-

---

231 Guido, from Città di Castello in Tuscany, was made Cardinal deacon of S. Maria in Via Lata by Honorius II, *Liber Pontificalis*, ii.327; Cardinal priest of S. Marco in 1134, he was elected pope as Celestine II in 1143, Zenker (1964), 83–4; Hüls (1977), 239. He had spent time at the Schools in France, was respected for his learning and left some fifty books to the cathedral of his home town, Malaczek (1981), 58–9.

232 There is a fuller account of these discussions in the *Vita Prima* of Bernard of Clairvaux, Bk II.vi.43–6, in MPL 185, cols 293–5, which (unlike Falco) reported the sensational recognition by the much-respected supporter of Anacletus, Peter of Pisa, of the justice of Innocent's case. He seems to have been particularly swayed by Bernard's argument that how could almost all the churchmen of Christendom be wrong in supporting Innocent, while the few who still supported Anacletus by 1137 were somehow right. Despite his sincere change of allegiance and the support of St Bernard, Peter was deprived of his cardinalate at the Second Lateran Council in 1139, but restored by Celestine II in 1143, a sign of how much he was respected even by his erstwhile opponents. He died in 1145, *Letters of St. Bernard*, 353–4 no. 283; Palumbo (1942), 591–4; Malaczek (1981), 66.

233 Date also given by *Orderic*, v.508.

two days. Pope Innocent promptly gathered his forces and with help from his friends rose up valiantly against his enemies. Archbishop Rossemanus ordered all the bells of the city of Benevento to sound to mark the death of Anacletus.

In this year the above-mentioned emperor died in Tuscany while returning to his empire, and after his death Conrad was by a unanimous vote elected to the imperial position.[234]

The year 1138, the ninth year of the pontificate of the lord Innocent II, Supreme Pontiff, the month of March, first of the indiction. After the said Anacletus had died his cardinals took counsel with his brothers and sent to King Roger announcing the death of Anacletus and that, provided that it was agreeable to him, they would proceed to elect another pope. The king assented to their wish in order to hamper the party of the lord Pope Innocent, and gave them power to elect a pope. Once [the messengers] had returned to Rome their supporters gathered and in mid-March chose Cardinal Gregory as their intruded pope, whom they called Victor. But with the aid of God's mercy this heresy and invasion lasted for only a short time. Not many days had gone by when Anacletus's brothers, realising that events had so changed, made a volte-face and agreed to a treaty of peace with the lord Pope Innocent, and they and all the supporters of his opponent changed sides and entered into fealty to him.[235] That wicked man who had appeared with the name of Victor laid down the tunic and mitre and acknowledged Pope Innocent's commands. So the whole city of Rome exulted most joyfully and gloriously and with the help of God Pope Innocent brought unity and concord to the Church.

A few days later the pope took counsel and went to Albano, planning to gather an army and go to Duke Rainulf, but he was taken ill and was unable to go. Meanwhile King Roger had gathered his army and crossed the frontiers of Apulia, thinking to make subject to his power those cities of which he had been deprived by the emperor. Knowing of his arrival Duke Rainulf stirred up every part of Apulia to stand together in the face of his rage. Without delay they hastened at the double to the duke, and resisted the king's ferocity for nearly two

---

234 Lothar died at Breitenwang in the Tyrol on 1 December 1137. In reality, the election of Conrad III in January 1138 was more in the nature of a coup, masterminded by Archbishop Adelboro of Trier, and bitterly opposed by some of the other princes, notably Duke Henry of Bavaria, who as husband of Lothar's only child clearly hoped to succeed him.

235 *Chron. Cas.* IV.130, p. 607, suggested that Innocent achieved this through large-scale bribery, and with the promise that the cardinals of Anacletus would not be deprived of their positions.

months. Meanwhile, so we have been told, the aforesaid king accepted the lord Pope Innocent as his father and lord and sent orders to the city of Benevento and throughout every part of his kingdom that he be accepted as father and lord. We did indeed receive his letter and call Innocent father and lord.[236]

After this had taken place Rao of Fragneto showed himself as a rebel to the city of Benevento and King Roger and ordered the vines of the Beneventans to be cut down. The citizens took counsel and informed the king of Rao's depredations, asking him to rescue them from these perils as quickly as possible. The king immediately gathered his army and set out, and on his arrival stormed Montemarano and other *castella* and burned them. Then he came to Ceppaloni and together with the Beneventans besieged it. That same day he took the village, plundered the property of its peasant inhabitants and destroyed all their houses. The next day the turrets and walls of the *castellum* were surrendered into the king's hands. For fear of the king Rao of Fragneto and his wife had left there three days earlier and hastened to Duke Rainulf, along with Rao de lo Tufo and Henry of Sarno who had similarly fled from the king and abandoned their *castella*.[237] The citizens of Benevento immediately and humbly begged the king to grant them the *castellum* of Ceppaloni to destroy as an enemy of their city. What more? The king granted the people's petition and allowed them to demolish it. Without delay a great crowd of Beneventans hastened to destroy it, all the buildings of the *castellum* were razed to the ground and the whole city rejoiced at its destruction. For if I wished to describe all the cruel acts and dangers which we had suffered from the lords of that *castellum*, I would have neither the tongue to speak of them nor the style to describe them. Hence we praised God and gave thanks to the king, who had conceded that place to us to destroy.[238]

236 Only two documents survive from Benevento from this period, but it may be significant that these two, Museo del Sannio, Fondo S. Sofia, vol. 8 no. 36 (July 1138), *Più antiche carte di S. Modesto*, 23–4 no. 8 (March 1139), lack the papal pontifical years in the dating clause, reflecting the uncertain position in the city. From February 1140 onwards Beneventan documents were dated by the pontifical years of Innocent II, beginning with Museo del Sannio, Fondo S. Sofia, vol. 13 no. 5.

237 The manuscripts have *Orricus de Sarno*, but see here *Al. Tel.* II.55, and *Cod. Dipl. Verginiano*, iii.52–4 no. 214 (February 1134), 187–92 no. 245 (January 1138), in both of which Henry described himself as Count of Sarno. For his predecessors as count, Loré (2008), 63–5.

238 Ceppaloni was subsequently rebuilt, and was one of a number of fiefs granted by the king to Novellonus de Bussone, a baron from the principality of Capua who had gone over to the king's side, *Catalogus Baronum*, art. 955. Other lands of Rao of Fragneto were given to Bartholomew of Monteforte, son of the Rogerian loyalist Rao Pinella, *ibid.*, art. 355 (below, 331). Cuozzo (1984), 87, 265–6.

After this the king entered the frontiers of Capua and captured a *castellum* called Calvi.[239] Duke Rainulf meanwhile gathered his army and watched all the time for a chance to attack him and take his revenge. But the king, who was well-advised, pitched his camps in the mountains and in defensible places and thus circumvented the prudence and courage of the duke, who was much upset by this but gave no outward sign, for he could not show the anguish in his heart. Once again he was based at Alife, reckoning that the king would come there. The king however, retreating as we have said from the duke's staunchness, returned to the *castellum* of Calvi, and [then] ordered his tents to be pitched in the territory of S. Agata, planning to go to Benevento. Next he moved his army and pitched camp at Plancella, near Benevento, where he remained for two days.[240] Then he took counsel and retreated, crossed the River Calore with his army and pitched camp at Ponte Valentino where he remained for [a further] two days. However Duke Rainulf, who was prudent of mind, remained in the territory of Pietramaggiore, intending courageously and worthily to come to the rescue of the *castellum* of Apice which the king was threatening to besiege. The king begged the Beneventans that they would all hurry to assist him. Rossemanus, who was then the archbishop, for love of the king asked the citizens [to do this] and sent them to help him. However, hearing that the *castellum* of Apice had been reinforced by knights and prudent men, the king took counsel, raised camp and ordered an attack on the *castellum* of Pietrelcina, which he devastated with fire and the sword. Marching on from there he captured other *castella* and ordered them to be burned. He captured Ponte Landolfo, Fragneto, Campolattaro, Guardia and the city of Alife, and gave them to the fire.[241] The king's soldiers and the innumerable crowd of plunderers who followed him carried away, stole and despoiled all the property of the citizens and the ornaments of the churches, dividing them up between themselves as best they could. So reader, if you had been there, you would have been horrified by such desolation and confusion in the city, and you would have affirmed that there had not been such ruin and incendiarism meted out to Christians since the time of the Greeks and pagans.[242]

239 Calvi was the seat of a bishopric, 13 km. NW of Capua.

240 Perhaps Chianchello, 11 km. S of Benevento, although this identification is not certain.

241 All these places are about 20–25 km. NW of Benevento, apart from Alife, which is a further 20 km. away in the same direction. After capturing them, the king continued northwards into the Molise plateau.

242 The burning of Alife was also noted by the *Annales Casinenses*, ad. an. 1138, MGH SS xix.309.

After he had ravaged the city of Alife, the king set his army in motion once again and marched into the territory of Venafro, intending to subject the cities there to his power. Right away the king personally gave the cruel order that the city of Venafro be attacked and stormed; the citizens defended themselves and their city as best they could. Seeing their steadfastness, the king cruelly carried out his threat and ordered the city to be stormed. As a consequence of sin, that city, strongly fortified and full of riches, was at once captured and the goods of all the citizens and a great quantity of valuables were captured by their enemies, divided up among them and reduced to nothing. Men, women and children fled into the mountains leaving all their property in the hands of thieves and plunderers, and thus the city and its fortifications passed into the power of the king. Hearing of this cruelty, Presenzano, Roccaromana and the other *castella* round about accepted the king's authority. After doing this the king returned to Benevento and camped at the *castellum* of Paduli on 12th September. Duke Rainulf meanwhile, who had been unable to resist the king, remained disconsolately in the region of Alife. The king marched on and went to the city of Melfi, thinking to make it submit to his power, but he was unable to do this and so turned round and marched against the *castellum* of Tocco. He at once ordered wooden machines to be constructed, with which to destroy the towers and walls of the *castellum*, and in consequence some of the towers were destroyed. Duke Rainulf kept a close and daily watch on the king to prevent him from invading the lands of Count Roger of Ariano. However the people of the *castellum*, seeing the king's strength and fury, surrendered themselves into his power, and the *castellum* of Tocco passed into the king's lordship on 29th September after he had besieged it for eight days. After this had taken place the king raised his camp and came to Benevento during a period of heavy rain. He himself pitched camp at the church of St Peter the Apostle near the city,[243] while the whole of his army was quartered in Benevento itself and remained there for three days. The rain at this time was quite terrible and it became very dangerous to travel and impossible to find supplies for the army while doing so; hence, as we have said, the army stayed in the city of Benevento to replenish itself. The king himself entered Benevento on 4th October and carefully visited the churches and palaces of the city and the *curia* of the pope.

Once his army was resupplied he moved out of the city and camped

243 The nunnery of St Peter without the walls, south of the River Sabato, for which see note 97.

near the *castellum* of S. Severo.[244] Then he marched to the *castellum* of Morcone and brought it under his power, and having done this he captured the *castellum* of S. Giorgio and Pietramaggiore. Hearing this Count Roger of Ariano abandoned the *castellum* of Apice, and gave all the villeins there permission to obey the king. He himself entered the city of Ariano, confident that there he would receive help from Duke Rainulf, for he was absolutely determined not to submit to the king's will. The king at once obtained fealty over Apice. He himself stayed for four days at the *castellum* of Tammaro.[245] Collecting together his army the duke approached Ariano, guarding it from any attack by the king. Thus the two worked against one another. After this the king left the *castellum* of Tammaro and hurried towards the territory of Melfi, then he marched to the strongly-fortified *castellum* of Sant'Agata and secured possession of that and the neighbouring *castella*. The duke meanwhile took over the city of Melfi to prevent any attempt by the king to seize it. Realising that Duke Rainulf was continually forestalling him and his men and protecting the cities of Apulia, the king took counsel, furnished the *castella* which he had captured with knights and men-at-arms and ordered them to be carefully guarded, and went himself to Salerno, planning to return to Sicily, from which he had been absent for a long time.[246] The duke went to Bari and visited the coastal areas, encouraging all the people to gather their forces and at a suitable moment take up arms to resist the king. They unanimously and enthusiastically declared themselves ready to do this.

The year 1139 from the Incarnation of the Lord, and the tenth year of the pontificate of the lord Innocent II, Supreme Pontiff and Universal Pope, the month of March, second of the indiction. In this year the afore-mentioned Pope Innocent celebrated a synod at Rome on 8th April.[247] Innumerable archbishops, bishops and abbots attended this

---

244 San Severo, now disappeared, was in the Val Fortore, NE of Benevento, near S. Marco dei Cavoti, D'Angelo, *Falcone*, 268. It should not be confused with San Severo near Foggia in the Capitanata.

245 Tammaro no longer exists; it was near Paduli railway station (like many south Italian stations, some way off the town it theoretically serves) by the River Calore, 10 km. E of Benevento, D'Angelo, *Falcone*, 268.

246 By the end of 1138 the fighting had switched to Irpinia and northern Apulia, the region to the west of Benevento was securely in Roger's hands, and the process of establishing a royal administration there was already under way. In March 1139 a royal chamberlain, Hugh Mansellus, was holding a court at Montesarchio in the Caudine Valley, *Più antiche carte di S. Modesto*, 23–4 no. 8.

247 The Second Lateran Council, for which Robinson (1990), 138–9; for the canons promulgated, Mansi, *Concilia*, xxi.525–33.

holy meeting; and there, among the other matters which were enacted
with the help of the Holy Ghost, in the presence of all the Catholic
men who were gathered together there, Pope Innocent bound King
Roger and all his followers with the chains of anathema. In this year
Duke Rainulf, of whom we have made mention above, was taken ill
with a burning fever and left this world at Troia on the last day of
April. William, the venerable Bishop of the city, and all its clergy and
people in floods of tears laid him honourably to rest in the cathedral. O
what lamentations from everyone invaded the city, virgin and widow,
young and old of both sexes, and knights! If I should try to describe
it properly there would be neither time nor space to do so. The people
of Bari, Trani, Melfi, Canosa and all the other towns under his rule
and trusting in his protection abandoned consolation, tore their hair,
beat their breasts and wore out their knees, with far more than the
customary mourning, for they lamented a most pious duke and father
of all, who laying aside vindictiveness had ruled over his duchy with
sweetness and humanity. What more? Even his bitter enemies had
compassion for his death and lamenting his [lost] prudence were
moved to tears. Almost the whole of Italy incessantly recounted his
probity and his battles. However, hearing that Duke Rainulf, that most
warlike and magnanimous of men, had departed this world, King
Roger was filled with vanity and pride and rejoiced more than seemed
humanly possible. Forgetting that we all die, he rejoiced and was puffed
up, reckoning that he could gather an army, invade Apulia and make
it submit in fealty to his command. What more? Seven ships full of
men-at-arms and carrying a great sum of gold and silver were made
ready, and on 25th May he sailed to Salerno. The clergy and people of
Salerno at once received him with many *laudes* and hymns resounding.
The king sent letters without delay to all those who dwelt round about,
instructing them to take up their arms and flock to him. They received
these letters and obeyed his order; then after raising his army the king
came to Benevento and hastened to attack his enemies.

In this year, on 29th May the mountain situated near the city of Naples
erupted in fire and flames for eight days, in such a way that the cities
and *castra* nearby were mortally afraid, and from this fire a black and
horrible ash was thrown up and the wind carried this ash as far as
Salerno, Benevento, Capua and Naples. The fire was seen for eight
days, and many citizens of Benevento, including the writer of this work,
collected the ash, which could be seen on the ground for a month.[248]

---

248 'Monte Vesuvio erupted with great fire, which was followed by ash of such density that

And when, as said above, King Roger had collected his army he speedily marched on the count's city, and fiercely besieged it until he had secured it under his rule.[249] The count sought flight and went to Troia. Then the king gained control over all the cities and *castra* of the Capitanata. Moreover the duke, the king's son, brought all the cities of Apulia and the coast under his rule, promising them peace and security. He was not however able to secure the well-fortified city of Bari, because the prince of that city had kept with him 400 knights, in addition to the 50,000 inhabitants. Realising that he was unable to capture the city of Bari, the duke went with his army to his father King Roger, who was bivouaced in the neighbourhood of Troia, and once they had joined forces they planned together how they could force the city of Troia to submit to their power. Count Roger of Ariano was stationed four miles from the city with 700 knights, prepared to fight to the death. The citizens of Troia were ready to defend their city along with those persons from other places who had fled there from fear of the king. Seeing the city garrisoned by men of such courage, the king sent 200 knights to the nearby *castellum* of Vaccarizza,[250] and himself marched with the duke his son and their army against Count Roger's city of Ariano. The king at once besieged the city and ordered wooden engines for assaulting it to be constructed. The citizens and the knights who were with them were however not a bit afraid of what was being done; 200 knights and 20,000 armed men had been brought into the city. Seeing it so prepared and garrisoned the king ordered camp to be struck, and convulsed with fury ordered that the vines, olives and other trees be cut down and all their crops be devastated, and leaving the city remained thus in its vicinity for two more days.

At the same time Pope Innocent heard of the death of Duke Rainulf and greatly mourned him. He took counsel, left the city of Rome with an army of a thousand horsemen and a very large force of infantry and

---

it darkened the whole sky, and this covered the entire region as far as the principality and Calabria. It began on 29 May, and diminished little by little, covering the ground for thirty days and nights, with the dust being blown about by the wind, before ceasing on the day of the Apostles Peter and Paul [29 June]', *Annales Cavenses*, MGH SS iii.192.

249 The count here is Roger of Ariano. Which city this was is at first sight puzzling. One would assume it to be Ariano, but Falco describes the siege and capture of this town a little later in the narrative. The passage would, however, make sense if Ariano surrendered to Roger before his attack on Troia, but later returned to the count's side when the troops mentioned below arrived, thus forcing the king to besiege it again.

250 In 1109 the lord of this *castrum* (7 km. NE of Troia) was Defensor son of William, but by 1156 it was owned by the Bishop of Troia, Cod. Vat. Lat. 13491, document no. 10; *Chartes de Troia*, 48–9.

came to S. Germano.[251] When he learned that the pope had departed the city, King Roger sent envoys to him seeking peace and promising to be obedient to the pope's command and his requests. The pope received the king's envoys honourably and sent two cardinals to him outlining an agreement for peace and good relations, and inviting the king to hasten to S. Germano. What more? The king received these cardinals properly and honourably, abandoned the city of Troia which he was besieging and together with the duke his son and his army force-marched to meet the pope. Envoys from both sides negotiated the terms of the peace. The pope though sought from the king [the return of] the principality of Capua, which he had unjustly confiscated from Prince Robert. The king absolutely refused to return the principality, and in consequence they argued together for eight days. After this, the king gathered up his army and marched into the lands which are called those 'of the sons of Burrellus'.[252] He made some of the *castra* of these lands surrender to his power. When the pope and those with him found out that the king had moved to that area, he ordered that a *castrum* called Gallucio should be attacked and laid waste. The king was immediately informed that the pope was attacking this *castellum*. What more? The king force-marched to the territory of S. Germano where the pope was staying. The awful rumour of the king's arrival flew rapidly about and the king's *castra* at once took heart. Hearing of the king's arrival, the pope, Prince Robert and the forces of the Romans ordered their camps to be struck and moved to a safer place. However, the duke, the king's son, found out about the pope's retreat and set up an ambush with nearly a thousand knights. They charged out against the pope's knights who, realising the scale of the trap they were in, turned tail and fled, fleeing as fast as they could in several directions. The prince, Richard of Rupecanina and many of the Romans escaped; many however of the knights and footmen died in the river, and we have heard that many others were captured by the king. Pope Innocent followed after his men as though it was safe. Alas, a band of knights suddenly attacked and captured him. Dividing up all his treasure and ornaments among themselves, they took him to the king. They brought him as a captive, loaded with insults, to the tent which the king had sent for him, and subsequently the chancellor Haimeric and the cardinals were [also] brought prisoners there. Pope

---

251 The town at the foot of Monte Cassino, now (since 1863) called Cassino, which lay on the *Via Latina*, the Roman road which was the principal route between Rome and Capua in the Middle Ages.

252 For this extended kin-group, see *Al. Tel.* II.69, note 124, above. The Landulf Burrellus whom Falco mentioned earlier was probably a member of this family.

Innocent was captured on 22nd July. O what lamentation and depths of sorrow took hold of the minds of the faithful and the papal cities! If I wanted to describe it properly I would have neither time nor space to do so! What more? The king at once sent envoys to Pope Innocent, whom he was holding captive, begging him more humbly than one would have thought possible to grant him the hand of peace and concord. Seeing himself isolated and deprived of military support, the pope assented to the king's prayers and petitions. Agreements and privileges were confirmed on each side and on 25th July the king, and his sons the duke and the prince came into the pope's presence, flung themselves at his feet and begged for mercy, and bowed to his authority. They immediately swore on the Gospels to do fealty to St Peter and to Pope Innocent and his canonically chosen successors, and [also] to other things which were written down. He gave the Kingdom of Sicily to King Roger by banner, and granted to his son the duke the Duchy of Apulia and to the prince his other son the Principality of Capua. The day on which the pope confirmed the peace with the king was that on which the feast of St James the Apostle was celebrated, 25th July.[253] After this the pope celebrated a solemn mass and preached at length of the steadfastness of the peace. Everyone was transported by delight and an abundance of joy, praising the Heavenly King for the conclusion of peace and rejoicing in the hand of concord. Hearing that peace had been concluded and that the king was now obedient to the pope's will, the people of Benevento were seized with such joy and exultation that if I were to describe it all I would run out of time and words.

After peace was concluded with the king, the pope entered Benevento on 1st August. The people of Benevento received him with great honour and devotion, and rejoiced so greatly that they might have been seeing St Peter in the flesh. The king camped outside the city after accompanying the pope up to the Porta S. Lorenzo. That same day at Vespers he entered the city and climbed up to the *curia* of the lord pope. He stayed there with him for a little while, then went to the cathedral and the basilica of St Mary and entered St Bartholomew the Apostle's to pray for his salvation. He went into the monastery of St Sophia and prostrated himself before the altar of St Mercurius. Then he went to the monastery cloister and inspected the dormitory and refectory, and commending himself to the monks' prayers he left the city by the Porta Somma and returned rejoicing to his camp. However Rossemanus, who had fought continually against the pope and had been consecrated

253 See below 310–12 for Innocent's bull granting Roger the kingdom.

Archbishop by Peter Leone, was expelled from the city. The wretched man hurried to the lord king.[254] After this the lord pope destroyed the *castellum* which Rossemanus had had built at the Porta Somma. In these days the citizens of Naples came to Benevento and submitted their city in fealty to the lord king. They approached the duke his son and bowed their necks in fealty to him.[255]

Meanwhile the king set his army in motion and went to Troia and made that city submit to his power. The Bishop of Troia, by name William, and the people of the city sent envoys to the king asking that he enter the city and count them unequivocally among his *fideles* and friends. The king received the envoys, but he said to them that 'I will not enter the city while that traitor Rainulf remains among you'. Those who had been sent to him returned to the city and immediately made the king's intention clear to everyone. Although the citizens were much upset by the king's response, they ordered four knights to break open the tomb, remove Duke Rainulf's body and carry it outside the city, so that the king's anger should be assuaged and he would enter the city peacefully. The duke's enemies ordered one of the knights, called Gallicanus, who had been one of his most faithful followers, to break open the coffin and remove with his own hands the putrefying body. They did this both as an insult to the dead duke and to cause Gallicanus pain. Gallicanus was forced by fear and to avoid incurring the king's wrath to carry out the duke's poor bones, as we have described, as though he and the others were happy to do this. O horror! The duke's enemies immediately fastened a rope around the corpse's neck and dragged it through the streets up to the city's citadel, then they turned round and went to the charcoal workings outside the city where there was a filthy stagnant ditch, into which they sank the duke's body. O what an amazingly evil action! Fear and horror straightaway invaded the whole city, and everyone, both friends and enemies of the duke, wished for death. I testify to the Eternal King, Judge of the Centuries, that we have never read of such a ghastly thing having happened in previous generations or [even] among pagans. How could such cruelty as this profit the king's authority? What victory or royal glory did it lead to? But desiring to satisfy his rage against one on whom he could not exercise it while he was alive, he did it when he was dead. Indeed, while

254 Rossemanus was subsequently given the church of St Lucy at Syracuse, Garufi, *Documenti inediti*, 41–2 no. 16; White (1938), 203–4.

255 These two sentences were omitted from D'Angelo's Latin text, but not from the Italian translation, D'Angelo, *Falcone*, 224–5. Prof. D'Angelo informs me that this was his mistake, and I have translated this passage from Del Re, *Cronisti*, 247.

the duke lived the king did not dare to approach his battle line, even if he had ten thousand armed men and the duke only a few. When he saw what had happened, his rage was to some extent mitigated. But let us return to the subject. Hearing of what had happened, the king's son the duke bravely went to his father, reproached him for the manner of the deed and begged his father that the duke who had been so dishonoured be granted burial. The king favoured his son's prayer and ordered that the body be handed over for burial. After these events the people of the city waited for him to go in to them as he had promised. However, he did not wish to enter the city of Troia, but raised his camp and went to Bari which he besieged by land and sea.

When the pope entered the city of Benevento he quashed every ordination made by Peter Leone and Rossemanus. On the day of the Assumption of St Mary[256] and on the Passion of St Bartholomew[257] he went down to the cathedral and formally celebrated a solemn mass, and having done this the pope, who had often received appeals from the Romans, took the road on 29th September and with the Lord's help returned to Rome. In this year Archbishop Gregory of Benevento, who had been consecrated by Pope Innocent, entered the city on 2nd September,[258] and the lord pope appointed the Cardinal deacon Guido as Rector of Benevento. Hearing of the lord Pope Innocent's arrival the people of Rome went out together to meet him and welcomed him honourably and very joyfully, then they urged him to break, on their advice, the peace which he had concluded with King Roger. The pope absolutely refused to agree to their request; for he said that it had been pleasing to the Lord that his capture had led in this way to peace. And when, as has been said above, the king was besieging the city of Bari, Pope Innocent, who was then in the city of Benevento, sent the Bishop of Ostia, a very venerable man, to Bari to advise the people of the city to bow their necks in fealty to the king and obey his commands.[259] As they were proud of spirit and puffed up with pride the people of Bari would not allow the bishop to enter the city and refused to listen to what he had to say. What

256 On 15 August.

257 24 August.

258 For Gregory as archbishop, see Rome, Università 'La Sapienza', De Donato, 49–50 no. 13 (1140, month uncertain); *Più antiche carte della cattedrale*, 196–202 nos. 65–6 (April 1141, April 1142).

259 Alberic, Cardinal Bishop of Ostia 1138–48, a French Cluniac, formerly Prior of St Martin-des-Champs and Abbot of Vezelay, was often employed as a legate: to England in 1138, to Antioch in 1139–40 and to France from 1144. He was a close friend of Peter the Venerable and highly regarded by Bernard of Clairvaux. He died at Verdun in 1148. Zenker (1964), 15–20.

more? The bishop returned and told the lord pope of the fierceness and high spirits of the people of Bari, and, as said, the lord pope returned to Rome. Realising the pride of the people of Bari, King Roger ordered wooden engines and nearly thirty [siege] towers to be made in order to break down the walls and defences of the city. After these machines had been built he ordered them to be pushed up near the city wall and very soon the walls of the city had been breached and its towers overthrown. The palaces of the city which were near the wall on the inside were also damaged and lying in ruins. They suffered this fearful havoc for two months, August and September, during which hunger and thirst also became acute. A loaf of bread was sold for six *romesinae* and they ate, so we have heard, horseflesh. Finally, partly through famine and partly because of the sedition which had arisen among the people, Jaquintus, the prince of the city, sent some of the citizens and Roger of Sorrento to the king offering freely to surrender the city to him provided that when peace was made they should have a guarantee of safety from him, and that the king should return those of the city he held captive to them, while they would similarly release the king's men whom the city held. This treaty and its terms were acceptable both to the king and the city, and with the agreement of the people of the city peace was made, and after oaths had been given the peace treaty was ratified. After this had happened there appeared a certain knight whom the prince of the city had ordered to be blinded. He threw himself at the king's feet and begged him to render justice to him against the prince who had deprived him of the light of his eyes. The king was immediately suffused with rage and moved more than one would have thought possible. He ordered the judges of Troia, Trani and Bari to be summoned at the double to give their verdict on the agreement which the king had made with the city of Bari, namely whether the captives on both sides should be returned safe and unharmed. What more? It was decreed by the judges of Bari that Prince Jaquintus, who had had the man blinded, and his counsellors were at the king's mercy. The prince, his counsellors Guaiferius and Abiut and their associates immediately confessed in the king's presence that it was on [respectively] their order and advice that this man had been deprived of the light of his eyes. The king promptly ordered the prince, the men named and ten others to be hanged, ten others to be blinded and mutilated and other prominent citizens to be arrested and held in chains, and their goods to be confiscated. So he inflicted on the city of Bari an unheard-of revenge. Such fear and horror invaded the city that neither man nor woman dared to go out into its squares and streets. They invoked the mercy of the Saviour with tears and sighs that he should deign to help them in their affliction. Having done this the king took counsel and split up his army; he himself went to Salerno on 5th October and there dealt with matters of business and things which needed doing. The afflictions and persecutions of the city of Bari occurred during the first week of October. When the king arrived at Salerno he deprived his enemies of all their lands and forced them on oath to go north of the Alps. This they did. He ordered that a ship be prepared and his opponent Count Roger of Ariano and his wife be sent prisoner to Sicily, and thus securing vengeance on his enemies, he himself sailed on a warship to Sicily on 5th November.[260]

On 22nd January of this year, at cockcrow, there was a great earthquake, so serious that we thought our houses would collapse. As we have said above, after Pope Innocent had recovered the city of Benevento he appointed as rector of the city Guido, deacon of the Roman See and a man of discretion distinguished by his virtuous way of life.[261] He remained in the city as rector up to 1st March. Then the pope sent another rector, the subdeacon John, a relative of his, and Guido went back to Rome.[262]

The year 1140 and the eleventh year of the pontificate of the lord Innocent, the month of March, third of the indiction. In this year King Roger sent his son Anfusus, Prince of the Capuans, with a large army of knights and infantry beyond the city of Pescara to subjugate that province to his power. The prince took his army as his father had ordered, and made great efforts. He went past Pescara, captured a large number of the *castella* and villages in that area, plundered them and consigned some to the fire. A few days later the king ordered his son Duke Roger with 1,000 knights and a large force of infantry to go to the prince's help. The duke united with the prince his brother and subjected that province, which is close to the frontiers of Rome, in great fear to their rule. As a result Pope Innocent was much disturbed, and on the advice of the Romans sent cardinals to them telling them not to invade

---

260 Count Roger must have later been released and exiled, since in April 1144, along with Robert II of Capua, he was present at the imperial court at Würzburg, *Conradi III et Filius eius Henrici Diplomata*, ed. F. Haussmann (MGH Diplomatum Regum et Imperatorum Germaniae 9, Vienna 1969), 176–7 no. 99.

261 This was not Guido di Castello (see note 231), who had been promoted to be a cardinal priest in 1134, but probably Guido, Cardinal deacon of SS. Cosma and Damiano 1132–49, who had been Pope Innocent's legate in Spain 1134–7, and later was legate in Germany and papal chancellor, Zenker (1964), 146–8.

262 Perhaps John Paparo, appointed Cardinal deacon of S. Adriano by Celestine II in December 1143, and promoted in 1151 to be Cardinal priest of S. Lorenzo in Damaso, Zenker (1964), 79–82.

the lands of others and not to infringe the frontiers of Rome. They wrote back to the pope in reply that they were not seeking the property of others but they wished only to recover lands which belonged to the principality.

While these and other things were happening, the king had ships prepared and came to Salerno in the middle of July.[263] He wanted to find out what had been done by his sons the duke and the prince whom, as I have said above, he had sent out with armies. At the same time he also intended to hold discussions with the lord Pope Innocent. The king took counsel and left Salerno, approaching the city of Benevento with an escort of 200 knights. He had a long and thorough conference with the then Rector of Benevento, John, subdeacon of the Roman See, and other Beneventans about the peace and best interests of the city, and its fealty to the pope. Then he moved on and went to Capua. After staying there for only a few days dealing with various matters of business he went on to S. Germano.[264] There he took counsel and sent messengers to the duke and prince his sons, telling them to return to him; for the king had heard that Pope Innocent was much disturbed and upset by their invasion of the province. The duke and prince received the messengers and returned to their father, leaving all the towns which they had captured furnished with everything they might need. After this the king sent envoys to the pope, informing him humbly that he wished if at all possible to speak with him and to put an end to their many different problems. However, the pope took counsel and wrote back that both because of the exigencies of the time and other urgent business he would be unable to meet him. The king in consequence gathered up his army and went back to Capua, and after staying there for a little while dismissed his troops and gave everyone permission to return to their homes. The king himself rode with 500 knights to Pescara, which, as we have said above, had been captured by his sons.[265] Then, after travelling round the whole of the region which his sons had conquered and making a careful study of everything there, he came to the city of Ariano where he held a court with his nobles and

263 Roger was at Palermo on 25 April 1140, when he issued the foundation charter for his palace chapel of St Peter, *Roger II Diplomata*, 133–7 no. 48.

264 The king visited Montecassino on 28 July, *Annales Casinenses*, MGH SS xix.309, where the date was given as 28 March (impossible since he was still in Sicily). For the correct date, Caspar (1904), 540.

265 Roger was near Chieti (15 km. S of Pescara) on 27 August, when he issued a privilege for the abbey of Casauria, *Roger II Diplomata*, 139–40 no. 49. The (problematic) chronicle of the abbey of St Stephen *ad Rivum Maris* claimed that Roger issued a privilege for this house in the diocese of Marsia in August 1140, *Roger II Diplomata*, deperdita no. 79.

bishops and dealt with a large number of different matters. Among the other dispositions which he made there he promulgated a terrible edict, hated throughout Italy and leading to death and poverty, namely that nobody dwelling in his kingdom should receive *romesinae* or pay them in any transaction, and on the worst possible advice he introduced his own money; the ducat, worth eight *romesinae*, which was reckoned to have been struck far more of copper than of silver. He also introduced copper *follares*, three of which were equivalent to one *romesina*.[266] All the people of Italy suffered and were reduced to poverty and misery by this horrible money, and as a result of these oppressive actions hoped for the king's death or deposition.

After introducing this money and these evil edicts the king gathered together his knights and went to Naples. The Archbishop of Naples, whose name was Marinus, ordered all the clergy of the city to be summoned, announced the king's arrival to them, and encouraged them and the citizens to greet the king joyfully and in the proper manner. The knights and citizens of the city went out through the Porta Capuana into what they call the Neapolitan Field, welcomed the king with more honour and care than one would have believed possible and escorted him up to the Porta Capuana. The priests and clergy of the city then went out through that gate and led him into the city with hymns and *laudes* rising to the heavens. Four noblemen held the reins of the king's horse and his stirrups there, and four more led him to the cathedral. Reader, if you had seen the number of people pouring into the squares, and the widows, married women and virgins leaning out of the windows, you would have been amazed and would have said that no other emperor, king or prince had ever been received with such honour and joy in the city of Naples. What more? After this ecstatic welcome the king dismounted at the cathedral and was entertained in the archbishop's chamber. The next day he rode all through the city and round the outside. The king then went in a ship that had been made ready to the *castellum* of the Holy Saviour near to the city, and summoning the citizens of Naples there he dealt with various issues

266 These *romesinae* may have been silver pennies of Rouen [see *Al. Tel.*, III.8 and note 132]. Despite Falco's strictures, the new ducats contained at least as much silver (about 50%) as the old Byzantine *miliaresia*. It was only under William I that the silver content was reduced. The new coins, clearly meant to remedy a shortage of lower-denomination coins that became more and more marked after the Norman conquest of Byzantine Apulia, remained in use until c.1166, though their circulation appears to have been mainly limited to Apulia. Thereafter they were largely replaced by silver pennies from the north. Martin (1991), 460–3; Travaini (1995), 55–60, 210–224.

to do with the liberty and interests of the city.[267] He gave to every knight five *modia* of land and five villeins, and promised that if life was granted to him he would reward them [further] with generous gifts and possessions. Meanwhile, during the middle of the night the king had had the entire outside of the city of Naples measured, for he wished to know what its circumference was. By careful measurement he found out that it was 2363 paces. Having found out what the distance was, he asked the people of the city who were gathered together before him, seemingly out of love, whether they knew how many paces the circumference of the city measured. They confessed, more amazed than one would have thought possible, that they did not know. As though he had derived his answer from studying, the king then informed them of the length of their city's perimeter. As a result the whole city declared that the king was wiser and more learned than his predecessors, and they were amazed how he had known what the answer was since the city had never before actually been measured as the king had arranged!

After all this had happened the king hurried to Salerno and after staying there for a few days took ship and putting to sea on 4th October sailed to Palermo. His son the duke remained in Apulia and the prince his other son stayed at the city of Capua. And when, as we said earlier, King Roger had introduced his [new] money he sent a message to John, subdeacon of the Roman See and Rector of Benevento, and to the citizens asking that they accept this money within the city. On hearing this, the rector was amazingly downcast. He replied that he could not accept such money without the pope's permission, particularly since its introduction had been to the detriment of the whole of Italy. Finally the rector took counsel and informed the pope of the king's edict, asking him to send instructions as to what should be done about this issue. Hearing this Pope Innocent lamented more than one would have believed possible and was amazed at the appalling actions of King Roger. He immediately sent letters to the Beneventans which read as follows: 'We have heard from you and from others who have informed us of the truth of what the king has done and of the introduction of his new coins; as a result we order you not to be frightened or upset by such things for they are transitory and they can soon be

267 This was on an island, now the site of the Castel dell'Ovo (in its present form dating from the Angevin period) and linked to the S. Lucia district of Naples by a modern causeway. It was the seat of a monastery dedicated to the Holy Saviour, existing in the ninth century (perhaps earlier) and last attested in 1132. The monks were later transferred to a monastery in the city, dedicated to St Peter; they were certainly there in 1164, *Italia Pontificia*, viii.461–2. Falco's reference to the *castellum* would suggest the monks were moved and the island fortified between 1132 and 1140, most likely during the siege of 1135–6.

changed. Besides we are every day watching out for your interests'. These letters were received and read, and we gave thanks for what had occurred and breathed more easily for a while. After this Pope Innocent sent to King Roger telling him that all the people of Italy and elsewhere were lamenting because of the introduction of this money, and how they had been brought to suffer famine. ... [*the extant MSS end here*].

[The Ferraria Chronicle, probably based on Falco, continues][268]

In 1142, which was the thirteenth year of this same Innocent, the pope sent a message to the king that he had no right to choose the pastors of churches and he should desist from this presumption. To which the king responded thus, that: 'From the time of Duke Robert Guiscard, and in that of Duke Roger and Duke William until now this has been the custom, from which I do not in any way wish to desist, rather I want to hold firmly to it'.

In 1143, which was the fourteenth year of this same pope, certain citizens of Tripoli in Barbary arrived who promised to surrender this city and rule over it to King Roger, if he would send people there, which he confirmed [that he would do] on oath. The king believed them and sent 300 well-armed knights with their horses and supplies. Thus the admiral George arrived and laid siege to the city from three sides. However, he was unable to capture it, because the men who had promised to give it up acted treacherously, for they did not keep the promises they had made.

In this same year Pope Innocent fell sick. He advised the cardinals that to avoid schism when he died they should elect one of five candidates whom he named as the father of the world, placing before their eyes how many murders had resulted from the previous dissension. And he immediately gave them 40,000 marks, which he ordered them to use for the defence of the Church. After doing this he migrated to the Lord on 24th September. He had ruled for thirteen years, seven months and eight days. Guido di Castello succeeded him, who took the name Celestine, who ruled for five months and fifteen days.[269]

Meanwhile the king wanted the pope to confirm the kingdom to him, as had once been conceded by his predecessor. He strove to obtain this, not by requests and persuasion but by giving him no alternative, and he hoped to attain this for himself by the betrayal of the Beneventans. What more? He took away the immunity which he had granted to them in the time of Anacletus and that of Innocent, when he had freed the Beneventans from the exactions, dues and services to which they had been made subject by the Normans. He also got the neighbouring barons to harass the townspeople unmercifully. The Beneventans sent envoys to the king to beg him to observe the immunity which he had given them. The king sent Robert his chancellor to Benevento to inspect his

268 Translated from *Chron. Ferraria*, 27–8.
269 For him, see note 231 above.

privilege, but the latter not only read it but retained it, nor would he return it before it had been copied and shown to the king.[270] The chancellor then left Benevento, taking the privilege with him without permission [*inlicentiatus*]. The citizens were harassed and made to suffer – indeed they were afraid to go outside the town. The Archbishop of Benevento set off to see the pope, but was arrested while on his journey by Thomas of Finocchio.[271] The pope was informed of the harassment that was visited upon the Beneventan people and by which they were every day afflicted.

In 1144, which was the first year of this same lord Pope Celestine, Cardinal Octavian and the Roman consul Cencius Frangipani on the orders of the pope went to the king to negotiate a peace between him and the pope. They set off, but while they were at Palermo with the king and before they could settle anything about those matters which they had proposed, the king was informed of the moment and day when Pope Celestine had died, and that Cardinal Gerard had succeeded him, who was called Pope Lucius.[272] Hearing this, the king was pleased and rejoiced in no small way. He summoned Cardinal Octavian and the consul Cencius, who had come on this legation, to him, and said: 'Tell me why you have come to us and what you wish to seek from us'. They showed the pope's letter to him and explained the reason for their journey. Hearing this, the king explained to them that Pope Celestine had died on 8th March and how Gerard the former chancellor had succeeded him, who had taken the name Lucius.[273] Hearing this, they were amazed and sad. The king then sent a message through them to the lord Pope Lucius, that he was greatly pleased by his promotion and that he would welcome a meeting with him. On the day chosen, 4th June, they met for this meeting in the church of St Paternianus at Ceprano,[274] where the king and his sons, the duke and prince, prostrated themselves on the ground and kissed the pope's feet, and then received the kiss on the mouth and proclaimed themselves to be his servants. And after the celebration of the holy mass, the king gave [the pope] a gold coronet: his sons offered a vessel of gold and two wonderfully decorated silk *pallia*. Then, after the blessing was given and a banquet had taken place, a peace agreement was negotiated. For the pope sought the principality of Capua from the king and his sons. The king and his sons, however, demanded that property which this same pope held from the principality; and so they negoti-

---

270 The Englishman Robert of Selby, chancellor from 1137, who died c.1151, Brühl (1978), 46–7.

271 He was the son of Hugh the Infant, and was later recorded as a royal justiciar in August 1154, *Più antiche carte di S. Modesto*, 24–8 no. 9 (June 1144); Museo del Sannio, Fondo S. Sofia, vol. 13 no. 11.

272 For Cardinal Gerard, see note 140 above.

273 The Ferraria Chronicle adds 'who sat eleven years [*recte* one year] and five months', and a marginal note says, 'he is said to have been from Bologna' – these appear to be later additions.

274 Ceprano was on the border between the principality of Capua and papal territory.

ated from midday until evening, but were unable to agree on a peace. Indeed, not only did they not agree, but their differences grew greater. What more? They remained around there for almost two weeks, and every day the king's army grew stronger. Finally they departed in discord; the pope returned to Rome and the king went back to Sicily. After this his sons besieged Veroli and ravaged its vines and fields, and they captured and sacked various *castella* in the Campagna.[275] The king now came back with a fleet and laid siege to the town of Terracina, but was unable to take it. His sons captured Marsia, Amiterno and all the land as far as Rieti, which town Robert the chancellor of this same king later burned down. And Duke Roger and Prince Anfusus of Capua [both] died during their father's lifetime, to his grief.[276] The king took as his wife the sister of Count Hugh of Molise and engendered from her a son named Simon, whom he appointed as prince of Capua.[277] Wishing in the meantime to gain the kingdom of Africa and Tripoli in Barbary, the king granted the truce which he had refused between his sons and Pope Lucius while the latter were alive, and confirmed that for seven years he would not molest the Beneventans nor the borders of the Romans.[278]

275 Veroli is 18 km. NW of Ceprano, within papal territory.

276 Anfusus died on 10 October 1144, but Duke Roger only on 2 May 1149 [see below, *Romuald*, note 34]: this sentence thus probably was the work of the later Cistercian chronicler rather than of Falco.

277 Falcandus, however, makes clear that Simon was illegitimate, born *ex consuetudinaria matre*, and suggests that Roger wished to make him Prince of Taranto rather than Capua, *Falcandus*, 51 (*Tyrants*, 104–5). Given Simon's involvement, apparently as an adult, in the conspiracy against William I in 1161, he was probably born before 1144. If his mother was the sister of Count Hugh, it is possible that her virtue was the price paid for his restoration after falling foul of the king in 1135 (he was the former Count of Boiano; the comital title, though not the actual county, changed after his restoration). Some years later, c.1150/1, Count Hugh was seeking to marry an illegitimate daughter of King Roger, Adelaide, *The Historia Pontificalis of John of Salisbury*, ed. M. Chibnall (London 1956), 80–2.

278 See the letter of Pope Lucius to Abbot Peter of Cluny, 22 September 1144, below 312, which makes clear that agreement was reached *before* the death of Prince Anfusus. While the mention of the Beneventans suggests that this passage was based upon the now-lost ending of Falco's work, it would appear to have been reworked by the subsequent author.

ROMUALD OF SALERNO, CHRONICON SIVE ANNALES, 1125–54

In the year from the Lord's Incarnation 1125, fourth in the indiction, there now succeeded Honorius II, of the Lombard nation, formerly archdeacon of Bologna, afterwards cardinal, then Bishop of Ostia, who was called Lambert. Following the precedents [*statuta*] of his predecessors, he invested Duke William by banner with the duchy of Apulia and received liege homage and oath from him. Although Duke William was much loved by his barons and men, he was however held to some extent in contempt by them for his kindness and patience. They instigated dispute between him and his liege man and paternal cousin, Count Roger of Sicily. When peace and concord had several times been negotiated between the duke and count, they once again stirred up war and discord between them. And since the said duke was a liberal and generous man and paid out whatever he could find to his knights, he was first of all forced by necessity to place Calabria in pledge to the count for 60,000 bezants. Afterwards he sold to him the half of Palermo which belonged to him by hereditary right. Finally, when he was unable to have a son by his wife, he received a great deal of money from the above-mentioned count and at Messina instituted him as heir to the duchy of Apulia and all his land. He confirmed to the church of Salerno all that his grandfather Duke Robert and his father Duke Roger had given to it, and added to this the greater part of the Jewry.[1] On dying he left the *castrum* of Olevano and all Pastina to the church.[2] He died, as we all must, at Salerno at the age of thirty, in his eighteenth year as duke, in the year of the Lord's Incarnation 1127, on the Feast of St Nazarius in the month of July [28th July], fifth in the indiction. He was buried at Salerno in the tomb of his father in the church of the Apostle St Matthew, which Duke Robert his grandfather had completely [re]

---

1 Roger Borsa granted the Jewry of Salerno to the archbishopric in 1090, L.A. Muratori, *Antiquitates Italiae*, i (Milan 1738), 899–900. William confirmed this donation in October 1121, *Pergamene Salernitane 1008–1784*, ed. L. Pennacchini (Naples 1941), 57–9 no. 12. See Loud (2007a), 317, 516–17.

2 The only deathbed donation of which we have details is that to Cava [see above, *Al. Tel.* I.1, note 2]. Some of the lands in this bequest may have been at Olevano, 22 km. E of Salerno, in the region described in the charter, but the archbishopric had owned it since at least the mid-eleventh century, Taviani-Carozzi (1991), 961–9; Ramseyer (2006), 141–2. Garufi, *Romuald*, 214n, suggested that Pastina was near Amalfi.

built. Duke William was of middle height, graceful of body, a daring and energetic knight, well-versed in the art of war, generous, humble, kindly and patient, affable to all, pious and merciful and much loved by his men, greatly honouring the churches of God and their ministers. Hearing of the death of Duke William who had instituted him as his heir, Count Roger immediately came with his galleys to Salerno and was honourably received by the Salernitan citizens, to whom he confirmed their tenements, possessions and ancient customs, receiving them as his men. He left however the citadel [*turris maior*] in their power. He was anointed as prince in this same city by Bishop Alfanus of Capaccio.[3] Then he went to Reggio where he was raised to the duchy of Apulia, and so returned to Sicily.

In the year of the Lord 1127, sixth in the indiction, in the month of September Bohemond the younger sailed to Antioch and was made prince in his father's stead.[4] He left all his cities in Apulia to his relation Count Alexander to rule them in his place. In this year Count Roger of Sicily was excommunicated by Pope Honorius since he did not permit the bishops of Sicily to come to Rome. He was once again excommunicated by the pope because he had improperly seized the title of duke for himself without consulting the Roman pontiff.[5]

---

3 Alfanus is attested as Bishop of Paestum [Capaccio] 1100–34; see for example Cava, *Arm. Mag.* D.25, D. 27, G.34, Romuald here uses the title of the see employed in his own time; although the bishop had been based at Capaccio since the mid-eleventh century, the title of Bishop of Paestum continued in use until c.1150. One of the first documents to use the new title is Cava, *Arca* xxix.26 (October 1155).

4 Correctly 1126.

5 *Manuscripts B and C of the Chronicle add this paragraph as a marginal addition here. It was probably inserted shortly after Archbishop Romuald's death.* 'In the year from the Incarnation of the Lord 1127, sixth of the indiction. In this year Bohemond the son of Prince Bohemond was summoned by the people of Antioch that he might rule over Antioch in the place of his father. He left all the cities of Apulia which he held to the lord Count Alexander, for the latter to hold them in his place, and he putting to sea with fourteen galleys and six other merchant vessels, and with a picked host of young men, he travelled to Antioch. In the month of June in the same indiction, while the *castellum* of Oggiano was under siege by the counts of Calabria, namely Alexander of Senise and Robert of Grandmesnil, and many others, by the order of Count Roger of Sicily, there also arrived no small host of knights and Saracen infantry [sent] by this same Count Roger. Roger the husband of Judith was resisting them from within with a group of most valiant knights. Suddenly one day, with the sun in the east, Roger of Terlizzi and Robert Ricinnus charged upon them with a picked band of knights, and so shattered them that there was none of them who did not either put to flight, bound as a captive or perished through the sword of the victor. The number of dead among the Saracens and the other infantry is not recorded, although it is said that the whole camp was dripping with blood as though it was water. All their equipment was given over to destruction and plunder.' Roger of Terlizzi (in northern Apulia, 10 km. SW of Molfetta) was the son of Count Godfrey of Molfetta (*fl.* 1089–1105) and is attested between February 1120 and 1131, *Le Pergamene della cattedrale*

The next year he entered Apulia with a great army. Pope Honorius knew that the said duke wished on his own authority to usurp for himself the duchy of Apulia, the investiture and lordship of which belonged to him through the legitimate right of his predecessors. He went to Apulia and, along with Prince Robert of Capua and Count Rainulf of Airola,[6] the duke's brother-in-law, and with the counts of Conversano, Prince Grimoald of Bari and the other Apulian barons, marched against him in an attempt to drive him out of Apulia.[7] Duke Roger however was a wise and clever man, and being unwilling to expose his forces to battle

---

di Terlizzi (971–1300), ed. F. Carabellese (Codice diplomatic barese iii, Bari 1899), 58 no. 41 and 62–3 no. 45; Chartes de Troia, 198 no. 57 (November/December 1130). Robert Ricinnus was present at a ducal court at Troia in November 1123, Chartes de Troia, 175–7 no. 46. Alexander, lord of Senise in Lucania, appears in two charters of the Greek monastery of Carbone, in 1093 and 1100, Gertrude Robinson, 'The History and Chartulary of the Greek monastery of St Elias and St Anastasius of Carbone', Orientalia Christiana 14 (1929), 200–6 nos. 14–15, although it is possible that the Alexander of 1129 was a son or other relative rather than the same man.

6 Rainulf was also called Count of Airola by the Liber Pontificalis, ii.322. Airola, in the Valle Caudina, 20 km. SW of Benevento, was one of a number of towns in his extensive dominions.

7 Another marginal note in MSS B and C adds: 'In the year from the Incarnation of the Lord 1128, seventh of the indiction. In the month of May of this year Count Roger, after mustering a multitude of horse and foot, crossed over from Sicily and marched in haste to Apulia. His army comprised 2,000 knights and 30,000 infantry, and it is said there were 50,000 archers. Nobody could count the vast number of oxen, sheep, pigs and other animals. When he arrived he seized all the lands which Judith held with her husband Roger, that is Tursi, Oggiano, Pisticci, Craco and all the towns and villages round about, and he laid siege to the castellum of Sant'Arcangelo. On seeing this Geoffrey, the son of the lord Count Alexander, came out and sought pardon from him, which was freely granted to him. In this same year and indiction, in the month of November, Pope Honorius came to the city of Troia and held a synodical assembly with the bishops, abbots and counts of Apulia. Count Roger was once again excommunicated, and all his accomplices in his arrogance with him.'

A second marginal note in these MSS continues: 'In the year of the Lord 1132 [sic: this must in fact be 1128], eighth of the indiction, in the month of September, after Duke Roger had made Brindisi subject to his power and built a citadel [turris] therein, and [then] returned to Sicily, Count Tancred arrived to besiege that citadel. He strove by every means to capture it, but as the fortress seemed to him to be impregnable he became very angry. He is said to have sworn that should he ever be able to capture it nobody who was in that fortress would be spared, but that he would have some hanged, others burned or buried alive. But this oath was to his detriment rather than benefit, for when the guards and defenders of the citadel became aware of this oath directed against them they encouraged each other to fight and die bravely rather than wishing to surrender. After making no progress with his siege he took advice and reined in his anger. When Prince Grimoald of Bari arrived, Tancred tried to persuade the garrison with honeyed words to surrender the citadel to him and Grimoald. Tancred and his men [then] left to besiege Gallipoli, which he did. In December the aforesaid prince captured the citadel, but through kindness rather than ferocity, and he allowed the garrison to leave unharmed with their goods.'

with them, he shut himself and his army up in strong and well-defended places where he stayed for a long time. His opponents became bored and were forced by shortages to split up and return to their own homes. Seeing himself deserted by the barons the pope returned to Benevento. Duke Roger followed him there, envoys were exchanged and they came to an agreement by which Roger did liege homage and swore an oath to him, and the pope invested him by banner with the duchy of Apulia on the bridge over the Sabato. After doing this Pope Honorius returned to Rome and Duke Roger went back to Sicily. He came once again to Apulia the next year, made peace with the said barons and Prince Robert of Capua, and recovered control of the citadel of Salerno.[8]

8 *Marginal note in MSS B and C*: 'In the year of the Lord 1129, eighth of the indiction, Duke Roger sailed from Sicily, came into Apulia and marched on Taranto. Then he reached Nardò with a great army, for it is said that he had 3,000 knights, and up to 6,000 infantry, archers and Saracens. Finding that Nardo had been abandoned he took it, allowing it to be completely plundered and destroyed. Indeed he ordered that the blood of Christians be cruelly shed by the Saracens, who killed old men, struck down and transfixed with their swords boys torn from their mothers' breasts, and slew priests standing next to altars and the Cross. They scattered the sacraments of the Church, that is the holy chrism, in order to mock them, and trampled them underfoot; they ravished women in front of their husbands, and the duke ordered that the survivors be bound and transported to Sicily. Then he went with his savage army to Brindisi, and in the month of June he placed this under siege by land and sea. He had a very high tower built before it from long beams, bound together with iron chains and protected by hides and osiers, overtopping the walls of the aforesaid city. But siege engines of this sort brought him no profit nor harmed the men of Brindisi, for Geoffrey son of Count Alexander and Richard lord of Chiaromonte, who were within, likewise built catapults and machines with which they soon completely destroyed the tower. Seeing that his skill could in no way prevail, and with the entire army suffering from hunger, he had the tower set on fire and returned to Taranto.' For Alexander and his brother Richard of Chiaromonte, who were among the leading lords of Lucania, Trinchera, *Syllabus*, 105–6 no. 80 (November 1116), Robinson, 'Chartulary of Carbone', 262–72 nos. 29–30 (September 1125, April 1130/1), Trinchera, *Syllabus*, 144–5 no. 110 (1131). For this family, who came originally from Clermont-sur-Oise in the Beauvaisis, Ménager (1975b), 275–84.

Another note adds: 'In the month of June in the year 1129, eight of the indiction, the galleys of Duke Roger blockaded the city of Bari, making entering or leaving the city impossible for any of the barks and vessels of the Bariots. It is said that were some forty to sixty fast galleys [there]. Arriving with his army, the duke captured Salpi in the month of August, and Ruvo, [the latter] so it is said through the treachery of the citizens. And since lord Tancred was suffering from bodily illness, and was also being threatened by the attack of Duke Roger, at last in high summer, that is on 10 August, he, along with his brother the lord Count Alexander and the lord Grimoald who led the principality of Bari, made peace with the said Duke Roger, also returning the lands taken by them, that is Gravina to Robert, Aquaviva and Cornulo …. to the priors of the lord Saint William.' The last sentence is clearly incomplete. Robert of Gravina was one of those who, in June 1132, swore on behalf of the king to respect the rights of the citizens of Bari, *Roger II Diplomata*, 54–6 no. 20 [= *Cod. Dipl. Barese* v.137–9 no. 80]. The reference to St William of Vercelli, founder of Montevergine (d.1142), is difficult to explain. Was some property returned to this abbey itself, or (more likely) did its superiors act as 'honest brokers' to facilitate the return of property to its owners?

Afterwards, on the advice of the barons and people, he had himself anointed and crowned in Palermo as King of Sicily. After securing the royal throne he came with a fleet and a great army to Salerno, closely invested Amalfi, Ravello and Scala, captured them after a long siege, and thus subjected these cities and their castles to his rule.

At this time Bohemond, son of Prince Bohemond, was killed in battle against Damascus. His body is said to have been buried headless.[9]

After this [Roger] returned to Apulia and besieged Bari which surrendered to him, and he then carried off to Sicily its prince, Grimoald, and the wealthy and noble citizens who had opposed him. Meanwhile Pope Honorius died in the sixth year of his pontificate, in the year 1130, eighth in the indiction. On his death schism arose in the Roman church. The larger and wiser part of the cardinals chose as pope Gregory, of the Roman nation, Cardinal deacon of S. Angelo, who was called Innocent II. The other part of the cardinals raised as pontiff a noble Roman citizen, Peter son of Peter Leone, Cardinal deacon of St Nicholas de Carcere, who was called by them Anacletus. He however had the forces of his relatives, and with their help and support subjected almost the whole of the City to his rule. Since he could not remain in the City, Innocent, on the advice and with the help of the Frangipani, secretly went down the Tiber to the sea and sailed to Pisa in a Pisan galley. He was honourably welcomed by its citizens, and remaining in that city for some little time he celebrated a solemn council there. Then he went on to Gaul and was there recognised by King Louis of France and all

---

A further marginal note continues: 'In the month of September in the year from the Incarnation of the Lord 1130 [*recte* 1129], ninth of the indiction, in the month of September, after Duke Roger had made all the cities of Apulia subject to his lordship, that is Troia, Siponto, Monte Gargano and Trani, with all the *castella* and villages situated round about them, he came to Melfi. He had all the counts of Calabria, Apulia, Salentino, Bruttium [*Brizie*], Lucania and Campania, summoned there, as well as the bishops and abbots; and he ordered all the counts that they should be ever faithful to himself and to his sons Roger and Tancred and obey their instructions, nor should they permit or consent to there being theft and robbery in their lands. And after these orders had been confirmed on oath, he returned to Sicily in the month of October.'

9 This was in February 1130. See above, *Al. Tel.* I.12, note 21.

A final marginal note in MSS B and C adds: 'In the year from the Incarnation of the Lord 1131, tenth of the indiction. The aforesaid Duke Roger instructed all the bishops of the various provinces of Calabria, Apulia and Campania to muster in the province of Sicily on the day of the Lord's birth in the month of December, and on the order of Pope Calixtus [*sic*] they anointed him as king and placed a royal crown on his head, and they ordered everyone to call him king. At this time Bohemond the son of Prince Bohemond was killed in battle near Damascus. His body was found headless, and was buried in the monastery of St Mary which is near the Sepulchre of our Redeemer, on the right side of that Sepulchre. [This happened] in the month of February.'

the western Church. After securing his rule over the City Anacletus sent a messenger to King Roger of Sicily, who recognised him. With his authority Anacletus entered Apulia and celebrated a council at Melfi.[10] He often sent messengers to the said king asking that he might have a meeting with him, and that he should do homage to him as was customary. But the latter, a wise and astute man with an eye for the future refused to meet and talk with him. After remaining for some little time in Apulia Anacletus therefore returned to Rome, and he remained there up to the end of his life.

Meanwhile Prince Robert of Capua and Count Rainulf of Airola, with other counts and barons of Apulia, raised a rebellion against King Roger. On ascertaining this King Roger gathered together a fleet and a great number of knights and foot soldiers and came to Salerno. At the River Scafati in the territory of Nocera he fought with Prince Robert of Capua and Count Rainulf and was defeated. He fled and took refuge at Salerno. Afterwards, gathering his strength again he returned once more to Apulia. He laid siege to the counts of Conversano, stormed their cities and *castella*, and sent some of them prisoners to Sicily. After a little time had passed, he came with a great army to the Terra di Lavoro, captured and ravaged Nocera, destroyed Aversa, and occupied Capua and almost the whole of the Terra di Lavoro. The Prince of Capua took refuge in Naples along with Count Rainulf. Since the king was unable to capture that city, partly because of its site and partly because it was well-garrisoned, he disposed his troops in Aversa and other neighbouring places and had them attack it continually and lay waste [its environs]. Prince Robert of Capua went to Pisa to implore the Pisans' help, leaving at Naples Sergius the *Magister Militum* and duke of that city and Count Rainulf. Afterwards he came back to Naples with a great Pisan fleet and greatly strengthened the daring and bravery of the barons who were in Naples. The Pisan galleys went to Amalfi and finding it unfortified and unprepared captured and plundered it. King Roger was at this time in the Terra di Lavoro and hearing of this he sent his army against the Pisans who still remained in the Amalfitan district, put them to flight, putting many of them to the sword and so rescued the city. The beaten Pisans fled first to Naples and then returned to Pisa. However King Roger, a careful and prudent man who in carrying out his designs preferred to use craft rather than force, attacked his enemies fiercely, now in the Terra di Lavoro and then in Apulia, and brought some of

---

10 This is a mistake for Canosa, where Anacletus held a council on 9 November 1130, Baumgartner (1897), 576–8; *Italia Pontificia* viii.38.

them round to his side by threats and fear, and some indeed by gifts and promises. Realising that they could no longer resist the king, Prince Robert of Capua, Count Rainulf and some others among the barons fled to the German Emperor Lothar, humbly begging his help to recover their lost lands, claiming that Apulia and Sicily were legally subject to his empire. After driving these enemies and rebels from his kingdom and putting them to flight, King Roger held the whole country, except for Naples which he was unable to capture, in peace and tranquillity. He had as a young man when he was still count married Elvira, daughter of the King of Spain, by whom he had many children: Roger whom he appointed Duke of Apulia, Tancred whom he made Prince of Taranto, Anfusus whom he appointed Prince of Capua, William and Henry. He also had one daughter by this wife.[11]

Meanwhile after remaining in France for a little while, Pope Innocent came to Germany and was received by the Emperor Lothar and all his princes with the utmost glory and devotion. On the advice and the continual urging of the pope and also much affected by the prayers and tribulation of the exiles from Apulia, the emperor entered Italy with a great army, and came, along with Pope Innocent, into Apulia by way of Ancona. He ordered Prince Robert of Capua, along with Count Rainulf, the other exiles and a section of his army to invade the Terra di Lavoro, and he instructed the galleys of the Pisans to go to their assistance. The emperor occupied the whole of Apulia without resistance. Indeed King Roger realised that he was unable to withstand the emperor because the greater part of his barons and cities had deserted him. So he strongly fortified his cities and *castra*; he himself and his army followed the emperor one or two days behind attacking the cities and castles [*castella*] which the emperor had taken, and he sent frequent messengers to the imperial army, winning over his princes through promises and bribes to support and favour him.[12] The Prince of Capua and Count Rainulf entered the Terra di Lavoro, secured both it and the Duchy of Amalfi by force and coming to Salerno with a great force of knights and the Pisan galleys laid siege to it. However the citizens of Salerno, who from antiquity had continued faithful to their lords, remained loyal as was traditional, and manfully resisted them. King Roger's chancellor, Robert, was then at Salerno with a force of royal knights and many barons, and they, as well as the Salernitan citizens,

11 Roger also had several illegitimate children, including a daughter Adelaide, who married Count Hugh of Molise, and a son Simon whose mother was Count Hugh's sister, *Tyrants*, 86–7, 104–5.

12 Literally, 'to his love and grace'.

made freqent sorties against the army of the prince and the Pisans and fought bravely against it. After they had besieged the city for nearly a month and had been unable to find any means to capture it, the emperor was summoned from Apulia and he and the pope arrived with his army. Robert the chancellor, a well-advised and sensible man, feared that if it should happen that the city was stormed by the emperor then the cause of King Roger would suffer irreparable damage, and so on the barons' advice he told the citizens of Salerno on the king's behalf to come to an agreement with the emperor and to safeguard himself and the royal knights who were in the city. Obeying his instructions the citizens made peace with the emperor and gave him a large sum of money, arranging that the 400 knights who were in the city should retire unharmed with their gear to King Roger. However the chancellor, the barons and a few of the knights took refuge in the citadel. After peace had been made the proud and over-excited Pisans started to molest and inflict injuries on the people of Salerno. The latter could not bear their pride, and seizing their weapons rushed upon them, burning in their very presence the huge wooden castle which they had constructed to attack the city. The Pisans were furious, and as a result deserted the emperor, who had failed to assist them. Afterwards they made peace with King Roger.

Once he had gained control of the city, and taking hostages from the inhabitants for the money, the emperor departed and pitched his camp at S. Severino. There he took counsel with the pope and his barons and decided to make Count Rainulf Duke of Apulia. But because of this a great quarrel arose between the pope and emperor. The pope claimed that the investiture of the duchy of Apulia rightly belonged to the Roman pontiff, and that his predecessors had strictly exercised this right for a long time previously. The emperor on the contrary asserted that this rightfully belonged to the empire and that the duchy of Apulia ought to be subject to imperial authority. But, since each of them was in the course of a journey and thus on both sides they were then lacking evidence and documents, this dispute could not be fully resolved and so by mutual consent they came to an agreement as follows: that the pope and emperor [together] should invest Count Rainulf with the duchy of Apulia by banner, and that afterwards when they had a suitable place and time the claims of both parties should be fully examined and investigated and the dispute justly resolved. That was what was done, for they invested Count Rainulf with the duchy of Apulia with the pope holding the upper part of the banner and the emperor the lower part. Once this was done the emperor returned to Germany. Innocent however entered

Rome and was honourably received by the Frangipani and certain other nobles. Not long afterwards Anacletus breathed his last.[13]

Hearing that the pope and emperor had retired, and strengthened by his 400 knights who had come from Salerno, King Roger arrived at the city and was welcomed by the Salernitan citizens with the utmost devotion. He attacked and destroyed Nocera without delay, seized the whole Terra di Lavoro, took Capua at sword point and burned it. Then he came to an agreement with Sergius the *Magister Militum* of Naples and enlisted him in his army. Sending his columns on from there towards Apulia he recovered the whole of the Terra Beneventana and the Capitanata. Count Rainulf, who was trying to be called duke, learned of this and raised an army of knights and a huge force from the coastal cities and attacked him at Rignano.

A peace settlement between them was discussed for a long time, with Abbot Bernard of Clairvaux acting as mediator, but sin made it impossible to conclude this, and a fierce battle resulted. Duke Roger, the king's son, was in the thick of the fight, gallantly attacked the forces opposing him and drove them back in flight as far as Siponto. However the king, who was in the rear and largest division, abandoned his soldiers and fled, and in consequence many thousands of men were captured or killed. Sergius, the *Magister Militum* of Naples, died of a sword thrust. The king rode all night and reached Salerno, whose citizens, as was their custom, received him dutifully. He remained in that city for a little while, and garrisoned his cities and *castella* with knights and infantrymen. It was now that William, from Ravenna, the archbishop-elect of Capua, was elected in the church of Salerno.[14] Then, after securing Naples and taking measures for and organising the places in that region, the king returned to Sicily with his sons Duke Roger and Prince Tancred.

When summer came he returned to the Terra di Lavoro with a great army and fleet. Pope Innocent, who had secured the City on the death of Anacletus, raised a powerful army from the Romans and Campanians, and entered the king's territory. He occupied S. Germano and nearly all

13 Innocent was in Rome by 1 November 1137, J-L 7856–8. Anacletus died on 25 January 1138 [above, 230].

14 For William's election as archbishop of Capua, *Al. Tel.* III.31–2. Since he is still referred to as archbishop-elect he had not yet received consecration, hence there was no canonical problem in his now being elected to a different see. He is first attested as Archbishop of Salerno (i.e. having received consecration) in February 1140, Salerno, Archivio diocesano, Mensa Archiepiscopalis, *Arca* I no. 45, and he died on 7 July 1152, *Necrologio di S. Matteo*, 92.

the Land of St Benedict,[15] and besieged the *castrum* of Gallucio. Hearing this King Roger sent his son Duke Roger of Apulia against him with a mighty army. He arrived and raised the siege of the *castrum*, defeated the Romans and captured the pope and many of the Roman nobles with him. The king, who had followed behind him, wanted to approach the pope's feet in an appropriately humble manner. The latter, a stern and steadfast man, at first refused to receive him. Finally, after envoys had scurried between them negotiating a peace treaty, he took the advice of the cardinals and, because of the many Roman citizens who had been captured with him, he accepted the king back into his grace, received an oath and homage from him, and invested him by banner with the kingdom of Sicily and the duchy of Apulia.

At that time Count Rainulf, who called himself duke, died at Troia as a result of being bled. Now also Monte Vesuvio threw forth iron-coloured and reddish dust in such quantities that it reached Naples, Capua and Salerno. The king brought Pope Innocent with due ceremony to Benevento, and then with his permission left, went to Troia and captured it. Afterwards he invested Bari, which surrendered to him after a long siege. He had Jaquintus, who called himself Prince of Bari, and many others hanged. Richard of Chiaromonte was killed there. Alexander his brother fled to Romania.[16] And thus the most mighty King Roger, having overcome and destroyed enemies and traitors, gloriously and triumphantly returned to Sicily and held his realm in the utmost peace and tranquillity. Pope Innocent returned to Rome and held that peacefully and tranquilly. Not long afterwards Lothar, the Emperor of the Germans, died and Conrad succeeded him in the empire. Similarly, Louis, King of the French, died and was succeeded in his kingdom by his son Louis.[17]

King Roger however established peace and good order in his kingdom, and to preserve that peace instituted chamberlains and justiciars throughout the land, promulgated laws which he had newly drafted and removed evil customs from their midst. And, since he was great of heart and always full of ambition, he was by no means contented just with the lordship of Sicily and Apulia. He prepared a great fleet and sent it with many knights to Africa which he captured and held. He stormed Sousa, Bône, Gabes, Sfax and Tripoli, and made them subject

---

15 The *Terra Sancti Benedicti* was the land of Montecassino, an extensive block of territory around the monastery, and ruled by the abbot as a privileged and exempt franchise.

16 For Richard and Alexander, see note 8 above.

17 Louis died at Paris on 1 August 1137.

to his rule.[18] For his honour and convenience he made peace with the King of Babylon.[19] At this time John, Emperor of Constantinople, was wounded by a poisoned arrow and died at Antioch.[20] His son Manuel succeeded him in his empire. The latter sent envoys to King Roger to arrange a marriage between the two sides. To complete this alliance the king sent suitable envoys to the emperor, who kept them talking there for a long time in the usual way, and afterwards had them flung into prison.[21] The king was in consequence furious and had many galleys and ships made ready at Otranto, which he sent to Romania with counts and a large army. They arrived and ravaged Corfu and many other islands, took Corinth and Thebes at sword point, plundered them and carried off a great deal of money and silken textiles. On another occasion King Roger sent the Admiral Salernus with his fleet to Romania, who met the great fleet of the emperor at Cape Malea, bravely fought and defeated the Greeks there, and brought back the Despot Angelos, master of the fleet and the emperor's blood relative, and many others prisoner to Sicily.[22]

Meanwhile Pope Innocent died at Rome and was buried at the Lateran

18 Tripoli was captured in 1146, Mahdia, Sfax and Sousa in 1148; Tunis (not mentioned here) probably paid tribute. Thus most of the coast of Tunisia (Ifriqiyah) was under Sicilian control. The dependence of this region on imported Sicilian grain undoubtedly facilitated these conquests, as did internal divisions in the towns. Abulafia (1984), especially 32–5; see also Matthew (1992), 57–9; Houben (2002), 79–84; De Simone (2002), and especially Metcalfe (2009), 166–70. For a Muslim account of the capture of Gabes and Mahdia, *The Chronicle of Ibn al-Athir for the Crusading Period, 1146–93*, 13–14, 18–20.

19 That is the Fatimid Caliph of Egypt, either al-Amir (1101–30) or al-Hāfiz (1130–49). The excellent diplomatic relations between Sicily and Egypt had begun with an Egyptian embassy in 1123, and George of Antioch had been sent on an embassy to Cairo in 1126. Reform of the central Sicilian administration, c.1145, also drew heavily on Fatimid models. Johns (1993), especially 145–7; Johns (2002).

20 He died after a hunting accident in Cilicia (not Antioch) on 8 April 1143.

21 According to the contemporary Byzantine historian John Cinnamus it was Roger who made this proposal, for a marriage between one of his sons and a Byzantine princess. Manuel sent an embassy to Palermo, headed by a certain Basil Xeros, but what led Manuel to react badly was his ambassador's recognition that Roger was of equal status to the emperor (presumably therefore Basil had accorded Roger the title of *Basileus*), *Deeds of John and Manuel Comnenus, by John Kinnamos*, 75–6.

22 These events took place late 1147–early 1149. The campaign, and in particular the fighting on Corfu, was described in detail in *Deeds of John and Manuel Comnenus, by John Kinnamos*, 76–82. For this, and especially the attacks on Corinth and Thebes, the later account of Niketas Choniates is also useful, *O City of Byzantium. The Annals of Niketas Choniates*, trans. H.J. Magoulias (Detroit 1984), 43–52. The Byzantine and Venetian sources claimed that the battle off Cape Malea was a victory for their side. See Chalandon (1907), ii.135–45; Houben (2002), 84–6, Kislinger (2009), 58–62. The Admiral (Emir) Salernus later witnessed a privilege of William I for the archbishopric of Palermo in December 1157, *William I Diplomata*, 60–4 no. 22.

in the thirteenth year of his pontificate, in the year of the Lord's Incarnation 1143, seventh of the indiction.[23] Guido, of the Tuscan nation, previously cardinal priest, succeeded him, and took the name Celestine II. He was unwilling to confirm the peace which had been made between Pope Innocent and King Roger, and called it into question. He died in the sixth month of his pontificate.[24] To him there succeeded Gerard of Bologna, formerly Cardinal priest of S. Croce and chancellor, who was called Lucius II. When King Roger heard of the election of Pope Lucius he greatly rejoiced, because the latter had been his spiritual father [*compater*] and friend. He immediately sent envoys to the pope, and coming by sea to Gaeta met him at Ceprano. They negotiated about peace between them for a long time, but were unable to come to an agreement because of the opposition of the cardinals. As a result the angry king returned to Sicily. At the king's order his son Duke Roger of Apulia invaded the Campania with a great army, overran and plundered it as far as Ferentino, and then went back to Apulia.[25] Pope Lucius returned to the City. Not long afterwards the Roman people appointed Jordan son of Peter Leone as *Patricius* and for the first time created senators in the City. Pope Lucius however died in the eleventh month of his pontificate, in the year 1145 from the Lord's Incarnation, eighth of the indiction.[26] He was succeeded by Bernard, of the Pisan nation, formerly monk of Clairvaux and Abbot of St Anastasius, then cardinal priest, who was called Eugenius III.[27] He left the city because of the uprising of the senators and people, and was solemnly consecrated at the monastery of Farfa. Then he journeyed to Gaul and was honourably received by Louis the younger, King of the French, and all the Gallic church. He celebrated a general council at Rheims.[28]

At that time King Conrad of the Germans journeyed to Jerusalem with a huge army of knights and footmen, and coming to Constantinople was honourably received by the Emperor Manuel, partly through fear and

---

23 On 24 September 1143. The problems with the Romans, which Romuald discusses later, had already begun before Innocent's death, Partner (1972), 180.

24 On 8 March 1144, *Liber Pontificalis*, ii.385.

25 Cf. *Annales Casinenses*, MGH SS xix.310. A seven-year truce was agreed in autumn 1144; in a letter soon after to Abbot Peter of Cluny, Pope Lucius made clear he had wanted a permanent peace, see below, 312.

26 On 15 February 1145, *Liber Pontificalis*, ii.386.

27 Little is known of his career before he became pope. He became the first abbot of the new Cistercian house of SS. Vincent and Anastasius (Tre Fontani), just south of Rome, in 1140, but we do not know even what his titular church was as a cardinal, Zenker (1964), 184–7.

28 The council began on 21 March 1148; canons in Mansi, *Concilia*, xxi.711–20. The most detailed account is in *The Historia Pontificalis of John of Salisbury*, 4–41.

partly because he had married his sister-in-law. The emperor showed himself kindly and generous enough towards King Conrad, as is the Greek custom, gave him many gifts and promised that he would provide guides for the march and supplies of food. But, after King Conrad and his army crossed the Arm of St George,[29] supplies for him and the army were not forthcoming; it is said, on the prompting and order of the emperor. Due to this shortage of food the army began to grow weaker and distintegrate. On discovering this, the Turks attacked them fiercely and defeated the Germans, weakened as they were by hunger and the hardships of the march; they put many of them to the sword and reduced many [others] to miserable slavery. The emperor [Conrad] lost the greater part of his army and arrived at Jerusalem with only a handful. King Louis of the French followed King Conrad with a great army of knights and infantry in the same year and by the same route; he too was similarly received and deceived by the Emperor Manuel. After he had crossed the Arm of St George, since he had believed the specious promise of the emperor that he and his army would find supplies of food, and that food was lacking, he lost the greater part of his army, partly through hunger and partly in battle, and arrived at Jerusalem with only a small force. So it happened that, in consequence of sin and because of the trickery and evil of the Greeks, these two powerful and noble princes both lost their armies and dissipated the honour and good reputation of the Christians. They stayed at Jerusalem for a little while to pray; then Conrad returned to Germany via Constantinople, the King of France however went back home via Apulia. King Roger received him ceremoniously, gave him many horses and gifts, and ordered him to be honourably escorted through his territory.[30]

Pope Eugenius remained in France for some time and then returned to Italy, making his base at Tusculano.[31] Gathering troops he ordered them to attack and punish the disobedient Romans. Hearing of the pope's arrival King Roger sent envoys to him, and despatched some of his knights to serve him. While the aforesaid pope was dwelling at Tusculano the King of France arrived there on his way back from Jerusalem. Remembering the benefits and honour accorded to him in France by the king, the pope received him with great reverence and honour as was proper, gave him many gifts and let him return to his homeland

29 The Hellespont (modern Dardanelles).

30 Cf. *Historia Pontificalis*, 60–1.

31 Eugenius crossed the Alps towards the end of May 1148. He spent the rest of that year in northern Italy, was at Viterbo from 30 December until late March 1149, and then at Tusculano from 8 April (J-L 9331) until the end of November, when he finally returned to Rome.

in peace.[32] King Roger ordered the archbishops and bishops of his land to be consecrated by Pope Eugenius; he sent frequent envoys to him to negotiate a peace, but was unable to secure this. But since, as Scripture says, 'whom the Lord loveth he chasteneth, and scourgeth every son whom he receiveth',[33] after Almighty God brought King Roger many propitious successes and raised him up, he inflicted adversity upon him by the blows of paternal pity, lest his great success exalt his mind more than would be proper and bring him to pride. For first his illustrious queen Albidia, from whom he had had so many sons, died, and her only daughter. Then the Prince of Taranto, Prince Anfusus of the Capuans and Henry died. Finally his eldest son Duke Roger of Apulia died in the year from the Lord's Incarnation 1149, twelfth of the indiction.[34] He was a handsome man and a mighty soldier, pious, kindly, merciful and much loved by his people. Despite being afflicted with so many blows, King Roger sustained these punishments from his Pious Father with an undaunted spirit, and thus showed himself firm between prosperity and adversity, neither puffed up more than was proper by success nor cast down by adversity. For although he was weighed down by a multiplicity of griefs, he gave in public the appearance of being consoled and his face pretended that he had overcome his grief; for his consolation he bestowed consolation on his kingdom and denied his enemies any means of injuring him. And since he had left only William, Prince of the Capuans, fearing that he might lose him too through the fragility of the human condition, he married Sibilia, daughter of the Duke of Burgundy, who not long afterwards died at Salerno and was buried at Cava.[35] He took as his third wife Beatrice, daughter of the Count of Rethel, by whom he had a daughter who was called Constance.[36] A couple of years before he died he had his son William, Prince of the Capuans, anointed as King of Sicily, and ordered that he should rule alongside him.[37]

---

32 *Historia Pontificalis*, 61–2.

33 Hebrews, 12: 6.

34 Tancred died about 1138, Anfusus on 10 October 1144, Henry about 1145 and Duke Roger on 2 May 1149; Houben (2002), 95–6. For the deaths of Duke Roger and Prince Anfusus, *Necrologio di S. Matteo*, 60, 158, both entries give the day and the year; although Chalandon (1907), ii.171–2, argued that Roger died in 1148, the year stated by the *Annales Casinenses*, MGH SS xix.310.

35 She died on 16 September 1150, *Necrologio di S. Matteo*, 136.

36 Constance was born after her father's death. Beatrice died on 30 March 1185, *Romuald*, 231n, from the necrology of Palermo cathedral.

37 William was crowned at Easter 1151, without consulting the pope, who according to John of Salisbury 'took it ill, but oppressed by the evils of the time could offer no resistance', *Historia Pontificalis*, 68–9.

Meanwhile, after remaining for some considerable time at Tusculano, Pope Eugenius made peace with the Romans and was welcomed back to Rome with the greatest honour by the senators and all the Roman people. What is more he bound the populace to him by gifts and alms, so that he could for the most part arrange the City as he wished. If envious death had not snatched him from their midst, he would have deprived the senators newly created by the people of that little river of their usurped dignity. At that time King Conrad of the Germans died, and his nephew Frederick succeeded him in his kingdom.[38] Not long afterwards Pope Eugenius died at Rome and was buried at St Peter's, in the [eighth] year of his pontificate.[39] Conrad from the Roman nation succeeded him, an old man, full of days, formerly cardinal priest, then Bishop of Sabina and vicar of the Roman Church, who was called Anastasius, in the year from the Lord's Incarnation 1153.[40]

Meanwhile King Roger possessed his realm in peace and tranquillity. Since in neither peace nor war did he know how to be idle, he ordered a very beautiful palace to be built at Palermo, in which he constructed a chapel floored in astonishing stone, which he covered with a gilded roof, and endowed and beautified with various ornaments.[41] And lest this great man should at any time lack pleasures either aquatic or pastoral, he created a pleasure garden at a place which was called Favara, with many canals and streams, into which he ordered different types of fish, brought from many different regions, to be introduced. He had another beautiful and splendid palace constructed next to this pleasure garden. He had some of the hills and woods which are round about Palermo enclosed with a stone wall, and ordered a delightful and well-stocked park made, planted with all sorts of trees, and in it he had deer, roebucks and wild boars kept. And he had a palace in this park to which he ordered water to be brought by underground pipes from the clearest of springs.

38 Conrad III died on 15 February 1152. Frederick was elected at Frankfurt on 4 March, *The Deeds of Frederick Barbarossa, by Otto of Freising*, 111, 115–16.

39 According to the *Liber Pontificalis*, ii.387, Pope Eugenius died at Tivoli on 8 July 1153. Romuald's account of his last years simplifies a complex situation. His agreement with the Romans in November 1149 was, in the words of Paolo Brezzi, 'an unstable compromise', and he faced a further rebellion in the city in November 1151, Brezzi (1947), 334–9; Partner (1972), 183–7.

40 Conrad was a Roman who had been appointed Cardinal priest of S. Pudentiana by Paschal II as far back as 1114, and promoted to be Cardinal Bishop of Sabina in 1128, Zenker (1964), 46–8; Classen (1968); Tillman (1972), 325–30; Hüls (1977), 128–9, 201.

41 The Palatine Chapel was formally founded in April 1140, *Roger II Diplomata*, 133–7 no. 48. However, construction may have begun as early as 1132, Demus (1950), 25–6. See also Loud (2007a), 328–9.

So this wise and careful man enjoyed these aforesaid pleasures as the nature of the season suggested; for in winter, and in Lent because of its profusion of fish, he dwelled at the Favara palace; while in the summer he made the fiery season's heat bearable at the Parco, and diverted his mind from his many cares and the strain of his duties by a moderate amount of hunting. And although the king himself was possessed of great wisdom, ingenuity and was most careful, he also gathered men of wisdom of different sorts from the various parts of the earth and took counsel with them. For he brought George, a man of mature wisdom, foresight and care, from Antioch, and made him his Great Emir [*ammiratus*], and through his advice and prudence he obtained many victories on land and sea.[42] He appointed Guarin and Robert, learned and prudent clerics, in succession as his chancellor.[43] And if he could find proven and wise men, whether from his own land or born elsewhere, laymen or clerics, he had them around him, and promoted them to honours and riches as their individual merits suggested. Finally he made Maio, a young man originating from Bari, who was both fluent of speech and prudent and careful, first *scrinarius*, then vice-chancellor and eventually chancellor.[44] He created many new counts in his kingdom, had the city of Cefalù built, in which he had the splendid and beautiful church of the Holy Saviour constructed at his own expense, to which he made subject the city and its service.[45]

Towards the end of his life, allowing secular matters to be neglected and delayed, he laboured in every conceivable way to convert Jews and Saracens to the faith of Christ, and endowed converts with many gifts and resources. He ordered the church of St Nicholas, Messina, to be built, in large part at his own expense, although it could not be completed in his lifetime.[46] He had a silver panel, made at his own

---

42 For George, see above, *Al. Tel.* II.8.

43 Guarin was chancellor 1132–7; Robert was firmly attested as chancellor from February 1140, although Romuald implies that he was already holding this office in 1137; he died c.1151, Brühl (1978), 44–7, and see above, *Al. Tel.* III.3, and *Falco*, note 267.

44 Maio was *scrinarius* (literally 'archivist') from October 1144, *Roger II Diplomata*, 183–97. He was probably vice-chancellor from 1149, *ibid.*, 224–8 no. †78 (a forgery, but drawing on a genuine document), and was noted as chancellor in an Arabic document of 1152/3, Johns (2002), 309. However, given that the chancellor Robert was mainly employed as governor on the mainland, Maio may well have been in day-to-day charge of the chancery throughout the last decade of Roger's reign, Loud (2009), 793–4.

45 Most of this church was built between 1131 and 1148, although the west front was not finished until the thirteenth century, White (1938), 189, 201; Demus (1950), 3–24.

46 This was a new cathedral for the city, built on a different site from that founded by Roger I (for which, *Malaterra*, III.32, p. 77). Roger II's foundation was only consecrated in 1197, at which time its dedication was changed to the Blessed Virgin Mary, *I Diplomi della cattedrale*

expense, placed before the altar of St Matthew in Salerno as a memorial to his name, and every time he came to Salerno from Sicily he customarily offered one or two precious cloths to the Salernitan church. But since 'it is impossible to remain at the summit',[47] and as punishment for the sins of the whole kingdom, after so many victories and successes the most glorious King Roger died of a fever at Palermo and was buried in the cathedral of that city, in the fifty-eighth year of his life, the second month and fifth day, on the 27th February, in the twenty-fourth year of his reign, in the year from the Lord's Incarnation 1152 [*sic*], first of the indiction.[48] King Roger was large of stature, corpulent, leonine of face, somewhat hoarse of voice; wise, far-seeing, careful, subtle of mind, great in counsel, preferring to use his intelligence rather than force. He was very concerned to gain money, hardly very prodigal in expending it, fierce in public but in private kindly, generous with honours and rewards to those faithful to him, but inflicting injuries and punishments on those disloyal. He was more feared than loved by his subjects, dreaded and feared by the Greeks and Saracens.

[*The Paris and Rome manuscripts of the* Chronicon, *BN MS Latin 4933 (manuscript C of the Garufi edition) and Biblioteca del Capitolo di S. Pietro, E.22 (manuscript B) contain the following addition, which was probably not written by Romuald, or whoever the compiler of the main chronicle was, but may date from the very early thirteenth century.*]

That the world may acknowledge clearly how King Roger was wholeheartedly catholic, and how he burned with zeal and enthusiasm for the Christian faith, the evidence of the following events makes clear.[49]

King Roger had a certain eunuch called Philip, whom the king valued and trusted because of his good service to him. Having found him faithful in deed and reliable in carrying out his business, he gave him precedence over everybody in his palace and appointed him as master of his household. As time went on Philip grew ever more valued and regarded, to such an extent that the king made him admiral of his fleet and sent him with it to Bône, which he took at sword point and sacked, before returning in triumph and glory to Sicily.

---

di Messina, ed. R. Starrabba (Documenti per servire alla storia di Sicilia, Ser. I.1, Palermo 1876–90), 43 no. 32.

47 Lucan, *De Bello Civili*, 1.70.

48 Actually 1154.

49 For discussion of what follows, Houben (2002), 109–13; Johns (2002), 215–17; Metcalfe (2009), 166–70.

But since he showed himself ungrateful to his creator for the benefits
he had received, and returned evil for good towards the Celestial King,
he rightly incurred the anger and indignation of the temporal monarch.
For under the cloak of the Christian name he served as a soldier of
the devil, and while pretending to behave as a Christian he was both
by conviction and behaviour completely a Saracen. He hated Christians and greatly loved pagans. He entered Christian churches unwillingly, but more frequently visited the synagogues of the evil doers and
provided them with oil to fuel their lights and other things which they
needed. He totally rejected Christian traditions; he continued to eat
meat on Fridays and in Lent, he sent envoys with gifts to the tomb of
Mahommed and commended himself to the prayers of the priests of
that place.

These and other of his wicked acts, committed under the shade of the
Christian name, came to the ears of King Roger. The latter, filled with
zeal for God but acting with his usual wisdom, had Philip summoned
to his court to answer for the aforesaid crimes. Trusting in the grace
and love of the king, he replied to his accusers with spirit and claimed
that the charges which had been made against him were false. However,
thanks to Divine justice, his accusers proved through the testimony
of trustworthy witnesses that what had been said was true. Once he
realised that he would be found guilty, and fearing the king's justice,
Philip began to seek pardon and beg the king for mercy, and promised
that in future he would be a genuine Christian. Then the king was lit
up by the flame of the faith. He burst into tears and said: 'My faithful
subjects, you should know that my heart is filled with deep grief, and
racked by anger, in that this servant [*minister*] of mine, whom I raised
from boyhood as a catholic, has because of his sins been revealed as a
Saracen, and as a Saracen has sheltered under the name of our faith
while he practised the works of the infidel. If he had indeed offended
our Majesty in other matters, if he had stolen part, even a large part,
of our treasure, then in memory of his past services he would still
have merited and obtained grace and pardon. But since by what he has
done he has chiefly offended God, and has given to others material and
example for sin, I could not pardon either my own son or one of my
close relations for such an injury to our faith and offence to the Christian religion. In this verdict the whole world will come to realise that
I am consumed by love for the Christian faith and I will not hesitate to
punish even my servants for injuries to it. Let the laws therefore rise up,
our government arm itself with the sword of equity, and let them cut
down the enemy of the faith with the sword of justice, and through this

the unbelievers shall be struck with terror'. Then the counts, justiciars, barons and judges who were there present, acknowledging the justice of what the king said, gathered together and considered the issue for a long time, and then pronounced this sentence: 'We have decreed that Philip, who has brought the Christian name into disrepute and under a pretence of the faith has led the life of the infidel shall be burned by the avenging flames. He who has been unwilling to receive the fire of charity shall incur the [actual] fire of burning. Let no relics of this most wicked man remain, but be turned into ashes by temporal fire while he goes to be burned for ever by the eternal fire'. Then, on the orders of the justiciars, his feet were bound to a wild horse and he was violently dragged to a lime pit which was in front of the palace; his feet were freed from the horse and he was thrown into the middle of the flames and immediately burned. All those who were accomplices and sharers in his iniquity were also given death sentences.[50]

It was thus most clearly revealed by this affair that King Roger was a most Christian and catholic prince, who to punish an injury to the faith, did not spare his own chamberlain whom he had brought up, but handed him over to the flames for its honour and glory.

---

50 The execution of Philip took place in the month of Ramadan 548AH (20 November–19 December 1153), as described by *The Chronicle of Ibn al-Athir for the Crusading Period, 1146–93*, 63–4, based on the lost Zirid chronicle of Ibn Shaddād.

GERMAN SOURCES FOR THE REIGN OF KING ROGER

The Annals of Erfurt 1135–7[1]

[These annals, covering the reign of Lothar of Supplinburg, 1125–37, were written by a monk of the monastery of St Peter of Erfurt, in Saxony, who may have been called Werner. The visit of the Greek envoys described here was also recorded by the so-called 'Saxon Annals', which gave a lengthy account of the expedition into southern Italy in 1137, also translated below.]

[1135] The emperor held his court at the city of Merseburg on the feast of St Peter in Chains [1 August]. … There came to the emperor at this same time a duke and a bishop sent by the King of Greece, with envoys from the Doge of Venice, asking for and seeking his judgment against a certain Roger, Count of Sicily, who had seized Africa (which is acknowledged to be the third part of the world) from the King of Greece, through force of arms and along with the pagans, and made it subject to his rule.[2] [Then] placing upon himself a royal diadem he had usurped the name of king, despoiled the Venetians and taken away from them various goods worth 40,000 talents. And he had alienated the whole of Apulia and Calabria from the Roman Empire, and committed other acts contrary to law and right. In consequence a large fleet was promised by the envoys to assist the army of the emperor, as well as innumerable regiments of soldiers, and a plentiful supply of money in gold and silver to finance these forces. Who could describe with how many and great gifts the Lord honoured the emperor at that time? The envoys from Greece brought gold and precious stones, with purple cloths of various shades, and many strong spices up to now unknown in this land. …

[1136] The emperor travelled to Italy a second time, and through Divine grace enjoyed wonderfully good fortune in his affairs. Indeed he

---

1 Translated from S. Petri Erphesfutenses Annales Continuatio, in *Monumenta Erphesfurtensia, Saec. XII, XIII, XIV*, ed. Oswald Holder-Egger (MGH SRG, Hanover 1899), 41–3.

2 As Houben (2002), 78–9, notes, this was a considerable exaggeration at this period, when King Roger's African conquests had barely begun, and the Byzantine Empire had anyway not held this region for many centuries. Was this entry actually written after the major North African conquests in 1146–8?

captured by force of arms Apulia, which Duke Roger of the Sicilians had formerly invaded, and he restored it to the jurisdiction of the Apostolic See. In this expedition Archbishop Bruno of Cologne died, and is buried in the city of Bari in Apulia.[3] ...

[1137] The Emperor Lothar returned from Italy, but when he entered the frontiers of Germany and while the princes were awaiting his arrival at Würzburg, he was taken ill and ended his days – his death ending his just rule over the whole kingdom. His body was carried back to Germany by the Empress Richenza, and was buried at the abbey of Königslutter, which he had built, on 31st December in the presence of the Saxon and Thuringian princes.[4]

The Saxon Annals[5]

[These annals, a lengthy account of German history from 741 to 1139, were written between 1148 and 1152. The identity of the author is unknown, though he almost certainly came from eastern Saxony. Scholars of a previous generation identified the author as Arnold, Abbot of Berge from 1119 and Abbot of Nienburg (in the diocese of Halberstadt) from 1134, who died in 1164. However, the most recent editor of the text considers this identification unlikely, not least because these two monasteries were only occasionally mentioned in the text. The earlier sections of these annals are almost entirely derivative, although they display very wide reading, and the use of a very large number of earlier historical works, on the part of the author. The earlier sections rely especially on the work of Regino of Prüm, Thietmar of Merseburg and Ekkehard of Aura. Only the account after 1124, which is very favourable to Lothar and his son-in-law Henry the Proud of Bavaria, is of much independent value, and even that may have been heavily dependent on a now lost set of Annals from Paderborn.]

[1135] The emperor celebrated the feast of St Peter in Chains at Nienburg and the feast of St Lawrence [10 August] and the Assumption of St Mary [15 August] at Merseburg. There came there the dukes

---

3 Bruno [II], Archbishop of Cologne 1131–7, son of Count Adolf III of Berg, died on 29 May 1137 (see below).

4 Lothar had converted Königslutter (between Brunswick and Heldensleben in Saxony), previously a house of canonesses, into a Benedictine monastery c.1135, *Annalista Saxo*, p. 599.

5 Translated from *Annalista Saxo*, 599, 602, 606–10.

of Poland and Bohemia and their leading men,[6] and the ambassadors of the Greek emperor bringing honourable gifts with them, requesting peace and friendship with the emperor, and seeking help against the tyrant Roger who had greatly harmed part of the Roman Empire and the land of the Greeks. Having rewarded them as was proper, he sent them back home, accompanied by his ambassadors Bishop Anselm of Havelburg and others.[7] ...

[1136] The Emperor Lothar held a general court and gloriously celebrated the Assumption of St Mary at Würzburg;[8] from there he intended to travel to Italy to re-establish imperial power there, in particular against Roger the tyrant of Sicily, who had seized many towns in Apulia and kept them under his authority with towers and other fortifications. Thus he summoned the princes of the various regions and their followers, who swore a long time prior to the aforesaid expedition [to take part]. The chief among them were the archbishops Bruno of Cologne, Adalbero of Trier and Conrad of Magdeburg,[9] with many other bishops and abbots, and Duke Henry of Bavaria, Duke Conrad the brother of Duke Frederick of Swabia,[10] and Conrad Margrave of Saxony,[11] with a great crowd of other princes and nobles. Having therefore settled the affairs of the German kingdom for the time being, the emperor set out on his journey with those named above, nor did he permit his army to plunder. ...

6 Bolesław III 'Wrymouth', Duke of Poland 1102–38; Sobiesław I, Duke of Bohemia 1125–40.

7 Anselm, Bishop of Havelburg 1129–55, and Archbishop of Ravenna 1155–8, a Premonstratensian and one of the leading scholars of the day, who went on a second diplomatic mission to Constantinople in 1154; for whom see Lees (1998), especially 42–7 on this first embassy.

8 On 15 August. Lothar was at Würzburg two days earlier, when he issued a privilege for the abbey of Stavelot, *Lothar Diplomata*, 144–6 no. 93.

9 Adalbero, Archbishop of Trier 1131–52; his family were lords of Montreuil, near Verdun in Lotharingia. He was commemorated by two biographies, one in verse, the other (by a cleric called Baldric) in prose, *Gesta Alberonis Metrica and Gesta Alberonis Archiepiscopi*, ed. Georg Waitz, MGH SS viii.236–60. According to the latter, 251, he was summoned to provide 100 knights for the expedition to Italy, but brought only 67. His service in the 1136/7 campaign was praised in *Conradi III Diplomata*, 43 no. 26 (May 1139). Conrad, Archbishop of Magdeburg 1134–42, son of Count Gebhard II of Querfurt (killed fighting the Bohemians in 1126), was a cousin of the Emperor Lothar. For his election, *Annalista Saxo*, 597, and for his pontificate Claude (1975), ii.39–53. For these archbishops and Lothar, see also Petke (1985), 234, 245–7, 254–7.

10 The future King Conrad III (1138–52), his brother Duke Frederick (d.1145) was the father of the future emperor, Frederick Barbarossa (1152–90).

11 Conrad of Wettin (d.1157) whom Lothar, as duke of Saxony, had helped to succeed to the margravate of Meissen in 1124, and whom he had then also appointed as Margave of Lausitz in 1131.

[Lothar crossed the Alps via the Brenner Pass, meeting the nobles of northern Italy near Verona on 22 September. A lengthy account follows of his dealings with the cities of northern Italy over the winter of 1136/7.]

[1137] ... The emperor celebrated Easter at Fermo,[12] and then shifted his camp to Ferentillo, the inhabitants of which, who were preparing to rebel, he drove from the town. Here [too] dispute arose between the Saxons and Bavarians, in which Archbishop Conrad and his vassals [*fideles*] were despoiled, but with the help of the Margrave Conrad the Bavarians were defeated, plundered and put to flight. A noble called Nithard was killed [there].

Then having sorted out matters in [the Kingdom of] Italy, the emperor entered Apulia. He held a court [*placitum*] near the River Tronto where he received into his grace and took homage from the margraves Thomas and Matthew, with their lord the palatine [count?] William, a very illustrious man.[13] Then he went through the frontier of this palatinate to the city of Castelpagano, a town with a citadel rendered impregnable both because of its natural elevation and man-made fortifications. Everybody was very keen to take this, but the townspeople willingly surrendered because of their hatred for Roger and the heavy oppression they had received from the citadel. As a result the terrified garrison were forced to surrender. Their commander, Richard, returned to Roger not long afterwards, and the latter ordered him to be blinded. However a certain other man called Richard, who received the citadel from the emperor as his successor, promised to betray it to Roger in the hope of financial reward. When the money was paid the latter ordered him to be hanged next to it, not unjustly, as a reward for his treachery.

Meanwhile the emperor sent Duke Conrad with part of the army to storm the *castellum* of Rignano, the inhabitants of which came out with cries of terror and surrendered. Duke Conrad went from there to Monte Gargano and besieged it for three days until the emperor arrived with his army and attacked the town and its citadel. One of the garrison who surpassed all the others in courage and daring was killed, and all the others surrendered. From the church which is above this *castellum*, hidden away near the mountain top, they took a great store of gold, silver, and precious stones and textiles which Duke Simon of

12 On 11 April. On Good Friday (9 April) Lothar issued a privilege at Fermo for a monastery in Milan, *Lothar Diplomata*, 184–5 no. 115.

13 Count William of Loritello. The *placitum* was probably that referred to in *Chron. Casauriense*, 886.

Dalmatia had deposited there.[14] After humbly praying to the Archangel Michael, the emperor went on to Troia, then to Canne and after this to Barletta. The citizens of this last town dared to sally forth against the army to show off their courage; many of them were killed and many others captured, most of whom had their noses and other members cut off – the others fled and just managed to escape back into the town. However, the emperor was content with the defeat he had inflicted upon them, and hurried onwards, abandoning an attack upon these towns to another time. When he later returned the citizens were so afraid that they left them deserted of their own accord and fled away to various places.

The emperor then went to Trani, the inhabitants of which received him joyfully. They first of all went out to him, then encouraged by his good faith towards them, they destroyed Roger's citadel. Thirty-three of the latter's ships appeared, sent by him as a protection for his men, but of these eight sank and their crews were lost. The rest immediately disappeared in flight. There, on the fourth day before Pentecost, Archbishop Bruno of Cologne had himself bled; three days later he suddenly died.[15] Hugh was put in his place.

Meanwhile Duke Henry of Bavaria, whom we mentioned earlier, was sent by the emperor along the Via Cassia to assist Margrave Engelbert.[16] He arrived in the plain of Mugello where he defeated Count Guido (who had rebelled against the margrave), and destroying three of his *castella* he forced him to be reconciled to his lord. He then took him along to Florence which he besieged and forced to surrender. Then he marched through Pistoia to San Genesio. He attacked and subdued its inhabitants and those of the *castellum* of Fucecchio who were [also] in rebellion, and he destroyed the tower at Capiano as it was a den of thieves who wickedly plundered travellers. Then he set off for Lucca, a hard and difficult march on which many men were lost, and prepared to besiege that city, but some bishops and the Abbot of Clairvaux acted as mediators and the duke was bought off with a large sum of money. The citizens were however forced into this by their fear of the Pisans, for the latter were their [habitual] enemies who had taken this opportunity to seek the duke's aid to destroy both the city and Monte S. Maria where the citizens had hoped to take refuge. After this sum was

---

14 The famous pilgrim shrine of St Michael on Monte Gargano.

15 On 29 May.

16 Engelbert of Spanheim, from the family of the Dukes of Carinthia, whom Lothar had appointed as Margrave of Tuscany in 1135. He was then quite young: he died in 1173.

paid the duke moved his camp to Siena which he attacked, ravaging the countryside round about. He destroyed another nearby *castrum*, and then directed his march towards the town of Grosseto, to which he sent envoys to claim the service customarily owed to the emperor. They were however greeted with contempt and threatened both that stones would be thrown at them and that they would be attacked in the open field. Because of this he laid siege to the town on all sides. He attacked with his siege engines a very strongly fortified *castrum* which put up a fierce resistance, and captured it, which led the town's inhabitants to become so frightened that they surrendered. There the duke met Pope Innocent, whom he received honourably, took with him as he went from city to city, and lent him his support against his adversaries. He went to Viterbo where the majority [of the citizens] favoured Innocent but the more resolute supported Peter Leone. He first destroyed the nearby town and 'imperial market' of S. Valentino; and at last the people of Viterbo, heeding the pope's warnings and terrified of the duke, surrendered themselves and paid 3,000 talents. However a tremendous dispute arose there between the pope and the duke, for the former claimed this money for himself because of his ownership of the city, while the latter claimed it by the laws of war.[17] They then went on to Sutri where they deposed the bishop as a supporter of Peter Leone, and they substituted in his place his chaplain, Abbot John of Fulda [?*Vuldensis*].

The duke then marched through Roman territory and into the Campania where he laid siege to Montecassino and forced it to surrender. He then marched on to Capua. But when he decided to lay siege to it, its prince (who had accompanied him on the expedition) gave him 4,000 talents to preserve the city unharmed. He proceeded onwards, destroying those of the neighbouring towns and *castella* which had dared to rebel, and finally they arrived at Benevento. Its citizens threatened them in a hostile manner, but the duke defeated them, killing many and capturing even more. He restored the pope to his position there. The latter deposed two cardinals who had taken part in the schism of Peter Leone and had them confined to a monastic cloister. The duke marched on to Troia, plundered it and took a number of prisoners. He and the pope then sought out the emperor who at that time, that is before the feast of Pentecost, had entered Bari and was encamped there around the very strong citadel which Roger had built to hold down the city. The army launched vigorous attacks upon it with siege engines. There were heavy casualties on both sides, but for a long time they could not

---

17 Innocent II was at Viterbo from 26 March until 17 April 1137, J-L 7832–36.

take the citadel. There Count Siegfried was hit by an arrow and killed.[18] Finally, after working hard with a number of machines, the emperor's knights and the Bariots managed to undermine the walls of the towers and made them collapse. Having penetrated inside they killed [almost] everyone there; only a few were taken prisoner.

On the day of Pentecost, as the pope celebrated a solemn mass at Bari in the presence of the emperor, bishops and princes, a golden crown was seen descending from the sky over the monastery of St Nicholas.[19] Over it was a dove, and under it a thurible with incense was borne, and going before it two lighted wax candles were seen. Also, Archbishop Bruno of Cologne was solemnly buried there: in his place Hugh, the dean of that church was appointed and there he received pontifical benediction and his *pallium* from the pope.[20]

Roger sent messengers seeking the emperor's grace, and he promised him a huge sum of money and to hand over his son to him as a hostage if the emperor would grant the principality of Apulia to his other son. However the emperor was more concerned with the peace of the Church than with money, and he flatly refused to hand over that province to a semi-pagan tyrant.

After spending four weeks at that city the emperor returned to Trani and then went to Melfi.[21] Forty armed knights made a sortie from the town into the hills to scout, but they were surprised by the army. Some were killed and the rest fled. Seeing this, the citizens went out to help them, but 300 more were killed, others captured, and the rest turned tail. As the emperor began the siege the next day the citizens surrendered.

At that time in Germany Archbishop Adalbert of Mainz died and most of that city was burned down. Adalbert the younger received the archbishopric.[22] In that year many places were devastated by fire,

18 Count Siegfried of Heinsburg.

19 Pentecost was on 30 May. His presence at Bari that day is also mentioned by the *Annales Magdeburgenses*, MGH SS xvi.186. The church of St Nicholas was founded in 1087 to house the saint's relics taken from Myra by Bariot seamen.

20 Hugh of Sponheim, dean of Cologne since 1127 and also Provost of St Maria, Aachen, since 1129, Petke (1985), 259.

21 Innocent II can be attested at Bari from 30 May until 21 June 1137, J-L 7839–44.

22 Adalbert [II] of Saarbrücken, Archbishop of Mainz 1109–37, was a key political figure in early twelfth-century Germany, and had been one of those most responsible for the election of Lothar as king in 1125. He died on 23 June 1137. After some delay he was succeeded by his nephew, Adalbert [III], archbishop 1138–41, whom Anselm of Havelberg commemorated in a verse biography, written very shortly after his death, *Vita Adelberti II Mogunti*, in *Bibliotheca Moguntina*, ed. Philip Jaffé (Bibliotheca Rerum Germanicarum 3, Berlin 1866), pp. 565–603.

namely Mainz, Speyer, Strassburg and the monasteries and most of
the town of Goslar. The monk Richbert of the cell of Wanlefsrode was
murdered.

The Emperor Lothar celebrated the feast of the Apostles [29 June] at
Melfi. There Archbishop Hugh of Cologne had himself bled, and four
days later, on 30th June, he died. He was buried in the abbey there.[23]
The emperor made his camp in the hills around Melfi, where some
people stirred up a great disturbance with the intention of killing the
pope, cardinals and the [Arch]bishop of Trier. Those involved thought
that they intended to prolong the time of their stay in every single
place and by doing this delay their own return home. The emperor was
woken up by the riot, mounted his horse and intervened, punishing
the guilty severely. Coming down from the hills he went to the royal
abbey of Vulture where he was honourably received,[24] gave gifts there
and went on to Potenza where he appointed the Bishop of Regensburg as chancellor to replace the Archbishop of Cologne.[25] Then he
sent on Duke Henry, the Margrave Adalbert[26] and other valiant men to
besiege Salerno. They reached there, but having very few archers, they
were unable to get through the narrow pass. They sent an envoy to the
Pisans to request archers with whom they might drive the enemy away
from the pass.

At that time the Pisans had on the emperor's behalf attacked the mighty
and most powerful city of Amalfi and made it subject to the empire.
They then launched an attack on Naples to liberate it from Roger, who
had been besieging it for a long time and had reduced it to a catastrophic
state of hunger. But hearing of their arrival and of the siege of his
city, he had hastened to relieve that and had abandoned the aforesaid
[city of] Naples. The Pisans then arrived there and sent the duke 500
archers. Gathering together their ships, along with eighty Genoese and
300 Amalfitan vessels, they blockaded Salerno from the sea with their
huge force. The duke meanwhile fixed his camp in the plain outside
the city. Though large numbers of their enemies often came out, they
drove them back every time they made a sortie. The duke forced those
attacking him to take refuge back in the city with many killed and a

---

23 Cf. *Annales Magdeburgenses*, MGH SS xvi.186, which also record the death of Bishop
   Adalbero of Basel.

24 The abbey of SS. Peter and Michael on Monte Vulture.

25 Heinrich of Wolfrathausen, Bishop of Regensburg 1132–55, who later took part in the
   Second Crusade.

26 Probably Alberto Malaspina, Margrave of Liguria.

smaller number captured. Once they had joined forces with the Pisans, they launched heavy attacks both by land and sea, while the emperor travelled from Potenza via Avellino and captured the *castrum* of San Severino before arriving at Salerno. The Pisans built at great expense a wonderful siege engine which threw stones and demolished the walls and towers of the city, which led to its capture.

The Assumption of St Mary [15 August] was celebrated there, and the emperor returned to San Severino where he and the pope argued for a considerable time as to which of them would grant rule over Apulia to the man seeking it; but finally they decided that they would both grant it to Duke Rainald [*sic*]. They then went to Benevento where they consulted with the duke about settling various matters in Apulia. They urged him to recruit as many German knights as he could [to fight] against Roger, so that their strength of heart and endurance in military campaigns might reinforce the bravery of the Latins.

Soon he had gathered some 800 of them, and they returned to Melfi under the command of Richard, Reginald's [*sic*] brother,[27] and Alexander.[28] They arrived at Acerenza which Alexander captured from William by a ruse, namely by a rumour that the emperor was coming. The garrison fled in fear and the knights captured the *castrum* and pursued the fleeing William whom they captured and hanged. They also took his wife and another 300 of Roger's knights, as well as 200 whom they captured in the town. After doing this, they were helped by the Bariots and the people of other nearby towns to rescue Monopoli which had been besieged by Roger. They besieged Brindisi with the same army, the inhabitants handed over the town, and they stormed and captured the citadel, drowning its garrison and capturing twenty-five ships.

The emperor however went from Benevento to Capua, and then across the Campania to Montecassino, the unworthy abbot of which he deposed and substituted another in his place. He restored to this church many estates and *castella* which it had lost, partly by force and partly through legal judgment. Here the bishop of Concordia died and was buried.[29] The emperor then went to Palestrina, where the town sited below [the citadel] was a nest of robbers who plundered the pilgrims going to the tombs of the Apostles. The knights attacked the town with a great force of archers and captured it, along with the citadel;

27 That is, Richard of Rupecanina, brother of Duke Rainulf.
28 Probably Alexander of Chiaromonte.
29 Herman, Bishop of Concordia (in the Veneto) 1121–37.

the citizens were driven out, and they took away the vast plunder that
had been amassed there. Count Giso of Hesse died and was buried at
Palestrina.[30] From there passing Tivoli, they went to Farfa, where the
emperor restored many *castella* and estates to the abbot of the church
there, which had been violently stolen by Peter Leone and others.[31] The
army also captured a certain great and opulent town that lay near there,
whose inhabitants had resisted and insulted it, and set fire both to the
town and to its citadel. No small number of men perished in various and
violent ways. After this the pope with the agreement of the emperor
and princes honourably left them.[32]

*[The account continues with Lothar's journey back through northern Italy to
the Alps, where he died at Breitenwang on 3 December 1137.]*

30 Giso V, Count of Gudensberg 1122–37.

31 Atenulf, Abbot of Farfa 1125–44, had been elected with the support of Honorius II and
   had been a supporter of Innocent II during the papal schism; in return the latter had made
   him a cardinal. Hence it was hardly surprising that Anacletus and his supporters had taken
   over much of the abbatial property. See Stroll (1997), 248–54.

32 Before they parted, Innocent issued a privilege for the archbishopric of Magdeburg on 2
   October 1137, Claude (1975), ii.43.

THE MONTECASSINO CHRONICLE
OF PETER THE DEACON[1]

(96) After ruling over his duchy for almost sixteen years, Duke William died, and the whole family line descended from Robert Guiscard ended with him. On his death Roger, the son and heir of the late Count Roger of Sicily, brother of the aforesaid Duke Robert Guiscard, occupied the duchy. The pope marched with an army against him, but finally they came to an agreement and he confirmed the duchy to him. At this time Prince Jordan died and his son Robert succeeded him in the princely office.[2] The latter granted a privilege to this monastery, remitting the *dazio* owed by the men of Casa Gentiana, concerning escheats, [granting?] twenty *modia* of land in the territory of S. Mauro ad Casale, and including fishing rights both in the sea and the river throughout the territory of Castel Volturno, [confirming] what had been given by his father Jordan II, his uncles Richard II and Robert, his grandfather Jordan and great-grandfather Richard. He also allowed men to come to live on the land of St Benedict and granted other things to the monastery. A penalty of 100 pounds of gold was placed on this.[3] Also Count Robert of Molise had a privilege drawn up for this monastery, concerning a half share of the *castrum* of Serracapriola, which is under the jurisdiction of the diocese of Larino, placing on this a penalty of 100 pounds of gold.[4] Furthermore Duke Roger gave a privilege to St Benedict [confirming] what Duke Robert and his wife Sichelgaita, and Duke Roger and his son William, had given in Apulia, Calabria, the principality of Salerno and Amalfi, and the concessions of princes, barons and others of the faithful. This was done in the year 1130 by the hand of Warner, Dean of Mazzara, and had a penalty of 300 pounds of gold placed upon it.[5]

(97) Meanwhile Pope Honorius departed this life, and Gregory, Cardinal

---

1 The following extracts comprise *Chron. Cas.* IV.96–106, and IV.127–8, pp. 556–68, 603–4.

2 On 19 December 1127, *Necrologio di Cod. Cas. 47*, 43.

3 Gattula, *Accessiones*, 242–3 (March 1128).

4 Leccisotti (1947), 89–90 (June 1128). The use at this date of the title 'Count of Molise', which is in the charter text, is suspicious, and suggests that this document may have been forged or interpolated.

5 *Roger II Diplomata*, 40–2 no. 14 (issued at Palermo on 30 December 1129).

deacon of Sant'Angelo, was elected as Pope Innocent II and Peter, Cardinal priest of St Calixtus, as Pope Anacletus. Innocent however remained in the City with the bishops and cardinals who supported him only for a little time. He then travelled to the city of Pisa, leaving Bishop Conrad of Sabina as his vicar in the City.[6] Meanwhile Peter granted a crown to Duke Roger of Apulia, confirming to him by a privilege the principality of Capua and the duchy of Naples, along with Apulia, Calabria and Sicily, and by appointing him king attracted him to his party. He ordered the bishops and abbots in the area under his jurisdiction to do homage to him. At this same time Prince Robert, whom we mentioned above, had a privilege drawn up for this place, as he had done before, assigning it 50 *tarì* from the forest and the harbour of the mill which is at Cazoli on the River Volturno, along with harbour [rights] on both banks of the river.[7] After this the aforesaid prince went to Pisa, and King Roger marched on the principality. Because of this the prince furnished himself with a Pisan fleet and came to Naples. The Aversans submitted to his rule. But when King Roger marched against him he fled, and the king reduced Aversa to ashes and gave the Principality of Capua to his son Anfusus. (At this time Archbishop Hubert of Pisa, the legate of the Apostolic See, made a privilege for this monastery concerning St George de Baray and St Maria de Gennos.)[8] Pope Innocent entered the land of the Swabians and Lotharingians. He was met by King Lothar near Liège, followed the ancient custom in confirming the staff and ring to him and also granted the land of Countess Matilda to him.[9] King Lothar then came to Rome, received his crown from Innocent, and went home again. While in his view (as I think) the whole Roman world was quiet and peaceful and its subjects lay under his rule, he received regular letters from Pope Innocent at

---

6 For Conrad of Sabina, see *Romuald*, note 40, above.

7 Gattula, *Accessiones*, 245–6 (March 1132), although the terms of the document are slightly different from those given here. The *tarì* was a gold coin of Islamic origin, equivalent to a quarter dinar, minted at Amalfi from the 960s and at Salerno from c.1012, which was the principal monetary unit of the Campania region, and indeed of much of the kingdom of Sicily during the twelfth century. See Travaini (1995), 16–22, 153–82; Loud (1999c), 819–20.

8 This privilege was issued in 1135 to end a dispute between these Sardinian churches, *Italia Pontificia*, x.431–2 no. 6; full text in Erasmo Gattula, *Historia Abbatiae Casinensis* (Venice 1733), 353.

9 They met on 22 March 1131, *Annalista Saxo*, 593; *Annales Magdaburgenses*, MGH SS xvi.183–4. While Innocent was ready to excommunicate Lothar's opponents Frederick of Swabia and his brother Conrad (later King Conrad III), the emperor's wish to recover the right of investing bishops with ring and staff (surrendered by Henry V in the Concordat of Worms in 1122) was *not* granted.

Pisa, urging him to defend the crown of the Roman Empire from the
enemy's yoke and, as a truly energetic and clement Caesar to free the
Church from schism and restore it to peace, concord and unity. In the
year 1135 he raised a really immense army drawn from the whole
Roman Empire, and together with his wife the Empress Richenza he
entered Italy. Meanwhile terror and foreboding infected southern Italy,
and everybody asked everybody else what they ought to say or do.

(98) While this was going on the royal chancellor, Guarin, ordered
Joscelin, who was then in charge at Capua, to summon the Abbot of
Cassino[10] and when he arrived immediately to arrest him. However the
abbot learned of this and refused to come, sending back a message that
it was impossible for him to leave at this time. The chancellor became
more and more suspicious of him, and sent orders that he should come
to meet him at Capua as fast as possible, so that they might discuss
affairs of state with the barons of that land. However the abbot was now
in fact very ill, and because of this he refused to go to him. When he
recovered, before Christmas, he sent two brothers to the lord chancellor,
then staying at Benevento, with instructions to exaggerate the seriousness of his illness. The chancellor replied that after the celebration of
the feast the abbot should come to him at Capua, otherwise he himself
would come to the abbot. The brothers returned on the feast of St John
the Evangelist[11] and told everyone what they had heard. During their
journeys to and fro they had made inquiries about this summons among
the friends and subjects [*fideles*] of the monastery; the only answer
which they had heard was that the chancellor sought to arrest the abbot.
So the latter, who did not know what to do in this predicament, feigned
illness. The chancellor then came to Cassino as he had announced,
accompanied by the archbishop-elect of Capua[12] and Joscelin.

Meanwhile the bishop-elect of Aquino,[13] goaded by envy and intoxi-
cated by the poison of evil, sent a squire [*scutifer*] with a message to the
royal chancellor that the Abbot of Cassino was making preparations not
on their behalf, but rather against their interests, in order to receive the
Emperor Lothar and Pope Innocent. Even if they did not believe he was
telling the truth, they should demand the monastery of Cassino from
the abbot: if the latter surrendered it they would know that he was lying,

---

10 Seniorectus, Abbot of Montecassino 1127–37.

11 On 27 December.

12 William – see *Al. Tel.* III.31 [above, 118].

13 Guarin, Bishop of Aquino 1137–48. Aquino, 10 km. W of Montecassino, was the seat of
the diocese immediately bordering the *Terra Sancti Benedicti*.

but if he refused they could see for certain that he spoke the truth. But the man who delivered this letter knew what it contained. He went to the monastery and revealed what was in it to the abbot. The latter was given the letter by the squire, and on reading it found there just what he had been told. The chancellor arrived at San Germano with the elect of Capua and Joscelin, and Guarin, the elect of Aquino, came to them with the same purpose. They then sent deceitful orders to the abbot, telling him not to make excuses but to come down to them to arrange urgent matters of state, but he replied that he could not come because of his illness. However, he did send some of the senior men of the monastery to the chancellor, who in the latter's presence reproached the elect of Aquino for his aforesaid actions and demonstrated that he had been wholly and completely untruthful. When the elect denied that he had done this, they showed the letter and read out its contents in detail. He was then dumbfounded and had no idea how to make a rational response. However the royal representatives ignored what had occurred and, feigning anger, started to make frivolous remarks to the Cassinese [monks], insofar as they allowed the elect of Aquino to assert on oath that he had not come for this purpose, nor should credence be given [to the letter]. But a little while later those who 'conceived mischief'[14] compounded their evil by arresting the man who had carried the letter, torturing him and depriving him of his eyes. However, the elect who was afraid – indeed terrified by the angry threats of the townspeople – was escorted out of the city by Joscelin and returned to Aquino.

(99) At this same time a certain brother named John was paying his debt to nature and lay without the power of moving or speaking. Suddenly he revived and told them that he had seen Father Benedict and a multitude of deceased monks standing in the church when King Roger had entered this same church to carry off all the treasure from the church of Cassino. But when the king had reached the steps of the main church, the dead men who were some distance away in the church had rushed upon him and killed him. After he had said this, he added that: 'You should undoubtedly know that I have been speaking truthfully, for you should know that I shall soon leave this world. For if I live on after this, you will indubitably know that what I have told you is false'. After saying this, he fell asleep. Thus a certain brother: we who were present at this vision and keep it in our memory see that it has been all but completely fulfilled, for we see that almost all the treasure of this place has been taken away through the action of King Roger. All

14 Job, 15:35.

this took place on the Vigil of the Epiphany.[15]

(100) After this the abbot and brothers decided that twelve of the senior members of the monastery should go barefoot to the town, where the aforesaid chancellor and the archbishop-elect of Capua were staying, and beg them humbly for a breathing space during which the brothers who were in the obediences might be summoned, that they might discuss the issue with them as one and thus be able to provide a suitable response about the above matter. Once this decision had been taken, the whole congregation followed them with groans and lamentation right up to the monastery gate. After they had departed, the [remaining] brothers went back to the church of St Benedict. Who can describe how many tears were shed there? For everyone prostrated themselves on the ground and struck their heads on the pavement, begging the Lord with heartfelt lamentation, that in his mercy He might spare this place. Then turning to Blessed Benedict as if they saw him present, they said: 'Most worthy and holy Father, who after going the way of all flesh are more present to your disciples than if you were still alive, you have promised that you will be here in the future. Thus we adjure your holiness through the Father, the Son and the Holy Spirit that, just as you promised us, you will protect this place and defend it from all evils'. After this the brothers took up the wood of the life-giving Cross,[16] the arm of the holy Apostle and Evangelist Matthew and [that] of Maurus the holy Confessor of Christ,[17] and decided to process with litanies through the churches situated within the monastery. When they had made their prayers of supplication and praise to the Lord in the church of St Martin and finished their farewells, they left and went to the church of St Stephen.[18] Then one of the brothers went before them to open the doors of the basilica, but he found them bolted, for the brother who looked after that church was one of those twelve who

---

15 On 5 January. Roger confiscated the abbey treasures in 1143, *Annales Casinenses*, MGH SS xix.310.

16 This relic was brought from Jerusalem c.990 by Leo, brother of Aligern, Abbot of Monte-cassino 949–86, and enclosed in a silver reliquary by Abbot Theobald (1022–35/7), *Chron. Cas.* II.11, 53; pp. 189, 265. For this, Willard (1976).

17 A disciple of St Benedict, mentioned by Gregory the Great, *Dialogi Libri IV*, ed. U. Moricca (FSI, Rome 1924), II.3–4, 6–8, pp. 84–7, 89–93, whose life and *translatio* was written by Abbot Odo of Glanfeuil in the ninth century, and then added to and emended by Peter the Deacon, Caspar (1909), 50–2; Bloch (1986), ii.972–3, 982–9, 1025–33.

18 The church of St Martin within the precinct had been rebuilt during the 1070s by Abbot Desiderius, and that of St Stephen, located outside the monastery gate, under Abbot Oderisius I (1087–1105) being re-dedicated in 1103, *Chron. Cas.* III.34, IV.23, pp. 409–10, 490.

had gone to the chancellor, and he had forgotten to leave the key of the church but had taken it with him.

The man who had gone ahead to open the church returned, told them what had happened and said that the people who had previously set out ought to return. Meanwhile everyone else was running about and similarly discovering locked doors. However, the brother who was carrying the cross was unaware of what had happened. Exhorting those who were following him, he came to the doors of the church, and through Divine assistance the doors opened as soon as the handles were touched. Hence they rejoiced in some small measure and gave thanks to God, and then with complete devotion and heartfelt contrition began once more the interrupted litanies and returned to the church of Father Benedict, and so they performed the masses of the day with lamentation and sadness. And at that time those words spoken by the Prophet were fulfilled: 'the day of your rejoicing shall be turned to lamentation'.[19]

When the brothers who had been sent to the chancellor came to that place where Father Benedict had spoken once a year with his sister,[20] the dean and those who had gone with him earlier on the same mission learned of their coming and sent a message back to the monastery telling them that because of what they had done the chancellor was rather roused to anger than inclined to mercy. For, after hearing that the brothers were processing through the churches of Almighty God with the arm of St Maurus begging for mercy, the chancellor became puffed up by pride and started to utter many threats against the monks, saying that he would 'cut off their garments in the middle, even to their buttocks',[21] and their lips and noses, and like another Nicanor he uttered words of blasphemy against God and his saints,[22] saying that the hope which the monks had in Benedict and Maurus was in vain and would rather bring them harm than be to their advantage. After this, he became furiously angry and sent letters to the inhabitants of the Campania, Samnium, Apulia, Lucania and Calabria, instructing them to come as speedily as they could with all sorts of war engines to besiege and capture the monastery of Cassino. Realising that the chancellor

19 Tobit, 2:6.

20 For this, Gregory the Great, *Dialogi*, II.33, pp. 125–6. The church on this spot, dedicated to St Scholastica, had almost certainly been destroyed by Muslim raiders in 883, and its site has not been identified, although it was clearly close to the main monastery, Bloch (1986), ii.647.

21 II Samuel, 10:4.

22 Cf. I Maccabees, 7:34–8.

was planning his death and the seizure of the abbey, the abbot discussed the matter with a very few people and sent a message to Landulf of San Giovanni,[23] who was at that time supporting the emperor, telling him to come and receive the monastery of Cassino under his protection, and to defend it against those who sought to seize it. Since this could not be done by day, the message was sent during the night. Oaths were made on both sides, and on the third day after the feast of the Epiphany, which was a Friday,[24] the knights of the aforesaid Landulf were brought into the monastery, and its fortifications were handed over to them. After this Landulf himself arrived at Cassino, bringing the utmost reassurance to the abbot and brothers, and greatly unsettling their enemies. When the chancellor heard of Landulf's arrival, he abandoned the town of Aquino where he had been staying, crossed the River Liri at Sant'Angelo in Theodice and went to Mignano, where he was taken seriously ill.[25] There he ordered a notary to write letters to the effect that everyone who dwelt in King Roger's kingdom should come to capture the monastery of Cassino. But while he was busy trying to achieve this, he suddenly died. Thereafter the abbot decided with the brothers that for three days they should beg for the clemency of Almighty God, that he might out of his overflowing pity grant peace and safety to the abbey of Cassino. And since they could not observe silence because of the noise and disturbance of these days, they decreed that for three successive nights the whole Psalter should be sung in the church after Compline. But before they began this three-day period, the abbot rose up in chapter and according to the custom of the monastery sought pardon and made confession of his faults. Similarly all the brothers after him confessed that they had failed in their observance of the rule of Father Benedict, and then the abbot granted them pardon for all the excommunications made in the abbey of Cassino, and absolved them for any matter in which they had offended.

(101) During these days a certain brother named Bonus, tired out after the early morning service in the church of the blessed protomartyr Stephen, fell asleep. The blessed Benedict 'made himself known unto

---

23 Lord of S. Giovanni Incarico in the upper Liri valley 20 km. W of Montecassino, with which he was closely allied, he came of a family of Lombard nobles who had collaborated with the Normans. He apparently married Peter the Deacon's sister. He died in September 1143. Hoffmann (1971a), 64–73.

24 On 8 January.

25 Sant'Angelo in Theodice, 5 km. S of Montecassino, was one of the most important *castella* in the *Terra Sancti Benedicti*, though its inhabitants were sometimes restive under abbatial rule, e.g. *Chron. Cas.* II.68, IV.79, pp. 305, 543–4. Mignano, 18 km. SE of Montecassino, was the site of the encounter between King Roger and Innocent II in July 1139.

him in a vision'[26] and said: 'You have suffered great inconvenience and disturbance, and huge damage to your property through your actions, but "be strong in the Lord, and in the power of his might",[27] since soon my house will be restored and returned to its original condition. I order you beseech the most blessed Maurus most fervently in your prayers, since through his intervention you will undoubtedly be freed from the pressing danger and disturbance'. With these words he disappeared. The brother awoke and told the abbot and brothers everything that he had seen and heard. The brothers in chapter decided unanimously that every Sunday on the entry to the church after the antiphon to the blessed Benedict they should add the antiphon to the blessed Maurus, and similarly on all feast days in which the collect was said, so that his antiphon and prayer were said on all these days. Meanwhile all our lands except for the *castrum* of Cassino abandoned their fealty to the abbot and brothers.[28] The men of the *castrum* of Sant'Angelo were the instigators and the cause of this process, for they were the first to receive the monastery's enemies within their *castrum* and they began the attack on the abbey of Cassino. After this Bertulf the *mansionarius*, who was a German, and Atenulf, known as the Marsian, were because of this sent to the Emperor Lothar. Then all the obediences throughout the Campania, Piceno, Samnium, Lucania and Calabria were seized and taken away from the jurisdiction of the abbey of Cassino. The chancellor who was the cause and agent of this evil met his end in Salerno, on the seventeenth day after he had come here on the eve of the Ephiphany, calling out 'Benedict and Maurus, why are you killing me?' After he had repeated this many times over, he left this life.[29]

(102) At this time a certain brother Crescentius, of the Roman nation, saw in a vision a lake of great size and the colour of fire, the waves of which seemed to be carried up to Heaven; and in these waves he saw the chancellor's soul being raised up high into the air and then plunged once more into the lower depths. He saw two monks standing next to this lake, and he was asked by them whose soul it was that he saw being afflicted with such awful suffering. The brother replied that he did not know. To this the one who seemed to be the older of the two replied, saying: 'This is the soul of Guarin the chancellor, and the reason that he

26 Numbers, 12:6.

27 Ephesians, 6:10.

28 The *castrum* of Cassino was probably S. Pietro in Monasterio, at the southern foot of Monte Cassino and about 2 km. from S. Germano, a settlement that was abandoned in the early sixteenth century.

29 On 21 January 1137.

is suffering so much is because of the disturbance and tribulation which he has caused to the monastery of Cassino'. The brother then asked him who he himself was, who could explain such matters. The other replied that he was Brother Benedict. The brother woke from his dream and was adamant that he had seen and heard this, invoking God and his saints as witnesses. Meanwhile some of our people, against the abbot's wishes, started to negotiate a peace agreement with those who were of the king's party, with Bishop Richard of Gaeta acting as intermediary.[30] So it happened that an oath was made by the obedientiaries on behalf of the brothers that there would be a peace agreement, and oaths were sworn by the other side [too] that there would be a peace. Thus the quarrelling and disturbance were suddenly set at rest – but more of this in the proper place.

(103) On the third day after these events had taken place, the aforesaid abbot was overcome by illness and finished his life on 4th February.[31] The dean had discussions with the brothers all through the night that he passed away as to how, before the news of his death became known, the men of the above-mentioned Landulf, who were garrisoning the monastery, might be got rid of. To this end they paid off their commanders and secured a safe-conduct from the royal bailiffs to allow them and their men to depart unharmed. At midday they marched out of the monastery with their weapons and returned to their homes. This was made possible because up to that moment the abbot's death had been kept secret. With the ninth hour now approaching, the burial office was celebrated and he was brought to the right-hand side near the entrance to the cemetery, next to the step, where the four pupils of the Blessed Benedict rest.

(104) But let us return to the matter in hand, from which I have wandered. While the abbot's coffin was [still] in the church, knights arrived, sent by Joscelin, the chamberlain of the Principality of Capua, ordering that nobody should presume to discuss the election of a new abbot without him being present. So it was postponed, while the monks complained and bickered until his eventual arrival. When he did come, they showed him the instructions of Father Benedict, as set out in the privileges, for the election of an abbot.[32] He replied

[marginal handwritten note: auth/ pow bner church]

---

30 Richard is attested as bishop 1124–37.

31 Cf. *Necrologio di Cod. Cas.* 47, 61.

32 The right of free election of the abbot had been confirmed to Montecassino in a whole series of papal privileges, notably by Nicholas II in 1059, Alexander II in 1067, Urban II in 1097, Paschal II in 1105 and 1112, and Calixtus II in 1122. See Cowdrey (1983), 56–9; for a full list of the privileges, *ibid.*, introduction, xli, table 1. The right of freely electing

that nothing which had been shown was of any value at the present time: 'Either wait until instructions [come] from my lord King Roger; or alternatively, hand over the fortress of Bantra[33] and then choose whomever you wish, provided that he first does fealty to the king'. But when the brothers said that they could not do this, he raised an army and confiscated all the *castra* of the monastery of Cassino from its jurisdiction.

This crisis had lasted for some six days when the brothers gathered together at the monastery on the feast of St Scholastica,[34] and discussed the election of an abbot. They were divided into [two] parties, one of which wanted to elect Rainald of Collimento (who afterwards held office as abbot), the other group supported Rainald of Etruria. After lengthy debate it became clear in the end to the senior monks [*priores*] that there was a split over the election, and so they sent messengers to [both] King Roger and to the Roman pontiff, then living at Pisa, informing them of what had happened to the monastery of Cassino and asking for their advice concerning this matter. But after both parties had absolutely refused to give way to the other, the supporters of Rainald of Collimento seized their candidate, placed him in the seat of Father Benedict and appointed him as abbot, even though the other group opposed this and refused to accept it. Indeed the others were extremely angry, and they secretly sent a messenger to Bertulf the *mansionarius* and Atenulf, the brothers of the monastery of Cassino whom Abbot Seniorectus had sent as envoys to the Emperor Lothar, informing them that Seniorectus had passed from this world and that this same Rainald had been elected, but in a disorderly and uncanonical manner, and against their wishes. They begged them to request the emperor and the pope, on behalf of the whole congregation, not to give their assent to Rainald's election and to appoint as abbot of the monastery of Cassino someone else from their ranks, claiming that they would rather destroy the monastery, or abandon it, rather than accept that man as abbot. When Rainald was fully informed of this, he made a secret peace deal with Joscelin and the other partisans of the king, [by which] he did fealty to the king and they confirmed the position of abbot to him. He then received the oath from the monastery's peasant tenants [*coloni*],

---

the abbot was also stressed in some of the forged documents of earlier popes produced in the early 1130s by Peter the Deacon, notably in a supposed bull of Pope Zachary of '748', *Italia Pontificia*, viii.121 no. †22.

33 Rocca Bantra (now Rocca d'Evandro), on the eastern edge of the *Terra Sancti Benedicti*, 14 km. SE of Montecassino.

34 On 10 February.

and was confirmed in the Cassinese abbacy by the son of Peter Leone, whose subdeacon he was.[35]

Meanwhile, the envoy who was carrying the letter arrived at Ravenna where the emperor was then staying, and he and his letter were brought to the Emperor Lothar by the aforesaid brothers.[36] They told him of what had happened to the church of Cassino, which was subject to the Roman emperor, how Abbot Seniorectus had died and how Rainald, who had done fealty to King Roger, had been chosen as abbot against the wishes of the majority, which had led to some of the brothers leaving the monastery to escape the hands of their enemies, and of all the disasters that had occurred. After they had burst into tears, to the distress of his courtiers, [they explained] that the abbey of Cassino had fallen into confusion and that all this had occurred because of its loyalty to the Roman Empire, in which (after God and Father Benedict) the church of Cassino placed all its trust. The Emperor Lothar was moved by compassion, and by the knowledge that the church of Cassino had been under the protection of his predecessors, but much more by his hatred for King Roger whom he considered the most deadly enemy of his empire. This made him more favourably disposed towards the brothers, and observing the decree which had been instituted by Pepin and Charlemagne he appointed them according to ancient custom to be among the chaplains of the Roman Empire.[37] Then he summoned the dukes, princes and margraves of the empire, told them of the benefits granted by his predecessors to the abbey of Cassino, and accused the aforesaid Rainald, charging him with being an avowed enemy of the Roman Empire since he had received confirmation of his abbatial position from an enemy of the empire, ignoring, and in contempt of, the emperor, from whom the church of Cassino had received towns, *castra* and all its property.

(105) At that same time Duke Henry of Bavaria, the emperor's son-in-law, on the latter's instructions and together with Pope Innocent, entered the Campania.[38] They pitched camp in the plain next to Monte Cassino,

---

35 That is, by Anacletus II.

36 Lothar was at Ravenna in mid-February 1137, having earlier celebrated the Purification of the Virgin Mary on 2 February at San Cassiano, near Imola, *Annalista Saxo*, 605.

37 These 'decrees' were only mentioned in the *Epitome Chronicorum Casinensium*, purportedly a ninth-century work, but in fact a forgery of Peter the Deacon, for which Caspar (1909), 111–21.

38 Henry 'the Proud', Duke of Bavaria from 1126, leader of the powerful South German Welf family, had married Lothar's daughter (and only child) Gertrude in May 1127. Innocent issued a bull from near Anagni, in the papal Campagna, 60 km. from Montecassino, on

and sent the pope's chaplain Richard, himself a monk of Cassino, to the monastery, telling them that if they were willing to receive them and show their obedience to Pope Innocent, then the latter would to the best of his ability cherish them as sons, brothers and companions, and they would always treat the monastery of Cassino as being under the protection and defence of the emperor. But Rainald would not lend his ear to this. The brothers wanted more than anything to drive him out of the monastery, if they were given the opportunity, but Rainald summoned them to chapter and persuaded them to remain loyal to King Roger and preserve their obedience to the son of Peter Leone, who would not fail to help them. Then he told them that he had received the abbot's position from them, not from anyone else. He would resign the abbacy on their command, if they so wished, but if they did not he would keep the post. All this was said with his mouth, not with his heart. For he had already sent in secret to Gregory, son of Atenulf of San Giovanni, telling him to come with his army to Cassino through the wood of Terelle, so that with the assistance of his troops he could hold on to the monastery in defiance of pope, duke and monks.[39]

When Gregory arrived, he and the abbot-elect made a sworn alliance. The defences of the monastery were handed over to him, and he and his knights launched a sudden attack on the pope's envoys. After he had put them to flight, he greatly heartened his men. But meanwhile the pope's representatives went to the town next to the mountain, forced the citizens to swear fealty to the emperor and thus returned to the camp. However, Rainald shut himself up in the monastery with Gregory, cutting down the crops and destroying everything that was outside the abbey, to ensure that nothing was left to feed either men or their horses. Some eleven days had passed when the duke, seeing not only that the property of the monastery of Cassino was being ruined but also that time was slipping away with these skirmishes, took counsel and summoned Rainald. He received a golden chalice and hostages in lieu of 400 pounds from him, and [in return] confirmed the abbot's position to him in the emperor's name, provided that he remained loyal to the latter. Giving safe-conduct to him and his men, he ordered that the emperor's banner be carried into the church of the Blessed Benedict, and then with great ceremony it was installed on the tower next door

---

6 May, J-L 7837, so they probably arrived near Monte Cassino two or three days later, marching down the Via Latina.

39 This Gregory, also known as Gregory *Paganus*, was a cousin of Landulf of S. Giovanni, who also held land in the papal Campagna, Hoffmann (1971a), 67–70. Terelle was on the northern slopes of Monte Cairo, some 7 km. NW of the monastery.

to the church. The next day he struck his camp and marched with his huge army on the town of Capua. There Rao the son of Rahel and Godfrey of Aquila appeared and submitted themselves and their men to the commands of the pope, Prince Robert and Duke Henry.[40] When the Capuans realised that the barons were all flooding over to the pope and duke, they flung themselves on the ground and sought pardon. This was granted to them, and they surrendered themselves, their property and their city to the lordship of these rulers. Once this had occurred, the entire Capuan principality abandoned its obedience to Roger and its men threw themselves at the pope's feet, promising to obey all his instructions. Many went over to them because of the friendship which they had with Prince Robert; some because of the reputation of these leaders and because of the rewards and benefices that they hoped they might receive from them; many because they considered them to be their rightful lords.

After restoring the Principality of Capua to Prince Robert, the emperor's son-in-law Henry and Pope Innocent pitched camp with their mighty army at the bridge of San Valentino next to Benevento. The duke and pope then sent envoys into the town with instructions that, unless the inhabitants wished to incur apostolic anathema and imperial wrath, they should surrender Benevento into their hands and go out into the market place outside the town. However, those in the city who were of the party of Peter Leone refused, and the envoys of Pope Innocent got nowhere. Negotiations broke down and they were expelled from the city, for Roger's knights then stationed in the town would not consent to any agreement. The latter soon mustered 500 knights and 3,000 infantry, and prepared their army to attack those outside the town. Because of this, the pope in his wrath against the Beneventans cast them out from the ranks of the Church, and ordered the duke and his army to march against them. But when the duke's squires [*scutiferi*] in the front line retreated, he realised that events were in the balance. He ordered his knights to cross the river, climb the hill on which the town was built and force an entrance through the *Porta Aurea*. There was however dispute within the city concerning what was going on, with some people saying that the town should be surrendered to Pope Innocent and that they should obey St Peter and his vicar as their forefathers had

---

40 Rao son of Rahel was lord of Teano, *Chron. Cas.* IV.44, p. 512; Gattula, *Accessiones*, 229 (April 1112), Gattula, *Historia*, 395 (March 1140); Cuozzo (1984), 237–8; Godfrey, who was lord of Sessa Aurunca and later (seemingly after 1139) Count of Fondi, was Rao's son-in-law; for him *Chron. Cas.* IV.90–1, pp. 551–3; *Cod. Dipl. Caietanus* ii.250–1 no. 323 (May 1132). Godfrey died on 14 January 1148, *Necrologio di S. Matteo*, 8.

done, while others said no and were determined to resist. Meanwhile the knights crossed the river and reached the town. When the Beneventans saw how their enemies had marched against them, they withdrew from the battle and sought safety in flight. Those of the duke's side instantly pursued them and entered the town with them, and it was in this way that they received the surrender of Benevento. Once they had gained this city, they marched on that of Troia in Apulia. This was surrendered by its citizens without a fight, and the nearby towns, the Gargano region and Siponto went over to their obedience.

(106) Meanwhile, at the same time the Emperor Lothar left Ravenna and restored his rule over the provinces of Umbria, Emilia, Flaminia and Piceno, reducing the towns there to obedience under the jurisdiction of the Roman Empire, and overthrowing those that resisted. When he came to the monastery of St Martin on the Saline, he was met by Transmund, provost of the Holy Liberator, who entreated him on behalf of the Cassinese congregation to order the return to the Blessed Benedict of its property in that region which had been alienated.[41] Lothar then marched his army against Bari, which is the capital of all Apulia, pitched his tents there and was welcomed by the townspeople. He began a full-scale attack upon the very strong citadel which King Roger had built. After attacking its rampart for a long time with his siege engines, and with heavy casualties on both sides, finally and with great difficulty he captured it and reduced it to the ground. He restored the rights of the Roman Empire over all the cities of Apulia, and after doing this he went to the town of Melfi in Apulia to rendezvous with the duke. After arriving there, he led his army to Salerno and ordered it to besiege it. During this time Bertulf and John, [two] brothers of the abbey of Cassino, charged the men of Siponto before this same emperor of imposing their rule over a wood belonging to the monastery which had been placed under the jurisdiction of its hospital.[42] The emperor heeded their prayers and granted them a sealed charter in which he ordered them to allow this wood to remain unharmed and in the hands of the monastery of Cassino then and in the future, unless they wished to incur his imperial wrath, and he placed a penalty of 1,000 *bizantei* on this, should they be tempted to infringe this decree.[43]

41 The Holy Liberator monastery on Monte Majella was the chief Cassinese dependency in the Abruzzi.

42 The abbey's pilgrim hospice on Monte Sant'Angelo, set up in 1098–1100, *Le Colonie Cassinesi in Capitanata* ii *Gargano*, ed. T. Leccisotti (Miscellanea Cassinese 15, 1938), 29–34 nos. 1–2.

43 This document no longer survives.

[A lengthy account follows of how Abbot Rainald and a delegation of monks were summoned to meet the emperor and Innocent II at Lagopesole in Lucania, where for more than a week in July 1137 they were examined about and criticised for their support of Anacletus. Peter claimed to have acted as the abbey's spokesman, and gave a detailed account of his debates with Cardinal Gerard of S. Croce, acting as Innocent's spokesman, and with 'a certain Cistercian abbot', who was almost certainly Bernard of Clairvaux. The monks were eventually allowed to return to Montecassino. Two months later pope and emperor came to the monastery, and although the emperor was sympathetic to the monks and initially hesitant, Innocent insisted that Rainald be deposed from his abbatial position, which sentence was pronounced on 18 September 1137. Further dispute followed as to whether the monks might make a free election of a new abbot, or whether they should be guided in their choice by Innocent's representatives. The emperor, we are told, supported the monks, and Pope Innocent eventually gave way and allowed them to elect whom they liked. The monks then chose Guibald, Abbot of Stavelot, a distinguished German abbot who had played a prominent role in the imperial army and was much favoured by Lothar, but who had also seemingly impressed the Cassinese monks by his appeals for calm and decorum amidst their troubles. He was duly installed as abbot, and left behind when the German army headed north. He was, however, in an increasingly vulnerable position as King Roger recovered the mainland.][44]

(**127**) ... But let me now return to the subject, from which I have digressed. It became known on reliable information that the former abbot, Rainald, had crossed the Straits of Messina with King Roger. He gathered an army from his relations and friends, and winning over the citizens he secured entry to S. Germano, intending to climb up the mountain the next day to seize the monastery and recover the abbacy. Abbot Guibald sent Landulf of S. Giovanni from the monastery to fight against him, and the latter came to the town, defeated Rainald and his supporters and put them to flight, and set fire to the town. He returned to Guibald up at the monastery after capturing many people and killing more. Meanwhile King Roger marched against the city of Capua, accompanied by a formidable army; he set fire to it and forced it to surrender. After discussing the matter with the brothers Abbot Guibald sent envoys to Roger, who was then still based at Capua, seeking peace

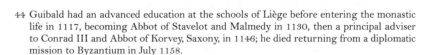

---

44 Guibald had an advanced education at the schools of Liège before entering the monastic life in 1117, becoming Abbot of Stavelot and Malmedy in 1130, then a principal adviser to Conrad III and Abbot of Korvey, Saxony, in 1146; he died returning from a diplomatic mission to Byzantium in July 1158.

from him and promising friendship. Roger ignored these overtures and sent the envoys, who had achieved nothing, back to the abbot with a message that no arrangement or agreement would be possible while an abbot who had been installed by the emperor remained in the abbey of Cassino; furthermore if by any chance Guibald should fall into his hands he would without a shadow of doubt execute him by hanging. Guibald was terrified by these awful threats. He abandoned the abbey of Cassino to the guardianship of Landulf of S. Giovanni, and on the night of 2nd November he fled with an escort provided by Landulf, without the brothers' knowledge, giving the brothers permission to elect as abbot whomever they wished.

(128) Twelve days having now passed after Guibald's flight, the brothers gathered together and after calling upon the grace of the Holy Ghost, they elected Rainald, a monk of this monastery, a man most distinguished in his observation of the Rule, behaviour and good qualities, and notable for his knowledge, both human and divine. He was descended from the most noble family of the counts of Marsia, from the province of Valeria, and he had been given to St Benedict as an oblate in the third *lustrum* of his life during the time of Oderisius II.[45] He outshone all his contemporaries through his great moral seriousness, honesty and constancy, so that this saying of the Lord could rightly be said of him, 'I will show him how great things he must suffer for my name's sake'.[46] For peoples and kingdoms conspired against him, and as one might say the whole world rose up against him, but 'putting on the helmet of salvation and the breastplate of faith',[47] and guarded by the protection of Father Benedict, he counted as nothing the traps of his enemies and those envious of him. Moreover at that time King Roger had recovered all the towns and *castra* right up to the bounds of the Cassinese abbey lands and made them subject to his most powerful and very harsh rule, but the abbot refused to agree to any deal with him, even though Roger wished this. The king then sent envoys to the abbot threatening to destroy the towns and *castra* belonging to the monastery, and had this announced both to the monks and to all the people.

---

45 Oderisius II, Abbot of Montecassino 1123–6, was deposed after a dispute with Honorius II; see Loud (2007a), 220–2. If Peter was correct, Rainald would be 10–15 at this period, in his mid-twenties in 1137. The counts of Marsia (the 'Attonid' family) were major benefactors of Montecassino, and two previous abbots had been members of this family: Oderisius I (1088–1105) and Gerard (1112–23), Howe (1997), 142–8, 185–8.

46 Acts, 9:16. Rainald (II), abbot 1137–66, was granted the rank of cardinal by Innocent II in 1141.

47 I Thessalonians, 5:8.

Then indeed, as is usually the case in such matters, the common people first raged savagely, and then their fury was changed into fear, and they all fled with their wives and children to the monastery of Cassino. Not long afterwards the aforesaid king sought an agreement with the monks of Cassino and in the meanwhile granted a truce so that all those who had fled through fear of him might return with their families to their homes.

THE CHRONICLE OF ST CLEMENT
OF CASAURIA

[*The chronicle of St Clement of Casauria, the wealthiest and most important monastery in the Abruzzi, was written by a monk called John Berard and completed about 1182. It provides a vivid picture of the king's takeover of this region in 1140, and of the advantages this might give and problems it might pose for vested interests there, as well as the chronicler's sense of the protection of his house by its patron saint. The chronicler, however, welcomed Roger as the bringer of peace and order.*][1]

[*after 1136*] Count Robert of Manopello, the son of Richard, had after the death of his father been restrained, at least to some extent, from evil for fear of his mother. But after his mother had rendered her debt to nature, this wicked son, engendered by a wicked father, exceeded the evil of his father by his own evil conduct, and he began to commit many hostile actions against the Blessed Clement and his house.[2] He was received as a guest by Abbot Oldrius,[3] who even allowed him to use his own chamber. After he had feasted and was stuffed full of food, he had the abbot summoned and with great arrogance and pride demanded that the latter hand over custody of the tower in the island's *castellum*, doing this not as a request but with menaces.[4] When the abbot made absolutely clear to him, in every way, that he could not do this, he [still] insisted that this tower should be handed over to him at once, and threatened that if this was not done he would destroy the church and lay waste all its land. What should the abbot do? He had to hand it over, whether he wanted to or not, and was very sad, greatly regretting that he had ever allowed the count inside the cloister walls. Those indeed whom the count stationed in the tower went about plundering as though they were scouts on the highway.[5] They seized the crop renders

Show of force

---

1 Latin text in *Chronicon Casauriense*, in *Rerum Italicarum Scriptores* ii(2), ed. L.A. Muratori (Milan 1726), cols. 886–92. For a fuller discussion of this source, see Loud (2005).

2 Robert was a minor when his father Richard died c.1105, Feller (1998), 753. For the vicissitudes of this county during the twelfth century, *ibid.*, 768–75. Richard was son of a Count Peter, who may have been Count Peter of Lesina, last attested in 1092, Loud (2000b), 253.

3 Oldrius, Abbot of Casauria 1127–52.

4 Casauria was built on an island in the Pescara River.

5 That is, ahead of an army in hostile territory.

and these agents of their mad lord raged furiously against the servants of Christ and St Clement.

The brothers did not wish to put up with this, and so they secretly sent two of the wisest among them, carrying the privileges of the emperors, to King Roger, who was then ruling in Apulia, to tell him of everything that had taken place, and to make tearful complaint about the count's tyranny and persecution. They received this reply from him – that they should return to the monastery as quickly as they could and they would be safe. If God should make this land subject to him, he would free the church, endow it from his property and bring help to the abbot and brothers. But when they at length returned, they were forced to live as exiles outside the monastery, in other people's houses in another district. Finally, through Divine mercy and the efforts of the abbot, the greed of the avaricious count was restrained by a bribe of two pounds of silver, and he permitted them to return home.

Not long afterwards, when the count had returned to the *castellum* of Manopello, the abbot presented himself to him [once again].[6] As they discussed the persecution that he had inflicted upon the monastery, it seemed to the count that the abbot was showing him insufficient respect in his replies. The angry count drew his sword and wanted to strike down the abbot, and if those who were present had not stopped him, he would have cut off the abbot's head – and granted the abbot what he greatly desired, to die for the sake of justice. Knowing that if he had dared to strike, he was safe in Divine help, the abbot had stretched out his neck and incited him, showing in this that he had no fear of death but rather hope of eternal life. The count, persevering in his madness, went back to Manopello, while the abbot, safer than he had been before, returned to his church. ...

[The chronicler then described a vision that appeared to two of the monks]

Meanwhile, King Roger had been crowned with a royal diadem, and undertaken rule over the kingdom of Sicily, the duchy of Apulia and the principality of Capua. He sent his son Anfusus, whom he had appointed as Prince of Capua, to the county of Chieti with a great army, and secretly ordered him diligently to seek out the counts of Manopello, who were the enemies of St Clement, and send them alive to him. When the counts found out what the aforesaid prince had been ordered to do by his father, they fled in secret, for they were able to resist him neither

---

6 Manopello is 11 km. E of the abbey of Casauria, and 14 km. SW of Chieti.

in one place nor another. When they fled, they lost both their own land and what they had acquired, and they ended their lives in foreign lands, as they deserved. From now on the church of St Clement could concentrate on the religious life in [a time of] abundant peace; its temporal property was increased by the care of a good shepherd, who watched out every day to advantage the flock which had been committed to him.

Biblical reference [handwritten marginal note]

At that time, the lord God decreed that that the most serene and victorious King Roger, whom Divine Grace had endowed with wisdom and courage much greater than that of all other mortal men, would visit the abbey of Pescara. Certain persons attacked the lord Abbot Oldrius, denouncing him, and saying that he had acted against the king in receiving the *castellum* of Bolognano[7] from the counts of Manopello who had fled and their representatives, even though this legally belonged to St Clement, and the land of the fugitive counts ought not to be denied to the king. But the abbot placed his trust in God and St Clement, and was in no way afraid. He resolutely held on to the *castellum* until the king came to the lands of the monastery. The latter pitched camp on the plain below Tocco and next to the Pescara river, and there he and his army remained for three days. The abbot took counsel and went to the king the very next day, to placate him with prayers and gifts, even intending to offer him money for the aforesaid *castrum*. He and all the brothers spent the night in the church, reciting the psalter with genuflections, litanies and prayers before the most holy body of St Clement. When day broke, they sang the morning hymns, and then he set off on horseback with some of the brothers to travel to the king. One of these brothers set off with the others, but was left behind on the way. He was hurrying after the abbot when an old man with the grey hair of age but of beautiful aspect appeared before him, standing on the bridge before the island gate, and clad as a pilgrim with the shell and staff, saying:

> Tell the abbot that he may safely go to the king, and he should take care not to offer him any money, for he will freely give you what you seek, and more than that.

The monk said: 'how do you know that?' He replied: 'because I was this night at the king's council, when he was discussing how to benefit your monastery'. The monk rejoiced in these words, and said to him: 'you shall be blessed for bringing good news. Go into the monastery and receive its charity'. He replied: 'I shall do so, for I am accustomed

---

7 Bolognano was 4 km. SE of the monastery.

to dwell there and to have its charity. Go with my blessing'. The monk now hurried off to rejoin the abbot and tell him about these events, but he wondered to himself how that man could know the king's secrets, since he appeared to be a pilgrim and a poor man, and men of this type were not accustomed to be admitted to the counsels, nor even into the halls, of kings. He turned round, and seeking to know the truth about his words, went all around the monastery, but was quite unable to find him, or even to catch sight of him. Hence those who had that night been praying with him were of the opinion that the messenger of this good fortune had been St Clement.

The lord Abbot Oldrius went to the king, and exercising his humility, he found such grace from him, a man who was so terrifying that he could even force mountains to tremble before his face, that the latter spoke to him with great kindness, not so much as a lord but rather as though a servant, and as a son to a father. Without delay he gave him what he sought, not for money but out of good will. The king was humble with the humble, and meek with the meek. He showed more respect to the serenity of his face, which seemed angelic in appearance, than to the silk garments of the wealthy and noble. He adjudged others to be vile and of no price compared with his merits, heaped praises upon him, holding him to be above all the other church pastors of his kingdom, and saying that he was solely devoted to the service of God's religion, not to amassing a host of friends. The king would receive nothing from him apart from the gift of prayers; he was instead generous to the church of St Clement from his own property, giving it three *castella*, whose names are Bolognano, Casale Plano and Colle Odoni, and a privilege of liberty and protection against its enemies, and of grace, reverence and honour against them. He promised to guard and augment the abbey and its property as though it was one of his special possessions.

[The text of Roger's privilege then follows, dated August 1140][8]

On the following day, namely 28th August 1140, this same glorious king devotedly visited the monastery. Standing in prayer before the venerable cross of the choir, he heard the mass of St Clement. He was very complimentary about this picture.[9] He had his privilege read out to them in the cloister, and then he was given, at his most earnest request, a

---

8 *Roger II Diplomata*, 139–40 no. 49. The privilege in fact confirmed the abbey in possession of only a part of the territory it claimed or had once owned, and Casale Plano and Colle Odoni were later not listed among the abbey's *castella* in the *Catalogus Baronum*, Feller (1998), 65–6.

9 That is, the painting of St Clement on the cross.

small piece of the shoulder-bone of St Clement. He inspected the island, and left even more devotedly than he had arrived. He gave orders to the abbot that if any adversary should molest the church in any way, and if and when it was necessary for the church to ask for help, he should send one of his men, not a monk but a servant, to avoid burdening the church with [unnecessary] expense. This would be security enough, for whatever the abbot requested he would grant, since King Roger did not wish Abbot Oldrius to be harassed. Indeed, he instructed him to make the most of his old age inside the monastery, where he might pray night and day for the state of the realm and for his safety and that of his sons.

After this Bohemond, who had been recently appointed by the lord king to the county of Manopello, succumbed (as is customary) to the chattering of certain flatterers of new men. He wanted the monastery of St Clement to be made subject to him, and sought as best he could a means to accomplish this. So that he might have allies for his plans, he wooed the chancellor Robert with prayers and promises, to bring this about by offering dishonest testimony.[10] It happened that the count and Robert the chancellor were talking with the abbot. The latter restrained their demands with a humble response, saying to Robert:

> My lord, we have you as [our] guide and defender in this land, and we shall have no other mediator between ourselves and the lord King Roger than you, [so] we ask and beg you in the name of our Lord Jesus Christ, whose servants we are, that you do not allow the freedom and justice of this church, which it has up to now possessed, to disappear and to be destroyed. You should remember with what care and what sincere intent the lord king freed our church from every evil custom and exaction. He did not wish the servants of God who dwell there to be kept busy with outside business but that they should day and night be watchful in the divine service and pour out perpetual prayers for himself and his sons and for the safety of his kingdom. Now however this Count Bohemond (I do not wish to conceal [the name of] one whose actions gravely injure our soul) is hindering us from the contemplation of God. He is encouraging us to take up secular arms and demanding that we provide cavalry and infantry and large sums of money, which you should certainly understand that we are unable to supply. We are appointed for the service of the Lord; it is quite improper that we should desert this and follow worldly matters.

10 Robert of Selby, chancellor 1137–51. Bohemond was originally from Tarsia in Calabria, and held the county of Manopello 1140–57. For his eventual disgrace and loss of the county in the reign of William I, see *Tyrants*, 75–6; *Chron. Casauriense*, 895–7.

To this the count replied:

> Lord abbot, you say this because you do not know the changing ways of kings and the various problems of this land. Through Divine grace the lord king has many people who pray in his kingdom, but he does not have many to defend it. It is necessary for those who do defend it to take up their shields and protect those who pray, and we who can bear arms will not be able to fight for the kingdom if we do not have the means of subsistence. The lord king realises this, and has in the full understanding [of this] given the abbey of St Clement to me, as my predecessors held it, and he did this in the presence of the chancellor Robert, who heard and saw [what happened] when it was given to me. You ought, please, to believe the testimony of one who is not accustomed to lie about such matters.

Robert, as we have said above, supported these words of the count, and he agreed so as to terrify the holy man, and so he started to claim that he had heard and seen when the lord king granted the abbey [to the count]. The abbot remained as silent as possible and waited for what God would do about this although he did not know what that might be, since they spoke these treacherous words to him so as to force from him by fear what they were unable to obtain by right. God however was watching out for his servant, and not many days later all this was revealed to King Roger, who immediately wrote to the count in these words.

> I am greatly displeased that you, whom I placed as the protector and defender of my kingdom, should dare to disturb and worry the peace of my head, my own chamber, my charitable institution, and you may well be rendered the due reward for your presumption. You have acted foolishly towards the abbey and brothers of St Clement, whose prayers are my shield and helmet against all the strength of the enemy. Desist from this wickedness, or the appropriate punishment which has been prepared for you for your presumption will fall upon you. I say this to you, by my faith as a king, and my hope in my sons, that God grant me what I desire from them, that unless you desist, and do not presume to harass the monks any further as you have done, then I shall destroy you, and your name will vanish from among the sons of men from this present generation until the Last Judgment! I wish you to take this same letter which I have sent to you and have it read in the chapter, that it be heard by everyone, that they shall all know what my wishes were concerning the church of St Clement and those who live there.[11]

11 *Roger II Diplomata*, 144 no. †51. The text itself is an invention, probably by the chronicler. Brühl describes it as 'the product of monastic wishful thinking'.

The count did as the king ordered. He brought the royal letter and heard it read out in the presence of the abbot and brothers, and thereafter, for as long as Abbot Oldrius lived, he did not dare to molest either the abbot or the inhabitants of this place.

ROGER II AND THE PAPACY
SELECTED DOCUMENTS

Paschal II to Count Roger II of Sicily, 1117[1]

[While implicitly recognising the grant of special rights over the Church made by Urban II to Count Roger I, in this letter the pope issued a sharp reproof to the count for exceeding the bounds of this concession. The disquiet expressed in this letter, combined with several other occasions when the young count seemed to display a high-handed attitude towards the Church, may have helped to influence Honorius II's opposition to his succession as Duke of Apulia in 1127–8.][2]

Before the invasion of the Saracens the island of Sicily was for a long time a special possession [*familiaris*] of the Roman Church, so that the Roman pontiffs had there guardians of its patrimonies and representatives of its office. However, Divine grace granted your father the distinction of driving the Saracens from that island, through his efforts, and the efforts and blood of his men, which led the churches of God to be restored therein. As a result, so you have argued in your letters, my predecessor freely and generously conceded to your father [the right to act] instead of a legate.[3] We also have conceded to you, his successor, that if when a legate is sent there from our side [*ex latere nostro*], whom we consider truly to be our vicar, then those things which are decreed by him shall be put into effect through your endeavour. For we read that it is for this purpose that secular powers are provided for the Church; that what ecclesiastical humility cannot do, the secular authority shall accomplish through its coercive power. We have never read that judgment over the persons and dignities of churchmen has been granted to laymen or to religious.[4] Furthermore, what legate or vicar has ever usurped for himself the summoning of bishops to a synod? This is usually done through nuncios, sometimes by individual and sometimes by general letters. You should, dearest son, know your limitations, and since power has been given to you by

---

1 Latin text in *Le Liber Censuum de l'Église Romaine*, ed. P. Fabre and L. Duchesne (3 vols, Paris 1889–1952), ii.125–6.

2 For discussion, Loud (1985), 136–43; Loud (2007), 148–51.

3 In July 1098, *Malaterra*, IV.29, p. 108.

4 That is, to monks.

God, you should not act against the Lord's power. The Lord has so conceded power to the Roman Church that it cannot be taken away by men. Learn from those around you the example set by good rulers, that you try not to harm churches but to help them, not to judge or oppress bishops but to venerate them as vicars of God. What was given to the Church by your father of noble memory, Count Roger, should not be diminished by you, but rather increased. Do not try to go before God, but follow him, since with him as your guide you will not offend but will have the light of life. I order you to do this as to a very dear son; I advise this, that if you are obedient and submissive as you pledge yourself [to be], by having done this you will gain salvation. The Almighty Lord will through his kindness direct, preserve and guard you. Given at Anagni, 1st October.

Anacletus II's privilege to Roger II, authorising the creation of the kingdom of Sicily, 27 September 1130[5]

[*The late fourteenth-century manuscript which preserves this text (Cod. Vat. Ottobon. Lat. 2940, fols. 18–19) records that the opening sentences were already impossible to decipher because of the age of the original manuscript. The Latin text which survives is virtually unpunctuated, and in places the meaning somewhat opaque. That the preservation of this important document has been so problematic is a sign of the* 'damnatio memoriae' *that overtook the pontificate of Anacletus after the conclusion of the papal schism.*]

[Your father, Roger I] zealously served the Church in many ways in the time of our predecessors the Roman pontiffs of distinguished memory Urban and Paschal. And your mother of happy memory, following nobly in the footsteps of her husband, and in return for the advantages given her by the Lord, took pains to honour most ceremonially this same Church of God and to sustain it with a generous hand. You yourself, to whom divine providence has granted greater wisdom and power than the rest of the Italian princes, have tried splendidly to honour our predecessors and to serve them generously. It is proper [then] to raise up your person and those of your heirs and to adorn them with permanent titles of grace and honour. Therefore we concede, grant and authorise to you, your son Roger, and your other sons following you in the kingdom as you shall decree, and to your heirs, the crown of the kingdom of Sicily, and Calabria, Apulia and all those lands which we

5 Latin text in Deér (1969), 62–4; also Hoffmann (1978), 173–5.

and our predecessors have granted and conceded to your predecessors
the dukes of Apulia, namely Robert Guiscard and his son Roger, to hold
and rule this kingdom in perpetuity, and to have by hereditary right
[*iure perpetuo*] all royal dignities and regalian rights. We decree that
Sicily shall be the capital of the kingdom [*capud regni*]. Furthermore
we authorise and concede that you and your heirs shall be anointed
as kings and at the appointed times crowned by the hands of those
archbishops of your land whom you wish [to do this], assisted if you
wish by other bishops of your choice. Also, we grant, concede and
consent that you, your sons and heirs shall have and possess in perpetuity all the concessions, grants and rights which our predecessors have
conceded and granted, and to which they have given their consent, to
your predecessors as dukes of Apulia Robert Guiscard, his son Roger,
and the latter's son William, and to you. We also grant to you and
your heirs and authorise [to rule] the principality of Capua with all its
appurtenances, as the princes of the Capuans have held it in the past
and [as they do] at the moment. We grant and confirm the honour of
Naples and its possessions and the aid of the men of Benevento against
your enemies. Kindly assenting to your repeated requests, we concede
to the Archbishop of Palermo and to his successors and the Palermitan church the consecrations of three of the bishops of Sicily, namely
those of Syracuse, Agrigento and Mazzara or Catania, on condition
that they shall suffer no damage to their dioceses or possessions from
the Archbishop of Palermo or the Palermitan church. We reserve our
full rights over the other two bishops. We concede, grant and authorise
these our concessions, as laid out above, to you, your sons and heirs, to
hold and possess in perpetual right, provided that you shall have sworn,
or they shall have sworn, homage and fealty to us and our successors,
which you shall do, or they shall do, at the time sought by us and at a
place safe for you, unless it shall be remitted by us or our successors, [in
which case] they [i.e. your successors] shall not on this account suffer
loss of honour, dignity or their land.[6] You and your heirs will however
pay the census, namely the 600 *scifati*[7] which you ought to pay every
year to the Roman church, if you are requested [to do this]. If you are
not so requested, you shall pay what is requested, but no case shall be
made about the rest left unpaid. If indeed in future any ecclesiastical or

6 Here I accept the modification to the text suggested by Hoffmann (1978), 159–60, to read
  nisi per nos et successores nostros remanserit. As he points out, this makes the 1130 text accord
  more closely with the later bull of 1139.

7 This was the south Italian name for Byzantine gold *nomisma*, derived from the borders
  [*scifae*] along the edges of these coins, Grierson (1971).

secular person tries to breach this our concession, then unless he makes suitable satisfaction, he shall be struck by the sword of anathema. Let the peace of our Lord Jesus Christ be on all those observing these our conditions, amen.

I Anacletus, Bishop of the Catholic Church
I Matthew Eudoxie priest
John, son of Peter Leone, Consul of the Romans[8]
Roger his brother
Peter son of Uguccio
Cencius ...
... son of Guido
Peter Leone of Fondi
Abucio
John Habdiricio
Milo ....

Dated at Benevento by the hand of Saxo, cardinal priest and chancellor of the Holy Roman Church,[9] 27th September, ninth [year] in the indiction, in the year from the Lord's Incarnation 1130, [first] year of the pontificate of our lord Pope Anacletus II.

Anacletus II's privilege to the Bishop of Messina, 1131[10]

[In the autumn of 1131 Anacletus undertook a structural re-organisation of the Church on the island of Sicily, probably at the request of the king, dividing the island into two church provinces, with the see of Messina promoted to be an archbishopric, and creating two new bishoprics to become its suffragan sees, along with the existing bishopric of Catania. However, after the conclusion of the schism these (perfectly sensible) arrangements became a dead letter since Innocent II and his immediate successors would not accept the legitimacy of any actions of Anacletus – Messina therefore reverted to being a simple bishopric, and the Curia refused to recognise the two new bishoprics of Lipari and Cefalù. A final solution to these problems came only in 1166, when Alexander III, then in dire need of Sicilian support against the hostile German Emperor

---

8 John was brother of Anacletus.

9 Saxo, Cardinal priest of S. Stefano in Monte Celio from 1116, one of the most senior members of the papal college at the 1130 schism, came from Anagni in the papal Campagna; he helped negotiate the Concordat of Worms in 1122, along with Lambert of Ostia, later Honorius II, Hüls (1977), 206–7.

10 Latin text in P.F. Kehr, 'Nachträge zu den Papsturkunden Italiens I', *Nachrichten der K. Gesellschaft der Wissenschaften zu Göttingen, Phil-Hist. Klasse* (1905), 332–3 no. 6.

Frederick Barbarossa, sanctioned the creation of the province of Messina, shorn of Catania, which was made directly dependent on the papacy.][11]

Anacletus, bishop, servant of the servants of God, to his venerable brother Bishop Hugh of Messina and his canonically appointed successors in perpetuity.[12] A request made from pious intention should be fulfilled by being given assent, so that sincere devotion shall shine forth and the useful matter requested can be put into clear effect. Since therefore our illustrious and glorious son King Roger has most devotedly requested from us and the Roman Church that, for the honour of the kingdom which we have with the generosity of the Apostolic See conceded in perpetuity to him and his sons, we ought to constitute the church of Messina as an archbishopric, we have mercifully decided to agree to the advice and prayers of our venerable brother bishops and cardinals. Therefore, our dearest brother in Christ Hugh, we promote you to be an archbishop and constitute the holy church of Messina, now the seat of a bishop, to be henceforth an archbishopric, and to have three bishoprics subject to it, namely those of Catania, Lipari and Cefalù, that in future you and your successors shall have the authority, power and dignity of an archbishop over these aforesaid churches and their bishops, as the holy canons describe metropolitans having over their suffragans.[13] This is however on condition that the three aforesaid bishoprics shall not suffer loss either of their property or of their parishes from you and your successors, and also saving all concessions and privileges granted to our glorious son Roger and his heirs by the Roman Church. If indeed in future any ecclesiastical or secular person shall knowingly try to dare to act against this document detailing our decision, if he shall not have made proper satisfaction after a second or third warning then he shall be deprived of all power, honour and dignity, and should know that he shall undergo divine judgment for the sin which has been committed and suffer punishment at the Last Judgment. However, let the peace of our Lord Jesus Christ be upon all those properly observing this; they shall enjoy the fruits of their good deed and at the Last Judgment shall find eternal peace. Amen, amen, amen.

I Anacletus, Bishop of the Catholic Church,
I Crescentius, Cardinal priest of SS. Marcellino and Pietro,[14]

---

11 White (1938), 89–90, 96–7, 189–90, 196; Loud (2007), 225, 229, 234–5.

12 Hugh, Archbishop of Messina 1131–4.

13 At the same time Anacletus raised the Benedictine abbey of Lipari and King Roger's new Augustinian foundation at Cefalù to be bishoprics, *Italia Pontificia*, x.357 no. 4, 364 no. 1.

14 See above, *Falco*, note 107.

I John, Cardinal priest of the Holy Pastor Pudentiana,[15]
I Amatus, Cardinal priest of S. Eusebio,[16]
I Gregory, Cardinal deacon of S. Eustachio,[17]
I Silvius, Cardinal deacon of S. Lucia,[18]
I Rainald, Cardinal deacon of S. Vito.[19]

Dated at Priverno by the hand of Saxo, cardinal priest and chancellor of the Holy Roman Church, 14th September, ninth [year] in the indiction, in the year from the Lord's Incarnation 1131, second year of the pontificate of our lord Pope Anacletus II.

Roger II's privilege to the Pierleone family, 28 January 1134[20]

[This privilege shows the close links between King Roger and the family of Anacletus II. The financial subsidy was clearly intended to support the family's position in Rome, which must have been weakened by the Emperor Lothar's visit to the city with Innocent II in the summer of 1133. The special status of this privilege, which survives in the original (now in the Vatican Library),[21] is shown by its physical form: it was written in golden ink on purple parchment, one of only two surviving diplomas of King Roger to have been accorded such treatment. (The other was the foundation charter for the Palatine Chapel in Palermo from April 1140.) The model for this, and for the use of the gold bull

15 John Dauferius, from Salerno, was made Cardinal deacon of S. Nicola in Carcere Tulliano in 1123, the only south Italian cardinal appointed by either Calixtus II or Honorius II. He supported Anacletus in the disputed election of 1130; soon afterwards Anacletus promoted him to be Cardinal priest of S. Pudentiana. He later defected to the side of Innocent II, who re-appointed him to his former cardinal diaconate. He was last attested in April 1134, and probably died not long afterwards. Zenker (1964), 110–11; Hüls (1977), 240–1.

16 One of the new cardinals appointed by Anacletus, and attested from September 1131 to October 1136, but nothing else is known about him, Zenker (1964), 110.

17 A cardinal from 1110 and one of those who elected Gelasius II in 1118, it appears he was regarded as the senior cardinal deacon in 1130. He was last attested in December 1137, Hüls (1977), 227.

18 He signed Anacletus's letter to the German king immediately after his election, so perhaps he was already a cardinal before the death of Honorius, Hüls (1977), 230–1.

19 Another new cardinal appointed by Anacletus; nothing else is known of him, Zenker (1964), 183.

20 Latin text in *Roger II Diplomata*, 98–101 no. 35; first published by Kehr (1901), 258–9, also in Deér (1969), 69–71.

21 This document was still in the hands of the Pierleone family until at least the later sixteenth century, Kehr (1901), 256–7. It was subsequently acquired by the Barberini family, whose manuscripts were transferred to the Vatican Library in 1902.

as a seal, came from the chancery of the German emperors, where such treatment was similarly accorded to a very few especially high-status documents, though the ultimate inspiration came from the Byzantine Empire.][22]

In the name of the Lord God Eternal and our Saviour Jesus Christ. In the year from His Incarnation 1134, twelfth in the indiction. While we were staying in utmost felicity in our palace, John son of the late Peter Leone, consul of the Romans, came into the presence of our majesty, and called to mind the benefits and honours which our father and mother of happy memory, and ourselves, had out of abundant generosity conferred upon his father, brothers and himself. Then of his own accord he offered us his service and liege homage, that of his undersigned brothers and nephews, namely Leo, Roger, Jordan and Guido, and his nephews Peter, Huguccio and Gratian, and oversight of all their fortresses, castles and houses. He asked insistently, tried assiduously and not only he but our own vassals [*homines*] begged the clemency of our power that this request be granted. Hearing his petition, and having ascertained what he wanted, and on the advice of those faithful to us, we have decreed that assent be given to his request. For we have decreed and ordered to be observed in perpetuity that the aforesaid honourable and distinguished men and their heirs shall do liege homage and liege fealty to us and to our heirs, against all men and women; they shall receive safely and securely in their *castella* and fortresses us, our heirs, people and money; they shall make war against all our enemies, if it shall be required of them, whenever and wherever it shall be necessary, without fraud or deceit, or anything that will be of harm to us or our heirs. They shall give security on oath, at a time and a place that we or our heirs will nominate to them or their heirs, or we shall have nominated. In consequence, at the same time we have, by the exercise of our generosity, promised to give them from our palace treasury (if they shall request it) 240 ounces of gold, according to the weight used at our court, every year, or an equivalent income from property, and seven horses and two Ethiopians, on condition that the privilege of donation that our father and we once made to their father and them shall remain in force. The oath shall be in this form: 'I swear and give assurance to you, my lord Roger, by the grace of God mighty King of Sicily and Italy, to the lord duke Roger, your son, and to all your heirs, …'.

---

22 Brühl (1977), who points out that in Byzantium such 'purple' documents were almost always diplomatic letters rather than privileges. Western examples were listed by Kehr (1901), 253–4, most notably Otto I's celebrated privilege to the Roman Church in February 962.

So God and this holy Gospel help me. To strengthen and confirm this our concession, we have ordered that this privilege be drawn up by the hand of Henry, archdeacon of Palermo and our chaplain, and have instructed that it be sealed with our gold seal.

Dated at Palermo, fifth day before the Kalends of February, since the chancellor is absent.

From the *Acta* of Innocent II's Council of Pisa, June 1135[23]

A sentence of general excommunication is promulgated against all those who in future shall bring merchandise by land or sea to Sicily or Apulia, that they might sell it there, and [on those] who shall travel there in order that they might serve the tyrant Roger, who has been separated from the Church, or his men, [to continue] until he shall return to the unity of the faith. However, to those who shall go by land or sea against him and Peter Leone for the liberation of the Church and shall labour faithfully in this same service, that same remission is made which Pope Urban decreed at the Council of Clermont to all those travelling to Jerusalem for the liberation of Christians.

In this same council, Peter Leone, and his brothers and supporters, have been excommunicated, and the ordinations made by these same schismatics have equally been condemned. Furthermore, the aforesaid Roger of Sicily, the Bishop of Albi, Count Alfonso of Toulouse[24] and many others have been bound by this same chain of anathema.

Innocent II's privilege to Roger, authorising the creation of the kingdom, 27 July 1139[25]

[Since Innocent denied that Anacletus was a legitimate pope, it followed that he could not recognise the latter's creation of the kingdom of Sicily. Hence, although after his capture at Gallucio in 1139 he was forced to acknowledge the legitimacy of that kingdom, his bull confirming its existence was phrased to imply that this was his own original creation. Nevertheless, its terms were very similar to those of the bull of Anacletus in 1130.]

23 Latin text in Girgensohn (1971), 1099–1100.

24 Humbert de Geraud, Bishop of Albi, and Alfonso Jordan, Count of Toulouse (d. 1148), Girgensohn (1971), 1092–3.

25 Latin text in Deér (1969), 74–5; Hoffmann (1978), 175–7.

Innocent, bishop, servant of the servants of God, to his most dear son in Christ Roger, illustrious and glorious King of Sicily and to his heirs in perpetuity. It is right and proper that the bride of Christ, the holy and apostolic Roman mother church should love with sincere affection those whom He has chosen from on high by the dispensation of Divine counsel for the rule and safety of the people, and has properly endowed with prudence, justice and other splendid virtues, and should promote them from high rank to even higher position. It has indeed been proven by clear evidence that your predecessor Robert Guiscard, Duke of Apulia, that valiant [*strenuus*] and faithful knight of St. Peter of distinguished memory, manfully fought against the mighty and powerful enemies of the Church, and left to his posterity the worthy memory of his name and an example of probity that should be imitated. Furthermore your father Roger, of illustrious reputation, was through warlike endeavours and pitched battles an undaunted adversary of the enemies of the Christian name, and a diligent propagator of the Christian religion, and as a good son he rendered service in many ways to his mother, the holy Roman Church.[26] In consequence of this, our predecessor the wise and religious Pope Honorius, knowing that your noble self was descended from the aforesaid distinguished family, hoping for much from you, and believing that you were endowed with prudence, strengthened by justice and suitable to rule the people, greatly cherished you and promoted you to higher rank. We therefore follow in his footsteps, and placing hope and trust in you, as a person who will be valuable and useful to the holy Church of God, we grant to your excellency and confirm by apostolic authority rule over Sicily, which has undoubtedly been a kingdom, for it is called this in ancient histories, and which was conceded to you by this same predecessor of ours. We grant to you the duchy of Apulia, which he also bestowed upon you, and furthermore we add through the power of our favour the whole of the principality of Capua. And, that you may devote yourself more keenly to the love and service of Blessed Peter, Prince of the Apostles, and of us and our successors, we have extended this grant of all these things, that is the kingdom of Sicily, the duchy of Apulia and the principality of Capua,[27] to your heirs, who shall do liege homage and swear fealty, as you have sworn, to us and to our successors, unless it shall be remitted by us and our successors, namely at a suitable time and a place that is safe

---

26 Similar sentiments to justify the creation of the kingdom were expressed in the foundation charter of the Palatine Chapel in April 1140, *Roger II Diplomata*, 133–7 no. 48, at 136.

27 From now on this became the official title of the kingdom, whereas until then Roger's documents had described him as 'King of Sicily and Italy', Kehr (1934), 42–3.

and not suspicious, and serviceable both to us and to them. We shall with the help of God maintain them with regard to those things that have been granted. Even if this [homage] shall be remitted by them, these same heirs of yours shall nevertheless continue to hold what they were holding, without diminution.[28] As has been agreed, a census of 600 *scifati* shall be paid every year by your heirs to us and our successors, unless perhaps some hindrance intervenes – and even if this obstruction remains, it shall nevertheless be paid [once more]. Dearest son, it is of importance that you show yourself devoted and humble for the honour and service of the holy Roman Church, your mother, and thus behave for its advantage and your own, so that the Apostolic See may rejoice in so devoted and glorious a son, and may be at peace in his love. If however any ecclesiastical or secular person shall dare to act against this our concession, then until he shall make suitable satisfaction for his presumption, he shall incur the wrath of Almighty God and of the blessed Apostles Peter and Paul, and until he shall repent he shall be struck by the sentence of anathema. Amen. I Innocent, bishop of the Catholic Church. I Alberic, bishop of Ostia,[29] etc. Dated in the territory of Mignano by the hand of Haimeric, cardinal deacon and chancellor of the holy Roman Church,[30] on 27th July, in the second indiction, in the year from the Incarnation of the Lord 1139, and in the tenth year of the lord Pope Innocent II.

From a letter of Pope Lucius II to Abbot Peter of Cluny, 22 September 1144[31]

We wish to inform you that the Almighty Lord has visited us with His grace; He has chastised us, and is chastising us, but he has not given us up to death. Through His mercy we are getting better, and we hope to recover our good health in a little while. We have agreed to a meeting with the King of Sicily, and since we have been unable to conclude a lasting peace with him to the honour of God and His Church, however much he attempt to force us with his violence, we have concluded a truce with him.

---

28 As Hoffmann (1978), 162–3, pointed out, this clause seems to have been a concession to the king, and indeed somewhat more favourable to him than the equivalent clause in the Treaty of Benevento in 1156, which definitively settled Sicilian–papal relations.

29 See above, *Falco*, note 249.

30 See above, *Falco*, note 134.

31 Latin text from MPL, 179: 905, *epistola* no. 64.

From the Treaty of Konstanz, 1153[32]

The lord king [Frederick I] will have one of his *ministeriales*[33] of the kingdom swear on his behalf, and the same man will promise, giving faith with his own hand in the hand of the lord pope's legate, that he [the king] will make neither treaty nor peace either with the Romans or with Roger of Sicily without the free consent of the Roman Church and the lord Pope Eugenius, or of his successors who wish to keep the terms of the undersigned agreement with King Frederick. And he will work with the forces of the kingdom to subjugate the Romans to the lord pope and the Roman Church, as they were a hundred years back.

32 Latin text in MGH *Constitutiones et Acta Publica*, i.201 no. 144.

33 *Ministeriales* were a peculiarly German institution, unfree knights, who were thus especially closely tied to their lords. 'Household knights' is a possible English translation, but even this does not convey the full implications of their dependent status. The Staufen rulers of Germany increasingly relied on their royal and family *ministeriales* as agents of their rule. The literature on the subject is vast, but for a very helpful brief introduction, Arnold (1986).

THE ASSIZES (OR CONSTITUTIONS) OF KING ROGER

Text of Cod. Vat. Lat. 8782, fols. 91ʳ–94ᵛ¹

[This collection of laws is the earlier of two related texts purporting to contain the legislation of King Roger. As explained in the introduction, this text contains genuine legislation of King Roger and may be a law code promulgated in the 1140s, although certainly not at the meeting at Ariano in 1140 mentioned by Falco. Most of these laws are also in the Montecassino MS of Roger's assizes (in a different order); nearly all of them were repeated, attributed to King Roger, in Frederick II's Liber Augustalis of 1231. The footnotes identify these instances and the sources of the laws in the Codex and Digest of Justinian and other texts of Roman law.]

It is right and proper, barons, that we should not be presumptuous either concerning ourselves or about the condition and merits of our whole kingdom, and that if we have received anything from the generosity which has resulted from Divine grace, then we should repay these Divine benefits through which we have our strength with humble service, lest we be entirely ungrateful for such great favour. If then holy God has through His mercy laid our enemies low and restored peace, and if He has made our kingdom whole once again by means of His most gracious tranquillity,[2] both in matters fleshly and spiritual, we are compelled to renew the paths of both justice and piety, when we see that these have become miserably crooked. This very thing which is called inspiration we have received by a gift from the Giver himself, when he says: 'By me kings reign, and legislators decree justice'.[3] For we consider that nothing is more pleasing to God than if we straightforwardly offer Him that which we have learnt Him to be, namely mercy and justice. In this oblation the office of kingship claims for itself a certain privilege of priesthood; from this a certain wise man skilled in the law calls

---

1 Translated from G.M. Monti, 'Il testo e la storia esterna delle assise normanne', in *Studi di storia e di diretto in onore di Carlo Calisse* (Milan 1940), i.295–348 [repr. Monti (1945), 83–184]. This, the most useful available edition, has parallel texts of the Vatican and Montecassino MSS and relevant clauses of the *Liber Augustalis*.

2 Phraseology reminiscent of *Romuald*, above 264, Houben (2002), 138.

3 Proverbs, 8:15.

the interpreters of the law priests.[4] Therefore we who through His
grace possess the authority of justice and law ought in part to improve
them and in part redraft them, and those of us who have secured mercy
should in all matters handle them more mercifully and interpret them
in a more kindly way, especially where their severity contains a degree
of inhumanity.[5] And we do not claim this on the basis of pride, as if we
were more just or more moderate than our predecessors in the establishment or interpretation of laws through our vigilance, but because
we have erred in many things[6] and, because we are more inclined to err,
we take the view that it is appropriate that those who do wrong should
be spared in keeping with the moderation that is appropriate to our
times. For the Holy One himself has instructed us as follows, saying:
'Be ye also merciful as your Father also is merciful';[7] and the King and
Prophet says: 'All the paths of the Lord are mercy and truth';[8] and
without doubt we shall take the view that he who has given judgment
without mercy shall receive judgment without mercy.[9] We therefore
desire and order that you should faithfully and enthusiastically receive
the provisions which we make public in the present code whether they
have been promulgated by us or [simply] re-enacted.

I About the interpretation of laws

We order that the laws newly promulgated by our majesty, mitigating
through piety excessive harshness and thus encouraging benevolent
rule, and elucidating what is obscure, should be fully observed by all.
Because of the variety of different people subject to our rule, the usages,
customs and laws which have existed among them up to now are not
abrogated unless what is observed in them is clearly in contradiction
to our edicts here.

II About the privilege of holy churches

Let all those subject to our power know that it shall always be our
intention to protect, defend and augment in every way the churches
of God, for which the Lord Jesus Christ shed his blood, as our predecessors were at pains to do, with their traditional generosity. As a
result many and uncountable benefits have always been granted by

4 *Digest*, I.1.1.

5 Cf. *Digest*, I.3.18 and I.3.25.

6 James, 3:2.

7 Luke, 6:36.

8 Psalm 25:10.

9 Cf. James, 2:13.

God to their advantage. Thus we shall defend and guard inviolate all the property and possessions of the holy churches which have been entrusted to our custody, after that of God and the saints, with the temporal sword which has been granted to us by God. We commend this to [our] princes, counts, barons and all our faithful subjects, who should know that whomsoever should attempt to violate our decree shall incur the wrath of our majesty.[10]

III General admonition

We advise princes, counts, greater and lesser barons, archbishops, bishops, abbots, and all those who have subject to them citizens, burgesses, peasants and men of any sort, that they should treat them decently and show themselves merciful, particularly when collecting the tax [*adiutorium*] owed, they should demand this in moderation, for [by doing this] they render thanks to God and great joy to us, under whose power and rule Divine providence has subjected both prelate and subject. If this should be neglected, it will be examined by our solicitude with a view to reforming for the better what has been done ill.[11]

IV About royal property

We desire that our princes, counts, all barons, archbishops, bishops and abbots should know that whoever holds any property great or small from our *regalia* can in no way and by no ingenuity alienate, grant or sell, or diminish in whole or in part anything belonging to our regalia in such a way that our regalian rights are diminished or abolished or suffer any injury.[12]

V About the sale of holy relics

We permit no one to sell or barter relics of martyrs or of any other saint. If anyone shall presume to do this, and the price has not yet been fixed, then nothing shall follow, if the vendor wishes to agree with the purchaser; if, however, money has been paid, restitution shall not be made to the purchaser, who is to hand [them] over to the fisc. It shall be the concern of our providence to punish anyone daring to infringe

---

10 Cassino Assize 1 (in Codice Cassinese 468, for which see the introduction, pp. 42–3 above).

11 Cassino Assize 2.

12 Cassino Assize 3; *Liber Augustalis*, III.1, trans. Powell (1971), 105. Cahen (1940), 120, suggested that this law especially aimed to protect the military service owed to the crown from fiefs, since in 1230 Frederick II, legislating on alienations from fiefs, expressly mentioned it, *Liber Augustalis*, III.6, trans. Powell (1971), 108.

this, and, with the advice of the bishops, to place the relics where it shall be most suitable.[13]

VI Concerning flight to a church

We order by the present law, which shall, God willing, remain in force in perpetuity, that in all parts of our kingdom nobody in flight of whatsoever condition shall be expelled or dragged out of the most holy churches, nor shall anyone because of them exact from the venerable bishops or *yconomi*[14] that which is owed by them. Anyone who shall endeavour or do this shall be faced with capital punishment or the loss of all their property. Meanwhile food shall not be denied to the fugitives. However, if a serf or *colonus* or serf of the glebe shall have fled from his lord or shall have fled with stolen property to holy places, he shall be returned to the lord with the property which he has taken, that he may be punished according to the nature of the crime which he has committed, or, if intercession has occurred, restitution shall occur piously and freely.[15]

VII About not violating the privileges of churches

Whosoever shall dare to violate the privileges of a holy church shall, once the offence is removed, pay compensation according to the harm done to the church; if he shall not be able to pay the fine to which he is condemned, the matter shall be committed to the judgment of the king or the arbitration of his officials. Nevertheless he shall be subject to the providence of the king and the arbitration of his officials about the scale of the offence.[16]

VIII About the privilege of bishops

The bishops shall not be compelled to give testimony except in ecclesiastical or state cases, when authorised by necessity or royal authority. Priests shall not be compelled to make corporal oath in [secular] matters. We order that deacons, subdeacons and below placed as ministers to the holy altar shall be strangers to vile restrictions, and we quite prohibit that priests, though not the others, be subject to personal servile dues [*angaria*].[17]

13 Cassino Assize 4 (first sentence only).

14 *Yconomi* were administrators of church property; in cathedrals, usually a canon, Loud (1985), 209–10.

15 Adapted from *Codex* I.12.6, this may also draw on *Digest*, I.6.2; also part of Cassino Assize 4.

16 *Codex*, I.3.16.

17 *Codex*, I.3.6–7, also part of Cassino Assize 4.

IX Concerning illicit conventicles

We forbid illicit conventicles to be celebrated outside a church in private houses; under threat of the immediate demolition of the house if its lord has knowingly received clerics in it who celebrate new and unruly conventicles.[18]

X About serfs wishing to become clerics

No bishop should presume to ordain serfs [*adscriptitii*] without the desire and assent of the persons to whose right and power they are subject, nor [somebody] from another diocese [*parrochia*] with letters of commendation either from a bishop or from their own chapter, following the institutes of the canons.

If those with whom they are enrolled [as serfs] should be convicted of having received any reward for having given permission for their ordination, they will lose the right of adscription and the one who has given the money shall be degraded from his orders and sold with all his property on behalf of the fisc.

It so happens that on sacred occasions wickedness obstructs sacred desires and disturbs the service of God and the ministry of the Church. But no evil should be allowed to hinder our laws at any time. If, for example, there shall have been priests assigned to a church in the country or in a village, and after their deaths others must be substituted, and the lords of the country place or village refuse to allow the bishop to make a substitution from among the serfs, especially when the bishop is looking for a suitable person from among these serfs; it appears worthy and most just to our clemency that on the just petition of the Church the lord of the serfs should be corrected by the law. But the sons of a deceased priest should be returned to the condition of serfs, without any appeal.[19]

XI About the rape of virgins

If anyone presumes to rape holy virgins veiled by God, even for the purpose of marriage, he shall suffer capital punishment, or other penalty which royal censure shall decree.[20]

---

18 *Codex*, I.3.15; the first sentence only in Cassino Assize 5.

19 *Codex*, I.3.16; first sentence, Cassino, Assize 6; whole section, *Liber Augustalis*, III.2, trans. Powell (1971), 105–6.

20 *Codex*, I.3.5; Cassino Assize 8; *Liber Augustalis*, I.20, trans. Powell (1971), 23.

XII[21]

No Jew or pagan shall dare either to buy or sell Christian servants, or to possess them by any title [whatsoever], or to hold them as a pledge. If he should presume to do this, all his property will be confiscated to the fisc and he shall become the servant of the Court. If he should by some wicked trick or persuasion have the servant circumcised or make him deny his faith, then he shall be punished by capital penalty.[22]

XIII About those apostatising

We curse thoroughly those who apostatise from the Catholic faith. We pursue them with vengeance. We despoil them of all their goods. We withdraw the protection of our laws from those who break a promise or vow, we abolish their right of inheritance and cancel their every legitimate right.[23]

XIV About jesters

Players and those who make jokes by bodily writhing shall not use in public either the habits of virgins dedicated to God or monastic or clerical vestments. If they should do so they shall be publicly flogged.[24]

XV About wards and orphans

Through considerations of piety, many privileges are confirmed by ancient laws to wards and orphans, which through passage of time have fallen into disuse. We entrust and favourably commend [these laws] to our judges since their abandonment is intolerable. In addition we settle the equity of the laws on women, who are not less disadvantaged by the fragility of their sex. We order that they should be aided from the depths of piety both by us and by our officials, as is right and proper.[25]

XVI About those unworthily aspiring to the priesthood

No one should dare to seek the dignity of the priesthood by paying

21 Untitled.

22 *Codex*, I.10; Cassino Assize 6 (part 2).

23 *Codex*, I.7.1; Cassino Assize 9; *Liber Augustalis*, I.3, trans. Powell (1971), 10–11.

24 *Codex* I.4.4 (first promulgated by Theodosius the Great in 394); Cassino Assize 7. Pennington (2006) suggests that the punishment, not allowed by Roman Law, drew on clerical precedent, from Gregory the Great on.

25 Cassino Assize 10 is a shortened version of this section. *Liber Augustalis* II.41, trans. Powell (1971), 98, has the second sentence only. A judge at Bari referred to this law when sanctioning the sale of a house by a woman in need in May 1167, *Codice diplomatico Barese* i *Le Pergamene del duomo di Bari (952–1264)*, ed. G.B. Nitto de Rossi and F. Nitti de Vito (Bari 1897), 96–8 no. 50. Houben (2002), 139.

money, and they should receive disgrace and punishment [in recompense] for the price paid as soon as this [crime] is by their own action detected. For he who seeks this honour by such an importunate and impudent manner should be deprived of it.

XVII About those who commit sacrilege

There should be no dispute about the judgment, plans, decrees or deeds of the king, for to dispute his judgments, decrees, deeds and plans, or if he whom he has chosen or appointed is worthy, is comparable to sacrilege.[26] Many laws have punished sacrilege most severely, but the penalty must be moderated by the decision of the one who is judging, unless perhaps the temples of God have been openly and violently despoiled, or gifts and sacred vessels have been stolen at night, for in that case the crime is capital.[27]

XVIII About the crime of treason

Whosoever should start a plot, whether with one knight or with many, or on his own, or should give an undertaking or oath to a plot, that plans and prepares the murder of one of the illustrious men who are among our councillors and advisers – they have by their wish to commit evil chosen for themselves severe legal punishment. The culprit should be struck down by the sword as guilty of treason and all their property should be confiscated by the state. Their sons should indeed receive no benefit whether by our generosity or by legal right. Let death be a blessing to them and life a punishment. If however anyone shall have denounced what has been done by the conspirators without delay, he shall promptly receive pardon and grace.[28]

The crime of treason also encompasses those who discuss and attack the reputation of the king after his death, so that anyone who should do or be a party to this will from that day on be treated as a criminal and have no protection, but everything that they have shall be sold according to the laws of the fisc.[29]

He who shall purge a relative of a crime deserves succession to them.

All those by whose advice hostages escape, citizens are armed, plots

26 Cf. here the trial of Richard of Mandra in 1168, *Tyrants*, 194.

27 First sentence from *Codex*, IX.29.2; second loosely based on *Digest* XLVIII.13.6, a law of 380, may show knowledge of *Digest*, VII.1.4. Cassino Assize 11 is a shortened version; *Liber Augustalis* I.4–5, trans. Powell (1971), 11.

28 *Codex*, IX.8.5; Cassino Assize 12.

29 *Codex*, IX.8.6.

are fomented, tumults excited, magistrates killed, men desert from the army or flee from the enemy, allies are betrayed, military formations are cloven asunder by wicked tricks, battles lost, fortresses abandoned, help denied to allies and other things of this type [done], shall be considered guilty of this crime, as will he who spies on, corrupts or publishes the king's counsels, as well as he who knowingly gives shelter and renders assistance to the enemies of the kingdom.[30]

XIX About new knighthood

Consenting to divine justice, we approve what must be approved and reject the contrary. For just as the good must not be exasperated, so the evil should not be benefited. Therefore we order and propose this edict, that if someone should seize new knighthood contrary to the happiness, peace and integrity or our kingdom, will lose completely the name and profession of knight, unless perhaps he is descended from the stock of a knightly family. We order the same about those who receive the order of any profession, as for example if they obtain the authority of a judge or the office of a notary, or others similar.[31]

XX About forgers

A person who alters royal letters, or seals what he has written with a spurious seal, should suffer capital punishment.[32]

XXI About coining money

We impose capital punishment on and confiscate the property of those coining adulterine money or knowingly receiving it; we inflict this penalty [also] on those conspiring [in this]. We deprive those who shave gold or silver coins, dye them, or in anyway diminish them, of their property and their lives.[33]

XXII

Where a case of forgery occurs, diligent inquiry shall follow promptly, with proofs, witnesses, comparison of scripts and other indications of the truth; not only shall the accuser be examined for proofs, but the judge shall be the arbiter between both parties, that when all the evidence finally agrees he shall impose sentence, When proved, capital

---

30 *Digest*, XLVIII.4.4.

31 Cassino Assize 31; *Liber Augustalis*, III.59, trans. Powell (1971), 141.

32 Cassino Assize 14; *Liber Augustalis*, III.61, trans. Powell (1971), 141.

33 First sentence, *Codex*, IX.24.1–2; second sentence, *Digest*, XLVIII.10.8; incorporated in Cassino Assize 14; *Liber Augustalis*, III.62–3, trans. Powell (1971), 142.

punishment shall follow, if a punishment of that magnitude is merited, or another penalty depending on the seriousness of the offence.[34]

XXIII About a forged document

Whosoever uses a false document unwittingly shall not be punished for the crime of forgery. Whoever furnishes a falsehood with witnesses should be punished with the penalty for forgery.[35]

XXIV About the concealment of wills

Someone who removes, conceals, destroys or alters wills and public instruments shall be subject to the same penalty. If anyone destroys his father's will, in order to succeed as though to one [who died] intestate, shall be deprived of the inheritance from his father.[36]

XXV About public officials

The status of the person aggravates or diminishes the punishment for fraud. Officials of the state or judges who have, during their period in office, stolen public revenues [are guilty of] the grave crime of embezzlement and shall be punished capitally, unless royal piety spares them.[37]

 royalty has authority to change

XXVI About public properties

Anybody who has allowed public property to be lost or diminished through his own negligence should be considered guilty and liable through his own person and property, at the discretion of royal piety. Anybody who knowingly gives assent to what has been done shall be liable to the same legal penalty.[38]

XXVII About the legitimate celebration of marriages

Since it belongs to the care and solicitude of the kingdom to draft laws, govern the people, instruct them in morals, extirpate evil customs,[39] it seems right and equitable to our clemency to rescind by the sternness of our edict a certain evil custom which, as though some damage or

34 *Codex*, IX.22.22.

35 First sentence, *Codex*, IX.22.3; whole section is contained within Cassino Assize 14; *Liber Augustalis*, III.64–5, trans. Powell (1971), 142.

36 First sentence, *Codex*, IX.22.4; second sentence, *Digest*, XLVIII.10.26; whole section in Cassino Assize 14; *Liber Augustalis*, III.66–7, trans. Powell (1971), 142–3.

37 Draws on *Codex*, IX.28.1; Cassino Assize 19; *Liber Augustalis*, I.36, trans. Powell (1971), 34.

38 Second sentence, *Codex*, IX.28.1; Cassino Assizes 19–20; *Liber Augustalis*, I.36(b), trans. Powell (1971), 34.

39 'Romuald' uses a very similar phrase about Roger's legislation, see above, 259.

pestilence, has for a long time and up to the present crept into use by part of our people, to prevent burgeoning vices spreading to the rest. For it is contrary to custom, inconsistent with what is laid down by the holy canons, and unheard of to Christian ears to desire to contract matrimony, to procreate legitimate progeny and bind oneself indissolubly to a consort, unless seeking the favour and grace of God in these matters of marriage and 'concerning Christ and the Church' as the Apostle says',[40] by confirming the sacrament through the priestly ministry. Thus we decree by the present law, which (God willing) shall last in perpetuity, that it is necessary for all those wishing to contract a legitimate marriage to have the marriage solemnly celebrated after the betrothal and each for his own measure and comfort to take the path to a church and priestly blessing.

rel. auth over marriage

After the examination he shall place a ring of price and they shall submit to priestly prayer, if they wish to bequeath succession [to their property] to their future heirs. Otherwise they should know that they are acting against our royal precept and would have no legitimate heirs either by will or by intestacy from those born to an illicit marriage contrary to our law; the women would have no right to the dowers proper for those legitimately married. We relax the rigour of this law to all those who have already contracted marriage at the time of its promulgation. We also relax the chain of this necessity for widows desiring to [re]marry.[41]

XXVIII About adulteresses

Moved by the piety to which we owe our whole being, we decree by the present general law that whenever a charge of adultery or fornication is put before those who, through our foresight and enactment, control our laws, they should pay no attention to status, but should clear-sightedly note the conditions and ages, and investigate the state of mind [of the parties] to establish whether [it was] of set purpose or from advice received or because of the perils of youth that they have rushed into the act, or whether they are fallen women; [to establish] whether the women's financial means are weak or strong, and whether they have

40 Ephesians, 5:32.

41 Cassino Assize 16; *Liber Augustalis*, III.74–6, trans. Powell (1971), 145, with some changes in wording. Parts of this assize may be dependent on a law of Leo VI of 907. Express reference was made to this assize in two wedding contracts from Ruvo, in Apulia, in August 1171 and January 1180: the latter saying 'Our wedding now having been celebrated according to the lawful, solemn and holy ceremonies laid down by the lord king Roger', *Codice diplomatic Barese* ix *Documenti storici di Corato (1046–1327)*, ed. F. Beltrani (Bari 1927), 71–3 no. 63, at 72; cf. *Le Pergamene di Conversano*, 261–3 no. 125.

been motivated by wilfulness or by a particularly unhappy marriage; in order that, once all these factors have been investigated, proven and clarified, either a more lenient or a more severe sentence may be passed on the crimes committed, not on the basis of the severity of the law but on that of the balance of fairness. For, if we proceed in this way, justice will tally perfectly with divine justice; nor will we be departing from that divine verdict, 'with what measure ye mete, it shall be measured to you once again'.[42]

The harshness of the laws has been softened so that she shall not, as once, be struck down by the sword but that the property belonging to her shall be subject to confiscation, if she shall have no legitimate children from this marriage or another. For it is most unjust that those who were born at a time when the law of the marriage was legally preserved should be defrauded of their inheritance. And she should certainly not be handed over to her husband whose anger would imperil her life, but rather the punishment for the violation of a marriage should be slitting of her nose, which [punishment] has been most sternly and cruelly introduced. However neither her husband nor her relations should be permitted to harm her further. If her husband is unwilling that such a penalty be inflicted on her, we will not allow a crime of this sort to go unpunished, and we order her to be publicly flogged.

Whosoever allows his wife to be wanton with debauched men while he looks on or by his arrangement cannot easily accuse her in court, since he who consents to what he could forbid opens the way to fraud.

We shall not condemn everyone who has a suspect wife as a pimp; for who rightfully disturbs the peace of another's marriage? But if we learn clearly that someone has a lascivious wife, we shall immediately from this time hold her worthy of strict punishment, and we condemn him to the penalty of infamy. Known prostitutes shall not be thought worthy to observe these laws and shall stand absolutely immune from the judicial punishments for adultery and fornication.[43]

XXIX About the same issue

A woman who has frequently exhibited her body for sale and revealed herself publicly as a prostitute is freed from accusation of this crime [i.e. of adultery]; however, [while] we prohibit violence to be done to her, we forbid her to dwell among women of good reputation.

---

42 Matthew, 7:1.

43 This last paragraph, *Codex*, IX.9.2 and 28.

An adulterer and an adulteress cannot be charged together. Each should be charged separately and the outcome of the matter awaited; for if the adulterer is able to clear himself, the woman is free and need make no further defence. If, however, he shall be found guilty, then let the woman in turn be accused. The law does not make a choice of who should be first tried, but if both are present then the man shall be tried first. Divorce [*repudium*] must always be permitted in this accusation, and neither violence nor detention should be employed.[44]

XXX About pimping

We decree by the present law that madams, namely those who solicit the chastity of another, which is the worst type of crime, should be punished as adulteresses. We punish mothers who prostitute their virgin daughters and abandon the bonds of marriage as madams; thus their noses should be slit. For it is cruel and inhuman for them to sell the chastity of their own offspring. But if a daughter prostitutes herself and the mother only consents, the matter shall be left to the decision of the judge.[45]

XXXI About the violation of marriage

If our royal majesty's providence refuses in any way to permit one of our barons to invade the *castrum* of another within the bounds of our kingdom, or to plunder it, to make an armed attack on it or to take anything from it by fraud, to prevent him by this act depriving him of its property; then by how much more do we hold him punishable if he should presume to violate the marriage of a fellow and neighbour? It seems that the law must not tolerate this. Therefore we decree that if anyone shall be accused to us of such a deed, and it be clearly proved, they shall be deprived of all their property.

If a husband catches his wife in the very act of adultery, then he shall be allowed to kill both the wife and the adulterer, provided that it is done without any further delay.[46]

XXXII About adultery

The legal penalty for pimping binds a husband who shall seize his wife caught in the act of adultery but has allowed the adulterer to get away,

---

44 Again draws on *Codex*, IX.9.2, 28; Cassino Assize 17; *Liber Augustalis*, III.77–8, trans. Powell (1971), 146.

45 *Liber Augustalis*, III.79–80, trans. Powell (1971), 146.

46 Cassino Assizes 22–3; last sentence only in *Liber Augustalis*, III.81, trans. Powell (1971), 147; cf. for this also *Prochiron Legum*, ed. F. Brandileone and V. Puntoni (FSI, Rome 1893), XL.8, p. 318.

unless however the latter escaped through no fault of his own.[47]

XXXIII About those failing to make an accusation

He who receives back his wife after the crime of adultery has been proved seems to have abandoned the accusation, and thus cannot raise any further charge.[48]

XXXIV About injuries inflicted on private persons

What is fully in agreement with law and reason is indeed welcome to all, and what is not agreeable to all on grounds of equity is manifestly unpleasing. For it is not to be wondered at if, when something which God has most carefully and properly placed in man is negligently and contemptuously held in no account by wrong judgement, the wise man and lover of honesty is rightly indignant. For is it any more absurd that a stricken mare be compensated when its tail is cut off, and when a most respectable man be deprived of his beard? Therefore on the suggestion and plea of the subject people of our kingdom, and realising the defects of its laws, we pronounce this law and edict, that if any ordinary person be deliberately and intentionally deprived of their beard, then those convicted of having done this shall have the following penalty imposed, namely a fine of six golden royal *solidi*. If, however, this was done in a fight, without being planned beforehand, then they shall be fined three *solidi*.[49]

XXXV About injuries inflicted on *curiales*

Judges should most diligently observe that they consider the dignity of *curiales* in any case of injury; and that they impose sentence according to the quality of the persons, both of those who were injured and of those who inflicted the injury, and where and when such a rash act was committed. They shall impose sentence according to the quality of the persons; for strictly speaking injury was done by them not to the persons themselves, but in fact should be seen as an offence to the royal dignity.[50]

---

47 *Codex*, IX.9.2; *Digest*, XLVIII.5.30.

48 *Digest*, XLVIII.5.41; Cassino Assize 24; *Liber Augustalis*, II.11, trans. Powell (1971), 75.

49 Cassino Assize 32 is a shortened version of this section.

50 Cassino Assize 13 (slightly shortened), *Liber Augustalis*, III.40, trans. Powell (1971), 127.

XXXVI About those wishing to become physicians

Whosoever in the future desires to become a physician should present himself to our officials and judges, for an examination according to their judgment. But, if he should rashly take this for granted, let him be consigned to prison and all his property confiscated. For this had been arranged so that subjects of our kingdom shall not be put at risk through physicians' inexperience.[51]

XXXVII About kidnappers

Whosoever knowingly sells a free man shall be subject to this legitimate penalty, that the person sold shall be redeemed from his property and that the criminal himself shall become a slave of our court, and the rest of his property shall be confiscated. If the man who has been sold cannot be redeemed, then the criminal should be handed over as a slave to the victim's parents, and his property awarded to the court. In any case where the man who has been sold shall return, the criminal shall become a slave of the court, and his sons born after this case shall be subject to the court in perpetual slavery.[52]

XXXVIII About robbers

He who, thinking his life to be in danger, shall kill an attacker or robber, ought not to fear blame for his action.[53]

XXXIX About children and madmen

If a child or madman shall kill a man without evil intent, he shall not be held accountable. For the one is excused by reason of innocence, the other by their unfortunate condition.[54]

XL About theft

He who shall kill a nocturnal thief shall remain unpunished, if the latter could not be arrested while the hue and cry was raised.[55]

---

51 *Codex*, X.52.10; *Liber Augustalis*, III.44, trans. Powell (1971), 130.

52 This draws on *Digest*, XLVIII.15.1, 4 and 15; Cassino Assize 25; *Liber Augustalis*, III.82, trans. Powell (1971), 149. The *Prochiron Legum*, XXXIV.4, p. 235, dealt with this crime, but its penalty was the loss of a hand.

53 *Codex*, IX.16.2; Cassino Assize 26.

54 *Digest*, XLVIII.8.12, also in Basil I's *Prochiron*, c. 80.

55 *Digest*, XLVIII.8.9; cf. *Prochiron Legum*, XL.4–5, p. 317.

XLI About arsonists

Whosoever sets a house on fire by deceit should suffer capital punishment as an arsonist.[56] In criminal matters the intention shall be taken into consideration, not the result; for there is no difference between someone who kills and one who seeks to cause death.[57]

XLII About those who throw things

Whosoever hurls himself down from on high and kills a man, and whoever incautiously and without shouting a warning hurls a branch or throws a stone or some other implement and kills a man, shall be subject to capital penalty.[58]

XLIII About poison

Whosoever gives, sells or possesses evil or harmful medicines which affect the mind, or poisons, shall be subject to capital penalty. Whoever prepares a love potion or some other harmful food, even if he harms no one, shall not go unpunished.[59]

XLIV If a judge neglects his duty

If a judge receives money and then declares someone guilty of a crime and of death, then he shall be subject to capital punishment. If a judge fraudulently and deceitfully hands down a sentence contrary to the laws, then he shall lose his judicial authority without hope of recovery, be branded with infamy and all his property shall be confiscated. However, if he makes a mistake in sentencing through ignorance of the law, he shall be punished for his simplicity of mind and be subject to our royal mercy and foresight.[60]

---

56 *Digest*, XLVIII.19.28, c. 12; Basil I, *Prochiron*, c. 18; Cassino Assize 27; *Liber Augustalis*, III.87, trans. Powell (1971), 149.

57 *Digest*, XLVIII.8.14–15.

58 *Digest*, XLVIII.8.7; included in Cassino Assize 26; *Liber Augustalis*, III.88, trans. Powell (1971), 149.

59 First sentence, *Digest of Justinian*, XLVIII.8.3; second sentence, *Digest*, XLVIII.19.38, c. 5; Cassino Assize 29; *Liber Augustalis*, III.69–70, trans. Powell (1971), 143.

60 Cassino Assize 30; *Liber Augustalis*, II.50, trans. Powell (1971), 103, with the order of the sentences changed, the last sentence being placed first. Pennington (2006) suggests that the title, although only the title, was taken from the Roman Law, perhaps *Digest*, V.1.15, or XLIV.7.5.4. If correct, this is important evidence for the compiler(s)' wider knowledge of the *Corpus Iuris Civilis*.

THE CATALOGUE OF THE BARONS

Extracts

[The 'Catalogue of the Barons' was a register of the military obligations of the mainland provinces of the kingdom of Sicily (excluding Calabria), compiled in the last years of the reign of King Roger c.1150, and revised and updated c.1167/8. The first few entries here show this process of revision. The extracts translated here comprise sections of the Catalogue from the duchy of Apulia (articles 345–56, 383–425), the principality of Salerno (articles 437–54), the principality of Capua (articles 806–50) and the Abruzzi (articles 1030–52, 1217–22). The only known manuscript of the Catalogue was written in the later thirteenth century, and some of the mistakes and apparent omissions may be due to later copyists,[1] although in some cases it appears that information was still to be provided when the list was drawn up. The translation below reproduces the text as written on the manuscript, rather than trying artificially to strip away the alterations of 1167/8 to reconstruct the original text of 1150.]

The Land of Benevento[2]

344: Count Roger of Buonalbergo[3] has said that his demesne in the *Terra Beneventana* [is as follows]: from Apice a fief of six knights, from Buonalbergo a fief of four knights, from S. Severo a fief of three knights. Together his own fief has thirteen knights, and with the *augmentum* he has offered thirty-one knights, fifty sergeants and two crossbows.

These are his barons.

345: Robert of Monte Malo holds from the fief of Thomas of Finocchio Joa, Palata and S. Giovanni Maitin, which is a fief of three knights, and

---

1 The manuscript was one of those destroyed when the contents of the Archivio di Stato of Naples, which had been transferred for safety to a villa at Nola, were burned as a reprisal by a Wehrmacht unit in September 1943. Evelyn Jamison produced her subsequent edition from photographs of this manuscript, taken pre-war.

2 This headline may be a later insertion, the object being to distinguish the fiefs of the Count of Buonalbergo in this region from those he held in the principality of Capua, which were listed later, arts. 806–7.

3 Roger's name was inserted by the revisers of 1167/8 for that of his father Robert, who died before 1154. For the family, see below, note 70.

with the *augmentum* he has offered six knights.[4]

346: Robert de Marca has said that he holds from him Reino which is a fief of one knight, and Mallerius de Marca holds Pesco which is a fief of one knight, and with the *augmentum* he has offered four knights.[5]

347: Savarinus de Terra Rubea holds Tammaro from this same fief of Thomas, which is a fief of two knights, and Terra Rubea which is a fief of two knights, and with the *augmentum* he has offered eight knights.

348: Bartholomew of Pietrelcina holds from this same man Pietrelcina, which so he has said is a fief of one knight, and with the *augmentum* he has offered two knights.[6]

349: Rao Pinellus holds Fragneto from him, which is so he has said a fief of one knight, and with the *augmentum* he has offered two knights.[7] Together there are from the aforesaid fief of Thomas of Finocchio which he holds from the aforesaid Count Roger with the *augmentum* twenty-two knights.

350: Gerard de Greci holds Greci from the aforesaid count, which is a fief of three knights, and Savignano a fief of one knight, and Ferrara a fief of two knights. Together from his own fief [there are] six knights, and with the *augmentum* twelve knights and twelve sergeants.[8]

351: The wife of [Robert] Potofranculus and [the wife of] William Potefranco [who are] his sisters hold Monte Calvo which is a fief of four knights and Ginestra which is a fief of one knight, and with the *augmentum* they have offered ten knights.[9]

---

4 Thomas of Finocchio himself was not listed at this point, but much later under the principality of Capua, arts. 982 *et seq.*, presumably because his own demesne lands to the west of Benevento were deemed to be within its borders, whereas Buonalbergo and the fiefs subject to it east of Benevento were undoubtedly in the duchy.

5 This may either be the Robert attested from 1122 to 1137 who appears at several points in Falco's chronicle, see *Falco*, above, note 164 there, or his son of the same name, attested 1175–81. Malgerius was brother of the first and uncle of the second. See Loud (1997), 285, 291, 296 (genealogical chart). Pesco Sannita is 12 km. N of Benevento, Reino a further 8 km. N of that.

6 See above, 202, and note 165.

7 He was the father of Bartholow Monteforte, below, art. 355. His fief was Fragneto l'Abbate.

8 Son of Brian of Greci, and nephew of Abbess Bethlem of S. Maria di Porta Somma, Benevento; see above, 161, and Jamison (1934). Gerard was later a royal justiciar, in 1163, and both he and his brother Brian were still alive in July 1177, *Chartes de Troia*, no. 94.

9 Robert of Potofranco was named by Falco as one of the barons of the Count of Ariano in 1137 (above, 228); his wife, whose name we do not know (presumably now a widow) was also *domina* of Montefalcone, *Catalogus Baronum* art. 323.

352: Godfrey son of Paganus of Montefusco has said that he holds from this same count Monterone which is a fief of one knight, and Campolattaro which is a fief of one [knight?], and Santa Croce and the villeins that he holds in Apice [form] a fief of one knight, and with the *augmentum* he has offered six knights.[10]

353: Robert of Monte Malo has said that he holds in chief from this same count S. Giorgio which is a fief of three knights, and Guasto which is a fief of one knight, and with the *augmentum* he has offered in all eight knights and ten sergeants.

354: Robert of Molinara has said that he holds Molinara which is a fief of two knights, and with the *augmentum* he has offered four knights and ten sergeants.

355: Bartholomew of Monteforte holds from the fief of William of San Fraymundo, which he holds from this same count, namely Fragneto which is a fief of one knight, and with the *augmentum* he has offered two knights.[11]

356: Hugh son of Rainald son of William has said that he holds on demesne Sant' Eleuterio which is a fief of three knights, and Castelpagano which is a fief of two knights, and with the *augmentum* he has offered twelve knights and eighty sergeants.

[...]

383: Count Godfrey of Lesina holds in chief from the lord king Bantia, which Henry de Ollia used to hold, which so he said [is] a fief of four knights, and with the *augmentum* he has offered eight knights.[12]

384: Marsilius holds from this same count Chieuti, which is so he said a

---

10 His father Paganus, identified as the royal constable of Montefusco, witnessed a donation to Montevergine by the widow of a man from Montefusco killed fighting for the king at the battle of Rignano in 1137, *Cod. Dipl. Verginiano*, iii.179–82 no. 243.

11 He was the son of Rao Pinellus (for whom see above, art. 349), as revealed in a donation of his to the church of St Matthew at the Porta Aurea in Benevento in 1180, Benevento, Museo del Sannio, Fondo S. Sofia, vol. 13 no. 19. Fragneto (Monforte) had been held by Rao of Fragneto (above, 232); since he was an opponent of the king, it had presumably been confiscated from him and given to Bartholomew, son of one of Roger's supporters.

12 This entry comes from the revision of 1167/8. Henry de Ollia, a royal justiciar and Godfrey's father, was still alive at the time of the original compilation c.1150. This Norman family was from Oully-le-Tesson (Calvados), Ménager (1975b), 338; Cuozzo (1984), 97–8. For Godfrey, who succeeded to Henry's justiciarate, *Additamenta ad Chronicon Casauriense*, RIS ii(2).1010–11 (January 1164); *Cod. Dipl. Tremiti*, iii.324–7 no. 117 (October 1175). He was appointed Count of Lesina after the disgrace and imprisonment of the incumbent count, William, c.1156, for which *Tyrants*, 75. Bantia was near S. Severo in the Capitanata; the settlement no longer exists.

fief of two knights, and with the *augmentum* he has offered four knights.[13]

385: Matthew de Guandalino holds from him Loreto and Monte Calvo, which is so he said a fief of four knights, and with the *augmentum* he has offered eight knights.

386: The Bishop of Civitate for San Leucio one knight and a half, and with the *augmentum* he has offered three knights and fifteen sergeants.

387: Count Godfrey of Lesina so he has said [holds] Lesina [which] is a fief of eight knights, and Apricena is a fief of four knights, and Ripalta a fief of two knights. Together from his own fief there are fifteen knights and in his *augmentum* there are seventeen knights. Together between fief and *augmentum* he has offered thirty-two knights and 100 sergeants; and as Raymond son of Frachaldus testified this same Count Godfrey holds the *casale* of San Trifone, a fief of one knight, and with the augmentum he has offered two knights.[14]

388: The wife of William of Crevonzone made known through her vassal [*homo*] Benedict that she holds San Nicandro which is a fief of two knights and Roccetta which is a fief of one knight, and with the *augmentum* she has offered six knights and ten sergeants.[15]

Together from the demesne and service of the said Count, from his own fief there are eighteen knights and from the *augmentum* both of the demesne and of the service twenty knights. Altogether there are thirty-eight knights and 110 sergeants.

389: Item, Hugh son of Rahel holds the *casale* of San Pietro Veterano which Matthew of San Pietro and Benjamin used to hold, which is a fief of one knight, and with the *augmentum* he has offered two knights.[16]

---

13 He and his brother Richard also held fiefs in the Abruzzi, as vassals of the Count of Manopello, *Catalogus Baronum*, arts. 1014, 1017. Marsilius made a donation to Holy Saviour Abbey, Monte Majella, in 1144, Cuozzo (1984), 296. Chieuti is in the northern Capitanata, 16 km. W of Lesina and 8 km. from the Adriatic coast.

14 Again, this entry comes from the revision of 1167/8.

15 This entry too probably comes from the revision, since William was still alive in July 1153, when he was one of the witnesses to a legal case involving the abbey of Tremiti, held at Vieste, one of the justiciars presiding being Henry de Ollia, *Cod. Dipl. Tremiti*, iii.297–9 no. 107. The family name was Norman, deriving from Gravenchon (Seine-Maritime), Ménager (1975b), 318. Sannicandro Garganico (the modern form of the name) is 20 km. E of Lesina. In March 1174, this *castello* was held by William son of Manerus, *Cod. Dipl. Tremiti*, iii.322–4 no. 116.

16 This is part of the revision; the original holders were listed in *Catalogus Baronum*, arts. 365–6, as vassals of the Count of Loritello; they were thus probably involved in his rebellion in 1154–6, and their fiefs were confiscated, Cuozzo (1984), 90–1.

390: Count Philip of Civitate according to what he has said about what he holds in the duchy: Civitate is a fief of ten knights, Monterisi a fief of three knights, Monte Rotaro a fief of one knight, Montilari a fief of three knights, and Deliceto a fief of three knights. Together from the demesne of the said count there are twenty knights, and his *augmentum* is twenty knights. Altogether there are forty knights and forty sergeants.[17]

These are his barons

391: Roger de Parisio holds from this same count Castellucio, which is a fief of two knights, and with the *augmentum* he has offered four knights and four sergeants.[18]

(Avellino)

392: Count [Roger] of Aquila[19] said that his demesne which is in the principality is a fief of twenty knights, and at Riardo a fief of one knight;[20] and at Avellino there is a fief of sixteen knights which he holds in the duchy, and at Mercogliano is a fief of two knights, and at Capriglia a fief of two knights, and at Sant'Angelo a fief of two knights. Together from his own fief there are forty-six knights, and in his *augmentum* there are forty-five knights. Together, between fief and *augmentum* he has offered eighty-eight [*sic*] knights and 100 sergeants.

These are his barons from the duchy

393: Boamund Malerba holds Summonte which is a fief of two knights, and with the *augmentum* he has offered four knights and ten sergeants.[21]

394: Robert de Tufo holds Montefredane which, so he has said, is a fief

---

17 This is also part of the revision; the Count of Civitate at the time of the original compilation was Robert son of Robert fitz Richard (for whose father, see above, *Al. Tel.* II.68, note 105 there). When and how Philip became count is unknown: he died before 1178, Cuozzo (1984), 66–7; Martin (1993), 720. All the places mentioned in this entry have now disappeared. Civitate was near the River Fortore, about 8 km. E of Serracapriola.

18 He was recorded as constable of Count Robert II of Civitate in January 1152, *Codice diplomatico del regno di Carlo I e Carlo II d'Angiò*, ed. G. Del Giudice, i (Naples 1863), appendix xxvii–xxviii, no. XI.

19 Count Roger of Avellino (d.1183); his name was another that was inserted when the Catalogue was revised in 1167/8, replacing that of his father Richard, who died in 1152.

20 These were in the principality of Capua, cf. art. 808 below, where the entry for Riardo (near Teano) is repeated.

21 Boamund Malerba, lord of Summonte, made a series of donations to the nearby monastery of Montevergine, *Cod. Dipl. Verginiano* iv.31–3 no. 308 (June 1152), 247–50 no. 366 (February 1158), and *ibid.*, v.124–6 no. 435 (December 1163), in the last of which he claimed to be 'born of a most noble family of the French'.

of two knights, and with the *augmentum* he has offered four knights and ten sergeants.[22]

395: Roger of Fragneto holds Grottolella and Salza which are fiefs of two knights, and with the *augmentum* he has offered four knights and ten sergeants.[23]

Together from both the demesne fief and the service of the said count there are forty-nine knights, and in his *augmentum* both from the demesne and the service there are fifty-one knights. Together there are in all 100 knights and 130 sergeants, and if the necessity of war shall demand it he can have more than have been promised.

From this same constabulary. Richard son of Richard under the constabulary of Guimund of Montellari.

396: [The son of][24] Guimund of Montellari said that he holds Castellucio which is a fief of two knights, and with the *augmentum* he has offered four knights.

397: Raho de Rocca Troia said that he holds the third part of a knight, and with the *augmentum* he has offered himself.[25]

398: Armarus said that he holds half the fief of a knight in Foggia, and with the *augmentum* he has offered one knight.

399: Maynardus de Grano said that he holds Prisurgio which is a fief of one knight, and with the *augmentum* he has offered two knights and two sergeants.[26]

400: John de Boctio said that he holds twenty commended men in Castiglione, and with the *augmentum* he has offered one knight.[27]

---

22 He witnessed a donation of Count Roger of Avellino to Montevergine in August 1167, *Cod. Dipl. Verginiano*, v.261–4 no. 474.

23 He was son of Hugh of Castello Cripta, *Cod. Dipl. Verginiano*, iii.327–9 no. 279 (1144); for him see *ibid.*, v.328–31 no. 494 (March 1169).

24 This is an insertion from the revision of 1167/8. For Guimund as a royal justiciar, *Le Colonie Cassinesi in Capitanata* iv *Troia*, ed. T. Leccisotti (Miscellanea Cassinese 29, Montecassino 1957), 96–9 no. 30 (1156).

25 His father John was *stratigotus* (ducal bailiff) of Troia in 1123; Raho himself was advocate (legal representative) for the Bishop of Troia in September 1144, and later, in March 1159, a royal justiciar, *Chartes de Troia*, 175–7 no. 46, 219–21 no. 67, 241–4 no. 76. His son Lucas was similarly a royal justiciar, *ibid.*, 263–5 no. 87 (1170).

26 He witnessed several charters at Troia between 1154 and 1162, *Chartes de Troia*, 226–31 no. 70–1, 241–4 no. 76, 249–51 no. 80.

27 John de Boccio in fact held his property at Castiglione as a vassal of the abbey of Montecassino, although this was the subject of considerable dispute. A court held by Duke Roger of Apulia judged that he owed tithe to Montecassino in March 1147; subsequently John came to a separate agreement (undated, but probably in 1148) with Abbot Rainald about

401: Leo of Foggia said that he holds a few commended men and has offered one knight.[28]

The Bishop-elect of Troia[29]   The Abbot of Orsara[30]

The Abbot of St. Nicholas of Troia[31]   The Abbot of Vulture[32]

The Bishop of Melfi

402: The Bishop of Melfi holds Gaudiano and has there from the demesne a fief of two knights, and in service a fief of two knights, and with the *augmentum* he has offered eight knights and 100 sergeants.[33]

The Abbot of Banzi[34]

403: Jordan son of James of Andria holds half of Pietrasicca, which is one fief, and with the *augmentum* he has offered two knights. The other half is in the demesne of the lord king.

---

this, which included provision for his sons to succeed him and made express reference to the service of one knight to the king. This agreement was renewed after John's death by his sons, in December 1156; this document refers to a further court case heard on the instructions of King Roger at Troia in the presence of the Count of Civitate and the justiciar Guimund of Monte, thus presumably before 1154, *Colonie Cassinesi in Capitanata* iv *Troia*, 93–5 nos. 27–8, 96–9 no. 30.

28 He was a royal chamberlain who was one of the witnesses to the agreement between the sons of John de Boccio and Montecassino in 1156.

29 This must be Hugh, attested as bishop-elect in 1144–7, hence this entry comes from the original Catalogue: his successor William [III], bishop 1155–75, had long since been consecrated by the time of the revision of 1167/8, Cuozzo (1984), 107.

30 St Angelo of Orsara, in the diocese of Troia, was founded c.1120 by Spanish monks, and retained a long-standing link with the kingdom of Leon, Hiestand (1991).

31 This Benedictine abbey in Troia was first mentioned in a papal privilege for the bishopric in 1067, *Chartes de Troia*, 106–7 no. 14 [*Italia Pontificia*, ix.203 no. 5]. A legal case of 1184 refers to a now-lost privilege of King Roger for this abbey, which may have dated from 1129, *Roger II Diplomata*, deperdita no. 84.

32 St Michael on Monte Vulture, in the diocese of Rapolla, which began life in the tenth century as a community of Greek hermits, later became a Benedictine house, *Italia Pontificia*, ix.502–3. Roger issued a privilege for this abbey in September 1141, *Roger II Diplomata*, deperdita no. 62.

33 Duke Roger Borsa had given this *casale* [unfortified village] to the bishop in December 1096, although his charter stipulated that nothing was to be owed in return for this, Ughelli, *Italia Sacra*, i.923–4.

34 This would appear to have been inserted here in error, for the abbey of Banzi, in Lucania, had been listed earlier, *Catalogus Baronum*, art. 87: 'The abbot of Banzi, so William of Rapolla said, holds Banzi from this same county [of Andria], which is a fief of three knights, and with the *augmentum* he has offered seven knights'. The abbey probably owed service because it had recently purchased the *castello* of Banzi, Loud (2007a), 349–50.

Sant' Agata

These are the knights of Sant'Agata holding a fief.[35]

404: Landulf son of Peter Aguinardus holds, so he said, a fief of two knights, and with the *augmentum* he has offered four knights.[36]

405: Gualeramus, so he said, holds a fief of one knight, and with the *augmentum* he has offered two knights.[37]

406: Richard son of Brinus holds a fief, so he said, of one knight, and with the *augmentum* he has offered two knights. Together there are from Sant' Agata … knights holding fiefs, and there are thirty not holding fiefs. Rainald Fraihaldus ought to make inquiry about these.[38]

Bovino

407: According to Richard de Calvello, the knights of Bovino having fiefs are nine.

The knights of Bovino not having fiefs are twenty. Matthew the Chamberlain ought to write to the Curia about their names and tenements.[39]

Ascoli

These are the knights of Ascoli from the demesne of the Holy Trinity of Venosa.

408: The Abbot of the said Holy Trinity of Venosa has offered for all his land and his tenement thirty knights and 230 sergeants for the help of the great expedition, and the customary sergeants which the Curia is accustomed to have from the half of Ascoli which belongs to the said church.

409: From Corneto of Holy Trinity of Venosa. From S. Giovanni in Fronto on behalf of the Abbot of Holy Trinity of Venosa. From Valle

35 Sant'Agata di Puglia.

36 His father Peter claimed to be the successor to Hoel the Breton as lord of Sant'Agata in June 1143, Martini (1915), 57–8 no. 19.

37 He was a witness to a charter of Count Robert II of Civitate to the abbey of Torremaggiore in January 1152, for which see above, note 18 to art. 391.

38 A royal chamberlain, cf. *Catalogus Baronum*, arts. 118–24, and above art. 387.

39 For Matthew, *Catalogus Baronum* art. 627, where we are told that he holds only fifteen villeins, but with the *augmentum* renders one knight. Matthew can be attested between 1137 and 1149, though most of the evidence relating to him comes from the charters of the monastery of St Maria of Calvello, now only known through the notebooks of the seventeenth-century antiquary G.B. Prignano. He did, however, in his official role as chamberlain, witness a restitution of tithes to the bishopric of Troia in September 1144, *Chartes de Troia*, 219–21 no. 67. See Cuozzo (1984), 170–1. This entry thus clearly comes from the original Catalogue.

Sorbi of this same abbot. From Orta of this same abbot. From Acqua-bella of this same abbot. From Barrano of this same abbot.[40]

The Abbot of St. John in Lama[41]

The Abbot of Holy Trinity Cava[42]

From St. Peter de Olivola and St. James of Lucera[43]

From Montefusco

410: Guerrarius of Montefusco has said that he holds in demesne a fief of one knight, and he holds a fief of two knights in service, and with the *augmentum* he has offered both for himself and from his men six knights.[44]

411: Herbert son of Milo Paganus, so Guerrarius has said, holds in demesne a fief of one knight, and in service a fief of one knight, and with the *augmentum* he has offered three knights.[45]

412: Raynerius son of Guimund and Brienus his brother, so they have said, hold a fief of one knight, and with the *augmentum* they have offered two knights.

---

40 Acquabella was given to Venosa by Robert Guiscard in 1063; the abbey acquired most of the other properties in the 1090s from Duke Roger Borsa or the counts of the Principate, Loud (2007a), 351. Holy Trinity, Venosa, was founded in the 1040s by Drogo de Haute-ville, elder brother of Robert Guiscard, who made it the mausoleum of his dynasty. Its twelfth-century history was chequered, and it was reformed by monks from Cava in the 1140s; see Houben (1995), especially 135–65; and Loud (2007a), 84–90, for its eleventh-century significance.

41 An earlier notice, *Catalogus Baronum* art. 376, said that this abbey, on the southern slopes of the Gargano massif, founded in the early eleventh century, owed four knights, and with the *augmentum* eight and 100 sergeants. King Roger issued a (now-lost) privilege for this abbey in 1134, *Roger II Diplomata*, deperdita no. 44.

42 Benedictine abbey, founded near Salerno c.1020 and much favoured by the Norman Dukes of Apulia and their nobles; by this time it was one of the wealthiest monastic houses in southern Italy, see Loud (1987); Ramseyer (2006), 159–92; Loré (2008).

43 These were both dependencies of Cava, being given to it in 1083 and 1086 respectively, Loud (1987), 150.

44 He was the son of Accardus of Montefusco, one of the barons who on the orders of the Count of Ariano swore not to exact customary dues from Benevento in 1137 [above, 225], *Cod. Dipl. Verginiano*, 235–8 no. 256 (December 1139). He later became Constable of Montefusco, *ibid.*, iv.55–8 no. 315 (1153), hence his testimony with regard to the other fief holders there.

45 In June 1161 he gave a garden at Montefusco to two brothers, for the good service they had rendered him. He subsequently became constable of Montefusco and a royal justiciar, and was still alive as late as 1195. *Cod. Dipl. Verginiano*, v.16–18 no. 405, vi.273–6 no. 572, x.289–91 no. 988. His father Milo Paganus witnessed a donation by Eternus, lord of Montefusco, to Montevergine in June 1135, *ibid.*, iii.80–4 no. 220.

413: Niel son of Pipinus holds a fief of one knight, and with the *augmentum* he has offered two knights.

414: Tancred of Molise along with his wife the daughter of Hugh the Brown holds in demesne a fief of one knight, and he holds in service a fief of five knights, and with the *augmentum* he has offered both on his own behalf and from his men twelve knights.[46]

415: William son of Raoul, so Guerrerius has said, holds in demesne a fief of one knight, and in service a fief of one knight, and with the *augmentum* he has offered both on his own behalf and from his men four knights.

416: Constantine, so Guerrerius has said, holds a fief of two knights, and with the *augmentum* he has offered four knights.[47]

417: Robert son of Girard holds a fief of one knight, and with the *augmentum* he has offered two knights.

418: Raho de Brae, so he has said, holds a fief of one knight, and with the *augmentum* he has offered two knights.

419: Gibel, so Guerrerius has said, holds a fief of one knight, and with the *augmentum* he has offered two knights.

420: Guimund son of Paganus, so he has said, holds a fief of one knight, and with the *augmentum* he has offered two knights.

421: William son of Alexander Corbolinus has said that he holds a fief of one knight, and with the *augmentum* he has offered two knights.

422: Basuinus holds a fief of one knight, and with the *augmentum* he has offered two knights.

423: Tancred of Cantalupo holds the fief which was that of Tancred de Cripta, which William Buccafollis held, which is so he says a fief of one knight, and with the *augmentum* he has offered two knights.[48]

424: Landulf son of Andrew holds from him the fief that was held by Tadeus de Greca, a fief of one knight, and with the *augmentum* he has

---

46 Tancred and his wife Amelina made a donation to Montevergine in April 1174, *Cod. Dipl. Verginiano*, vi.273–6 no. 572.

47 Probably the Constantine son of Roger of Montefusco who made a donation to Montevergine in December 1139, *Cod. Dipl. Verginiano*, iii.239–43 no. 257; he was still alive in January 1166, *ibid.*, v.201–4 no. 457.

48 Tancred of Cantalupo had married the daughter of Tadeus de Greca, *Cod. Dipl. Verginiano*, iv.200–3 no. 353 (February 1157), who was thus the granddaughter of the Constable Landulf de Greca. He was still alive in April 1174, when he witnessed a charter of Tancred of Molise [see above, note 46]. William Buccafollis is attested in March 1144, *Chartes de Troia*, 215–17 no. 65.

offered two knights. From both the demesne and service of this same Tancred he has offered with the *augmentum* four knights.

425: The son of Helias of Montefusco has said that he holds ten villeins, and with the *augmentum* he has offered one knight.

From Montefusco there are with the *augmentum* forty-nine knights.

[...]

(From the Principality)[49]

The constabulary of Lampus of Fasanella.

437: William son of Henry of S. Severino has said that his demesne of S. Severino is a fief of eight knights, and from Cilento [he has] a fief of six knights. Together from his own fief [there are] fourteen knights and his *augmentum* [is] fourteen knights. Together there are from both fief and *augmentum* twenty-eight knights and eighty armed infantrymen, whom he has offered.[50]

438: This same William has said that Montoro is a fief of thirteen knights and his *augmentum* is thirteen knights. Together from fief and *augmentum* he offers twenty-six knights from Montoro.[51]

Together there are both from his own fiefs of S. Severino, Cilento and Montoro twenty seven knights and his *augmentum* [is] twenty-seven knights.[52] Between fief and *augmentum* he offers fifty-four knights and eighty infantrymen.

These men hold from him

439: Florius [*sic*] of Camerota holds Corbella[53] which is, so he says, a

---

49 A later insertion.

50 Henry of S. Severino died on 31 August 1150, *Necrologio di S. Matteo*, 124. William was apparently a minor when his father died, and for some years thereafter his lordship was under the administration of his mother Fenicia, Cava, *Arca* xxix.92 (May 1157), xxx.71 (January 1162). William was forced to flee into exile in 1162, and only restored c.1167, just before the revision of the Catalogue. He subsequently served as a royal justiciar 1179–87, *Falcandus*, 78, 131 [*Tyrants*, 129, 182–3]; Portanova (1976), 329–39; Cuozzo (1984), 120–2.

51 While William was in exile, and perhaps even after his return, Montoro (10 km. S of Avellino on the road to Salerno) appears to have been in the hands of William, lord of Atrepalda (5 km. E of Avellino), Cava, *Arm. Mag.* H.44 (January 1166), I.4 (March 1169). *Falcandus*, 131, however suggests that it was claimed by William of San Severino's cousin, Count Robert of Caserta. William had recovered Montoro by November 1169, Cava, *Arca* xxxiii.44. Portanova (1976), 339.

52 A marginal annotation corrects this from twenty-eight.

53 'Florius' is a copyist's error, probably for Roger. Roger of Camerota, lord of Corbella, was one of the witnesses to a legal case between Abbots Falco of Cava and Cosmas of Pantano

fief of two knights, and with the *augmentum* he offers four knights (for
another fief of one knight, once that of Roger Russus, which the lord
king has given to him, and with the *augmentum* two knights).[54]

440: William of Pistiglione holds Castelluccio, which so he has said is
a fief of two knights, and with the *augmentum* he offers four knights.[55]

441: Robert son of Trogisius de Cripta with his mother holds S. Giorgio,
which so he has said is a fief of two knights, and with the *augmentum* he
offers four knights.[56]

442: The Court holds what Lampus of Fasanella held, namely in Corneto
a fief of two knights, in [each of] Trentinara, Magliano and Selefone a
fief of one knight, and with the *augmentum* it offers ten knights.[57]

443: Guido of Trentinara holds from this in service a fief of one knight,
and with the *augmentum* he offers two knights.[58]

---

at Agropoli in January 1144, Cava, *Arca*, xxv.56, and subsequently his fief in Cilento was
held by his son Godfrey, Cava, *Arca*, xxxii.96 (May 1168), xxxiv.22 (April 1172). For
Florius, see below, art. 454.

54 The section in parentheses was probably a marginal note in the original MS, which a
copyist subsequently entered into the text.

55 William held other fiefs in the principality directly from the king, from which he owed
seven knights, and with the *augmentum* sixteen knights and forty-six sergeants, *Catalogus
Baronum*, arts. 466–7. He was first recorded in June 1142, when he granted Cava the
monastery of S. Angelo of Selvanera, seemingly in return for the burial of his father Rao
in the monastery, Cava, *Arm. Mag.* G. 36, 38. He was a royal justiciar in 1159, although
he had apparently ceased to serve as such by October 1161, Robinson (1930), 68 no. 45;
Cava, *Arca*, xxx.46; *Arm. Mag.* H.38; and towards the end of his long life he supported
the conquest of Henry VI, being last recorded in April 1195, Clementi (1953/4), 355–6.
Cuozzo (1984), 123–4.

56 He was the second of the three sons of Trogisius of Grottaminarda (25 km. SE of
Benevento), who was a major landowner in the region along the eastern frontier of the
principality of Salerno; for him see *Catalogus Baronum*, arts. 708–18. S. Giorgio (16 km.
SW of Avellino) was the dower of his mother, Mabilia of S. Severino, who died on 18
February 1173, *Necrologio di S. Matteo*, 26. Robert appears already to have been in posses-
sion of this during his mother's lifetime (or he rendered the service on her behalf). He was
a benefactor of the Cava dependency of St John at Roccapiemonte (2 km. S of S. Giorgio),
Cava, *Arm. Mag.* I.25 (February 1181), I.35 (March 1182).

57 Lampus, a Lombard, son of a Count Guaiferius, married a woman from the kin-group of
the former Lombard princes of Salerno. He seems to have acquired his land at Corneto
from his brother-in-law Jordan, Cava, *Arm. Mag.* G.14 (October 1134), G. 24 (March 1137).
Lampus was a royal justiciar in the principality in 1143–51, and also a royal constable
when the Catalogue was first drawn up. Cuozzo suggests, plausibly but without definite
proof, that he lost his fiefs because he was involved in the revolt of Count William III of
the Principate in 1155/6, Jamison (1913), 365–8; Cuozzo (1984), 125–7; Cuozzo (1995),
110–14. Loud (1987), 162, gives a genealogical chart. For other fiefs of Lampus, *Catalogus*,
arts. 487–9.

58 This entry is also part of the revision of 1167/8 since Guido was the successor to Robert
of Trentinaria, whose deathbed will, dated 3 October 1156, survives, Cava, *Arm. Mag.*

444: Ascittinus of Sicignano holds from this in service a fief of one knight, and with the *augmentum* he offers two knights.[59]

There are seven knights doing service from his own fiefs, and with the *augmentum* he offers fourteen knights and thirty sergeants.[60]

445: (The Court) Gragnano which is a fief of one knight, and its *augmentum* is two knights and fifty armed infantrymen.

446: James Guarna brother of the lord Robert, Archdeacon of Salerno, holds Castellione, which so he has said is a fief of two knights, and with the *augmentum* he offers five knights and 100 sergeants.[61]

447: Landulf de Manso holds Lettere, which so he has said is a fief of two knights, and with the *augmentum* he offers four knights.[62]

448: Guaymar of Rotunda, for Rotunda which he holds, and for what he has in Acerno, which is a fief of three knights, and with the *augmentum* he offers six knights and fifty sergeants,[63] and for half of Vietri,[64] a fief of one knight and a half, and with the *augmentum* he offers three knights and fifteen sergeants.

449: Guido of Acerno for what he holds in Acerno and in Giffoni, which

---

H.27, Ughelli, *Italia Sacra*, vii.400–1. It is unclear whether they were related; no son was named in Robert's will. Trentinara is on a hilltop 6 km. SE of Capaccio on the northern edge of the Cilento massif.

59 He was presumably a descendant of the Ascittinus of Sicignano, attested in 1085–6, Houben (1995), 278; Cava, *Arm. Mag.* C.1 (assuming that the latter document, an early thirteenth-century forgery, was based on a genuine model; for this Carlone (1984), 26–8). Sicignano d'Alburni overlooks the Tanagro valley 50 km. E of Salerno.

60 This entry appears to be unaltered from the original Catalogue of c.1150.

61 Castellione is now Castellemare di Stabia, on the bay of Naples. James [Jacobus] Guarna, died on 19 June 1177, his brother Robert, archdeacon of Salerno on 15 January 1180 *Necrologio di S. Matteo*, 8, 84. They came from one of the leading families of Salerno, being among the (at least) eight children of Peter Guarna (d.1157), who had been *Stratigotus* (governor) of the city in 1125. This entry probably comes from the original Catalogue of 1150, since otherwise it is odd that there was no mention of his most notable relation, his brother Romuald, who became Archbishop of Salerno in 1153. Garufi, introduction to *Romuald*, pp. v–x; Cuozzo (1984), 128–9; Loud (2000b), 305 (genealogical chart).

62 He was son of a Count Alfanus and died before May 1183, by which time his wife Itta had re-married, to Lucas Guarna, lord of Mandra, another brother of Archbishop Romuald, Cava, *Arm. Mag.* L.2. However, the assumption of Cuozzo (1984), 129, that he only acquired Lettere (on the Amalfitan peninsula, 6 km. E of Castellamare di Stabia) in 1168 appears unjustified, although it is possible that it had previously been held by Philip Mansellus, active at the royal court in 1161, for whom *Tyrants*, 103.

63 Marginal correction, fifteen. The translation of this entry reproduces the clumsy phraseology of the Latin.

64 Vietri di Potenza, 25 km. W of Potenza, not Vietri sul Mare near Salerno. Later entries reveal that Guaymar held a half-share in Vietri, the other half held by a man called Accardus, *Catalogus Baronum*, arts. 477, 479.

so he has said is a fief of three knights, and with the *augmentum* he offers six knights and fifty sergeants.[65]

450: Philip Guarna holds so he has said a fief of one knight which Roger of San Mango used to hold, and with the *augmentum* he offers two knights and six sergeants.[66]

451: Alfanus of Castellamare has himself said that his whole fief in Castellemare is a fief of three knights, and Torricella [is one] of one knight and a half, and what he holds in Cilento is a fief of one knight, and with the *augmentum* he offers eleven knights and eleven sergeants.[67]

452: Marinus Brancaccio of Naples holds the fief which Fulk of Tivilla held, which is so he has said a fief of four knights, and with the *augmentum* he offers eight knights and fifteen sergeants.[68]

453: Arrabitus of Cuccaro has said that he holds Cuccaro which is a fief of four knights, and with the *augmentum* he offers eight knights and twenty sergeants.

454: Florius of Camerota has said that his demesne is a fief of twelve knights, and with the *augmentum* he offers twenty-four knights and fifty sergeants.[69]

[...]

65 Marginal correction, fifteen. Acerno and Giffoni were both in the mountains to the east of Salerno. Guido and Guaymar of Rotunda were brothers, Cuozzo (1984), 130.

66 He was another brother of Archbishop Romuald, who died on 30 June 1187, *Necrologio di S, Matteo*, 88; Cuozzo (1984), 131 (who corrects Garufi's erroneous transcription). He acted as legal guarantor to his brother Lucas when the latter sold his and his wife's share of a church to Cava in 1183, Cava, *Arm. Mag.* L.2.

67 Alfanus gave a church to Cava in December 1144, Cava, *Arm. Mag.* G. 43; he was subsequently a royal chamberlain in the principality of Salerno 1151–8, and acted as administrator of the county of the Principato after the arrest of Count William II c.1156. He may well have been the Alfanus who was entrusted with escorting Elizabeth of Champagne to Sicily, where she was to marry Duke Roger of Apulia, the king's eldest son, in 1140, *Letters of St. Bernard*, 351 no. 279, but this cannot be confirmed. Jamison (1913), 392–4; Cuozzo (1984), 131–2; Cuozzo (1995), 102, 260–1. This Castellamare was at the mouth of the River Alento; Torricella no longer exists but was further up the river valley, below Monti della Stella.

68 Marinus was one of several co-owners who gave Cava the church of St Gregory *de Regionario* in Naples in June 1150, Cava, *Arm. Mag.* H.8. Fulk of Tivilla (a name derived from Théville, dépt. Manche) and his brother Simon were among those who witnessed a lease by the abbot of St Nicholas, Capaccio, in April 1146 (among the other witnesses were Lampus of Fasanella [above, art. 442]), Cava, *Arca*, xxvi.45.

69 He had a long career as a royal justiciar in three different circuits from 1150 until 1189, in the principality of Salerno, the principality of Capua and the Val di Crati in northern Calabria. He was also one of the ambassadors who negotiated the marriage of King William II with a daughter of Henry II of England in 1176. See now Loud (2008), 396–9, which adds new evidence to the accounts in Jamison (1913), 366–7; Cuozzo (1984), 133–4.

(Count Robert of Buonalbergo)

806: Count Robert of Buonalbergo has said that he holds in demesne in the principality of Capua Suessula Pantana which is a fief of eight knights, and his part of Acerra is a fief of five knights, and Maranello which is a fief of seven knights. Together from his own demesne fief there are twenty knights, and there are twenty knights in the *augmentum*. Together between his own fief and the *augmentum* forty knights and two crossbowmen.[70]

This is the baron of this same count who holds from him.

807: Raynald Musca holds from him a fief of four knights[71] and there are four knights in his *augmentum*. Together between fief and *augmentum* he has offered eight knights. Together from both the demesne and service of the aforesaid Count Robert there are from his own fiefs twenty-four knights. Together between the fiefs of the demesne, of service and the *augmentum* there are forty-eight knights and two crossbowmen.[72]

(Count Richard of Aquila)

808: Count Richard of Aquila has said that his demesne at Calvi is a fief of twenty knights, and Riardo is a fief of one knight. Together there are twenty-one knights, and in the *augmentum* there are twenty-one knights. Together between fief and *augmentum* there are forty-two knights.[73]

---

70 Robert de Medania, whose family originally came from Anjou, son of Geoffrey de Medania, lord of Suessula and Acerra, and Sica, grand-daughter of Prince Guaimar IV of Salerno. His grandfather Robert was a prominent figure in the entourage of the princes of Capua between 1091 and 1108; Robert (II) first appeared in May 1118, witnessing a donation of his father to the abbey of St Lawrence, Aversa, *Cod. Dipl. Aversa*, 25–7 no. 17. His parents' marriage may have been annulled; his mother was (later?) married to Roger of San Severino, and in March 1125 Robert witnessed a donation to the abbey of Cava by his half-brother, Henry of San Severino, Cava, *Arm. Mag.* F.36. He was probably granted the county of Buonalbergo in the early 1140s; he died before June 1154. Ménager (1975b), 370–1; Cuozzo (1984), 220–1; Loud (1996), 330, with a genealogical chart.

71 A correction was inserted in the MS. Originally this read three.

72 On Raynald, who came from a prominent baronial family in the principality of Capua, and who was one of those who changed sides and joined the king in 1135, see Cuozzo (1984), 220–1; Loud (1985), 163–4, and for a genealogical chart of his family, *ibid.*, 251. Raynald can be found in the sources from 1126 to 1169. See also below, arts. 839–42, for his lordship in the Valle Caudine.

73 Richard of Aquila, Count of Avellino, who died on 24 September 1152, *Necrologia di S. Matteo*, 142. He married Magalda, great-niece of King Roger, daughter of Adelicia of Aderno. His family originally came from L'Aigle (dépt Orne), Ménager (1975b), 320–1. For a genealogical chart of the family, Loud (1996), 335. Calvi was the seat of a bishopric, 13 km. NW of Capua; Riardo is 5 km. N of Calvi.

These are his barons.

809: John de Baios holds a fief of one knight, and with the *augmentum* he has offered two knights.

810: Hector de Thora holds a fief of two knights, and with the *augmentum* he has offered four knights.

811: William Guaius holds a fief of one knight, and with the *augmentum* he has offered two knights.

812: Marinus of Capua holds a fief of two knights, and with the *augmentum* he has offered four knights.

813: Amicus of Rivo Matrice holds a fief of one knight, and with the *augmentum* he has offered two knights.[74]

814: Raul de Actia holds a fief of one knight, and with the *augmentum* he has offered two knights.

815: Simon Joscelin holds a fief of two knights, and with the *augmentum* he has offered four knights.

816: William Blosseville holds a fief of one knight, and with the *augmentum* he has offered two knights.[75]

817: (The brother of)[76] William son of Blardinus holds a fief of one knight, and with the *augmentum* he has offered two knights.

818: Richard Brunellus holds a fief of one knight, and with the *augmentum* he has offered two knights.

819: (The son of) Ursus de Regina holds a fief of one knight, and with the *augmentum* he has offered two knights.

820: Gloriosus holds a fief of one knight, and with the *augmentum* he has offered two knights.

821: (The son of) Godfrey Scallone holds a fief of one knight, and with

---

74 He witnessed a donation of Count Richard of Avellino to Montecassino in December 1149, Gattula, *Accessiones*, 256, and he was still alive in 1171, when he testified in a dispute about water rights between the people of the towns of Sessa Aurunca and Teano; his evidence then included his witnessing a grant by King Roger, Ughelli, *Italia Sacra*, vi.553–4. Rivo Matrice, near Pontecorvo in the Liri Valley, was abandoned towards the end of the Middle Ages.

75 The family came from near St Valéry in the Pays de Caux. His ancestor, also William, had briefly been duke of Gaeta in the early years of the twelfth century, Ménager (1975b), 299–300, Loud (1985), 91. Abbot Rainald II of Montecassino complained to King Roger about his illegal seizure of lands and serfs belonging to the abbey at Pontecorvo, as revealed in a subsequent judgement of William I in 1155, *William I Diplomata*, 16–19 no. 6.

76 An insertion during the revision of 1167/8.

the *augmentum* he has offered two.[77]

822: Manasses holds a fief of one knight, and with the *augmentum* he has offered two.

Together from his own fief eighteen knights, and from the *addoamentum* eighteen.[78] Together between fief and *augmentum* [there are] thirty-six knights.

823: The Abbot of Cassino has offered in the great expedition sixty knights and 200 sergeants.

(Count Jonathan of Carinola)

824: Count Jonathan as he himself has said holds in the principality of Capua Carinola which is a fief of fifteen knights, Airola which is a fief of five knights, and San Martino which is a fief of five knights. Together there are from his own fief from his demesne a fief of twenty-three knights, and there are twenty-seven knights in his *augmentum*. Together between fief and *augmentum* fifty knights and fifty sergeants.[79]

These are the barons of this same Count Jonathan who hold from him in the principality.

825: (William de Avenabulo holds this), so he has said, from this same count in Aversa a fief of two knights and in his *augmentum* there are three knights. Together between fief and *augmentum* five knights. (The said William de Avenabulo holds this),[80] and this same Simon has in service a fief of nine knights, and his *augmentum* is nine knights. Together between the fief and the *augmentum* of Simon there are eighteen knights. Together between the demesne and service of the said Simon there are from his own fiefs eleven knights, and from the *augmentum* twelve knights. Together, between demesne, service and *augmentum* he has offered twenty-three knights.[81]

---

77 Probably the Roger Scallone who witnessed a donation of Count Roger of Avellino to Montevergine in March 1174, *Cod. Dipl. Verginiano*, vi.259–65 no. 569. Godfrey Scallone witnessed charters at Aversa in May 1143 and March 1150, *Cod. Dipl. Aversa*, 83 no. 47, 101 no. 57.

78 *Addoamentum* is a substitution by the thirteenth-century copyist for *augmentum*. This is the only place in the MS where he uses this later term.

79 The calculation here is eccentric, since the total from his demesne fiefs comes to twenty-five knights, not twenty-three. But since the *augmentum* usually comprised a doubling of the knight service, a total for the two combined of fifty would appear correct. Count Jonathan (d.1162) was also Count of Conza in the principality of Salerno, cf. *Catalogus Baronum*, arts. 694–701. Genealogical chart of the family, Loud (1996), 333.

80 The words in brackets are subsequent notes, presumably inserted in the 1167/8 revision.

81 This Simon was the original holder of these fiefs, Simon of Sora, recorded as one of the

These hold from William de Avenabulo, as this same William and Matthew de Avenabulo have said.

826: Odo Peregrinus holds from William de Avenabulo, so he has said, a fief of one knight, and with the *augmentum* there are two knights.[82]

827: Raul son of Jordan holds from William de Avenabulo, so he has said, a fief of one knight, and with the *augmentum* there are two knights.

828: William son of Humphrey holds two fiefs from him, and with the *augmentum* he has offered four [knights?][83]

829: Nicholas son of Matthew of Monfici holds from this same William a fief of one knight, and with the *augmentum* he has offered two knights, and he holds another fief in chief from the lord king.[84]

830: William son of Umbertus holds from this same William a fief of one knight, and with the *augmentum* there are two knights.

831: Aymarius of Naples holds from this same William a fief of one knight, and with the *augmentum* there are two knights.

832: Pandulf de Alaysi holds from this same William a fief of one knight, and with the *augmentum* there are two knights.[85]

833: Peter Cacapice, Constable of Naples,[86] holds from this same William de Avenabulo a fief of one knight, which William of St. Flaymundo was

---

barons of Aversa in several charters from the cathedral there from 1143 to 1150, *Cod. Dipl. Aversa*, pp. 83, 95, 99, nos. 48, 55, 57; he was murdered by some of his own men in 1156. His son, who rebelled against William I, was eventually reinstated by the regency government in 1167, but his fiefs in Aversa had by then been regranted to William de Avenabulo. *Annales Ceccanenses*, MGH SS xix.284–5. Cuozzo (1984), 226–8. The de Venabulo, a Norman family from near Les Andelys on the Seine, had been prominent in Aversa since the later eleventh century, Ménager (1975b), 351; Loud (1985), 89. William de Avenabulo was last recorded in April 1168, *Cod. Dipl. Aversa*, 159 no. 89.

82 Odo witnessed several charters from Aversa between 1164 and 1168, including a donation of William de Avenabulo to the cathedral chapter in March 1165, *Cod. Dipl. Aversa*, 150–2, 153–60 nos. 85, 87–9.

83 He witnessed a sale to Aversa cathedral in May 1144, *Cod. Dipl. Aversa*, 85–6 no. 49.

84 Matthew, attested in charters 1143–51, held a fief of two knights at Aversa, *Catalogus Baronum*, art. 880. Nicholas witnessed donations of his father to churches in Aversa in December 1146 and May 1151, *Cod. Dipl. Aversa*, 103–5 no. 60; 327–8 no. 10. The surname was presumably derived from the French Montfichet.

85 He also held a small fief in Salerno, *Catalogus Baronum* art. 516, and died on 6 October 1159, *Necrologio di S. Matteo*, 152.

86 Several relations of his also held fiefs in Aversa, and he held one fief there directly from the king, *Catalogus Baronum* arts. 902–4. His son John made a donation to Aversa cathedral in 1198, *Codice diplomatico svevo di Aversa*, ed. C. Salvati (Naples 1980), 6–8 no. 3.

holding;[87] he had held *Viveriis*,[88] but this same William de Avenabulo claimed that this Peter Cacapice with his fief should serve the lord king in chief.

834: Robert Ingressus holds, as he himself has said, Rocca de Albano from the aforesaid count, which is a fief of two knights, and with the *augmentum* he has offered four knights and ten sergeants.[89]

(Curia)

835: Bartholomew Burrell, so his father Marius has said, holds from this same count all the land that was that of Gregory Paganus, namely ...[90]

836: Landulf of Aquino, so Atenulf of Caserta has said, holds from the same count Alvito and Campoli and a quarter of Aquino, which [are] fiefs of ten knights, and with the *augmentum* he has offered twenty knights and thirty sergeants.[91]

837: Raynald Buccavitellus has said that he holds Gallinaro from the same Count Jonathan, which is a fief of three knights, and with the *augmentum* he has offered six knights and six sergeants.[92]

838: Pandulf holds in Nocellato in the lands of Carinola a fief of two knights, and with the *augmentum* he has offered four knights.

839: Raynald Musca said that he holds in demesne in the valley of Arienzo a fief of four knights, and with the *augmentum* he has offered

87 William de Fraymundo (the usual spelling) was a tenant-in-chief and also a vassal of the count of Buonalbergo in the *Terra Beneventana*, *Catalogus Baronum*, arts. 355, 382, 978. He died before 1160; his son, another William, succeeded to some but not all of his fiefs, Cuozzo (1984), 96, 253–4.

88 No place of this name can be identified, and Jamison, *Catalogus Baronum*, 152n, speculated that it might refer to a game reserve in the marshes to the west of Aversa near the Lago di Patria.

89 He witnessed a donation to Montecassino, made at the monastery, in July 1145, Dormeier (1979), 263–5 no. 11.

90 The paragraph breaks off at this point without specifying the fiefs concerned. Marius Burrell (or Borell), a relative of the Counts of Sangro, later took part in the rebellion against William I and Maio of Bari in 1160/1 and was forced to flee the kingdom, *Falcandus*, 29, 78 [*Tyrants*, 83, 129].

91 Landulf was a descendant of the former princely family of Aquino. He also had a fief at Sette Fratti, in the mountains to the north of Monte Cassino. Atenulf of Caserta also held land at Suessa Aurunca. See *Catalogus Baronum*, arts. 934, 1009.

92 He also held fiefs at S. Giovanni Incarico and Isola del Liri, both on the northern border of the kingdom, the former from the Count of Fondi and the latter directly from the king, *Catalogus Baronum*, arts. 1000, 1012. He was one of a court at Suessa Aurunca which heard various complaints by the Abbot of Montecassino in February 1167, Gattula, *Accessiones*, 262–4.

twelve knights and 100 sergeants and ten crossbowmen, and he has said that eleven vassals [*vavassores*] of his who hold eleven knights' fees from him will give with the *augmentum* twenty-two knights.

These hold from the aforesaid Raynald Musca.

840: William Fillarinus holds Rocca from him which is a fief of two knights, and with the *augmentum* he has offered four.[93]

841: Fulk the chaplain and Robert son of Scaldus hold from this same William a fief of two knights, and with the *augmentum* they provide four knights.

842: Roalt and Jordan hold from the aforesaid William two very poor knights' fees, for which with the *augmentum* they both serve.

Together from the demesne and service of the said Raynald Musca there are from his own fiefs twenty-one knights, and in the *augmentum* there are twenty-four knights. Together between fief and *augmentum* he has offered forty-four knights, 100 sergeants and ten crossbowmen.

(The Court at Aversa)[94]

843: Robert de Lauro has said that he holds Lauro, which is a fief of four knights, and in his *augmentum* there are six knights. Together between fief and *augmentum* he has offered ten knights and ten sergeants.[95]

844: Landulf Burrell has said that he holds Strangolagalli which is a fief of one knight, and with the *augmentum* he has offered two knights.[96]

845: William of Monteforte has said that he holds in demesne Monteforte, which is a fief of two knights, and that he holds Avellino and Mercogliano, a fief of three knights, and from Forino with what he holds in Sarno there is a fief of one knight, and from Alito there is a fief of one knight. Together there is a fief of seven knights, and in the *augmentum* there are seven knights. Together from fief and *augmentum*

---

93 His son Godfrey gave the abbey of Cava a tithe of all his revenues from Oraczano, where he was then living, in April 1187, Cava, *Arm. Mag.* L.26.

94 Later note.

95 A member of the powerful S. Severino clan, he was subsequently, before 1159, appointed Count of Caserta, and from 1171 until his death on 31 August 1183 was one of the two master justiciars who ran the royal government on the mainland, Cuozzo (1984), 271–5; Tescione (1990), 35–45, and for a genealogical chart of the family, Loud (1987), 160.

96 Probably another member of the large kin-group of the Burrell counts of Sangro, Landulf was later, in 1165, a royal constable, and like Amicus of Rivo Matrice (above, art. 813) testified in 1171 that he had witnessed King Roger granting water rights to the people of Suessa, Ughelli, *Italia Sacra*, vi.553–4; Cuozzo (1984), 232–3.

he has offered fourteen knights and fifteen sergeants.[97]

846: Godfrey his son, so he has said, holds in Aversa a fief of one knight and three very poor knights each having a half fief. Together there are two knights' fees, and with the *augmentum* he has offered five knights.

847: Baldwin Longueville, so he has said, holds in Aversa a fief of one knight, and with the *augmentum* he has offered two knights.[98]

848: Roger de Pede Larrone holds in Aversa a fief of one knight, and with the *augmentum* he has offered two knights.

849: Matthew de Avenabulo has said that he holds in Aversa a fief of two knights, and with the *augmentum* he has offered four knights.[99]

850: And Robert Caramannus holds from him a very poor fief. Together there are five knights.

[...]

1030: Count Robert of Aprutium[100] has said that he holds in demesne from the lord king, in [the county of] Penne, Atri which is a fief of ten knights; and in Aprutium Santo Flaviano which is a fief of ten knights,[101] and Contraguerra which is a fief of four knights, and Civitella which is of three knights, and Campoli which is of five knights and Montorio which is of five knights; and in Ascoli he holds Aquaviva which is a fief of two knights together with Torre which is similarly in Ascoli. Together from the demesne of the aforesaid Count Robert [there are] fiefs of forty-four knights, and in his *augmentum* there are seventy-six.[102] Together between fiefs and the *augmentum* of his demesne the aforesaid count has offered 120 knights and 200 sergeants.

These men hold from the aforesaid Count Robert of Aprutium.

97 William, lord of Monteforte Irpino, attested from 1109 onwards, died between February 1162 and March 1163, when he had been succeeded by his son Godfrey; see *Cod. Dipl. Verginiano* v.35–8 no. 411, 68–71 no. 420. He was son of Richard and grandson of a certain Rao *normannus*, Ménager (1975b), 264–5; Cuozzo (1984), 233–4.

98 He died before September 1158, when his widow Maria is mentioned, *Cod. Dipl. Aversa*, 126–9 no. 73, at 127.

99 He was the brother of William de Avenabulo (above, art. 825), first recorded in May 1143. He served as a royal justiciar, c.1162 to 1171, *Cod. Dipl. Aversa*, 83 no. 47, 120–1 no. 70; Tescione (1990), 160–2, appendix no. 2.

100 Son of Count Atto V of Aprutium, attested from 1120 until 1155, in April 1148 acting as royal justiciar in the region, Jamison (1913), 457–61 no. 6; Cuozzo (1984), 306–7. This and subsequent entries concern the Abruzzi region which King Roger and his sons took over in 1140.

101 Modern Giulianova, on the Adriatic coast at the mouth of the River Tordino.

102 Marginal correction, sixty-six.

1031: Berard of Castellone so he has said holds from the aforesaid Count Robert in Aprutium Baezano which is a fief of three knights; and in Ascoli he holds Faraone which is a fief of one knight. Together there are four knights, and in his *augmentum* there are eight knights;[103] together between fief and *augmentum* he has offered twelve knights and twenty sergeants.[104]

1032: William Colonellus and James his brother hold in Aprutium Colonella, which so they have said is a fief of two knights. Together between fief and *augmentum* [there are] four knights and eight sergeants.

1033: Walter Raynaldi holds from the aforesaid count in Aprutium S. Omero, which as he has said is a fief of four knights, and Aquaviva which is of one knight. Together there are five knights, and with the *augmentum* there are ten knights and twenty sergeants.[105]

1034: Oderisius of Corropoli holds from him in Aprutium Corropoli, which so he has said is a fief of two knights, and with the *augmentum* he has offered four knights and eight sergeants.

1035: Hugozonus holds in Aprutium Ripa Gualterana, which so he has said is a fief of two knights, and Torricella which is of one knight; and in Ascoli he holds Collutum which is a fief of one knight, and Luco which is a fief of one knight. Together there are five knights, and with the *augmentum* he has offered ten knights and twenty sergeants.

1036: Richard Bagnadinus and Odemundus his nephew hold in Aprutium Rocca Camilliana, which so they have said is a fief of two knights, and half of Poggio and S. Croce which is a fief of one knight. Together there are three knights, and with the *augmentum* he has offered six knights and twelve sergeants.

1037: Huguizonus Leguitarius holds in Ascoli Leguitario which is a fief, so he has said, of two knights, and in his *augmentum* there are two knights. Together between fiefs and *augmentum* he has offered four knights and eight sergeants.

1038: Landulf Cerboni holds on the far side of the River Tronto Monte S. Paolo, which so he has said is a fief of two knights, and with the *augmentum* he has offered four knights and eight sergeants.

---

103 These figures were originally entered as five and seven respectively, and subsequently corrected.

104 Berard held other fiefs as a subtenant of Walter and Berard Gentile in Penne, *Catalogus Baronum*, arts. 1191, 1194. He belonged to a large kin-group, who were often at odds with the abbey of St Clement, Casauria, *Chronicon Casauriense*, 884–5, 896.

105 S. Omero is just to the north of the River Salinello, about 12 km from the coast and 20 km. SE of Ascoli Piceno. Aquaviva no longer exists.

1039: Walter Enganna Contem holds on the far side of the River Tronto Monte Donnulo, which so he has said is a fief of two knights, and with the *augmentum* he has offered four knights and eight sergeants.

1040: Acto Muczani holds in Ascoli for the aforesaid Count Robert Mucciano, which so he has said is a fief of one knight, and with the *augmentum* he has offered two knights and four sergeants.

1041: Bagnolinus of Macchia, so he has said, holds from the same count in Ascoli Macchia, which so he has said is a fief of one knight, and with the *augmentum* he has offered two knights and four sergeants.

1042: Acto Todini holds in Aprutium from the same count Bellante, which he has said is a fief of four knights, and Ripa which is a fief of two knights, and half of Colli and a third part of Speltino which is a fief of one knight, and S. Angelo which is a fief of half a knight. Together there are seven and a half knights, and in his *augmentum* there are nine and a half knights; together between fief and *augmentum* he has offered seventeen knights and thirty sergeants.[106]

These hold from the said Ato Totini. [*sic*]

1043: Acto de Ripa Candone holds from him Ripa Candone, which so he has said is a fief of one knight, and with the *augmentum* he has offered two knights and four sergeants.

1044: Acto of Patecciano so he has said holds from this same Acto Todini Patecciano which is a fief of one knight, and he holds two parts of Speltino which is of half a knight, and with the *augmentum* he has offered three knights and six sergeants.

1045: William de Andrea holds from this same Acto Todini Arenario which is so he has said a fief of one knight, and with the *augmentum* he has offered two knights and four sergeants.

1046: The lords of Montecchio hold from the said Acto in Aprutium a fief of one knight in Montecchio, and with the *augmentum* they provide two knights and four sergeants.

1047: Todemarius Gualterii with his relations holds in Aprutium Tizzano with his tenement, Rocca Tetonesca, Morricone and Monte S. Pietro, which so he has said is a fief of seven knights, and with the *augmentum* he has offered fourteen knights and twenty-seven sergeants.[107]

---

106 Atto son of Todinus witnessed a grant of enfeofment by Bishop Guido of Aprutium in 1123, *Il Cartulario della chiesa teremana*, ed. F. Savini (Rome 1910), 83–4 no. 48.

107 Jamison notes that this entry appears to be in the wrong place, and that Todemarius and his family, the Totoneschi, were tenants of the Bishop of Aprutium (Teramo) rather than

1048: Raynald Alberticii with his associates holds from the aforesaid Acto Folignano, which so he has said is a fief of one knight, and with the *augmentum* he has offered two knights and two sergeants.[108]

1049: Berard de Nicolao holds Selvapiano, which is so he has said a fief of one knight, and with the *augmentum* he has offered two knights and four sergeants.

1050: Ramfredus of Nereto holds in Nereto a fief of half a knight, and with the *augmentum* he has offered one knight and two sergeants.[109]

1050 [*sic*]: Cono Guictonis holds in Aprutium Poggio, which so he has said is a fief of two knights, and with the *augmentum* he has offered four knights and eight sergeants.[110]

1051: Walter of Poggio holds Cantalupo which is a fief of one knight, and with the *augmentum* he has offered two knights and four sergeants.[111]

1052: James and Raynald so they have said hold Ripa which is a fief of three knights, and Poggio which is a fief of three knights. Together they are a fief of six, and in the *augmentum* there are six knights; together between fief and *augmentum* they have offered twelve knights and twenty-four sergeants.

[...]

(The Abbot of St. Clement in Pescara)

1217: Oderisius, Abbot of St. Clement in Pescara, which is in the county of Manopello, holds in Chieti Fara and Insula which is a fief of one knight, and holds in Chieti Bolognano which is a fief of one knight; and he holds in Penne Alanno which is a fief of two knights; and he holds in the county of Aprutium Guardia which is a fief of two knights, and Arolla which is a fief of one knight. Together there are fiefs of seven knights, and with the *augmentum* he has offered thirteen knights and

---

of the counts of Aprutium; see for example the charter of enfeoffment of 1123 by Bishop Guido II, *Cartulario della chiesa teremana*, 85–8 no. 49.

108 Subsequently corrected to four sergeants.

109 He may well have been a sub-tenant of the Bishop of Aprutium; in August 1121 Fanto-linus of Nereto gave his share of the *castellum* of Nereto (3 km. W of Teramo; no longer exists) to the bishopric with the consent of his overlords Count Henry and Matthew of Aprutium, *Cartulario della chiesa teremana*, 74–5 no. 40, 78–9 no. 42.

110 Cono was one of those who consented to the confirmation by the counts of Aprutium to Bishop Berard in 1122; he was forced by the Emperor Lothar to abandon his claims to property of Casauria in 1137, *Cartulario della chiesa teremana*, 78–9 no. 42, *Chron. Casauriense*, 886. Entry no. 1050 is repeated twice in the edition.

111 He also held a number of holdings from the Bishop of Aprutium, *Cartulario della chiesa teremana*, 67 no. 34.

eighteen sergeants.[112]

1218: The Abbot of St. Stephen on the Sea Shore [*in Rivo Maris*], so he has said, holds from the lord king Regolceti which is a fief of two knights, and Osento which is a fief of one knight. Together there are four fiefs, and with the *augmentum* he has offered eight knights and eight sergeants.[113]

These hold from this same Abbot of St. Stephen on the Sea Shore.

1219: Robert Bordinus holds from this same abbot in Chieti the *casale* of San Salvatore which is a fief of one knight, and with the *augmentum* he provides two knights.[114] Together from the demesne and service of the said abbot there are from his own fiefs six knights, and with the *augmentum* he has offered twelve knights and eight sergeants.

1220: Robert Altini holds Scerni in Chieti from this same abbot which is a fief of one knight, and with the *augmentum* he has offered two knights.

(The Bishop of Aprutium)

1221: Bishop Guido of Aprutium has said that he holds in Aprutium Teramo and San Benedetto, Forcella,[115] Caprafico, Lavarone, Ripa and Tortoreto, and a certain tenement in San Flaviano,[116] and Collevecchio and Miano with its tenement, and a certain tenement in Montorio; and in Penne he holds Lucum, which so he has said are fiefs of ten knights, and with the *augmentum* he has offered twenty-four knights and forty sergeants.

1222: Bishop Berard of Forcone has said that he holds Civita di S. Massimo in Forcone which, so he has said, is a fief of one knight, and

---

112 The abbey of St Clement of Casauria, founded by the Emperor Louis II c.872–3: Oldrius (Oderisius) was abbot 1127–52, dying on 12 December 1152, *Chron. Casauriense*, 893. Most of the possessions listed here were very close to the abbey; *Insula* was the island in the Pescara River where it was sited; Bolognano, 3 km. SE of the monastery was one of three *castella* confirmed to the abbey by King Roger in August 1140, *Roger II Diplomata*, 139–40 no. 49. Alanno was 8 km. NE of the monastery.

113 Benedictine abbey near the mouth of the River Osento, and about 7 km. S of the mouth of the River Sangro. Its origins are shrouded in obscurity, but may date back to the ninth century. According to the abbey chronicle, King Roger confirmed these two *castella* to this house circa September 1140, *Roger II Diplomata*, deperdita no. 79, a reference that Brühl accepts as genuine, although this chronicle presents many suspicious features and may be a later forgery. For what is known about the abbey, *Italia Pontificia*, iv.281–2.

114 Now the village called Casalbordino, about 6 km. S of the abbey.

115 Guido (II), Bishop of Aprutium 1123–54, had received the *servitum* from Forcella from Count Matthew of Aprutium in 1128, *Cartulario della chiesa teremana*, 110–11 no. 61.

116 Modern Giulianova.

the *casale* of S. Massimo which is [a fief] of one knight.[117] Together
they are fiefs of three knights, and with the *augmentum* he has offered
six knights and twelve sergeants.

---

117 Bishop Berard received a privilege from King Roger at Salerno in November 1147, Caspar
    (1904), 568 no. 210.

THE BOOK OF ROGER
BY ABÛ 'ABDALLÂH AL-IDRÎSÎ

[*This geographical treatise, describing the known world of the mid-twelfth century and completed shortly before the death of King Roger in February 1154, was written for the king by an Arab prince descended from the family of the Prophet, and also related to the rulers of the Maghreb, who appears to have arrived in Sicily in 1139. To accompany his treatise, al-Idrîsî compiled maps and created a silver planisphere showing the seven regions ('climes') of the world in accordance with Ptolomaic geography. In his work, he claimed, he sought to satisfy the king's wish to know more about the various countries of the world, as well as the details of his own kingdom and its routes and resources. Nevertheless, our author's work was not as original as was once thought, drawing in particular upon a 'Book of Curiosities' written about a century earlier, as well as upon the tenth-century geographer Ibn-Hawqal.[1] al-Idrîsî's work was subsequently praised, and used, by a number of late medieval Arabic writers, notably the Damascus prince Abû'l-Fidâ (d.1331) and perhaps the most important Islamic historian of the later Middle Ages, Ibn Khaldûn (d.1406). The extracts translated below, from the introduction to the work and from Book IV, eulogise Roger II and his father, and then al-Idrîsî begins his account of the island of Sicily by describing Palermo, and continues to cover Messina and its environs, while another brief extract describes the bay of Naples and the Amalfitan peninsula.*

These extracts were originally translated from Henri Bresc and Annliese Nef, Idrîsî. La Première géographie de l'Occident (Paris 1999), pp. 58–60, 306–10, 312–13, 378–9, but Dr Alex Metcalfe of the University of Lancaster has kindly checked my version against the Arabic text.]

The best subject that can interest an observer, because it inspires him with thoughts and ideas, is the great King Roger, glorious through God and powerful through the power of the latter, King of Sicily, Italy, Lombardy and Calabria, supporter of the *imâm* of Rome and of the Christian religion. He is superior to the King of the *Rûm* through the extent and the rigour of his power. He runs his government as he wishes, decreeing or forbidding what takes place. He renders justice according to the dictates of his religion, submitting himself to equity.

1 Metcalfe (2009), 262–4.

He takes his subjects under the protection of his generosity and his grace. He holds the reins of his kingdom in the tightest manner and he submits the unfolding of his reign to the best order and the most beautiful of harmonies. He has conquered lands in the east as in the west. He has bent the necks of tyrants of his religion both far and near. He has an army that abounds in men and equipment, and numerous fleets benefiting from help of every sort. What we have experienced and the information available attest this, both what we have seen and what we have heard. Is there any distant objective that this king has not gained and about which he is not informed? Is there any difficult endeavour in which he has not succeeded and does not render possible? Moreover the course of events runs in accordance with his efforts and his will, so that happiness is granted him, and depends on his will in every event. His supporters always enjoy the honours of complete victory, while his enemies suffer humiliating defeats, one after another. For how many degrees of glory has he established solid bases! For how many great projects has he had the moons arise, to appear [like] the light which shines upon their regions and transforms gardens into magnificent parks and marvellous plantations. Furthermore, he combines nobility of character and nobility of descent, the beauty of his actions and the beauty of his morality. To this one adds his bravery of heart, the clarity of his intellect, the profundity of his spirit, the width of his discernment, the strength of his mind, his organisation and perspicacity in the vicissitudes of fate, an ability that comes from a very sure understanding of affairs. The objectives that he seeks, he obtains like arrows [hitting] a target; problems he resolves; the whole of his government rests upon him and his sleeps are like vigils. His judgments are most just, and his presents are like overflowing seas or torrential rainstorms.

As to the mathematical and applied sciences that he knows, these cannot be counted, nor are there limits to them; he is exceptionally accomplished and excels in every one. He brings about astonishing inventions and encourages marvellous new things to which no other king before him has given rise, nor has he just inspired them. His inventions appear clear to those who look upon them, one can point them out and prove them clearly. They are spread through the cities, their renown extends towards the horizons and in every region. We dispense with listing them precisely and in detail, or in treating of them in other than general terms. However, if we were to take care to describe them, setting them down in writing and enumerating them, we would be amazed before the marvels that he had invented, because their interpretation is miraculous and their range is striking. But who has ever counted grains of sand and arrived at a total?

One example of the sublime nature of Roger's knowledge and of his high and elevated instincts is that he wanted to know his lands in a wide-ranging and exacting way, relying on certain and proven information, even though the components of his realm are widespread, that the duties of those involved in his government are many, and that provinces of [mainland] Italy whose inhabitants have submitted to his power and might have recognised his authority. He wanted to know the bounds of these regions, the ways by land and sea, the climate in which they are situated, and the seas and gulfs that are found there.

[...]

It was in the year 453 from the Hégirah[2] that the most illustrious, the most valiant, the most powerful and the most brilliant of kings, Roger son of Tancred, the best of the Frankish kings, conquered the principal towns of Sicily, and with the help of his companions started to reverse the tyranny of its governors and to destroy their troops. He did not cease until he had dispersed the assembly of its governors, overthrown the tyrants who defended the island, attacking them night and day before bringing death and perdition to them; and he did not cease to wield his sword and lance against them, until he had rendered himself master of the whole island by his victories, and had conquered Sicily, district by district, unceasingly taking over the frontier zones [taghr]; and all that in the space of thirty years. Once the country was subject to his authority and he had established his royal throne, he extended the benefits of his justice to the inhabitants; he respected their religion and laws; he guaranteed to them the preservation of their property and their lives, both to them and to their families and children. It was thus that he governed during his lifetime, up until his death, of which the term was fixed by destiny, and that took place in the year from the Hegirah 494, while he found himself in the fortress of Mileto in Calabria, where he was buried.[3]

He left as his heir his son, the great king who carried the same name as his did he, and who followed in his footsteps. Roger, in fact, put into effect the methods of government and exalted the magnificence of the kingdom; he gave lustre to the royal position and their due place to

2 AD 1061, a date confirmed by Christian sources, but only for the start of the invasion of Sicily.

3 November 1100–October 1101.

affairs of state, to which he has devoted great attention, accomplishing praiseworthy actions to promote justice and security. His merit was such that kings have made themselves subject to his rule, showing by clear signs that they supported and followed him, entrusting him with the keys to their states, and coming from every part to him, desirous of putting themselves in the shade of his throne and benefiting from his protection and clemency. The consideration, the glory and the grandeur of his rule have not ceased to be augmented from day to day, up until the time when we are writing the present work.

As for Sicily, of which there is discussion, it is an island of pre-eminent position, vast dimensions, numerous localities, numberless charms and immense advantages. If we were to try to enumerate these qualities in detail and to describe its overall state locality by locality, we would find ourselves faced with a glorious plan, but disposing of limited means. We shall then explain succinctly enough to make this clear to the reader, and we shall come to the conclusion that we have proposed for ourselves.

This island, at the time at which we are writing, is under the rule of the great King Roger. It comprises 130 localities, towns or fortresses, without counting the agricultural estates, villages and other places. We shall deal first of all and in particular with the coastal regions, limiting ourselves to them to the exclusion of all others, and proceeding in this manner to return to the point from which we departed. Then we shall undertake the description of the localities, of the fortified towns and of the vast inhabited region in the interior of the island, point by point and one place after another, with the help of God the most high.

The first of these towns is Palermo, a city that is both most remarkable for its grandeur and most illustrious for its importance, among the most celebrated and prestigious centres of preaching in the world. It is endowed with qualities that confer upon it an unequalled glory and combine beauty and nobility. The seat of government from ancient times and during the early days of Islam, it is from there that fleets and armies departed on military expeditions, and it is to there that they returned, as indeed they still do today.

This town is on the coast; it has the sea to the east, and is surrounded by high and massive mountains. The shore in this region is pleasant and laughing – it is orientated towards the east. The town is endowed with magnificent buildings, which welcome travellers and flaunt the beauty of their construction, the skill of their design and their marvellous originality.

Palermo is composed of two parts: the section called the Cassaro, and the suburb. The Cassaro [al-Qasr] is the ancient walled town, renowned throughout the entire world; it is organised around three streets. Along the central street one finds fortified palaces, high and noble residences, and many mosques, hostels, bath houses and the warehouses of great merchants. As for the two others, one also finds splendid palaces there, lofty and sumptuous buildings, and plenty of bath houses and hostels. It is there that the grand mosque is situated, or at least the building that fulfilled that function in the past, and which is today returned to that condition in which it was formerly.[4] It uplifts the spirits by its marvellous construction, and by the originality of the motifs which have been invented, chosen and executed for its pictures, gilding and inscriptions.

As for the suburb [al-Rabad], it comprises another town and it surrounds the first on every side. One finds there the old town that carries the name of Khâlisa ['the elect'], where in the days of the Muslims the Sultan and the upper classes resided. One finds there also the sea port and the arsenal for the construction of ships.

The town is traversed on every side by watercourses and springs; fruits grow in abundance; its buildings and walks are so beautiful that it is impossible for the pen to describe them or for the mind to imagine them; everything is a real seduction for the eye.

The Cassaro, which has just been mentioned, is among the best defended and most lofty of fortified towns; it can resist attacks and is in fact impregnable. At its highest point is a fortress, built recently for King Roger and composed of enormous blocks of cut stone covered with mosaics. The walls of the Cassaro are high and well situated, its towers and guard posts are of very solid construction, like the various palaces and halls that it shelters. These last are decorated with the most marvellous calligraphic motifs and covered with remarkable paintings. All travellers attest the splendour of Palermo and describe it in exaggerated terms. They claim expressly that there are not outside Palermo any buildings more magnificent that it has, homes more noble, a palace more imposing or houses more agreeable.

The suburb that surrounds this ancient fortified town, that has recently been mentioned, is very large. It contains a great number of houses, hostelries, bath houses and shops. It is surrounded by a perimeter wall, a ditch and a wide open space. Within the latter there are many gardens, splendid parks, and canals with fresh running water coming from the

4 That is, it has once again become the Christian cathedral.

mountains that surround this plain. Outside and to the south flows the River Abbâs [Oreto], which works a very large number of mills that suffice for the needs of the town.

To the east of Palermo, and at one day's distance, one finds the fortress of Termini, which is on a promontory that overlooks the sea.[5] It is among the most imposing of fortresses and on one of the largest sites. It is surrounded by a curtain wall, and one sees there the remains of ancient monuments and buildings, among which one notes an amphitheatre of magnificent construction, that attests the power of the person who built it. One finds also a recently fortified quarter and two beautiful bath houses, next door to one another, on top of an ancient building.

To the west is a most agreeable district known under the name of Trabia, where the watercourses turn numerous mills; there is a plain and great fields there. A type of vermicelli is produced there, which is exported in great quantity to the rest of the world, to Calabria, to the Muslim provinces and into Christian countries. The river of Termini flows there,[6] the water of which is excellent, and in spring one fishes for the fish known under the name of *rây* [shad]. The port is devoted to the fishing of a great fish called tuna.

Twelve miles from there is the fortified town of Brucato [*Bû Ruqqâd*], which is on high, surrounded by numerous fields under cultivation and endowed with a market.[7] Its revenues are notable, water is abundant and there are mills, gardens and numerous orchards. All around are huge estates and good fields. It is two miles from the sea. From there to Roccella [*Sahkrat-al-Hadîd*],[8] a little village and castle, on top of the said rock that juts out into the sea, is a dozen miles. Towards the interior one can see a sandy plain, fertile fields and lands perfectly cultivated.

From there to Cefalù is a short journey.[9] The fortified settlement of Cefalù is on the coast. It resembles a town; one finds there markets, baths and mills. These last are inside the town, on a sweet and fresh water course, from which the inhabitants drink. Cefalù is on a rock that is next to the sea and benefits from a good harbour where people land

---

5 Termini Imerese, just over 30 km. E of Palermo.

6 The River Sulla.

7 Brucato was destroyed in the fourteenth-century wars and the site abandoned, Backman (1995), 32.

8 'Iron rock'; modern Campofelice di Roccella lies a little inland.

9 About 12 km.

from all around. The locality is populous and a fortress overlooks it. This is built on the summit of steep mountain and is all but inaccessible, so difficult is the climb.[10]

From there to the fortified village of Tusa is a short journey. It is of ancient construction, located on a steep site, and surrounded by a prosperous countryside. The settlement and its suburb are at the top of an isolated mountain, which one can only reach by difficult paths that are not well-known. Roundabout, one finds an excellent and fertile land, on a wide plain and with excellently cultivated fields which yield a good return. Tusa is about two miles from the sea.[11]

[… al-Idrîsî's description continues eastwards along the north coast of Sicily]

From Milazzo to Messina is a short journey. The town of Messina is in the eastern corner of the island and is surrounded by mountains on the western side. The coast here is pleasant; its territory is fertile and one finds orchards and gardens which produce fruit in abundance. It is surrounded by excellent watercourses which turn numerous mills. It is one of the most remarkable and prosperous of localities, [and] a place of constant coming and going. Vessels are built here; others call here and moor, coming from every coastal district of Christendom. It is there that one finds congregated the greatest ships and that one encounters travellers and merchants from every sort of country, Christian and Muslim. Its markets are well-provisioned, the prices there are favourable and the wealth is striking. The mountains round about contain mines of iron, which is exported to neighbouring countries. Its harbour is entirely admirable, and is spoken of throughout the entire world because the largest vessels can moor there so close to the shore that one can transport by hand what is carried on the ships to dry land.[12]

Messina lies on the strait that separates Sicily from Calabria. The sea renders the passage difficult, above all because the wind blows in the opposite direction to the current, and because the water that enters the strait encounters that which is flowing out. In fact, he who is taken between the two can only be saved if God on High wishes it. The strait at its widest is ten miles and at the narrowest point three.[13]

---

10 The Spanish Muslim traveller Ibn Jubayr, who visited Sicily in 1184, recorded of this fortress that 'I have never seen any more formidable', *The Travels of Ibn Jubayr*, 344.

11 Tusa is 19 km. SE of Cefalù, as the crow flies, and 3 km. from the sea.

12 The same point was made by Ibn Jubayr, *Travels*, 339.

13 Ibn Jubayr thought that the Strait at its widest was only six miles, but gave an equally

From the town of Messina to Taormina one reckons a day's journey following the coast.[14] Taormina is a well-defended fortified settlement set on high. It is one of the most remarkable ancient fortified towns and one of the most noble ancient places. It is on a mountain that towers over the sea and is endowed with a fine harbour where ships come from all parts laden with cargoes of grain. One finds inns and markets there and it is the meeting point for all the caravans and travellers going to Messina. Roundabout one finds prosperous agricultural estates and fields perfectly cultivated, a gold mine and a mountain, known under the name of Tûr,[15] renowned for miracles and for the religious activities that take place there. Its watercourses allow numerous mills to turn, and one finds a small number of gardens there. A river flows there, crossed by a magnificent bridge, the building of which attests the skill of the designer and the power of the government which built it. One sees there an ancient Roman amphitheatre, the remains of which reflect a glorious rule and great power. Not far from there is a gold mine.

A day from there is Aci, [which is] by the sea shore.[16] It is one of those places where the buildings are ancient, and it is endowed with a market. The fields which surround it are perfectly cultivated, and the harvest is earlier than that in the rest of Sicily because of the heat of the climate. Pitch, tar, wood and many other things are obtained from there. To the west of this place rises the mountain known as the *Jabal al-Nâr*.[17]

[... *Later on, the author turns to the Italian mainland*]

Naples is a beautiful town, ancient, prosperous and filled with busy markets where one may carry out transactions because merchandise, and commodities in general, are abundant. From there to the port of Stabia, which has excellent mooring, deep water and is in a bay, at the mouth of a river whch runs year round and whose water is sweet, is thirty miles.[18]

Those who wish to travel directly by land to Amalfi must continue for fifteen miles. Between Naples and Stabia one notices the 'mountain of

---

vivid description of the treacherous conditions: the sea 'pours through like the bursting of a dam and, from the intensity of the contraction and the pressure, boils like a cauldron', *Travels*, 336.

14 About 45 km.

15 Either Castelmola or Monte Venerella, both mountains just to the north of Taormina.

16 Acireale, 30 km. S of Taormina.

17 'The mountain of fire', that is Mount Etna.

18 Actually about 26 km.

fire', a mountain that one does not climb because it continually vomits forth fire and stones.[19] Someone who wishes to follow the coast must go from Stabia to Sorrento, which is thirty miles.

Sorrento is built on a cape that juts out into the sea. It is a prosperous town where the houses are good and resources are abundant. It is surrounded by trees. It has a narrow harbour, in which boats cannot winter if they are not beached. Ships are built there. From there to cape *Râs M.n.tîra* is twelve miles;[20] then to the little port of Positano fifteen, and [thereafter] to the port town of Amalfi eighteen.

Amalfi is a prosperous town and has a harbour. It is fortified on the landward side but is easy to access from the sea. If one attacks it, one will take it. It is ancient and has fine surroundings. Its people are numerous and rich. From there to the river mouth of Vietri, a beautiful place where ships can find anchorage, is ten miles.[21] This river takes its name from a place situated on its upper reaches, which is fortified and only accessible at two points, and where one can find water and wood. From this river to Salerno, a remarkable town, with well-stocked markets and all sorts of goods, in particular wheat and other cereals, is two miles.

19 Monte Vesuvio.

20 *Râs M.n.tîra* [*sic*] is modern Punto Campanella.

21 By the modern coast road this is now about 20 km.; by sea about 14 km.

BIBLIOGRAPHY

Manuscript sources

Benevento, Museo del Sannio,

Fondo S. Sofia, vol. 8 no. 36; vol. 12 nos. 38, 42, 43; vol. 13 nos. 2, 4, 5, 11, 19; vol. 34 no. 3.

Cava dei Tirreni, Abbazia di S. Trinità,

Armarii Magni, C.1; D.25, 27; E.8, 9, 20, 21, 26, 32; F.20, 25, 34, 36; G.14, 24, 28, 34, 36, 38, 43; H.8, 21, 22, 27, 38, 44; I.4, 25, 35; L.2, 26.

Arcae, xxii.42; xxv.56; xxvi.45; xxix.26, 92; xxx.46, 71; xxxii.96; xxxiii.44; xxxiv.22.

Rome, Archivio Segreto Vaticano,

AA Arm. I.xviii.4999 no. 6.

Rome, Biblioteca Apostolica Vaticana,

Codice Vaticano Latino 13491 [a file of individual charters rather than a codex], nos. 10, 16.

Pergamene Aldobrandini, Cartolario I, nos. 39, 41, 51, 55, 56, 59.

[These were consulted in 1990, when they were still in the BAV; they have since been returned to the palace of the Principi Aldobrandini at Frascati.]

Rome, Università 'La Sapienza', istituto di paleografia,

De Donato, Vittorio (1952), 'Le Carte del XII secolo della biblioteca capitolare di Benevento' [typescript thesis].

Salerno, Archivio Diocesano,

Mensa Archiepiscopalis, Arca I, no. 45.

Printed primary sources

Alexandri Telesini Abbatis Ystoria Rogerii Regis Siciliae atque Calabriae atque Apulie, ed. Ludovica de Nava, with historical commentary by Dione R. Clementi (FSI 1991).

Annales Casinenses, MGH SS xix.303–20.

Annales Cavenses, MGH SS iii.185–96.

Annales Magdeburgenses, MGH SS xvi.105–96.

Annales Palidenses, MGH SS xvi.48–98.

[*Gli*] *Annales Pisani di Bernardo Maragone*, ed. Michele Lupo Gentile (RIS, Bologna 1930–6).

Anonymi Barensis Chronicon, RIS v.

Baumgartner, P.M. (1897), 'Ein Brief des Gegenpapstes Anaclet (II)', *Neues Archiv der Gesellschaft für altere deutsche Geschichteskunde* 22: 576–8.

Bertolini, Ottorino (1923), 'Gli Annales Beneventani', *Bullettino dell'istituto storico italiano per il medio evo* 42: 1–163.

[*Il*] *Cartulario della chiesa teremana*, ed. F. Savini (Rome 1910).

Catalogus Baronum, ed. E.M. Jamison (FSI, Rome 1972).

Chronica Monasterii Casinensis, ed. Hartmut Hoffmann (MGH SS xxxiv, Hanover 1980).

[*The*] *Chronicle of Ibn al-Athir for the Crusading Period from al-Kamil fi 'l-Ta'rikh, Part 2, The Years 541–589/1146–93: the Age of Nur al-Din and Saladin*, trans. D.S. Richards (Farnham 2007).

Chronicon Casauriense, auctore Iohanne Berardi, ed. Ludovico Antonio Muratori (RIS ii(2), Milan 1726), 775–916; and *Additamenta ad Chronicon Casauriense*, ibid., 917–1018.

Chronicon Ignoti Monachi Cisterciensis Sanctae Mariae de Ferraria, ed. Λ. Gaudenzi (Naples 1888).

Chronicon Sanctae Sophiae (Cod. Vat. Lat. 4939), ed. Jean-Marie Martin (FSI, Rome 2000).

Chronicon Vulternense, ed. V. Federici (3 vols, FSI, Rome 1924–38).

Codex Diplomaticus Caietanus (2 vols, Montecassino 1887–92).

Codice diplomatico barese (19 vols, Bari 1897–1950), volumes cited here:

> i, *Le Pergamene del duomo di Bari (952–1264)*, ed. G.B. Nitto de Rossi and F. Nitti de Vito (1897).

> iii, *Le Pergamene della cattedrale di Terlizzi (971–1300)*, ed. F. Carabellese (1899).

> v, *Le Pergamene di S. Nicola di Bari. Periodo Normanno (1075–1194)*, ed. F. Nitti di Vito (1902).

> ix, *Documenti storici di Corato (1046–1327)*, ed. F. Beltrani (1927).

Codice diplomatico pugliese (continuazione del Codice diplomatico barese),

> xx, *Le Pergamene di Conversano (901–1265)*, ed. G. Coniglio (1975).[1]

> xxi, *Les Chartes de Troia (1024–1266)*, ed. J-M. Martin (1976).

Codice diplomatico del monastero benedettino di S. Maria di Tremiti (1005–1237), ed. Armando Petrucci (3 vols, FSI, Rome 1960).

---

1 Most of the documents in this collection had been previously published in *Chartularium Cupersanense*, ed. D. Morea (Montecassino 1892). However, reference here has been made exclusively to the modern edition.

Codice diplomatico del regno di Carlo I e Carlo II d'Angiò, ed. G. Del Giudice, i (Naples 1863).

Codice diplomatico normanno di Aversa, ed. A. Gallo (Naples 1927).

Codice diplomatico svevo di Aversa, ed. C. Salvati (Naples 1980).

Codice diplomatico verginiano, ed. P.M. Tropeano (13 vols, Montevergine 1977–2001).

[*Le*] *Colonie Cassinesi in Capitanata* ii *Gargano*, ed. Tommaso Leccisotti (Miscellanea Cassinese 15, Montecassino 1938).

[*Le*] *Colonie Cassinesi in Capitanata* iv *Troia*, ed. Tommaso Leccisotti (Miscellanea Cassinese 29, Montecassino 1957).

Conradi III et Filius eius Henrici Diplomata, ed. F. Haussmann (MGH Diplomatum Regum et Imperatorum Germaniae 9, Vienna 1969).

[*The*] *Deeds of Frederick Barbarossa, by Otto of Freising and his Continuator Rahewin*, trans. C.C. Mierow (New York 1953).

Deeds of John and Manuel Comnenus, by John Kinnamos, trans. Charles M. Brand (New York 1976).

Deér, Josef (1969), *Das Papsttum und die süditalienischen Normannenstaaten 1053–1212*, Göttingen 1969.

Del Re, Giuseppe (1845), *Cronisti e scrittori sincroni napoletani*, i, Naples.

De Rebus Gestis Rogerii Calabriae et Siciliae Comitis, auctore Gaufredo Malaterra, ed. Ernesto Pontieri (RIS, 2nd edn, Bologna 1927–8).

[*The*] *Digest of Justinian*, ed. T. Mommsen and P. Krueger, trans. Alan Watson, vol. iv (Philadelphia 1985).

[*I*] *Diplomi della cattedrale di Messina*, ed. Raffaele Starrabba (Documenti per servire alla storia di Sicilia, Ser. I.1, Palermo 1876–90).

[*I*] *Documenti inediti dell'epoca normanna in Sicilia*, ed. Carlo Alberto Garufi (Documenti per servire alla storia di Sicilia, Ser. I.18, Palermo 1899).

[*The*] *Ecclesiastical History of Orderic Vitalis*, ed. Marjorie Chibnall (6 vols, Oxford 1969–80).

Elze, Reinhard (1973), 'Tre Ordines per l'incorazione di un re e di una regina del regno normanno di Sicilia', in *Atti del Congresso internazionale di studi sulla Sicilia normanna (Palermo 4–8 dicembre 1972)*, Palermo, 438–59.

Falco of Benevento, *Chronicon Beneventanum*, ed. Edoardo d'Angelo (Florence 1998).

Frutolfs und Ekkehards Chroniken und die anonyme Kaiserchronick, ed. F-J. Schmale and I. Schmale-Ott (Ausgewählte Quellen zur deutschen Geschichte des Mittelaters, Freiherr von Stein Gedächtnisausgabe, 15: Darmstadt 1972).

Fulcher of Chartres, *Historia Hierosolymitana (1095–1127)*, ed. Heinrich Hagenmayer (Heidelberg 1913); [translated as] Fulcher of Chartres, *A History of the Expedition to Jerusalem 1095–1127*, trans. Frances R. Ryan and H.S. Fink (1969).

[Erasmo] Gattula, *Accessiones ad Historiam Abbatiae Casinensis* (Venice 1734).

[Erasmo] Gattula, *Historia Abbatiae Casinensis* (Venice 1733).

Girgensohn, Dieter (1967), 'Documenti beneventani inediti del secolo XII', *Samnium* 40: 262–317.

Gregory the Great, *Dialogi Libri IV*, ed. U. Moricca (FSI, Rome 1924).

Guillelmi I. Regis Diplomata, ed. Horst Enzensberger (Codex Diplomaticus Regni Siciliae, Ser. I.iii, Cologne 1996).

Heinemann, Lothar von, *Normannische Herzogs- und Königsurkunden aus Unteritalien und Sizilien* (Tübingen 1899).

[*The*] *Historia Pontificalis of John of Salisbury*, ed. Marjorie Chibnall (London 1956).

Idrîsî. La Première Géographie de l'Occident, trans. Henri Bresc and Annliese Nef (Paris 1999).

Italia Sacra, ed. Ferdinando Ughelli (2nd edn by N. Colletti, 10 vols, Venice 1717–21).

[*The*] *Itinerary of Benjamin of Tudela*, trans. M.N. Adler (London 1907).

Kehr, Paul Fridolin (1901), 'Diploma purpureo di re Roggero II per la casa Pierleone', *Archivio della reale società romana di storia patria* 24: 253–9.

Kehr, Paul Fridolin (1905), 'Nachträge zu den Papsturkunden Italiens I', *Nachrichten der K. Gesellschaft der Wissenschaften zu Göttingen, Phil-IIist. Klasse*, 321–80.

[*The*] *Letters of St. Bernard of Clairvaux*, trans. Bruno Scott James (London 1953).

[*The*] *Liber Augustalis or Constitutions of Melfi promulgated by the Emperor Frederick II for the Kingdom of Sicily in 1231*, trans. James M. Powell (Syracuse, NY, 1971).

Liber de regno Siciliae e la Epistola ad Petrum Panormitane Ecclesie Thesaurium di Ugo Falcando, ed. G.B. Siragusa (FSI, Rome 1897).[2]

Liber Pontificalis, ed. L. Duchesne and C. Vogel (3 vols, Paris 1886–1957).

Liber Pontificalis prout extat in Codice Dertusensi, ed. J.M. March (Barcelona 1925).

[*Il*] *"Libro del capitolo" del monastero della SS. Trinità di Venosa (Cod. Casin. 334): una testimonianza del Mezzogiorno normanno*, ed. Hubert Houben (Galatina 1984).

Lotharii Diplomata, ed. E. von Ottenthal and S. Hirsch (MGH Diplomatum Regum et Imperatorum Germaniae, viii, Berlin 1927).

Loud, G.A., 'A calendar of the diplomas of the Norman Princes of Capua', *Papers of the British School at Rome* 49 (1981), 99–143.

---

2 English translation as: *The History of the Tyrants of Sicily by 'Hugo Falcandus', 1154–69*, trans. G.A. Loud and T.E.J. Wiedemann (Manchester 1998).

Monti, Gennaro Maria (1940), 'Il testo e la storia esterna delle assise normanne', in *Studi di storia e di diretto in onore di Carlo Calisse*, Milan, i.295–348 [reprinted in Monti, *Lo Stato normanno-svevo. Lineamenti e ricerche* (1945), below].

Monumenta Bambergensia, ed. Philipp Jaffé (Bibliotheca Rerum Germanicarum v, Berlin 1869).

Monumenta Corbeiensia, ed. Philipp Jaffé (Bibliotheca Rerum Germanicarum i, Berlin 1864).

Monumenta Erphesfurtensia, Saec. XII, XIII, XIV, ed. Oswald Holder-Egger (MGH, SRG, Hanover 1899).

Muratori, Ludovico Antonio (1738), *Antiquitates Italiae Medii Aevi*, i, Milan.

[*I*] *Necrologi Cassinesi I Il Necrologio del Cod. Cassinese 47*, ed. Mauro Inguanez (FSI, Rome 1941).

Necrologio del Liber Confratrum di S. Matteo di Salerno, ed. C.A. Garufi (FSI, Rome 1922).

L'Obituarium S. Spiritus della biblioteca capitolare di Benevento (secc. XII–XIV), ed. Alfredo Zazo (Naples 1963).

[*Le*] *Pergamene degli archivii vescovili di Amalfi e Ravello*, i, ed. Jole Mazzoleni (Naples 1972).

[*Le*] *Pergamene dell'archivio vescovile di Caiazzo (1007–1265)*, ed. C. Salvati, M.A. Arpago et alii (Caserta 1983).

[*Le*] *Pergamene di S. Giovanni Evangelista in Lecce*, ed. Michele Pastore (Lecce 1970).

[*Le*] *Pergamene normanne della Mater Ecclesia Capuana, 1091–1197*, ed. Giancarlo Bova (Naples 1996).

[*Le*] *Più antiche carte del capitolo della cattedrale di Benevento (668–1200)*, ed. A. Ciarelli, C. de Donato and V. Matera (Rome 2002).

[*Le*] *Più antiche carte dell'abbazia di San Modesto in Benevento (secoli VIII–XIII)*, ed. Franco Bartoloni (Rome 1950).

Prochiron Legum, ed. F. Brandileone and V. Puntoni (FSI, Rome 1893).

Regesta Imperii iv(1), *Lothar III*, ed. J.F. Böhmer and W. Petke (Mainz 1995).

Regesta Pontificum Romanorum ad annum MCXCVIII, ed. P. Jaffé, S. Loewenfeld *et alii* (2 vols, Leipzig 1885–8).

Regesto di S. Angelo in Formis, ed. Mauro Inguanez (Montecassino 1925).

Reichenmiller, M. (1963), 'Bisher unbekannte Traumerzählungen Alexanders von Telese", *Deutsches Archiv für Erforschung des Mittelalters* 19: 339–52.

[*Die*] *Reichschronik des Annalista Saxo* (2000), ed. Klaus Naß (MGH SS xxxvii), Hanover.

Robinson, Gertrude (1929, 1930), 'The history and cartulary of the Greek monastery of St. Elias and St. Anastasius of Carbone', *Orientalia Christiana* 15 (1929), 121–276; 19 (1930), 5–199.

Rogerii II Regis Diplomata Latina, ed. Carl-Richard Brühl (Codex Diplomaticus Regni Siciliae, Ser. I.ii(1), Cologne 1987).

Romualdi Salernitani Chronicon, ed. C.A. Garufi (RIS, 2nd edn, Città di Castello 1935).

Sacrorum Conciliorum Nova et Amplissima Collectio, ed. J.D. Mansi, xxi (Venice 1776).

[*The*] *Travels of Ibn Jubayr*, trans. R.J.C. Broadhurst (London 1952).

Vita Barbati Episcopi Beneventani, ed. Georg Waitz, MGH Scriptores Rerum Langobardorum, 555–63.

Vita Norberti Archiepiscopi Magdaburgensis, ed. R. Wilmans, MGH SS xii.663–704.

Vita prima Sancti Bernardi, MPL 185, cols. 225–453.

William of Malmesbury, *Gesta Regum Anglorum*, ed. R.A.B. Mynors, R.M. Thomson and M. Winterbottam, vol. i (Oxford 1998).

William of Tyre, Chronicon, ed. R.B.C. Huygens (Corpus Christianorum, Continuatio Medievalis 63, Turnhout 1986); [translated as] *A History of Deeds done beyond the Sea, by William Archbishop of Tyre*, trans. Emily A. Babcock and August C. Krey (2 vols, New York 1941).

Secondary sources

[Items starred thus * also contain editions of source material]

Abulafia, David (1977), *The Two Italies. Economic Relations between the Norman Kingdom of Sicily and the Northern Communes*, Cambridge.

Abulafia, David (1983), 'The Crown and the economy under Roger II and his successors', *Dumbarton Oaks Papers* 37: 1–14.

Abulafia, David (1985), 'The Norman kingdom of Africa and the Norman expeditions to Majorca and the Muslim Mediterranean', *Anglo-Norman Studies 7 Proceedings of the Battle Conference 1984*, ed. R. Allen Brown, Woodbridge, 26–49.

Amari, Michele (1933–9), *Storia dei Musulmani di Sicilia*, 2nd (revd) edn by Carlo Alfonso Nallino, 3 vols, Catania.

Antonucci, G. (1933), 'Goffredo, Conte di Lecce e di Montescaglioso', *Archivio storico per la Calabria e la Lucania* 3: 449–59.

Arnold, Benjamin (1986), 'Servile retainers or noble knights: the medieval ministeriales in Germany', *Reading Medieval Studies* 12: 73–84.

Arthur, Paul (2002), *Naples, from Roman Town to City State*, London.

Asbridge, Thomas (2000), *The Creation of the Principality of Antioch 1098–1130*, Woodbridge.

Backman, Clifford R. (1995), *The Decline and Fall of Medieval Sicily. Politics, Religion and Economy in the Reign of Frederick III, 1296–1327*, Cambridge.

Beck, P. (1990), 'Archeologia di un complesso castrale: Fiorentino in Capitanata', in *Lo Scavo archeologico di Montarrenti e i problemi dell' incastellamento medievale. Esperienza e confronto*, ed. R. Francovich and M. Milanese, Florence, 137–54.

Becker, Julia (2004), 'Die griechischen und lateinischen Urkunden Graf Rogers I. von Sizilien', *Quellen und Forschungen aus italienischen Archiven und Bibliotheken* 84: 1–37.

Becker, Julia (2008), *Graf Roger I. Von Sizilien. Wegbereiter des normannischen Königreichs*, Tübingen.

*Bloch, Herbert (1986), *Monte Cassino in the Middle Ages*, 3 vols, Rome.

*Bloch, Herbert (1998), *The Atina Dossier of Peter the Deacon of Monte Cassino. A Hagiographical Romance of the Twelfth Century*, Rome.

*Blumenthal, Uta-Renate (1978a), *The Early Councils of Pope Paschal II*, Toronto.

Blumenthal, Ute-Renate (1978b), 'Opposition to Pope Paschal II; some comments on the Lateran Council of 1112', *Annuarium Historiae Conciliorum*, 10: 82–98.

Bresc, Henri (1987), 'La pêche dans l'espace économique normand', in *Terra e uomini nel Mezzogiorno normanno-svevo* (Atti delle settime giornate normanno-sveve, Bari 1985), ed. G. Musca, Bari, 271–91.

Bresc, Henri (1999), 'Le royaume Normand d'Afrique et l'archevêché de Mahdiyya', in *Le Partage du monde. Échanges et colonisation dans la Méditerranée médiévale*, ed. Michel Balard and Alain Ducellier, Paris, 347–66.

Bresc, Henri, and Nef, Annliese (1998), 'Les Mozarabes de Sicile (1100–1300)', in *Cavalieri alla conquista del Sud. Studi sull'Italia normanna in memoria di Léon-Robert Ménager*, ed. E. Cuozzo and J-M. Martin, Rome/Bari, 134–56.

Brezzi, Paolo (1947), *Roma e l'impero medioevale (774–1252)*, Bologna.

Brown, T.S. (1992), 'The political use of the past in Norman Sicily', in *The Perception of the Past in Twelfth-Century Europe*, ed. Paul Magdalino, London/Rio Grande, 191–210.

Brühl, Carl-Richard (1977), 'Purpururkunden', *Festschrift für Helmut Beumann zur 65. Geburtstag*, ed. K-U. Jäschke and R. Wenskus, Sigmaringen, 3–21.

Brühl, Carl-Richard (1978), *Urkunden und Kanzlei König Rogers II. von Sizilien*, Cologne.

Cahen, Claude (1940), *Le Régime Féodal de l'Italie Normande*, Paris.

Caravale, Mario (1966), *Il Regno normanno di Sicilia*, Rome.

Carlone, Carmine (1984), *Falsificazione e falsari cavensi e verginiani del secolo XIII*, Altavilla Silentina.

Caspar, Erich (1904), *Roger II. (1101–1154) und die Gründung der normannisch-sicilischen Monarchie*, Innsbruck.

Caspar, Erich (1909), *Petrus Diaconus und die Monte Cassineser Fälschungen. Ein Beitrag zur Geschichte des italienischen Geisteslebens im Mittelalter*, Berlin.

Chalandon, Ferdinand (1907), *La Domination normande en Italie et en Sicile*, 2 vols, Paris.

Cielo, Liugi R. (1995), *L'Abbaziale normanna di S. Salvatore de Telesia*, Naples.

Cilento, Nicola (1983), 'La «conscienza» del Regno nei cronisti meridionali', in *Potere, società e popolo tra età normanna ed età sveva* (Atti delle quinte giornate normanno-sveve, Bari–Conversano, 26–28 ottobre 1981), Bari, 165–84.

Classen, Peter (1968), 'Zur Geschichte Papst Anastasius IV', *Quellen und Forschungen aus Italienischen Archiven und Bibliotheken* 48: 36–63.

Claude, Dietrich (1975), *Geschichte des Erzbistums Magdeburg bis in das 12. Jahrhundert*, 2 vols, Cologne/Vienna.

*Clementi, Dione R. (1953/4), 'Some unnoticed aspects of the Emperor Henry VI's conquest of the Norman Kingdom of Sicily', *Bulletin of the John Rylands Library* 36: 328–59.

*Clementi, Dione R. (1965), 'Alexandrini Telesini "Ystoria Serenissimi Rogerii Primi Regis Siciliae", Lib. IV.6–10 (Twelfth-century political progaganda)', *Bullettino dell'istituto storico italiano per il medio evo* 77: 105–26.

Clementi, Dione R. (1968), 'The relations between the papacy, the Western Roman Empire and the emergent kingdom of Sicily and south Italy (1050–1156)', *Bullettino dell'istituto storico italiano per il medio evo* 80: 191–212.

Clementi, Dione R. (1991), 'Historical Commentary on the Libellus of Alessandro di Telese', in *Alexandri Telesini Abbatis Ystoria* [in printed primary sources above], 177–364.

Comparetti, Domenico (1908), *Vergil in the Middle Ages*, trans. E. Benecke, London.

Cowdrey, H.E.J. (1983), *The Age of Abbot Desiderius. Montecassino, the Papacy and the Normans in the Eleventh and Early Twelfth Centuries*, Oxford.

Cuozzo, Errico (1980), 'Prosopografia di una famiglia feudale normanna: I Balvano', *Archivio storico per le provincie napoletane* 98: 61–87.

Cuozzo, Errico (1984), *Catalogus Baronum. Commentario* (Fonti per la storia d'Italia, 101b), Rome.

Cuozzo, Errico (1989), *«Quei maladetti Normanni». Cavalieri e organizzazione militare nel Mezzogiorno normanno*, Naples.

Cuozzo, Errico (1995), *Normanni, nobiltà e cavalleria*, Salerno.

Cuozzo, Errico (1998), 'Intorno alla prima contea normanna nell'Italia meridionale', in *Cavalieri alla conquista del Sud. Studi sull'Italia normanna in memoria di Léon-Robert Ménager*, ed. E. Cuozzo and J-M. Martin, Rome/Bari, 171–93.

D'Angelo, Edoardo (2009), 'Intellettuali tra Normandia e Sicilia (per un identikit letterario del cosidetto Ugo Falcando)', in *Cultura cittadina e documentazione. Formazione e circolazione di modelli*, ed. Anna Laura Trombetti Budriesi, Bologna, 325–49.

De Francesco, A. (1909, 1910), 'Origini e sviluppo del feudalismo nel Molise fino alla caduta della dominazione normanna', *Archivio storico per le provincie napoletane* 34 (1909), 432–60, 640–71; 35 (1910), 70–98, 273–307.

Demus, Otto (1950), *The Mosaics of Norman Sicily*, London.

De Simone, Adelgisa (1999), 'Il Mezzogiorno normanno-svevo vista dall'Islam africano', in *Il Mezzogiorno normanno-svevo visto dall'Europa e dal mondo mediterraneo*, ed. G. Musca (Atti del tredicesime giornate normanno-sveve, Bari 21–24 ottobre 1997), Bari, 261–93.

De Simone, Adelgisa (2002), 'Ruggero II e l'Africa islamica', in *Il Mezzogiorno normanno-svevo e le Crociate*, ed. G. Musca (Atti del quattordicesime giornate normanno-sveve, Bari 17–20 ottobre 2000), Bari, 95–129.

*Dormeier, Heinrich (1979), *Montecassino und die Laien in 11. Und 12. Jahrhundert*, Stuttgart.

Erdmann, Carl (1927), 'Mauritius Burdinus (Gregor VIII)', *Quellen und Forschungen aus italienischen Archiven und Bibliotheken* 19 (1927), 205–61.

Falkenhausen, Vera von (1977), 'I Ceti dirigenti prenormanni al tempo della costituzione degli stati normanni nell'Italia meridionale e in Sicilia', in *Forme di Potere e struttura sociale in Italia nel medioevo*, ed. G. Rossetti, Bologna, 321–77.

Falkenhausen, Vera von (1980), 'I Gruppi etnici nel regno di Ruggero II e la loro partecipazione al potere', in *Società, potere e popolo nell'età di Ruggero II* (Atti delle terze giornate normanno-sveve, Bari, 23–25 maggio 1977), Bari, 133–56.

Falkenhausen, Vera von (1998), 'I diplomi dei re normanni in lingua greca', in *Documenti medievali greci e latini: studi comparativi (Atti del seminario di Erice, 23-29 ottobre 1995)*, ed. G. De Gregorio and O. Kresten, Spoleto, pp. 253–308.

Feller, Laurent (1998), *Les Abruzzes Médiévales. Territoire, Économie et Société en Italie Centrale du IXe au XIIe Siècle*, Rome.

Feller, Laurent (2002), 'The northern frontier of Norman Italy, 1060–1140', in *The Society of Norman Italy*, ed. G.A. Loud and A. Metcalfe, Leiden, 47–74.

Franke, Alexander (2008), 'Zur Identität des "Hugo Falcandus"', *Deutsches Archiv für Erforschung des Mittelalters* 64: 1–13.

Fuiano, Michele (1956), 'La Fondazione del Regnum Siciliae nella versione di Alessandro di Telese', *Papers of the British School at Rome* 24 (*Studies in Italian Medieval History presented to Miss E.M. Jamison*): 65–77.

Gallo, Alfonso (1938), *Aversa Normanna*, Naples.

*Garufi, Carlo Alberto (1910), 'Gli Aleramici e i normanni in Sicilia e nelle Puglia. Documenti e ricerche', in *Centenario della nascità di Michele Amari*, Palermo, i.47–83.

Gervasio, E. (1939), 'Falcone di Benevento e la sua cronaca', *Bullettino del istituto storico italiano per il medio evo* 54: 1–128.

*Girgensohn, Dieter (1971), 'Das Pisaner Konzil von 1135 in der Überlieferung des Pisaner Konzils von 1409', in *Festschrift für Hermann Heimpel zum 70. Geburtstag*, Göttingen, ii.1063–1100.

Goitein, S.D. (1967), *A Mediterranean Society. The Jewish Communities of the Arab World as portrayed in the Documents of the Cairo Geniza*, i *Economic Foundations*, Berkeley/Los Angeles.

Goitein, S.D. (1983), *A Mediterranean Society. The Jewish Communities of the Arab World as portrayed in the Documents of the Cairo Geniza*, iv *Daily Life*, Berkeley/Los Angeles.

Grant, Lindy (1998), *Abbot Suger of St. Denis. Church and State in Early Twelfth-Century France*, Harlow.

Grierson, Philip (1971), 'Nummi scyphati. The story of a misunderstanding', *Numismatic Chronicle*, Ser. VII.11: 253–60.

Guenée, Bernard (1973), Histoire, annales, chroniques. Essai sur les genres historiques au Môyen Age', *Annales. Economies, Sociétés et Civilisations* 28: 997–1016.

*Guillaume, Paul (1877), *Essai Historique sur l'Abbaye de Cava*, Cava di Tirreni.

Hiestand, Rudolf (1991), 'S. Michele in Orsara. Un capitolo dei rapporti-pugliesi-iberici nei secoli XII–XIII', *Archivio storico pugliese* 44: 67–79.

Hodges, Richard (1997), *Light in the Dark Ages. The Rise and Fall of San Vincenzo al Volturno*, Ithaca, NY.

*Hoffmann, Hartmut (1971a), 'Petrus Diaconus, die Herren von Tusculum under der Sturz Oderisius II von Montecassino', *Deutsches Archiv für Erforschung des Mittelalters* 29: 1–109.

Hoffmann, Hartmut (1971b), 'Chronik und Urkunden in Montecassino', *Quellen und Forschungen aus Italienischen Archiven und Bibliotheken* 51: 93–206.

Hoffmann, Hartmut (1973), 'Studien zur Chronik von Montecassino', *Deutsches Archiv für Erforschung des Mittelalters* 31: 59–162.

*Hoffmann, Hartmut (1978), 'Langobarden, Normannen, Päpste. Zum Legitimationsproblem in Unteritalien', *Quellen und Forschungen aus Italienischen Archiven und Bibliotheken* 58: 137–80.

Houben, Hubert (1995), *Die Abtei Venosa und das Mönchtum im normannisch-staufischen Süditalien*, Tübingen.

Houben, Hubert (1996), *Mezzogiorno normanno-svevo. Monasteri e castelli, ebrei e musulmani*, Naples.

Houben, Hubert (2002), *Roger II of Sicily. A Ruler between East and West* (trans. G.A. Loud and D. Milburn), Cambridge.

Houben, Hubert (2010), *Roger II von Sizilien. Herrscher zwischen Orient und Oksident*, Darmstadt, 2nd edn [first published in German in 1997, translated into English in 2002].

Housley, Norman (1985), 'Crusades against Christians: their origins and early development, c. 1000–1216', in *Crusade and Settlement. Papers read at the First Conference of the Society for the Study of the Crusades and the Latin East and presented to R.C. Smail*, ed. P.W. Edbury, Cardiff, 17–36.

Howe, John (1997), *Church Reform and Social Change in Eleventh-Century Italy*.

Dominic of Sora and his Patrons, Philadelphia.

Hüls, Rudolf (1977), *Kardinäle, Klerus und Kirchen Roms 1049-1130*, Tübingen.

Jahn, Wolfgang (1989), *Untersuchungen zur normannische Herrschaft in Süditalien (1040–1100)*, Frankfurt.

Jamison, Evelyn M. (1913), 'The Norman administration of Apulia and Capua, more especially under Roger II and William I, 1127–1166', *Papers of the British School at Rome* 6: 211–481 [also available as a separate monograph, Aalen 1987].

*Jamison, Evelyn M. (1929), 'The administration of the County of Molise in the twelfth and thirteenth centuries', *English Historical Review* 44: 529–59 [reprinted in Jamison 1992].

*Jamison, Evelyn M. (1932), 'I Conti di Molise e di Marsia nel secoli XII e XIII', in *Atti del convegno storico abruzzese-molisano*, Casalbordino, i.73–178 [reprinted in Jamison 1992].

*Jamison, Evelyn M. (1934), 'The Abbess Bethlem of S. Maria di Porta Somma and the barons of the Terra Beneventana', in *Oxford Essays in Medieval History presented to Herbert Edward Salter*, Oxford, 33–67.

Jamison, Evelyn M. (1939), 'Some notes on the *Anonymi Gesta Francorum* with special reference to the Norman contingent from south Italy and Sicily on the First Crusade', in *Studies in French Language and Medieval Literature presented to Professor Mildred K. Pope*, Manchester, 183–208 [reprinted in Jamison 1992].

*Jamison, Evelyn M. (1959) 'The significance of the early medieval documents from S. Maria della Noce and S. Salvatore di Castiglione', in *Studi in onore di Riccardo Filangieri*, 2 vols, Naples, i.51–80 [reprinted in Jamison 1992].

Jamison, Evelyn M. (1971), 'Additional work on the Catalogus Baronum', *Bullettino dell'istituto storico italiano per il medio evo* 83: 1–63 [reprinted in Jamison 1992].

Jamison, Evelyn M. (1992), *Studies on the History of Medieval Sicily and South Italy*, ed. Dione Clementi and Theo Kölzer, Aalen.

Johns, Jeremy (1993), 'The Norman Kings of Sicily and the Fatimid Caliphate', *Anglo-Norman Studies* 15 *Proceedings of the Battle Conference 1992*, ed. Marjorie Chibnall, 133–59.

Johns, Jeremy (2002), *Arabic Administration in Norman Sicily. The Royal Dīwān*, Cambridge.

Kamp, Norbert (1980), 'Der unteritalienische Episkopat im Spannungfeld zwischen monarchischer Kontrolle und römischer "libertas" von der Reichsgründung Rogers II. bis zum Konkordat von Benevento', in *Società, potere e popolo nell'età di Ruggero II* (Atti delle terze giornate normanno-sveve, Bari, 23–25 maggio 1977), Bari, 99–132.

Kehr, Paul Fridolin (1926), 'Zur Geschichte Viktors IV (Octavien von Monticelli', *Neus Archiv der Gesellschaft für ältere deutsche Geschichteskunde* 46: 53–85.

Kehr, Paul Fridolin (1934), *Die Belehnungen der süditalienischen Normannen-*

fürsten durch die Päpste (1059–1192), Berlin.

Kislinger, Ewald (2009), 'Giorgio di Antiocha e la politica marittima tra Normanni e Bizanzio', in *Giorgio di Antiocha. L'Arte della politica in Sicilia nel XII secolo tra Bizanzio e l'Islam* (Atti del Convegno, Palermo 2007), ed. M. Re and C. Rognoni, Palermo, 47–63.

*Leccisotti, Tommaso (1947), 'Antiche prepositure Cassinesi nei pressi del Fortore e del Saccione', *Benedictina* 1: 88–133.

Lees, Jay T. (1998), *Anselm of Havelberg. Deeds into Words in the Twelfth Century*, Leiden.

Loew, Elias Avery, and Brown, Virginia (1980), *The Beneventan Script. A History of the South Italian Minuscule*, 2nd edn, Rome.[3]

Loré, Vito (2008), *Monasteri, Principi, Aristocrazie. La Trinità di Cava nei secoli XI e XII*, Spoleto.

Loud, G.A. (1981a), 'How "Norman" was the Norman conquest of southern Italy?', *Nottingham Medieval Studies* 25: 13–35 [reprinted in Loud 1999a].

*Loud, G.A. (1981b), 'The Norman counts of Caiazzo and the abbey of Monte-cassino', in *Monastica i. Scritti raccolti in memoria del xv centenario della nascità di S. Benedetto 480–1980* (Miscellanea cassinese 44, Montecassino 1981), 199–217 [reprinted in Loud 2000a].

Loud, G.A. (1985), *Church and Society in the Norman Principality of Capua 1058–1197*, Oxford.

Loud, G.A. (1987), 'The abbey of Cava, its property and benefactors in the Norman era', *Anglo-Norman Studies 9 Proceedings of the Battle Conference 1986*, ed. R. Allen Brown, Woodbridge, 143–77 [reprinted in Loud 1999a].

Loud, G.A. (1991), 'The abbots of St. Sophia, Benevento in the eleventh century', *Quellen und Forschungen aus Italienischen Archiven und Bibliotheken* 71: 1–13 [reprinted in Loud 2000a].

*Loud, G.A. (1993), 'The genesis and context of the Chronicle of Falco of Benevento', *Anglo-Norman Studies 15 Proceedings of the Battle Conference 1992*, ed. Marjorie Chibnall, Woodbridge, 177–98 [reprinted in Loud 2000a].

Loud, G.A. (1996), 'Continuity and change in Norman Italy: the Campania during the eleventh and twelfth centuries', *Journal of Medieval History* 22: 313–43 [reprinted in Loud 1999a].

*Loud, G.A. (1997), 'A Lombard abbey in a Norman world: St. Sophia, Benevento, 1050–1200', *Anglo-Norman Studies 19 Proceedings of the Battle Conference 1996*, ed. Christopher Harper-Bill, Woodbridge, 273–306 [reprinted in Loud 2000a].

Loud, G.A. (1999a), *Conquerors and Churchmen in Norman Italy*, Aldershot.

Loud, G.A. (1999b), 'William the Bad or William the Unlucky? Kingship in Sicily 1154–1166', *Haskins Society Journal* 8: 99–113.

---

3 Revised edition of a book first published in 1914; Loew changed his name to Lowe.

Loud, G.A. (1999c), 'Coinage, wealth and plunder in the age of Robert Guiscard', *English Historical Review* 114: 815–43.

Loud, G.A. (2000a), *Montecassino and Benevento in the Middle Ages. Essays in South Italian Church History*, Aldershot.

Loud, G.A. (2000b), *The Age of Robert Guiscard. Southern Italy and the Norman Conquest*, Harlow.

Loud, G.A. (2002), 'The papacy and the rulers of southern Italy, 1058–1198', in *The Society of Norman Italy*, ed. G.A. Loud and A. Metcalfe, Leiden, 151–84.

Loud, G.A. (2005), 'Monastic chronicles in the twelfth-century Abruzzi', *Anglo-Norman Studies* 27 *Proceedings of the Battle Conference 2004*, ed. J. Gillingham; 101–31.

Loud, G.A. (2007a), *The Latin Church in Norman Italy*, Cambridge.

Loud, G.A. (2007b), 'History writing in the twelfth-century kingdom of Sicily', in *Chronicling History. Chroniclers and Historians in Medieval and Renaissance Italy*, ed. Sharon Dale, Alison Williams Lewin and Duane J. Osheim, University Park PA, 29–54.

*Loud, G.A. (2008), 'New evidence for the workings of the royal administration in mainland southern Italy during the later twelfth century', in *Puer Apuliae. Mélanges offerts à Jean-Marie Martin*, ed. E. Cuozzo, V. Déroche, A. Peters-Custot and V. Prigent, Paris, 395–417.

Loud, G.A. (2009), 'The chancery and charters of the kings of Sicily (1130–1212)', *English Historical Review* 124: 779–810.

Luttrell, Anthony (1975), 'Approaches to medieval Malta', in *Medieval Malta. Studies on Malta before the Knights*, ed. A.T. Luttrell, London, 1–70.

Malaczek, Werner (1981), Das Kardinalskollegium unter Innocenz II. und Anaklet', *Archivum Historiae Pontificiae* 19: 27–78.

*Mallet, Jean, and Thibaut, André (1984), *Les Manuscrits en Écriture Bénéventaine de la Bibliothèque Capitulaire de Bénévent*, vol. i: *Manuscrits 1–18*, Paris.

Martin, Jean-Marie (1974), 'À propos de la Vita de Barbatus, évêque de Bénévent', *Mélanges de l'École Française de Rome. Môyen-Age–Temps Modernes* 86: 137–64.

Martin, Jean-Marie (1980), 'Les communautés d'habitants de la Pouille et leur rapports avec Roger II', in *Società, potere e popolo nell'età di Ruggero II* (Atti delle terze giornate normanno-sveve, Bari, 23–25 maggio 1977), Bari, 73–98.

Martin, Jean-Marie (1987), 'Le travail agricole: rythmes, corvées, outillage', in *Terra e Uomini nel Mezzogiorno Normanno-svevo*, ed. Giosuè Musca (Atti delle settime giornate normanno-sveve, Bari, 15–17 ottobre 1985), Bari, 113–57.

Martin, Jean-Marie (1993), *La Pouille du VI au XII Siècle*, Rome.

Martin, Jean-Marie, and Noyé, Ghislaine (1982), 'La cité de Montecorvino en Capitanate et sa cathédrale', *Mélanges de l'École Française de Rome. Môyen-Age–Temps Modernes* 94 (1982), 513–49.

*Martini, M. (1915) *Feudalità e monachismo cavense in Puglia i Terra di Capitanata (Sant'Agata di Puglia)*, Martina Franca [only volume published].

Matthew, Donald J.A. (1981), 'The Chronicle of Romuald of Salerno', in *The Writing of History in the Middle Ages. Essays Presented to Richard William Southern*, ed. R.H.C. Davis and J.M. Wallace-Hadrill, Oxford, 239–74.

Matthew, Donald J.A. (1992), *The Norman Kingdom of Sicily*, Cambridge.

Matthew, Donald J.A. (2004), 'Semper fideles. The citizens of Salerno in the Norman kingdom', in *Salerno nel XII secolo. Istituzioni, società, cultura.* (Atti del Convegno internazionale, Raito di Vietri 1999), ed. P. Delogu and P. Peduto, Salerno, 27–45.

Ménager, L-R. (1959), 'L'institution monarchique dans les états normands de l'Italie. Contribution à l'étude du pouvoir royal dans les principautés occidentales, aux xiᵉ–xiiᵉ siècles', *Cahiers de civilisations médiévales* 2: 303–31, 445–68.

Ménager, L-R. (1960), *Ammiratus – Αμηράζ. L'Émirat et les origines de l'amirauté (XIᵉ–XIIᵉ siècles)*, Paris.

Ménager, L-R. (1969), 'La législation sud-italien sous la domination normande', in *I Normanni e la loro espansione in Europa nell'alto medioevo* (Settimane di studio del centro italiano di studi sull'alto medioevo 16, Spoleto), 439–96.

Ménager, L-R. (1975a), 'Pesanteur et etiologie de la colonisation normande de l'Italie', in *Roberto il Guiscardo e il suo tempo* (Relazioni e communicazioni nelle Prime Giornate normanno-sveve, Bari, maggio 1973), Rome: 189–214.

Ménager, L-R. (1975b), 'Inventaire des familles normandes et franques émigrés en Italie méridionale et en Sicile (XIᵉ–XIIᵉ siècles)', in *Roberto il Guiscardo e il suo tempo* [1975a as above]: 259–390.

Metcalfe, Alex (2009), *The Muslims of Medieval Italy*, Edinburgh.

*Monti, Gennaro Maria (1945), *Lo Stato normanno-svevo. Lineamenti e ricerche*, Trani.

Morris, Colin (1989), *The Papal Monarchy. The Western Church from 1050 to 1250*, Oxford.

Murray, Alan V. (2009), 'Norman settlement in the Latin kingdom of Jerusalem, 1099–1131', *Archivio Normanno-Svevo* 1: 61–85.

Oldfield, Paul (2009), *City and Community in Norman Italy*, Cambridge.

Oldoni, Massimo (1980), 'Realismo e dissidenza nella storiografia su Ruggero II: Falcone di Benevento e Alessandro di Telese', in *Società, potere e popolo nell'età di Ruggero II* (Atti delle terze giornate normanno-sveve, Bari, 23–25 maggio 1977), Bari, 259–83.

Palumbo, Pietro (1942), *Lo Scisma del MCXXX*, Rome.

Palumbo, Pietro (1963), 'Nuovi studi (1942–1962) sullo scisma di Anacleto II', *Bullettino dell'istituto storico italiano per il medio evo* 75: 71–103.

Partner, Peter (1972), *The Lands of St. Peter. The Papal State in the Middle Ages and the Early Renaissance*, London.

Pennington, Kenneth (2006), 'The birth of the *Ius Comune*: King Roger's legislation', *Rivista internazionale di diritto commune* 17: 23–60.

Petke, W. (1985), *Kanzlei, Kapelle und Königliche Kurie unter Lothar III (1125–1137)*, Cologne/Vienna.

*Petrucci, Armando (1959), 'Note di diplomatica normanna I, I documenti di Roberto di Basunvilla, II Conte de Conversano e III Conte di Loritello', *Bullettino dell'istituto storico italiano per il medioe evo* 71: 113–40.

Poole, Reginald Lane (1934), 'The beginning of the year in the Middle Ages', in his *Studies in Chronology and History*, ed. Austin Lane Poole, Oxford, 1–27.

Portanova, Gregorio (1976), 'I Sanseverino dal 1125 allo sterminio del 1246', *Benedictina* 23: 319–63.

*Pratesi, Alessandro (1955), 'Note di diplomatica vescovile beneventana, II', *Bullettino dell'archivio paleografico italiano*, n.s. 1: 19–91.

Ramseyer, Valerie (2006), *The Transformation of a Religious Landscape. Medieval Southern Italy, 850–1150*, Ithaca NY.

Reisinger, Christoph (1992), *Tancred von Lecce. Normannischer König von Sizilien 1190–1194*, Cologne.

Reuter, Timothy (1983), 'Zur Annerkennung Papst Innocent II: eine neue Quelle', *Deutsches Archiv für Erforschung des Mittelalters* 39: 395–416.

Reuter, Timothy (1996), 'Vom Parvenü zum Bundnispartner: das Königreich Sizilien in der abendländischen Politik des 12. Jahrhunderts', in *Die Staufer im Süden. Sizilien und das Reich*, ed. Theo Kölzer, Sigmaringen, 43–56.

Rivera, Cesare (1919), 'Per la storia dei Borelli, Conti di Sangro', *Archivio storico per le provincie napoletane* 44: 48–92.

Robinson, Ian S. (1990), *The Papacy 1073–1198. Continuity and Innovation*, Cambridge.

Scaduto, Mario (1947), *Il Monachesimo basiliano nella Sicilia medievale. Rinascita e decadenza sec. XI–XV*, Rome.

Scandone, F. (1956), 'Roccasecca. Patria di S. Tommaso di Aquino', *Archivio storico di Terra di Lavoro* 1:33–176.

Schilling, Beate (1998), *Guido von Vienne – Papst Calixt II.* (MGH Schriften 45), Hanover.

Schmale, Franz-Josef (1961), *Studien zum Schisma des Jahres 1130*, Cologne/Graz.

Schmeidler, Bernhard (1905–6), 'Über die Quellen und di Entestehungszeit der Chronicon S. Mariae de Ferraria', *Neues Archiv für altere Deutsches Geschichtskunde* 31: 13–57.

Schütz, Walter (1995), *Catalogus Comitum. Versuch einer Territorialgliederung Kampaniens under den Normannen von 1000 bis 1140 von Benevent bis Salerno*, Frankfurt.

Schwartzmaier, Hans (1968), 'Zur Familie Viktors IV', *Quellen und Forschungen aus Italienischen Archiven und Bibliotheken* 48: 64–79.

Servatius, Carlo (1979), *Paschalis II. (1099–1118). Studien zu seiner Personen und seiner Politik*, Stuttgart.

Skinner, Patricia (1995), *Family Power in Southern Italy. The Duchy of Gaeta and its Neighbours, 850–1139*, Cambridge.

Skinner, Patricia (2002), 'The Tyrrhenian coastal cities under the Normans', in *The Society of Norman Italy*, ed. G.A. Loud and A. Metcalfe, Leiden, 75–96.

Stroll, Mary (1987), *The Jewish Pope. Ideology and Politics in the Papal Schism of 1130*, Leiden.

Stroll, Mary (1997), *The Medieval Abbey of Farfa. Target of Papal and Imperial Ambitions*, Leiden.

Takayama, Hiroshi (1989), 'Familiares Regis and the royal inner council in twelfth-century Sicily', *English Historical Review* 104: 357–72.

Takayama, Hiroshi (1993), *The Administration of the Norman Kingdom of Sicily*, Leiden.

Taviani-Carozzi, Huguette (1991), *La Principauté lombarde de Salerne, IXᵉ–XIᵉ Siècles. Pouvoir et société en Italie lombarde méridionale*, 2 vols, Rome.

Tescione, Giuseppe (1965), 'Roberto conte normanno di Alife, Caiazzo e S. Agata dei Goti', *Archivio storico di Terra di Lavoro* 4: 9–52.

Tescione, Giuseppe (1990), *Caserta medievale e i suoi conti e signori*, 3ʳᵈ edn, Caserta.

Tillmann, Helene (1972), 'Ricerche sull'origine dei membri del collegio cardinalizio nel XII secolo II/1 Identificazione dei cardinali del secolo XII di provenienza romana', *Rivista di storia della chiese in Italia* 26: 313–53.

Tramontana, Salvatore (1977), 'Popolazione, distribuzione della terra e classe sociali nella Sicilia di Ruggero II il Gran Conte', in *Ruggero il Gran Conte e l'inizio dello stato normanno* (Relazioni e communicazioni nelle Seconde Giornate normanno-sveve, Bari, maggio 1975), Rome, 213–70.

Travaini, Lucia (1995), *La Monetazzione nell'Italia normanna*, Rome.

Trombetti Budriesi, Anna Laura (1992), 'Sulle Assise di Ruggero II', in *Unità politica e differenze regionali nel regno di Sicilia*, ed. C.D. Fonseca, H. Houben and B. Vetere, Lecce, 63–83.

Twyman, Susan (2002), *Papal Ceremonial at Rome in the Twelfth Century*, London.

Vehse, Otto (1930–1), 'Benevent als Territorium des Kirchenstaates bis zum Beginn der Avignonesischen Epoche, I Bis zum Ausgang der Normannischen Dynastie', *Quellen und Forschungen aus Italienischen Archiven und Bibliotheken* 22: 87–160.

White, Lynn T. (1938), *Latin Monasticism in Norman Sicily*, Cambridge MA.

Wieruszowski, Helene (1963), 'Roger II of Sicily. *Rex Tyrannus* in twelfth-century political thought', *Speculum* 38: 46–78.

Willard, Henry M. (1976), 'The Staurotheca of Romanus at Monte Cassino', *Dumbarton Oaks Papers* 30: 55–64.

Zazo, Alfredo (1956), 'I Beni della badia di S. Sofia in Benevento nel XIV secolo', *Samnium* 29: 131–86.

Zazo, Alfredo (1959), 'Le Chiese parrocchiali di Benevento del XII–XIV secolo', *Samnium* 32: 60–83.

Zecchino, Ortensio (1980), *Le Assise di Ruggiero II. Problemi di storia delle fonti e di diretto penale*, Naples.

Zema, D.B. (1944), 'The houses of Tuscany and of Pierleone in the crisis of Rome in the eleventh century', *Traditio* 2: 155–75.

Zenker, Barbara (1964), *Die Mitglieder des Kardinalkollegiums von 1130 bis 1154*, Würzburg.

INDEX